I frequently delve into the archives of Jonathan's *Apostolic Theology* blog to find help with my own theological questions. To have this practical resource in one volume is invaluable. Jonathan's ability to take complex issues and make them seemingly straightforward is a gift to the church. That teaching gift comes to the fore when he writes comprehensively like this. His logical reasoning means that you not only gain clear understanding of what the church believes but also why accepting one doctrine necessitates the exclusion of others. This approach future-proofs the book as it helps us to see the heresies of the past and how they frequently resurface under a new guise to subtly draw us away from the true revelation of Jesus. Nowhere is that more clearly seen than in the chapters on the personhood of Christ, where Jonathan skilfully explains Jesus Christ as 'God the Son in his own flesh', whilst demonstrating the inadequacy of our salvation when we deviate to the slightest degree from the biblical God-Man. *Apostolic Theology* is an immensely helpful and accessible resource that you will refer to time and time again, I recommend it to you with supreme confidence.

Mark Chenery
Bradford Area Apostle, Apostolic Church UK
Chairman, ActionOverseas

Review of the chapter on Christ's Incarnation:

Jonathan Black takes us on a tour of key scriptures and important thinkers from church history, steering us through heresies and councils, hymnody and creeds. The destination is the truth that from the manger to the ascension, the person in action is God the Son himself. Jonathan leads us to wonder at the glory of Jesus Christ, but also leads us to great enjoyment and comfort, showing how all this was 'for us and for our salvation'. I hope many will read and benefit from this rich but accessible introduction to the incarnation.

Daniel Hames
Curate, St Aldates Oxford
Lecturer in Systematic & Historical Theology, Union School of Theology

Review of the chapter on the Baptism of the Holy Spirit:

In this chapter, Jonathan Black has mixed the grand theology of this subject with the pastoral care required for its necessary application. To be 'filled with the Spirit' is not just an intellectual exercise worth exhausting ourselves over, or an experiential phenomena worth revelling in. It is more - a Trinitarian, eschatological, breaking-in on a believer's life: assuring us, empowering us, loving us, lifting us. Oh to be 'filled with the Spirit.' On this, a most Pentecostal of subjects, Jonathan Black, helps us through the issues, with his characteristic precision, to reflect upon and add to some great writings on this theme. You are heartily encouraged to read and absorb this, and, far more, reach up to the One who desires that you be 'filled with the Spirit.'

Craig Hopkins
Pastor, The Apostolic Church, Brackla Tabernacle, Bridgend, Wales

Review of the chapter on Sons in the Son: Theosis and Adoption

In this chapter, Jonathan Black provides an accessible and instructive orientation to the Apostolic doctrine of salvation, and especially its focus on believers' deifying transformation through Spirit-effected union with Christ. No doubt, many readers will be surprised by what Black describes. But he takes pains to show that the doctrine is not only deeply biblical but also vibrantly resonant with traditional Evangelical and Patristic teaching. Black's careful work is sure to bring to light aspects of Apostolic spirituality and theology that have never been fully appreciated, and just so to provoke readers both inside and outside the global Pentecostal movement to new lines of theological reflection and construction.

Chris Green
Associate Professor of Theology, Pentecostal Theological Seminary, Cleveland, Tennessee

Review of the chapter on the Resurrection of Christ:

It was a great delight to get stuck into the chapter on the Resurrection of our Lord. Jonathan has the gift of getting right to the heart of the matter without skimping in arguments grounded in the Word of God. In an age where the Lord's resurrection is no longer very politically correct, Jonathan powerfully and relevantly reminds us that Christ's resurrection is the essential foundation of the message of the Good News and of the Christian faith. I can't wait to get a copy of the full book for my holiday reading!

Éric Maréchal
President, The Apostolic Church, Belgium

Review of the chapter on Christ's Abiding Intercession:

The writer has opened up the subjects of this chapter in such a way as to encourage the reader's interest to know more. The concept of Christ being busy on behalf of His children is well worth meditating upon. Although English is not my first language I was able to grasp the truths being discussed and indeed enjoyed being taken deeper in my understanding of these truths. We should be grateful to God for this kind of writing which brings Apostolic theology to the more ordinary person. I look forward to being able to read the whole book.

Peter Washen
General Secretary, The Apostolic Church, Malawi

Review of the chapter on The Eternal Son:

Jonathan Black is clearly captivated with the glory of the eternal Son. Let him draw you, biblically and passionately, to see the Saviour afresh. You won't be disappointed.

Glen Scrivener
Evangelist, Speak Life
Author of *321: The Story of God, the World and You*

Apostolic Theology

A Trinitarian, Evangelical, Pentecostal
Introduction to Christian Doctrine

Jonathan Black

For

Dad & Mum
John & Sharon
Alan & Sandra
David & Eunice

And for Matthew

CONTENTS

Full indices available online at www.apostolictheology.org/bookindex

Foreword

Warren Jones
(Former National Leader of the Apostolic Church UK)

For some time, I have eagerly anticipated the publication of this book of Apostolic Theology, and on its arrival, my expectation has not been disappointed. On the contrary, I have been thrilled with this contemporary exposition of the truths 'most surely believed among us'

This volume appears at an important time in the history of our movement. As we go through an era of structural change to meet the demands of the twenty-first century, it ensures we remain anchored to the firm rock of scripture and are not 'blown about with every wind of doctrine'; that we are built on the unchanging truth of God's Word, not on the shifting sands of the prevailing post-modern culture.

The book is set out on the traditional pattern of our eleven tenets covering a wide range of biblical truth; but even with the breadth of its scope, this is no cursory, superficial skimming of issues Each truth is dealt with in scholarly depth, with illuminating insight and a Christo-centric focus.

Jonathan Black is well suited by his academic training to deal with these theological matters; but he wears his erudition lightly, and is able, in his role as Teacher, to communicate truth with a clarity and profound simplicity that makes his work eminently readable. Each subject is carefully referenced and abounds with scriptural evidence for the truth being discussed. This is, however, no cold academic treatise, but rather, a work of warm devotion by a man who loves Jesus and is committed to the Apostolic fellowship. He has produced for our generation what Pastor W.A.C. Rowe accomplished for previous generations through his book *One Lord One Faith*.

The volume will, I believe, have many uses: It will act as a defence of those vital truths at present under attack in modern theological circles. It will provide a resource for serious Bible study by those charged with the responsibility of leading study groups. It will be a rich mine of material and inspiration for preachers as they seek to bring to our congregations the challenge of living out God's Word in our contemporary society. But most of all, it will bring to us immense spiritual delight as, making it a part of our devotional life, we scan its pages purely for the joy of discovering more about our Lord Jesus Christ. Here is water to swim in.

My sincere hope is that it will find a wide readership and know a circulation beyond denominational boundaries. In particular, I pray that it will inspire a new generation to embrace biblical truth and devote their best energies to the worship and service of the One to whom all Scripture bears witness.

Warren Jones
Swansea
July 2016

Preface

'If then you were raised with Christ, seek those things which are above, where Christ is, sitting at the right hand of God. Set your mind on things above, not on things on the earth.' (Col. 3:1-2)

The Lord Jesus Christ our Saviour has shed His blood for us, conquered death, hell, sin and the devil, and is now seated at the right hand of the Father on high, from where He pours out the Holy Spirit upon the Church which is His Body, until He comes again to judge the living and the dead.

The outpoured Holy Spirit draws the Church to lift her eyes and set her mind on things above. But what are these things above? Jesus Christ the Lord enthroned at the right hand of the Father and pouring out the Holy Spirit, that's what's above. And that's what we're to fix our eyes on. On Jesus, our King of Glory and of Grace. On Jesus, the Lamb slain from the foundation of the world and who lives. On Jesus, who lives and reigns with the Father in the unity of the Spirit, one God, now and forever, Amen!

The Holy Spirit lifts our eyes to Jesus (*Jn 16:14*), and Jesus reveals the Father to us (*Jn 1:18*). And this is the life of the Church and of the Christian, to know the Father and the Son in the Spirit. 'This is eternal life, that they may know You, the only true God, and Jesus Christ whom You have sent' (*Jn 17:3*).

This book is to help you fix your eyes and set your mind on things above. This book is to help you grow in your knowledge of the Father and the Son in the Spirit. Don't be scared by the title or the size, because this is simply a book that looks at what the Triune God has told us about Himself in His Word, and what He has told us about ourselves and what He has done for us through the life, death, resurrection, and ascension of Jesus Christ, God the Son Incarnate.

Over a century ago, a glorious vision of Jesus Christ, Head of the Church, exalted far above all things, was what gave rise to the Apostolic Church. What started off as a handful of Welsh-speaking assemblies in rural Wales has, under the Headship of the Crucified, Risen and Ascended Christ, become a church of 15 million believers around the world. As part of the centenary celebrations this book is being published so that the biblical teaching which fuelled our last century might propel us forward into a new century, looking up to Jesus, our glorious Head, and out into His mission in the world in the power of the Holy Spirit.

My prayer is that the Head of the Church will use this book to equip, build up, comfort, and encourage His people, both in the Apostolic Church and beyond. Hopefully it will find some use among our brothers and sisters in other Pentecostal, charismatic, and evangelical movements as well, with whom we have so much in common through our common fellowship with the Father and His Son in the Spirit, through the shed blood of Jesus.

So, 'take up and read.' And 'seek those things which are above, where Christ is.'

Ascension Day, 2016

The Land of the Living Dead: Of Theologians, Footnotes and Old Welsh Hymns[1]

The Living Dead! (You can't do theology without them)

The world of theology is the world of the living dead, and necessarily so. You see, our temptation (to which we so easily succumb) is to make theology all about me and my Bible. Now, theology is about one of those things (the latter, just in case you were wondering), and it does involve both of those things. But it doesn't only involve me reflecting on Scripture. It also involves the living dead, whether I like it or not.

I am not alone

The living dead won't go away just because I pretend they don't exist. But if I pretend they don't exist, I'm perhaps more likely to be harmed than helped. If I pretend they don't exist, I can't distinguish between baddies and goodies (which is incredibly over-simplistic, I know, but hey, it works with the whole 'living dead' thing!).

You see the influence of the living dead isn't only powerful in theology, it's powerful in the prevailing philosophies of our culture, and cultures foreign and past as well. The ghosts of Kant and Hegel haunt Western thought. And beyond them lie the ghosts of Plato and Aristotle. Is your mind the foundation for what you believe? Behold, Descartes lives. Must everything submit to your powers of reason? There's zombie Kant. Do you think there's a division between spiritual truths and cold hard reasonable facts? Hello Galileo! Think that people get saved by responding to an altar call? Then meet Mr Finney who died in 1875. Convinced that it's contact with God or a decision for Christ that's important, not so much the historical events? Let me introduce you to Rudolph Bultmann. Love Myers-Briggs tests? Then you need to meet Carl Jung. And if you think it's

---

[1] I could have just called this bit 'A Note to the Reader,' but that would have been boring!

common sense that some things are just common sense and other things absurd, you might want to meet Thomas Reid.

My thoughts about the world are not mine alone. Whether I realise it or not, my thinking is influenced, and even shaped, by the living dead.

It's not good to be alone

The presence of the living dead is not a bad thing in itself. In fact, in principle, it's a good thing. We aren't supposed to shut ourselves off into our own private, interior world of thought. Thinking, and above all theological thinking, is a communal thing.

Theology is an ecclesial activity: it's done within the Church. But when we say church here, we don't mean one local assembly at one point in time, but rather the Body of Christ. In the creed, we confess belief in 'the communion of saints'. That means we're joined with those who have gone before us (just as those who will come after us will be joined with us) in fellowship through Christ in the Spirit. Ignatius, Irenaeus, Athanasius, Gregory of Nazianzus, Augustine of Hippo, Luther, Calvin, Cranmer, Owen, Edwards, Wesley, Whitefield, etc. aren't simply men of bye-gone ages; they're men to whom we're joined in fellowship in the one body of Christ. So their influence isn't just there in the cultural atmosphere like that of Aristotle and Hegel; their influence is something to which we should gladly expose ourselves, to learn from them, just as we willingly learn from those who are alive today.

If theology is an ecclesial activity, then it's an activity carried out in the communion of the saints. And that means, not only the living ones, but the dead ones too!

So what's all that got to do with this book?

The Ascended Christ, the Head of the Church, has given gifts of teachers to His Body (Eph. 4:11), not just now, but throughout the history of the church. So, if we only pay attention to the teachers who are alive today, we're ignoring the gifts which Jesus has given. And I have no intention of doing that in these pages. So as you read this book you'll meet lots of dead theologians (or teachers). But don't be tempted to ignore them because they lived long ago: they are gifts from Jesus to His Church, so benefit from some of these great gifts whom He has given.

Although you'll find some quotes from the living as we go along, most of the people I'll point you to have long died. And that's intentional. Most of the dead theologians you'll encounter in these pages come from one of three periods of church history. Firstly, you'll meet some of the great Church Fathers from the first few centuries of the church's life, during the age in which the Councils of the undivided church were held, and the creeds drawn up to defend the faith against false teachers.[2] These are men like Irenaeus, Athanasius, Gregory of Nazianzus, Cyril of Alexandria, Augustine, and John of Damascus.

Secondly, you'll meet the great Reformers of the Protestant Reformation, Martin Luther and John Calvin, through whom God brought a great gospel revival to Europe in the 16th century. We'll also encounter some of their successors in the years after the Reformation: the great continental theologians of Protestant Orthodoxy, Martin Chemnitz, Johann Gerhard, and Francis Turretin, as well as English Puritans such as John Owen and Richard Sibbes.

Finally, you'll get to meet some early Pentecostals. Pentecostalism is incredibly diverse and quickly spread all over the world, so I can't possibly give you a taste of all that diversity. But, I'm British, and this book was written for the centenary of one of the three original British Pentecostal denominations, so I'll mostly be introducing you to some of the early British Apostolics: men like D.P. Williams, Thomas Rees, W.H. Lewis, W.R. Thomas, and W.A.C. Rowe (although, along the way, we'll hear a few voices from Elim and AoG, the other two historic British Pentecostal movements, as well). If you're not an Apostolic or a British Pentecostal, then these voices will hopefully be interesting as one example of early Pentecostal thought. If, however, you are an Apostolic, then these voices are significant for us, even if the names have been forgotten, for this is the century of heritage we're celebrating.

Don't be scared away by the Footnotes

Introducing you to these voices from the past means there will be footnotes. But don't be scared off by that. Many of the footnotes are just there to tell

---

[2] These Councils are referred to as the Ecumenical Councils.

you where the quotations come from, so not everyone will need to spend much time in the footnotes. But some people might want to find out more, so the notes are there for them. Some chapters have quite a lot; some chapters don't have many at all. And I'm afraid that's all my fault. In some places I thought it was more important to draw your attention to what the church has had to say in the past, in other places there wasn't so much need. Sometimes that's because of which issues the Christian church has had to give more attention to in years gone by, because of false teachers who have come along to disturb the peace of the church and turn people away from the true faith in Christ. Other times, it's because there are important issues that maybe don't get talked about quite as much today, so I thought it would help you to see what the church had to say in the past.

Singing the Faith

Another thing you'll find as you read this book are bits of hymns and choruses along the way. One of the first academics to study Pentecostalism, Walter Hollenweger, argued that Pentecostal theology is usually passed on, not by 'the *summa theologica* but the song.'[3] In another place he wrote:

> Hymns are more decisive in their influence on the religious belief and practice of Pentecostals than is the literature of the Pentecostal movement. A Pentecostal lives with his hymns. He knows fifty or a hundred hymns, with several verses, by heart as well as innumerable choruses … The Pentecostal movement teaches people to sing who would otherwise remain dumb.[4]

The early Apostolics did write a lot more, doctrinally speaking, than many other Pentecostal movements; however, the hymns and choruses they sang still played a teaching role, passing on the faith as well as reflecting the content of their faith. So, throughout this book you find excerpts, not only from old Apostolic choruses[5] and the two English hymn-books of the

---

[3] W.J. Hollenweger, 'Charismatic and Pentecostal Movements: A Challenge to the Churches', in *The Holy Spirit*, ed. Dow Kirkpatrick (Nashville: World Methodist Council Tidings, 1974), 221.

[4] Walter J. Hollenweger, *The Pentecostals* (London: SCM, 1972), 464-465. Admittedly, many younger British Pentecostals no longer know so many hymns or even choruses by heart, yet still, what they sing has an enormous impact on what they believe, for good or ill.

[5] Mostly from among those printed in the *Gospel Quintet Chorus Books*.

Apostolic Church,[6] but also from the Apostolics' Welsh hymnbook, *Molwch Dduw*. Why the old Welsh hymns? Simply because most hymns written by the early Apostolics were written in Welsh. So these are not only the songs they sang, but the songs they wrote. In fact, a huge number of the hymns in *Molwch Dduw* were written by D.P. Williams. So, if Walter Hollenweger was right, these Welsh songs were the *summa theologica* of the Apostolic Church.[7]

A Last Note From Me About the Book (and a few Thanks)

This might be a rigorously written book, with its footnotes and dead theologians, but it isn't an academic book. (Although, if some academic theologians happen to read it, I hope they'll find some things of interest.)

All that remains now is for me to say thank you to all those who have helped and encouraged. These thanks are for far too many people to mention them all by name. But to all who have helped in any way with this project (including members of my church, my family, and two theologians who gave some helpful feedback on portions of the manuscript) I am incredibly grateful. And, of course, I am thankful to the Apostolic Church for entrusting me with the task of writing this book (a request which was made to me on my third day in the pastorate).

In 1951, the presbyteries of the Penygroes district asked for 'a book to be written on the Church Tenets, much more comprehensive' than the booklets they had available.[8] At the time, the request was deferred for future consideration. But I am sure the presbyteries which made the request continued to pray for such a book to one day be written. And I hope this book finally meets that request. Therefore, to those praying elders of Penygroes, and to all who have prayed for me in the course of this work, I am abundantly thankful.

---

[6] *Redemption Hymnal* and *Hymns at the Holy Table*. The *Redemption Hymnal* was jointly produced by the three original British Pentecostal denominations: the Apostolic Church, the Elim Pentecostal Church, and the Assemblies of God (AoG).

[7] I think Hollenweger's claim is a bit exaggerated, especially in regard to the Apostolic Church, but D.P. Williams' Welsh hymns definitely highlight things 21st century Western Pentecostals (British Apostolics included) rarely, if ever, sing about anymore. So they show us some things very dear to the hearts of early Pentecostals that we might have forgotten a bit about over the last century.

[8] *Apostolic Church Annual General Council, 1951*, Minute 61.

But my highest thanks go to Him about whom this book has been written, the Triune God: the Father who loves us and sent His Son to die for our sins, the Son who took on our flesh to live our life and die our death, that we might know eternal life in Him, and the Holy Spirit who unites us to Jesus by faith, making us well-beloved sons in the Well-Beloved Son, sharing in the Father's love for His Son in the joy of the Spirit.

Glory be to the Father, and to the Son, and to the Holy Ghost;
As it was in the beginning, is now, and ever shall be. Amen

Soli Deo Gloria.

Tenet 1

The Unity of the Godhead,
& Trinity of the Persons therein.

Chapter 1

The Triune God's Self-Revelation in Jesus

Theology isn't scary. Theology is simply speaking about God.[1] It's not a complicated academic discipline, but rather, theology is about what the Bible teaches, for the Bible is God's Word: God's revelation of Himself.

In fact, everyone is some sort of theologian. The question is will we be good theologians or bad theologians? A good theologian speaks a good word about God, by seeking, as far as possible, to say what God says about Himself. A bad theologian doesn't speak a good word about God, by instead rejecting God's own self-revelation and finding ideas about God elsewhere. 'Whoever does not know God as He has revealed Himself in His Word is making up for Himself an idol in his heart.'[2] Of course, there is only one perfect theologian: the Lord Jesus Christ, the Word of God Himself. The Incarnate Word is the only human being who perfectly speaks of God. But we who trust in Him seek to speak as truthfully as we can of the God of our salvation, as He renews our minds in the image of Christ who is the Truth.

So how can we be good theologians? To speak the truth about God, we must first know God. But how can we know God? We come to know God through the gospel.

What, therefore, is the gospel? The word *gospel* means *good news*, but what sort of good news brings us to know God? Mark begins His Gospel with these words: 'The beginning of the gospel of Jesus Christ, the Son of God' (*Mk 1:1*). He tells us right at the beginning that the gospel is good news about Jesus. It starts here, with His very identity: who He is. Jesus is the Christ, the Son of the Living God (*cf. Mt 16:16; Jn 6:69*). The gospel is the good news of a person: not simply news about a man called Jesus, but news of Jesus who is the Son of God.

The apostle Paul pens a succinct summary of this gospel of Jesus Christ the Son of God for the Corinthians:

> Moreover, brethren, I declare to you the gospel which I preached to you, which also you received and in which you stand, by which also you are saved, if you hold fast that word which I preached to you—unless you

---

[1] The word *theology* comes from the Greek words *Theos* (God) and *Logos* (Word).
[2] Johann Gerhard, *Loci Theologici*, Exegesis III §3 (ET p.268).

> believed in vain. For I delivered to you first of all [or, as of first importance] that which I also received: that Christ died for our sins according to the Scriptures, and that He was buried, and that He rose again the third day according to the Scriptures. (*1 Cor. 15:1-4*)

Paul tells the Christians in Corinth that it is by this gospel that they are saved. This good news is of first importance. This is the summary of the most important thing Paul taught them when he was with them in Corinth. And the reason it is so important is because, by this gospel, people are saved. But what is this gospel that saves? Once again, we see that the gospel is centred in a person: the Lord Jesus Christ. Yet, Paul's focus here is not only on the person of Christ, but on what He has done for us and for our salvation. 'Christ died for our sins … and rose again.' The gospel is the good news of Jesus and what He has done for us in His cross and resurrection. It's not only the news that Christ died, but that He died for our sins.

In his second epistle to the Corinthians, Paul summarises the gospel in another way. 'For He made Him who knew no sin to be sin for us, that we might become the righteousness of God in Him' (*2 Cor. 5:21*). Here we see that this good news is good news about the meaning of Christ's work. The gospel tells us how Jesus' sinless life and atoning death save us. Paul tells us of a great exchange: Christ took our sin, and in return we are clothed with His righteousness.[3]

So, the gospel is the good news of Jesus Christ, the Son of God, who died in our place for our sins and rose again from the dead. And the gospel bears fruit in the forgiveness of sin, in righteousness in Christ, and eternal life.

But what is eternal life? Jesus, in praying to His Father, tells us the answer: 'And this is eternal life, that they may know You, the only true God, and Jesus Christ whom You have sent' (*Jn 17:3*). Eternal life is knowing the Father and the Son. And when the Bible talks about knowing someone, it doesn't just mean knowing about them, but rather this is a relational knowledge. To know the Father and the Son means having a good relationship with them.

Therefore, to know eternal life, the most important questions that can be asked are: Who is the Father? Who is Jesus Christ? And how can we know them? These questions are the very essence of theology. And that's why theology is the most practical subject in the world!

---

[3] We'll look at all this in more detail later in the book.

How Can We Know God?

As we've seen, we come to know God through the gospel. That's how we know Him in terms of our experience, but let's step back a bit to see why that is. The way we know God is through His good news, because if we are to know God, He must reveal Himself. When we say God reveals Himself, we simply mean that God makes Himself known. And we need God to do the revealing: we need God to make Himself known to us. There are two reasons for that.

First, our minds are, without God, captive to sin.[4] Sin clouds our perception of things. 'The natural man does not receive the things of the Spirit of God, for they are foolishness to him; nor can he know them, because they are spiritually discerned' (*1 Cor. 2:14*), and 'the carnal mind is enmity against God' (*Rom. 8:7*).

Second, God is greater than us. Imagine you want to learn about caterpillars. Caterpillars are rather small things, so you could go out and collect lots of them. You could watch them and discover what they're like. You could even put them under a microscope to study them up close. If you want to know about caterpillars, you're big enough to discover them for yourself. Even if it was lion you wanted to learn about, a few of us could work together and safely trap and pen in a lion so we could examine it (from a safe distance). We wouldn't need the lion to reveal himself, because a few of us together are greater than the lion. In fact, by whole countries working together we can even get beyond this planet by sending astronauts to outer space to look at and examine the earth. Whether it's a lion, a caterpillar, or the earth, we can get outside it and beyond it to learn about it. But we can't do that with God! We can never get beyond God (*Acts 17:28*). We can never make ourselves greater than Him, to look down and examine Him from a safe distance. We cannot climb up to God; but He graciously comes down to us. But how?

---

[4] We'll look at that more when we consider Sin and Depravity in chapters 8 & 9.

Jesus is the Revelation of God

God has graciously come down to us in Jesus. Jesus Christ, God the Son Incarnate, is the Truth and Revelation of God. Christ Himself declared:

> I am the way, the truth, and the life. No one comes to the Father except through Me. If you had known Me, you would have known My Father also; and from now on you know Him and have seen Him … He who has seen Me has seen the Father. (*Jn 14:6-7, 9*)

Jesus, the Truth, is the only way to the Father. There is no other way to know the Father except through the Son who reveals Him. And, Jesus says, if we know Jesus, we know the Father too. Those who see Jesus, see the Father. We do not have to search somewhere beyond Jesus to find out what God is like. The Incarnate Son reveals the Father so perfectly, that to see Jesus is to see the Father. In other words, Jesus is the revelation of God.

Jesus speaks about this revelation in Luke's gospel:

> In that hour Jesus rejoiced in the Spirit and said, 'I thank You, Father, Lord of heaven and earth, that You have hidden these things from the wise and prudent and revealed them to babes. Even so, Father, for so it seemed good in Your sight. All things have been delivered to Me by My Father, and no one knows who the Son is except the Father, and who the Father is except the Son, and the one to whom the Son wills to reveal Him.' (*Lk 10:21-22; cf. Mt 11:25-30*)

Only God can know God. So the Father knows the Son perfectly, and the Son knows the Father perfectly. The only way we can know God is for one who is God to open this knowledge to us. The Father gives revelation 'to babes', but how does He do that? By delivering all things to the Son so that the Son reveals the Father perfectly to whom He will. And to whom does the Son will to reveal the Father? Not to the wise and prudent, who already have knowledge; but to 'babes', who gladly recognise their lack of knowledge and come willingly to Jesus to receive His revelation.

The apostle Paul also writes of Christ as the revelation of God. He tells the Corinthians that:

> it is the God who commanded light to shine out of darkness, who has shone in our hearts to give the light of the knowledge of the glory of God in the face of Jesus Christ. (*2 Cor. 4:6*)

This is how God wants us to know Him. This revelation in Christ is God's activity. He is shining the light of His knowledge into our hearts in Jesus. God is willingly revealing Himself and His glory in Jesus Christ. So it is 'in the face of Jesus Christ' that we human beings find 'the glory of God'. There is nowhere else where we can see God's glory, apart from the incarnate Son. Anything which claims to display the glory of God, but bypasses or ignores the incarnate, crucified and risen Son can be nothing but a counterfeit. Where there is no Jesus, there is no glory.

The writer to the Hebrews also shows us this connection between Jesus as the revelation of God and God's glory:

> [God] has in these last days spoken to us by His Son, whom He has appointed heir of all things, through whom also He made the worlds; who [is] the brightness of His glory and the express image of His person. (*Heb. 1:2-3*)

Jesus, the incarnate Son who has in these last days come into the world as the one through whom the Father speaks to reveal Himself, is the brightness of God's glory. Why is God's glory described as bright? In the Bible, the glory of the Lord is what He most essentially is, which is outgoing, radiating, life-giving love (*1 Jn 4:8-10*). God's glory is not an inward-focused idea of fame and power, but rather His outgoing love which shines forth, and is perfectly embodied, in Jesus Christ, the Incarnate Son, who goes out from the Father in love to draw us into their fellowship of love. This is the glory of the Lord.

Jesus is 'the express image' of God. He is not a different type of God from the Father. The Incarnate Son is not a God unlike the Father. No! Jesus Christ is the God who is just like the Father and who perfectly reveals the Father. If the Son is the express image of the Father, then the Father is exactly like the Son. 'The Father is seen in the Son, and the Son is seen in the Father, and the one shines in the other.'[5] We know what the Father is like, because He is just like Jesus. Therefore, our God is the Christ-like God. As Thomas Torrance put it:

> There is in fact no God behind the back of Jesus, no act of God other than the act of Jesus, no God but the God we see and meet in him. Jesus Christ is the open heart of God, the very love and life of God poured out to redeem humankind, the mighty hand and power of God stretched out to heal and

---

[5] Cyril of Alexandria, In Io. i.2 (ET 1:10).

save sinners. All things are in God's hands, but the hands of God and the hands of Jesus, in life and in death, are the same.[6]

Or, in the words of Scripture, 'He is the image of the invisible God, the firstborn over all creation' (*Col. 1:15*). The invisible God is visible in Jesus. So Jesus reveals the Father perfectly.

In the prologue to John's Gospel, the apostle emphasises this truth, that the Son is, and always has been, the revelation of the Father. 'No one has seen God at any time. The only begotten Son, who is in the bosom of the Father, He has declared Him' (*Jn 1:18*). Here we read that the only way to see God is to see Jesus, for Jesus is the revelation of God. The only way anyone has ever seen God is by seeing the Son. But what about people in the Old Testament (who lived before the incarnation of Christ)? There were certainly people who knew God in the Old Testament (for that's what salvation is – *Jn 17:3*), and there were even people who saw God. Abraham (*Gen. 18*), Jacob (*Gen. 32:30*), Moses (*Ex 33:11*), and Moses with Aaron, Nadab, Abihu and seventy of the elders of Israel (*Ex. 24:9-11*) are just a few examples from the first two books of the Old Testament of people who saw God. So how does that tie in with what Jesus and John have to say in the New Testament, that 'no one has seen God at any time', that only Jesus has revealed Him? How did they see God, if no one has seen God at any time? Jesus Himself gives us the answer: 'Your father Abraham rejoiced to see My day, and he saw it and was glad' (*Jn 8:56*). According to Jesus, Abraham saw Him. Abraham didn't just hear a promise of a far-off Messiah: he actually saw Him. So that's how Abraham saw the LORD. The LORD who came and met with Abraham under the terebinth trees at Mamre was the only begotten Son who is in the bosom of the Father and who declares Him.

And Jesus doesn't just tell us that Abraham saw him. Elsewhere in John's Gospel, Jesus says that Moses spoke of Him (*Jn 5:39-47*) and John tells us that Isaiah saw Him (*Jn 12:40-41*). How did Moses write of Jesus? Well, let's just take a few examples from the first half of Exodus. Moses wrote of how he met with the Angel of the LORD who spoke as the LORD at the burning bush (in other words, the LORD sent from the LORD).[7] And he wrote about how this LORD sent from the LORD delivered the people out of Egypt (*cf. Jude 5 ESV*). He wrote about the presence of the Angel of the LORD with the people in the pillar of cloud by day and the pillar of fire by night. He wrote of how the people saw the glory of the LORD who heard

---

[6] Thomas F. Torrance, 'The Christ Who Loves Us', *A Passion for Christ: The Vision that Ignites Ministry* (Eugene, Oregon: Wipf & Stock, 2010), 17.

[7] We'll look more at the identity of the Angel of the LORD in chapter 2.

their complaints against the LORD (*Ex 16:7*) and of the LORD who stood between him and the rock and was struck so that the people might drink of the waters of life (*Ex 17:6*). So, when Jesus says that Moses wrote of Him, He doesn't just mean that Moses included the odd Messianic prophecy – No! Moses saw Him. Moses spoke with Him. And whereas Moses didn't see the Father's face (*Ex 33:23*), He spoke with the Son 'face to face, as a man speaks to his friend' (*Ex 33:11*). 'No one has seen God at any time. The only begotten Son, who is in the bosom of the Father, He has declared Him' (*Jn 1:18*).

When did Isaiah see Jesus (*Jn 12:40-41*)? In the context John has just quoted from *Isaiah 6*, where Isaiah had seen 'the Lord sitting on a throne, high and lifted up, and the train of His robe filled the temple' (*Isa. 6:1*). Then John, after quoting *Isaiah 6:10*, John tells us, 'These things Isaiah said when he saw His glory and spoke of Him' (*Jn 12:41*). In the context, 'Him' very clearly refers to Jesus (*Jn 12:37-38*). So Lord high and lifted up whom Isaiah saw in the temple was none other than God the Son.

Just as Jesus is the revelation of God for us today, so Jesus was the revelation of God for Abraham, Moses and Isaiah. In telling us this about Abraham, Moses and Isaiah, John wasn't just taking three random figures from the Old Testament. Abraham was the father of the nation and the one with whom the LORD made His covenant. Moses was the one God used to lead the nation out of the bondage of Egypt and the one through whom God gave them the law. And Isaiah was the greatest of the writing prophets. These three men were revered and esteemed because of their great revelation of God. And yet even Abraham, Moses and Isaiah needed Jesus as revelation. The only reason they had great revelation of God was because they had Jesus.

So, by singling out Abraham, Moses and Isaiah, the Scripture shows us that, no matter who you are, no matter how great a prophet you might be, Jesus is still the only way to know the Father. There is no other way to God that bypasses Jesus. There is no other mighty revelation that will do instead of Jesus. Jesus is the revelation of God.

Let's just pause for a moment to think of some practical implications of the fact that Jesus is the revelation of God.

1.) *Jesus is the revelation of* **God**. Therefore, if you know Jesus, you really do know God. There isn't some mysterious God who hides behind Jesus. Jesus is not simply a starting-step on a journey to God Jesus is God who reveals God perfectly. To know Jesus is to know God. To see Jesus is to see the Father, for the Father is like Jesus. This means that the Christian life is a life of truly knowing our Christ-like God. It is not a life of service to, or fear of, a far-off, hidden deity. Rather, it's a life of fellowship with the One who has drawn near to us in Christ: the One who has loved us through the Cross of Christ. In the words of the great Reformer, Martin Luther:

> Let us go to the child lying in the lap of His mother Mary and to the sacrificial victim suspended on the cross; there we shall really behold God, and there we shall look into His very heart.[8]

2.) Jesus is **the** *revelation of God*. God has chosen to mediate all revelation through Jesus; therefore there is no revelation or knowledge of God apart from Jesus. Therefore all our thinking about who God is and what He is like must begin with Jesus. We can't start with some vague concept of deity and work our way from there to the Triune God. There is no other starting point for theology or for salvation. If we want to know the true and living God, we must look to Jesus and live. As Johann Gerhard put it: 'Whoever lacks a knowledge of Christ, the Son of God and our mediator, is without God – that is, he does not know the true God. (*Cf. Acts 17:30; Rom. 10:14; Gal. 4:8*.)'[9]

3.) **Jesus** *is the revelation of God*. So if we want other people to know God, we need to tell them specifically about Jesus. Mission and evangelism are all about Jesus Christ, for, unless people know Jesus, they won't know God. That means gospel preaching – the proclamation of Christ – is of vital importance. It's through proclaiming Jesus that we are a missional people.

The Trinitarian Truth

Jesus is 'the Truth' (*Jn 14:6*). So truth isn't a concept; it's a person. Yet at the start of his Gospel, John tells us that 'grace and truth came through Jesus Christ' (*Jn 1:17*). How can the truth come through Jesus if Jesus is the Truth? What is this truth that comes through Jesus? John gives us the answer in the next verse: 'No one has seen God at any time. The only begotten Son, who is in the bosom of the Father, He has declared Him' (*Jn 1:18*). The truth that

---

[8] Martin Luther, *Luther's Works*, 3:276-7.
[9] Gerhard, *Loci Theologci*, Exegesis III §6 (ET, p.269).

comes through Jesus is the knowledge of the Father. Jesus is the Truth because He makes the Father known; He is the revealing Word of the Father. In the words of one first generation Apostolic apostle and teacher, 'He is God's Word, by which God is expressing Himself to us.'[10]

However, the same apostle tells us that 'the Spirit is truth' (*1 Jn 5:6*). Jesus promised to send the Spirit of Truth (*Jn 14:17; 15:26; 16:13*) who will lead us into all truth (*Jn 16:13*). How does the Spirit lead us into the Truth? By testifying to Christ, who is the Truth (*Jn 15:26*). The Holy Spirit, who is the Spirit of Truth, is the Spirit of Jesus who leads us to Jesus, and so into all truth.

Truth, therefore, is Trinitarian. And the revelation of that truth is Trinitarian too. God the Father perfectly expresses and reveals Himself by sending out His Word in the power of His Spirit. Jesus is the Word of God (*Jn 1:1*) and the express image of the Father (*Heb. 1:3*). He who has seen Jesus, has seen the Father (*Jn 14:9*).

The Son makes Himself known by sending His Word in the power of the Spirit. What is the Word of Christ? It's Scripture (*Col. 3:16; Rom. 10:17*), and the purpose of Scripture is 'to make you wise for salvation through faith which is in Christ Jesus' (*2 Tim. 3:5*). So the purpose of the Bible is to reveal Jesus to us. And so that means, the Bible is a relational book. The Bible draws us to know Jesus who introduces us to the Father. Therefore, the main goal in reading the Bible is not learning facts or getting information. Rather, reading the Scriptures is to be a joy and delight, because through them we have fellowship with Jesus who is the source of all joy. Through the Bible we don't just get knowledge about God, but we actually know Him.[11]

The Spirit sends His Word in power to make Christ known. 'Then the word of God spread, and the number of the disciples multiplied greatly in Jerusalem, and a great many of the priests were obedient to the faith' (*Acts 6:7*). Filled with the Holy Spirit, the Church proclaims Christ biblically in her preaching and evangelism. Speaking words in the Spirit, the Church speaks the biblical Word of Christ who is the Word of the Father.[12]

---

[10] George Perfect, *Riches of Grace*, xii.1 (Sept. 1936), 176.

[11] We'll look at the doctrine of Scripture in much more detail in chapters 34 and 35.

[12] We'll look at both the threefold Word and the proclamation of the Word in chapter 35.

Creation and Revelation

Jesus is the Revelation of God. Yet the Scriptures tell us that 'the heavens declare the glory of God' (*Ps 19:1*). So how can the creation reveal God's glory? First, we must understand that the creation is not a different way that God can be known apart from Jesus. God is not known in two different ways. There is not a scientific knowledge of God that begins with our discoveries and works up to Him in addition to a faith knowledge that comes through the gospel of Jesus Christ. If that were the case, how could we be sure that they were both dealing with the same God? Yet, as we have seen already, due both to the sin which clouds our minds and God's greatness far beyond our capacities, we cannot climb up from earthly things to a knowledge of God. God is known only through His own self-revelation.

What is it that the heavens declare? They declare the glory of God. And the glory of God is found in the face of Jesus Christ (*2 Cor. 4:6*). The heavens do not declare another way of knowing God; the heavens point us to the only way of knowing God. They point us to Jesus who is the glory and revelation of God.

All creation gives glory to the Son. In the book of Revelation, the praise of the Lamb is the song of all creation. John heard 'every creature which is in heaven and on the earth and under the earth and such as are in the sea, and all that are in them' crying out in praise:

Blessing and honour and glory and power
Be to Him who sits on the throne,
And to the Lamb, forever and ever! (*Rev. 5:13*)

'What may be known of God is manifest' in the creation, 'for since the creation of the world His invisible attributes are clearly seen, being understood by the things that are made, even His eternal power and Godhead' (*Rom. 1:19-20*). Creation does not merely hint at the existence of God; creation displays whatever there is that may be known of Him. Even the invisible qualities of God, His eternal power, and His Godhead may be seen in the creation. But who is this God of which creation speaks? He is the Triune God of Scripture. (We must not swap the Triune God for simply a solitary powerful creator when we read *Romans 1*.) He is the Father who reveals Himself in His Word, the Son. This is the God of whom creation speaks, yet, dead in our sins, we do not understand what it is saying. It is our sin which blocks our ears to the true cry of salvation, declaring the glory of God in Jesus (*Rom. 1:18*). But our deafness cannot change the cry, for 'All things were created through Him and for Him' (*Col. 1:16*). All have heard the gospel Word of Christ, Paul says, for the heavens have declared Him 'to the ends of the world' (*Rom. 10:18; Ps 19:4*). As the great Athanasius said, mankind:

> could look up into the immensity of heaven, and by pondering the harmony of the creation come to know its Ruler, the Word of the Father, Whose all-ruling providence makes known the Father to all … Yet men, bowed down by the pleasures of the moment and by the frauds and illusions of the evil spirits, did not lift up their heads towards the truth.[13]

As Paul put it in Romans, although the Son of the Father is declared by the heavens, sinful humanity 'suppress the truth in unrighteousness' (*Rom. 1:18*). It is sin that keeps our heads bowed down, our eyes closed, and our ears blocked to the glory of God in Jesus Christ which the heavens declare. But those who have received God's salvation in Christ have theirs ears and eyes opened, and may lift up their heads to see how the creation glorifies the Saviour and points us to Him.

Jesus teaches us how the revelation of creation speaks of Him in John's Gospel. He speaks of seeds, telling us:

> The hour has come that the Son of Man should be glorified. Most assuredly, I say to you, unless a grain of wheat falls into the ground and dies, it remains alone; but if it dies, it produces much grain. (*Jn 12:23-24*)

This is why seeds are so important (cf. the attention given to seeds in the creation account in *Gen. 1:11-13*). Seeds were created through the Son and for the Son. They were created to work in the way they work in order to point to the death and resurrection, leading to a fruitful harvest, of God the Son incarnate. Seeds speak to us of Jesus and what He has done for us. And so seeds declare the glory of God.

The Triune God created the heavens and the earth for Jesus. He created the world as the place where He would accomplish His eternal purpose in Christ. And He created it in such a way that the whole creation would glorify Jesus and point us to Him.

---

[13] Athanasius, *On the Incarnation*, 12.

Grace and Revelation

We don't discover God; He reveals Himself to us. We don't climb up to God; He graciously descends to us. Revelation is God's work, not ours. It is by His grace, not our efforts that we come to know the Father and the Son in the Spirit. By grace, we meet Jesus in His Word and He reveals the Father to us. By grace, we meet Jesus in His Word and He brings us to know the Father. And this is eternal life – knowing the Father and Jesus Christ whom He has sent (*Jn 17:3*).

Chapter 2

The Eternal Son

At the centre of the Christian faith stands the Word who was in the beginning with God and who is God (*Jn 1:1*). This Eternal Word is the 'only begotten Son' who reveals the Father to us (*Jn 1:18*).[1] So right at the beginning of John's Gospel we read that the only begotten Son who was with the Father in the beginning is God the Word. And this is the central relationship of the Christian faith: the eternal relationship between God the Father and His Word, God the Son.

The Deity of Christ

Let's start by looking at the deity of the Son – the fact that the Son is God. As we have just seen, this is clearly stated in the opening verse of John's Gospel: 'In the beginning was the Word, and the Word was with God, and the Word was God.' This shows us both that the Son (the Word) is God and that He is distinct from the Father ('the Word was with God'). Yet this is far from the only mention we have in Scripture of the deity of the Son. So let's have a look at the wider picture the Bible presents of the Deity of Jesus Christ, God the Son.[2]

The Lamb Upon the Throne

When we think of God, we often think of Him as the mighty Creator. Naturally, when human beings think of Him, they think of His power and authority (*Rom. 1:20*). And what greater symbol of God's mighty power and authority could there be than His throne? Yet at the centre of God's throne there is the Lamb who was slain and lives (*Rev. 5:6; 7:17*). So Jesus, 'the Lamb of God who takes away the sin of the world' (*Jn 1:29*) is at the centre

---

[1] Some manuscript traditions read 'only begotten God' in *John 1:18*, yet this still shows us that He is the Son as He is begotten.

[2] Space won't allow us to look at everything the Bible has to say about the Deity of Christ, but we'll focus on a few of the major lines of biblical evidence.

of God's throne. Christ the Lamb is at the centre of God's rule, of God's authority, of God's power, of God's Kingship. And this isn't a temporary exaltation to the throne, for 'to the Son [God] says: "Your throne, O God, is forever and ever; A sceptre of righteousness is the sceptre of Your kingdom"' (*Heb. 1:8*). Jesus Christ is permanently seated on the throne of God.

And to be seated with God on His throne demonstrates that Jesus shares equally in the power and authority of God. But, if it is Jesus who reveals God, who has revealed that Jesus is at the centre of God's throne? Jesus Himself reveals it.[3] These Scriptures which speak of the Lamb at the centre of the throne come from the book of Revelation, which begins: 'the Revelation of Jesus Christ, which God gave Him to show His servants' (*Rev. 1:1*). Furthermore, it was 'the first voice which [John] heard ... like a trumpet speaking' (*Rev. 4:1*) which took him up into the throne room of heaven to see the Lamb upon the throne; and that first voice he had already described:

> I heard behind me a loud voice, as of a trumpet, saying, 'I am the Alpha and the Omega, the First and the Last' ... Then I turned to see the voice that spoke with me. And having turned I saw seven golden lampstands, and the midst of the seven lampstands One like the Son of Man ... And when I saw Him, I fell at His feet as dead. But He laid His right hand on me, saying to me, 'Do not be afraid; I am the First and the Last. I am He who lives, and was dead, and behold, I am alive forevermore. Amen.' (*Rev. 1:10-13, 17-18*).

The voice that spoke with John was Jesus, the One 'who lives, and was dead' and who is 'alive forevermore'. So Jesus took John into the throne room of heaven to see the Lamb upon the throne. It is Jesus who reveals Himself at the centre of God's throne.

In fact, this isn't the first time that Jesus reveals this. During His trial before the Sanhedrin, the high priest asked Jesus 'Are You the Christ, the Son of the Blessed?' (*Mk 14:61*) and Jesus replied 'I am. And you will see the Son of Man sitting at the right hand of the Power, and coming with the clouds of heaven' (*Mk 14:62*). The high priest's reaction wasn't good: 'Then the high priest tore his clothes and said, "What further need do we have of witnesses? You have heard the blasphemy! What do you think?" And they all condemned him to be deserving of death' (*Mk 14:63-64*). Jesus' reply about where He would sit and how He would return was enough to

---

[3] We will turn our attention to the relationship between Christ (the Eternal Word of God) and Scripture (the written word of God) in chapter 35.

infuriate the high priest and have him condemn Christ for blasphemy. So clearly, for the high priest and the Sanhedrin, the place where Jesus would sit and the way in which He would return was a very strong claim indeed.

In fact, Jesus' answer to the high priest in *Mark 14:62* is a combination of two Old Testament Scriptures, both of which speak of the reign of God. The first of these Old Testament Scriptures has to do directly with God's throne: 'The LORD said to my Lord, "Sit at My right hand"' (*Ps. 110:1*). Jesus' words to the high priest at His trial aren't the only New Testament reference to this verse. (In fact it is one of the favourite Old Testament verses of the New Testament writers.) Jesus had already spoken of this verse in *Mark 12:35-37*, asking how the Christ could be both David's son and David's Lord. Through that question Jesus was pointing out that the Messiah would be much more than a king descended from David. The Messiah would be a King much greater that David who would sit on YHWH's throne.[4] So, when Jesus answered the high priest's question by citing *Psalm 110:1*, the high priest heard clearly that Jesus was not watering down the Messianic hope, but declaring Himself to be the long-promised King greater than David who would share the throne of YHWH. In other words, Jesus was boldly proclaiming His equality with God.

The second Old Testament verse to which Jesus refers in His answer to the high priest is *Daniel 7:13*: 'behold, One like the Son of Man, coming with the clouds of heaven!' But what does Jesus mean with this reference? To the high priest and members of the Sanhedrin, who would have known well the Old Testament Scriptures, the meaning would have been clear from its Old Testament context. Daniel saw a vision of the Ancient of Days seated on His throne, surrounded by the heavenly host (*Dan. 7:9-10*).

> And behold, One like the Son of Man,
> Coming with the clouds of heaven!
> He came to the Ancient of Days,
> And they brought Him near before Him.
> Then to Him was given dominion and glory and a kingdom,
> That all peoples, nations, and languages should serve Him.
> His dominion is an everlasting dominion,
> Which shall not pass away,
> And His kingdom the one
> Which shall not be destroyed. (*Dan. 7:13-14*)

---

[4] YHWH is the name of God, usually translated 'LORD' (in small capitals) in our English Bibles (and occasionally in older translations by 'Jehovah').

The Son of Man receives 'dominion and glory and a kingdom' from the Ancient of Days. So when Jesus quotes this Scripture to the high priest concerning Himself, He is telling the high priest that He is the One who receives 'dominion and glory and a kingdom' from the Ancient of Days. And this kingdom is a universal kingdom for 'all peoples, nations and languages [will] serve Him'; and it is an everlasting kingdom 'which shall not pass away … which shall not be destroyed.' This then is not simply an image of a divine right of kings (a king receiving his kingdom from God under His authority and rule), but rather this is a sharing in God's universal and everlasting kingship. In other words, it means the same as being seated with God on His throne.

So, Jesus is telling the high priest that He is equal to God and shares equally in God's rule and reign. Jesus is particularly speaking to the high priest concerning what will happen. The New Testament epistles confirm that Jesus has indeed now sat down at the right hand of God. Paul writes that God 'raised [Christ] from the dead and seated Him at His right hand in the heavenly places, far above all principality and power and might and dominion, and every name that is named, not only in this age, but also in that which is to come' (*Eph. 1:20-21*). So Jesus is not only exalted to heaven, but exalted above everything else. He is seated in equality with God in His rule over all creation.

In Hebrews we read that Jesus has 'sat down at the right hand of the Majesty on high' (*Heb. 1:3*), that He is 'seated at the right hand of the throne of the Majesty in the heavens' (*Heb. 8:1*), and that He has 'sat down at the right hand of the throne of God' (*Heb. 12:2*). Although we could read these statements as if Jesus sat down to the right hand side of God's throne, the description of the throne room of heaven which the book of Hebrews gives us makes it clear that there is only one throne. The heavenly throne room is described in terms of the Holy of Holies, and so the only place to sit is on the one throne of God (which in the earthly Holy of Holies was represented by the Ark of the Covenant).

So, the throne on which Christ sits is God's own throne. It is called 'the throne of God and of the Lamb' in *Revelation 22:1* and again in *22:3*. So in these verses it isn't simply a matter of Jesus sitting on God's throne, but rather the throne belongs to God and to the Lamb equally. The Father's throne is the Son's throne and the Son's throne is the Father's throne. They are so united that *Revelation 22:3* can continue by saying 'and His servants shall serve Him', referring to both God and the Lamb with the single singular pronoun 'Him'. The word 'serve' here means religious service or worship, and so that means that God and the Lamb are seated upon the throne in equality, receiving equal worship.

All Hail the Lamb

In fact, that isn't the first time that John records the worship of the Lamb upon the throne. When John was taken to the heavenly throne room, he saw the worship of the heavenly host around the throne:

> Worthy is the Lamb who was slain
> To receive power and riches and wisdom,
> And strength and honour and glory and blessing! (*Rev. 5:12*)
>
> Blessing and honour and glory and power
> Be to Him who sits on the throne,
> And to the Lamb, forever and ever! (*Rev. 5:13*)

The heavenly hosts worship both God and the Lamb. Yet later, John falls down to worship before the feet of an angel, but the angel stops him, saying: 'See that you do not do that! I am your fellow servant, and of your brethren who have the testimony of Jesus. Worship God! For the testimony of Jesus is the spirit of prophecy' (*Rev. 19:10*; see also *Rev. 22:9*). The angel will not accept worship, because God alone is worthy to be worshipped and adored. Yet the heavenly host gladly worship the Lamb seated on the throne.

And this is not the only Scriptural example of the worship of Jesus. During His earthly ministry, Jesus' disciples at times worshipped Him.[5] A clear example can be seen when Jesus walked on the water. After He got into the boat we read, 'Then those who were in the boat came and worshipped Him, saying, "Truly You are the Son of God"' (*Mt 14:33*). Unlike the angel who later appeared to John, Jesus does not refuse His disciples' worship.

At the end of Matthew's Gospel we see another clear instance of the disciples worshipping Jesus. The occasion is when the disciples see the risen Christ, just before He gives them the Great Commission. 'When they saw Him, they worshipped Him; but some doubted' (Matthew 28:17). Here they encounter the Lamb who was slain and lives and bow before Him in worship. And, rather than rebuking them for an inappropriate act, Jesus

---

[5] The Greek word for worship is used many times with Jesus as its object in the gospels (particularly in Matthew's gospel). However, the word can either refer to bowing down to show respect or bowing down in worship. The meaning must be determined by the context.

confirms that they doing the right thing, declaring 'All authority has been given to Me in heaven and on earth' (*Mt 28:18*).[6]

And as the disciples on that mountain worship the Lamb that was slain and lives, they join with the heavenly host worshipping around the throne. In fact, not only do the angels of heaven worship the Lamb, but God actually commands them to worship the Lamb. 'But when He again brings the firstborn into the world, He says: "Let all the angels of God worship Him"' (*Heb. 1:6*). This worship of Jesus must be right, for God Himself has commanded it.

The Bible makes very clear that only God is to be worshipped. The first and second of the Ten Commandments state:

> I am the LORD your God, who brought you out of the land of Egypt, out of the house of bondage. You shall have no other gods before Me. You shall not make for yourself a carved image—any likeness of anything that is in heaven above, or that is in the earth beneath, or that is in the water under the earth; you shall not bow down to them nor serve them. For I, the LORD your God, am a jealous God. (*Ex 20:2-5*).

Jesus Himself said 'You shall worship the LORD your God, and Him only you shall serve' (*Mt 4:10*, quoting *Deut. 6:13*).

Throughout the Old Testament, God's holy jealousy is seen, as He is depicted as a jealous husband while Israel, His unfaithful wife, plays the harlot with foreign gods (*e.g. Judges 2:16-17; 8:27, 33; Hos. 1-3; Ezek. 16; Ezek. 23*). Worship of anyone other than the true and living God is spiritual adultery.

Yet, the heavenly host openly worship Jesus the Lamb before the throne of God. Unlike the worship of anyone else, the worship of Jesus is not spiritual adultery. In fact, God welcomes and invites the worship of Jesus in His very own heavenly throne room. And so the worship of Jesus does not contravene the Ten Commandments. Quite the opposite! Jesus is 'the LORD [their] God who brought them up out of the land of Egypt.'[7] In fact, it is through the worship of Christ the Lamb that we can worship God seated on the throne. As Jesus said, 'No one comes to the Father except through Me' (*Jn 14:6*).

---

[6] The words 'but some doubted' likely refer not to doubting the resurrection (for on other occasions Jesus alleviates such doubts by demonstrating the reality of His risen body; cf. *Lk 24:36-43; Jn 20:20, 24-29*), but rather to doubting whether such worship was appropriate.

[7] cf. *Jude 5* in ESV and NA[28]. The same can be seen from a study of the book of Exodus; it is the Angel of the LORD who speaks as the LORD (the LORD sent from the LORD) who leads them up out of Egypt.

The same Scriptures which affirm that only God is to be worshipped also ascribe all glory and honour to Jesus Christ (*e.g. Heb. 13:20-21; 1 Pet. 4:11; 2 Pet. 3:18; Rev. 1:5-6; 5:12-13*) and that this worship of Jesus is God's desire and brings God great glory.

> Therefore God also has highly exalted Him and given Him the name which is above every name, that at the name of Jesus every knee should bow, of those in heaven, and of those on earth, and of those under the earth, and that every tongue should confess that Jesus Christ is Lord, to the glory of God the Father. (*Phil. 2:9-11*)

The true and living God alone is to be worshipped (and no one else), yet Jesus is worshipped according to God's desire and to God's glory. So Jesus is equal to God in glory, honour and worship.

The LORD is salvation

The heavenly host in John's vision proclaimed the wondrous deeds of Christ as they worshipped Him.

> You are worthy to take the scroll,
> And to open its seals;
> For You were slain,
> And have redeemed us to God by Your blood
> Out of every tribe and tongue and people and nation,
> And have made us kings and priests to our God;
> And we shall reign on the earth. (*Rev. 5:9-10*)

Jesus is the One who redeems and reconciles. He is the One who makes His people kings and priests to God. In other words, Jesus is the One who saves. Yet throughout the Scriptures the clear refrain is that 'salvation belongs to the LORD' (*Ps 3:8; cf. e.g. Rev. 7:10; 1 Chron. 16:23; 2 Chron. 6:41; Ps 18:2, 46; Ps 68:20*). More than that, His salvation is how He reveals Himself to be LORD (YHWH/Jehovah). He reveals His name 'the LORD' to Moses at the Burning Bush in the context of His coming to save His people from the bondage of Egypt (*Ex 3:14-16*). The LORD tells Moses that He had not given the full revelation of this name ('the LORD') to Abraham, Isaac and Jacob (*Ex 6:3*). Yet Abraham 'called on the name of the LORD' (*Gen. 13:4*), spoke to the king of Sodom of 'the LORD, God Most High' (*Gen. 14:22*), and addressed God in prayer as 'LORD God' (*Gen. 15:2*). What then does the LORD mean when He says to Moses, 'by My name LORD I was not known to them' (*Ex 6:3*)?

Clearly the word 'LORD' was known and was known to be God's name. Yet, for the Hebrews a name was much more than a label. Abraham may have known the name as a label or form of address for God, but what he did not know was the significance of the name. As Calvin puts it, 'Nor does God by "His name" in this passage mean syllables or letters, but the knowledge of His glory and majesty, which shone out more fully and more brightly in the redemption … than in the commencement of the covenant.'[8] The new significance that Moses and his generation learnt of the name 'LORD' was in the great work of redemption which the LORD would work for them 'with an outstretched arm and with great judgments' (*Ex 6:6*). It was the reality they would sing on the other side of the Red Sea, that 'the LORD is my strength and song, and He has become my salvation' (*Ex 15:2*). The LORD is salvation and salvation is of the LORD.

When we come to the throne room of heaven in Revelation, we find the heavenly host worshipping Jesus as Saviour. And this doesn't come as a surprise, for by that stage we have seen the salvation of Jesus Christ. The entire Old Testament points toward Christ and His saving work and prepares the way for us to understand it when He comes. The four gospels show us the eternal Son of God who willingly takes on our humanity and lives a human life in the human world for us and our salvation. We see His perfect obedience in life and death, His mighty victory at the Cross as He sheds His blood for our redemption, and His glorification as He rises, ascends and makes intercession for us. And as we see all this, we too cry out in worship with the heavenly host, 'Worthy is the Lamb!'

Christ's finished work for us and our salvation displays His identity as the God who saves. Even His name declares the truth of who He is: Jesus means 'the LORD is salvation'. During His earthly ministry, Samaritans recognised Him as 'the Saviour of the world' (*Jn 4:42*). In the Acts, Christ was preached as Saviour (*Acts 5:31; 13:23*). Paul calls Him 'the Saviour, the Lord Jesus Christ' (*Phil. 3:20*; see also *Eph. 5:23; 2 Tim. 1:10; Titus 1:4; 2:13; 3:6*). Peter and John both join Paul in explicitly calling Christ 'Saviour' (*2 Pet. 1:1; 1:11; 2:20; 3:2; 3:18; 1 Jn 4:14*). And not only is He called the Saviour, but He is also called salvation. When Mary and Joseph took Jesus to present Him in the temple, Simeon declared to God, 'my eyes have seen your salvation' (*Lk 2:30*). What Simeon's eyes had seen was the baby Jesus himself, but the revelation Simeon received was that seemingly helpless child was in fact Himself God's long promised salvation. Jesus is salvation and salvation is of Jesus. The LORD is salvation and salvation is of the LORD.

---

[8] John Calvin, *Commentaries on the Last Four Books of Moses*, 1:127-128.

Once again the book of Exodus will lead us forward, for there these last two sentences are reconciled in full. When Moses encounters the burning bush where the LORD calls him and reveals His name, it is 'the Angel of the LORD [who] appeared to him from the midst of the bush' and speaks with him (*Ex 3:2*). And yet, this Angel of the Lord speaks to Moses as the Lord: 'I am the God of your father … I AM WHO I AM' (*Ex 3.6, 14*). The Angel of the LORD reveals the LORD and the Angel of the LORD is the LORD.[9]

And more than that, the Angel of the LORD brings the salvation of the LORD. The Angel of the Lord says, 'I have surely seen the oppression of my people … So I have come down to deliver them … I will certainly be with you' (*Ex 3:7-8, 12*). And this promise of the Angel to go with them is fulfilled as the Angel of the LORD leads them out of Egypt in the pillar of cloud by day and pillar of fire by night (*Ex 14:19; Num. 20:16; Judges 2:1*) and would ultimately lead them into the promised land (*Ex 23:20,23; 32:34; 33:2; Judges 2:1*).

So in Exodus, the salvation of the LORD is brought by the Angel of the LORD: the Angel who reveals the LORD and who is the LORD. Who is this Angel? He is the LORD sent from the LORD to reveal the LORD and to redeem as LORD. He is God sent from God, God who reveals God, and God who is salvation.[10] Jude identifies this saving LORD sent from the LORD even more precisely as 'Jesus, who saved a people out of the land of Egypt' (*Jude 5*, ESV).

So, right back in Exodus in the Old Testament's great act of redemption, we see how it is true both to say the LORD is salvation and Jesus is salvation, for Jesus is the LORD sent from the LORD who reveals the LORD and saves His people. Jesus is salvation, for Jesus is the LORD.

Jesus Christ is Lord: The Son and the Names of God

Jesus is the LORD. So Jesus bears the covenant name of God. Yet God does not share His name and His glory with those who aren't God: 'I am the LORD, that is My name; and My glory I will not give to another'

---

[9] The Angel is even simply referred to as 'the LORD' several times (*Exodus 3:4, 7; 4:2, 4, 6, 10, 11, 14*) and as 'God' (*Exodus 3:4, 11, 13, 14, 15*). We'll return to the Angel of the LORD later in the chapter.

[10] *Exodus 23:20-21* makes it very clear that this is not a created angel like all other angels, but rather God Himself, for God's 'name is in Him'. Thus the Angel of the Lord shares the name of the Lord, and so shares His glory: He is God.

(*Isa. 42:8*). Being called 'LORD' isn't a mark of honour given to Jesus; no, He is called LORD because he *is* the LORD.

And it is not only in the Old Testament that we see Jesus' identity as the Lord. At the beginning of each of the four gospels we read of John the Baptist's ministry preparing 'the way of the LORD' (*Mt 3:3; Mk 1:3; Lk 3:4; Jn 1:23*). Each of the gospels is citing the prophecy of *Isaiah 40:3* and attributing to Jesus the covenant name of the LORD.

After Christ's ascension, the early disciples weren't slow to call upon Him as Lord.[11] Even before Jesus poured out the Holy Spirit upon them on the day of Pentecost, they had begun to address Him in prayer as Lord (*Acts 1:24*; see also Stephen's prayer in *Acts 7:59-60* for prayer addressed to Jesus as Lord). When Jesus appears to Saul on the Damascus road, it is 'the Lord' who speaks to him: 'Then the Lord said, 'I am Jesus, whom you are persecuting' (*Acts 9:5*). And already by that time the disciples were speaking of Christ as 'the Lord Jesus' (*Acts 9:17*).

Paul frequently wrote of Jesus as Lord.[12] In *Romans 10:13* Paul cites *Joel 2:32*, 'whoever calls on the name of the LORD shall be saved.' The LORD Paul is referring to in the context is the Lord Jesus: in *verse 9* he writes of salvation for those who 'confess with your mouth the Lord Jesus and believe in your heart that God has raised Him from the dead'.

This calling on the name of the LORD is applied to Jesus again in *1 Corinthians 1:2*: the saved are those 'who in every place call on the name of Jesus Christ our Lord'. Paul appropriates a few other important Old Testament truths about the LORD in the same passage and applies them to Jesus: 'the day of the Lord' (e.g. *Joel 1:15*) becomes 'the day of our Lord Jesus Christ' (*1 Cor. 1:8*) and 'the name of our Lord Jesus Christ' takes on the role of the name of YHWH (*1 Cor. 1:10*). At the end of *1 Corinthians 1* Paul quotes from *Jeremiah 9:23-24*, 'He who glories, let him glory in the LORD' (*1 Cor. 1:31*), and again Paul applies this Old Testament Scripture about YHWH to the Lord Jesus; we glory in the LORD because 'Christ Jesus … became for us wisdom from God – and righteousness and sanctification and redemption' (*1 Cor. 1:30*), and Paul glories in the LORD by preaching, not 'with excellence of speech', but by proclaiming 'Christ and Him crucified' (*1 Cor. 2:1-2*). 1

---

[11] Up until now our references to Lord have been either from the Old Testament or New Testament quotations of the Old Testament, and hence 'LORD' in small capitals, signifying that the Hebrew word used is YHWH. In the Greek of the New Testament, however the same word is used for both YHWH and lord, so we use 'Lord' without the small capitals. Not every use of 'Lord' in the New Testament is equivalent to YHWH; the context must determine the meaning.

[12] We will only refer to a few of these passages where Paul calls Jesus 'Lord'.

Corinthians 2 closes by equating 'the mind of the LORD' (*Isa. 40:13*) with 'the mind of Christ' (*1 Cor. 2:16*).

One final example taken from Paul's letters is to be found in *Philippians 2:9-11*. The culmination of this Scripture is that 'every tongue should confess that Jesus Christ is Lord, to the glory of God the Father' (*Phil. 2:11*). Although the word 'Lord' here isn't a quotation from an Old Testament passage about YHWH, it is clear that Lord here means YHWH. Every knee is to bow and every tongue to confess at this name. Not only does this combination point to the absolute Lordship of Christ, but is actually a reference to an Old Testament Scripture where YHWH declares that 'there is no other God besides me ... for I am God and there is no other' (*Isa. 45:21-23*). According to Isaiah, 'every knee shall bow, every tongue shall take an oath' before YHWH. Paul says exactly the same thing about the name of Jesus.

Philippians 2:9-11 also tells us that Christ has 'the name which is above every name'. Given the biblical context, that can be none other than the name YHWH, the LORD. Together with the allusions to *Isaiah 45:21-23*, this confirms that the confession here is that Jesus Christ is YHWH.

Paul is not alone among the epistle writers in calling Jesus the LORD. Peter also applies Old Testament Scriptures about YHWH to Jesus. In *1 Peter 2:3* he writes, 'if indeed you have tasted that the Lord is gracious', alluding to *Psalm 34:8*, 'Oh, taste and see that the LORD is good'. The following verse makes clear that Peter is talking about the Lord Jesus, 'a living stone rejected by men, but chosen by God and precious' (*1 Pet. 2:4*).

So the New Testament writers unashamedly apply the covenant name of the LORD to Jesus. But this is nothing new, for the Old Testament writers had already done the same thing.[13] It was the early Christians' knowledge of the Old Testament Scriptures which allowed them so readily to confess Jesus Christ as LORD.

And not only do the New Testament writers apply the covenant name of the LORD to Jesus, but they also simply call Him God. John opens His gospel with the proclamation that 'the Word was with God, and the Word was God' (*Jn 1:1*) and closes it with Thomas' confession before the risen Saviour, 'My Lord and my God!' (*Jn 20:28*).[14] The blood of Jesus, which He shed for His church, is called God's own blood (*Acts 20:28*). The Father

[13] Note our discussion of the Angel of the LORD who is the LORD, above. See also *Genesis 19:24; Exodus 33:7-11, cf. 20-23; Exodus 34:9; Isaiah 48:12-16*.

[14] There is another chapter of John's gospel after Thomas' exclamation, but this is certainly the climax.

Himself addresses the Son as 'God' in *Hebrews 1:8* (quoting from *Ps 45:6*). According to the New Testament, Jesus Christ is 'our God and Saviour' (*Titus 2:13; 2 Pet. 1:1*).

At the beginning of John's vision, Jesus announced Himself as 'the Alpha and the Omega, the First and the Last' (*Rev. 1:10*). Yet, 'the First and the Last' is the name of the King and Redeemer of Israel, the God beside whom there is no other God (*Isa. 44:6*).

Through His exalted position on God's Throne, the worship and honour He receives, the salvation He gives, and the names and titles He shares with the Father, the New Testament is very clear that Jesus Christ is true God of true God. The Son is God.

The Deity of the Son in the Old Testament

So far we've mostly concentrated on the Scriptures which speak of the Incarnate Christ in the New Testament. However, God the Son did not begin to be with the incarnation. For, right from the beginning, 'the Word was with God, and the Word was God' (*Jn 1:1*). And so the deity of Christ is not a new teaching of the New Testament, but rather a doctrine proclaimed in all the Scriptures. Thus the Old Testament, in its own right, teaches the deity of the Son.

The Angel of the LORD

One of the chief ways we see God the Son in the Old Testament is as the Angel of the LORD, of whom we've briefly made mention above. The Hebrew word for 'angel' literally means 'messenger' or 'sent one', so it isn't limited to the spiritual beings we call angels in English. Therefore *the Angel of the LORD* means *the Messenger of the LORD* or *the Sent One from the LORD*. So, the word 'Angel' doesn't mean that this is a created being.

Rather, the Scriptures point in another direction entirely. This Angel is not only sent from the LORD, but is called the LORD. At the first appearance of the Angel of the LORD, Hagar calls Him 'You-Are-the-God-Who-Sees'. But the Scripture does not say that she gave this divine name to the Angel who spoke to her, but to 'the LORD who spoke to her' (*Gen. 16:13*). Hagar recognised that this was not merely an angel, but rather the Angel who is the LORD Himself, the Messenger of LORD who is the LORD, the Lord sent from the LORD.

The Angel of the LORD shares the Honours of God

The Angel of the LORD (*Ex 3:2*), who is God and the LORD (*Ex 3:4*) appeared to Moses in the burning bush. And when Moses drew near, the Angel told him to 'take [his] sandals off [his] feet, for the place where [he was standing was] holy ground' (*Ex. 3:5*). So Moses was to draw near to the Angel of the LORD in the burning bush in adoration and worship.

When the Angel of the LORD appeared to Gideon, Gideon brought an offering and set it before Him, and the Angel of the LORD accepted the offering, proving to Gideon that He was indeed the LORD (*Jdgs 6:18-24*). When Manoah worshipped the LORD in the presence of the Angel of the LORD, the Angel accepted His worship, ascending in the flame just as He had done with Gideon, and then Manoah realised that He had seen God (*Jdgs 13:15-23*).

Although the title 'the Angel of the LORD' is not used in the book of Joshua, someone who matches the description of this Angel does appear. Joshua encountered the 'Commander of the army of the LORD' who came to him as a Sent One from the LORD and as His Messenger (*Josh. 5:13-15*). Just as when Moses encountered the Angel of the LORD at the burning bush, the Commander told him to take off his sandals 'for the place where you stand is holy' (*Josh. 5:15*), and when Joshua saw the Commander, he 'fell on his face to the earth and worshiped' (*Josh. 5:14*).

So, in the Old Testament we see that there is One who is sent from God as His Messenger, called the Angel of the LORD and the Commander of the LORD's army, who is worshipped as God, and who (unlike created angels) willingly receives worship as God.

The Angel of the LORD shares the Attributes of God

From the removal of the sandals from the feet of Moses and Joshua we can see that the Angel of the LORD is holy (*Ex 3:5; Josh. 5:15*). And the Angel also displays the omniscience of God in His words to Moses, saying, 'I have surely seen the oppression of My people who are in Egypt, and have heard their cry because of their taskmasters, for I know their sorrows' (*Ex 3:7*).

We can also see His divine knowledge in His encounter with Hagar. He knows who Hagar is, where she is, and where she has come from (*Gen. 16:7-8*). He knows that she is pregnant, and that the child in her womb is a son (*Gen. 16:11*). Hagar responds to the Angel's divine knowledge by calling 'the name of the LORD who spoke to her, You-Are-the-God-Who-Sees' (*Gen. 16:13*) in recognition of the fact that she had seen the one who 'sees' her. To Hagar, the Angel also revealed Himself as the source of life, for He told her, 'I will multiply your descendants exceedingly, so that they shall not be counted for multitude' (*Gen. 16:10*).

The Angel of the LORD shares the Names of God

As we've seen, Hagar calls the Angel of the LORD 'God', while Moses, narrating the incident calls Him 'LORD' (*Gen. 16:13*). The Angel calls Himself 'the LORD' when speaking to Abraham after providing the ram to be sacrificed instead of Isaac on Moriah (*Gen. 22:16*) and 'God' when talking to Jacob, both in his dream, and after wrestling with him (*Gen. 31:11-13; 32:28*). Even though the title 'Angel of the LORD' isn't used at that encounter in *Genesis 32*, we know it is the Angel, because Hosea tells us so:

> [Jacob] struggled with God.
> Yes, he struggled with the Angel and prevailed;
> He wept, and sought favour from Him.
> He found Him in Bethel,
> And there He spoke to us—
> That is, the LORD God of hosts.
> The LORD is His memorable name. (*Hos. 12:2-5*)

There Hosea tells us that this Angel with whom Jacob wrestled is the LORD God of Hosts Himself.

Later, at the end of his life, Jacob would bless his grandsons. And the blessing he gave them was the blessing of the God of Abraham, Isaac and Jacob. So who is the God of Abraham, Isaac and Jacob? According to Jacob, it's the Angel of the LORD. Jacob prayed:

> God, before whom my fathers Abraham and Isaac walked,
> The God who has fed me all my life long to this day,
> The Angel who has redeemed me from all evil,
> Bless the lads. (*Gen. 48:15-16*)

Here Jacob 'confidently and self-consciously confess[es] the divinity of the God who is sent by God.'[15] The God who redeemed Jacob, the Saving God of Abraham, Isaac and Jacob, is the Angel of the LORD.

In the exodus from Egypt, the Angel of the LORD led the children of Israel in a pillar of cloud by day and a pillar of fire by night, and yet it was the LORD Himself who 'went before them by day in a pillar of cloud to lead the way, and by night in a pillar of fire to give them light, so as to go by day and night' (*Ex 13:21; cf. Ex 14:19; Jdgs 2:1-4*). In the New Testament we are told another name for this Angel of the LORD who is the LORD who delivered Israel from Egypt: Jude tells us that it was 'Jesus, who saved a people out of the land of Egypt' (*Jude 5 ESV*).[16]

After the exodus, the LORD speaks to Moses about the Angel of the LORD:

> Behold, I send an Angel before you to keep you in the way and to bring you into the place which I have prepared. Beware of Him and obey His voice; do not provoke Him, for He will not pardon your transgressions; for My name is in Him. But if you indeed obey His voice and do all that I speak, then I will be an enemy to your enemies and an adversary to your adversaries. For My Angel will go before you and bring you in to the Amorites and the Hittites and the Perizzites and the Canaanites and the Hivites and the Jebusites; and I will cut them off. (*Ex 23:20-23*)

Not only is the Angel occasionally called by the name of the LORD, but the name of the LORD is in Him. 'One cannot separate the name YHWH from the reality of YHWH; thus, he is also YHWH [as] is also shown in the fact that this angel has the power to absolve and retain sin as well as the ability to speak as YHWH.'[17] The One who is sent from God possesses the very name of God Himself, and in keeping with that name, His voice is to be obeyed, it is His prerogative to forgive or retain sin, and He is the one by whom the Lord will act to cut off the enemies of His people, and to bring

---

[15] Paul Blackham, 'The Trinity in the Hebrew Scriptures', in Paul Louis Metzger, ed., *Trinitarian Soundings in Systematic Theology* (London: T&T Clark, 2005), 42.

[16] Although manuscript tradition underlying the *New King James Version* reads 'Lord' rather than 'Jesus', the preceding verse still makes it very clear that this Lord is indeed Jesus: 'For certain men have crept in unnoticed, who long ago were marked out for this condemnation, ungodly men, who turn the grace of our God into lewdness and deny the only Lord God and our Lord Jesus Christ. But I want to remind you, though you once knew this, that the Lord, having saved the people out of the land of Egypt, afterward destroyed those who did not believe.' (*Jude 4-5*).

[17] Charles A Gieschen, 'The Real Presence of the Son Before Christ: Revisiting an Old Approach to Old Testament Christology', *Concordia Theological Quarterly*, 68.2 (2004), 116.

them into their promised inheritance. The Angel of the LORD is the LORD whose voice is the voice of the LORD and who fulfils all the promises of the LORD.

At the other end of the Old Testament, Malachi tells us of this divine Angel:

> Behold, I send My messenger,
> And he will prepare the way before Me.
> And the Lord, whom you seek,
> Will suddenly come to His temple,
> Even the Messenger of the covenant,
> In whom you delight.
> Behold, He is coming,
> Says the Lord of hosts. (*Mal. 3:1*)

Although our English translation doesn't use the word 'Angel', it is the same Hebrew word which is translated 'Messenger' here. So the Angel of the LORD is the Messenger of the Covenant, but even more significantly, He is the Lord whom we seek. This time it's not LORD (*YHWH/Jehovah*), but Lord (*Adonai*). Yet, although the word Lord (*Adonai*) can be used of both God and human beings, here it clearly does refer to God, for this Lord, who is the Angel of the Covenant, 'will suddenly come to His temple.' And this Lord, who is the Angel of the Covenant, is very clearly the Lord Jesus. For the first 'messenger' in *Malachi 3:1*, the one who prepares the way for the Lord, is John the Baptist (*cf. Mt 11:10; Mk 1:2; Lk 1:76; 7:27*) who prepared the way for Christ the Lord.

The Angel of the LORD shares in the Deeds of God

The Angel of the LORD does things that only God can do. In Deborah's song of victory, she sings of how the Angel of the LORD pronounces the curse of God's judgment (*Jdgs 5:23*). And when the LORD promised Hezekiah, through the prophet Isaiah, that He would 'defend this city, to save, for [His] own sake' (*2 Kgs 19:34*), He sent the Angel of the LORD to carry out His judgment against Sennacherib's army (*2 Kgs 19:25*).

But, not only does the Angel of the LORD carry out God's judgment; He also brings God's salvation. Jacob worshipped the Angel of the LORD as the one who 'redeemed [him] from all evil' (*Gen. 48:15-16*). The Angel of the LORD is also the one who forgives sin (*Ex. 23:31*). In judgment, redemption and the forgiveness of sins, the Angel does the things that only God can do.

The Angel of the LORD is the LORD, yet distinguished from the LORD

Although the Angel of the LORD is identified as the LORD Himself, both by name and by the demonstration of His deity in His honours, attributes, and deeds,[18] He is also distinguished from the LORD. We've seen this, for example, in *Exodus 23:20-23* where the LORD speaks about the Angel of the LORD. When David sinned by taking a census of Israel, the LORD sent judgment in the form of a plague through the Angel of the Lord:

> And when the angel stretched out His hand over Jerusalem to destroy it, the LORD relented from the destruction, and said to the angel who was destroying the people, 'It is enough; now restrain your hand.' And the angel of the LORD was by the threshing floor of Araunah the Jebusite. Then David spoke to the LORD when he saw the angel who was striking the people, and said, 'Surely I have sinned, and I have done wickedly; but these sheep, what have they done? Let Your hand, I pray, be against me and against my father's house.' (*2 Sam. 24:16-17*)

Here the LORD speaks to the Angel of the LORD as a distinct person. In Zechariah we see the distinction the other way round, in that the Angel of the LORD speaks to the LORD:

> Then the Angel of the LORD answered and said, 'O LORD of hosts, how long will You not have mercy on Jerusalem and on the cities of Judah, against which You were angry these seventy years?' (*Zech. 1.12*)

At times the Angel can be called the LORD, and yet at times He can be distinguished from another distinct person called the LORD. We'll look at this phenomenon again below, as it can be seen elsewhere in the Old Testament, beyond the Angel of the LORD passages.

---

[18] We've used those particular words as headings to help you remember the evidence for the deity of the Angel of the LORD using the acronym HAND: *Honours, Attributes, Names, Deeds.* Arranging the evidence for the deity of Christ into these four categories is traditional, dating at least back to the Reformation, but the acronym for ease of remembering comes from Robert M. Bowman and J. Ed Komoszewski, *Putting Jesus in His Place: The Case for the Deity of Christ* (Grand Rapids: Kregel, 2007). We'll use the acronym again when we think about the deity of the Holy Spirit in chapter 4.

The Angel of the LORD is God the Son

The Angel of the LORD is the LORD, yet He is a distinct person from the LORD. So who is the Angel of the LORD? The New Testament identifies Him for us. Jude, the brother of Jesus, identifies the Angel of the LORD who saved a people out of Egypt as Jesus (*Jude 5*). Just as in *Exodus 23:21*, He is the one who did not pardon the transgressions of those who did not believe, but 'afterward destroyed' them (*Jude 5*). Likewise, Paul writes that the Israelites tested 'Christ' in the wilderness (*1 Cor. 10:9-10*). Who was it that the Israelites provoked in the wilderness? It was the Angel of the LORD (*Ex 23:20-21*).[19]

Yet, the identification of the Angel of the LORD with God the Son does not only rely on a few explicit statements in the New Testament. It is the Son who is the visible 'image of the invisible God' (*Col. 1:15*). When Gideon (*Jdgs 6:22-23*) and Manoah (*Jdgs 13:22*) see the Angel of the LORD, they are afraid they will die, for they know that no one can see the invisible God and live. Yet the LORD comforts Gideon and tells him he won't die, and the LORD accepts Manoah's offering, which gives Manoah's wife grounds to assure her husband that they won't die. No one can see the invisible God and live, yet they have seen the God who can be seen: the image of the invisible God. And it is always the Word and Son of the Father who is His visible image and who reveals Him, for 'no one has seen God at any time. The only begotten Son, who is in the bosom of the Father, He has declared Him' (*Jn 1:18*).

Even the title 'the Angel of the LORD' is significant in pointing us to His identity as God the Son, for it means 'the Sent One from God' (*cf. Jn 3:34; 6:29; 8:42; 10:36; 17:3*) and so 'it refers to a divine Person who sends the One who bears the title. It is a title that contains within itself the Father and the Son.'[20]

So, the New Testament tells us of specific deeds of the Angel of the LORD that they were the deeds of Christ. Those who saw the Angel of the LORD in the Old Testament saw the God sent from God in whom the invisible God is visible. It has always been the Son who has revealed God.

---

[19] Paul goes on to identify Jesus as the Lord who sent the serpents and had Moses set up the bronze serpent for the healing of the Israelites (*Num. 21:4-9*). NB Jude and Paul have no qualms about referring to the pre-incarnate Son as 'Jesus' or 'Christ'.

[20] Paul Blackham, 'The Trinity in the Hebrew Scriptures', *Trinitarian Soundings in Systematic Theology*, 41.

And even the very title 'the Sent One from God' matches what Jesus says about Himself. There can be no doubt that the Angel of the LORD, who is the LORD distinct from the LORD is God the Son who reveals the Father. And this is no novel reading of the Old Testament; this is what the Christian church has confessed from its earliest days.

Some Testimonies from Church History on the Identity of the Angel of the LORD

Although the historic Christian reading, from the earliest days of the history of the church, has been that the Angel of the LORD is God the Son, in recent years this understanding of the Scriptures has been widely attacked.[21] Therefore, in addition to the biblical case we have just seen, let's have a look at a few testimonies from the history of the church, to remind us that this is no novel idea.

Justin Martyr looks back to the Exodus and sees the Angel of the Lord who spoke to Moses in the burning bush as the one who became incarnate of the Virgin:

> Of old He appeared in the shape of fire and in the likeness of an angel to Moses and to the other prophets; but now in the times of your reign, having, as we before said, become Man by a virgin, according to the counsel of the Father, for the salvation of those who believe in Him.[22]

Gregory of Nyssa, and His brother Basil of Caesarea both understood the burning bush in the same way:

> For we too say plainly, that the prophet, wishing to make manifest to men the mystery concerning Christ, called the Self-Existent Angel, that the meaning of the words might not be referred to the Father, as it would have been if the title of Existent alone had been found throughout the discourse ... even so we affirm that the true Word that was in the beginning, when He announces the will of His own Father, is styled Angel (or Messenger), a title given to Him on account of the operation of conveying the message. And as the sublime John, having previously called Him Word, so introduces the further truth that the Word was God, that our thoughts might not at once turn to the Father, as they would have done if the title of God had been put first, so too does the mighty Moses, after first calling Him Angel, teach us in the words that follow that He is none other than the Self-Existent Himself, that the mystery concerning the

---

[21] The rejection of the teaching that the Angel of the LORD is God the Son is not an altogether new development, and can be traced back at least as far as Augustine.

[22] Justin Martyr, *First Apology*, lxiii.

Christ might be foreshown, by the Scripture assuring us by the name Angel, that the Word is the interpreter of the Father's will, and, by the title of the Self-Existent, of the closeness of relation subsisting between the Son and the Father ... Accordingly, He Who through Himself reveals the goodness of the Father is called Angel and Word, Seal and Image, and all similar titles with the same intention. For as the Angel (or Messenger) gives information from some one, even so the Word reveals the thought within, the Seal shows by Its own stamp the original mould, and the Image by Itself interprets the beauty of that whereof It is the image, so that in their signification all these terms are equivalent to one another.[23]

It is clear to all, that wherever the same person is called both angel and God, it is the Only-Begotten who is declared, who manifests Himself to human beings from generation to generation and announces the will of the Father to His saints. Thus He who to Moses gave Himself the name 'He who is,' is to be thought of as none other than God the Logos, who in the beginning is with God.[24]

At the Reformation, Martin Luther taught this presence of the Son in the Old Testament:

Thus it follows powerfully and irrefutably that the God who led the people of Israel out of Egypt and through the Red Sea, who guided them in the wilderness through the pillars of cloud and fire, who nourished them with heavenly bread, and who performed all the miracles Moses describes in his book, who also brought them into the land of Canaan and then gave them kings and priests and everything, is therefore God and none other than Jesus of Nazareth, the Son of the Virgin Mary, whom we call Christ our God and Lord ... And, again, it is he who gave Moses the Ten Commandments on Mount Sinai, saying, 'I am the Lord your God who led you out of Egypt; you shall have no other gods.' Yes, Jesus of Nazareth, who died for us on the cross, is the God who says in the first commandment, 'I, the Lord, am your God.'[25]

Later Lutherans, such as Abraham Calov, argued that the identification of the Angel of the LORD with God the Son was a mark of orthodoxy, and still today some Eastern Orthodox theologians argue that this was 'an essential aspect of the theological presuppositions of all Ecumenical Councils concerning the person of Christ.'[26]

---

[23] Gregory of Nyssa, *Against Eunomius*, xi.3

[24] Basil of Caesarea, *Refutation of Eunomius' Apology*, ii.18; translation from John S. Romanides, 'Jesus Christ – The Life of the World', WCC-Orthodox Consultation, Damascus, February 1982.

[25] Martin Luther, 'Last Words of David', *Luther's Works* 15:313-314.

[26] John S. Romanides, 'Jesus Christ – The Life of the World.'

The Son

The Angel of the LORD is not the only name given to God the Son in the Old Testament. In fact, the Son is even explicitly referred to as the 'Son'. In *Psalm 2*, the Son of the LORD speaks:

> I will declare the decree:
> The LORD has said to Me,
> You are My Son,
> Today I have begotten You. (*Ps 2:7*)

The New Testament makes clear that this Psalm is speaking of Christ the Son (*Acts 13:33; Heb. 1:5; 5:5*). According to the Psalm, it is those who put their trust in the Son, and embrace Him, who are blessed (*Ps 2:12*). This Son is the Lord's Anointed (*Ps 2:2*) who will receive the nations as His inheritance and rule over the ends of the earth (*Ps 2:8-9*). It is the Son who will pour out the wrath of God upon those who do not fear the Lord and trust in His Word; yet, He is the refuge of 'those who put their trust in Him' (*Ps 2:10-12*). Therefore, this Son exercises divine prerogatives; He does the things only God can do. And the picture of this Son in *Psalm 2* corresponds perfectly with what we are told of Christ in the New Testament.

In the book of Proverbs, Agur, the son of Jakeh, utters wisdom, telling Ithiel and Ucal that the Holy One cannot be known by human beings own understanding and learning, but only by God's own pure words (*Prov. 30:1-6*). And one of the precise reasons Agur gives for our need of God's Word is that, without it, we will not know 'what is His name, and what is His Son's name' (*Prov. 30:4*). The God who 'is a shield to those who put their trust in Him' (*Prov. 30:5*), according to Agur, is the Holy One who has a Son.

Isaiah calls the promised Messiah *Son*. 'For unto us a child is born, unto us a Son is given' (*Isa. 9:6*). He will be born as a child, but before His birth He is already a Son to be given by the LORD. And this Son is called 'Mighty God.' The Son given from God is Himself the Mighty God, which fits perfectly from the Old Testament truth of the Angel of the LORD who is sent from God and is Himself God, and with the New Testament truth of the person of Jesus Christ.

The Word of the LORD

In the Old Testament, the Word of the Lord repeatedly comes to people and speaks.[27] Yet 'too often this designation is understood as an abstraction rather than as a title for YHWH's visible image that is much like the Angel [of the LORD].'[28]

The first appearance of the Word of the LORD who comes speaking in this way is to Abram (*Gen. 15:1*). However, it is a vision, not a voice by which the Word comes to Abram. Abram sees the Word who comes and speaks: the Word is visible, active, and personal. Abram and the Word engage in two-way conversation (*cf. Jer. 1*). '*The Word of the LORD came to me, saying*' is clearly not simply a formula to introduce a mental voice, for the Word of the LORD is referred to as 'He' and He takes Abram outside before speaking to him again (*Gen. 15:5*).

Genesis 15 is the great Old Testament passage to which the New Testament points us to teach justification by faith alone. And yet, in doing that, it shows us precisely in whom that faith is placed. For the LORD in whom Abram believed 'and He accounted it to him for righteousness' (*Gen. 15:6*) is the one with whom he has been speaking: the Word of the LORD. Justification by faith alone has always been in Christ alone.

The Word of the LORD in the Old Testament is not merely the utterance of syllables. Rather the LORD appears by the Word of the LORD (*1 Sam. 3:21*). For the Word of the LORD is His Voice by which He made all things (*Gen. 1; Ps 33:6*) and which walked with Adam and Eve in the Garden (*Gen. 3:8*). The New Testament tells us plainly that the Word of the LORD is none other than the Son of the Father (*Jn 1:1, 14; Rev. 19:12-13*).[29]

---

[27] *Gen. 15:1, 4; 1 Sam. 15:10; 2 Sam. 7:4; 24:11; 1 Kgs 6:11; 16:1; 17:2, 8; 18:1; 21:17; 28; 2 Kgs 20:4; 1 Chron. 22:8; 2 Chron. 11:2; Isa. 38:4; Jer. 1:4, 11, 13; 2:1; 13:3, 8; 18:5; 24:4; 28:12; 29:30; 32:6, 26; 33:1, 19, 23; 34:12; 36:27; 37:6; 43:8; Ezek. 3:16; 6:1; 7:1; 11:14; 12:1, 8, 17, 21, 26; 13:1; 14:2; 15:1; 16:1; 17:1, 11; 18:1; 20:2, 45; 21:1, 8, 18; 22:1, 17, 23; 24:1, 15, 20; 25:1; 26:1; 28:1, 11, 20; 29:1, 17; 30:1, 20; 31:1; 32: 1, 17; 33:1; 23; 34:1; 35:1; 36:16; 37:15; 38:1; Jonah 1:1; 3:1; Hag. 2:20; Zech. 1:1; 4:8; 6:9; 7:8.* In the later prophets (e.g. Haggai) it seems that this may have become an expression to refer to words, but in other Scriptures this is clearly not the case (e.g. Jer. 1).

[28] Gieschen, 'The Real Presence of the Son', 122.

[29] We'll return to the Son as the Word of God in chapter 35.

The Two Called Jehovah

Just as we see the Angel of the LORD called the LORD (*YHWH/Jehovah*) and yet relating to a distinct person who is called the LORD (*YHWH/Jehovah*), there are also several Old Testament Scriptures which show this relationship between two persons who are both called the LORD (*YHWH/Jehovah*) without referring to either of them as the Angel.

In *Genesis 18-19*, the LORD, along with two angels, comes to visit Abraham. (The one who speaks to Abraham is clearly identified as the LORD in *Gen. 18:13-14, 17, 20, 22*). The LORD remains and speaks further with Abraham, telling him of the coming destruction of Sodom and Gomorrah, but the two angels depart for Sodom. There they find Lot, and warn him to flee the coming destruction. But when the destruction comes, we read that 'the LORD rained brimstone and fire on Sodom and Gomorrah from the LORD out of the heavens' (*Gen. 19:24*). Here the Scripture tells us of the LORD who brings the judgement on earth from the LORD in heaven. There is a clear distinction of persons between the LORD who spoke to Abraham on earth and rained judgment on Sodom, and the LORD in heaven. Here we see 'two LORDs in the one verse.'[30]

Again in *Exodus 33* we see the same phenomenon. In *verses 7-11* we read of how 'the LORD spoke to Moses face to face' (*Ex. 33:11*). Yet a few verses later the LORD says to Moses 'you cannot see my face; for no man shall see my face and live' (*Ex. 33:20*). In this chapter we encounter both the LORD who can be seen and the LORD who cannot; both the invisible LORD, and the LORD who is the visible image of the invisible LORD (*cf. Col. 1:15*). Further examples of the two called the LORD can be found in *Exodus 34:9*, *Micah 2:12-13* (*cf. v.3*), and *Zechariah 2:10-12*.

The Two Called God

We've already seen that the Son given in *Isaiah 9:6* by God is called the Mighty God. The promise of the Messiah is the promise of God sent by God. Another example is found in *Psalm 45*, where the glorious King is called God, and yet is anointed by God:

---

[30] Paul Blackham, *Genesis*, (London: Biblical Frameworks, 2006), 56

> Your throne, O God, is forever and ever;
> A sceptre of righteousness is the sceptre of Your kingdom.
> You love righteousness and hate wickedness;
> Therefore God, Your God, has anointed You
> With the oil of gladness more than Your companions. (*Ps 45:6-7; cf. v.2*)

Conclusion: The Son who is God sent from God in the Old Testament

The evidence we've just examined[31] demonstrates that the one God of the Old Testament, besides whom there is no other (*Isa. 44:6; 45:5-6; 21*), is the LORD who sends the LORD. The true and living God has always been the Triune God, and so God the Son was living and active in Old Testament times. The Lord has always revealed Himself by the Word of the Lord (*1 Sam. 3:21; Jn 1:18*). In other words, the deity of the Son is not a new teaching in the New Testament; we can already see the Son who is the LORD sent from the LORD in the Old Testament. And already in the Old Testament, it is the Son who reveals the Father.

---

[31] Along with more; see e.g. the appearances of the glory of the LORD in the Old Testament as well as the figure of the Wisdom of the LORD.

Chapter 3

The Eternal Father

The Lord Jesus Christ, the Eternal Son and Word of the Father, is, as we have seen in the last chapter, God. Yet Jesus also speaks of the Father as His God (*Jn 20:17; Mt 27:46; Mk 15:34; Rev. 3:12*). In fact, when the New Testament uses 'God' as a name, it is nearly always referring to the Father.[1] As Paul writes to the Corinthians, 'there is one God, the Father, of whom are all things, and we for Him; and one Lord Jesus Christ, through whom are all things, and through whom we live' (*1 Cor. 8:6*). This is the faith of the Christian Church: 'I believe in one God the Father Almighty … and in one Lord Jesus Christ, the only-begotten Son of God … and I believe in the Holy Ghost, the Lord and giver of life.'[2]

Jesus tells us that He is in the Father and the Father is in Him (*Jn 17:21, 23*). Moreover, He said, 'I and My Father are one' (*Jn 10:30; cf. Jn 17:22*). Jesus' first hearers knew exactly what He was saying, for at that statement they 'took up stones again to stone Him' (*Jn 10:31*). Jesus was declaring His equality with the Father and the Father's equality with Him. With the word *one* Christ declares the identity of substance of the Father and the Son, while at the same time, with the word *are*, He speaks of the distinction of person between the Father and the Son. The Father and the Son are one, yet the Father is not the Son, and the Son is not the Father. Therefore, as Athanasius and Cyril of Alexandria, the church's great teachers on the person of Christ, taught, *whatever is said of the Father is said of the Son except that the Son is not the Father*.[3]

Of this oneness between the Father and the Son, Cyril of Alexandria writes elsewhere:

> He beautifully corresponds in every detail … to the form of the one who begat him; indeed, he genuinely depicts in himself the one who begat him, the one from whom he exists. However, he will not for that reason lose his own subsistence, nor will the Father lose his. Neither will their complete likeness cause any confusion of the hypostases so that we understand the

---

[1] This is when the Greek word *Theos* is used with an article, and so as a proper noun.

[2] Nicene Creed

[3] Athanasius, *Contra Arianos*, 3.3-6; Cyril of Alexandria, *Dialogues on the Trinity*, III 465 a-d (Sources Chrétiennes edition, vol. ii, 21-23).

Father who begat to be the same in number as the Son who was begotten of him. We will confess the identity of nature for both, but the proper subsistence of each one surely follows so that we should think of the Father as really the Father, and the Son as the Son.[4]

The Father is just like the Son and the Son is just like the Father. The only difference is that the Father is not the Son and the Son is not the Father. The Father and the Son are distinct persons and yet they are perfectly one.

For D.P. Williams and the early Apostolics, this is 'the basic truth of the Christian faith ... that God is the Father, and that He has a Son within His essence, eternally.'[5] In the early church, Cyril of Alexandria said exactly the same thing: 'He [the Father] has this offspring [the Son] present in Him, substantially by His nature.'[6] This relationship between the Father and the Son is the very heart of the Christian faith, and from this relationship between the Father and the Son flows our salvation and the whole of the Christian life.

The Father is Not a Father without the Son

God's very identity is to be the Father. He has always been the Father and will always be the Father. For the early Apostolics, this was 'the most glorious' thing about God.[7] However, this is often not the first thing people think about when they think about God today. When radical atheists speak of their disbelief in God, the God they describe is usually not a loving Father pouring out His love upon His eternal Son in the joy of the Spirit. Rather, they might speak of a god who is most fundamentally a ruler, or a law-giver, or a powerful creator. Often even well-meaning Christians end up speaking of God as if one of these were His fundamental identity. The Triune God does rule and reign, He has spoken His law, and He did create the heavens and the earth out of nothing, but none of those are His

---

[4] Cyril of Alexandria, *In. Io.* i.2, (ET 1:10). We'll look at the words the Church has used to express Trinitarian truth, like subsistence and hypostasis in chapter 6. For now, what you need to know is that both words refer to 'person' when it comes to the Trinity.

[5] D.P. Williams, *The Trinity*, 1:77.

[6] Cyril of Alexandria, *Dial. Trin.* ii.460.e (Sources Chrétiennes, Vol. 1, p.352).

[7] D.P. Williams, *The Trinity*, 1:77.

fundamental identity. Fundamentally, and above all else, He is the Father who loves His Son in the unity of the Spirit.

The early church also had a problem with people thinking of God in ways other than Father. At the start of the fourth century, Arius, a presbyter in Egypt, insisted that the most fundamental identity of God was that He was the origin and cause of everything else, but that He Himself was not caused by anything else. Therefore, instead of calling God 'Father', Arius wanted to call Him 'Unoriginate.' But, when you start to rename and redefine God in terms other than those in which He has revealed Himself in Scripture, it leads to problems. A son, to be a son, receives his being from someone else (in the case of God the Son, He eternally receives His being by being begotten of the Father). But that didn't meet Arius' definition of God as Unoriginate. So Arius denied the deity of the Son and His equality with the Father. Instead he considered the Son to be the first creation of the Unoriginate (the Father), far above all other creatures, yet even further below God. This was all summed up with Arius' infamous dictum, 'there was a time when he was not.'

Now, Arius' arguments might seem a bit obscure to us, but his heresy caught on quickly and spread rapidly in the fourth century. Even after the First Ecumenical Council of the undivided church (the Council of Nicaea) condemned it as heresy, Arianism continued to thrive. How did it find such success? To a large extent, because it was a heresy spread by song. Arius composed a collection of easily-learnt songs (called the *Thalia*) which spread his false teaching throughout the length and breadth of the church. One ancient writer tells us that, with his songs, Arius, 'by degrees seduced the minds of the unlearned by the attractiveness of his songs to the adoption of his own impiety.' In other words, people picked up the Arian heresy through the words they were singing.[8]

Athanasius, the great champion of orthodoxy and life-long opponent of Arianism, began his great anti-Arian work *Contra Arianos* (*Discourses Against the Arians*) by focusing on these songs. He compares the *Thalia* of Arius to the dance of Herodias' daughter 'reeling and frolicking in his blasphemies against the Saviour.'[9] However, Athanasius didn't only criticise the heretical songs; he thoroughly demolished the heretical theology.

---

[8] And today still, popular worship songs might just as easily spread false and dangerous doctrines through the church. Therefore, we should take care to ensure that the songs we sing reflect the biblical truth.

[9] Athanasius, *Contra Arianos*, 1.2.

One of Athanasius' great arguments against Arianism lay in recognising the difference of approach to God. Athanasius knew that Jesus is the revelation of God. Arius, however, insisted that (as he thought the Son was a creature and not God) the Son was incapable of truly knowing God. Therefore, for Arius, the Son could not be the revelation of God. Instead, Arius looked for the revelation of God in His powerful deeds, and particularly in His causation of all things. Athanasius saw the great difference in their theologies of revelation and saw how significant the impact of this was on their understanding of God. And, rather than conceding the terms of debate to Arius, he insisted that Arius had to shift, and look in the right place for the revelation of God. Athanasius argued: 'it would be more godly and true to signify God from the Son and call him Father, than to name God from his works alone and call him Unoriginate.'[10] The Father-Son relationship is primary, and causation and creation can only be understood in light of the Father and His Son. Jesus is the revelation of God, and so by looking to Jesus, the eternal Son, we must see the fundamental identity of God as 'the Father [who] has a Son within His essence, eternally.'[11]

The very names 'Father' and 'Son' show us that we cannot think of the Father and the Son in isolation from one another. As Cyril of Alexandria straightforwardly puts it, 'The Father is Father because He has begotten the Son; the Son, for His part, is Son because He is begotten of the Father.'[12] You can't have the Son without the Father, nor can you have the Father without His Son. Their very names imply their eternal relation and communion. And the names Father and Son also point to their equality of being and their oneness:

> He is called Father because of the Son, so how could he be thought of as Father if the Son is not Son by nature? But this is absurd. God is the true Father. All the Holy Scriptures indeed cry this out. Therefore, the one who is from him by nature is completely Son. And if so, he is not inferior. Since he is Son, he is of the same substance.[13]

---

[10] Athanasius, *Contra Arianos*, 1.34.
[11] D.P. Williams, *The Trinity*, 1:77.
[12] Cyril, *Dial. Trin.* i.415a (Sources Chrétiennes ed., Vol. 1, p.214)
[13] Cyril, *In Io.* i.3, (ET 1:15).

The Love of the Father who is Love

'God is love' (*1 Jn 4:8*). In words so simple, yet so profound the Scriptures tell us who God is. John does not write that God is loving, but that He is love. This is not one attribute of God among many; this is the identity of God. But who is this God who is love? He is the one who 'has sent His only begotten Son into the world, that we might live through Him' (*1 Jn 4:9*). The God who is love is the God who 'loved us and sent His Son to be the propitiation for our sins' (*1 Jn 4:10*). When John writes that God is love, He is not writing directly of the Trinity (although it is true that loving communion is of the essence of the Three-in-One), but of the Father. God the Father, who sent His Son, is love. Love is His very identity. His love did not come into being in time with the creation of human beings or angels. He is love, has always been love, and will always be love. And this is possible only because He has never been, and will never be, without His Son and His Spirit. The true and living God is the Father who eternally loves His Son in the Spirit. As D.P. Williams emphasised, 'God is not a monad, isolated and alone, but exists … in three Persons in the eternal essence … Three Persons, not one apart or outside the other.'[14] If God were a monad, isolated and alone, He could not be love, for He would have had no one to love from all eternity. But, because the Triune God is three persons – the Father, the Son, and the Holy Spirit – from all eternity, there is an eternal love between the three within the heart of the Trinity, with no beginning or end.

So the very identity of God in the Scriptures is the Father who is love. Without someone to love and without someone to father, He could not be who He is. And so God must have 'a Son within His essence, eternally.'[15] And Jesus tells us of the Father's love for the Son from all eternity. He prays to His Father, saying 'You loved Me before the foundation of the world' (*Jn 17:24*). Again and again, the Scriptures speak of the Father's love for the Son (*Jn 3:35; 5:20; 10:17; 15:9*). The Son is the one in whom the Father delights (*Isa. 42:1*). Yet, in Jesus' high priestly prayer on the night of his arrest, He makes clear that this love is an eternal love, with which the Father loved Him even before the foundation of the world. God has always been the Father who loves His Son in the Spirit. He was the loving Father before He was the Creator. 'The Father, then, is the Father of the eternal Son, and he

---

14 D.P. Williams, *The Trinity*, 1:66.
15 D.P. Williams, *The Trinity*, 1:77.

finds his very identity, his Fatherhood, in loving and giving out his life and being to the Son.'[16]

The Father Begets the Son and the Son is Begotten of the Father

What makes the Father the Father and the Son the Son if the only difference between the Father and the Son is that the Son is not the Father and the Father is not the Son? Cyril of Alexandria tells us quite simply: 'The Father is Father, and not Son, because He begets; the Son, in turn, is Son, and not Father, because He is begotten.'[17] We call this doctrine – that the Father eternally begets the Son and the Son is eternally begotten of the Father – *the eternal generation of the Son*. Cyril highlights the importance of this doctrine of eternal generation, for 'there would be no Father, nor any Son either, unless there is a begetter and a begotten.'[18]

Yet, despite Cyril's warning, and despite the fact that the doctrine of the eternal generation is enshrined in the Nicene Creed itself, a number of recent evangelical theologians have tried to jettison the doctrine.[19] But, as Fred Sanders points out, this is not a good change:

> Is it really necessary to affirm these eternal relations of origin? I believe it is. The doctrine of the Trinity is not something we have learned from general logical principles, from natural revelation, or from common sense. It is a truth about God that is only made known by special revelation. As a result, Trinitarian theology needs to handle its knowledge in a particularly careful way. Above all, the doctrine of the Trinity should not be stated in a way that goes one step beyond what God has revealed. The secret things belong to the Lord! Evangelical Protestants are likely to be good guardians of that boundary line. But there is another boundary line marking off the opposite error; we should also take pains to ensure that we make the most of everything that has been revealed. Trinitarian information is a precious

---

[16] Michael Reeves, *The Good God: Enjoying Father, Son and Holy Spirit* (Milton Keynes: Paternoster, 2012), 9.

[17] Cyril, *Dial. Trin.* i.416.c (Sources Chrétiennes ed., Vol. 1, p.218).

[18] Cyril, *Dial. Trin.* ii.431.e (Sources Chrétiennes ed., Vol. 1, p.266).

[19] Technically, to jettison this creedal doctrine is formally heretical. Someone may argue a case for this from Scripture, as several evangelicals have attempted to do, but they must also admit at the same time that what they are arguing for is a departure from the accepted orthodox Trinitarian doctrine of the Christian church. Unfortunately several of the most popular and widely used evangelical systematic theologies of recent decades take such a revisionist approach.

theological commodity, and we should never be found falling short of receiving what God has made known. The things revealed belong to us and to our children forever! Eternal divine sonship is revealed, and calling it eternal generation has been the classic Christian way of ensuring that we keep a firm grasp on the meaning of sonship. Trinitarian theology affirms this about God the Trinity: the Son and the Spirit stand in particular relationships to the Father, and those relationships are relationships of origin. The Son and the Spirit come from the Father and always have.[20]

So let's have a closer look at some of the biblical teaching on the Father's begetting of the Son and the Son's generation from the Father.

Back in the Old Testament, the Psalms sing of how the LORD has begotten His Son. The Son, speaking in the middle section of *Psalm 2*, says:

> I will declare the decree:
> The LORD has said to Me,
> 'You are My Son,
> Today I have begotten You. (*Ps 2:7*)

The New Testament takes up this verse and makes clear that this is Christ the Son who is begotten of His Father (*Acts 13:33; Heb. 1:5; 5:5*). When is this 'today' in which the Father begets the Son? Paul links this Psalm with the resurrection of Christ in his sermon in *Acts 13:33*. However, he is not tying the 'today' of begetting to the day of resurrection. For already in the Psalmist's day, the Father had said to the Son 'today I have begotten You.' Rather, Paul points to the resurrection of Jesus Christ as the great declaration of His identity as the Son (*cf. Rom. 1:1*); and this identity as Son is His begottenness of the Father. The 'today' in which the Father speaks to the Son is an eternal 'today'. The Son does not suddenly begin to be the Son of the Father; He has always been and will always be the Son of the Father, and so He is begotten eternally with an eternal generation.

In the New Testament, Jesus speaks of His eternal generation, teaching that 'as the Father has life in Himself, so He has granted the Son to have life in Himself' (*Jn 5:26*). The Son has life in a different way from any created being. Created beings receive life from God, but it is always a life in dependence on God for its existence and a derivative life. God the Father's life is not dependent or derivative; He 'has life in Himself.' This is the eternal life of God, not the derivative life of a created being. Yet the Son has this life from the Father. 'John in this verse is speaking of the full and perfect

---

[20] Fred Sanders, *The Deep Things of God: How the Trinity Changes Everything* (Wheaton: Crossway, 2010), 92-93.

bestowal or sharing of the divine life from the Father to the Son.'[21] As Augustine says, by this Christ 'wants it to be understood that the Father has begotten him.'[22]

John explicitly teaches that the Son is 'born of God' in his first epistle. 'We know that anyone born of God does not continue to sin; the One who was born of God keeps them safe, and the evil one cannot harm them' (*1 Jn 5:18 NIV*). The saving Son is the one who was born of God the Father, eternally begotten by Him.

Five times in John's writings Jesus is called the 'only begotten' (*Jn 1:14, 18; 3:16, 18; 1 Jn 4:9*). Although a number of twentieth century commentators and even some Bible translations[23] have abandoned the translation 'only begotten' for the Greek word μονογενής (*monogenes*), there is strong evidence that the traditional translation ('only begotten') is the correct one. This was certainly the understanding of the earliest post-Biblical readers of the New Testament. Justin Martyr and Theophilus of Antioch in the second century, and then Tertullian, writing at the end of the second century or beginning of the third, all understood this word as referring to the only begotten.[24] The context of its occurrence in Scripture also points to the traditional translation.[25] Thus, that the Son is begotten of the Father is not only the language of the Creed, but the very language of Scripture.

So, the Scriptures teach that the Son is begotten of the Father, and this is what the Christian Church throughout the world and throughout the centuries has confessed. We believe:

> In one Lord Jesus Christ, the only-begotten Son of God,
> Begotten of his Father before all worlds,
> God of God, Light of Light,
> Very God of very God,
> Begotten, not made,

[21] Kevin Giles, *The Eternal Generation of the Son: Maintaining Orthodoxy in Trinitarian Theology* (Downers Grove: IVP, 2012), 86.

[22] Augustine, *De Trinitate*, 1.4.26 (ET p.89).

[23] The NIV, for example, has opted for 'one and only' instead of 'only begotten.'

[24] Justin Martyr, *First Apology*, 23; *Dialogue with Trypho*, 105; Theophilus of Antioch, *Theophilus to Autolycus*, 2.10; Tertullian, *Against Praxeas*, vii.

[25] For discussions of this internal textual evidence for the meaning 'only begotten', see John V. Dahms, 'The Johannine Use of **Monogenēs** Reconsidered', *New Testament Studies*, 29.2 (April 1983), 222-232; Robert Letham, *The Holy Trinity: In Scripture, History, Theology, and Worship* (Phillipsburg: PRP, 2004), 385-386; John M. Frame, *The Doctrine of God* (Phillipsburg, New Jersey: PRP, 2002), 710-711.

Being of one substance with the Father.[26]

The Son is the Only-Begotten God who is God of God. 'Such is the teaching of sacred Scripture, but as to the manner of the begetting … this is beyond understanding.'[27] The Scriptures simply tell us that the Son is begotten of the Father, but they do not describe the precise nature of this begottenness in any detail.

> When we say that He [the Only Begotten Son] is before all ages, we mean that His begetting is outside of time and without beginning, for the Son of God was not brought forth from nothing into being … Actually, He was always with the Father, being begotten of Him eternally and without beginning. For the Father never was when the Son was not but the Father and the Son begotten of Him exist together simultaneously, because the Father could not be so called without a Son.[28]

Cyril of Alexandria shows us that the Father's begetting of the Son who is always with Him and in Him upholds the full deity of the Son and His full equality with the Father:

> The Son exists in the Father and from the Father. He did not come into existence from outside of the Father or in time but exists in the substance of the Father. He radiates out from that substance like beams from the sun or heat from a fire. These sorts of examples show that one thing can be begotten of another but still always be with it and inseparably attached to it. The one cannot exist in itself apart from the other, yet the integrity of its own nature is truly preserved … Therefore, as these examples show, the fact that something is 'in' what it is from does not take away the fact that the two are 'with' each other. Instead, the 'in' shows that the begotten offspring always coincide with the sources that begat them and that they share in one nature with them, so to speak. The same holds true for the Son. If he is thought and said to be in the Father and with the Father, that does not mean the Son will be alien or foreign or in second place after the Father. Instead, he will always be in him and with him and radiating from him according to the ineffable mode of divine generation.[29]

Or, as Michael Reeves put it much more recently:

> The Father is never without the Son but, like a lamp, it the very nature of the Father to shine out His Son. And likewise, it is the very nature of the Son to be the one who shines out from his Father. The Son has His very

---

26 *Nicene Creed*

27 John of Damascus, *De Fide Orthodoxa*, i.8 (ET p.182).

28 John of Damascus, *De Fide Orthodoxa*, i.8 (ET p.178).

29 Cyril of Alexandria, *In Ioh.*, i.i (ET 1:8).

being from the Father. In fact, he *is* the going out – the radiance – of the Father's own being. He is the Son.[30]

The very identity of God the Father is to be the Begetter of the Son. This is who He eternally is, and this is the only way we can know Him, through His only begotten Son.

The Monarchy of the Father

Related to the doctrine of the Father's eternal generation of the Son, but distinct from it, is the doctrine of the monarchy of the Father. The monarchy of the Father means that the Father is the one source and fountain of deity.[31] 'The Father, rather than the divine essence, is the origin or cause of the divine nature in the Son and the Spirit.'[32] This means that the unity of the Trinity is found, not in an abstract divine essence, but in the Father Himself. The danger of losing the monarchy of the Father, and grounding the unity of the Trinity in the divine essence instead is that the one essence ends up overshadowing the three persons and they 'find themselves more or less swallowed up in the nature or essence.'[33]

The biblical basis for the doctrine of the monarchy of the Father is found in the way the New Testament uses the name 'God', not for a substance beyond the three persons of the Trinity, but for the Father. Both Peter and Paul write of 'the God and Father of our Lord Jesus Christ' (*1 Pet. 1:3; Rom. 15:6; 2 Cor. 1:3; 11:31; Eph. 1:3; Col. 1:3*). Paul's letters often open with a greeting from 'God our Father and the Lord Jesus Christ' (*Rom. 1:7; 1 Cor. 1:3; 2 Cor. 1:2; Eph. 1:2; Phil. 1:2; Col. 1:2; 1 Thess. 1:1; 2 Thess. 1:1-2; Philemon 3.*) Paul even tells us that 'there is one God, the Father' (*1 Cor. 8:6*). Even Jesus calls the Father 'the only true God' (*Jn 17:3*). The Father is the one

[30] Michael Reeves, *The Good God*, 9.

[31] For the doctrine of the monarchy of the Father among the early Apostolics, see D.P. Williams, *The Trinity*, 1:48, 56; W.R. Thomas, *The Paraclete*, xxix; W.R. Thomas, *On Ephesians*, 214.

[32] Robert Letham, *The Holy Trinity: In Scripture, History, Theology, and Worship* (Phillipsburg, New Jersey: PRP, 2004), 251.

[33] Vladimir Lossky, *The Mystical Theology of the Eastern Church* (London: James Clarke, 1957), 57.

God who begets the Son and breathes out the Spirit who are eternally one with Him. The one God is 'the Father, loving and giving life to his Son in the fellowship of the Spirit.'[34] So the unity of the Godhead is not found in something other than the three persons, but in the Father from whom the Son is begotten and the Spirit proceeds. As Gregory of Nazianzus put it:

> The three have one nature … the ground of unity being the Father, out of whom and towards whom the subsequent persons [i.e. the Son who is begotten of the Father, and the Spirit who proceeds from the Father] are reckoned.[35]

So the Father is 'the one God of the Bible by being the ground of the unity of the three persons.'[36] Or, in the words of D.P. Williams. 'the oneness of the Trinity [is] in the one God and Father.'[37] But remember it is as the Father that He is the one God and ground of unity of the Trinity: as the Father who is never without His Son and His Spirit, whose very identity is found in His fatherhood of the Son.

As we've already seen, Jesus teaches in *John 5:26* that the Father 'has granted the Son to have life in Himself.' A few verses earlier, Christ says that 'the Son can do nothing of Himself, but what He sees the Father do; for whatever He does, the Son also does in like manner' (*Jn 5:19*). The Son receives both His life and His will and activity from the Father (for the Father, Son and Holy Spirit share one will and activity) and so He is fully equal to the Father, for He, not only can do, but does do all the things which the Father does.

Cyril of Alexandria tells us, 'the Father is the beginningless beginning of the Son's nature, so to speak, but only in the sense of source because the Son's existence is "from" the Father.'[38] So the Father's monarchy does not mean that the Father is greater, more exalted, or somehow more divine than the Son and the Spirit. His monarchy is in terms of source and does not in any way impinge on the absolute equality of the Father, Son and Spirit in their deity, glory and honour. Gregory of Nazianzus cautions us about misunderstanding the monarchy of the Father:

> I should like to call the Father the greater, because from him flows both the Equality and the Being of the Equals (this will be granted on all hands), but

---

[34] Reeves, *The Good God*, 20.

[35] Gregory of Nazianzus, *Oration 42.15*

[36] John Zizioulas, *Communion and Otherness* (T&T Clark: London 2006), 118.

[37] D.P. Williams, *The Trinity*, 1:56.

[38] Cyril of Alexandria, *In Ioh*. i.1 (ET 1:8).

> I am afraid to use the word Origin, lest I should make Him the Origin of
> Inferiors, and thus insult Him by precedencies of honour. For the lowering
> of those Who are from Him is no glory to the Source. Moreover, I look with
> suspicion at your insatiate desire, for fear you should take hold of this
> word Greater, and divide the Nature, using the word Greater in all senses,
> whereas it does not apply to the Nature, but only to Origination. For in the
> Consubstantial Persons there is nothing greater or less in point of
> Substance.[39]

Jesus does say in *John 14:28*, 'My Father is greater than I.' But this does not
mean of a greater nature. As Athanasius shows us, 'it is that the Son too says
not, "My Father is better than I," lest we should conceive Him to be foreign
to His Nature, but "greater," not indeed in greatness, nor in time, but
because of His generation from the Father Himself, nay, in saying "greater"
he again shows that He is proper to His essence.'[40] When Jesus says 'My
Father is greater than I,' He is speaking in terms of source, and so pointing
us to the monarchy of the Father. The Son and the Spirit are, in their nature,
the Equals of the Father, whose equality finds its source in the Father. As we
confess in the Athanasian Creed:

> And in this Trinity none is before, or after another; none is greater, or less
> than another. But the whole three Persons are coeternal, and coequal. So
> that in all things, as aforesaid; the Unity in Trinity, and the Trinity in
> Unity, is to be worshipped. He therefore that will be saved, let him thus
> think of the Trinity.

While maintaining the absolute equality of the three persons of Father, Son
and Holy Spirit with regards to their deity, eternity, and glory, the doctrine
of the monarchy of the Father also helps us to make sense of the order
which we see in the Trinity. The technical word for this order is *taxis*. We'll
come back to the subject of *taxis* in chapter 5.

The Only Begotten Son who is in the bosom of the Father reveals the
Father to us. The Son, who has enjoyed the love of His Father from all
eternity, brings us to the Father, so that we can know His Father as our
Father, and so enjoy the eternal life which is to know the Father and His Son
in the Spirit.

---

[39] Gregory of Nazianzus, *Oration 40 (On Holy Baptism)*, 43.

[40] Athanasius, *Contra Arianos*, 1.58; see also Basil of Caesarea, *Against Eunomius*, 1.25;
Gregory of Nazianzus, *Oration 30.7*.

Chapter 4

The Eternal Spirit

At Jesus' Baptism, as the Father spoke of His love for the Son, a dove descended from heaven. But this was no ordinary dove. The Scriptures tell us that the dove which alighted upon Christ was none other than the Holy Spirit (*Mt 3:16; Mk 1:10; Lk 3:22; Jn 1:32*). In our baptism too, we recognise this same Holy Spirit, as we are plunged under the water 'in the name of the Father, and of the Son, and of the Holy Spirit' (*Mt 28:19*). But what, or who, is this Holy Spirit who is so closely connected to the Father and His Son?

The Holy Spirit is a Distinct Divine Person

In the book of Acts, we read of the coming of the Holy Spirit with tongues of fire and with the sound 'of a rushing mighty wind' (*Acts 2:2-3*). Jesus' promise had been that the disciples would receive power at the Spirit's coming (*Acts 1:8*). But we must pay careful attention to the Biblical presentation of the personality of the Holy Spirit, for He is not merely a power sent from God. The Spirit is not simply the activity of the Father and the Son in the created world. Rather, the Holy Spirit is Himself a person, like the Father and the Son.

Speaking in the First Person

As a person, the Holy Spirit can say 'I'; he speaks in the first-person. When Paul and Barnabas were called to the apostleship, the Holy Spirit spoke in prophecy, and the Scripture tells us: 'the Holy Spirit said, "Now separate to Me Barnabas and Saul for the work to which I have called them"' (*Acts 13:2*). Here the Holy Spirit is not simply the divine power by which the prophet speaks, but rather, the Holy Spirit Himself speaks in His own person. He does not speak impersonally of separating these apostles 'to God'; He speaks personally, telling them to separate these new apostles 'to

Me'. Later in Acts, we see that the prophet Agabus does not merely speak words under the power of the Spirit, but rather, the words he speaks in prophecy are the Holy Spirit's own words. And so Agabus can say, 'thus says the Holy Spirit' (*Acts 21:11*), for the Holy Spirit Himself speaks as a person.

Personal Actions

And speaking in the first person is not the only personal action of the Holy Spirit. The Holy Spirit teaches (*Jn 14:26*) and testifies (*Jn 15:26; Rom. 8:16*). He leads (*Rom. 8:14*), helps (*Rom. 8:26*), and intercedes (*Rom. 8:26-27*). The Holy Spirit reveals things of the future (*1 Tim. 4:1*) and calls to the ministry (*Acts 13:2; 20:28*). He has a mind (*Rom. 8:27*) and He wills (*Heb. 2:4*).[1] These are not the activities and properties of a mere force or power sent from God. These are the actions of a person.

The Holy Spirit can be Grieved and Sinned Against

An attribute, such as power, cannot be grieved, but a person can. And the Holy Spirit can be grieved, for we are warned, 'do not grieve the Holy Spirit of God' (*Eph. 4:30*). The children of Israel, in the Old Testament, 'rebelled and grieved [God's] Holy Spirit' (*Isa. 63:10*). In this, they sinned against Him. As did Ananias and Sapphira in the New Testament (*Acts 5:3*). Jesus also tells us that it is possible to blaspheme the Holy Spirit (*Mt 12:31-32*). The fact that the Spirit can be sinned against, grieved, and blasphemed, demonstrates that He is a divine person.

The Holy Spirit Has Appeared in Visible Form

At Jesus' baptism, the Holy Spirit appeared in bodily form as a dove (*Lk 3:22*), and on the Day of Pentecost, He was seen in the form of tongues of fire (*Acts 2:3-4*). As Francis Turretin points out:

---

[1] The will of the Holy Spirit is one with the will of the Father and the Son. Strictly speaking the will belongs to the nature, while the person wills. Yet only one of the divine persons of the Holy Trinity can will with the one divine will. An attribute of God, such as His power, cannot will. See the discussion of Monothelitism in chapter 11.

It belongs to persons (not to attributes or accidents) to assume visible forms and to appear in or with or under such forms. Nor without absurdity can anyone say that the justice or mercy of God or any other virtue manifested itself by visible form … Hence under the visible form there must have been some subsistence (which the text asserts was the Holy Spirit and expressly distinguishes from the persons of the Father and the Son in the baptism of the Saviour).[2]

Distinction from the Father and the Son

Jesus distinguishes the Holy Spirit from both Himself and His Father. On the night of His arrest, Jesus told His disciples, 'I will pray the Father, and He will give you another Helper, that He may abide with you forever' (*Jn 14:16*). The 'another Helper' (or 'another Paraclete') is another of the same kind. (Koine Greek used different words for *another of the same kind* and *another of a different kind*.) So, this Paraclete, who will be sent from the Father in response to the prayer of the Son, is a Paraclete of the same kind as the Paraclete who is already with them. And who is this first Paraclete? It's Jesus Himself. The second Paracelte is coming because Jesus, the first Paraclete is going (*Jn 16:7*). And Jesus is explicitly called our Paraclete in *1 John 2:1*. So, this Paraclete, which is the Holy Spirit, is a Paracelte of the same kind as Jesus. Jesus is a divine person, so the Paralete must also be a divine person. A mere power from God could not be a Paraclete of the same kind as Christ. As John Chrysostom put it: 'But if the Spirit were inferior to the Son, the consolation would not have been adequate; and how could He have said, "It is expedient for you?" [*Jn 16:7*].'[3]

The Holy Spirit, our Paraclete, is of the same kind as Jesus. Yet He is also distinct from Jesus, and from the Father, for Jesus will send this Paraclete from the Father, the Paraclete proceeds from the Father, and the Paraclete testifies of the Son (*Jn 15:26*). Therefore, the Holy Spirit cannot be another way of speaking of the Father or the Son. He is not only a divine person, but also a distinct third divine person. We also see this at Jesus' baptism, in the words spoken at our baptism (*Mt 28:19*), and in the apostolic benediction – 'the Grace' (*2 Cor. 13:14*).

---

[2] Francis Turretin, *Institutes of Elenctic Theology*, 1:304.
[3] John Chrysostom, Homily I on Acts i.1,2.

The Deity of the Holy Spirit

Having seen that the Holy Spirit is a person (rather than a power, activity or attribute of God) and that He is a distinct third person (rather than another way of speaking of the Father or the Son), we can now look at the biblical evidence that this third person is God, just as the Father is God and the Son is God.[4]

The Holy Spirit shares in the Honours of God

The Holy Spirit, according to the Nicene Creed, 'with the Father and the Son together is worshipped and glorified.' Thus, Christians confess that the Holy Spirit shares equally with the Father and the Son in the honours due to God. But what does the Bible have to say about the honours of the Holy Spirit?

Firstly, the Holy Spirit is worshipped as God. We baptise 'in the name of the Father, and of the Son, and of the Holy Spirit' (*Mt 28:19*), and baptism is an act of worship. So the name into which we are baptised is the name of Him whom we trust and the name of Him whom we worship. So, baptism in the Triune name displays our faith in and worship of the Triune God: Father, Son and Holy Spirit. Therefore, as we worship the Triune God in the sacrament of baptism, we worship and glorify the Holy Spirit. Athanasius says that:

> Just as there is one baptism given in Father, Son and Holy Spirit, and just as there is one faith in the Trinity (as the Apostle said), so too the Holy Trinity, which is identical with itself and united in itself, has nothing in it that belongs to things which have come into existence. This is the indivisible unity of the Trinity, and there is one faith in it.[5]

In other words, the faith and worship of the Father, Son and Holy Spirit together, displayed in the sacrament of baptism, shows us that the Father, Son and Holy Spirit are equal in deity and that none of them are created

---

[4] I've used the same way of laying out the evidence that we used to look at the deity of the Angel of the LORD to make it easy to remember using the acronym HAND.

[5] Athanasius, *Letters to Serapion on the Holy Spirit*, 1.30.2

beings. The worship of the Holy Spirit in the sacrament of baptism shows us that He is God.

Furthermore, we glorify God in our bodies, not only as we are gathered to Word and Sacrament to worship Him, but at all times, for our bodies are 'the temple of the Holy Spirit' (*1 Cor. 6:19-20*). The God whom we glorify in our bodies must be the same God who dwells in us as His temple for Paul's argument here to make sense. And so that means we must glorify the Holy Spirit in our bodies, whose temples our bodies are. In all our lives we are called to serve and worship God the Holy Spirit (together with the Father and the Son), whose temples we are, and glorify Him in our bodies.

Paul points us to a Trinitarian worship including the Holy Spirit in his letter to the Philippians. 'For we are the circumcision, who worship God in the Spirit, rejoice in Christ Jesus, and have no confidence in the flesh' (*Phil. 3:3*). We worship the Father, in the Spirit, rejoicing in the Son. Augustine saw this verse as a very strong and direct statement of worship to the Holy Spirit, and hence of His deity:

> But the place which makes it most evident that the Holy Spirit is not a creature is the one where we are bidden not to serve the creature but the creator (*Rom. 1:25*) – serve, no in the sense in which we are bidden to serve one another in charity … but in the sense in which only God is served … hence the name 'idolaters' for those who offer to images the service owed to God. As regards this service it is said *The Lord your God shall you adore, and him only shall you serve* (*Dt 6:13*) … then the Holy Spirit is certainly not a creature, since all the saints offer him such service, according to the apostle's words, *For we are the circumcision, serving the Spirit of God* (*Phil. 3:3*), which in the Greek is *latreuontes* ['worshipping'].[6]

The Church also invokes, or calls upon, the Holy Spirit in worship and prayer. In 'the Grace' we pray, invoking the Holy Spirit for His communion or fellowship (*2 Cor. 13:14*). As the great Puritan theologian, John Owen, noted, the apostle John invoked the Holy Spirit for grace and peace for the seven churches of Asia (*Rev. 1:4*).

> The principal respect that we have unto him immediately, in our worship of him under the New Testament, is as he is the author of these various gifts and graces. So John, saluting the churches of Asia, prayeth for grace for them from God the Father, and from 'the seven Spirits which are before his throne,' Rev. i.4; that is, from the Holy Spirit of God considered in his care of the church and his yielding supplies unto it, as the author of that

---

[6] Augustine, *De Trinitate*, 1.13. Augustine does go on to note some textual variants here, which explain why our English translations tend not to match exactly with Augustine's Latin version of *Phil. 3:3*.

perfection of gifts and graces which are, and are to be, bestowed upon it.
So doth the number of 'seven' denote.[7]

As we trust in His grace and peace, call upon Him for grace and peace, and rejoice in the grace and peace which we receive from Him, we worship and glorify the Holy Spirit in the unity of the Trinity.

Finally, the possibility of dishonour of the Holy Spirit demonstrates that He shares in the honours of God, for He can be blasphemed (*Mt 12:32*). Blasphemy is a sin of dishonour against the true and living God (*cf. Ex. 20:7*), so the only way that the Holy Spirit can be blasphemed is because His name is highly exalted as the name of the living God. It is only because His name is so highly honoured due to His deity that He could be blasphemed.

The Holy Spirit shares in the Attributes of God

The Holy Spirit is the 'Holy' Spirit and 'the Spirit of Holiness' (*Rom. 1:4*). Yet, it is the Lord God Almighty 'alone' who is holy (*Rev. 15:3-4*). God's people are holy only by sharing in His holiness in Christ through the Holy Spirit (*1 Cor. 1:30; Rom. 15:16*). The Spirit, however, does not share the holiness of another, but is Himself holy. We are sanctified, but He is the sanctifier. Athanasius shows us that this reveals the deity of the Holy Spirit, for 'he who is not sanctified by another, nor participates in sanctification, but is himself the one who is participated in, the one in whom all creatures are sanctified' cannot be a created being, but must be God who alone is holy.[8] Didymus the Blind wrote that:

> Since the Holy Spirit is different from those whom he sanctifies, he does not share a single nature with the other creatures who receive him. But if his nature is different from those other creatures and he subsists in his own essence, it is clear that he is not created and not made ... his nature is different from all created beings.[9]

Therefore, His holiness demonstrates that He is 'of the same substance' (*homoousios*) with the Father and the Son.[10]

Yet, holiness is not the only attribute of God in which the Holy Spirit shares. The Spirit shares in the eternity of God, for it was 'through the

---

[7] John Owen, *Pneumatologia*, in *The Works of John Owen*, 1:133.
[8] Athanasius, *Letters to Serapion on the Holy Spirit*, 1.23.1
[9] Didymus the Blind, *On the Holy Spirit*, 29; cf. 10-15.
[10] Didymus the Blind, *On the Holy Spirit*, 81.

eternal Spirit' that Jesus Christ 'offered Himself without spot to God' (*Heb. 9:14*). He shares in the truth, wisdom, and grace of God, for He is called 'the Spirit of Truth' (*Jn 14:17*), 'the Spirit of Wisdom' (*Deut. 34:9*) and 'the Spirit of grace' (*Heb. 10:29*). There is none good but God alone, and yet the Holy Spirit is God's 'good Spirit' (*Neh. 9:20; Ps 143:10*), sharing fully in the divine attribute of goodness.

The Scriptures also show us that the Holy Spirit is omnipresent: He is present everywhere. David asks:

> Where can I go from Your Spirit?
> Or where can I flee from Your presence?
> If I ascend into heaven, You are there;
> If I make my bed in hell, behold, You are there.
> If I take the wings of the morning,
> And dwell in the uttermost parts of the sea,
> Even there Your hand shall lead me,
> And Your right hand shall hold me. (*Ps 139:7-10*)

Athanasius explains what this omnipresence means, by first pointing to the omnipresence of the Son:

> So, the Son is everywhere. Because he is in the Father and the Father in him … But creatures are in the places assigned to them … But if the Son is everywhere because he is not in places assigned to him but in the Father, and if he is not a creature because he is outside of all things, then it cannot follow that the Spirit is a creature, because he is not in places assigned to him but fills all things and is outside of all things. For thus is it written: *The Spirit of the Lord has filled the world* [Wisdom of Solomon 1:7]. And David sings in the psalm: *Where can I go from your Spirit?* [Ps 139:7]. For he is not in a place but outside all things and in the Son, as the Son is in the Father. For this reason then he is not a creature.[11]

Athanasius helps us to see that the omnipresence of the Triune God is to be understood in personal terms, through the mutual indwelling of the Father, Son and Holy Spirit.

The Holy Spirit is almighty God for He shares in the attribute of omnipotence. He is called the Spirit of might (*Isa. 11:2*). In His power, He performs 'mighty signs and wonders' (*Rom. 15:19*). The power of the Holy Spirit is the same power as the power of the Father and the Son. We can see that His power is the very power of God by comparing the same account in two of the gospels. In Luke's Gospel, Jesus says that it is by 'the finger of God' that He drives out demons (*Lk 11:20*), but in the parallel passage in

---

[11] Athanasius, *Letters to Serapion on the Holy Spirit*, 2.13.2-3

Matthew's Gospel, Jesus says that He casts out demons 'by the Spirit of God' (*Mt 12:28*). Therefore, the power of the Spirit of God is the power of the finger of God. In other words, the Holy Spirit's power is God's very own power. Didymus the Blind points out that 'without a doubt the finger is ascribed to the substance of him whose finger it is.'[12] In other words, if the power of the Holy Spirit is the same power as the finger of God, then the Holy Spirit must be consubstantial (*homoousios*) with God the Father.

The Holy Spirit also shares in the divine attribute of omniscience, for He knows all things (*Isa. 40:13-14; Rom. 11:34*). Not only does He know everything within the created order of the heavens and the earth, but the Holy Spirit also knows everything concerning God Himself, for 'no one knows the things of God except the Spirit of God' (*1 Cor. 2:10-12*). The Spirit knows the things that only God can know.

The Holy Spirit Shares the Names of God

The Holy Spirit also shares in the names of God. For a start, he is called God. When Peter confronts Ananias over his sin, he asks him, 'Ananias, why has Satan filled your heart to lie to the Holy Spirit?' (*Acts 5:3*). In the next verse, however, Peter tells Ananias that he has 'not lied to men but to God' (*Acts 5:4*). In one breath Peter can speak of lying to the Holy Spirit, and in the next breath He can call the same divine person 'God'. We see the same thing through the lips of David in the Old Testament. In his last words, David introduced a prophecy by saying:

> The Spirit of the LORD spoke by me,
> And His word was on my tongue.
> The God of Israel said,
> The Rock of Israel spoke to me. (*2 Sam. 23:2-3*)

Here David calls the same divine person 'the Spirit of the LORD', 'the God of Israel', and 'the Rock of Israel'. So David calls the Holy Spirit God. Ezekiel does something very similar, telling us that 'the LORD God' fell upon him, but then revealing that this LORD God is 'the Spirit' (*Ezek. 8:1-3*).

The Holy Spirit is also called by the covenant name of God – the LORD (YHWH or Jehovah). In Judges we read of how 'the Spirit of the LORD came mightily upon' Samuel (*Jdgs 15:14*). Yet, in the next chapter, when Samuel discovers that the Spirit has departed from him, we read that 'the

---

[12] Didymus the Blind, *On the Holy Spirit*, 88.

LORD had departed from him' (*Jdgs 16:20*). So the Spirit is the LORD. In Hebrews, 'the Holy Spirit says' that the children of Israel tested and tried him in the wilderness (*Heb. 3:7-9*), yet in Exodus, when He is tempted by the children of Israel, He is called the LORD (*Ex. 17:7*).

The Holy Spirit is called by the name of 'the Lord' in the New Testament as well. Paul writes to the Corinthians:

> Now the Lord is the Spirit, and where the Spirit of the Lord is, there is freedom. And we all, with unveiled face, beholding the glory of the Lord, are being transformed into the same image from one degree of glory to another. For this comes from the Lord who is the Spirit. (*2 Cor. 3:17-18*, ESV)

Finally, the Holy Spirit shares in one name with the Father and the Son. Jesus commanded His disciples to baptise 'in the name of the Father and of the Son and of the Holy Spirit' (*Mt 28:19*). Not in their names, but in their name. And so Father, Son and Holy Spirit is *the* name of God. And in the Bible, names are not merely labels by which to address people, but rather they reveal someone's identity. So, the very identity of the true and living God is Father, Son and Holy Spirit.

The Holy Spirit performs the Deeds of God

The Holy Spirit does deeds which only God can do. The Father created all things through the Holy Spirit (*Gen. 1:2; Job 26:13; Ps 33.6*), and by the Spirit He preserves and upholds His creation (*Job 33:4; Ps 104:30*).

When the Spirit speaks, the words which He speaks are the word of God. The Holy Spirit revealed to the aged Simeon 'that he would not see death before he had seen the Lord's Christ' (*Lk 2:26*). Yet, on the day that Simeon finally did see Jesus the Saviour, he 'blessed God' (*Lk 2:28*) saying 'Lord, now You are letting Your servant depart in peace, according to Your word' (*Lk 2:29*). So the word of the Holy Spirit (*v.26)* is the word of God (*v.28*) and the word of the Lord (*v.29*). The Spirit also inspired the God-breathed Scriptures (*2 Pet. 1:21; cf. 2 Tim. 3:16*).

The Holy Spirit was active in the saving works of Christ. In the incarnation, the Holy Spirit came upon Mary as the power of the Most High overshadowed her (*Lk 1:35*). At the cross, it was 'through the eternal Spirit' that the Incarnate Son 'offered Himself without spot to God' (*Heb. 9:14*).

And now the Holy Spirit is involved in the divine work of salvation, as he applies to us the redemption purchased by Christ. It is the Holy Spirit who regenerates us. In reply to Nicodemus' question about how someone could be born again, Jesus said:

> Most assuredly, I say to you, unless one is born of water and the Spirit, he cannot enter the kingdom of God. That which is born of the flesh is flesh, and that which is born of the Spirit is spirit. Do not marvel that I said to you, 'You must be born again.' The wind blows where it wishes, and you hear the sound of it, but cannot tell where it comes from and where it goes. So is everyone who is born of the Spirit. (*Jn 3:5-8*)

Paul also tells us that our regeneration is through the 'renewing of the Holy Spirit' (*Titus 3:5*). As Jesus says, 'it is the Spirit who gives life' (*Jn 6:63*).

The Holy Spirit also sanctifies believers (*Rom. 15:16; 1 Pet 1:2*). In fact, the Trinitarian nature of our salvation is seen in that 'God from the beginning chose you for salvation through sanctification by the Spirit and belief in the truth' (*2 Thess. 2:13*). The Father has chosen us for salvation through faith in Christ (who is the Truth) and by the sanctification of the Holy Spirit. So the Holy Spirit is set alongside the Father and the Son in the work of our salvation. Finally, in the glorious culmination of our salvation on the last day, the Holy Spirit will be involved in our resurrection from the dead. For, 'if the Spirit of Him who raised Jesus from the dead dwells in you, He who raised Christ from the dead will also give life to your mortal bodies through His Spirit who dwells in you' (*Rom. 8:11*).

The Holy Spirit also accomplishes the deeds that only God can do in the Church. The Holy Spirit sets apart apostles and makes elders, so it is the Holy Spirit who calls to the ministry and who reveals to the Church these calls (*Acts 13:2; 20:28*). Yet, it is God alone who calls to His service (*1 Tim. 1:1; Rom. 1:1; Heb. 5:4*). The Holy Spirit also sends out His servants on His gospel mission (*Acts 13:4*), yet it is the Lord who sends out 'labourers into His harvest' (*Mt 9:38*). As Didymus the Blind says:

> If those whom Christ sent to evangelize and baptize the nations are those whom the Holy Spirit placed in charge of the Church and the Father appointed by his decree, there can be no doubt that the Father, Son and Holy Spirit have a single activity and approval. It follows from this that the Trinity has the same substance.[13]

So the Holy Spirit does the things only God can do. He shares in the honours, attributes, names and deeds of God, and therefore, He can be none other than God Himself. Thus the Holy Spirit is the true and living God, and

---

[13] Didymus the Blind, *On the Holy Spirit*, 105

the Holy Spirit is a third person distinct from the Father or the Son. The God of the Bible, and the God of the Christian faith is the Triune God: Father, Son and Holy Spirit – one God in three persons.

The Procession of the Holy Spirit

The Holy Spirit, who is the Spirit of the Father and the Spirit of the Son, is God. But what is the relationship between God the Holy Spirit and the Father and the Son? We've already looked at the monarchy of the Father, and we've already seen that the Son is eternally begotten of the Father, as God from God. So what of the Holy Spirit's relation of origin?

Is the Holy Spirit begotten like the Son? No, He is not begotten, for if He were there would be two Sons. The Holy Spirit is 'neither made, nor created, nor begotten; but proceeding.'[14] The doctrine of the Spirit's procession takes its name from its Scriptural basis in *John 15:26*, where Jesus told His disciples: 'But when the Helper comes, whom I shall send to you from the Father, the Spirit of truth who proceeds from the Father, He will testify of Me.' Christ told them that He would, after His ascension, send the Spirit. But, continuously, the Spirit proceeds from the Father. Just as the generation of the Son is an eternal generation, so too the procession of the Spirit is an eternal procession. John of Damascus writes:

> Only the Son is begotten, for He is begotten of the substance of the Father without beginning and independently of time. And only the Holy Ghost proceeds: not begotten, but proceeding from the substance of the Father. Such is the teaching of sacred Scripture, but as to the manner of the begetting and the procession, this is beyond understanding.[15]

That last sentence from the Damascene is very important to remember: the eternal generation of the Son and the eternal procession of the Spirit are things which we cannot understand or explain. We cannot imagine what it is like be eternally begotten or to eternally proceed. Yet, we confess these truths because they are revealed by Holy Scripture, and so by these words

---

[14] *Athanasian Creed*
[15] John of Damascus, *De Fide Orthodoxa*, i.8 (ET p.182).

we signify the distinction between the three persons of the Godhead.[16] The Father is like the Son and the Spirit in every way, except that He is neither begotten nor proceeding. The Son is the like the Father and the Spirit in every way, except that He is begotten. The Spirit is like the Father and the Son in every way, except that He proceeds.

> The Son is not the Father; there is *one* Father, yet he is whatever the Father is. The Spirit is not the Son because he is from God; there is *one* Only-Begotten. Yet whatever the Son is, he is. The three are a single whole in their Godhead and the single whole is three in personalities.[17]

These relations of origin 'serve to express the hypostatic [personal] diversity of the Three'[18] while upholding their unity as the one God in three persons.

Outgoing Love Requires a Third Person

In the middle ages, a Scottish monk joined a French abbey on the banks of the river Seine. His name was Richard and the institution he joined was the Abbey of Saint Victor, so ever since, he's been known as Richard of Saint Victor. This abbey was one of the most prestigious schools of theology in the twelfth century, and Richard was one of its most prestigious sons.

Richard gave himself to contemplation of the Trinity and set out to demonstrate why God must be the Triune God. If God were only one person, he concluded, God could not be love, for none can possess love 'in the truest sense of the word if he loves himself exclusively.' True love must be 'aimed at someone else' and so 'if a multiplicity of persons is absent, there can be no place for charity-love.'[19] But Victor wasn't satisfied just with an explanation for the plurality of persons in the Godhead; he wanted to think about why our God is Father, Son and Holy Spirit, and not just Father and Son. His conclusion was that perfect love between two persons would be so exclusive that it wouldn't be an outgoing love that reaches down to us.

---

[16] Space precludes discussion of the *Filioque*: the question of whether the Spirit proceeds from the Father and the Son, or from the Father alone. This is the creedal issue which, since the middle ages, has divided the Eastern and Western Churches.

[17] Gregory of Nazianzus, *Oration* 31.9 (ET p.123).

[18] Vladimir Lossky, *In the Image and Likeness of God*, (Crestwood: SVS, 1974), 79.

[19] Richard of Saint Victor, *On the Trinity*, 3.2

Actually, when two reciprocally loving [persons] hug each other with the greatest desire and enjoy their mutual love very much, the supreme happiness of one consists of the intimate love of the other and conversely, the prime joy of the latter, resides in the love of the former.[20]

Therefore, as the true and living God is not a grasping, self-absorbed God, but rather a God who overflows in love towards His people, there has to be a third person – the Holy Spirit – in the Godhead for the perfect love of God to be this delightful outgoing love for us.

If we want both of them to be able to communicate delights as such, they necessarily have to have another one to be loved in the same manner. Consequently, as we have said, if the two [persons] who love each other are so generous to be willing to communicate every perfection of theirs, it is necessary that both of them require with equal desire and for the same reason a third [person] to be loved in the same fashion. [It is also necessary that they] possess him, according to their desire, in the fullness of their power.[21]

This is why the Triune God is the God of creation and the God of salvation: because from all eternity He has been the Father, Son and Holy Spirit, who delight to share their perfect love. And through the Holy Spirit, we are caught up into the love of the Triune God, as the Spirit unites us by faith to Christ, who 'is the true Son, and so when we receive the Spirit we are made sons,'[22] and share in the love of the Father for His Son (*Eph. 2:18; Jn 17:23*).

---

[20] Richard of Saint Victor, *On the Trinity*, 3.15

[21] Richard of Saint Victor, *On the Trinity*, 3.15

[22] Athanasius, *Letters to Serapion on the Holy Spirit*, 1.19.5

Chapter 5

The Holy Trinity

In the United Kingdom, fewer than ten percent of people go to church, yet two thirds of the population say they believe in God. The question is, who is this God in whom they say they believe? As we've seen, Jesus is the revelation of God. So the only true God is the God revealed by Jesus. And very often, He is nothing like the God in whom people say they do or don't believe.

In the last few chapters we've seen that Jesus Himself is true God from true God, begotten of the Father from all eternity. And we've seen as well that Jesus brings us to His Father as our Father and our God. The one God and Father who eternally loves His Son in the fellowship of the Spirit is the God whose very identity is love. And Jesus pours out God the Holy Spirit, breathed out by God the Father, who glorifies the Father in the Son. We've seen that Jesus is God, the Father is God, and the Holy Spirit is God. We've seen that the Son is not the Father and the Father is not the Son. The Spirit is not the Son and the Son is not the Spirit. The Father is not the Spirit and the Spirit is not the Father. And yet these three are one: 'one God in Trinity, and Trinity in Unity.'[1]

To know the true and living God is to know the Holy Trinity. This is who God is: the Father who eternally loves His Son in the unity of the Spirit. Johann Gerhard reminds us that we cannot think of God apart from the Trinity:

> Whoever does not know the mystery of the Trinity does not know God as He has revealed Himself in His Word nor does he know the definition of God given in the Scriptures. Therefore he is straying from the true God and does not know God Himself. ... For whoever does not know God as He has revealed Himself in His Word is making up for himself an idol in his heart.[2]

The God of the Bible, and the God of our salvation, is the Triune God.

---

[1]*Athanasian Creed*; For 'these three are one', see *1 Jn 5:7*. As this *Comma Iohanneum* is such a highly disputed text, I'll make mention of it only here in a footnote, and not base any Scriptural argument upon it.

[2] Gerhard, *Loci*, Exegesis III §3 (ET p.268).

The Revelation of the Trinity in the Life of Christ Incarnate

Jesus is the revelation of God. Therefore Jesus revealed the Triune God in His life on earth. After being left behind in the temple at the age of twelve, He said to Mary and Joseph, 'Did you not know that I must be about My Father's business?' (*Lk 2:49*). This was not simply a commonplace way for a child to speak of God. Jesus specifically calls Him 'My' Father. And, Luke emphasises for us that Mary and Joseph 'did not understand the statement which He spoke to them' (*Lk 2:50*). They did not understand Him, because these were not the words of a typical child speaking of God, but the words of the child who was like no other child: the incarnate Son of God speaking of God His Father. In the previous chapters we've already looked at some of the things Jesus said which revealed the Father and the Spirit. But here let's focus on two events in the incarnate life of Christ which reveal to us the Triune God.

The Revelation of the Trinity in the Transfiguration of Christ

Years later, on Mount Tabor, Jesus revealed the Trinity in another way entirely. Having taken Peter, James and John 'up on the mountain to pray' (*Lk 9:28*), Jesus was transfigured in their sight.

> As He prayed, the appearance of His face was altered, and His robe became white and glistening. And behold, two men talked with Him, who were Moses and Elijah, who appeared in glory and spoke of His decease which He was to accomplish at Jerusalem. (*Lk 9:29-31*)

When the disciples awoke from sleep, 'they saw His glory' (*Lk 9:32*). But that was not the end, for 'a cloud came and overshadowed them … and a voice came out of the cloud, saying, "This is My beloved Son. Hear Him!"' (*Lk 9:34-35*). There, Jesus stands shining in the radiance of His glory on the mountain. The disciples eyes are opened to see the reality of the glory which is always Christ's, for He is always the radiance and brightness of the Father's glory (*Heb. 1:3*) But as the glory of the Son is seen it is seen in His relationship of sonship with the Father. Jesus shines with the brightness of the Father's glory and the Father announces His love for His Son. And the

Son stands with His disciples under the Father's declaration of love, in the bright cloud which is the Holy Spirit.[3]

It's not that Peter, James and John see Jesus speaking to two strangers in a patch of fog. They know who these two men are (*Lk 9:33*). They know that Jesus is speaking with Moses and Elijah. And they know the significance of the cloud (*cf. Lev. 16:2*). Moses was the mediator of the old covenant. Elijah was a mighty prophet standing at the head of a long line of prophets. These were two significant servants of God: two men who had known mighty revelation of God. So, when the disciples hear a voice in the cloud in the presence of Moses and Elijah, they would know exactly who was speaking. This was the voice of God Himself, saying 'This is my beloved Son. Hear Him.' The voice in the cloud identifies Jesus as God's Son, not a messenger like Moses or Elijah. He is the Beloved Son of the Father, and so this mighty revelation of the transfiguration of Christ displays to us the eternal relationship of love which exists between the Father and His Son in the Spirit. The Father tells the disciples to 'hear' His Beloved Son. Jesus is the revelation of God, and so we must hear Him to hear what God has to say about Himself and about His great salvation. So, through His transfiguration, Jesus reveals, not only Himself in His glorious radiance, but His Father too, in the unity of the Spirit. In His transfiguration, Jesus reveals the Trinity.

The Revelation of the Trinity in the Baptism of Christ

Yet the transfiguration is not the first such revelation in the incarnate life of Christ. At the very outset of His public ministry, Jesus came to the Jordan to be baptised by John. And in His baptism, Jesus revealed the Holy Trinity.

> When all the people were baptized, it came to pass that Jesus also was baptized; and while He prayed, the heaven was opened. And the Holy Spirit descended in bodily form like a dove upon Him, and a voice came from heaven which said, 'You are My beloved Son; in You I am well pleased.' (*Lk 3:21-22*)

Here at the baptism of Jesus, the Father declares His love for His Son, and the Holy Spirit descends visibly upon the Son. The Holy Spirit is poured out as a visible anointing upon the Anointed One (the Christ). At Jesus' baptism

---

[3] Thomas Aquinas, *Summa Theologiae*, 3a.45.5, *ad*. 2.; Gregory Palamas, *Discourse on the Holy Transfiguration*.

we see what Mark sums up as the gospel at the beginning of His Gospel: 'The beginning of the gospel of Jesus Christ, the Son of God.' The title Christ (from the Greek) or Messiah (from the Hebrew) means 'Anointed One.' So, in His baptism, we see the clear demonstration of the identity of the one who is God's good news. He is 'Jesus Christ'; in the Spirit's descent as a dove, He visibly 'christs' or anoints the Son. Jesus is 'the Son of God'; in the Father's declaration of love He announces that Jesus is His Son. And this is for us very good news indeed.

It is impossible for there to be an anointed one, without an anointer and an anointing. As Irenaeus, a disciple of a disciple of the apostle John, pointed out:

> Indeed, in the name of Christ is implied He who anoints, and He who is anointed, and the ointment with which He is anointed. And so it is the Father who anoints, and the Son is anointed in the Spirit who is the Ointment. This the Word says through Isaias, *The Spirit of ... God is upon me, because He has anointed me* [Isa. 61:1], by which he points out the Father who anoints, and the Son who is anointed, and the Ointment which is the Spirit.[4]

Basil of Caesarea put it like this: 'For the naming of Christ is the confession of the whole [Trinity], since it is clear that God is the one anointing, the Son is the one anointed, and the Spirit is the anointing.'[5] The very title and name 'Christ' points us not only to who Jesus is, but also to His Father and His Spirit. The title 'Christ' points us to the whole Trinity. And so the very identity and title of Jesus reveals the Triune God.

And at His baptism, the Christ reveals the Trinity. Not only does the baptism of Christ reveal the fact of the Trinity, but also the relationship which exists between the Father, Son and Holy Spirit. As Jesus stands in the waters of the Jordan, while the Father speaks and the dove descends, there we see the Father, Son and Holy Spirit together in love, fellowship, and united in their purpose and will. The Father declares His love for the Son in the Spirit. The three rest together in that moment in the Jordan in perfect loving fellowship and communion. Not only does the Father declare His love for the Son, but He also says that He is well pleased in Him. The Father takes pleasure in His Son; He delights in Him. The Father is speaking Scriptural words over His Son here, quoting from *Isaiah 42:1*: 'Behold! My Servant whom I uphold, My Elect One in whom My soul delights!'

---

[4] Irenaeus, *Against Heresies*, 3.18.3
[5] Basil of Caesarea, *On the Holy Spirit*, 12.28

(Matthew's Greek version reads, 'Behold! My Servant whom I have chosen, My Beloved in whom My soul is well pleased!: *Mt 12:18*). This is a word of rejoicing over the Son. The Father loves His Son, delights in Him and rejoices over Him. That this is a quotation from the Old Testament shows us that this joy did not only begin with the incarnation. And this loving joy and delight is certainly not just beginning now at Christ's baptism in the Jordan. This is the eternal relationship between the Father and the Son (*cf. Jn 17:24*).

But Isaiah also shows us that this love, joy and delight is not limited to the Father and the Son. For when the Lord, in Isaiah, speaks of 'the one in whom My soul delights,' He then immediately goes on to declare, 'I have put My Spirit upon Him' (*Isa. 42:1*). This joy and delight is shared by the Father and the Son with the Holy Spirit. Which is exactly what we see at Jesus' baptism.

Why did the Holy Spirit descend in bodily form like a dove? A dove is not a random creature in Scripture. Back in *Genesis 8*, Noah sent out a dove from the ark at the end of the flood. 'Then the dove came to him in the evening, and behold, a freshly plucked olive leaf was in her mouth; and Noah knew that the waters had receded from the earth' (*Gen. 8:11*). When the dove returned with the fresh olive leaf, those aboard the ark knew that there was dry land once again. Now they knew that they had been carried safely through the judgment and out on the other side into a new abundant life. So the dove brought them great joy. The dove brought them the joy that, for them, the judgment was over. And the dove brought them the joy of a new life.

Like the dove on Noah's ark, the Holy Spirit is the bringer of joy. He brings us the joy of assurance that Christ has carried us safely through judgment through His death on the cross and out on the other side into new life through His resurrection from the dead. But the Holy Spirit does not only begin to be the bringer of joy after the creation of the world and in relation to human beings. He has always been the Spirit of joy.[6] The Father has always loved His Son in the joy of the Holy Spirit.

And so in the baptism of Jesus we see the Trinity for what it really is: not a complicated problem of mathematics or philosophy, but the Father, Son and Holy Spirit united together in loving, joyful fellowship. In the waters of the Jordan we see that the Triune God is the Father loving His Son in the Spirit.

---

[6] Note the frequent connection between the Holy Spirit and joy and delight in the Scriptures: *Ps 51:12; Isa. 42:1; Lk 10:21; Acts 13:52; Rom. 14:17; 15:13; Gal. 5:22; Phil. 3:3; 1 Thess. 1:6.*

And, in Jesus' baptism, we see that the Father, Son and Holy Spirit are not only one in their being of loving fellowship, but also one in purpose and will. This is the outset of Jesus' public ministry which will culminate in the cross. In fact, Jesus' baptism is even more tightly linked to the cross than just the beginning of a series of events which will ultimately lead there (*Mt 20:22; Mk 10:38; Lk 12:50*).[7] So, through the revelation of the Trinity in this inaugural step towards the cross, we see that the Father, Son and Holy Spirit are united in their will and purpose for Jesus' sinless life and atoning death for us and for our salvation. The substitutionary life and work of Christ is not something the Son does independently, on His own, as if there were some division between the will and purpose of the Father and the Son. The Son has willingly come as our propitiation, sent by the Father in love (*1 Jn 4:10*). 'The Son can do nothing of Himself, but what He sees the Father do' (*Jn 5:19*). And it is 'through the eternal Spirit' that the incarnate Son 'offered Himself without spot to God' on the cross of Calvary (*Heb. 9:14*). The revelation of the Trinity in Jesus' cross-linked baptism declares the unity of will and purpose of the Triune God in the atoning work of the incarnate Son for us and for our salvation. At Jesus' baptism we see that the Triune God loves us to the degree that one of the Trinity would suffer in the flesh.

And, as Johann Gerhard pointed out in the years after the Reformation, this revelation of the Trinity at the outset of Jesus' ministry has an ongoing impact in focusing the message of the Church.

> This occurred when Jesus was 30 years old and was about to begin His ministry of preaching in these lands, because it was at this age that the Levitical priests formerly would be admitted to the public ministries. Therefore this theophany was not merely the solemn confirmation of the ministry of the Messiah but also a brief summary of that doctrine which would be preached in the Church in the time of the New Testament.[8]

The revelation of the Trinity in the waters of the Jordan continually reminds the Church of her message and the theme of her preaching. The Church is to proclaim the Word of the Lord: to proclaim the Beloved Son with whom the Father is well pleased. The Church is to make known the God who is the loving Father who pours out His eternal love upon His Son in the joy and unity of the Holy Spirit. The Church is to proclaim the Triune God revealed in Jesus Christ.

---

[7] We'll return to Jesus' baptism and look at this aspect more in chapter 13.

[8] Gerhard, *Loci*, Exegesis III §75 (ET p.333).

At Jesus' baptism in the Jordan we have a mighty revelation of the Triune God: three persons, distinct from one another (the Son in the water, the Spirit descending, and the Father speaking), yet united perfectly together in joyful loving fellowship. This is our God.

The Triune God is Love

What was God doing before the foundation of the world? Before the foundation of the world, the Father was pouring out His love upon the Son in the joy of the Holy Spirit (*Jn 17:24*). 'God is love' (*1 Jn 4:8*) and so His love has no beginning and will never have an end. As we've seen in chapter 3, when John writes 'God is love', He is writing about the Father. Yet because the Father is love, and eternally loves His Son in the Spirit, love is also the very essence of the Trinity. As Thomas Torrance puts it:

> This is what the doctrine of the Holy Trinity supremely means, that God himself is Love ... for God's Being is an eternal movement in Love, and consists in the Love with which the Father, the Son and the Holy Spirit ceaselessly love one another.[9]

The identity of the Trinity is found in the eternal fellowship of love between the Father, Son and Holy Spirit, and so 'the essence of the Triune God is love.'[10]

On Not Three Gods

Three distinct persons are revealed to us in the waters of the Jordan, but not three Gods. Jesus Himself quotes from the Shema (*Dt 6:4*). When one of the scribes asked Him about the greatest commandment, Jesus answered:

---

[9] Thomas F. Torrance, *The Christian Doctrine of God*, (London: T & T Clark, 1996),162-163.

[10] D.P. Williams, *The Sanctuary of the Christian Life* (Manchester: Puritan Press, 1948), 21, cf. 76; cf. D.P. Williams, *The Trinity*, 1:16; cf. W.R. Thomas, *On Ephesians*, 145. Even D.P. Williams' Welsh hymns point to the love between the Father, Son and Holy Spirit as the essence and eternal life of the Trinity. E.g. *Molwch Dduw*, 394 and 185.

> The first of all the commandments is: 'Hear, O Israel, the Lord our God, the Lord is one. And you shall love the Lord your God with all your heart, with all your soul, with all your mind, and with all your strength.' This is the first commandment. (*Mk 12:29-30*)

The Scriptures of both the Old and New Testaments are clear: there is only one true God and He is the LORD. Moses, who saw the Lord Jesus face to face (*Ex 33:11*) told the children of Israel that 'the LORD Himself is God; there is none other beside Him … The LORD Himself is God in heaven above and on the earth beneath; there is no other' (*Dt 4:35, 39*). The prophet Isaiah gives the most extended treatment of God's oneness in the whole of the Scriptures in *Isaiah 43-45*.[11] The constant refrain in these chapters is 'I am the LORD and there is no other; there is no God besides me' (*Isa. 45:5*). Yet, startlingly, in the midst of this emphatic declaration of the uniqueness of the one true God, we read:

> Thus says the LORD, the King of Israel,
> And his Redeemer, the LORD of hosts:
> I am the First and I am the Last;
> Besides Me there is no God. (*Isa. 44:6*)

There is no God other than the one God who is the LORD, and the Redeemer. And this Redeemer is also called the LORD (the LORD of hosts). Even within the Bible's most extended passage on the uniqueness of the one true God, we find a possible indication[12] of distinction within the one God between the LORD and the LORD, which, as we saw in chapter 2, is one of the ways in which we see the presence of the Son in the Old Testament. Isaiah's God besides which there is no other, is the Father together with His Son. Elsewhere in his prophecies, Isaiah shows us that the LORD the Redeemer who is from the LORD is anointed with the Spirit of the LORD (*Isa. 61:1*: the one who is speaking is the LORD; cf. context of *Isa. 60:22* and *Isa. 61:8*) and we know that this LORD who is speaking is the Son (*cf. Lk 4:16-22*). Isaiah's God, besides whom there is no other, is the LORD who anoints the LORD with the Spirit of the LORD. Isaiah's God, besides whom there is no other, is the Triune God.

---

[11] There are 10 references to the uniqueness of the one true God in this section of Isaiah (*Isa. 43:10-11; 44:6, 8, 24; 45:5, 6, 14, 18, 21, 22*).

[12] There is a way of reading this without the distinction, which is taken up in the NIV translation. However, the declaration 'I am the First and I am the Last' is certainly applied to the Son elsewhere in Scripture (*Rev. 1:17-18; 2:8*).

And the same God whom Isaiah spoke of, is the God who is revealed in the baptism of Christ. So what we see in Jesus' baptism isn't three Gods in very close cooperation. No, not at all. What we see in Jesus' baptism is the one God who is Father, Son and Holy Spirit: the Father who eternally loves His Son in the joy of the Spirit.

But, if the One God is three persons united in love, how do we guard the unity of the Godhead, and avoid drifting off into a heretical tritheism? Four doctrines guard the unity of the three persons united in love: two which we've already seen (the *monarchy of the Father*[13] and the *relations of origin*[14]), as well as two which we'll look at now (*perichoresis* and the *inseparable operations*).[15]

Perichoresis

The Father, Son, and Holy Spirit are perfectly united in love. They are also perfectly united in purpose, in will and, in action. All of that is centred in Jesus and the Father's great love for His Son. So these are not three separate and divided persons, each getting on with their own agendas. The Father, Son and Holy Spirit are one God, unitedly acting together in love.

In John's Gospel, Jesus reveals to us how He and the Father, together with the Spirit, are so united in will, purpose, and action and how they are fully involved in one another's works, so that 'the Son can do nothing of Himself, but what He sees the Father do; for whatever He does, the Son also does in like manner' (*Jn 5:19*). Likewise, the Spirit 'will not speak on His own authority, but whatever He hears He will speak' (*Jn 16:13*). How is this so? It is so, because the Father, Son and Holy Spirit mutually indwell one another.

When Philip asked to be shown the Father, Jesus answered:

> Have I been with you so long, and yet you have not known Me, Philip? He who has seen Me has seen the Father; so how can you say, 'Show us the Father'? Do you not believe that I am in the Father, and the Father in Me?

---

[13] See chapter 3.

[14] We've looked at the eternal generation of the Son in chapter 3, and the procession of the Spirit in chapter 4.

[15] Together with all of this there is the doctrine of *consubstantiality*, or the *homousion*, which we shall look at in chapter 6.

> The words that I speak to you I do not speak on My own authority; but the
> Father who dwells in Me does the works. Believe Me that I am in the
> Father and the Father in Me, or else believe Me for the sake of the works
> themselves. (*Jn 14:9-11; cf. Jn 10:38*)

To see the Son is to see the Father because the Father is in the Son and the
Son is in the Father. The Father dwells in the Son and the Son dwells in the
Father. Later in John 14, Jesus tells His disciples, 'I will not leave you
orphans; I will come to you … If anyone loves Me, he will keep My word;
and My Father will love him, and We will come to him and make Our home
with him' (*Jn 14:18, 23*). When the Son comes to us, the Father comes too, for
the Father dwells in the Son and the Son dwells in the Father. But not only
that, the context of Jesus' statements here is His teaching on the coming of
the Paraclete: the Holy Spirit. It is when the Holy Spirit comes to us (*Jn
14:16-17*) that Jesus will come to us (*Jn 14:18*) and the Father and Son will
make their home with us (*Jn 14:23*). This then points to the mutual
indwelling, not only of the Father and the Son, but of the Father, Son and
Holy Spirit. When the Holy Spirit comes to dwell in us, the Father and the
Son come to dwell in us in and with Him, because the Father and the Son
dwell in the Holy Spirit and the Holy Spirit dwells in the Father and the Son
(see also *Rom. 8:9-10; 1 Cor. 2:10-12; Eph. 2:22*). This is the doctrine of
perichoresis.[16]

Because of this mutual indwelling of perichoresis, the Father, Son and
Holy Spirit are united:

> So as not to be confused, but to adhere closely together, and they have
> their circumincession [perichoresis] one in the other without any blending
> or mingling and without change or division in substance.[17]

Those are the words of John of Damascus, writing in 8th century Syria.
About nine hundred years later in Germany, Johann Gerhard wrote of this
perichoresis of the Trinity:

> There is no one of these persons outside another, nor can we know,
> worship or call upon one of them without also at the same time knowing,
> worshipping, or invoking the others too. … But now the persons of the
> Trinity are related to each other in such a way that one of them is not

---

[16] Also sometimes called *circumincession*, and occasionally *mutual interpenetration*.
[17] John of Damascus, *De Fide Orthodoxa*, i.8 (ET p.187).

> outside another because of the consubstantiality and mutual interpenetration [perichoresis] of the persons.[18]

The Father is always in the Son and the Son is always in the Father. The Son is always in the Spirit and the Spirit is always in the Son. The Spirit is always in the Father, and the Father is always in the Spirit. You cannot divide the three persons of the Triune God, for they eternally mutually indwell one another. The three are one in their perichoresis.

Inseparable Operations

As the Father, Son and Holy Spirit mutually indwell one another in perichoresis, and so are never apart from one another, each person of the Trinity is at work in all of God's external works (*opera ad extra*).[19] Traditionally the church has summed up this doctrine with the Latin expression *opera Trinitatis ad extra indivisa sunt*: 'the external works of the Trinity are indivisible.' We can see this illustrated in how the Bible regularly attributes the works of God to each of the three persons of the Trinity. The Father creates (*Gen. 1:1*) through the Son (*Jn 1:3; Col. 1:16*) in the Spirit (*Gen. 1:2; Ps 33:6*). The Father saves (*Jn 3:16; 2 Tim. 1:8-9*) through the Son (*Jn 3:16; 2 Tim. 1:9-10*) in the Spirit (*Titus 3:5; 1 Pet. 1:2; Jn 3:3-5*).

The revelation of the Trinity in the baptism of Jesus in the waters of the Jordan also reveals the inseparable operation of the Triune God, for there the mission of God for the salvation of sinners in Christ through his sinless life and atoning death, is seen to belong equally to the Father, Son and Holy Spirit. As Cyril of Alexandria frequently said, 'all things are by (or from) the Father, through the Son, in the Holy Spirit.'[20] Or in the words of Gregory of Nyssa, in the Trinity there is:

> one motion and disposition of the good will which is communicated from the Father through the Son to the Spirit … Every operation which extends from God to the Creation … has its origin from the Father, and proceeds through the Son, and is perfected in the Holy Spirit.[21]

---

[18] Gerhard, *Loci*, Exegesis III §4 (ET p.268).

[19] *i.e.* external to the three-in-one life of the Triune God.

[20] Cyril of Alexandria, *Thesaurus* 580D; *Dial. Trin.* VI 596d; *In Io.* several times, e.g. *In Io.* I.9; see Hans Van Loon, *Dyophysite Christology of Cyril* (Brill, 2009), 204.

[21] Gregory of Nyssa, *On Not Three Gods* (*Ad Ablabius*)

Trinitarian Taxis

The shape of the inseparable operation – from the Father, through the Son, in the Spirit – together with the doctrine of the monarchy of the Father point us to the *taxis* of the Trinity. *Taxis* speaks of an order within the Trinity. That order is from the Father, through the Son, by the Spirit, and it is not a reversible order.[22] As Gregory of Nazianzus tells us, in the Trinity, 'the union is the Father from whom and to whom the ordering [*taxis*] of persons runs its course.'[23] Singaporean Pentecostal theologian, Simon Chan, explains this Trinitarian *taxis*:

> Monarchy also implies order (*taxis*), but order does not mean subordination but a way of relating within the Trinity that distinguishes Father from the Son and from the Spirit … The relationship is always *asymmetrical* … There is a *hypostatic* hierarchy, but not a moral or essential hierarchy in God … Hierarchy becomes a problem only when the other is seen as essentially or morally inferior, not when what is brought forth is essentially the same with the one who caused.[24]

This Trinitarian taxis means that 'while the Father loves the Son and the Son loves the Father, there is a very definite shape to their relationship. Overall the Father is the lover, the Son is the beloved … In his love [the Father] will send and direct the Son, whereas the Son never sends or directs the Father.'[25]

Jesus reveals our God to us, and the God He reveals is the Father, who pours out His love upon His Son in the Spirit. This is the God we see in the brightness and cloud of Mount Tabor at the transfiguration, and this is the God we see in the waters of the Jordan. And ultimately, this is the God we see at the cross of Mount Calvary.

---

[22] We pray and worship by the Spirit, through the Son, to the Father (*Eph. 2:18*), but that is our order of approach – the order in which God brings us from the outside in – not the order within the internal Triune life of the Three-in-One.

[23] Gregory of Nazianzus, *Oration 42.25*

[24] Simon Chan, *Pentecostal Ecclesiology* (Blandford Forum: Deo, 2011), 108-109.

[25] Michael Reeves, *The Good God*, 10.

Chapter 6

Confessing the Trinitarian Faith:
Speaking the Ineffable

The God of the Bible is the Father who eternally loves and gives life to His Son in the unity of the Spirit. The God of the Bible is the Triune God. God is not a single, solitary monad, all alone before He created the heavens and the earth. Neither are there three Gods. The Christian faith is faith in the God who is Three-In-One: the Triune God.

> We worship one God in Trinity, and Trinity in Unity; Neither confounding the Persons; nor dividing the Essence. For there is one Person of the Father; another of the Son; and another of the Holy Ghost. But the Godhead of the Father, of the Son, and of the Holy Ghost, is all one; the Glory equal, the Majesty coeternal. Such as the Father is; such is the Son; and such is the Holy Ghost. The Father uncreated; the Son uncreated; and the Holy Ghost uncreated. The Father unlimited; the Son unlimited; and the Holy Ghost unlimited. The Father eternal; the Son eternal; and the Holy Ghost eternal. And yet they are not three eternals; but one eternal. As also there are not three uncreated; nor three infinites, but one uncreated; and one infinite. So likewise the Father is Almighty; the Son Almighty; and the Holy Ghost Almighty. And yet they are not three Almighties; but one Almighty. So the Father is God; the Son is God; and the Holy Ghost is God. And yet they are not three Gods; but one God. So likewise the Father is Lord; the Son Lord; and the Holy Ghost Lord. And yet not three Lords; but one Lord. For like as we are compelled by the Christian verity; to acknowledge every Person by himself to be God and Lord; So are we forbidden by the catholic[1] religion; to say, There are three Gods, or three Lords.[2]

In the last few chapters we've seen that the Threeness and Oneness of the Triune God is not some sort of mathematical puzzle or philosophical speculation, but rather the reality of the one God who eternally exists in loving communion. But now we turn to the question of how we speak of God as Three-In-One. How can God be both one and three? God is both three and one, but He is not three in the same way in which He is one; and He is not one in the same way in which He is three.

---

[1] On the word *catholic*, see chapter 28.

[2] *Athanasian Creed*

It is often said that the Trinity was a doctrine which gradually developed over the first few centuries of the history of the Christian church. Yet, strictly speaking, that's not the case at all. From the very beginning the church worshipped the God who is Three-In-One; what took a few centuries to work out was how to speak of God's Threeness and Oneness in a way which was clear and which guarded against false teachings about the Triune God. Finally the church settled on the formula *one being; three persons*. These aren't perfect terms (and the church has never claimed that they are perfect) but they are terms which allow us to speak the unspeakable. Augustine reminds us:

> Yet when you ask 'three what?' human speech labours under a great dearth of words. So we say three persons, not in order to say that precisely, but in order not to be reduced to silence.[3]

When we speak of the Triune God as *one being, three persons*, we are attempting to speak the ineffable. As the emperor Gratian put it to Ambrose: 'We speak about these things not in the way we ought but in the way we can.'[4]

The Vocabulary of the Trinity

The vocabulary which the church developed to speak the ineffable is not necessarily all that transparent to us in the 21st century. So let's examine these words which the church uses to confess its faith in the Triune God.[5]

Three Persons

The Triune God is three persons, but He is not three people. Even in that strange plural we use for the persons of God, we have an indication that divine personhood and human personhood are not identical. Especially in the West, when we think of human beings, we tend to think of a person as

---

[3] Augustine, *De Trinitate*, 5.9
[4] Cited in Martin Chemnitz, *Loci Theologici*, 1:102.
[5] As the quotations from Augustine and Gratian above remind us, we cannot precisely define these words, for we are trying to speak what cannot be spoken.

an individual, and so we often think of a person independently of others.[6] Yet it cannot be so with the Triune God, for the Father, Son, and Holy Spirit mutually indwell one another and so are never one without the other. The Son is eternally begotten of the Father, and the Spirit is eternally proceeding. So we can never think of the Trinitarian persons independently of one another. The Father, Son and Holy Spirit are eternally three persons in loving relation.

There are traditionally two alternative words for person in Christian theology: *hypostasis* (from Greek) and *subsistence* (from Latin).

One Being

The Triune God is one being. The Greek word *ousia* gets translated into English as being, essence or substance. The problem is that, to the 21st century mind, substance sounds a bit like some sort of 'stuff' out of which something is made. But God is not made out of 'stuff.' There isn't something called holiness or eternity out of which God is formed. So we must guard against such a notion of substance as a thing.[7]

Rather, an *ousia* (*being/substance/essence*) was, in the thought of the early church, simply *something about which something can be said*. Therefore *being* is the most straightforward and transparent English equivalent, as an *ousia* is simply *that which is*. As Athanasius pointed out, the Triune God 'has His being beyond all substance and human discovery,'[8] therefore, we cannot base our idea of the one *ousia* of the Triune God on any other concept we have of *being* or *substance*. There is nothing like our God.

Johann Gerhard gives a classical explanation of the *ousia* of God as:

> an essence one in number and undivided, common to the three persons of the Godhead. This is not in the three persons partially, as if part of it were in the Father, part in the Son, and part in the Holy Spirit, but the entire

---

[6] Of course, a human person is never really fully independent of others, but is just a reflection of our western individualism.

[7] Which is why I've generally chosen to use the translation *being* rather than *substance*. However, it is important to be aware that, in Trinitarian terms, substance means the same as being, for the traditional English translation of *homoousios* (which we'll look at below) is *consubstantial* ('of the same substance').

[8] Athanasius, *Contra Gentes*, 2; Torrance's translation of this passage reads 'beyond all being and human conception of being'; Thomas F. Torrance, *The Christian Doctrine of God*, 116.

essence is in the Father, the entire essence is in the Son, and the entire
essence is in the Holy Spirit because of infinity and immateriality.[9]

As Gerhard notes, the being of God is not divided between the three
persons. As the Scriptures teach, 'all the fullness of the Godhead' dwells in
the Son (*Col. 2:9*). And the same is true of the Father and of the Spirit, for the
three persons who are the one being of the Godhead mutually indwell one
another perfectly and fully in perichoresis. Whatever the Father is, the Son
(who is begotten of Him) and the Spirit (who proceeds), also are. The
Father's being is the being of the Son and of the Holy Spirit. The *ousia* of
God does not exist beyond or outside of the three persons of the Trinity. The
one being of God consists of the three persons eternally united in loving
communion, for the true and living God has 'no true being, apart from
communion.'[10]

The Trinitarian theology of the Apostolic Church has always
highlighted this. The one being of God can only be found in the loving
communion of the three persons.[11] The very being of the Father is love, and
this is the one being of the Triune God.[12] Therefore, 'the essence [*ousia*] of
the Triune God is love.'[13] Love is 'the essence of His nature, the quality of
His Divine substance.'[14] His being is the eternal loving fellowship of the
three persons.[15]

Homoousios: The Basic Truth of the Christian Faith

'The basic truth of the Christian faith,' wrote D.P. Williams, is 'that God is
the Father, and that He has a Son within His essence, eternally.'[16] This is the
truth of the *homoousion*: that the Son is *homoousios* (*consubstantial*; of the same

---

[9] Gerhard, *Loci*, Exegesis III §48 (ET p.303).

[10] John Zizioulas, *Being as Communion* (London: Darton Longman & Todd, 1985), 17; cf.
Basil of Caesarea, *Ep. 38.4*.

[11] D.P. Williams, *The Trinity*, 1:47, 66.

[12] D.P. Williams, *The Trinity*, 1:17, 65.

[13] D.P. Williams, *The Sanctuary of the Christian Life* (Manchester: Puritan Press, 1948), 21,
cf. 56.

[14] D.P. Williams, *The Trinity*, 1:16.

[15] D.P. Williams, *The Trinity*, 1:66. Cf. *Molwch Dduw*, 394, 185 & 305; Cf. W.R. Thomas, *On
Ephesians*, 145.

[16] D.P. Williams, *The Trinity*, 1:77.

ousia/essence/substance/being) with the Father. And the Holy Spirit is *homoousios* with the Father and the Son. The reality of the *homoousios* shows us both that the Triune God is one, and that He is three. He is one, for the Father, Son and Spirit are of the same being; He is three for, as Basil the Great pointed out, 'nothing can be *homoousios* with itself, but one thing is *homoousios* with another.'[17] So, the word *homoousios* tells, us not only that the Father, Son and Holy Spirit are one being, but also that they are eternally distinct from one another. Let's have a look at some of the implications of this vital doctrine that the Father, Son and Holy Spirit are *homoousios*: that the true and living God is the Holy and Consubstantial Trinity.

Without the homoousion we would have no true revelation of God

Jesus reveals God perfectly because He is *homoousios* with the Father. We can have complete confidence in the revelation of God we receive in Jesus Christ, because:

> What is said of the Father, is said in Scripture of the Son also, all but His being called Father. For the Son Himself said, 'All things that the Father has are Mine' [*Jn 16:15*]; and He says to the Father, 'All Mine are Yours, and Yours are Mine' [*Jn 17:10*].[18]

And so when we see Jesus, we see the Father (*Jn 14:9*), for Jesus is the consubstantial revelation of the Father. Without the homoousion, 'we would be left completely in the dark about God. God would be for us no more than an absolute blank, of which we can neither think nor speak.'[19] But, because Jesus is consubstantial with the Father, He reveals the Father as He truly is. Our God is the Christ-like God, and can be none other than the Christ-like God, because of the homoousion.

> The homoousion asserts that God is eternally in himself what he is in Jesus Christ, and, therefore, that there is no hidden God behind the back of Jesus Christ, but only he who is made known to us in Jesus.[20]

---

[17] Basil of Caesarea, *Ep. 52.3* (*To the Canonicæ*)

[18] Athanasius, *De Synodis*, 49

[19] Thomas F. Torrance, *The Trinitarian Faith*, 133.

[20] Thomas F. Torrance, *The Trinitarian Faith*, 135.

Without the homoousion we would have no access to God

Ephesians 2:18 tells us that it is through Jesus that we have access 'by one Spirit' to the Father. However, if the Son and the Spirit were not homoousios with the Father, how could they give us access to the Father? It is because the Spirit and the Son are one with the Father that in the Son, by the Spirit, we have access to the knowledge of God and into the Father's relationship with His Son in the Spirit.[21] Only God can give access to God. We cannot climb up to Him; He must reach down to us, which the Father does in His consubstantial Son and through His consubstantial Spirit.

Without the homoousion we would know nothing of the love of God

God's love is given to us in the Son who gave Himself for us (*1 Jn 4:9-10*) and we experience the love of God poured out in our hearts by the Holy Spirit whom He gives us (*Rom. 5:5*). However, if the Spirit and the Son were not one with the Father, then the love of Christ and the love of the Spirit would not be God's own love. As Torrance puts it:

> In fact, there would be no revelation of the love of God but, on the contrary, something that rather mocks us, for while God is said to manifest his love to us in Jesus, he [would] not actually [be] that love in himself.[22]

Without the homoousion we would have no true Mediator between God and man

It is because Jesus Christ is *homoousios* with the Father that He can be the one Mediator between God and man. Christ did not stop being consubstantial with the Father in the incarnation. It is the Incarnate Son who said 'I and My Father are One' (*Jn 10:30*). And so the Incarnate Son is *homoousios* with the Father. Therefore, Christ is our true Mediator, for He is both one with the Father, and one with us: 'consubstantial with the Father according to the Godhead, and consubstantial with us according to the Manhood.'[23]

---

[21] See chapter 23.
[22] Torrance, *The Trinitarian Faith*, 134.
[23] *Definition of Chalcedon*

Homoousios with the Father, the Incarnate Son does what the Father does, joined with the Father in the inseparable operation of the Triune God. As the Father has been working, so Jesus, who is one with Him, has been working (*Jn 5:17*), 'for whatever He does, the Son also does in like manner' (*Jn 5:19*). Therefore, when the Son acts to save, He truly acts as the Mediator of the Father, and so mediates God's salvation. As Athanasius noted, 'through the Son is given what is given; and there is nothing but the Father operates it through the Son; for thus is grace secure to him who receives it.'[24]

Without the homoousion we would not know the saving grace of God

Because Jesus is one with the Father, the grace which has appeared in Jesus Christ is the grace of God Himself (*2 Tim. 1:9-10*). Therefore, 'God himself is the content of his saving grace in Jesus Christ. In Jesus Christ the Giver of grace and the Gift of grace are one and the same, for in him and through him it is none other than God himself who is savingly and creatively at work for us and our salvation.'[25] Torrance continues:

> What about the passion and sacrifice of Christ in which, as our Lord claimed, he gave himself for the redemption of mankind? What would be the message of the Cross if Christ and God were ultimately divided there, Christ only a creature on earth, and God infinitely removed in the exaltation of his divine being? How could the great reconciling exchange have taken place unless it was God himself who in his infinite loving-kindness had come in Jesus Christ to make our nature, our sin and our death his own, in order to save us.[26]

Therefore, the homoousion is vital to our salvation and to the gospel itself. The one who died on the cross for our sins is true God, of one being with the Father and the Spirit. In the words of the Heidelberg Catechism, only He who is true God 'might bear, in his manhood, the burden of God's wrath, and so obtain for and restore to us righteousness and life.'[27] Therefore, as Gregory of Nyssa pointed out, to reject the homoousion 'is nothing short of a plain denial of the message of salvation.'[28] Our salvation rests upon the Holy and Consubstantial Trinity.

---

[24] Athanasius, *Contra Arianos*, 3.12
[25] Torrance, *The Trinitarian Faith*, 138.
[26] Torrance, *The Trinitarian Faith*, 142.
[27] *Heidelberg Catechism*, 17.
[28] Gregory of Nyssa, *Against Eunomius*, 1.15

Trinitarian Heresies

Having spent the last few chapters looking at the Biblical teaching on the Trinity, and now having looked at the vocabulary the church developed to guard and teach the Trinitarian truth, let's have a brief look at some of the ways that people have strayed from this truth over the course of the church's history.

The Ancient Trinitarian Heresies

Denying the Three Persons: Modalism

Modalism is a modern name for a group of ancient heresies which stressed the absolute oneness of God. The ancient church knew these heretical groups under names like the *Noetians* and the *Sabellians*.[29] As John of Damascus tells us of the Noetians, they 'maintained that the Father and the Son and the Holy Ghost were the same.'[30] The modern term modalism comes from their idea that the one God, who knew no eternal distinction of persons, revealed himself to human beings in three successive modes. Hence, 'Father' was the mode in which he revealed himself in creation and the giving of the law. 'Son' was the mode in which he revealed himself in the incarnation of Christ for the salvation of the world. And 'Holy Spirit' was the mode in which he revealed himself in the application of salvation. So the God of the modalist heresies was not eternally Father, Son, and Holy Spirit, but these were just three ways he revealed himself to humanity.

Denying the Equality of the Three Persons: Subordinationism

Subordinationist heresies came in a number of varieties and frequently cropped up, bringing with them huge problems, in early church history. What ties together this group of heresies is that they each denied the full equality of being of the three persons. Some, such as the *Ebionites*, claimed

---

[29] John of Damascus, *On Heresies*, 57, 62 (ET pp.125-126).
[30] John of Damascus, *On Heresies*, 57.

that Jesus was just a human being.[31] Others, like *Arianism*, made Him much higher than humans, but much lower than God: the first and greatest creature, but a creature nonetheless.[32] Yet others, namely the *Pneumatomachi* ('fighters against the Spirit') upheld the deity of the Son, but denied the deity of the Spirit.

Denying the One Being: Tritheism

Tritheism is the heresy which denies the unity of the Godhead, and instead erroneously sees the Father, Son and Holy Spirit as three Gods. However, there was no significant tritheist threat to the ancient church, and only a very small number of individuals have ever been charged with Tritheism. At the present time, the major trithesitic group is the Church of Jesus Christ of Latter Day Saints (*i.e.* Mormonism), which believes in 'God, the Eternal Father, and in His Son, Jesus Christ, and in the Holy Ghost,'[33] but maintains that these are three separate beings.[34]

A Modern Trinitarian Heresy: Oneness Pentecostalism

A new Trinitarian heresy arose in North America in the early years of Pentecostalism, and persists today around the world. 'Jesus-Only' or 'Oneness Pentecostalism' sometimes appropriates to itself the name 'Apostolic', but it is in no way related to the Apostolic Church which considers the Trinity to be 'the most essential article of the Christian faith.'[35] As Fred Sanders notes, 'it is a disturbing fact that the most vigorous form of anti-trinitarianism currently on the market is to be found within the sphere of conservative evangelicalism.'[36]

Unlike Unitarians, Oneness adherents accept the deity of Christ, however, the only way they can account for the relationality between Christ

---

[31] At the time of the Reformation, Socinianism would take this view, and nowadays it's widespread among theological liberalism.

[32] Modern-day parallels can be found in the teaching of the Jehovah's Witnesses.

[33] *Articles of Faith of the Church of Jesus Christ of Latter Day Saints*, 1.

[34] E.g. *Doctrine and Covenants* 130:22; *History of Joseph Smith* 1:17.

[35] Thomas Rees, *The Unity of the Godhead and the Trinity of the Persons Therein*, Tenets of the Apostolic Church Vol. 1, 15.

[36] Fred Sanders, 'Oneness Pentecostalism: An Analysis', *The Scriptorium Daily*, 3rd May 2014, http://scriptoriumdaily.com/oneness-pentecostalism-an-analysis/

and God (due to their disbelief in the distinct persons of the Father and the Son) is through an essentially Nestorian Christology, with the human 'Christ' relating to the God who is incarnate within him.[37]

The anti-trinitarianism of the Oneness Pentecostals is of another kind. They argue that God is 'absolutely one' and 'without distinction of persons.'[38] Jesus, Oneness teaching maintains, 'is the one name that fully reveals the one God in his salvific work as Father, Son, and Holy Spirit.'[39] Their theologians claim that 'the Father is the Holy Ghost'[40] and that 'Jesus is the Father.'[41] Therefore, they view 'Father, Son, and Holy Spirit as manifestations of the one God rather than three eternal persons.'[42] The three names 'can only denote different aspects or roles,' only 'describe God's relationships to man,' not His eternal identity, and are 'not the only [titles] God has.'[43] In this, Oneness Pentecostalism is a form of modalist heresy (although it differs from the ancient forms of modalism). These 'Jesus-Only' advocates claim that the Nicene Creed, with its Trinitarian faith, is rooted in Hellenistic philosophy and pagan infiltration of the church after Constantine.[44] Instead they maintain that 'Jesus is not the incarnation of one person of a trinity but the incarnation of all the identity, character, and personality of the one God.'[45] Altogether, Oneness theology is 'a form of modalism, which, unlike Sabellianism, affirms the presence of all three manifestations simultaneously, rather than in successive epochs of salvation history.'[46]

These teachings however deny what we have learnt from the Scriptures to be the very identity of the true and living God. For Oneness Pentecostals God cannot eternally exist in love, for, before the creation of the world, there was no one for him love. The God of Oneness Pentecostalism is not the God whose very identity is the One who pours out His love on His Son in the Spirit.

---

[37] Frank D. Macchia, 'The Oneness-Trinitarian Pentecostal Dialogue: Exploring the Diversity of Apostolic Faith', *Harvard Theological Review*, 103.3 (July 2010), 338, 345. For the dangers of the Nestorian heresy, see below, chapters 11-13.

[38] 'Oneness-Trinitarian Pentecostal Final Report', 34.214.

[39] 'Oneness-Trinitarian Pentecostal Final Report', 13.207.

[40] David K. Bernard, *The Oneness of God* (Antioch, Tenn.: Word Aflame, 2003), 129.

[41] Bernard, *Oneness of God*, 66.

[42] 'Oneness-Trinitarian Pentecostal Final Report', 13.207.

[43] Bernard, *Oneness of God*, 134.

[44] Bernard, *Oneness of God*, 255-283.

[45] 'Oneness-Trinitarian Pentecostal Final Report', 37.215.

[46] D.A. Reed, 'Oneness Pentecostalism', *New International Dictionary of Pentecostal and Charismatic Movements*, 942.

Furthermore, if the God of Oneness Pentecostalism is not eternally a Father in loving communion with His Son in the Spirit, then the revelation of God received from this modalistic God is not a true revelation. Oneness theology denies 'the basic doctrine of the Christian faith … that God is the Father, and that He has a Son within His essence, eternally.'[47] Thus they deny that there is a Son who is like the Father in every way (except being Father), and so can truly reveal the Father. For Oneness adherents claim that 'the Sonship – or the role of the Son – began with the child conceived in the womb of Mary.'[48] The 'Son', in oneness terms, refers to 'the humanity of Jesus Christ' and to God as he shows himself through that humanity.[49] Therefore the Oneness 'Son' is not, strictly speaking, one with the Father. The *homoousion* is denied (for it necessitates distinction of persons), and the Oneness God reveals himself in a way which does not correspond to who he supposedly is. Fred Sanders highlights that:

> The fundamental problem of all forms of modalism is this: if God, in order to reveal Himself, becomes something other than what He is, then He has not revealed Himself but has revealed something else. In this case, if God emerges from a state of being a non-modal and non-interpersonal being to become a modal, interpersonal being in the story of Jesus, then He has not revealed His true non-modal, non-interpersonal self. He has revealed instead a Father-God who has interpersonal fellowship with Himself in the modal person of the incarnate God, Jesus Christ. But according to Oneness theology, that interpersonal fellowship of Father and Son is precisely the thing He is not. So the unipersonal God attempts to reveal Himself but instead reveals an interpersonal divine being.[50]

Oneness Pentecostalism then is not merely another variety of Pentecostal denomination; it is a serious heresy. As Fred Sanders concludes, it may be evangelical, but it is not Christian.[51]

Unlike American Pentecostals, for whom Oneness teaching caused a great controversy, the early British Apostolics did not have much interaction with this heresy. However, in the 1920s an elder was excommunicated for baptising in the name of Jesus only (one of the marks of Oneness practice),

---

[47] D.P. Williams, *The Trinity*, 1:77.

[48] Bernard, *Oneness of God*, 101.

[49] Bernard, *Oneness of God*, 134.

[50] Fred Sanders, 'Oneness Pentecostalism: An Analysis.' Sanders is a serious Trinitarian theologian, and his assessment of Oneness theology is one of the most perceptive in dealing with the key issues.

[51] Evangelical in the sociological sense, but outside the bounds of orthodox Christianity. This is not to deny that there may be saved people in Oneness churches, but 'the churches they are in are not Christian churches.' Fred Sanders, 'Oneness Pentecostalism: An Analysis.'

and refusing to baptise in the name of the Father, Son and Holy Spirit. For the Apostolics, this was a denial of 'the basic doctrine of the Christian faith' and so any teaching or worship contrary to the doctrine of the Trinity was such a dangerous false teaching that it could only be dealt with by excommunication.[52]

The Unsuitability of Illustrations of the Trinity

Quite often people try to use illustrations of things in the natural world to 'explain' the three-in-oneness of the Trinity. But, in reality, these illustrations never work. And most of the time they just end up teaching ancient heresies rather than the true Trinitarian faith.[53]

Let me show you the problem with one common analogy: we'll look at why the Trinity is not like water in any way. For the sake of clarity, the (heretical) faulty illustration is a comparison of the Trinity to water, which has three forms - liquid, ice and steam. But the Trinity is not like that at all, and here's why:

The same water cannot be liquid, ice and steam at the same time, all the time.

God is Father, Son and Holy Spirit at the same time, and He is always, has always been, and will always be Father, Son and Spirit at the same time, all the time. But that's not what water, ice and steam are like. Water is sometimes liquid, sometimes ice, and sometimes steam, but never all three at the same time. So that's not like God. In fact, this is the ancient heresy of Modalism, falsely teaching that the one God sometimes manifests Himself as Father, sometimes as Son, sometimes as Spirit.

---

[52] The elder in question was first given the opportunity to repent and amend his teaching and practice, but he refused and stubbornly maintained his heresy, leading to excommunication.

[53] For a fun, yet scathing, example of this, see 'St Patrick's Bad Analogies' by Lutheran Satire. https://youtu.be/KQLfgaUoQCw

Liquid, ice and steam cannot mutually indwell one another.

You can't split God into three and find Father, Son and Spirit – they aren't three parts of God. The consubstantial Father, Son and Holy Spirit mutually indwell one another in perichoresis. The Father is in the Son and the Spirit, the Son in the Father and the Spirit, and the Spirit in the Father and the Son. The unity of the three is not found in sharing the same molecular make-up like liquid, ice and steam all being H_2O. After all, there is no molecular make-up for God.

Now this mutual indwelling works in the Trinity, for the Father, Son and Holy Spirit are one in purpose and will - they're not trying to pull apart. But you can't have mutual indwelling with water, ice and steam. For steam and liquid melt ice. Ice liquefies steam. The three destroy one another, so they are not like the Triune God.

There's no love lost between liquid, ice and steam.

Our God – the Triune God – is the Father eternally loving His Son in the Spirit. Our God is three persons united in love. That's the very heart of the doctrine of the Trinity. It's not a maths problem of how three can be one, but rather the very identity of our loving God.

Liquid, ice and steam don't love one another. It's not that they dislike one another either. It's simply that they don't have any personal relationship. So not only does comparing God to water remove the love from the very core of His being, but it also strips Him of His personal existence. God is not a thing. He's not a 'what' but a 'who'. And 'who' He is is the Father eternally loving His Son in the Spirit, which is very different from liquid, ice and steam.

So there you have it. Not only does the water illustration introduce a heresy (Modalism) rather than the biblical Trinity, but it also robs God of His true oneness found in the loving relationships of mutual indwelling between the Father, Son and Spirit and transforms the loving personal God from a 'who' into an impersonal 'what'.

That's just one of the common analogies, but the others are equally problematic, and so, I think it's best we conclude with Gregory of Nazianzus: 'So, in the end, I resolved that it was best to say "goodbye" to images and shadows, deceptive and utterly inadequate as they are to express the reality.'[54]

The Trinity: the Centre of the Christian Faith and the Doctrine from which all Doctrines Flow

As we have seen in the last few chapters, the Trinity is not simply one aspect of the truth about God. Rather, the Trinity is the very identity of the true and living God, who is eternally the Father who loves His Son in the joy of the Holy Spirit.

Why is the Trinity so important? It's so important because it's who our God is. This is the God who saves; the God in whom we trust; the God to whom we pray; the God we worship; the God we're called to be like. And He is the God who is overflowing, outgoing love: the Father who delights in His Son in the love of the Spirit.

So, the Trinity isn't just something to tick off for orthodoxy before moving onto the next doctrine. No. The Triune identity of the living God is 'the most essential article of the Christian faith.' Therefore, 'it is absolutely necessary to believe in the Trinity ... before we can fully grasp and appreciate the other doctrines of our faith.'[55] All Christian doctrine flows out from the Trinity. And the whole of the Christian life flows out from the Trinity too.

The early Apostolics grasped this centrality of the Trinity. They weren't at all ambiguous or unclear when it came to God's identity: He is the Triune God and can't be thought of in any other way. 'God is not a monad, isolated and alone, but exists in three Persons in the eternal essence', writes D.P. Williams. The Father-Son relationship in the Spirit is 'the basic truth of the Christian faith.' And so 'the essence of the Triune God is love. They are one in essence because they are one in love.' And how is this Triune God known? 'The Son of God has always been the Revealer and the Mediator between God and man.' 'Jesus is the Son of the Father's love. God's love is not a sentiment, not an emotion: it is a Person ... a Man. That Man is Jesus.'[56]

---

[54] Gregory of Nazianzus, *Oration 31.33* (Fifth Theological Oration, On the Holy Spirit).
[55] Thomas Rees, *The Unity of the Godhead and the Trinity of the Persons Therein*, Tenets of the Apostolic Church Vol. 1, 15.
[56] All those quotations are from D.P. Williams.

So there you go, for D.P. Williams, the identity of God, and the very foundation of the Christian faith, is that He is the Father who eternally loves His Son in the Spirit. And this God reveals Himself and His love to us only in the Person of His Son.

The Father overflows toward us in love, sending the Son of His love as the propitiation for our sins (*1 Jn 4:8-10* — see there how God's very nature as love is tied so closely to the Incarnation and Atonement and how we see that God is love through Jesus dying as the propitiation for our sins). The initiative is His (*1 Jn 4:10*). He is not waiting for us to climb up to Him by discovering his will for our success and walking in it. No! He knows that we're not a success! He knows that we've failed. And yet He loves us, and comes in the Person of the Son to save us. We don't climb up to Him; He stoops down to us and lifts us up.

But how does He lift us up? By taking us down. Down into death, and then up into resurrection. Down through the law and up with the gospel. Down in repentance and up in faith. Down in ourselves, and up into Jesus.

And then, raised up in Jesus, we know loving fellowship with the Triune God. He invites us into His life and His love. Unlike the powerful Monad who remains 'isolated and alone', the Triune God is never alone (after all, He is three Persons united in love from all eternity). But even beyond the fellowship of the three Triune Persons, He has chosen never to be alone, for He has chosen from all eternity to be God for us, and through Jesus, God with us.

So that means the true God — the Triune God, doesn't give mere stuff. No; He gives us Himself! And so we know Him, and that is eternal life (*Jn 17:3*).

The Trinity shapes everything!

Tenet 2

The utter depravity of human nature,
the necessity for repentance and regeneration
& the eternal doom of the finally impenitent.

Chapter 7
Creation & Humanity

Creation and the Out-going Love of the Triune God

The Triune God has no beginning or end. His creation, however, did have a beginning. 'In the beginning God created the heavens and the earth.' (*Gen. 1:1*). The heavens and the earth, and all that are in them, are not co-eternal with the Father, Son and Holy Spirit. Thus the Bible distinguishes all of reality into, on the one hand, the Creator and, on the other, His creation. Christians must always maintain this Creator-creature distinction, and 'distinguish God from all creatures.'[1] The Triune God eternally exists, independently of anything else. The heavens and the earth (the temporal creation) exist in complete dependence upon God their Creator. The Triune God has brought them into existence *ex nihilo* (out of nothing) and so they owe their existence to Him and Him alone.

But if the Triune God eternally exists independently of anything else, there was no necessity for Him to create the heavens and the earth. He did not need to create the world to be who He is or to be happy. For God is not dependent upon creation. He is already perfect in Himself and so lacks nothing. God is not constrained to create. Therefore, He didn't create unwillingly or begrudgingly. The Triune God wanted to create the world and everything in it. So why did the Father, Son and Holy Spirit so willingly create the heavens and the earth, with all that are in them, including you and me?

From all eternity, God has been the Father who loves His Son in the unity of the Holy Spirit. Therefore from all eternity God has been three persons united in love. The Father delights in loving His Son in the Spirit. And from all eternity He has been the life-giving God, for the Father eternally begets His Son. So it is in keeping with His character that He should turn out from Himself to give life and love. Creation, then, is the Triune God's act of free love. God creates in love to have creatures to love. The Cambridge Puritan preacher, Richard Sibbes, put it like this:

---

[1] Caspar Olevianus, *De substantia foederis* (1585), 1.1.5.

> If God had not a communicative, spreading goodness, he would not have
> created the world. The Father, Son and Holy Ghost were happy in
> themselves, and enjoyed one another before the world was. Apart from the
> fact that God delights to communicate and spread His goodness, there had
> never been a creation or redemption.[2]

The Father, Son and Holy Spirit were happy in themselves. The Father
enjoyed His loving fellowship with His Son so much that He wanted to
share the goodness of it with others. So, the Father who loves His Son in the
Spirit created us to love His Son in the Spirit too and to share with the Son
in the goodness of the Father's love (*Jn 17:26*).

This means that the Father created *for* the Son. Creation is *for* Christ.
Paul explicitly states this: 'All things were created through Him [i.e. the Son]
and for Him' (*Col. 1:16*). The Son is the 'heir of all things' (*Heb. 1:2; Ps 2:8;
Deut. 32:8-9*). So Christ is not simply a rescue plan for creation. Christ is the
true purpose of creation.

In Ephesians, Paul tells us that God has an eternal purpose for creation,
and this purpose is centred in the Lord Jesus Christ:

> having made known to us the mystery of His will, according to His good
> pleasure which He purposed in Himself, that in the dispensation of the
> fullness of the times He might gather together in one all things in Christ,
> both which are in heaven and which are on earth—in Him. (*Eph. 1:9-10*)

The Father so loves His Son that He creates the world in order to have a
people to love His Son, to be united to the Son, to be filled with the Son, and
to share in the glory of the Father's love for the Son. The Swedish theologian
Gustaf Wingren (drawing from Irenaeus) put it like this:

> the Son of God ... exists *before* man, and, indeed, when man is created, he is
> created through the Son and *for* the Son, so as to reach His destiny in the
> Son, his Saviour ... and since the Saviour existed before man came into
> being, it was proper that something to be saved should come into being,
> lest the Saviour should exist by Himself alone.[3]

The heavens and the earth and everything in them were created, and
continue to exist, for the Lord Jesus Christ, the eternal Son and Word of the
Father. The purpose of everything that exists is found in Him and Him

---

[2] Richard Sibbes, 'The Successful Seeker', *The Complete Works of Richard Sibbes*, 6:113.
[3] Gustaf Wingren, *Man and the Incarnation: A Study in the Biblical Theology of Irenaeus*
(Eugene: Wipf and Stock, 2004: Original Swedish, 1947), 5-6.

alone. Athanasius stated it simply and memorably: 'It is not He who was created for us, but we are created for Him.'[4]

God's Two Hands: God created by His Word and Spirit

The opening verses of Genesis tell us how God created the heavens and the earth:

> In the beginning God created the heavens and the earth. The earth was without form, and void; and darkness *was* on the face of the deep. And the Spirit of God was hovering over the face of the waters. Then God said, 'Let there be light'; and there was light. (*Gen. 1:1-3*)

God spoke His creation into being as His Spirit hovered over the face of the waters. The Father spoke His Word in the Spirit, and what He said came to pass. So the Father created through His Word and His Spirit. God's work of creation was a Triune work. As Irenaeus put way back in the second century, 'For with [the Father] were always present the Word and Wisdom, the Son and the Spirit, by whom and in whom, freely and spontaneously, He made all things.'[5]

It is not only in *Genesis 1* that we see the involvement of the Son and the Spirit in creation. The Psalmist rejoices in the Lord, for 'By the word of the Lord the heavens were made, and all the host of them by the breath of His mouth' (*Ps 33:6*). The word for 'breath' is the same as the word for 'Spirit': the same word used in *Genesis 1:2* of the Holy Spirit at the beginning of the creation. So the Psalmist describes poetically what Moses has already told us in the creation narrative.

Elsewhere, the Psalmist connects the Holy Spirit's work with both creation and renewal of the creation (*Ps 104:30*). Job's friend, Elihu, also acknowledges the role of the Holy Spirit in creation: 'The Spirit of God has made me, and the breath of the Almighty gives me life' (*Job 33:4*).

The apostle John tells us that 'all things were made through' the eternal Word and Son of the Father, 'and without Him nothing was made that was made' (*Jn 1:3*). And Paul confirms that, not only were all things created for the Son, but also 'all things were created through Him' (*Col. 1:16*). The

---

[4] Athanasius, *Contra Arianus*, II.31
[5] Irenaeus, *Against Heresies*, 4.20.1

writer to the Hebrews tells us that it was through His Son that the Father 'made the worlds' (*Heb. 1:2*).

Didymus the Blind pointed out what the participation of the Son and the Spirit in God's work of creation shows us about their identity:

> The Holy Spirit's activity is the same as that of the Father and the Son, and that a single substance is implied by the same activity, and, vice versa, that those who are [the same in substance] do not have an activity that is diverse.[6]

So the participation of the Son and the Spirit in God's work of creation shows us that the Son and the Spirit are consubstantial – the same in substance – with the Father. The Father, Son and Holy Spirit are one God and it is this Triune God who creates.

The Doctrine of Man

At the end of His work of creation, the Triune God created man. 'So God created man in His own image; in the image of God He created him; male and female He created them.' (*Gen. 1:27*). 'Man' (or 'mankind') is the name which God gave to the human race when they were created (*Gen. 5:1-2*). As with all creation, God was under no necessity to create mankind. So why were we created?

Man Created for Fellowship with the Triune God

The LORD God created man in a different way from all other creatures. 'And the LORD God formed man of the dust of the ground, and breathed into his nostrils the breath of life; and man became a living being' (*Gen. 2:7*). The LORD God who stooped down to form Adam from the dust, is the same LORD God who spoke with Adam face to face (*Gen. 2:15-17, 22; 3:9*) and who came to walk with Adam and Eve in the Garden in the cool of the day (*Gen. 3:8*). Bearing in mind that 'no one has seen God [the Father] at any

---

[6] Didymus the Blind, *On the Holy Spirit*, 145

time' (*Jn 1:18*), and that the LORD God who walked in the Garden is also called 'the Voice of the LORD God' and 'the presence [or face] of the LORD God' (*Gen. 3:8*), we can see that this is God the Word and Son of the Father who stooped down in love to form Adam from the dust of the ground, and to make a bride for him out of his wounded side. For as John tells us, though no one has seen the Father at any time, 'the only begotten Son, who is in the bosom of the Father, He has declared Him' (*Jn 1:18*). So God created man (both male and female) personally through the presence of the Son.

Yet, not only was the Son personally present to create man, but He also breathed into man His Holy Spirit. The Word and Son of the Father breathed into Adam's nostrils 'the Spirit of life' (*Gen. 2:7*). As Hebrew uses the same word for both breath and spirit/Spirit, this verse has been interpreted in a number of ways in the history of the church. Some have read it simply as the giving of life through the beginning of breathing. Others have read it as the granting of the soul to man.[7] While these two views probably predominate today, one of the most ancient Christian understandings of *Genesis 2:7* points to something else entirely. The early church noted the similarity between the Son's breathing upon Adam (His creation) in *Genesis 2:7*, and the Son's breathing upon His new creation in *John 20:21-22*. In *John*, when Jesus breathes upon His disciples, He says 'Receive the Holy Spirit' (*Jn 20:22*). The parallel between the two passages suggests that when Jesus breathes out into His people, what they receive is not mere breath (or even their natural soul), but rather the Holy Spirit who proceeds from the Father and the Son.

Cyril of Alexandria expresses this understanding of the Son's breathing of the Spirit into Adam:

> Seeing that [Adam] ought not to be merely rational with an aptitude for doing good and right but also a participator in the Holy Spirit, [the Son] breathed into him, so that he might have brighter marks of the divine nature within him, the breath of life. This is the Spirit furnished through the Son to rational creation.[8]

> Since sin has had dominion over all because of Adam's transgression (Rom. 5.14), the Holy Spirit departed and evil took place on this account.[9]

---

[7] Augustine, *City of God*, 13.24
[8] Cyril of Alexandria, *On the Solutions to Dogmatic Questions*, 2
[9] Cyril of Alexandria, *Scholia on the Incarnation of the Only Begotten*, 1

So, when He formed Adam from the dust of the ground, the LORD God gave him the Holy Spirit, and so brought him to share in the loving fellowship of the Holy Trinity.

True life is a gift of God through the Son in the Spirit. What we see here in this ancient understanding of *Genesis 2:7* is that it wasn't a case of natural life existing first and then eternal life coming along later. The life Christ offers came first. God's intention for mankind was to enjoy life in Christ and full of the Spirit.

Then, when the Word had created man, he placed him in the Garden of Eden. It was the Lord God who planted the Garden. The Lord didn't make Adam plant a garden and work his way into it. Rather, the Word planted it, and gave it as His gift to Adam. So Adam got into the Garden because of Jesus' work, not his own work. In complete contrast to the creation myths of the nations surrounding Israel, the true and living God didn't create human beings for them to provide for Him. Rather, the Lord God created human beings for Him to provide for them, as the giver of life, the over-flowing fountain of love, and the God of all grace. In Eden He provides a home and food; but there He also provides His love, fellowship and presence.

So Adam had everything he needed to enjoy life, and to enjoy it in all its fullness in the presence and fellowship of the loving Triune God. And this wasn't down to anything he had done, but all because of what the Triune God had done for him. Right from the outset the Lord shows us that life – fullness of life, life in relationship with the Father, Son and Holy Spirit – (which is what the Scriptures call eternal life) – isn't something we gain because of how good we are, or because of anything good we do. This life is only received as God's free gift, not because of anything we do, but all because of what Jesus has done.

The Garden of Eden was much more than a garden: it was a temple. It was a place of God's presence and where people met with God. The Bible doesn't call Eden 'the Garden of Adam', but 'the Garden of God' (*Ezek. 28:13; 31:8-9*) or 'the Garden of the LORD' (*Gen. 13:10; Isa. 51:3*). The Triune God didn't just make a nice Garden for Adam to live in, but He planted this Garden for Adam to live in His presence – in God's home. Eden was a foretaste of heaven on earth. And Adam and Eve met with God there (*Gen. 3:8; 2:19*). So the Garden was God's own garden, His home, and in it He met with man. Therefore, the Garden of Eden was a temple.

In fact, it's not that the Garden of Eden looks like a temple, but rather, it's the temple that looks like the Garden of Eden. Think of Solomon's temple and the tabernacle before it. How were they decorated? With gold and precious stones. Nearly everything in the tabernacle was covered in gold (*e.g Ex 25:11-13, 17-18, 24-31; 36-39; 26:6, 29-3, 37*) and even the High Priest's garments were covered with precious stones (*Ex 28:9-30*). And gold and precious stones are exactly what we find in Eden (*Gen. 2:12; Ezek. 28:13*).

The temple was decorated with trees, flowers and pomegranates (*Ex 28:33; 39:24-25; 1 Kgs 7:18-20, 42; 2 Kgs 25:17; 2 Chron. 3:16; 4:13*), and with its lampstand in the shape of a tree (*Ex 25:31-36*). In Ezekiel's vision of the new temple, trees were growing along the river coming out of the temple (*Ezek. 47:7, 12*). And so the temple and tabernacle point us back to the trees and plants of the Eden, with the Tree of Life standing in the centre (*Gen. 2:9*).

The temple and tabernacle were also decorated with angels. There were cherubim on top of the Ark of the Covenant (*Ex 25:18-22*), and cherubim woven into the curtain (*Ex 26:1, 31; 36:8, 35*). There in the Holy of Holies, the cherubim were depicted as the guardians of God's sanctuary. And that's just what happened when Adam and Eve were exiled from the Garden sanctuary: 'So He drove out the man; and He placed cherubim at the east of the garden of Eden, and a flaming sword which turned every way, to guard the way to the tree of life' (*Gen. 3:24*).[10]

So, the Garden of Eden was a temple where man lived in God's presence and God met with man. This was God's plan for man in creation. Man was created to live in the presence of the Triune God and enjoy fellowship with Him. And that is the life which will be enjoyed for all eternity by those who come to God through faith in Jesus Christ. The Scriptures tell us that we are only 'pilgrims and strangers' (*Heb. 11:13*) on this earth; this world is not our home. Our true home is the Garden-Temple: the place where God dwells – the place where we will enjoy all eternity in the loving presence of the Father, Son and Holy Spirit (*Rev. 22:1-5*).

Man Created after the Image and Likeness of God (The Imago Dei)

On the sixth day of creation, the Triune God created man, saying:

> 'Let Us make man in Our image, according to Our likeness; let them have dominion over the fish of the sea, over the birds of the air, and over the cattle, over all the earth and over every creeping thing that creeps on the earth.' So God created man in His own image; in the image of God He

---

[10] Note also rivers (*Gen. 2:10-14; cf. Ps 46:4; Joel 3:18; Ezek. 47; Rev. 22:1*) and mountains (Eden is on a height as rivers flow down from it *Gen 2:10; also Ezek. 28:14; cf. Ps 48:1; Ezek. 20:40; Dan. 9:20*) as connections between the Garden of Eden and the tabernacle/temple.

created him; male and female He created them. Then God blessed them,
and God said to them, 'Be fruitful and multiply; fill the earth and subdue
it; have dominion over the fish of the sea, over the birds of the air, and over
every living thing that moves on the earth.' (*Gen. 1:26-28*)

The first thing the Lord declares about the creation of mankind, is that man
is to be made after the image and likeness of God. 'Image' and 'likeness'
should be understood as synonyms, referring to the same thing. So, in
Genesis 1:27, Scripture can refer to this simply 'in the image of God', and in
Genesis 5:1, simply 'in the likeness of God.' Of all the creation, only mankind
is said to be made in the image and likeness of God, and so the image of
God (*imago dei*) sets mankind apart from the rest of God's creation (see also
Gen. 9:6; Jas 3:9). It is not animals, nor even angels, who have been made in
the image and likeness of God, but human beings.

But what is the image of God? It is clear from *Genesis 1* that both men
and women are made in the image of God, and that being created in God's
image is connected with Gods' blessing. However, *Genesis 1* doesn't exactly
specify the content of the *imago dei*, and so discussions of the image which
begin with the creation of man have led to a variety of suggestions as to
what characteristic of human beings constitutes the *imago dei*. However,
Scripture suggests another starting point, rather than the creation of man, by
which we can understand the image of God. For Scripture tells us that Jesus
is the Image of God (*2 Cor. 4:4*). 'He is the image of the invisible God, the
firstborn over all creation' (*Col. 1:15*). So, Jesus Christ is the Image who
makes the invisible God visible. And He is not a poor image: not a pale
imitation. Rather, the Son is 'the brightness of [the Father's] glory and the
express image of His person' (*Heb. 1:3*). Jesus Christ the Son is the exact
Image of God.

So, mankind was not created *as* the image of God, for the Image of God
is the eternal Son, begotten of the Father from all eternity. Instead mankind
was created *after* the image of God, *in* His image, *according to* His likeness.
The great Athanasius put it like this:

> But, in fact, the good God has given them a share in His own Image, that is,
> in our Lord Jesus Christ, and has made even themselves after the same
> Image and Likeness. Why? Simply in order that through this gift of God-
> likeness in themselves they may be able to perceive the Image Absolute,
> that is the Word Himself, and through Him to apprehend the Father;

which knowledge of their Maker is for men the only really happy and blessed life.[11]

What, then, was God to do? What else could He possibly do, being God, but renew His Image in mankind, so that through it men might once more come to know Him? And how could this be done save by the coming of the very Image Himself, our Saviour Jesus Christ? Men could not have done it, for they are only made after the Image; nor could angels have done it, for they are not the images of God. The Word of God came in His own Person, because it was He alone, the Image of the Father, Who could recreate man made after the Image.[12]

Only Jesus Himself is the true Image of God. Human beings were created after the image, and so once again this highlights how mankind was made for a relationship with the Father through His Son, the true Image of God.

Adam was never created the image or likeness of God, and neither can his race be of themselves. But, said Irenaeus, in reference to Colossians 1:15, 'the image of God is the Son, according to whose image was man made'. Adam was created in the image of God, or as 'the image of the Image'. He was created to be the type of Jesus Christ, who is the revelation and reality of the true being of mankind. It was only with the visible appearance of the true Image in the incarnation that Adam, created to be like Christ, could be perfected after the Image and Likeness of God.[13]

That mankind was created after the image of the 'One who imaged Elohim', D.P. Williams taught, shows us that we were created 'dependent on God' with Christ as our 'treasure-house,' and so the goal of our salvation is to be conformed to the image of the Son (*Rom. 8:26-30*). The Purpose of God for mankind is 'the perfection of the Body [of Christ] on His Image … that the Body may grow in the fullness of Christ, complete on His image.' [14] So the Welsh Pentecostal echoes the second-century Church Father, Irenaeus, who tells us that 'the image of God is the Son, according to whose image was man made; and for this reason, He appeared in the last times, to render the image like himself.'[15]

---

[11] Athanasius, *On the Incarnation*, 11.

[12] Athanasius, *On the Incarnation*, 13; See also Irenaeus, *Adv. Haer.*, 3.18.1 (ET pp.87-88).

[13] Michael Reeves, '"Know Thyself "? A Lesson in Christological Anthropology from Irenaeus of Lyons', *Whitefield Briefing*, 9.6 (Dec. 2004).

[14] D.P. Williams, *Riches of Grace*, xiii.5 (May, 1938), 386, 391, 394.

[15] Irenaeus, *Demonstration of the Apostolic Preaching*, 22. Cf. Irenaeus, *Adv. Haer.* 3.18.1.

Man Created as a Physical and Spiritual Being

Human beings are composite creatures, made up of both a physical part (the body) and a non-physical part (the soul or spirit).[16] The distinction between body and soul is perhaps seen most clearly at death, for James defines physical death in terms of the separation of these two parts of man's being: 'the body without the spirit is dead' (*Jas 2:26*).

The Bible frequently and repeatedly uses the words 'soul' and 'spirit' as interchangeable synonyms. We can see this very clearly in the *Magnificat*, when Mary says:

> My soul magnifies the Lord,
> And my spirit has rejoiced in God my Saviour. (*Lk 1:46-47*)

Here 'soul' and 'spirit' are set in parallel. Much as English poetry is frequently marked by rhyme, parallelism was one of the most frequent marks of the poetry of Israel. We find lots of Hebrew parallelism in the Psalms, where there are two (or more) lines that are roughly the same length, roughly similar in terms of grammar, and about the same subject. While there are a few different ways such parallels are used by Hebrew poets, the most common is where the two lines use different words to say the same thing. And that's what Mary is doing at the beginning of the *Magnificat*.[17] She's using 'soul' and 'spirit' as two different ways of saying the same thing.

We can also clearly see 'soul' and 'spirit' used as interchangeable synonyms in John's Gospel. Praying to His Father about His impending crucifixion, Jesus says 'now my soul is troubled' (*Jn 12:27*), yet in the very next chapter, at the Last Supper, John tells us that Christ 'was troubled in spirit' (*Jn 13:21*) as He told His disciples that one of them was about to betray Him. The same thought is being expressed in these two incidents, yet John happily interchanges the words 'soul' and 'spirit.'

This equivalence between the words 'soul' and 'spirit' is probably seen most clearly between death and the resurrection of the dead. (We'll look at

---

[16] 'The words "soul" and "spirit" are certainly used separately in Scripture, yet they are not kept entirely distinct, being sometimes used interchangeably.' (Samuel M. McKibben, 'The Utter Depravity of Human Nature', *Tenet Booklet 2*, 7.)

[17] The Magnificat is, of course, recorded in Greek, not Hebrew, but maintains the Semitic features of its original speaker, Mary, who was a Hebrew (no matter which language she used when she originally spoke these words).

the intermediate state in chapter 10 below, but here what's important to know is that during this period of awaiting the resurrection, the bodies of believers rest in the grave while the immaterial part of the their being is in heaven with Christ.) The writer to the Hebrews calls the inhabitants of heaven in this intermediate state 'the spirits of just men made perfect' (*Heb. 12:27*), whilst John refers to them as 'souls' (*Rev. 6:9; 20:4*). The same variety of words is seen in Scripture's description of what happens at death: at times death is referred to as the departure of the soul (*Gen. 35:18; Lk 12:20*), while at others it is the giving up of the spirit (*Ps 31:5; Lk 23:46; Jn 19:30; Acts 7:59; Jas 2:26*).

Man created as Male and Female (and the Doctrine of Marriage)

When the Lord God created mankind in His image and likeness, the Scripture tells us, 'male and female He created them' (*Gen. 1:27*). 'He created them male and female, and blessed them and called them Mankind in the day they were created' (*Gen. 5:2*). After the summary of the Lord God's creative work of the six days, Genesis then gives a fuller account of the creation of mankind as male and female.

> And the Lord God said, 'It is not good that man should be alone; I will make him a helper comparable to him.' ... And the Lord God caused a deep sleep to fall on Adam, and he slept; and He took one of his ribs, and closed up the flesh in its place. Then the rib which the Lord God had taken from man He made into a woman, and He brought her to the man.
> And Adam said:
>> 'This is now bone of my bones
>> And flesh of my flesh;
>> She shall be called Woman,
>> Because she was taken out of Man.'
> Therefore a man shall leave his father and mother and be joined to his wife, and they shall become one flesh. (*Gen. 2:18:21-24*).

The account of the creation of man as male and female is intertwined with God's institution of marriage (*Gen. 2:24; cf. Mt 19:5-6; Mk 10:7-8; Eph. 5:31*). Thus, marriage was instituted by God as part of His 'good' creation, and the Lord Jesus (and the rest of the Scriptures) root all marriage in God's establishment of marriage at the creation of Adam and Eve. So marriage is a gift of the Triune God, given to mankind in creation by His loving revelation.[18]

Yet, marriage is greater than simply a loving gift of God to mankind; it is also a holy mystery and gracious revelation of the great love of Christ for His Bride, the Church (*Eph. 5:32*). So marriage cannot be changed or altered in any way without attacking, suppressing, and rejecting the revelation of Christ's love for His Church. This holy mystery and revelation portrays the union between Christ, the loving husband, and the Church, His Bride who submits to and receives His love. So the roles of husband and wife within this mystery and revelation are not one and the same, nor are they interchangeable (*Eph. 5:23-24*): in reflecting this holy mystery, husbands are called to 'love [their] wives as Christ loved the Church and gave himself for her,' (*Eph. 5:25*) and wives are called to 'submit to [their] own husbands, as to the Lord' (*Eph. 5:22*).

Being both inseparable from God's creation of man as male and female, and a holy mystery which reflects the union of Christ the Bridegroom with His Bride, the Church, in distinct and non-interchangeable roles, marriage must be the union of one man and one woman. Therefore, it is impossible for a true marriage in the sight of God to exist between two men or two women, and such would be an attack on the Gospel mystery of our Lord Jesus Christ's giving of Himself over to death to redeem His sinful Bride.

As a mystery, reflecting the exclusive union between Christ and His Bride, marriage is to be an exclusive relationship between only one man and only one woman. Therefore, in the seventh commandment, the Lord declares, 'thou shalt not commit adultery' (*Ex. 20:14; Deut. 5:18*).

Christ teaches that marriage is life-long. 'What therefore God hath joined together, let not man put asunder' (*Mt 19:6*). Marriage is not a private contract between two individuals to be determined as they see fit, but a holy covenant in the sight of God. So, being effected by the Triune God, this marriage bond cannot be broken by man: neither by the man and wife themselves, nor by the ruling authorities, whether of church or state. That means a legal divorce does not un-marry in the sight of God or His Church.

As an unbreakable bond, marriage is a life-long estate, ordinarily breakable only by death. It's because the bond of marriage ends at death that widows and widowers are free to remarry in the Lord (*1 Cor. 7:39*; see

---

[18] The language and content of this and subsequent paragraphs on marriage draws heavily from *The Doctrinal Position of the Apostolic Church on Marriage* due to my work in drafting the *Doctrinal Position*. See the *Doctrinal Position* for further detail on the doctrine of marriage and the official stance of the Apostolic Church in the United Kingdom.

also *Mt 22:29-30*). This means that divorce is contrary to God's design for marriage as a life-long union. Jesus teaches that divorce was not from the beginning, but rather it exists only due to the hardness of mankind's hearts (*Mt 19:8*). So, divorce exists as a result of mankind's sinfulness.

Divorce attacks the holy mystery of marriage and the gospel to which it points: the gospel of Christ's permanent, exclusive, and irrevocable self-giving in unmerited love and grace to His Bride. It attacks the Gospel picture in marriage of Christ's great loving forgiveness for His Church; attacks the Gospel picture of Christ the Bridegroom 'who did not come to be served, but to serve, and to give His life a ransom for' His Bride (*Mk 10:45*); attacks the Gospel picture of Christ the Bridegroom who lived and suffered throughout His earthly life, not for His own sake, but for the sake of His Bride; and attacks the Gospel picture of the Bride who finds joy and satisfaction, not in herself, but in her heavenly Bridegroom. Therefore, although due to the hardness of men's hearts divorce may extraordinarily be permitted in areas tightly defined by the Word of God, those who belong to Christ as their heavenly Bridegroom should avoid it where at all possible, seeking the gospel path of forgiveness and reconciliation.

The Word of God also closely connects sexual union with marriage, as the 'one flesh' union. While the expression 'one flesh' does not refer only to sexual union, this is a significant aspect of it, and marriage is ordinarily consummated in sexual union.

Sexual Union is God's good gift to a husband and wife united in marriage. Sex is part of God's good creation and is His gift, and so sex is right, good, and to be enjoyed within the context in which God has given it. And that context is the marriage of one man to one woman. Thus the only appropriate context for sexual union is within the bond of marriage, and so all sex outside the marriage of one man to one woman is sin (e.g. *Mt 15:19; Mk 7:21; Gal. 5:19; Eph. 5:3; Col. 3:5; Lev. 18:22; 20:13; Rom. 1:24-28; 1 Cor. 6:9-11; 1 Tim. 1:9-10; 1 Cor. 6:13-20; Ex. 20:14; Deut. 5:18; Prov. 6:32; Mt 5:27-28; Lk 16:18; Gal. 5:19; Gen. 34:1-7; Deut. 22:25-27; Ex. 22:19; Lev. 18:23; 20:15-16; Deut. 27:21*).

Children are a significant part of God's good design for marriage. From the beginning, in God's marriage of Adam and Eve, the first couple, He blessed them and charged them to 'be fruitful and multiply' (*Gen. 1:28*). The Scriptures tell us that children are a gift and blessing from the Triune God (*Ps 127:3-5; Ps 128:3-6*), and in God's good design and purpose, the blessing of children is intended as a blessing and crown upon the marriage of one man and one woman. We should always remember that it is the Lord God who opens and closes the womb (*Gen. 20:18; 29:31; 30:22; 1 Sam. 1:5-6*). When a married couple experiences the pain of childlessness, the Church should support, grieve with, and pray for them.

Because marriage is 'a great mystery' which speaks 'concerning Christ and the Church' (*Eph. 5:32*), it points us to the Gospel, for it speaks to us of Christ who gave Himself, through His Incarnation and Atonement, for His Church (*Eph. 5:25*). Yet this loving self-giving, even unto death, was not due to the perfection or righteousness of the Church, but rather in order to cleanse and sanctify her (*Eph. 5:26-27*), and so the mystery of marriage should always point us to the Good News that God justifies the ungodly only through the blood and righteousness of Jesus. Therefore Christians should not enter into the estate of Holy Matrimony on the assumption of perfection, but rather in rejoicing in the great grace of God in Christ Jesus and eager to show grace and forgive, as we have been forgiven.

The Ongoing Care of the Triune God for His Creation: The Providence of God

The Triune God did not abandon His creation once He had made it. He is not like a giant watch-maker in the sky who winds up creation at the beginning and then leaves it be to run its course. Rather, He upholds and sustains His creation at every moment. As John Chrysostom said: 'For as a ship cannot stand firm in the billows without a pilot, however strong and well-equipped she may be, all the less can the universe stand firm without God's care and guidance.'[19] Or, in the words of Augustine of Hippo:

> For He is not like someone who goes away after he has built the structure of a building, and his work stands though he has stopped and gone away. The world could stand for barely a blink of an eye if God would take His guidance away from it.[20]

The Creator of the heavens and the earth continually upholds and sustains His creation (*Job 12:9-10; Acts 17:24-25*). This is God's work of providence. It is because the Triune God has 'established the earth' that it

---

[19] John Chrysostom, *Ephesians*, Homily 19.
[20] Augustine, *On the Literal Interpretation of Genesis*, 4.12

continues to abide, but only according to His ordinances and as His servant (*Ps 119:90-91*). The Lord Jesus, the eternal Son and Word of God, upholds 'all things by the word of His power' (*Heb. 1:3*), for 'in Him all things consist' (*Col. 1:17*). The creation continues to exist, and owes its dependence for each moment, upon the Lord Jesus Christ, for it is only in Him that all things are held together.[21]

---

[21] Alas, the limits of space preclude a more detailed discussion of the doctrine of Providence.

Chapter 8

Sin & Adam

What is Sin?

Sin was not part of the original creation which the LORD God called 'very good' (*Gen. 1:31*). Rather, sin was introduced into God's good creation in Genesis 3 with the Fall. Here at the very beginning of sin we can see the nature of what sin is.

Sin is Unbelief

Adam and Eve sinned by eating of the fruit of the tree of the knowledge of good and evil (*Gen. 3:6*). Eating of fruit was not sinful, for the LORD God had freely given them the fruit 'of every tree of the garden' for food (*Gen. 2:16*), except for that one tree (*Gen. 2:17*). So it was not eating, but rather eating contrary to God's Word which was the sin. Therefore, eating the fruit was not itself the first sin. The first sin was rejecting the Word of the LORD. The LORD had spoken saying, 'but of the tree of the knowledge of good and evil you shall not eat, for in the day that you eat of it you shall surely die' (*Gen. 2:17*). Yet Adam and Eve did not have faith in His Word. Instead, disbelieving the Word of the LORD, they ate of the fruit of the forbidden tree.

The disbelief and rejection of God's Word involved at the root of this first sin can be seen both in the Serpent's temptation and in Eve's response. The very first words of the Serpent are an attack on the Word of the LORD: 'Has God indeed said…?' (*Gen. 3:1*). The Serpent begins his temptation of Eve by questioning the Word of God, and he continues by directly contradicting the Word of God, telling Eve 'you will not surely die' (*Gen. 3:4*). The Serpent never directly invites Eve to eat of the forbidden fruit; what he invites her to do, both indirectly through questioning and directly by contradiction, is to disbelieve and reject the Word of the LORD.

Eve's response demonstrates the same underlying reality of unbelief. 'So when the woman saw that the tree was good for food, that it was pleasant to the eyes, and a tree desirable to make one wise, she took of its fruit and ate (*Gen. 3:6*). She examines the tree and its fruit in light of her own reasoning, rather than in light of the Word of God. She places her own reasoning in a place of higher authority than the Word which God had spoken. She stops trusting in God's Word and rejects it in favour of her own assessment.

Although Genesis gives us less description of what happens when Adam eats of the fruit, the same is clear. Adam disbelieves and rejects the Word of the LORD, the Word which he, perhaps unlike Eve, had heard directly from the mouth of God (*Gen. 2:16-17*).

What we find in the account of the Fall in *Genesis 3* then is unbelief and distrust of the Word of the LORD at the root of human sin. Thus sin is the opposite of faith. The ancient church recognised this. Fulgentius of Ruspe wrote that Adam 'committed sin by faithlessness'[1] and Prosper of Aquitaine argued that 'if Adam had not first lost his faith, he would not have lacked all the other works; for by believing the devil, he did not believe in God.'[2] At the Reformation, Luther wrote that 'the main and real sin is unfaith, despising God, which is what takes place when a man does not fear, love, and trust in God as he certainly should.'[3] In the Post-Reformation period, Johann Gerhard argued that it was 'clear that Eve had already sinned with her unbelief when she was snatched up into the whirlpool of pride' and ate the forbidden fruit, concluding that 'the root and beginning of all unrighteousness is unbelief.'[4] The Apostolic Church also sees sin as the opposite of faith, defining the first sin as 'the unbelief of our first parents in God's Word.'[5]

Yet Genesis is not the only book of the Bible to teach that sin is the opposite of faith. Writing to the Romans, Paul defines sin as 'whatever is not from faith' (*Rom. 14:23*).[6] Thus 'unfaith at the bottom of the heart', as Luther

---

[1] Fulgentius of Ruspe, *First Letter to the Scythian Monks* (*Ep.17*), para. 43.

[2] Cited in Gerhard, *Loci* XII §27

[3] Paul Althaus, *The Theology of Martin Luther* (Philadelphia: Fortress, 1966), 145, citing WA 31¹, 148.

[4] Gerhard, *Loci* XII §27

[5] *Catechism upon the Tenets of the Apostolic Church*, ii.12.

[6] This reading of Rom. 14:23 goes back at least to Augustine (*Contra Julianum* 4.32; *Lectures on the Gospel of John*, NPNF, Vol.8, 353.) and was championed at the Reformation by Martin Luther (*Bondage of the Will*, Packer ed., 300; *Lectures on Galatians*, LW 27:76; *Preface to the Epistle to the Romans*). Among modern commentators, Douglas Moo rejects this reading of Rom. 14:23 while still maintaining the validity of the theological point (*The Epistle to the Romans*, NICNT, 863), while Lenski and Thomas Schreiner emphatically embrace the position of

explains it, is the 'root and source of all sin.'[7] At the beginning of Romans, Paul tells us that 'the just shall live by faith' (*Rom. 1:17*). Now he tells us that 'whatever is not from faith is sin' (*Rom. 14:23*), thus pairing faith with righteousness and unfaith with sin. Just as sin is the opposite of righteousness, so too it is the opposite of faith, for the righteous 'live by faith.'

The writer to the Hebrews makes a similar connection. 'Without faith it is impossible to please Him' (*Heb. 11:6*). As a result, where there is no faith, God is not pleased with any action. Where there is no faith, there is sin. Sin, once again, is seen to be the opposite of faith.

Earlier in Hebrews, the writer looks back to the sin of the Israelites in the Wilderness after the Lord had delivered them from slavery in Egypt (*Heb. 3:12-19*). The root of their sin (*v.17*) and disobedience (*v.18*) was found in unbelief (*v.19*). A hard heart of sin (*v.13*) and rebellion (*v.15*) is 'an evil heart of unbelief in departing from the living God' (*v.12*). Sin is unbelief, and the rebellion and disobedience which flow from it. Thus, as unbelief, sin is the opposite of faith.

But we mustn't think of this faith which is the opposite of sin as a good quality inherent in a person. Rather, faith is always faith in the true God who saves and in His Word. Adam and Eve disbelieved the Word of the LORD. They stopped trusting in the LORD God who spoke with them and who walked with them in the coolness of the Garden. Faith cannot be abstracted from the Word (or Voice) of the LORD who walked in the Garden. Jesus makes this very clear in John's Gospel. Teaching about the coming of the Holy Spirit, Jesus says that 'when He has come, He will convict the world of sin … because they do not believe in Me' (*Jn 16:8-9*). Once again, unbelief is seen at the root of what sin is. The Holy Spirit convicts people of sin because they don't believe. But this lack of faith is a specific lack of faith: they don't believe in Jesus Christ. Sin, then, is the opposite of faith in Jesus, the Living Word of God.

The wrath of God is the penalty for sin (e.g. *Isa. 13:9*), yet John tells us that the wrath of God abides on whoever does not believe in the Son.

> He who believes in Him is not condemned; but he who does not believe is condemned already, because he has not believed in the name of the only begotten Son of God. … He who believes in the Son has everlasting life;

Augustine of Luther (Lenski, *The Interpretation of St Paul's Epistle to the Romans*, 854; Schreiner, *Romans*, 739).

[7] Althaus, *Theology of Martin Luther*, 145, citing WA,DB 7, 6; LW 35, 369.

and he who does not believe the Son shall not see life, but the wrath of God abides on him. (*Jn 3:18, 36*)

So, the punishment for sin falls on those who do not have faith in Jesus. This means that either one has faith in Christ or else one is in sin (and thus under its punishment). Therefore, sin is the opposite of faith in the Lord Jesus.

Sin is man curved in on himself (Homo Incurvatus in Se)

Another way the Christian church has historically described sin is 'man curved in on himself' *(homo incurvatus in se)*. Instead of looking out to Christ in faith, in sin we turn away from him to gaze at ourselves (*cf. Prov. 12:8; Jer. 17:9; Rom. 7*). In the ancient words of Augustine, 'sin is a turning away from the Creator and a turning toward inferior, created things.'[8] Or in the Pentecostal words of D.P. Williams, sin is turning 'toward everything that is evil and devilish, and away from God and all that is good and true … [sin] is] deficiency of love to God and man … preference of self to God … sin is always a departure from God.'[9]

Martin Luther wrote:

> Our nature has been so deeply curved in upon itself because of the viciousness of original sin that it not only turns the finest gifts of God in upon itself and enjoys them … indeed, it even uses God himself to achieve these aims, but it also seems to be ignorant to this very fact, that in acting so iniquitously, so perversely, and in such a depraved way, it is even seeking God for its own sake.[10]

Having turned away from the Lord and His Word in sin, we turn in on ourselves, so that the sinner's ultimate aim is 'to enjoy oneself in one's works, and to adore oneself as an idol.'[11] Instead of the outward focuses, relational life of knowing the Father in the Son and filled with the Spirit for which we were created, in sin we turn inward and close ourselves off from the relationships for which we were made.

---

[8] Augustine, *Ad Simpl.*, 1.1
[9] D.P. Williams, *Riches of Grace* x.4 (March 1935), 131, 134.
[10] Martin Luther, *Luther's Works*, 25:291.
[11] Martin Luther, *Heidelberg Disputation*, Proof 7.

Sin is Lawlessness

John writes that 'sin is lawlessness' (*1 John 3:4*). We can see this aspect of sin in the Garden of Eden when Adam and Eve eat the forbidden fruit. God had spoken His command ('of the tree of the knowledge of good and evil you shall not eat' – *Gen. 2:17*), and so Adam and Eve broke the law which He had spoken. Yet, as we have seen, their lawless act was rooted in the deeper reality of unbelief. So how does John's definition of sin as lawlessness fit together with Paul's definition of sin whatever doesn't come from faith?

For a start, we should note that John, in his Gospel, has already pointed to sin as unbelief (as we have seen above in *John 3:18, 36; 16:8-9*). So his statement that 'sin is lawlessness' is not in competition with his understanding of sin as not believing in Jesus Christ. Sin as lawlessness sits within the context of sin as unbelief, for unbelief in Christ leads inevitably to the rejection of and rebellion against the law of God.

Not having faith in Jesus Christ is the breaking of the first commandment: 'I am the LORD your God, who brought you out of the land of Egypt, out of the house of bondage. You shall have no other gods before Me.' (*Ex. 20:2-3.*) It was the Lord Jesus who 'saved the people out of the land of Egypt' (*Jude 5*), therefore the first commandment calls for an honouring of the Lord Jesus as God, and to truly honour Him as God means having faith in Him. As Martin Luther put it, 'to have a God is nothing other than trusting and believing Him with the heart.'[12] Thus the unbelief which is at the root of sin is a form of lawlessness in that it is a breaking of the first commandment.

Luther argued that all the other commandments hinge on the first. 'Where the heart is rightly set toward God and this commandment is observed, all the other commandments follow.'[13] So, the breaking of the other commandments flows from breaking the first. In other words, lawlessness flows out from unbelief.

---

[12] Martin Luther, *Large Catechism*, Part 1: First Commandment.
[13] Ibid.

In Adam's Fall, Fell We All

Adam's sin was the greatest sin in the history of the world. That might seem like rather a hyperbolic statement to the modern mind, as we think of a comparison between eating fruit and genocide, and yet it is not hyperbole by any means, for every genocide (as well as every other sin) flows from Adam's eating. Unlike us, Adam didn't have a sinful nature, so he could have avoided eating the forbidden fruit through continued faith in Christ. And, unlike our sins, Adam did not sin only for himself, but rather he also sinned for us, in our place, resulting in our guilt and bondage to sin. So, Adam's sin was the greatest sin of all. As Johann Gerhard put it:

> Adam represented the whole human race; he had been created in the greatest integrity and uprightness, and thus he was able to obey the command of God without any difficulty. In these respects the sin of Adam was more serious than all the sins of his descendants.[14]

Adam's Fall wasn't only Adam's Fall, but the Fall of the whole human race. (There has only ever been one man who did not fall in Adam: the Lord Jesus Christ, the last Adam.) And so every one of us is affected by Adam's sin. In Adam's Fall, fell we all; for in Adam's sin, we all sinned (*Rom. 5:12*). Fulgentius of Ruspe put it like this: 'In that man, all who could not sin of their own accord sinned before being born.'[15]

Augustine vs. Pelagius

At the end of the 4th and beginning of the 5th Centuries, a British (or possibly Irish) monk called Pelagius began teaching in Rome that 'the statement that all sinned in Adam, was not made because of the sin which is derived from one's birth, but because of imitation of him.' Pelagius refused to believe that we all sinned in Adam's first sin, but instead traced the sinfulness of human beings to their following of Adam's bad example. As a result, Pelagius insisted that 'it is possible for a man to be without sin', as it is for each

---

[14] Gerhard, *Loci*, XII §40
[15] Fulgentius of Ruspe, *First Letter to the Scythian Monks*, para. 26.

individual to fall his own fall in imitation of Adam. (However, Pelagius did concede that everyone does sin, even if it were theoretically possible not to fall into sin.) He maintained that Adam's posterity are 'not more infirm than he' and insisted that babies were born without sin. ('Why seek Him [for infants]? They are whole.')[16]

Pelagius didn't believe that our souls had any connection to Adam. Instead, he thought that God created each soul immediately: that our souls didn't come from our parents in any way. Therefore, as a new creation of God, each soul would be good. There would be no way for the soul to be affected by sin at the time of its creation at the beginning of a particular human being's life.

So, if human beings were born with sinless souls unconnected to Adam, then each person's fall into sin would be a matter of their own free will (a key aspect of Pelagius' thought). Pelagius insisted that 'a man always is in a state that he may sin, or may not sin, so as to own ourselves always to be of a free-will.'[17]

In AD 411, Pelagius and some of his disciples arrived in North Africa, fleeing from Rome after it had been sacked by the Vandals. There he would cross paths with Augustine, the great bishop of Hippo.

While Pelagius placed huge emphasis on free will at the centre of his thought, Augustine instead looked to the grace of God. Augustine saw the primary problem of Pelagius' view of sin and free will as undermining the work of Christ on the Cross, for if to sin or not to sin is merely a choice of the human free will, then humans could save themselves by obedience to the law rather than by fleeing to Christ crucified as our only salvation.

> If this nature of the human race born from the flesh of that one transgressor can be capable by itself of fulfilling the law and attaining perfect righteousness, it ought to be sure of its reward … But if that was possible or is possible, then I too say what the Apostle said with regard to the law, 'Christ has died in vain' (Gal. 2:21) … If righteousness comes about through nature, then Christ has died in vain! But if Christ has not died in vain, then the whole of human nature can be justified and redeemed from the perfectly just anger of God, that is, from punishment, in no other way than by faith and the mystery of Christ's blood.[18]

---

[16] All quotations in this paragraph are from Pelagius, *De Natura*.

[17] Pelagius, *Confession of Faith*.

[18] Augustine, *Nature and Grace*, 2

Augustine further responds to Pelagius' rejection of the inherited consequences of Adam's sin by pointing both to Jesus' name and the reason that He came into the world.

> The Lord Jesus was called Jesus precisely because he saved his people from their sins, and the Lord Jesus stated, 'It is not those who are in good health who need a physician, but those who are sick. I came not to call the righteous, but sinners.' For this reason the Apostle too says, 'It is a reliable message worthy of complete acceptance that Christ Jesus came into the world to save sinners' (1 Tim. 1:15) … We seek such a great physician to help even the little ones, and this fellow [Pelagius] says, 'What are you seeking? Those for whom you are seeking a physician are in good health.'[19]

So, while Pelagius viewed sin as an individual choice, Augustine saw that sin is something much deeper: something rooted in human nature as a result of Adam's Fall. Writing of *Romans 5:12*, Augustine argues that 'if the Apostle had wanted to mention the sin that entered this world, not by propagation, but by imitation, he would have called its originator not Adam, but the devil.'[20] Instead, 'Adam bound his progeny in the penalty of death and damnation; by sinning he corrupted them in himself as their root.'[21]

The Heresies of Pelagianism and Semi-Pelagianism

Augustine's Gospel preaching and clear biblical teaching prevailed over the errors of Pelagius. The Council of Carthage condemned Pelagianism as heresy in AD 418 and the anathema was confirmed by the Council of Ephesus (the Third Ecumenical Council) in AD 431.

The views of a 5th Century monk might seem quite far removed from us today, but the heresy of Pelagianism which he spawned continues to have a great influence today (even where the name of Pelagius is unknown). Six points which were drawn up as charges against one of Pelagius' followers give us a simple summary of the Pelagian heresy:

1. Adam would have died, even if he had not sinned.
2. The sin of Adam injured himself alone, and not all mankind.

---

[19] Augustine, *Nature and Grace*, 23

[20] Augustine, *The Punishment and Forgiveness of Sins*, 9

[21] Augustine, *Enchiridion* Ch. 26, this translation taken from Gerhard *Loci* XII §40 as it is clearer than the NCP edition.

3. New-born children are in the same condition in which Adam was before the Fall.

4. It is not true that because of the death and sin of Adam all mankind die; neither is it true that because of Christ's resurrection all men rise again.

5. The Law leads to heaven as well as the Gospel.

6. Even before the coming of Christ there were men who were entirely without sin.[22]

The fifth and sixth points here show how the Pelagian view of sin and free will undermines the Gospel and diminishes the Cross of Christ, for, if all human beings are not dead in sin as a result of Adam's sin, then that means that they could attain salvation through their own good works in keeping the law, apart from the grace of God in the atoning work of Christ.[23]

At the time of the Reformation, the basic tenets of Pelagianism were still of such significant influence that the Reformers explicitly rejected them in their confessions of faith, specifically showing how Pelagianism related to salvation. The Lutheran *Epitome of the Formula of Concord*, for example, gives the following summary and rejection of Pelagianism:

> We likewise reject the Pelagian error, by which it is alleged that man's nature even after the Fall is incorrupt, and especially with respect to spiritual things has remained entirely good and pure *in naturalibus*, i.e., in its natural powers. (I.13)

> We reject also the error of the gross Pelagians, who taught that man by his own powers, without the grace of the Holy Ghost, can turn himself to God, believe the Gospel, be obedient from the heart to God's Law, and thus merit the forgiveness of sins and eternal life. (II.9)

Pelagianism is seen today when anyone insists that human nature is essentially good and that people can, of their own ability and free will, choose to come to God and live for Him. Often modern-day Pelagianism isn't put in quite those terms. Rather it might be expressed: 'God has put in you everything you need to live a victorious life. Now, it's up to you to draw it out.'[24]

---

[22] Deacon Paulinus of Milan's Points of Accusation against Coelestius.

[23] Pelagius himself insisted that he believed in the necessity of God's 'grace', but in reality redefined grace as free will (given by God in creation), the teaching of God's Law (so that we'd know what to obey) and the example of Christ's sinless life.

[24] Joel Osteen, *Become a Better You: 7 Keys to Improving Your Life Every Day*, as cited in Michael Horton, *Christless Christianity: The Alternative Gospel of the American Church*, 81. See pp.65-100 for Dr Horton's assessment of Osteen's theology as 'a sentimentalized version of the Pelagian heresy of self-salvation. But it is not Christianity.' (p.75). 'To the extent that it any

After the condemnation of Pelagianism, a softer version of the heresy emerged (known as Semi-Pelagianism), teaching that 'man by his own powers can make a beginning of his conversion, but without the grace of the Holy Ghost cannot complete it.'[25] Semi-Pelagianism was condemned as heresy at the Second Council of Orange in AD 529. Modern day Semi-Pelagianism is a perpetual danger. Unlike Pelagianism, Semi-Pelagianism can talk more about Christ and His Cross. However, Semi-Pelagianism sees salvation as God's response to our initiative. Modern day Semi-Pelagianism might sound like this: 'God's favour and blessing are on the other side of our obedience.' The words might be biblical words, but the order isn't. In the Bible, it is God who takes the initiative, granting us His favour and blessing in Christ, and our obedience comes in response to God's initiative in saving us in Jesus.

The so-called 'prosperity gospel' is a form of Semi-Pelagianism. Prosperity teachers claim that 'if you make up your mind … that you are willing to live in divine prosperity and abundance … divine prosperity will come to pass in your life. You have exercised your faith.'[26] That is a claim that faith begins with us, and then God responds to what we do (in making up our minds) with his blessings. And that is precisely the heresy of Semi-Pelagiansim. The 'prosperity gospel' is not merely an idiosyncratic aberration; it is a deceptive and dangerous heresy.

What does the Bible Teach about the Transmission of Sin?

The Bible teaches that we are not only born in sin, but conceived in sin. 'Behold, I was brought forth in iniquity, and in sin my mother conceived me' (*Ps 51:5*). In other words, we are sinners right from the beginning of our existence as individuals. Human beings are not innocent until they commit an evil deed. Rather, our evil deeds proceed from our sinful natures. Concerning 'man who is born of woman', Job asks rhetorically, 'Who can bring a clean thing out of an unclean?' and answers emphatically 'No one!' (*Job 14:1, 4*). So both David and Job point to sin as something passed on

---

theology at all, his message represents a convergence of Pelagian self-help and Gnostic self-deification.' (p.68).

[25] *Epitome of the Formula of Concord*, II.10. Although John Cassian, Vincent of Lérins, and the later Prosper are often called semi-pelagians, it is doubtful that they held to this heresy. Faustus of Riez, on the other hand, appears to have been a proper semi-pelagian. For more on this distinction, wait for the forthcoming work by Donald Fairbairn.

[26] Kenneth Copeland, *The Laws of Prosperity*, (Fortworth, Texas: 1974), 41.

through the generations. We are sinners because we have inherited our sinfulness and so are born sinners. This stands in stark contrast to the Pelagian view that 'new-born children are in the same condition in which Adam was before the Fall.'

Paul writes of the transmission of sin from Adam to us in *Romans 5:12*: 'Therefore, just as through one man sin entered the world, and death through sin, and thus death spread to all men, because all sinned.' Sin entered the world through one man, Adam, and thus spread to all men from him. But what does Paul mean when he writes 'because all men sinned.' When did all men sin? And what is the relationship between the sin of all men and the sin of Adam?

Pelagius argued that it is only when each one of us sins individually, after we've been born, that 'death spread to all men, because all sinned.' The connection with the one man, then, in the first part of the verse is to Adam's bad example which we eventually follow and sin.

Yet the context of *Romans 5:12* would suggest that Pelagius was wrong in his interpretation.

> Therefore, just as through one man sin entered the world, and death through sin, and thus death spread to all men, because all sinned—(For until the law sin was in the world, but sin is not imputed when there is no law. Nevertheless death reigned from Adam to Moses, even over those who had not sinned according to the likeness of the transgression of Adam, who is a type of Him who was to come. But the free gift is not like the offense. For if by the one man's offense many died, much more the grace of God and the gift by the grace of the one Man, Jesus Christ, abounded to many. And the gift is not like that which came through the one who sinned. For the judgment which came from one offense resulted in condemnation, but the free gift which came from many offenses resulted in justification. For if by the one man's offense death reigned through the one, much more those who receive abundance of grace and of the gift of righteousness will reign in life through the One, Jesus Christ.) Therefore, as through one man's offense judgment came to all men, resulting in condemnation, even so through one Man's righteous act the free gift came to all men, resulting in justification of life. For as by one man's disobedience many were made sinners, so also by one Man's obedience many will be made righteous. (*Rom. 5:12-19*)

For a start, Paul tells us explicitly here that the consequences come not from the billions of sins committed in imitation of Adam's sin, but rather as a result of the one sin of Adam. Many died 'by one man's offense' (*v.15*) and condemnation and judgment were the result of 'one offense' (*v.16*). By that 'one man's offense death reigned through the one' (*v.17*) and 'through one man's offense, judgement came to all men (*v.18*). It was 'by one man's disobedience' that 'many were made sinners' (*v.19*).

Thus in this passage we see five statements of cause and five statements of effect (*verses 12, 15, 16, 17 & 18*). Each of the effects is the same: the condemnation of death. This helps us to see that the five causes are also the same. *Verses 15, 16, 17 and 18* clearly refer to Adam's first sin, leaving us with *verse 12*, which tells us that all sinned. Now we can answer the question. How and when did all sin? All sinned in Adam's first sin.

Furthermore, Paul establishes a parallel here between the one man who sinned for many and the one man who obeyed for many. The first Adam sinned for us and the last Adam obeyed for us. The first Adam sinned in our place, dragging us all down with him into his death and condemnation. However, the last Adam died in our place, lifting us up into His life and righteousness. The parallel is drawn between Adam and Christ in such a way that, just as Christ is our saving Substitute and Representative, so too Adam was our sinning substitute and representative. So when did all sin (*Rom. 5:12*)? All sinned in Adam's first sin. Adam sinned as our representative and so we sinned in him. In Adam's fall, sinned we all.[27]

But how did we sin in Adam's first sin? The Scriptures do not directly answer that question and so the church has attempted to hold together what the Bible does say in various ways. As Augustine cautioned, 'Nothing is better known than original sin for preaching; for understanding, nothing is more mysterious.'[28] There are two main orthodox evangelical understandings: Federalism and Realism.

Federalism: Adam as our Covenant Head

The name *federalism* comes from the Latin word for covenant (*foedus*), because federalism sees the connection between us and Adam's sin in terms of Adam's covenant headship of the human race. The LORD God made a covenant with Adam on behalf of the whole of humanity (except for the Incarnate Christ). The Lord had only told Adam the commandment about not eating the forbidden fruit (before Eve had even been created), yet Eve

---

[27] This is very firmly the doctrine of the Apostolic Church. See e.g. *Catechism upon the Tenets of the Apostolic Church*, 2.12-13; *Asked and Answered: A Catechism of Apostolic Principles*, 2.a.4-6; *Fundamentals*, p.10; *Introducing the Apostolic Church: A Manual of Belief, Practice and History*, pp. 114-115.

[28] Augustine, *On the Catholic and Manichean Ways of Life*, i.22.

was guilty for breaking it. The commandment had been given to Adam as head of the human race, for all mankind. This explains why we fell in Adam and not in Eve (even though Eve sinned first). Eve only disobeyed for herself; Adam broke the covenant for all mankind. God made reference to this covenant when He rebuked Israel and Judah for their covenant-breaking through the prophet Hosea: 'like Adam they have transgressed the covenant' (*Hosea 6:7, ESV*). This covenant is often called the *Covenant of Works* or sometimes the *Covenant of Life*. The *Westminster Shorter Catechism* gives a helpful summary of this covenant:

> When God had created man, he entered into a covenant of life with him, upon condition of perfect obedience; forbidding him to eat of the tree of the knowledge of good and evil, upon the pain of death.
>
> The covenant being made with Adam, not only for himself, but for his posterity; all mankind, descending from him by ordinary generation, sinned in him, and fell with him, in his first transgression.[29]

Thus, according to federalism, we fell in Adam because he broke the covenant God had made with him on our behalf. Federalism is generally the understanding of the Reformed churches.

Realism: Adam as our Natural Father

Realism is a much older understanding of the transmission of sin, going all the way back to Augustine. (Federal theology developed in the post-Reformation period.) Realism sees us as actually having sinned in Adam (as opposed to Adam sinning for us as our covenant representative), because the whole of humanity was present in Adam as our first father. The whole human race existed (though not as differentiated individuals) in Adam as its head when he sinned. 'The total life of humanity was then in Adam; the race as yet had its being only in him.'[30]

A biblical example of this can be seen in *Hebrews 7:9-10*: 'Even Levi, who receives tithes, paid tithes through Abraham, so to speak, for he was still in the loins of his father when Melchizedek met him.' Levi would not be born for several generations after the time of Abraham, and yet the Bible says that he (and the tribe descended from him who would then receive the

---

[29] *Westminster Shorter Catechism*, Qs 12 & 16
[30] Augustus Strong, *Systematic Theology*, 619.

tithes) had paid tithes while 'still in the loins of' Abraham. The descendent acted in the ancestor generations before he was born. This is the realist understanding of how we sinned in Adam.

Psalm 51:5 and *Job 14:4* also lend their support to the realist understanding of the transmission of sin, for they point to sin as being passed on from one generation to the next, rather than directly from Adam (the covenant head) to each new generation. Johann Gerhard argued that these verses (along with *John 3:6*) demonstrate that 'original sin is propagated into all the descendants of Adam through carnal generation.'[31] Gerhard also argued that sin must pass from Adam into his descendants in the same way as his descendants come from him. 'Yet all people come from Adam by way of carnal generation. Therefore sin passes into all people by carnal generation.'[32]

Realism was the classical understanding of the transmission of original sin in the Western Church from Augustine to Luther and Calvin, and then on into Lutheran orthodoxy.

The Apostolic Church has traditionally held to a realist understanding of the transmission of original sin, as an inheritance from Adam through the intervening generations. However, at the same time it has accepted Christ's covenant headship. We fell 'through Adam, as our natural father and our covenant head.'[33]

Our Sinful Inheritance: The Effects of the Fall

Original Sin is the technical term for our sinful inheritance from Adam. But what is *original sin*? What are the effects of Adam's fall upon all subsequent generations? Adam's sin affects all his posterity in two ways: *original guilt* (the imputation of the guilt of Adam's first sin) and *original corruption* (or *utter depravity*).

---

[31] Gerhard, *Loci*, xii.98.
[32] Gerhard, *Loci*, xii.98.
[33] *Athrawiaethau Sylfeinol*, iii, 6. (Original Welsh: 'trwy Adda fel ein tad naturiol ac fel ein pen-cyfamodwr'.)

The Imputation of Adam's Sin

According to *Romans 5*, we die because of Adam's sin. This is the doctrine of *original guilt*, that we are counted guilty because of Adam's first sin. Paul writes that 'through one man's offense *judgment came* to all men, resulting in condemnation ... by one man's disobedience many were made sinners' (*Rom. 5:18-19*). Death (*Rom. 5:12-15*) is the judgment for those condemned under the guilt of sin. So *Romans 5* shows us that every human being is a sinner and condemned, not as a result of his own actions, but as a consequence of Adam's sin. All of Adam's posterity fell in him and are counted guilty because of Adam's sin.

The parallel that Paul draws in *Romans 5* between Adam and Christ shows that we are guilty in Adam in the same way that believers are righteous in Jesus. The righteousness of Christ is imputed to believers who are joined in union with Him. Likewise, the guilt of Adam's sin is imputed to all men who are united to him as their natural head and father. Because we were 'in Adam' when he sinned, his sin is imputed to us (cf. *Rom. 4:8; 5:13* which both speak of the imputation of sin).

But, some people might object, isn't it unfair of God to impute someone else's (Adam's) sin to us? There are two reasons why it isn't unfair at all. First, the realist understanding of the transmission of original sin means that we really were there sinning in Adam, and so share fairly in his guilt. Second, the parallel between Adam's sin and Christ's righteousness means that if we complain that the imputation of Adam's guilt is unfair, then we'd need to complain about the imputation of Christ's righteousness as well.

Utter Depravity

Guilt is not the only thing that we have inherited as a result of Adam's first sin. We have also inherited a *sinful nature* (also referred to as *utter depravity*). The expression utter depravity highlights the fact that the sinful nature affects every part of man. Due to the fact that our utter depravity is a result of Adam's sin, there is no time in our lives before we become totally depraved. The Psalms make this clear: 'The wicked are estranged from the womb; they go astray as soon as they are born' (*Ps 58:3*). In another Psalm David states: 'Behold, I was brought forth in iniquity, and in sin my mother conceived me' (*Psalm 51:5*). Thus even before we are born, right from the moment we are conceived, we have a sinful nature. From the very beginning of our existence we are utterly depraved.

This sinful nature consists of two parts: 1) *the lack of original righteousness,* and 2) *original corruption.*

The Lack of Original Righteousness

At the Fall, Adam and Eve lost the righteousness and holiness in which God had created them.[34] As a result, in God's 'sight no one living is righteous' (*Ps 143:2*). Paul states this lack of original righteousness memorably: 'there is none righteous, no, not one … there is no fear of God before their eyes … for all have sinned and fall short of the glory of God.' (*Rom. 3:10, 18, 23.*)

The lack of fear of the Lord entailed by the lack of original righteousness means that 'the natural man does not receive the things of the Spirit of God, for they are foolishness to him' (*1 Cor. 2:14*) and those who are under sin walk in darkness (*John 1:5; Eph. 5:8*).

Original Corruption

Human nature has not only been robbed of original righteousness by the Fall, but has also been corrupted in every aspect. Speaking to his disciples, Jesus said 'If you then, being evil, know how to give good gifts to your children, how much more will your heavenly Father give the Holy Spirit to those who ask Him.' (*Lk 11:13*). Here Jesus was not talking about evil actions, but rather an evil nature. The disciples, as human beings, were *evil*. One of those very disciples later wrote the warning that 'if we say that we have no sin, we deceive ourselves, and the truth is not in us' (*1 Jn 1:8*). Here John is also talking about our nature. He writes about *having* sin, rather than *doing* sins (which he warns about two verses later). As a result of Adam's sin, every member of the human race has received a corrupt, sinful nature.

The Bible teaches that it is because of this corrupt sinful nature that we are sinners. We sin because we are by nature sinners. It is not our sinful actions which make us sinners; rather, our sinful actions, thoughts and attitudes are the fruit of the fact that we are sinners by nature. 'For a good tree does not bear bad fruit, nor does a bad tree bear good fruit… an evil

---

[34] *Catechism upon the Tenets of the Apostolic Church,* 2.12.

man out of the evil treasure of his heart brings forth evil' (*Luke 6:43,45*). (We will discuss these actual sins that result from our sinful nature below.)

This sinful corruption of our nature is rooted deep in our hearts. At the time of the Flood, the Lord 'saw that the wickedness of man was great in the earth, and that every intent of the thoughts of his heart was only evil continually.' (*Gen. 6:5*). After the flood, He declared: 'I will never again curse the ground for man's sake, although the imagination of man's heart is evil from his youth; nor will I again destroy every living thing as I have done.' (*Gen. 8:21*). As the prophet Jeremiah declared, 'The heart is deceitful above all things, and desperately wicked; Who can know it?' (*Jer. 17:9*). This corruption rooted in our hearts affects every part of our nature: body, soul, and mind (*1 Cor. 15:50; Rom. 8:7; Eph. 2:3*). Paul confesses: 'in me (that is, in my flesh) nothing good dwells' (*Rom. 7:18*) and teaches that 'the carnal mind is enmity against God' (*Rom. 8:7*). Thus, it is not only our actions which are sinful, but also our thoughts, desires, attitudes, opinions, reasoning, and every other aspect of our being. If every aspect of our beings is affected by sin, that means that we have no spiritual good in us, for all that we are, and all that we do, is tainted by sin. 'All the faculties of the soul are corrupted by sin, all its powers are distorted by iniquity, its motives are polluted by selfishness, the understanding is darkened by ignorance, the will perversed by rebellion, and the affections ingrained by self-gratification.'[35]

Utter Depravity means Utter Inability

The condition into which the whole human race has fallen as a result of Adam's first sin is one of 'inability and hopelessness'[36] Sinful man now lives in a state of 'utter inability through any effort of his own to retrieve his lost position, neither can he regain the favour of God by any inherent goodness.'[37] Man cannot 'by his own power and endeavour please God … [for] his depraved nature renders this impossible, because it is, in itself, enmity against God.'[38]

Thus utter depravity means that we have no ability to do any spiritual good. 'There is none who does good, no, not one' (*Rom. 3:12*). Although we

---

[35] Fundamental Truths of the Apostolic Church, 2.i, *Guiding Principles*, 186.

[36] *Athrawiaethau Sylfeinol*, iii.6. (Original Welsh: 'anallu ac anobaith.')

[37] Fundamental Truths of the Apostolic Church, 2.i, *Guiding Principles*, 186.

[38] *Asked and Answered: A Catechism of Apostolic Principles*, 2.a.8. See also *Fundamentals*, 10.

may be able to do some things that appear good, they are not spiritually good as 'all our righteousnesses are like filthy rags' before God (*Isa. 64:6*). Everything we do is, to some degree, tainted by sin. This means that nothing that we do in our sinful state, no matter how good it may seem to us, is of any meritorious value in God's sight; it cannot earn His favour. 'Those who are in the flesh cannot please God.' (*Rom. 8:8*). In ourselves, we cannot do anything that will please the Triune God. Rather than being able to do good, unbelievers are slaves to sin (*John 8:34*). 'When you were slaves of sin, you were free in regard to righteousness' (*Rom. 6:20; cf. 2 Pet. 2:19*). This slavery to sin means a life separate from the righteousness of God, and so, while held captive in this bondage we cannot choose righteousness. This means that they cannot not sin. Instead, it is this slavery to sin which causes us to commit sins (*Jn 8:34*). Their wills are in bondage to sin and so, although they are free to choose their actions, they are not free to do what is good and pleasing to God. Paul describes this state as being 'dead in trespasses and sins' (*Eph 2:1*). Those who are dead in sin have no spiritual life in them and thus no possibility of any spiritual progress. Those who are dead cannot do anything to improve their state. Their only hope is for God to make them 'alive together with Christ' (*Eph 2:5*).

The utter inability which comes from this slavery to sin means that sinful man cannot by his own 'free will' choose to be saved. Back in the 6th Century, Fulgentius of Ruspe explained this by writing:

> As sin reigns, a man does indeed have free choice, but this is freedom without God, not freedom under God. That is, he is free of righteousness, not free under grace, and therefore he is free in the worst and most servile way, because he has not been set free by the free gift of the merciful God.[39]

Or, as Martin Luther put it during the Reformation:

> Let all the 'free-will' in the world do all it can with all its strength; it will never give rise to a single instance of ability to avoid being hardened if God does not give the Spirit, or of meriting mercy if it is left to its own strength. ... All the passages in the Holy Scriptures that mention assistance are they that do away with "free-will", and these are countless...For grace is needed, and the help of grace is given, because "free-will" can do nothing.[40]

John makes this point in the prologue to his Gospel, writing that salvation comes 'not of the will of the flesh, nor of the will of man, but of God' (*Jn*

---

[39] Fulgentius, *First Letter to the Scythian Monks*, para. 38.
[40] Martin Luther, *The Bondage of the Will*, 202, 270.

1:13). Therefore the Lord God must take the initiative and by His grace draw us to Christ (*Jn 6:44*) and open our hearts to receive the Word (*Acts 16:14*). Therefore, the utter depravity of human nature means that man needs God to grant him the gifts of repentance and regeneration.

Actual Sins

Actual sins are the results of our sinful nature. Just as 'a bad tree bears bad fruit' (*Matt. 7:17; Lk 6:43*), our sinful natures always manifest themselves through actual sins (*Matt. 15:19*), for 'all have sinned' (*Rom. 3:23*). This is not an obscure teaching. It is found all over the Bible. When King Solomon prayed at the dedication of the Temple, he stated clearly that 'there is no one who does not sin' (*1 Kgs 8:46*). Ecclesiastes notes that 'there is not a just man on earth who does good and does not sin' (*Eccl. 7:20*). James writes that 'we all stumble in many things' (*Jas 3:2*) and Paul quotes the Old Testament to declare that 'there is none righteous, no, not one … there is none who does good, no, not one.' (*Rom. 3:10, 12*). This means that we are all guilty of our own sins. Thus we merit death, not only as a result of Adam's sin, but also for our own actual sins.

Definition of Actual Sin

Actual sin can be defined as *any transgression of, or any lack of conformity to, the moral law of God* (cf. *1 John 3:4*).[41] This definition includes two important parts. Firstly, sin is transgression of God's law; thus anytime we disobey and break God's law, we sin. Sin is doing what God tells us not to do. Secondly, sin is any lack of conformity to God's law; thus anytime we don't do what we should do. Sin is not doing what God tells us to do. Therefore sin is not just certain actions, but can take the form of actions, words, attitudes, and desires.

---

[41] Cf. Augustine's definition of actual sin: 'it is a statement or a deed or a desire against the eternal law.' Augustine, *Contra Faustum*, 22.27. Cf. Also *Westminster Shorter Catechism*, 14.

The Three Causes of Actual Sin

What causes actual sin? The Bible shows us three causes. *1.) The corruption of our nature* which we have received from Adam's fall (*Matt. 15:19*). *2.) The suggestion of Satan*, who incited David to number the people of Israel (*1 Chr. 21:1*), who 'put it into the heart of Judas Iscariot' to betray Jesus (*John 13:2*), and who filled Ananias' heart to lie to the Holy Spirit (*Acts 5:3*). *3.) The stumbling blocks of the world (Matt. 18:7; Rom. 12:2*).

The first of these causes (our sinful nature) is the principle cause, and is always a cause of our actual sin. The devil and the world can suggest sin, but they cannot compel us to sin. Only our own utter depravity can do that. So we pray, 'from all the deceits of the world, the flesh, and the devil, Good Lord, deliver us.'[42]

The Difference between Sin and Temptation

As the causes of actual sin, the world, the flesh and the devil are also the three sources of temptation to evil. The Scriptures clearly distinguish between temptation to sin and sin itself.

> Let no one say when he is tempted, "I am tempted by God"; for God cannot be tempted by evil, nor does He Himself tempt anyone. But each one is tempted when he is drawn away by his own desires and enticed. Then, when desire has conceived, it gives birth to sin; and sin, when it is full-grown, brings forth death. (*Jas 1:13-15*)

According to James, temptation is the enticing of our sinful desires which when accepted gives birth to sin. Temptation may lead to sin (or it may lead to resisting sin), but it is not itself sin.

The Lord's Prayer also clearly distinguishes between temptation and sin. Jesus taught us to pray 'forgive us our trespasses,' and also to pray 'lead us not into temptation, but deliver us from evil' (*Matt. 6:12-13*). Therefore, trespasses and sins require forgiveness, but in temptation what we need is not forgiveness, but deliverance. So the Scriptures promise us a way of deliverance in temptation:

---

[42] From the Litany.

> God is faithful, who will not allow you to be tempted beyond what you are able, but with the temptation will also make the way of escape, that you may be able to bear it. Therefore, my beloved, flee from idolatry. (*1 Cor. 10:13-14*)

The temptation of Jesus also demonstrates to us the difference between temptation and sin. Christ was 'led up by the Spirit into the wilderness to be tempted by the devil' (*Matt. 4:1*) and 'was in all points tempted as we are, yet without sin' (*Heb. 4:15*). The Sinless Saviour remained sinless despite being tempted in every way and by the devil in person. So temptation cannot be the same as sin.

In temptation the strong are weak and the weak strong. Whoever falls into sin in temptation falls by his own fault, through relying on himself (rather than upon God's grace in Christ) as Peter did (*Matt. 26:33-36*). Those who rely on their own strength fall, but those who see their own weakness and fly instead to Christ for deliverance will overcome temptation solely through the grace of God (cf. *1 Cor. 10:12; 2 Cor. 12:9*).

The Sin Against the Holy Spirit

Jesus declared that 'every sin and blasphemy will be forgiven men, but the blasphemy against the Spirit will not be forgiven men. Anyone who speaks a word against the Son of Man, it will be forgiven him; but whoever speaks against the Holy Spirit, it will not be forgiven him, either in this age or in the age to come.' (*Matt. 12:31-32; cf. Mark 3:28-30; Lk 12:10*).This sin against the Holy Spirit is the one unforgivable sin.

According to Augustine, 'God wants to exercise us with the difficulty of the question concerning this sin, because in all of Holy Scriptures there is perhaps found no question greater or more difficult.'[43] Yet, pastorally, this is a question which must be faced, for it's a subject which raises fear among so many of Christ's sheep.

In Matthew's Gospel, Jesus says that he who blasphemes against the Holy Spirit 'will not be forgiven, either in this age or in the age to come.' In Mark's Gospel, He says that 'he who blasphemes against the Holy Spirit never has forgiveness, but is subject to eternal condemnation' (*Mark 3:29*). In each of the Gospels, Christ's words are directed against the Pharisees who were saying that Christ's miracles were performed through the power of

---

[43] Augustine, *Sermo 71*.

Beelzebub. The Pharisees were deliberately rejecting the truth of who Jesus is, and thus the truth of the gospel.

Why is this sin called the sin against the Holy Spirit? It cannot be against the Holy Spirit in respect to His person, for anyone who sins against the persons of the Father and the Son also sins against the person of the Holy Spirit, because the holy and consubstantial Trinity cannot be divided. Rather, this sin is called the sin against the Holy Spirit in respect to the Holy Spirit's ministry. The Holy Spirit's ministry is the giving of life through the gospel of Jesus Christ (*2 Cor. 3:8; John 16:14*). Therefore, to sin against the Holy Spirit, is to wilfully reject the Holy Spirit's ministry of giving life through the gospel of Jesus Christ, and then to attack that truth with blasphemy. This is the unforgiveable sin and the 'sin leading to death' (1 John 5:16).

Athanasius the Great reminds us of something very important when it comes to this unforgiveable sin:

> God did not say, 'He who blasphemes and repents will not be forgiven,' but 'He who blasphemes', that is, the person who remains in blasphemy, because there is no unforgiven sin in God's presence among those who repent in a devout and worthy manner.[44]

The Wages of Sin

Faith is looking to Jesus and Jesus is 'the Life' (*Jn 14:6*). So in faith we look to Jesus and live (*Jn 3:14-16; cf. Num. 21:8-9*). Those who know Christ in faith have eternal life (*Jn 17:3*). If sin is the opposite of faith, then sin is not looking to Jesus, but rather turning our gaze away from Him who is 'the Life' to the opposite: death.

And death is exactly the punishment for sin of which Adam was warned when the LORD God forbade him to eat of the tree of the knowledge of good and evil (*Gen. 2:17*). Paul tells us how this condemnation of death came not only upon Adam, but upon all mankind who have fallen into sin in him (*Rom. 5:12-21*).

---

[44] Athanasius, *Quaestiones ad Antiochum ducem*, 2:296.

We will give further consideration to death as the wages and penalty of sin in another chapter.

The Two Men: Sin and Salvation

If all humanity has fallen into sin in Adam and so merits death as the penalty of sin, then what hope is there for mankind? Paul tells us the answer: 'For since by man came death, by Man also came the resurrection of the dead. For as in Adam all die, even so in Christ all shall be made alive.' (*1 Cor. 15:21-22*). Just as sin and death come to us from Adam, so salvation and life come to us from Jesus (*Rom. 5:12-21*).

All humanity lives in one of these two men: either in Adam or in Christ. With Adam as our head, we share in his sin, guilt, and death. And we are all born 'in Adam'. But Christ saves by taking people out of Adam and uniting them to Himself instead. At the Cross, Christ made an end to our sin by dying our death. As Cyril of Alexandria put it, 'just as death conquered in Adam, so was it ruined in Christ.'[45] Now, 'in Christ' believers share in His righteousness and life. Born under sin and condemnation in Adam, yet saved 'in Christ', there is now no condemnation (*Rom. 8:1*).

---

[45] Cyril of Alexandria, *To the Monks of Egypt.*

Chapter 9

The Necessity for Repentance & Regeneration

Man's Need

Because man is utterly depraved, he needs what he does not have. He needs repentance and regeneration, but these are not things which he can produce for himself out of his own sinful nature. Rather these are gifts which man needs to receive from outside himself. These are the gifts of God, not the works of sinful man. When the second Tenet of the Apostolic Church speaks of 'the necessity for repentance and regeneration', it is expanding upon the meaning of the expression 'utter depravity'.[1]

A brief note is in order here on the structure of the Tenets of the Apostolic Church. Although Tenet 2 refers to regeneration and repentance, it doesn't talk about them positively (in a statement of what salvation is), but rather negatively, as what humanity needs, but doesn't have. The flow of the Tenets makes this even clearer; from here they go on to consider Christ's Incarnation and Atonement, and then the results of salvation. Thus any attempt to read Tenet 2 as a positive statement of salvation would mean a Christless, Pelagian soteriology, (which is very definitely ruled out by Tenets 3 and 4). So, 'the necessity for repentance and regeneration', has to be read as clarifying the concept of 'the utter depravity of human nature.' And this fits exactly with what we have already seen in the previous chapter about utter depravity. The overall flow of the Tenets points to a theology of the bondage of the will and divine monergism. The Tenets follow the classical Law-Gospel structure of Reformation Prostestant theology and proclamation: first God's Law shows us our sin (Tenet 2) and then Christ's Gospel proclaims the salvation the Law cannot provide (Tenets 3-4).

---

[1] *Catechism upon the Tenets of the Apostolic Church*, ii.19, 26-28; Fundamentals, 10-11.

God's Two Words: Law and Gospel

God's Law Shows Us Our Need of Salvation, but Provides No Power to Save

As D.P. Williams put it, 'the law would kill us and disqualify us.'[2] In the words of Martin Luther, 'the law brings the wrath of God, kills, reviles, accuses, judges, and condemns everything that is not in Christ.'[3] And that is precisely the job of the Law. God has not given His Law to give life, but to kill us and show us that we are dead with no hope other than to look to Christ and live (*Rom. 7:9-13*). The Law cannot save, but instead shows us our sinfulness so that we will come to Christ for salvation. 'By the deeds of the law no flesh will be justified in His sight, for by the law is the knowledge of sin' (*Rom.3:20*).

God's Law shows us our sin. As Paul explains it:

> What shall we say then? Is the law sin? Certainly not! On the contrary, I would not have known sin except through the law. For I would not have known covetousness unless the law had said, 'You shall not covet.' (*Rom. 7:7*)

The Law causes us to know our sin. Earlier in the epistle, Paul writes that God speaks by His Law so 'that every mouth may be stopped, and all the world may become guilty before God' (*Rom. 3:19*). It is not that the Law creates guilt before God, but rather that we know our guilt before God through the Law, for by the Law we recognise sin to be sin (*v.20*).

So the Law functions as a mirror, to show us our sin for what it really is.[4] And the Holy Spirit works through the proclamation of God's word of Law to convict of us of our sin (*John 16:8*) and of our need for Christ the Saviour. Therefore the Law is 'our tutor to bring us to Christ, that we might be justified by faith' (*Gal. 3:24*).

---

[2] D.P. Williams, *Riches of Grace*, iii.1 (March 1927), 23.

[3] Martin Luther, *Heidelberg Disputation*, Thesis 23.

[4] There are three biblical uses of the Law: 1) A Curb (to keep order in the world), 2) A Mirror (to show us our sin), and 3) A Guide (to show Christians the things in life which please God).

The Difference between the Law and the Gospel

D.P. Williams wrote that 'the law and the letter killed you; and you saw you were unable to fulfil it' but then Christ reveals Himself in His Gospel 'in grace'. The Law is 'hard and killing', but the Gospel brings 'blessing' and 'paradise'. [5] Martin Luther summed up the distinction between the two like this: 'The law says, "do this", and it is never done. Grace says, "believe in this", and everything is already done.'[6]

In a sermon on New Year's Day, 1532, Luther said:

> Distinguishing between the Law and the Gospel is the highest art in Christendom, one that every person who values the name Christian ought to recognize, know and possess. Where this is lacking, it is not possible to tell who is a Christian and who is a pagan or Jew. That much is at stake in this distinction … For the Law and the Gospel are indeed both God's word; but they are not the same kind of doctrine … the Law finds me, a sinner, and accuses and condemns me, while the Gospel says (Matt. 9:2), 'Be of good cheer, your sins are forgiven; you shall be saved.' … The Law makes demands of us and terrifies us. The Gospel gives to us, and consoles.[7]

In order to rightly distinguish between the Law and the Gospel, we need to recognise some of the differences between the two.[8] The Law is a humbling Word; it reveals sin, and so the Law brings condemnation, laying us low. The Law is an uncomfortable Word because it threatens sinners with punishment and shows us that what we deserve from God is His wrath.

But the Gospel is unlike the Law. Where the Law was an uncomfortable Word, the Gospel brings comfort. Where the Law was a threatening Word, the Gospel brings grace, forgiveness and joy. Where the Law kills, the Gospel brings life.

The Law tells us about ourselves, and what it tells us isn't good. It tells us how we've disobeyed. It tells us how we've missed the mark. It shows us the depths of our sin, and it shows us our just desserts.

But the Gospel tells us, not about ourselves, but about Jesus. The Gospel tells us how He obeyed perfectly for us. The Gospel tells us how He

---

[5] D.P. Williams, *Riches of Grace*, iii.1 (March 1927), 23.

[6] Martin Luther, *Heidelberg Disputation*, Thesis 26.

[7] Martin Luther, 'The Distinction between Law and Gospel: A Sermon.'

[8] For a much fuller account of the distinction between Law and Gospel, see C.F.W. Walther's Theses on Law and Gospel and their elaboration in C.F.W. Walther, *The Proper Distinction Between Law and Gospel*. For a shorter introduction to the distinction, see John T. Pless, *Handling the Word of Truth: Law and Gospel in the Church Today*.

lived the perfect life in our place. The Gospel tells us how Jesus bore the wrath of God which we deserved in His death on the Cross. And the Gospel tells us how He has been raised to life and ascended to the Father's right hand on our behalf. The Gospel isn't about us, it's about Jesus: and that's why the Gospel is good news.

And that's why we mustn't confuse Law and Gospel. For the Law is uncomfortable, but the Gospel is full of comfort, peace and joy. The Law kills, but the Gospel gives life. The Law is all about us, but the Gospel is all about Jesus. The Law shows us what we haven't done, can't do and won't do. But the Gospel shows us what Jesus has done and has completed. The Law says 'Do!', but the Gospel says 'Done!'

Those who are secure in their sins, not seeing their need to come to Christ in repentance, need to hear God's Word of Law. Those who are crushed under the weight of their guilt and the condemnation of the Law need to hear God's Word of Gospel. As Charles Spurgeon put it as he watched gospel churches slip down into moralism at the time of the Downgrade Controversy:

> There is no point on which men make greater mistakes than on the relation which exists between the law and the gospel. Some men put the law instead of the gospel; others put gospel instead of the law. A certain class maintains that the law and the gospel are mixed... These men understand not the truth and are false teachers.[9]

Even those who speak biblical words can be false teachers, as Spurgeon notes, if they fail to rightly distinguish the Law and the Gospel.

Repentance

What is Repentance?

Repentance is a matter of utmost importance in the Bible. In the New Testament alone the Greek verb meaning *to repent* is used 34 times and the Greek noun meaning *repentance* is used 24 times. The Old Testament talks of repentance even more. In fact, repentance is not simply a common

---

[9] Charles Spurgeon, *New Park Street Pulpit*, vol.1 (Pilgrim Publications, 1975), 285.

biblical expression, but it was also the theme of Christ's earthly preaching. When Mark introduces the beginning of Jesus' public ministry, he summarizes His message, writing: 'Jesus came to Galilee, preaching the gospel of the kingdom of God, and saying, "The time is fulfilled, and the kingdom of God is at hand. Repent, and believe in the gospel' (*Mk 1:14*). Then, after His Resurrection and before His Ascension, Jesus commissioned His disciples to preach the Gospel, telling them 'that repentance and remission of sins should be preached in His name to all nations' (*Lk 24:47*). Later Paul told the Ephesian elders that he testified 'to Jews, and also to Greeks, repentance toward God and faith toward our Lord Jesus Christ' (*Acts 20:21*). Thus repentance was an important aspect of Christ's preaching, an important part of what He commissioned the Church to preach, and an important part of the preaching of the apostles, such as Paul.

There are several reasons that the Scriptures place such emphasis on repentance. Firstly, it is the Lord's will that we repent: 'The Lord is not slack concerning His promise, as some count slackness, but is longsuffering toward us, not willing that any should perish but that all should come to repentance' (*2 Pet. 3:9*). In fact, this is not only His will, but also His commandment to us: He 'now commands all men everywhere to repent' (*Acts 17:30*). Thus God commands everyone to repent, and Christ has commissioned His Church to preach 'repentance and remission of sins' (*Lk 24:47*).

Furthermore, repentance is significant because, unless we repent, we will perish (*Lk 13:3, 5*). Repentance is unto life (*Acts 11:18*). As *2 Corinthians 7:10* teaches, repentance leads to salvation. Elsewhere we learn that this is because repentance is 'for the remission of sins' (*Mk 1:4*). Thus, unless we repent, we will remain in our sins and under the wrath of God. But what exactly is repentance?

Repentance is God's Gift

If man is utterly depraved, and thus incapable of doing any spiritual good or in any way contributing to his own salvation, how can he possibly repent? Is it not an impossible demand, given the fact that unbelievers are dead in their sins?

Indeed, being dead in their sins, unbelievers are incapable of repenting. Yet, God saves by His grace. Salvation, including our repentance, is wholly of God, and wholly by grace. The Bible teaches us that God gives repentance. Peter declared before the Sanhedrin that one of the reasons for which God had exalted Jesus was 'to give repentance to Israel' (*Acts 5:31*). When the believers in Jerusalem heard of the salvation of Cornelius and his household, 'they glorified God, saying, "Then God has also granted to the Gentiles repentance to life"' (*Acts 11:18*). Thus, whether of Jews or Gentiles, repentance is a gift given by God.   Paul also makes this point in His instruction to Timothy:

> A servant of the Lord must not quarrel but be gentle to all, able to teach, patient, in humility correcting those who are in opposition, if God perhaps will grant them repentance, so that they may know the truth, and that they may come to their senses and escape the snare of the devil, having been taken captive by him to do his will. (*2 Tim. 2:24-26*)

It is not Timothy who can cause those who are in opposition to repent, but rather God who can grant them repentance. This is an important lesson for us to remember. In evangelism, we do not have the power to convince or persuade someone to repent. Only God can grant the gift of repentance. Thus we must rely on Him and not on any powers of persuasion we may have. Our responsibility is to proclaim the gospel.

So, man in his own ability cannot repent. Being dead in sin, it is impossible for him to turn from sin.   Yet our gracious God grants repentance. If we have truly repented of our sins and been saved, it is only because of His gracious gift. Thus in all aspects of our salvation, even in repentance where we might seem to play the biggest role, all glory goes to God and to Him alone. Salvation is wholly of God, for it is only He who can save.

Throughout church history, the people of God have recognised that repentance cannot be a human work, but rather must be the gift of God. In the 6th Century, Fulgentius of Ruspe wrote:

> It is clear that a man receives from God penitence [repentance] leading to life so that he may begin to believe in God, [for] he cannot believe at all unless he receives penitence as a gift from the compassionate God. But what is man's penitence if not a change of his will? Therefore, God, who himself gives penitence to man, changes man's will.[10]

At the Reformation, John Calvin taught that repentance is 'conferred on us by Christ.'[11] The early leaders of the Apostolic Church also clearly taught

---

[10] Fulgentius, *First Letter to the Scythian Monks*, para. 34.
[11] John Calvin, *Institutes of the Christian Religion*, iii.3.1.

that repentance was God's gift.[12] William Cathcart, the missionary apostle to Australia, insisted that 'true repentance is wrought by [Christ].' [13] D.P. Williams insisted that no part of our salvation, including repentance, could be of human works or 'moral and religious efforts', for that 'would undervalue the purpose of the Cross, undermine the Atonement, and frustrate the Grace of God.'[14]

Repentance is turning from sin to Christ

There are two common misconceptions of repentance. First, some people mistakenly equate repentance with being sad or regretting. However, this is not the Scriptural view of repentance. Paul contrasts two different types of sorrow, writing that 'godly sorrow produces repentance leading to salvation, not to be regretted; but the sorrow of the world produces death' (*2 Cor. 7:10*). Here we see that some types of sorrow have nothing whatsoever to do with repentance and lead only to death. Even 'godly sorrow' is not equated with repentance, but rather said to lead to repentance. Godly sorrow, rather, would fit in the category of *conviction of sin*. It exists to show us our need for repentance. Thus we cannot equate repentance with sorrow or regret. Yet we do find that 'godly sorrow' is essential in bringing us to repentance.

The second mistaken notion of repentance is to confuse repentance with its fruits. The biblical concept of repentance is not a transformed life, but rather what leads to a transformed life. Repentance does not mean fixing our sinful lives; repentance means coming to Jesus for Him to crucify and bury our old sinful lives and raise us up with Him to a new life. Repentance is not a turning from works of sin to works of righteousness; it is a turning from sin to Jesus. So, having cleared up what repentance is not, we can now consider what repentance is.

The Greek word μετάνοια (*metanoia*) used in the New Testament for repentance, literally means a 'change of mind'. Yet the change of mind described in the Scriptures does not only involve the intellect but the whole person. Three aspects of repentance can be distinguished: 1) a change of thinking, 2) a change of feeling, and 3) a change of will.

---

[12] *Catechism upon the Tenets of the Apostolic Church*, ii.26.

[13] William Cathcart, *Riches of Grace*, xiii.5 (May 1938), 409.

[14] D.P. Williams, 'What the Apostolic Church Stands For', *Riches of Grace*, ix.2 (Nov. 1938), 68.

1) *Change of Thinking*. The first element in repentance involves our minds. In order to repent we must change our minds about sin, that is to say we must recognise that we are sinners. David gives an example of this in *Psalm 32:5*, writing 'I acknowledged my sin to You, and my iniquity I have not hidden.' Through this change of thinking we realize that we are guilty. The Bible refers to this as 'the knowledge of sin' and teaches us that it is through God's law that we receive this knowledge (*Rom. 3:20*). The law of God shows us that we have sinned against God and that we deserve punishment as the penalty of sin. God uses His law to bring about this change of thinking.

Although this change of thinking concerning sin is not enough by itself for true repentance, it is foundational to true repentance. We cannot truly repent of our sins without the 'knowledge of sin' in our lives. Thus, in order to be saved, we must recognise our need of salvation; we must recognise that we are guilty sinners before God and that we deserve only punishment. This means that, in our evangelism, we cannot neglect to speak about sin and guilt. People must see the true problem in their lives in order to turn from sin to God. We must point people to God's moral law, that they might see that they have not met His holy standards, and thus stand guilty before Him. This 'knowledge of sin' is a necessary element in true repentance.

2) *Change of Feeling*. The 'knowledge of sin' by itself may simply lead to fear. Thus more is needed in true repentance than simply a change of thinking. The next element is a change of feeling, which is sorrow for sin committed against a holy God. No longer do we simply recognise that we have sinned and stand guilty (the change of thinking), but we have a resulting godly grief. Again, David exemplifies this in *Psalm 32:3*, writing of his 'groaning all the day long.' David also demonstrates this sorrow throughout *Psalm 51*, which he wrote after his sin with Bathsheba. This is the type of sorrow which Paul had in mind when he wrote that 'godly sorrow produces repentance leading to salvation' (*2 Cor. 7:10*).

3) *Change of Will*. Even godly sorrow, necessary as it is, is not enough to constitute true repentance. After all, Paul wrote that 'godly sorrow produces repentance', not that it is in itself repentance. There is a third and final element which is necessary for true repentance. The change of thinking and change of feeling should lead to a change of will. This change of will involves an inward turning away from sin to seek forgiveness. This

aspect of repentance can be seen, as it results in 'fruits worthy of repentance' (*Matt. 3:8*). An example of this change of will can be seen in the Christians in Thessalonica who 'turned to God from idols to serve the living and true God, and to wait for His Son from heaven' (*1 Thess. 1:9-10*). Their repentance is seen in their turning from idols, and the fruits of that repentance are seen in their turning to the true and living God (*i.e.* faith). As Cyril of Alexandria put it, 'the fruit of repentance is, in the highest degree, faith in Christ.'[15] Thus the change of will in repentance is a turning away from sin to faith in Christ, as a result of changed thinking and feeling about sin.

Repentance and faith, then, go together. True repentance is believing repentance. True faith is repentant faith. The only true turning from sin is a turning to Christ. The very nature of sin itself makes this clear, for, as we have seen in the previous chapter, sin is essentially the opposite of faith in Christ. Therefore, to repent, by turning from sin to its opposite is to turn to Christ in faith. The New Testament demonstrates this by using the terms faith/believe and repentance sometimes together (e.g. *Acts 20:21; Mark 1:15*), and sometimes separately as synonyms one for the other (e.g. *Luke 15:7-10; Mark 2:17*).

Therefore, the early Protestants during the Reformation defined repentance as including faith:

> Now, repentance consists properly of these two parts: One is contrition, that is, terrors smiting the conscience through the knowledge of sin; the other is faith, which is born of the Gospel ... and believes that for Christ's sake, sins are forgiven, comforts the conscience, and delivers it from terrors. Then good works are bound to follow, which are the fruits of repentance. (*Augsburg Confession*, XII 2-6)

True repentance is the gift of God's grace whereby He turns us from our sin to Christ in faith for salvation, just as the embrace of his father turned the prodigal son away from his miserable condition to entrust himself once again to the father's love.

Why do we need the gift of repentance?

In our sin, all mankind are turned away from Christ (for that is the opposite of faith in Christ) and turned in on ourselves (*incurvatus in se*). This means

---

[15] Cyril of Alexandria, *In Luc*, Sermon vii.

that in our sinful state, we are turned away from Him who is the Life (*Jn 14:6*). If eternal life is to know the only true God through knowing Jesus Christ His Son (*Jn 17:3*), then the Triune God must intervene to turn us around, to turn us to Christ, so that we will know Him and live.

It is the living God who is the turner of hearts (*Prov. 21:11*). While men may turn hearts away from Christ (*1 Kgs 11:1-9*), only the Triune God can free hearts held captive in the bondage of sin and turn them to Christ (*1 Kgs 18:37*). Without God's gracious gift of repentance, we would remain in the death of slavery to sin.

Repentance and the Christian Life

Scripture does not describe repentance as a one-off act at the moment of conversion. Rather the whole of the Christian life is one of continually turning from sin to Christ. As Luther wrote in the first of the *95 Theses* he so famously nailed to the castle church door in Wittenberg at the outset of the Reformation: 'When our Lord and Master Jesus Christ said "Repent," he intended that the entire life of believers should be repentance.'

Regeneration

What is Regeneration?

The Lord Jesus told Nicodemus that 'unless one is born again, he cannot see the kingdom of God' (*Jn 3:3*). Regeneration is the fact of being born again or, as the Greek can also be translated, born from above. This new birth makes one a 'new creation' (*2 Cor. 5:17*) and so has an impact on the whole of one's life.

Regeneration is God's Work

The fact that regeneration means being born from above points to the truth that regeneration requires an outside source above us. It is not something that we can produce in ourselves. We have already looked at the Biblical teaching on sin and seen that all mankind are utterly depraved, 'dead in trespasses and sins' (*Eph. 2:1*). Being dead, we could not produce life in ourselves; that life had to come from an outside source. It is because man is dead in sin that Jesus said 'you must be born again' (*Jn 3:7*). A dead man is incapable of resurrecting himself.

The same passage in Ephesians which tells us that the unsaved are dead in sin also teaches how this death is replaced with life. 'But God, who is rich in mercy, because of His great love with which He loved us, even when we were dead in trespasses, made us alive together with Christ (by grace you have been saved)' (*Eph. 2:4-5*). It is God who regenerates. God alone, out of His rich mercy and grace gives us a new life in Christ. Peter confirms what Paul wrote: 'Blessed be the God and Father of our Lord Jesus Christ, who according to His abundant mercy has begotten us again to a living hope through the resurrection of Jesus Christ from the dead' (*1 Pet. 1:3*). To beget us again is to give us a new life, and God gives us this new life out of 'His abundant mercy'. Regeneration is wholly of the grace of God.

How does God regenerate us?

It is 'of His own will [that God] brought us forth by the word of truth' (*Jas 1:18*). Thus the will of God is the ultimate cause of our regeneration (cf. *Jn 1:13*) and He uses His Word to bring that regeneration about. Peter writes that we have 'been born again, not of corruptible seed but incorruptible, through the word of God which lives and abides forever' (*1 Pet. 1:23*), further clarifying that 'this is the word which by the gospel was preached to you' (*1 Pet. 1:25*). Thus, as the gospel is proclaimed, God uses His Word to regenerate us. It is God Himself who regenerates people, and so God Himself is present in the proclamation of the Word to regenerate. God acts through His Word by His Spirit, for He is the Triune God.

Peter tells us that it is 'through the resurrection of Jesus Christ from the dead' that we are 'begotten … again to a new hope' (*1 Pet. 1:3*). So the source of our new life in regeneration is the resurrection life of Jesus Christ. In regeneration, God makes 'us alive together with Christ' (*Eph. 2:5*). Our regeneration is found in Christ's resurrection.

Christ explained to Nicodemus that 'unless one is born of water and the Spirit, he cannot enter the kingdom of God. That which is born of the flesh is flesh, and that which is born of the Spirit is spirit' (*Jn 3:5-6*). Paul writes that God 'saved us, through the washing of regeneration and renewing of the Holy Spirit' (*Titus 3:5*). So, God regenerates by His Holy Spirit, yet He has appointed a means by which He acts in the Spirit, namely His Word: the preaching of the Gospel. God works by His Spirit through His Word. Word and Spirit belong together, just as the Son cannot be separated from the Holy Spirit (and neither can be separated from the Father from who they proceed). D.P. Williams summarised God's gracious work of regeneration by writing that 'the seed of the New Birth is miraculously (by the reception of the Word of faith and the Holy Spirit) implanted.'[16]

The Meaning of Regeneration

In regeneration, God takes us 'out of death into life, out of darkness into light, from Satan's possession to God's.'[17] The new birth is *1) A Re-Creation* which makes us *2) Alive to God*, grants us *3) Entrance into the Kingdom of God*, and *4) Enables us to perform good works* which are pleasing to God.

1) A Re-Creation. 'If anyone is in Christ, he is a new creation; old things have passed away; behold, all things have become new.' (*2 Cor. 5:17*). Regeneration is a new beginning which affects our whole being (*cf. Gal. 6:15*).

2) Alive to God. Through the new birth, God gives life in Christ to those who were dead in sins and trespasses (*Eph. 2:5; Col. 2:13*). Made alive to God, we are no longer alienated from Him (due to Christ's work of reconciliation), and are enabled to respond in faith to His grace toward us.

3) Entrance into the Kingdom of God. Excluded from the Kingdom of God since Adam and Eve sinned and were cast out of the Garden Kingdom, now through the new birth those who were under the power of darkness have been delivered into the Kingdom of the Son of God's love (*John 3:3; Col. 1:13*).

---

[16] D.P. Williams, *Riches of Grace*, xiv.5 (May 1939), 390.
[17] Thomas Jones, 'Eglwys Iesu Grist', *Riches of Grace*, i.1 (April 1916). Original Welsh: 'o farwolaeth i fywyd, o'r tywyllwch i'r goleuni, o feddiant Satan at Dduw.'

4) Enabled to Perform Good Works. Regeneration is the end of our utter inability. Not only are we lifted out of death and made new creatures in the Kingdom of God, but this new creation also means that we are now 'created in Christ Jesus for good works, which God prepared beforehand that we should walk in them' (*Eph. 2:10*). However, we must remember that this new ability is 'in Christ Jesus.' Even the saved do not have the ability to please God in themselves apart from the grace of God in Christ.

D.P. Williams summarised the Apostolic understanding of our need and God's provision of regeneration:

> The whole [human] race is deplorably sick; – Christ alone possesses the cure for its corruption and disease, and this is obtainable by His sacrificial Death and the shedding of His Blood. Thus we shall be liberated from sin and death, actually partaking of a new nature unto a new, deathless life.[18]

Hugh Mitchell defined and summed up regeneration as 'spiritual resurrection ... into a totally new quality of life.'[19]

Why do we need God's work of regeneration?

All mankind are born 'dead in trespasses and sins' (*Eph. 2:1*). The dead cannot give life to themselves. The dead cannot even seek God, for 'only the quickened soul seeks after God.'[20] Those who are 'dead to God [are] absolutely incapable of knowing God.'[21] Only the God of the Resurrection can give life to the dead. And so we need God to regenerate us through the resurrection of Jesus Christ (*1 Pet. 1:3*).

The Christian church has always recognised this need:

> But just as it was the case in natural birth that the divine work of forming the person altogether preceded the will of the person being born, so is it the case in the spiritual birth (by which we begin to put off "the old man, which is being corrupted by deceitful desires," so that we may put on "the new man, which is created in the righteousness and holiness of truth") that no one can acquire a good will by his own initiative unless his very mind (that is, our inner man) is renewed and remade from God.[22]

---

[18] D.P. Williams, *Riches of Grace*, v.2 (Nov. 1929), 81.
[19] Hugh Mitchell, 'The Necessity for Repentance and Regeneration', *Tenet Booklet 2*, 15.
[20] D.P. Williams, *The Sanctuary of the Christian Life*, 54.
[21] Hugh Mitchell, 'The Necessity for Repentance and Regeneration', *Tenet Booklet 2*, 15.
[22] Fulgentius, First Letter to the Scythian Monks, para. 39.

How does God save the Utterly Depraved

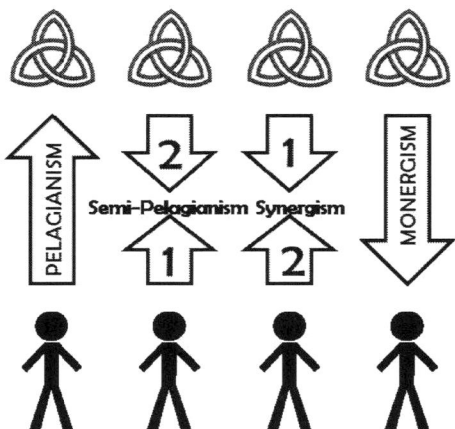

4 Views (2 Condemned Heresies)

The diagram above[23] attempts to set out four different understandings of salvation from the history of the church. We've already encountered two of these by name – Pelagianism and Semi-Pelagianism – and discovered that they've long been anathematised as heresies. The diagram helps us to see why. In both Pelagianism and Semi-Pelagianism salvation starts with man. In Pelagianism man attempts to climb up to God (and thus save himself). In Semi-Pelagianism man takes the first step up towards God and then God helps him the rest of the way. Clearly then, neither of these heretical doctrines is compatible with the doctrine of utter depravity.

That leaves two more approaches on the diagram: synergism and monergism (neither of which, you'll be glad to hear, has been condemned as heresy). So let's look briefly at each of these understandings of how God overcomes our sinful nature in salvation.

---

[23] The diagram below isn't original to me, but I have no idea who was the first to devise it. I suspect it's simply one of those diagrams that's floated around from one theology teacher to another for decades with its origins lost in the mists of time. Rather like a lot of old Pentecostal and Charismatic choruses.

Synergism

Synergism means that God and man work together in salvation (although, very importantly, God takes the initiative by His grace). This is the approach of Arminianism (including some Pentecostals) and also of Eastern Orthodoxy and Roman Catholicism. While some forms of synergism (including Eastern Orthodoxy and Roman Catholicism) reject the doctrine of utter depravity, other forms, including many Evangelical varieties of Arminianism, function within the context of utter depravity, so it is this form which we shall examine.

In order to hold together synergism with utter depravity, and accepting that God must take the initiative in our salvation by His grace, Arminian theology looks to the concept of *Prevenient Grace*. The word *prevenient* comes from Latin and means to come before. It refers to grace coming before salvation which enables the sinner to be saved. Due to the confusing and archaic nature of the word *prevenient* (even older writers referred to it as *'preventing'* grace), contemporary theologians who take this approach often use other terms, such as *enabling grace* or *pre-regenerative grace*.

Thomas Oden defines prevenient grace as 'the grace that begins to enable one to choose further to cooperate with saving grace.'[24] This is grace which comes before regeneration and which, unless resisted, would lead to regeneration.

In this type of theology, God is seen to take the initiative in our salvation, as this enabling grace is a work of the Holy Spirit, which opens the heart of the unregenerate to the truth of the gospel and which enables them to respond positively in faith. Prevenient grace involves three aspects, all of which are the work of the Holy Spirit:

1) Convicting
2) Persuading
3) Enabling

Those who believe in prevenient grace look for biblical support to *John 1:9* ('That was the true Light which gives light to every man coming into the world') as well as to the convicting work of the Spirit in *John 16:8*. (Other

---

[24] Thomas Oden, *John Wesley's Scriptural Christianity* (Grand Rapids, MI: Zondervan, 1994), 243.

passages occasionally cited include *Jn 1:4; 12:32; Rom. 1:20*.) Theologically, they draw arguments from the nature of God and of the Atonement.

Divine Monergism

Monergism means that it is God alone who acts by His grace to save, and so this position is often referred to in terms of God's 'sovereign grace.' This is the approach of Reformation Protestantism (the Lutherans and the Reformed) and is also the traditional understanding of the Apostolic Church. W.H. Lewis, for example, preached:

> The early Apostles and Evangelists thundered forth the utter depravity of human nature and the universal need of the New Birth. In unmistakable clarion notes they proclaimed the utter helplessness of man apart from the sovereign Grace of God and the efficacy of Calvary's blood.[25]

And D.P. Williams saw divine monergism as the only possibility for those who are dead in sin to be saved:

> Man is morally impotent to do anything toward his salvation. It is all given to the Holy Spirit. … There is strong opposition in the heart of man against God. The mind of the flesh is at enmity against God. This makes it impossible for man to turn to the Lord.[26]

Much earlier in church history, Fulgentius of Ruspe described God's sovereign grace in monergistic salvation like this:

> For "the Lord gives sight to the blind" [Ps. 146.8], actually making an unbeliever into a believer, a proud man into a humble one, a harsh man into a meek one, a fornicator into a chaste man, a malicious man into a kind one, a ferocious man into a peaceful one, a lover of the world into a lover of God and his neighbour, a plunderer of others' property into a liberal giver.[27]

---

[25] W.H. Lewis, 'The Body of Christ', *Riches of Grace*, 12.5 (May 1959), 134.
[26] D.P. Williams, *Justification*, 7.
[27] Fulgentius, *The Truth About Predestination and Grace*, 2.22.

The Biblical Case for Monergism

The Lord Jesus Christ declared that 'No one can come to Me unless the Father who sent Me draws him; and I will raise him up at the last day' (*Jn 6:44*). The only way to come to Christ for salvation is through the Father's drawing, and this drawing is not a mere prevenient grace which would enable us to look to Christ for salvation. Rather this drawing brings salvation, for those who are drawn to Christ by the Father will be raised up by Christ on the last day. The Father does not draw us to Christ as a preparatory work to enable us to opt for salvation, but rather the Father saves us by drawing us to Christ the Saviour. As Christ tells us in the next verse, 'therefore everyone who has heard and learned from the Father comes to Me' (*Jn 6:45*). It is God who is shown in Scripture to be the sole author of the new birth (*Eph. 2:4-5; 1 Pet. 1:3*), and the giver of faith and repentance (*Acts 3:16; 5:31; 11:18; Eph. 2:8-9; Phil. 1:29; 2 Tim. 2:24-26; 2 Pet. 1:1*). Christ has also declared that 'without Me you can do nothing' (*Jn 15:5*).

'God is faithful, by whom you were called into the fellowship of His Son, Jesus Christ our Lord' (*1 Cor. 1:9*). God's faithfulness is demonstrated not by inviting to or promising the fellowship of His Son, but by actually bringing people into that promised fellowship. In *2 Tim. 1:9* we see the parallel between God saving us and calling us; His call actually saves. *1 Pet. 2:9* tells us that we are to 'proclaim the praises of Him who called [us] out of darkness into His marvellous light.' This calling actually transports us out of the darkness and into God's light. As the next verse makes clear, obtaining mercy goes hand in hand with this call. *Acts 16:14* tells us of Lydia that 'The Lord opened her heart to heed the things spoken by Paul.' Lydia's heart isn't only opened to understand the gospel, rather God opens her heart to respond.

Divine monergism strongly proclaims that salvation is by grace alone (*sola gratia*). As Ephesians teaches, 'by grace you have been saved' (*Eph. 2:5*). It isn't simply that God is gracious and so He makes it possible for us to be saved. Rather, by His grace He actually intervenes and saves us.

Synergist Arguments against Divine Monergism and the Monergist Response

1) Since God commands men to repent and believe, they must have the ability to repent and believe. The great problem with this argument is that, if it were valid, it would not prove synergism, but Pelagianism. It was Pelagius himself who first argued that if God commanded something, man must have the ability to do it.[28] The Lord's commands to repent and believe do not presuppose our ability to fulfil them, but rather create that repentant faith in us (for 'faith comes by hearing', *Rom. 10:17*). We can prove that the Lord's word works in this way through the command He gave to Lazarus when he had been dead three days in the tomb: 'Lazarus, come forth' (*Jn 11:43*). A dead man in the tomb has no ability to come forth, yet the Lord's word in grace not only gave him some ability, but actually drew him out of the grave. The same can be seen when Peter said to the lame man at the Beautiful Gate, 'rise up and walk' (*Acts 6:3*). The lame have no ability to rise up and walk, and yet the Lord's word, spoken through the apostle Peter, lifted him to his feet and set him on his way 'walking, leaping, and praising God' (*Acts 6:8*). The same Jesus who commissions his church to go out and call all people to faith and repentance, also tells us that 'No one can come to Me unless the Father who sent Me draws him; and I will raise him up at the last day' (*Jn 6:44*).

2) Unless we assist in bringing about our repentance and faith, then our conversion would be by force and compulsion. However, monergism does not teach a robotic, forced conversion, but rather looks to the Scriptures which tell us that 'it is God who works in you both to will and to do for His good pleasure' (*Phil. 2:13*). The Lord does not force us to come to Him unwillingly for salvation, but rather He heals and renews our wills through regeneration so that we gladly and willingly believe and repent. As Augustine put it, 'God draws people by their own wills, but it is He who worked those wills.'[29] The early Protestants taught that 'God in conversion changes stubborn and unwilling into willing men through the drawing of the Holy Ghost.'[30] The early Apostolics agreed. In D.P. Williams' words, God's 'effectual calling operates on human choice.'[31]

---

[28] See e.g. the Confession of Faith of Pelagius, and Pelagius' trial at the Synod of Lydda, AD 415.

[29] Augustine, *On Admonition and Grace*, 14

[30] *Solid Declaration of the Formula of Concord*, ii.88

[31] D.P. Williams, *Sonship*, unpublished manuscript.

Chapter 10

Death & Hell

Death: The Penalty of Sin

The Bible teaches that death entered the world as a result of sin (*Rom. 5:12*). Even before he sinned, Adam had been warned that death would be the penalty for eating of the forbidden fruit (*Gen. 2:17*). Yet, Adam did not return to the dust on the same day he ate of the fruit. Rather, the LORD God pronounced judgment on him, in which he spoke of that day when, after a life of hard work, Adam would 'return to the ground … out of [which he was] taken' (*Gen. 3:19*). How could the LORD God tell Adam that he would die the day he would eat of the tree, and then on that day speak of a death many years away? The answer will be found by considering the different ways in which the Bible speaks of death and the consequences of sin.

Due to God's hatred of sin (*Deut. 25:16; Ps 5:4*), and sin's fundamental nature as the opposite of looking to Christ in faith, the consequences of sin include suffering the wrath of God and alienation from the true and living God. Both of these consequences can be seen in the case of Adam and Eve. After they had sinned, Adam and Eve hid from God due to their alienation from Him. Later God expelled them from the Garden of Eden, the place where they had enjoyed the special presence of God: thus again we see alienation. God's wrath is seen in the punishments and curses He metes out to Adam, Eve and the serpent. The Psalms give very strong warnings of God's wrath against sin:

> For You are not a God who takes pleasure in wickedness,
>> Nor shall evil dwell with You.
> The boastful shall not stand in Your sight;
>> You hate all workers of iniquity. (*Ps 5:4-5*)

> The LORD tests the righteous,
>> But the wicked and the one who loves violence His soul hates.
> Upon the wicked He will rain coals;
>> Fire and brimstone and a burning wind
>> Shall be the portion of their cup. (*Ps 11:5-6*)

When God made the covenant with Adam, He made clear how His wrath would be expressed in the penalty of sin: 'And the LORD God commanded the man, saying, "Of every tree of the garden you may freely eat; but of the tree of the knowledge of good and evil you shall not eat, for in the day that you eat of it you shall surely die"' (*Gen. 2:16-17*). Death is the penalty of sin.

The Bible speaks of death in three different ways: physical death, spiritual death and eternal death. *Physical death* is the separation of body and soul at the end of earthly physical life (*Jas. 2:26*). It is the common meaning of death in the world around us. God's curse on Adam after the Fall shows us that physical death is included in the consequences of sin: 'For dust you *are,* and to dust you shall return' (*Gen. 3:19*), and yet it does not exhaust the Scriptural meaning of death or the penalty of sin, for Adam did not die physically that day. Paul compares the death we receive from Adam with the resurrection of the dead in Christ: 'For since by man *came* death, by Man also *came* the resurrection of the dead. For as in Adam all die, even so in Christ all shall be made alive' (*1 Cor. 15:21-22*). Paul's argument here only makes sense if he is writing about physical death. Physical death is part of the penalty of sin.

Spiritual Death is the utter depravity of fallen humanity; it is the fact that we are born in bondage to sin, cannot do good in God's sight, and cannot do anything to improve our condition. We cannot seek God or His salvation, for 'there is none who seeks after God' (*Rom. 3:11*). We need Him to intervene and give us life in Christ (*Eph. 2:5*). This is the death which Adam died on the day he ate of the forbidden fruit and in which we are all born as Adam's descendants who fell in him.

Eternal Death is the final outcome of spiritual death. Those who do not come to faith in Christ and receive His salvation will suffer eternal death: unending punishment in Hell. This is the wrath of God (*Jn 3:36*). Hell, then, is not a mechanical consequence of sin. Rather, it is God's just judgment against sinful creatures through the expression of His wrath and displeasure (*Col. 3:6; Heb. 3:11*). (We will return to the topic of hell below.)

The penalty of sin includes these three forms of death, and so the only way to escape eternal death and the wrath of God is for our sins to be forgiven, and thus to be redeemed from the spiritual death which leads to eternal death and the wrath of God.

However, in the curse which is pronounced upon Adam and Eve (and the earth) after eating of the forbidden fruit, we see that death is not the only punishment for sin (*Gen. 3:16-19*). Theologians point to three types of punishment for sin:

1. 'The multiple calamities and miseries of this life' (*Gen. 3:15-19*)
2. 'Various ailments and, finally, bodily or temporal death' (*Gen. 3:19; Rom. 5:12*)
3. 'The wrath of God and eternal damnation' (*Eph. 2:3; Jn 3:36; Rom. 5:16, 18*)[1]

However, neither the calamities and miseries of this life, nor sicknesses and ailments function in the same way as death as the penalty of sin. Death is the direct and personal punishment for sin. 'The soul who sins shall die' (*Ezek. 18:4, 20*). We are all subject to death because we all sinned in Adam (*Rom. 5:12*), and so those who do not come to Christ for life will remain in death as the just punishment for their sins (*Jn 3:18, 36*).

The calamities and miseries of this life, including sickness and disease, do not necessarily follow directly and personally in the same way as death. Jesus taught His disciples this. Upon seeing a man born blind from birth, Jesus' disciples asked Him, 'Rabbi, who sinned, this man or his parents, that he was born blind?' (*Jn 9:2*). The disciples understood that infirmity and sickness has entered the world as a consequence of sin, and so assumed a direct causal connection (*i.e.* that a specific sin sinned by a specific person caused a specific infirmity). Yet Christ's response rejected such a direct causal connection: 'Neither this man nor his parents sinned, but that the works of God should be revealed in him' (*Jn 9:3*). Jesus was not denying that either the man or his parents were born in sin. Rather, what He was denying was the idea that a specific sin on the part of either the parents or their child caused his blindness. Infirmity and sickness, then, are part of the conditions in which we live in a fallen world as a result of the Fall, rather than (for the most part) being specific, personal punishments, for specific sins.[2]

Christ not only teaches this lesson with regard to infirmity and sickness, but also with regard to calamities and disasters:

---

[1] Johann Gerhard, *On Original Sin, Loci Theologici*, xii.122.

[2] There are occasions in Scripture when God uses sickness to punish sin (e.g. Miriam's leprosy in *Num. 12:10*; Elymas' blindness in Acts 12:8-11). There are also occasions where a disease is contracted as a direct result of a specific sin (e.g. a sexually transmitted disease might be caught through adultery).

> There were present at that season some who told Him about the Galileans whose blood Pilate had mingled with their sacrifices. And Jesus answered and said to them, 'Do you suppose that these Galileans were worse sinners than all other Galileans, because they suffered such things? I tell you, no; but unless you repent you will all likewise perish. Or those eighteen on whom the tower in Siloam fell and killed them, do you think that they were worse sinners than all other men who dwelt in Jerusalem? I tell you, no; but unless you repent you will all likewise perish.' (*Lk 13:1-5*)

Neither Pilate's massacre nor the collapse of the tower was the specific, personal punishment for a specific sin. Both of these tragedies, like the tragic disasters we know in our own time, were consequences of the Fall. The whole world lives under the consequences of sin, and the whole world eagerly awaits the final redemption from all sin's consequences.

> For I consider that the sufferings of this present time are not worthy to be compared with the glory which shall be revealed in us. For the earnest expectation of the creation eagerly waits for the revealing of the sons of God. For the creation was subjected to futility, not willingly, but because of Him who subjected it in hope; because the creation itself also will be delivered from the bondage of corruption into the glorious liberty of the children of God. For we know that the whole creation groans and labours with birth pangs together until now. (*Rom. 8:18-22*)

Death and the Christian

Until the day on which Christ returns for His people, everyone dies, whether believer or unbeliever. Yet that does not mean that everyone dies the same death. For believers are those who have been raised to new life through the resurrection of Christ. Regenerated, they no longer share in the spiritual death of Adam's family. Instead, the only death they know is a physical death: separation of body and soul (*Jas. 2:26*). The sting of death has been removed, for Christ has freed them from the penalty of sin through His death and resurrection. Therefore, Christ's redeemed, though they die physically, are not under the fearsome power of the grave, but instead the Lord Himself will receive them (*Ps 49:15*). For the Christian, at death 'the dust will return to the earth as it was, and the spirit will return to God who gave it' (*Eccl. 12:7*). (We refer to this period between death and the resurrection of the dead as *the intermediate state*.)

Jesus describes this in the story of the rich man and Lazarus (*Lk 16:19-31*). At death, the believing beggar Lazarus 'was carried by the angels to Abraham's bosom' (*Lk 16:22*). After death, Christ describes Lazarus as sharing in loving fellowship with Abraham (and thus the saints who have gone before) where he is comforted and does not share in any of the torments of Hades. He also describes it as impossible for those who are in 'Abraham's bosom' to pass over into the 'place of torment.' Therefore, there can be no fear of loss of salvation for the Christian after death.

Later in Luke's Gospel, we read the words of Jesus from the cross, when he promises the repentant and believing criminal who was being crucified alongside him, 'Assuredly, I say to you, today you will be with Me in Paradise' (*Lk 23:43*). By telling the man that this would occur 'today', Christ teaches us that there is no delay between death and the believer's entrance into Paradise. Although we await the sure and certain hope of the resurrection of the body, in the meantime the souls of believers pass immediately into the Paradise of Christ's presence at death.

Nor was Christ's presence in Paradise a one-off for that particular day. Paul confirms that death, for the believer, is 'to depart and be with Christ, which is far better' (*Phil. 1:23*). For, 'to be absent from the body [is] to be present with the Lord' (*2 Cor. 5:8*). The example of the martyr Stephen confirms this (*Acts 7:54-60*).

Therefore, John hears the heavenly voice which declares, 'blessed are the dead who died in the Lord' (*Rev. 14:13*). They are blessed, for they have entered into the presence of Christ where, as the Spirit proclaims, they 'rest from their labours' (*Rev. 14:13*).

In summary, at death, the souls of believers pass immediately into the paradise of the blessed presence of Christ the Lord, where they rest from their labours, share in God's comfort, and know loving fellowship with the saints who have gone before, while their bodies rest in the grave until the day of resurrection.

Yet, even the bodies of believers which rest in the grave are still united to Christ as they await that day of resurrection. Paul, writing of the resurrection of the dead at Christ's return, refers to the resurrection of 'those who are asleep' (*1 Thess. 4:15*). So, 'those who are asleep' refers to those who lie in the grave awaiting the resurrection (rather than to the souls of believers which rest in the comfort of paradise with the Lord), and of them the Scripture clearly states that they 'sleep in Jesus'. Thus, even the bodies of believers remain united to Christ after death. In fact, this union with Christ through the Spirit is what makes possible the resurrection of the body to eternal life (*Rom. 8:11*). As the great Puritan, Thomas Watson put it, 'the dust of believers is part of Christ's mystic body. The grave is a dormitory or place of rest to the saints, where their bodies quietly sleep in Christ, till they are awakened out of their sleep by the trumpet of the archangel.'[3] The *Westminster Shorter Catechism* gives a clear and succinct summary of the benefits which believers receive from Christ at death: 'The souls of believers are at their death made perfect in holiness, and do immediately pass into glory; and their bodies, being still united to Christ, do rest in their graves till the resurrection.'[4]

Against Purgatory

The Roman Catholic Church teaches a different destination for the people of God after death. According to the Catechism of the Catholic Church:

> All who die in God's grace and friendship, but still imperfectly purified, are indeed assured of their eternal salvation; but after death they undergo purification, so as to achieve the holiness necessary to enter the joy of heaven. The Church gives the name *Purgatory* to this final purification of the elect, which is entirely different from the punishment of the damned. … The tradition of the Church … speaks of a cleansing fire. … This teaching is also based on the practice of prayer for the dead.[5]

An older explanation of the Roman Catholic faith, the *Penny Catechism*, explained Purgatory through a series of questions and answers:

> *105. How are we in communion with the souls in purgatory?*
>
> We are in communion with the souls in purgatory by helping them with our prayers and good works: 'It is a holy and wholesome thought to pray for the dead, that they may be loosed from sins'. (2 Macc. 12:46)[6]

---

[3] Thomas Watson, *Body of Divinity*, ch. 41.
[4] *Westminster Shorter Catechism*, 37.
[5] *Catechism of the Catholic Church*, 1030-1032.
[6] 2 Maccabees is a book of the Apocrypha, which the Roman Catholic Church regards as Scripture, but Protestants do not recognise as Scripture.

106. What is purgatory?

Purgatory is a place where souls suffer for a time after death on account of their sins.

107. What souls go to purgatory?

Those souls go to purgatory that depart this life in venial sin; or that have not fully paid the debt of temporal punishment due to those sins of which the guilt has been forgiven.

108. What is temporal punishment?

Temporal punishment is punishment which will have an end, either in this world, or in the world to come.

109. How do you prove that there is a purgatory?

I prove that there is a purgatory from the constant teaching of the Church; and from the doctrine of Holy Scripture, which declares that God will render to every man according to his works; that nothing defiled shall enter heaven; and that some will be saved, 'as one who has gone through fire. (Matt. 16:27. Apoc. 21:27. 1 Cor. 3:15)[7]

So, from these Roman Catholic sources, we can see that Purgatory is supposed to be a place where the saved go upon death to prepare them for heaven by suffering for their sins in flames (which are different to the flames of hell).

At the Reformation, the Protestants rejected 'the Romish Doctrine concerning Purgatory' as 'a fond thing vainly invented, and grounded upon no warranty of Scripture, but rather repugnant to the Word of God.'[8] In keeping with the Reformers, the Apostolic Church rejects the Roman doctrine of Purgatory: 'Scripture in no wise refers to such a place, or suggests that works of merit or prayers of others will have any effect in lessening punishment or translating from hell to heaven.'[9]

We have already seen above that the Scriptures teach that the souls of believers pass immediately into Paradise and the presence of Christ at death, rather than into a place of flames, suffering, punishment and purification. As a result, in the second generation of the Reformation, when Martin Chemnitz examined the teachings of the Roman Catholics, he concluded that:

---

[7] *A Catechism of Christian Doctrine (The Penny Catechism)*, 105-109.
[8] *The 39 Articles*, Article 22.
[9] *Asked and Answered: A Catechism of Apostolic Principles*, 'The Last Things', Q.18.

> To such an extent, therefore, does the purgatory of the papalists militate against canonical Scripture that it is not able to stand unless the clearest statements of Scripture are criminally distorted and falsified. Therefore the fabrications of this purgatory are to be detested the more by us because, as is clear, they militate against Scripture and snatch away from us the sweet and very necessary consolation in the midst of death.[10]

There is, however, one canonical Scripture to which both the *Catechism of the Catholic Church* and the *Penny Catechism* refer concerning purgatory: *1 Cor. 3:12-15*. By superficiality of vocabulary, this Scripture might well appear relevant to the concept of purgatory: after all, Paul here speaks of fire, reward, loss, and of being saved. However, on closer examination, the inconsistency between this passage and purgatory becomes clear. The fire of which Paul writes tests 'each one's work, of what sort it is' (*1 Cor. 3:13*), whereas the fire of purgatory is supposed, not to test, but to punish and purify, and not to act upon works, but upon individuals. Furthermore, Paul's language throughout the passage is figurative ('gold, silver, precious stones, wood, hay, straw'). If the materials which are being tested by the fire are figurative, the most straightforward reading would be to understand the fire by which they are tested as figurative as well. Although this passage has been seized upon as a Scriptural support for purgatory, Paul is not here teaching anything like the concept of purgatory. Rather, this is an example of an already formed dogma searching (in vain) for a Scriptural support.

For, in fact, purgatory is a doctrine built on customary practice, rather than Scriptural support. As even the *Catechism of the Catholic Church* admits, the idea of purgatory is 'based on the practice of prayer for the dead.'[11] Here an unbiblical practice has led to an unbiblical dogma. The Roman Catholic Church finds support for prayer for the dead in 2 Maccabees 12:38-46. However, the book of 2 Maccabees is not canonical Scripture, but rather part of the Apocrypha. Yet, even if 2 Maccabees were canonical Scripture, what it presents regarding prayer for the dead is not the same as the Roman Catholic teaching. The dead for whom prayer is made in 2 Maccabees were idolaters who had entrusted themselves to an idol. Thus the prayer for the dead made by Judas and his men was a prayer for the salvation of those who had died in idolatry, not for the lessening of suffering of believers in purgatory. 2 Maccabees may possibly provide an interesting account of an unusual historical event, but it does not teach a doctrine of prayer for the purification of souls of the departed in purgatory.

---

[10] Martin Chemnitz, *Examination of the Council of Trent*, 3:315.
[11] *Catechism of the Catholic Church*, 1032.

The Apostolic Church, as with the churches of the Reformation, rejects the unbiblical practice of prayer for the dead. Prayer for the dead assumes that the living can influence the present state of those who have died, and thus ignores the Bible's teaching on the fixed state of the dead, on the blessedness of those who have died in Christ, on the 'great gulf' across which no one can pass between hades and paradise, and forgets that 'it is appointed for men to die once, but after this the judgment' (*Heb. 9:27*).

But purgatory is not only an unbiblical teaching and one built upon unbiblical customs. It is also a doctrine which contradicts the gospel of justification by faith alone through the finished work of Christ, and so purgatory is a teaching which 'shakes, perverts, and overthrows the chief articles of the heavenly doctrine.'[12]

The Roman Catholic concept of purgatory distinguishes between the guilt of sin and the temporal punishment of sin. The guilt of sin is said to be forgiven, but the sinner must still pay the debt of temporal punishment, either in this life or in the fire of purgatory. But such a concept is contrary to the biblical gospel of justification through the finished work of Christ, for Christ has not only released us from the guilt of sin, but has also taken the full punishment for our sins. Therefore the Protestant Reformers regarded purgatory as:

> overthrow[ing] from its foundations the article of our justification before God, which is the sum and purpose of all Scripture, and are an insult to the satisfaction made by the Son of God. For sin is simply not forgiven without satisfaction which completely, wholly, perfectly, and absolutely satisfies the law of God. But because such satisfaction is impossible for us, therefore God sent His Son "in the likeness of sinful flesh" that, having been made the Victim for sin, He might condemn sin, "in order that the just requirement of the law might be fulfilled," not *by* us but "in us" who are in Christ Jesus (Rom. 8:3-4). For He has been made righteousness for us by God (1 Cor. 1:30), and this is imputed to us through faith, because Christ was delivered for our trespasses (Rom. 4:25), that we might be made righteous by His obedience (Rom. 5:19), for He was made sin for us "so that in Him we might become the righteousness of God" (2 Cor. 5:21) ... Therefore to invent other expiations and redemptions in purgatory through alms and other intercessions of the living, or through the sufferings of those who are to be purified, is an insult to the blood of Christ ... [This] is blasphemy against the most perfect satisfaction of Christ, imputed to us by faith ... For if another propitiation and redemption from purgatory must be sought after death, then Christ's propitiation and redemption is not complete. If there is need for another cleansing through

---

12 Martin Chemnitz, *Examination of the Council of Trent*, 3:312.

fire after death in order to be saved, then the blood of Christ does not fully cleanse believers.[13]

Through the blood of Jesus, remission of the guilt of sin and of its punishment are both made at the same time. 'When the prodigal son returns, he is not subjected to torment but is at once received with joy. The sheep which has been found is not punished, but laid on the shoulder.'[14] Therefore, purgatory is to be rejected as an unbiblical teaching which is contrary to the gospel of the finished work of Christ.

The Intermediate State and the Unsaved

The unsaved, like the saved, die. The unsaved, like the saved, await the day of resurrection. So what happens to the unsaved between death and the final judgment? Just as the story of the rich man and Lazarus teaches us about the intermediate state for the saved (Lazarus), it also teaches us about the intermediate state of the lost (the rich man). The rich man is buried (*Lk. 16:22*), but the day of the final judgment and the resurrection of the dead has not yet come, as his brothers are still alive (*Lk. 16:27-31*). So this is clearly the intermediate state.

The intermediate state of the lost is described here as a state of 'torments in Hades' (*Lk. 16:23*) and these torments consist of 'flame' (*Lk. 16:24*) and also an awareness of missing out on the blessed state of comfort of the saved (the rich man is aware of Abraham and Lazarus and how they are not suffering). Furthermore, there is no possibility of moving from the torment of the flames to the blessedness of paradise, for, between the two, 'there is a great gulf fixed' (*Lk. 16:26*).

The souls of the unsaved, then, upon death, pass immediately into the torments of Hades, where they suffer for their sins in both the flames and the knowledge of their lack of blessedness and their alienation from the comfort of God. There is no possibility for salvation after death, nor for the unsaved dead to escape the flames of Hades into the paradise of God (*Heb. 9:27*).

---

[13] Chemnitz, *Examination of the Council of Trent*, 3:317-318.
[14] Chemnitz, *Examination of the Council of Trent*, 3:319.

The Final Judgment

The Lord 'has appointed a day on which He will judge the world in righteousness by the Man whom He has ordained' (*Acts 17:31*). On the final day, the Lord Jesus Christ will come to judge 'the quick and the dead'.[15] Jude records Enoch's prophecy:

> Behold, the Lord comes with ten thousands of His saints, to execute judgment on all, to convict all who are ungodly among them of all their ungodly deeds which they have committed in an ungodly way, and of all the harsh things which ungodly sinners have spoken against Him. (*Jude 14-15*)

Undoubtedly the most famous description of the final judgment can be found in John's vision in the book of Revelation:

> Blessed and holy is he who has part in the first resurrection. Over such the second death has no power, but they shall be priests of God and of Christ, and shall reign with Him a thousand years. … Then I saw a great white throne and Him who sat on it, from whose face the earth and the heaven fled away. And there was found no place for them. And I saw the dead, small and great, standing before God, and books were opened. And another book was opened, which is the Book of Life. And the dead were judged according to their works, by the things which were written in the books. The sea gave up the dead who were in it, and Death and Hades delivered up the dead who were in them. And they were judged, each one according to his works. Then Death and Hades were cast into the lake of fire. This is the second death. And anyone not found written in the Book of Life was cast into the lake of fire. (*Rev. 20:6, 11-15*)

The Scriptures speak frequently of this Day of Judgment, or Doomsday[16] (e.g. *Eccl. 12:14; Mt 10:15; 11:22-24; 12:36; 16:27; 25:31-46; Mk 6:11; Lk 10:14; 11:31-32; Acts 10:42; Rom. 2:25; 1 Cor. 4:5; 2 Cor. 5:10; 2 Tim. 4:1; Heb. 6:2*).

---

[15] This well-known expression comes from the Authorised Version of the Bible (i.e. the King James translation) and both the Apostles' and Nicene Creeds. 'Quick' means 'living.'

[16] *Doom* is an older English word for *judgment*.

Christ will be the Judge

Jesus taught that 'the Father judges no one, but has committed all judgment to the Son' (*Jn 5:22*). The Father has given the Son 'authority to execute judgment also, because He is the Son of Man' (*Jn 5:27*). Thus it is as the Incarnate God that Jesus Christ sits as Judge of the quick and the dead. Yet this judgment is not apart from the Father, for Jesus goes on to tell us, 'I can of Myself do nothing. As I hear, I judge; and My judgment is righteous, because I do not seek My own will but the will of the Father who sent Me' (*Jn 5:30*). The judgment of the Incarnate Son, then, is at one with the Father's judgment.

The great post-Reformation theologian Francis Turretin, explained the relationship of the judgment of the Father and the Son like this:

> Christ will be the Judge in that very visible nature in which he was condemned for us. For although judiciary power is common to the whole Trinity, still it will be specially exercised by the incarnate Son. Judgment is said to have been given him by the Father (Mt. 28:18; Jn. 5:22; Acts 10:42; 17:31) as being King of his church, the avenger of his elect, the most strict punisher of the wicked and rebellious, the Lord of all.[17]

It is 'the Lord Jesus Christ who will judge the living and the dead at His appearing and His kingdom' (*2 Tim. 4:1; cf. Mt 25:31; Acts 10:42; 17:31*).

Believers will be Judged

Christ taught of the Final Judgment as the judgment of the sheep and the goats:

> When the Son of Man comes in His glory, and all the holy angels with Him, then He will sit on the throne of His glory. All the nations will be gathered before Him, and He will separate them one from another, as a shepherd divides his sheep from the goats. And He will set the sheep on His right hand, but the goats on the left. (*Mt 25:31-33*)

Christ will then tell the sheep, 'Come, you blessed of My Father, inherit the kingdom prepared for you from the foundation of the world' (*Mt 25:34*). At the Final Judgment, believers will receive their eternal reward. Paul

---

[17] Francis Turretin, *Institutes of Elenctic Theology*, 20.vi.vii (ET 3:599).

confirms this, writing to Christians that 'we shall all stand before the judgment seat of Christ' (*Rom. 14:10*) and that 'we must all appear before the judgment seat of Christ, that each one may receive the things *done* in the body, according to what he has done, whether good or bad' (*2 Cor. 5:10*).

This judgment of believers is a judgment leading to reward (*Rev. 18:11*). The sheep receive the kingdom at the judgment. It is not a judgment which opens up the possibility of eternal condemnation, for there is 'now no condemnation to those who are in Christ Jesus' (*Rom. 8:1*).

The final judgment of believers is said by Scripture to be according to their works (*Mt 25:35-40; 2 Cor. 5:10*). This does not, however, mean that believers are saved by works. Rather, the good works of believers demonstrate their faith in Christ (*Jas. 2:14-20*). The salvation of believers is not due to the merit of their own good works (which, due to the utter depravity of sinful human nature, they could not even perform apart from salvation in Christ), but rather, they are saved because their names are written in the Book of Life (*Rev. 20:12, 15*).

The Scriptures only mention the good works of believers in connection with the Final Judgment, not their evil works. For, through justification in Christ, the evil works of believers have been cast into the depths of the sea, to be remembered no more (*Micah 7:19*).

Unbelievers will be Judged

Yet the judgment of the last day is not reserved only to believers. Rather, as John sees in his vision, 'the sea gave up the dead who were in it, and Death and Hades delivered up the dead who were in them. And they were judged, each one according to his works' (*Rev. 20:13*).

Just as good works demonstrate faith in Christ, so too evil works demonstrate unbelief and sin (*Mt 7:17-18*). Thus, unbelievers are said to be judged according to their works (*Eccl. 12:14; Mt 12:36; Jude 14-15; Rev. 20:13*), yet they are ultimately condemned because their names are not written in the Book of Life (*Rev. 20:15*) because they do not believe in Christ. 'He who believes in the Son has everlasting life; and he who does not believe the Son shall not see life, but the wrath of God abides on him' (*Jn 3:36*).

The Dutch theologian, Herman Bavinck, sums this up:

> The main issue in the final judgment is that of faith or unbelief. For faith in Christ is the work of God par excellence (John 6:29; 1 John 3:23). Those who believe do not come into judgment (John 5:24); those who do not believe

are already condemned and remain under God's wrath (John 3:18, 36). Therefore, the standard in the final judgment will in the first place be the gospel (John 12:48); but that gospel is not opposed to, and cannot even be conceived apart from, the law ... In the final judgment, therefore, the norm will be the entire Word of God in both its parts: law and gospel.[18]

In the judgment of that final day, the Lord Christ will say to those who are condemned, '"Depart from Me, you cursed, into the everlasting fire prepared for the devil and his angels" ... And these will go away into everlasting punishment, but the righteous into eternal life' (*Mt 25:41, 46*).

Hell: The Eternal Doom of the Finally Impenitent

First let's clear up a few issues of language. The goats were cast into 'everlasting punishment.' Our tenet speaks of 'eternal doom.' The two expressions mean the same thing, for doom is simply an older English word for judgment. The 'finally impenitent' are those who remain unrepentant and unbelieving until the end of their lives.[19]

What is this eternal doom – this everlasting punishment – of the finally impenitent? The word by which we know it best is *hell*.

What is Hell?

Hell is the place of the everlasting outpouring of the wrath of God. It is a 'living death' and 'the greatest of all torments in eternity.'[20] In hell, the finally impenitent undergo 'the fiery indignation' of the terrible wrath of God.[21]

---

[18] Herman Bavinck, *Reformed Dogmatics* (ET: Grand Rapids: Baker, 2008), 4:700.

[19] Thus, attempts which have been made in some countries to update the language of the Tenets of the Apostolic Church by replacing the words 'eternal doom' with 'eternal separation from God' do not express the same idea. Nor, as we shall see presently, do they carefully express biblical teaching. The original Welsh expression used to confess the faith of the Apostolic Church was 'cospedigaeth dragwyddol' (*eternal punishment*).

[20] John McGee, 'The Eternal Doom of the Finally Impenitent', *Tenet Booklet 2*, 24.

[21] Fundamental Truths, *Guiding Principles*, 189.

Hell is the place of God's active and just judgment

It is God who casts unrepentant sinners into hell (*Mk. 9:45, 47*). The punishment of hell actively comes 'from the presence of the Lord and from the glory of His power' (*2 Thess. 1:9*). This active punishment on God's part is just and righteous. 'It is a righteous thing with God to repay with tribulation those who trouble you … in flaming fire taking vengeance on those who do not know God' (*2 Thess. 1:6, 8*).

Hell is a place of everlasting punishment

At the final judgment, the wicked are cast into 'everlasting punishment' (*Mt 25:46*). Jesus describes hell as 'the everlasting fire' (*Mt 18:8*) and as 'the fire that shall never be quenched' (*Mk 9:43*). Paul writes of hell as 'everlasting destruction' (*2 Thess. 1:9*), the writer to the Hebrews tells us that 'eternal judgment' is an 'elementary' principle of the Christian faith (*Heb. 6:1-2*), Jude speaks of 'eternal fire' (*Jude 7*) and the Apocalypse tells us that the torment of hell lasts 'day and night forever and ever' (*Rev. 20:10; cf. 14:11*). Each of these descriptions of hell tells us that it is everlasting: there is no end to it.

Hell is a place of conscious torment

The punishment of hell does not merely consist in the absence of blessing. Rather, it is a place of active punishment through conscious torment. Christ teaches that hell is worse than earthly suffering (*Mk 9:43*: 'it is better for you to enter into life maimed, rather than having two hands, to go to hell') and worse than a horrific physical death (*Mk 9:42*: 'it would be better for him if a millstone were hung around his neck, and he were thrown into the sea').

The Lord Jesus describes the torment of hell as 'weeping and gnashing of teeth' (*Mt 8:12; 22:13; 24:51; 25:30; Lk 13:28*). It is an unquenchable fire (*Isa. 66:24; Mt 18:8; Mk 9:44, 46, 48; 2 Thess. 7-9; Jude 7; Rev. 14:10-11; 20:10, 15*).

In addition to the flames, this torment also includes seeing the saints in the blessedness of the kingdom of God, while knowing oneself to have been cast out (*Lk 13:28*).

> It is not a mere … punishment of loss, as if it consisted in a simple privation of good without any sense of evil. … the Scriptures describe

these punishments now privatively and negatively ... by the removal of all good, then positively and affirmatively ... The negative ... evils are separation from God and Christ and privation of the divine vision: in which is placed the happiness of the saints; separation from the angels and saints (between whom and the damned a great gulf ... is said to intervene); a privation of light, joy, glory, felicity and life, and of all good things of whatever kind they may be. On the other hand, the positive evils are manifold. These are adumbrated by pains and tortures, by torments, by groans and grief, by cries and wailings, by weeping and gnashing of teeth, by the gnawing worm, by the unquenchable fire and other things of like nature, which are accustomed to imply evils of all kinds in the soul as well as in the body.[22]

Hell is prepared for the devil and his angels

When Christ, the Just Judge, casts the wicked into hell on the Day of Judgment, He will declare, 'Depart from Me, you cursed, into the everlasting fire prepared for the devil and his angels' (*Mt 25:41*). Even as He casts the impenitent into the fires of hell, the Incarnate God proclaims that hell was not prepared for human beings, but for the devil. Although the unbelieving will spend eternity under the wrath of God in hell, this was not the purpose for which the Triune God created the human race: we were not created to be damned, but to be saved. As Peter proclaims, the Lord is 'not willing that any should perish but that all should come to repentance' (*2 Pet. 3:9*). This then highlights human responsibility (as opposed to an inscrutable divine decree) in who goes to hell. Those who are condemned to hell are condemned for their own fault: because they have 'not believed in the name of the only begotten Son of God' (*Jn 3:18*).

What Hell is Not

The Apostolic Church expresses the doctrine of hell in these three points:

1. That the finally impenitent on earth have no hope of eternal life. (Matt. 25:41-46; Rev. 20:12-15; Mark 9:43-48).
2. That the soul of man can never cease to exist. (Luke 20:35-36; Acts 24:15; Rev. 14:10-11).

---

[22] Turretin, *Institutes*, 20.vii.iv (ET 3:605).

3. That the punishment is eternal and irrevocable; there is no hope beyond the grave. (Mark 9:45-46. Cf. Rev. 19:20; 20:10; 21:8).[23]

These three statements rule out two false teachings regarding hell which had re-emerged in the early years of British Pentecostalism (and have again re-emerged among some Evangelicals and Pentecostals today): *Universalism* and *Annihilationism*.[24]

The False Teaching of Universalism

Universalism is a false teaching which claims that everyone will ultimately be saved. Many who hold to this teaching are motivated by the idea that eternal punishment is somehow contrary to the love of God. While some universalists simply reject the biblical teaching on hell, there are others who believe in a temporary hell (which will function as a sort of purgatory) accompanied by opportunities to repent and believe the gospel after death. Yet this is contrary to the biblical teaching that 'it is appointed for men to die once, but after this the judgment' (*Heb. 9:27*).

The False Teaching of Annihilationism

Annihilationism is the false teaching that the finally impenitent will cease to exist. Some annihilationists see this as happening after a period of

---

[23] Fundamental Truths, *Guiding Principles*, p.188.

[24] I am calling both Universalism and Annihilationism 'false teachings' as they are certainly both heterodox and rejected as errors by the Apostolic Church, the Protestant Reformers, and the vast majority of the Fathers of the undivided church. Arguably it is possible to go a step further and call both of these false teachings heresies, as the acts of the Second Council of Constantinople (the 5th Ecumenical Council of the undivided church) declare: 'If anyone says or thinks that the punishment of demons and of impious men is only temporary, and will one day have an end, and that a restoration (ἀποκατάστασις) will take place of demons and of impious men, let him be anathema.' Although scholars have raised several questions regarding this particular act of the Council and its specific reference (it is aimed at Origen and his teaching), it would appear to anathematise universalism, and thus make it a formal heresy, and possibly also to anathematise (at least certain forms of) annihilationism. Thus these two false teachings are not only certainly heterodox and erroneous, but also likely formally heretical. Within the context of the Apostolic Church, both have formally been declared heresies, and anyone who promotes these false teachings has 'no fellowship with us.' Any minister or officer who promotes these false teachings must 'leave their office.' *The Apostolic Church: Convocation of Apostles and Prophets at Bradford*, October 1929, 8-16.

punishment, others see it as happening immediately upon death, the annihilation itself being the punishment for sin.

Annihilationists point particularly to Scriptures which speak of the destruction of the wicked. John Stott argued that, 'it would seem strange ... if people who are said to suffer destruction are in fact not destroyed ... it is difficult to imagine a perpetually inconclusive process of perishing.'[25] Don Carson responded to Stott by writing:

> Stott's conclusion ... is memorable, but useless as an argument, because it is merely tautologous: *of course* those who suffer *destruction* are *destroyed*. But it does not follow that those who suffer destruction cease to exist. Stott has assumed his definition of 'destruction'.[26]

The words used in the Scriptures to describe 'destruction' or 'perishing' in hell, do not mean annihilation. Douglas Moss has examined the biblical usage of this vocabulary and concludes that 'in none of these cases do the objects cease to exist; they cease to be useful or to exist in their original intended state.'[27] Thus the biblical vocabulary is not compatible with annihilationism, but is fully compatible with the orthodox Christian doctrine of eternal conscious punishment.

Annihilationism is held by the Seventh Day Adventists, Christadelphians and Jehovah Witnesses. Additionally, in 1995 the Church of England Doctrine Commission's report, *The Mystery of Salvation*, rejected the historic doctrine of hell, claiming that 'hell is not eternal torment, but it is the final and irrevocable choosing of that which is opposed to God so completely and so absolutely that the only end is total non-being', thus allowing for annihilationism to be adopted among some Anglicans.[28]

Hell and the Presence of God

It has become increasingly common among evangelical Christians to speak of hell as separation from God. What most people generally understand by

---

[25] David L. Edwards & John R. W. Stott, *Evangelical Essentials: A Liberal-Evangelical Dialogue* (Downers Grove: IVP, 1988), 316.

[26] D.A. Carson, *The Gagging of God: Christianity Confronts Pluralism* (Grand Rapids: Zondervan, 1996), 522.

[27] See Douglas J. Moo, 'Paul on Hell', in Christopher W. Morgan & Robert A. Peterson, ed., *Hell Under Fire* (Grand Rapids: Zondervan, 2004), 104-105.

[28] The Doctrine Commission of the Church of England, *The Mystery of Salvation* (London: Church House Publishing, 1995), 199.

that statement is that hell is somewhere where God is not present. Yet this simply doesn't make sense. For the Sovereign God is omnipresent.

> Where can I go from Your Spirit?
> Or where can I flee from Your presence?
> If I ascend into heaven, You are there;
> If I make my bed in hell, behold, You are there. (*Ps 139:7-8*)

Not only is the Lord God omnipresent, but the Scriptures explicitly teach His presence in hell. The everlasting destruction of hell is punishment which comes 'from the presence of the Lord and from the glory of His power' (*2 Thess. 1:9*). John the Baptist prophesied of Jesus Himself as the one who 'will burn up the chaff with unquenchable fire' (*Mt 3:12*). Christ the Lamb shares in His Father's wrath (*Rev. 6:16-17*) and is Himself the gaoler of death and hell (*Rev. 1:18*). Most explicitly of all, Revelation 14:10 describes hell as being 'tormented with fire and brimstone in the presence of the holy angels and in the presence of the Lamb.' The wrath of God is poured out by the Triune God in His very presence in hell. Therefore, in the way the expression is normally understood, it is incorrect to say that hell is separation from the presence of God.

Given that 'the Lamb' is explicitly present in hell outpouring His wrath, is there any way we can speak of hell in terms of separation from God's presence? Yes, there is (but only if it is understood in a highly nuanced way). The Scriptures often speak of the presence of God in a way other than God's omnipresence (e.g. *Ex. 33:12-17*). Rather, the presence of God can refer to the blessed experience of the presence with His people. This is the 'comfortable presence' of God.[29] Hell, then, is separation from the comfortable presence of God. Instead, the finally impenitent in hell experience the uncomfortable presence of God as He pours out His wrath. When Christ tells the wicked to 'depart' (*Mt 7:23; 25:41*), therefore, it is not a

---

[29] Richard Sibbes defined the comfortable presence : 'That comfort that we shall have in heaven, in the presence of God, and of Christ, and his holy angels, is understood in some little way by the comfortable presence of God to the soul of a Christian, when he finds the Spirit of God raising him, and cheering him up, and witnessing his presence; as ofttimes, to the comfort of God's people, the Holy Ghost witnesseth a presence, that now the soul can say, God is present with me, he smiles on me, and strengtheneth me, and leads me along. This comfortable way God's children have to understand the things of heaven, by the first fruits they have here. For God is so far in love with his children here on earth, and so tender over them, that he purposes not to reserve all for another world, but gives them some taste beforehand, to make them better in love with the things there, and better to bear the troubles of this world.' Richard Sibbes, *A Glance of Heaven (or, A Precious Taste of a Glorious Feast)*, Second Sermon, *The Complete Works of Richard Sibbes*, Vol. 4, 168.

⟠ 172 *Apostolic Theology*

local departure from the omnipresent Christ, but rather they are cast out from communion with the Triune God through Jesus Christ the Son.

Significantly, the Bible will not allow us to make the mistake of dividing the Triune God when it comes to the doctrine of hell. Those who are 'tormented with fire and brimstone' in hell, are tormented 'in the presence of the Lamb' (*Rev. 14:10*). God mediates His judgment through the Son, so the Mediator of our salvation is also the Mediator of God's just judgement. As the great Gregory of Nazianzus, the Theologian, wrote: 'When all have known the Trinity, He is to some their illumination and to others their punishment.'[30]

---

[30] Gregory of Nazianzus, Orat. 2 *de pace*, cited in Gerhard *Loci*, Exegesis III §8.

Tenet 3

The virgin birth, sinless life,
atoning death, triumphant resurrection,
ascension, & abiding intercession
of our Lord Jesus Christ;
His second coming,
& millennial reign upon earth.

Chapter 11

The Incarnation

Salvation is of the Lord

Our Lord Jesus Christ is 'the only begotten Son of God, begotten of His Father before all worlds, God of God, Light of Light, very God of very God, begotten not made, being of one substance with the Father.'[1] So that is who has come into the world to bring us salvation – very God of very God. That is the only way that it could be, for salvation is not our climbing up to reach God, but rather His coming down in love to us. Salvation is the gift of God which we receive in the gift of the Son. And so, from first to last, salvation is of the Lord.

Christology (or the Doctrine of Christ) is, perhaps more than any other doctrine, steeped in history. Maybe that puts some people off, as reading about the Incarnation and the Doctrine of the Person of Christ often involves unfamiliar names in unfamiliar places at unfamiliar times in history. Indeed, we shall meet some of those names, but the reason we'll meet them is because they have already had to deal with questions that are still very important today. Perhaps the questions they faced might not always be the first ones we would think of, but that's all the more reason why we need to learn from those who have gone before us, for what so many of these great teachers of the faith saw was the vital connection between the questions of their day and the truth that salvation is of the Lord. Don't worry, we'll not be spending all our time with people from the past, but we will learn from their wisdom when we can. Ultimately the authoritative source for Christology is not in the words of dead theologians, but in the Bible. So as we approach the insights of the great Christological teachers of the past, we should remember that we come to them as interpreters of Scripture (for that is what they were) to be taught biblical truth.

---

[1] Nicene Creed ('being of one substance with' = *homoousios*). We've already seen this back in chapters 2 & 3.

The Word Became Flesh

John opens His Gospel by pointing us to the Word who was, in the beginning, with God and who was God (*John 1:1*). God the Word, John tells us, was the one through whom all things were created and the one who is both the true Life and true light (*John 1:3-4*). John uses language that is much more simple and much more familiar to us than the language of the great Christological teachers who would follow in the history of the Church (such as Athanasius), and yet the point he was making right from the outset of his Gospel account was just the same: Jesus Christ, the Word of God the Father, is and always has been true God. He has always existed together with the Father and is God just as the Father is God. In other words, Jesus the Word is of one being – *homoousios* – with the Father.

But John doesn't leave us there. Having established the identity of this Word of the Father, John goes on to make one of the most incredible statements that has ever been made: 'And the Word became flesh and dwelt among us, and we beheld His glory, the glory as of the only begotten of the Father, full of grace and truth' (*John 1:14*). Even the first few words of this verse make an incredible statement, for, as we have seen, John has already made very clear who this Word of whom writes is: God the Word, who is eternally with the Father. So what John is proclaiming here at the outset of His Gospel is the glorious reality of God become flesh. Incredible and glorious at the same time, this is the doctrine of the Incarnation of God the Son: a doctrine upon which the whole of the Christian faith rests.

We shall return to the words 'became flesh' in just a moment to examine what this entailed. But first let's briefly consider the rest of *John 1:14*. John tells us not only that the Word became flesh, but that He 'dwelt among us.' So the taking to himself of a human nature was not merely for the sake of experience. Rather, when the Word took on our flesh He also entered into the full experience of human life, including its relational and community aspects. He did not live a human life in isolation from human beings, but rather came at a specific time (*Luke 2:2*), in a specific place (*Micah 5:2; Matthew 2:1; Luke 2:4-7*), as a member of a specific family (*Matthew 1:1-17; Luke 3:23-38*). He had friends (*John 11:11; John 15:14-15*), a mother, brothers and sisters (*Matthew 12:46-47; 13:55-56; Mark 6:3; Luke 8:19-20; John 2:12; John 7:1-10; Acts 1:14; 1 Corinthians 9:5; Galatians 1:19*). Thus entering fully into human community, Christ the God-Man not only perfectly related to those around Him in love, but also fully experienced both the joys and the hurts of authentic human relationships in a fallen world.

John goes on to tell us that, when the Word became flesh and dwelt among us, 'we beheld His glory, the glory as of the only begotten of the Father.' Firstly then, in becoming flesh, Jesus did not lose anything of His glory as God the Word. It wasn't a case of being God before the Incarnation and then suddenly turning into a man instead. Nor was this a mixture of humanity and deity which diluted the glory of His deity. No; Jesus continued to be true God after the Incarnation, just as He was beforehand. He continued to be *homoousios* – of the same being – with the Father, and continued to share with Him in the full glory of the Godhead. Secondly, it is precisely in His Incarnation that we behold His glory. In other words, it is the Incarnate Christ who reveals God to us. We see Jesus as God in His Incarnation. We see the divine glory only through the one who has come in the flesh. Thirdly, this glory is 'as of the only begotten of the Father', which not only points us to how Jesus shares the Father's glory, but also to Jesus role in revealing not only Himself as true God, but also in revealing His Father to us (as John will go on to clarify further a few verses later – *John 1:18*). If this glory is the glory of the only-begotten Son, then it must point to the Father of the Son (for without the Father, there can be no only-begotten Son).

Finally then, John tells us that this Jesus, the Word who has become flesh, is 'full of grace and truth.' John doesn't tell us that the Word is full of grace and truth until he has told us that Word became flesh. Thus John points us to the Incarnate Christ as the source of grace and truth. (We'll come back to this in a later chapter when we consider what grace is.)

True Humanity

Let's return to John's first statement in *John 1:14*: 'the Word became flesh.' While we have already pointed out briefly that this is not a matter of what once was deity being transformed into flesh, nor of a diluted mixture of deity and humanity, let's now consider the question of what this does mean.

First, it will be helpful to consider the meaning of the word '*flesh*' here in *John 1:14*. Scripture uses the word '*flesh*' in significantly different ways in different places. Sometimes it's used to refer to our physical flesh as part of our bodies (e.g. 'flesh and bones' in *Luke 24:39*), sometimes it's used in contrast to Spirit to refer to our sinful nature (e.g. 'you are not in the flesh but in the Spirit' in *Rom. 8:9*), and sometimes, as we'll see here in *John 1:14*, it's used to refer to humanity. So we need to look at the context here to see how John is using the word. And when we do that, we see that John has just used this same word in the preceding verse, where he tells us that those who are born of God are not born 'of the will of the flesh' (*John 1:13*). *Flesh* is set on one side, along with blood and 'the will of man', in contrast to God on the other side. So what John is setting out here is a contrast between man and God. Being born again as children of God is not a human work – it is 'not of blood, nor of the will of the flesh, nor of the will of man' – but a divine work. So *flesh* in *John 1:13* refers to humanity, and *John 1:14* doesn't introduce anything to suggest that John is suddenly using flesh with a different meaning to how he has just used it.

This is also the way that John uses the word '*flesh*' later in his Gospel. In *John 17* Jesus prays to the Father and says 'You have given Him [Jesus, the Son] authority over all *flesh*, that He should give eternal life to as many as You have given Him' (*John 17:2*). Here again we see that John uses flesh to refer to humanity. The Father has not only given the Son authority over our bodies, but over humanity as a whole.

John is not the only Bible writer to use *flesh* in this way. Luke, in his Gospel, uses the word in this way, quoting from the prophet Isaiah: 'And all flesh shall see the salvation of God' (*Luke 3:6*). Again it's clear here that Luke and Isaiah aren't simply referring to the physical flesh of our bodies, but to humanity. Joel does the same in his famous prophecy of the last days: 'I will pour out my Spirit on all flesh' (*Joel 2:28*), as does the Psalmist (*Pss. 65:2; 145:21*).

So, when John writes that 'the Word became flesh' he doesn't just mean that Jesus took on a body of flesh and blood, but that Jesus took to Himself true humanity. In fact, John isn't the only writer to tell us of Jesus taking on flesh in this way. Paul declares that 'God was manifest in the flesh' (*1 Tim. 3:16*) and that Jesus 'was born of the seed of David according to the flesh' (*Rom. 1:3*).

Not Just the Appearance of Flesh

When Jesus took on humanity in the Incarnation, it was true humanity that He took to Himself, not just an appearance of humanity. In his first epistle John tells us:

> By this you know the Spirit of God: Every spirit that confesses that Jesus
> Christ has come in the flesh is of God, and every spirit that does not
> confess that Jesus Christ has come in the flesh is not of God. And this is
> the spirit of the Antichrist, which you have heard was coming, and is now
> already in the world. (*1 Jn 4:2-3*)

Already, by the time John was writing his first epistle, a dangerous heresy
had arisen that claimed that Jesus hadn't really come in the flesh, and so
John warns that this is the opposite of the Holy Spirit's word. If Jesus
hadn't truly come in the flesh, then there would have been no Incarnation,
and so no salvation.

John seems to be referring to the start of a heresy called Docetism
which claimed that Jesus only appeared to be human, and so His sufferings
were only in appearance.[2] Contrary to the Docetists, not only do we have
John's strong statement in *1 John 4:2-3* that to deny that Jesus has come in
the flesh is the spirit of Antichrist, but we also have plenty of biblical
evidence for the truth of Jesus' humanity and the reality of His human body.
For a start, we read clearly in both Matthew and Luke's Gospels that Jesus
was born (*Matt. 1:25; Luke 2:7*), and not only that, but Luke also describes for
us how Jesus grew up like all children (*Luke 2:40, 52*). When Jesus took on
true humanity, He willingly took on the limitations of the human body
faced by all of humanity. So He got hungry (*Matt. 4:2*) and thirsty (*John
19:28*). He grew tired (*John 4:6*). He even died, something that would have
been completely impossible for Him if He had only seemed to be human
(*Matt. 27:50; Mark 15:37; Luke 23:46; John 19:30, 33*).

Not a Transformation From Deity to Flesh

When the Word became flesh, He didn't stop being God. He didn't change
from one to the other. As Cyril of Alexandria, one of the greatest of all
teachers in the history of the Christian church on the doctrine of the person
of Christ, put it:

> When the Only Begotten Word of God became man he did not cast aside
> his being as God, for he remained what he was in the assumption of flesh.[3]

---

[2] The word *Docetism* comes from the Greek verb 'to seem'.

[3] Cyril of Alexandria, Homily Given at Ephesus on St John's Day in the Church of St
John. Translation in John McGuckin, *Saint Cyril of Alexandria and the Christological Controversy:
Its History, Theology and Texts* (Crestwood, NY: St Vladimir's Seminary Press, 2004), 281.

> Even in his humanity he remained God, and Lord of all, in so far as he was born in nature and truth from God the Father.[4]

> God the Word did not lay aside what He was when He assumed the flesh.[5]

The Fathers of the early church pointed to a parallel with two other Scripture passages (*2 Cor. 5:21 and Gal. 3:13*) which speak of Jesus becoming something to help explain what it meant for him to become flesh. Those Scriptures speak of how Christ was made 'sin for us' (*2 Cor. 5:21*) and became 'a curse for us' (*Gal. 3:13*), but in neither case did Jesus stop being what He was to be transformed into sin or a curse. Gregory of Nazianzus explained it like this:

> The text, then, 'The Word was made flesh' seems to me to be equivalent to speaking of his being made 'sin' and 'curse.' Not that the Lord was changed into these things – how could he have been? – but by accepting these things he 'assumed our acts of transgressions and carried our maladies.'[6]

The great Athanasius puts it like this:

> The Word himself was not converted into flesh and bones. This is what John meant by his saying, 'The Word became flesh' (Jn. 1.14), as can be ascertained from similar statements, such as that written by Paul: 'Christ became a curse for us' (Gal. 3.13). He did not himself become a curse, but he is said to have become a curse because he took the curse on himself for our sakes. Likewise he became flesh not by being changed into flesh, but because he assumed living flesh for our sake, and so became man.[7]

As well as this proper understanding of John's words, many of the Scriptures we looked at in chapter 2 which teach the deity of Christ specifically teach that the *Incarnate* Christ is God.

---

[4] Cyril of Alexandria, *Scholia on the Incarnation of the Only Begotten*, par. 4. Translation in McGuckin, *Saint Cyril of Alexandria and the Christological Controversy*, 294-335.

[5] Cyril of Alexandria, *Scholia*, par. 12

[6] Gregory of Nazianzus, *First Letter to Cledonius the Presbyter* (*Letter 101*), par. 12, translation in Gregory of Nazianzus, *On God and Christ: The Five Theological Orations and Two Letters to Cledonius* (Crestwood, NY: St Vladimir's Seminary Press, 2002), 162 (the last part here quotes the LXX of Isa. 53:4-5).

[7] Athanasius, *Letter to Epictetus*, par. 8, translation in McGuckin, *Saint Cyril of Alexandria and the Christological Controversy*, 385-386.

Hebrews 2:14

The writer to the Hebrews helps us to understand what John meant by 'the Word became flesh.'

> Inasmuch then as the children have partaken of flesh and blood, He Himself likewise shared in the same, that through death He might destroy him who had the power of death, that is, the devil (*Heb. 2:14*).

Here we read not only that Christ's Incarnation involved Him partaking of flesh and blood, but also that the flesh and blood which He shared was the same flesh and blood as that of 'the children', who in the context are those whom the Father has given to Christ (*Heb. 2:13*), those who are being sanctified (*Heb. 2:11*). In other words, the writer to the Hebrews is saying that the Incarnate Christ shares in the same flesh and blood as saved human beings. This is true humanity of which Christ partakes. Yet it is clear here that God the Son is not converted into a human being, but rather, while still being God, He 'partakes' and 'shares' true humanity. So the flesh of Christ is true humanity just like ours, and yet it is His flesh, His humanity.

Paul on the Incarnation

Paul also helps us understand *John 1:14* in two particularly important passages on the Incarnation. In *Philippians 2:5-11* he tells us that Christ Jesus, who was in the form of God and equal to God, 'made himself of no reputation, taking the form of a bondservant, and coming in the likeness of men … being found in appearance as a man' (*Phil. 2:7-8*). Here we see that it was the One who was with God in the beginning who 'became obedient to the point of death, even the death of the cross' (*Phil. 2:8*). The Incarnation was not a case of a man being taken up into being God; nor was the One who died on the Cross a new person made up from the joining together of man and God. Rather, in the Incarnation God the Son humbled Himself to take on our humanity. The person who was born in Bethlehem's manger, died on Calvary's Cross, and rose from Joseph's tomb was none other than God the Son, God the Word made flesh.

In *Romans 8:3* we read that God sent 'His own Son in the likeness of sinful flesh.' Again, it's God the Son in the flesh that we read about here.

Jesus is not a compound of God the Son plus a human nature; Jesus is God the Son Himself with His own human nature.

The Unassumed is the Unhealed

Very occasionally in the history of the church a great theologian and defender of the faith has coined an expression that so helpfully sums up some biblical teaching that it continues to be passed on as a useful tool in helping us gauge the biblical truth of people's teachings. *'The unassumed is the unhealed'* is one of these great expressions.[8] It was Gregory of Nazianzus who coined the phrase when writing to protect his flock against false teachers who denied that Jesus had a human soul or mind. Gregory's argument was that the whole of our humanity fell in Adam, and so the whole of our humanity needs to be saved. If Christ had only taken on part of our humanity, then only part of our humanity could be saved. If any aspect of our humanity was not assumed by Christ in the Incarnation, then it couldn't be healed by Him in salvation. Those who claim otherwise 'begrudge us our entire salvation.'[9]

The Biblical Case Against Apollinarianism: Jesus' Human Mind and Soul

The false teaching from which Gregory was seeking to protect his flock was known as Apollinarianism. The Apollinarians misunderstood when John wrote 'the Word became flesh', thinking that 'flesh' only referred to a body and so 'declared that He did not assume a mind' and 'denied that He assumed a soul.'[10] Apollinarianism was later condemned as a heresy, yet it isn't simply a matter of history, for as we have just seen, Gregory realised that this was a very important practical issue, as the Incarnation is so

---

[8] Gregory of Nazianzus, *First Letter to Cledonius the Presbyter (Letter 101)*, par. 5. Translation in Gregory of Nazianzus, *On God and Christ*, 158.

[9] Gregory of Nazianzus, *First Letter to Cledonius*, par. 5

[10] From John of Damascus' definition of the heresy of 'The Dimeorites , who are also called the Apollinarists', John of Damascus, *On Heresies*, 77. Translation in Frederic H. Chase, Jr., trans. *Saint John of Damascus: Writings*, The Fathers of the Church, Vol. XXXVII, (Washington D.C.: 1958), 131. Some Apollinarians went even further and claimed that Christ's body was not incarnate of the Virgin Mary, but rather 'consubstantial with the Godhead.'

intimately connected to our salvation. So let's have a look at what the Bible teaches about the human mind and soul of Christ.

Jesus' Human Mind

First of all, the Bible clearly presents Jesus with a human mind. We have already seen how Jesus grew like all human children, and when Luke tells us about Jesus growing up, it also tells us that 'Jesus increased in wisdom' (*Luke 2:52*). As God He is all-wise, so only in a human mind could He grow in wisdom. The writer to the Hebrews tells us that 'though He was a Son, yet He learned obedience by the things which He suffered' (*Heb. 5:8*). Again, this shows us that Jesus had a human mind, for as God He knows all things, so only with a human mind could He learn.

   Mark 13:32 is perhaps one of the most shocking verses in the Bible for us. And yet it's precisely in its shockingness that it shows us that Christ has a true human mind. There Jesus tells us, 'But of that day and hour no one knows, not even the angels in heaven, nor the Son, but only the Father.'[11] He's talking about the time of His return, and yet He Himself tells us that the Son doesn't know when it will be: only the Father does. Now, as God, Jesus knows all things, so this limitation in His knowledge points to the limitations He willingly assumed in His Incarnation. As the Word of the Father, the Father's knowledge is His. Yet, in the Incarnation He took on true humanity with all its limitations, including the limitation of a human mind. So, as God, Jesus knows what the Father knows, but in His humanity His knowledge is wilfully limited. In His humanity He, temporarily and willingly, does not make use of the omniscience that is His as God. This is just like what we have already seen with the fact that He 'increased in wisdom' and 'learned obedience.'

Jesus' Human Emotions

Moving on from merely considering the mind, we see in the Scriptures that Jesus also had true human emotions. At Lazarus' tomb, 'Jesus wept' (*John*

---

[11] Translations of the Bible based upon the critical text have a parallel to this verse in *Matthew 24:36*.

11:35).[12] Even before we read of Him weeping, we're told that, when He saw Mary weeping, 'He groaned in the spirit and was troubled (*John 11:33*). The Greek word used here expresses a strong emotion of anger, outrage or indignation. This passage is often turned to for proof of Jesus' human emotions. However, the text distinguishes between the weeping of Jesus and the weeping of the others by using different Greek words and this would appear to mark a contrast here in the types of tears; Mary and the others are weeping for Lazarus, but Jesus is not (for He knows that He is about to raise him from the dead). Rather Jesus is weeping over sin, death and unbelief, which is what caused His outrage in *verse 33*. In this case, it is not clear that this is an example of human (in contradistinction to divine) emotion in Jesus.[13]

We are on firmer footing in seeing Jesus' human emotions in Hebrews. Already we've seen how *Hebrews 5:8* shows us that Jesus had a true human mind, for 'He learned obedience', yet that verse also tells us that this was 'by the things which He suffered,' which shows us the human emotion of suffering on Jesus' part. The previous verse tells us more about his human emotions, for 'in the days of His flesh ... He had offered up prayers and supplications, with vehement cries and tears to Him who was able to save Him from death' (*Heb. 5:7*). The writer here describes Jesus' prayer life as impassioned, demonstrating the truth of Christ's true human emotions.

Another clear example is found in Matthew's Gospel. When a Centurion comes to Jesus seeking healing for his servant and saying, 'Lord, I am not worthy that You should come under my roof. But only speak a word, and my servant will be healed' (*Matt. 8:8*), Jesus famous response is preceded by a note of emotion: 'When Jesus heard it, He marveled, and said to those who followed, "Assuredly, I say to you, I have not found such great faith, not even in Israel!"' (*Matt. 8:10*). As God, Jesus could not be taken by surprise and so wouldn't marvel at the Centurion's words, so this clearly expresses human emotion in Christ.

Jesus' Human Soul

Having seen that the Bible refers to Jesus' human mind and human emotions, let's go on to look at what it says about His soul. Remember, the

---

[12] The word that's used for Jesus weeping is usually associated with shedding tears of lament and this is the only time it's used in the New Testament.

[13] Cf. Jesus' similar expression of emotion over the city of Jerusalem in *Matt. 23:37*.

Apollinarians claimed that Jesus didn't take on a human soul. Rather they thought that God the Word replaced the soul in Jesus. The Gospels, however, declare that Jesus did indeed assume a human soul (along with every other aspect of true humanity). In the Garden of Gethsemane He said to His disciples, 'My soul is exceedingly sorrowful, even to death' (*Matt. 26:38; Mark 14:34*). Earlier that week He had said, 'Now My soul is troubled, and what shall I say? "Father, save Me from this hour"? But for this purpose I came to this hour' (*John 12:27*). Both of these statements from Jesus not only refer to His soul, but also connect it with his human emotions. Likewise, Jesus makes a connection between His human emotions and His spirit at the last supper (*John 13:21*).

Peter also refers to Jesus' soul in his sermon on the day of Pentecost. First he quotes from *Psalm 16*, 'For You will not leave my soul in Hades, nor will You allow Your Holy One to see corruption' (*Acts 2:27*), which He tells is speaking of Christ (see *verse 25*). Peter then goes on to expound on this Scripture, telling us that David:

> foreseeing this, spoke concerning the resurrection of the Christ, that His soul was not left in Hades, nor did His flesh see corruption. This Jesus God has raised up, of which we are all witnesses. (*Acts 2:31-32*)

So Peter refers both to Christ's body (His flesh) and His soul, thus showing us that the Incarnation involved Christ assuming both a true body and a true soul.

As Gregory of Nazianzus so clearly summed it up, 'the unassumed is the unhealed.' If Christ had only assumed a body, if He had not taken to himself a true human soul with a true human mind and emotions, then salvation would only be for the body and there would be no salvation for our souls. But thanks be to God that the Lord Jesus Christ has assumed full humanity so that we may know a full salvation.

Dyothelitism: The Doctrine of the Two Wills in Christ

One of the more complicated controversies in the history of the doctrine of the person of Christ was the Monothelite controversy of the 7th century. We're not going to get into the details of the controversy here, but we will take a brief look at the doctrinal answer which emerged from it.

Monothelitism taught that there was only one will in Christ: the divine will. As a result of the 7th Century controversy, this was condemned as heresy at the Third Council of Constantinople in AD 680-681. The orthodox doctrine of the Christian church (known as *Dyothelitism*) is that Christ has two wills: one divine and one human.

So far removed in time, the Monothelite controversy may perhaps appear arcane, and even some evangelicals have advocated abandoning the doctrine. If we approach it from the perspective of 21st Century psychological ideas of personhood or even by wading into the depths of the (admittedly rather complicated) historical debate then we may indeed find the doctrine of dyothelitism arcane.[14] However, if we proceed in the direction from which we've started, hopefully we'll see why we need to hold on to this doctrine.

We have been thinking of Gregory of Nazianzus' helpful dictum 'the unassumed is the unhealed.' We have seen the need for the salvation of our will when we looked at the nature of sin and depravity. So, if salvation is for the whole of our being, including our will, then Christ must have assumed a full human nature, including a human will in order to save our will. But does the Bible teach that Christ assumed a human will?

Although the Scriptures may not speak so abstractly about Christ's human will as theology has been forced to since the Monothelite controversy, the Scriptures do provide plenty of evidence for the human will of the Lord Jesus. The Gospels frequently express human things that Jesus wanted to do: He 'wanted to go to Galilee' (*John 1:43*); 'He did not want to walk in Judea' (*John 7:1*); 'Then they departed from there and passed through Galilee, and He did not want anyone to know it' (*Mark 9:30*); He desired that His disciples might be with Him and behold His glory (*John 17:24*); and 'He would not drink' (*Matt. 27:34*).

Mark 7:24 tells us that 'from there He arose and went to the region of Tyre and Sidon. And He entered a house and wanted no one to know it, but could not be hidden.' Here we see a very clear example of Christ's human will, for the will in question here is not fulfilled. He didn't want anyone to know He was there, but yet He couldn't be hidden. As His divine will is omnipotent, this must be a reference to his human will.

In *Psalm 40:8* Christ speaks, saying 'I delight to do Your will, O my God.' (*Hebrews 10:6-7* confirms that it is Christ who is speaking here in this

---

[14] A significant contributing factor to what makes dyothelitism seem so arcane (other than the complicated name for the doctrine) is that many of the key texts haven't been translated. The most helpful book currently available in English on the controversy is Demetrios Bathrellos, *The Byzantine Christ: Person, Nature, and Will in the Christology of Saint Maximus the Confessor* (Oxford: Oxford University Press, 2004).

Psalm verse.) As Maximus the Confessor pointed out here, 'the Father is said to be Christ's God not according to Christ's being God, but according to His being man.'[15] Therefore this delighting to the will of God is an expression of the human will of Christ.

Finally then, we come to the verse which has often taken centre-stage in discussions of the will of Christ: His Gethsemane prayer, 'Not what I will but what you will' (*Mark 14:36*; cf. *Matt. 26:39,42*; *Luke 22:42*). Again, these words express the human will of Christ, for if they spoke of His divine will, they would imply that Christ as God has a different will to God the Father, which would attack the unity of the Trinity (on this point, see also *John 6:38*). But, if this is referring to the human will of Christ, is that not equally problematic, for does it not suggest that there are two contrary wills within the one person of Christ, destroying the unity of His person?

It is because of such questions that this text has long been at the heart of discussions of the two wills in Christ. Maximus the Confessor addressed this during the Monothelite controversy, arguing that Christ willed, both as God and as man, to do the will of the Father. So, according to Maximus, what was happening in Gethsemane was Christ deciding as man to obey God's will, and so overcoming that natural (and blameless) human will to avoid death. This then teaches us about how the two wills of Christ relate. Christ wills as God by His divine will, and willingly obeys as man by his human will, and so there is always full harmony between the divine and human wills of Christ.

The Hypostatic Union

So far we have seen that, in the Incarnation, the Word – God the Son – took to Himself true humanity without ever ceasing to be what He already was. So Christ is both true God and true man. Yet, how are the divine and human natures of Christ united? The answer is through what is called the hypostatic (or personal) union: God the Son has taken our humanity into His own person so that it is now the humanity of the Word and Son of God. So this means that it is the same One who is both God and man, and that whatever He does He does as both God and man.

---

[15] Maximus the Confessor, *Disputatio*, 324B-C

The Definition of Chalcedon

The union of the divine and human natures in the one person of Christ is usually explained with the Definition of Chalcedon. This was the outcome of the Council of Chalcedon of AD 451, which had been called to deal with the problem of those who claimed that there was only one nature in Christ (the heresy of monophysitism). The Definition states:

> Following, then, the holy Fathers, we all unanimously teach that our Lord Jesus Christ is to us:
> One and the same Son, the Self-same Perfect in Godhead, the Self-same Perfect in Manhood; truly God and truly Man; the Self-same of a rational soul and body; co-essential with the Father according to the Godhead, the Self-same co-essential with us according to the Manhood; like us in all things, sin apart; before the ages begotten of the Father as to the Godhead, but in the last days, the Self-same, for us and for our salvation (born) of Mary the Virgin Theotokos as to the Manhood; One and the Same Christ, Son, Lord, Only-begotten; acknowledged in Two Natures unconfusedly, unchangeably, indivisibly, inseparably; the difference of the Natures being in no way removed because of the Union, but rather the properties of each Nature being preserved, and (both) concurring into One Person and One Hypostasis; not as though He were parted or divided into Two Persons, but One and the Self-same Son and Only-begotten God, Word, Lord, Jesus Christ; even as from the beginning the prophets have taught concerning Him, and as the Lord Jesus Christ Himself hath taught us, and as the Symbol of the Fathers hath handed down to us.

The word 'same' appears in this short Creed eight times, always in reference to the identity of Jesus, either in the expression 'one and the same' or 'self-same.' Donald Fairbairn sums this up:

> Clearly the dominant affirmation of the definition is not that Christ consists of two natures but that Christ is one and the same. The one who is consubstantial [*homoousios*] with the Father is the same one who is consubstantial with us.[16]

According to the Definition of Chalcedon this one who is 'one and same' is the 'Son and Only-begotten God, Word, Lord, Jesus Christ.' In other words, the Chalcedonian Definition does not point us to a joining together of the two natures (human and divine), but to the one person who is both perfect God and perfect man: the one person of God the Son.

---

[16] Donald Fairbairn, *Life in the Trinity* (Downers Grove: IVP, 2009), 145.

> Neither the early church as a whole nor the Chalcedonian Definition in particular is affirming merely that Christ has two natures united into one person. Both the church and Chalcedon affirm that the person who possesses both divine and human natures is the eternal second person of the Trinity, the Son of God.[17]

The one person of Christ is not an adding together of a divine nature plus a human nature. Rather, in the incarnation, God the Son took to Himself true humanity so that the humanity of Christ is the humanity of God the Son. As the Athanasian Creed puts it, 'our Lord Jesus Christ, the Son of God, is God and man' and this is so 'by taking of the Manhood into God.' The One Person of Jesus Christ is not the adding together of divine nature and human nature, but the taking of human nature into God in the One Person of the Son.

For the early church, it wasn't enough to say that the Person of Christ had two natures, one human and one divine. It was even more important who that One Person of Christ is. He is not a new person made up from the adding together of the two natures, but the Person of God the Son, God the Word who was with the Father in the beginning.

T.F. Torrance sums it up like this:

> In the language of the Nicene Fathers it is he who came down from heaven and was made man for us and our salvation who is acknowledged to be of one and the same Being as God the Father, that is of the same equal Being as the eternal Father, while nevertheless distinct … from him as his only begotten Son. The incarnate Son, Jesus who was born of the Virgin Mary and crucified under Pontius Pilate, is none other than the eternal Son of God – the eternal Son of God, he who was begotten of the Father before all time, is none other than the incarnate Son, Jesus who was born of the Virgin Mary and crucified under Pontius Pilate.[18]

One of the biblical names given to Jesus Christ expresses this truth very succinctly. The prophet Isaiah foretold that the one born of the virgin would be called Immanuel (*Isa. 7:14*). Matthew takes up this promise in his Gospel and writes of its fulfilment in Jesus, adding the explanation of the name Immanuel: 'God with us' (*Matt. 1:23*). The one Matthew and Isaiah both refer to as Immanuel is the one who has come in the flesh and was born of the virgin. The testimony of both the Prophet and the Evangelist is that it was 'God with us' who was conceived in the womb of the Virgin Mary and

---

[17] Fairbairn, *Life in the Trinity*, 145.
[18] T.F. Torrance, *The Christian Doctrine of God,* 143-144.

born in Bethlehem's stable. That can only mean that the one person of Jesus Christ is the person of God of the Son Himself.

'If he had not suffered for us as a man, he would not have achieved our salvation as God.'[19]

These are the words of Cyril of Alexandria, writing at the outbreak of one of the most significant theological controversies in the history of the church. Cyril understood that the unity of the person of Christ was of the upmost importance for our salvation. Jesus could suffer, because He is man, but His sufferings could bring us salvation, because He is God. So it was essential that the One who suffered in our place be the God-Man; it was the Word who suffered according to His flesh.

The Problem of the Nestorian Heresy

Cyril's heretical opponent was Nestorius, the Archbishop of Constantinople. Nestorius and his friends insisted on a radical distinction between the human nature of Christ and the divine nature of Christ. They argued that it was only the human nature of Christ which was born of the Virgin Mary. Rather than the One Person who is the Son with His own humanity, Nestorius declared: 'we confess God in a man.'[20] He insisted that the two natures of Christ are 'separated in essence, but united by love.'[21] Nestorius (and his teacher, Theodore of Mopsuestia) did not understand the human nature of Christ as the Word's own humanity, but rather, they thought of it as 'the assumed man' and taught that this 'assumed man' was 'adopted' and 'indwelt' by God the Word.[22] Famously, Nestorius preached: 'I revere the one who is borne because of the one who carries him.'[23] In other words, his reverence for the man Christ Jesus was not because he recognised this man as God, but because he thought that this 'assumed man' had been 'assumed' and indwelt by God the Son. In the same sermon Nestorius said, 'God is within the one who is assumed.'[24]

---

[19] Cyril of Alexandria, *To the Monks of Egypt*
[20] Nestorius, *Sermon 8*
[21] Nestorius, *The Bazaar of Heracleides*, 1.1.58
[22] Nestorius, *The Bazaar of Heracleides*, 1.1.55-59
[23] Nestorius, *Sermon 9*
[24] Nestorius, *Sermon 9*

So, Nestorius separated the eternal Word and Son of the Father from the Jesus Christ. For him, the two were not the same at all. He insisted that one born of Mary and laid in the manger, was the 'assumed man', not the eternal Word. At the Council of Ephesus he angrily exclaimed, 'we must not call the one who became man for us, God ... I refuse to acknowledge as God, an infant of two or three months old.'[25]

We'll encounter Nestorius and his heresy again in some of the issues we'll look at in the next few chapters. But already we can see significant problems. For a start, the heresy of Nestorius doesn't fit well with what we've already seen from the Scriptures, that 'the Word became flesh' (*Jn 1:14*) and that the one 'for whom are all things and by whom are all things ... had to be made like His brethren' by sharing in their 'flesh and blood' (*Heb. 2:10-17*). Furthermore, the Scriptures explicitly tells us that it was 'the Son of God' and 'Lord of glory' who was crucified (*Heb. 6:6; 1 Cor. 2:8*). The Bible also uses the names and titles of Christ of the God-Man, not distinguishing between the natures.

> It is one person that the God-inspired scripture (both before and after the incarnation) designates as, Only Begotten, Word, God, Image, Radiance and Impress of the Father's Very Being, Life, Glory, Light, Wisdom, Power, Strong Right Hand, Most High, Magnificence, Lord of Hosts, and other such names which are truly fitting for the deity. And similarly one person (after the incarnation) that it calls, Man, Christ Jesus, Atonement, Mediator, First Fruits of the Dead, First Born from the Dead, Second Adam, and Head of the Body that is the Church. Both sets of titles apply to him. All are his, the first series as well as those which apply in these last times of this age. He is one, therefore, who was true God before the incarnation, and even in the manhood remained what he was, and is, and shall be. And so the one Lord Jesus Christ must not be divided up, as if there was a distinct man and a distinct deity. No, we say that Jesus Christ is one and the same, even though we recognise the difference of natures and keep them unconfused with each other.[26]

Two other key Scriptures to which Cyril of Alexandria pointed against Nestorianism were *John 19:7* and *Philippians 2:6-8*. In *John 19:7*, the reason

---

[25] From the *Acts of the Council of Ephesus*, Doc. 81, par. 6. Cited in John McGuckin, *Saint Cyril of Alexandria and the Christological Controversy* (Crestwood: SVS Press, 2004), 64. This statement of Nestorius was so shocking at the time that it was widely heard as a denial of the deity of Christ; but that is not how Nestorius intended it. Nestorius did not deny the deity of the Son; he simply wanted to stress the distinction and separation between the Son and the 'assumed man.' He was heretical, but Nestorius was no Arian.

[26] Cyril of Alexandria, *Scholia*, §13

given for Jesus' crucifixion is that 'He made Himself the Son of God.' Yet, as Cyril points out:

> He did not make himself God's Son; he is such in truth. For that reality is believed by us to belong to him not as something external, nor as something acquired or received by adoption, but as that which he is by nature ... For he was not a human being who made himself God's Son; the converse is true: being by nature and in truth Son of the God who is over all, he became a human being, in order that, by giving his own blood in exchange for the life of all, he might rescue all from both death and sin.[27]

Jesus does not lie, and so His claims to be the Son of God (*Mt 16:15-17; Mt 26:63-64; Lk 22:70; Jn 10:29-30, 36-38*) were not presumptuous: they were declarations of truth. So, He was crucified, not simply because He claimed to be the Son of God, but because He – the man Christ Jesus – was (and is) the Son of God.

Cyril also points us to how Paul contradicts Nestorius' teaching about the 'assumed man' who was adopted and indwelt by the Word in *Philippians 2*. For, there, the Scripture does not speak of a man who ascended 'to fullness from being someone empty, but rather the humbled himself from the divine heights and ineffable glory, not by being a humble man who was lifted up.' Cyril continues by writing that this shows that the Nestorians 'reverse the statements of the Incarnation and falsify the truth by rising up against all the divinely inspired Scriptures which know that he is God even after the Son became man and everywhere name him the one Son.'[28]

However, not only are there particular Scriptures which disprove the Nestorian heresy, but the overall theology of the Scriptures (the big picture of what they teach about Jesus and about salvation) also displays how big an error Nestorianism really is. Here, the problem of Nestorianism is twofold. Firstly, it would mean that the deity of Christ was nothing more than a divine indwelling. That would mean no Immanuel – God with us, for it would mean Jesus was not the direct personal presence of God in the world. Secondly, Nestorianism would make our salvation depend on someone who wasn't truly God. If Nestorius separated so distinctly between

---

[27] Cyril of Alexandria, *Festal Letter 24.3*. Translation in *St Cyril of Alexandria Festal Letters 13-30*, The Fathers of the Church, vol. 127, trans. Philip R. Amidon (Washington D.C.: CUA Press, 2013), 141-142. Cyril goes on here to show that the Incarnate Christ must be the true Son (not an adopted son) if we are to be adopted as sons in the Son and conformed to the image of the Son.

[28] Cyril of Alexandria, *Letter 55*, par. 25. Translation in *St Cyril of Alexandria Letters 51-110*, The Fathers of the Church, vol. 77, trans. John I. McEnerney (Washington D.C.: CUA Press, 1987), 24-25.

God the Son and the baby who lay in the manger, then there'd be just as big a separation between God the Son and the one who died on the cross. The Nestorian Christ who died would only be an 'assumed man' indwelt by the Son. He would not be God. But only God can save. As Cyril put it: 'If he had not suffered for us as a man, he would not have achieved our salvation as God.'[29] The one who suffered for us and our salvation is none other than God the Son in his own flesh.

> For God was in humanity. He who was above all creation was in our human condition; the invisible one was made visible in the flesh; he who is from the heavens and from on high was in the likeness of earthly things; the immaterial one could be touched; he who is free in his own nature came in the form of a slave; he who blesses all creation became accursed; he who is all righteousness was number among transgressors; life itself came in the appearance of death. All this followed because the body which tasted death belonged to no other but to him who is the Son by nature.[30]

Another Heretical Problem: Eutychianism

The Chalcedonian Definition responds to the Nestorian heresy. But it also responds to another heresy as well: *Eutychianism* (or *Monophysitism*). Eutyches, a presbyter of the church at Constantinople, taught that in the incarnation, the two natures (human and divine) came together into one nature in Christ (hence the name *Monophysitism*, from the words *monos*, 'one' and *physis*, 'nature'). Eutyches was overcompensating for the errors of Nestorius, by stressing the unity of Christ. However, his over-reaction took him into serious error. For, if Christ's human nature had been absorbed into His divine nature, and swallowed up in it like a drop of vinegar in the ocean (to borrow Eutyches' own analogy), then He would not be consubstantial (*homoousios* – of the same substance) with us.[31] He would not share in the same flesh and blood as us, and yet the Scriptures teach that He did, and that He had to be consubstantial with us to accomplish our salvation (*Heb. 2:14-18*).

---

[29] Cyril of Alexandria, *To the Monks of Egypt*
[30] Cyril of Alexandria, *On the Unity of Christ*, 61
[31] Eutyches himself recognised this and refused to confess that Christ was consubstantial with us. Many textbooks claim that Eutychianism would also mean that Christ was not consubstantial with the Father, but that would appear to be a logical conclusion of where Eutyches' teaching should logically have led, rather than anything he himself taught. Eutyches stressed the full deity of Christ and did not teach a *tertium quid*.

A Man in the Trinity

As we have seen, the one person of Christ is God the Son. John declares at
the start of his first epistle that the one 'which we have heard, which we
have seen with our eyes, which we have looked upon, and our hands have
handled' is the one who 'was from the beginning' and who is 'the Word of
Life … that eternal Life which was with the Father' (*1 John 1:1-2*). The one
who walked and talked with the disciples in Galilee was not someone
different from the eternal Son of God. It was not a Monophysite amalgam of
God the Son with human nature, nor was it a Nestorian human person
indwelt by the Son. Rather, John and the other disciples head and saw and
handled the eternal Word and Son of God Himself.

Speaking to Nicodemus, Jesus also identifies Himself as the very Son
Himself. 'No one has ascended to heaven but He who came down from
heaven, that is, the Son of Man who is in heaven' (*John 3:13*). According to
Jesus here, the Son of Man (that is, Jesus Himself) is 'He who came down
from heaven' and 'who is in heaven.' The person of Jesus Christ who is
speaking here to Nicodemus is not a different person from the person of the
Son who has eternally existed. It is not a man indwelt by the Son who
speaks to Nicodemus, but the Son Himself. The same Lord Jesus Christ is
both speaking to Nicodemus and in heaven. As Cyril of Alexandria put it,
'the same one was humbled and yet enthroned beside the Father.'[32]

Paul also teaches this in *Ephesians 4*, where he writes of Christ's
ascension. 'Now this, "He ascended"—what does it mean but that He also
first descended into the lower parts of the earth? He who descended is also
the One who ascended far above all the heavens, that He might fill all
things' (*Eph. 4:9-10*). The one who has now ascended on high is the same
one who descended from the heavens to 'the lower parts of the earth.' In
other words, Paul points to an identity of person from the one who has
always lived in heaven, through the incarnation and cross, to the ascension.
Making this even clearer, Paul quotes from *Psalm 68:18*:

> When He ascended on high,
> He led captivity captive,
> And gave gifts to men. (*Eph. 4:8*)

In its original setting in the Psalm, this verse speaks of God ascending
up on high. So, Paul is writing of the Lord Jesus as God who has descended

---

[32] Cyril of Alexandria, *Homily at Ephesus St John's*

to the manger and the cross and then ascended 'far above all the heavens.' The one who was born in Bethlehem, died on Calvary and ascended from the Mount of Olives is the eternal Son of God Himself. The blood of Jesus is God's own blood (*Acts 20:28*).

Therefore, if the one person of Christ is the person of God the Son, as the Scriptures teach and the Christian church confesses, then the second person of the Trinity is God the Son with His own flesh; the second person of the Trinity is the Incarnate Son, the God-Man. So, there is a man in the Trinity: the Man Christ Jesus. Hence, the Christian church confesses that 'one of the Trinity suffered in the flesh.' As the Fifth Council (the Second Council of Constantinople) decreed: *'If anyone does not confess that our Lord Jesus Christ who was crucified in the flesh is true God and the Lord of Glory and one of the Holy Trinity: let him be anathema.'*

Thus, everything Jesus Christ does, He does as the one person of God the Son with His own flesh. Everything the Incarnate Christ does He does as the God-Man. There are not some things He does as God and some things He does as man, for that would be to separate the two natures into two persons. Everything Jesus does he does as the one who is at the same time both God and Man. This is what we see with Jesus' miraculous signs in John's Gospel. The signs reveal that 'Jesus is the Christ, the Son of God' (*Jn 20:31*) because these are not miracles performed by a man but by God the Son in the flesh.

So, because everything Jesus does He does as the one person of God the Son with His own flesh, we can rightly sing with Charles Wesley:

> *Amazing love! how can it be*
> *That Thou, my God, should die for me?*[33]
> 　　*…*
>
> *God the invisible appears,*
> *God the Blest, the Great I AM,*
> *He sojourns in this vale of tears,*
> *And Jesus is His Name.*
>
> *…Our being's Source begins to be,*
> *And God Himself is born!…*
>
> *See the eternal Son of God*
> *A mortal Son of Man,*
> *Now dwelling in an earthly clod*
> *Whom Heaven cannot contain!*

---

[33] From Charles Wesley's hymn, 'And Can it Be', *Redemption Hymnal*, 324.

Stand amazed, ye heavens, look at this!
See the Lord of earth and skies
Low humbled to the dust He is,
And in a manger lies![34]

Wesley rightly has us sing that God was born and God has died, because the one person of Jesus Christ who was born in Bethlehem and died on Calvary is God the Son with His own flesh. One of the Trinity was born in the flesh and one of the Trinity died in the flesh.

Double Birth: The Two Begettings of the Son

Wesley has us sing language that can sound shocking unless we understand the true identity of the man Christ Jesus as the second person of the Trinity, and so he forces us to really think about the meaning of the incarnation as we sing 'Our being's Source begins to be, and God Himself is born.' How can being's Source begin to be? How can the eternal God be born? Yet that is the very truth of what has happened in the Incarnation of Christ. The One who is before all things, and through whom and for whom all things are created, began to be as a tiny baby in Mary's womb. God Himself, the Eternal Son and Word of God the Father, was born in a stable in Bethlehem. Wesley's startling language emphasises two glorious truths to us: the humility of God the Son in coming as a tiny baby, and the glory and majesty of the baby in the manger. The humility: God is a baby! The majesty: the Baby is God!

For the idea in Wesley's expression of 'being's Source begins to be and God Himself is born', there's a sort of theological shorthand: the double birth of the Word, or the two begettings of the Son. As John of Damascus wrote, 'our Lord Jesus Christ has one Person, two natures, and two begettings.'[35]

So how does the Word have a double birth? Well, first of all, who is the Word? He is God the Son. And the Son is born (or begotten) of His Father from all eternity. Now, that doesn't mean that there was a time before the foundation of the world when the Son was born. No. He has always existed along with the Father as His Well-Beloved Son. But to be the Son means to be born or begotten of the Father. But as there wasn't a time when He didn't

---

[34] From Charles Wesley's hymn, 'Glory Be to God on High'.
[35] John of Damascus, *De Fide Orthodoxa*, iii.12

exist, there wasn't a moment in time when He was born or begotten. Instead say He is eternally begotten of the Father.[36]

And yet this Son who is eternally begotten of God the Father, came Himself to be born at a particular moment in time in the stable in Bethlehem of the Virgin Mary. So He was born a second time. Once eternally, and once 2020 years or so ago in Bethlehem. We even confess this truth of the double-birth of the Son in the Nicene Creed: the Lord Jesus Christ was 'born[37] of His Father before all worlds … who for us men and for our salvation came down from heaven and was incarnate by the Holy Ghost of the Virgin Mary and was made man.'

And this double-birth is of great importance. During the fifth century this doctrine of the double birth was right at the heart of the Nestorian controversy. Nestorius and his supporters weren't prepared to say that it was the One who was eternally begotten of the Father who was born of Mary in Bethlehem. They wanted to distinguish between the Son of God and Jesus Christ. Their goal was not to deny the deity of Christ, but rather they were trying to introduce a significant distinction between His humanity and His deity. For them, Jesus of Nazareth was born once – of Mary, and God the Son was born once – eternally of the Father, yet the two came together in a union in Christ. So that meant Christ was a man plus the Son of God. And so the humanity of Christ was not the humanity of God.

Cyril of Alexandria was greatly alarmed by such talk. He wrote a letter to Nestorius, saying: 'The Word did not subsequently descend upon an ordinary man previously born of the holy virgin, but he is made one from his mother's womb, and thus is said to have undergone a fleshly birth in so far as he appropriated to himself the birth of his own flesh … We must not divide the One Lord Jesus Christ into two sons.'[38]

Why did this matter so much? Well, if it wasn't God the Word Himself who was born of Mary, but only a man who was subsequently endowed with the Word, then it wasn't God the Word who walked on the water, or touched the leper, or upon whose breast John leaned. It would only have been a man (albeit one peculiarly endowed with the Word) who did these things.

And so the prophecy of *Isaiah 7:14* – of Immanuel, God with us – wouldn't be fulfilled. God had promised His own personal presence. But if Jesus was simply a man upon whom the Word descended, we wouldn't

---

[36] We've looked at this above in chapter 3.
[37] Or 'begotten', depending on the translation.
[38] Cyril of Alexandria, *Second Letter to Nestorius*, pars. 5, 7.

have God's personal presence, only an indirect, mediated presence. As Donald Fairbairn puts it: 'Only if the Logos [the Word] was born twice could the Incarnation bring about God's direct, personal presence in the world.'[39]

And that would have an impact on our salvation. If Jesus who was born of Mary is the one who was eternally born of the Father, then it is God Himself who comes down to us to bring us salvation (which is what the Nicene Creed says). But if the one born of Mary wasn't the One begotten of the Father, then salvation is accomplished by a human being, not by God. Instead of being God's gracious descent to us, it becomes man's attempt to climb up to God. Jesus, then, becomes merely a help along the way, a giver of the grace which he has received in receiving the Word.

Cyril saw this danger. And Cyril knew that salvation was not our climbing up to God, but God's coming down to us in Jesus. Cyril knew that Jesus is not merely a help on our climb up, but rather that He is God Himself who has come down to lift us up. He is the Saviour who brings us into the family of the Triune God. And He can only do that because He is God: Jesus Christ is God the Word and Son of the Father who has become flesh for us and our salvation. It really was God in the manger.

Anhypostasia and Enhypostasia

The doctrine of the *anhypostasia* and the *enhypostasia* uses these two complicated words as shorthand to explain how the two natures are united in one person in the hypostatic union. We've already seen the word *hypostasis* when we looked at the terminology for the doctrine of the Trinity, so we've seen that it means person. So that means we can see that *anhypostasia* and *enhypostasia* are all about personhood. Literally, *anhypostasia* means 'no-person' and *enhypostasia* means 'in-person.' So the doctrine of the *anhypostasia* and *enhypostasia* says that the human nature of Christ was 'no-person' (*anhypostasia*) by itself, but was personalised 'in-the-person' (*enhypostasia*) of the Son. Christ's human nature did not have any independent existence or personhood apart from the incarnation. So, it wasn't a case of God the Son taking to Himself a human foetus which was already a person. The Triune God did not first create a child in the womb of Mary and then unite it to the Son. No. From the instant the human nature of Christ came into existence, it was precisely His human nature: the human

---

[39] Donald Fairbairn, *Grace and Christology in the Early Church*, 222.

nature of the eternal Word and Son of the Father. And that means that the humanity of Christ was never impersonal either, for it has always had its existence in the person of the Son.

John of Damascus put it like this: 'neither the soul nor the body [of Christ] ever had any person of its own other than that of the Word, and the Person of the Word was always one and never two.'[40] Rather:

> it was in the Person of the Word that the flesh subsisted, or, rather, had personality [*enhypostatos*], and it did not become an independently subsisting person in itself. For this reason, it neither lacks personality nor introduces another person into the Trinity.[41]

After the Reformation, Johann Gerhard expressed the same thing, writing that 'the assumed flesh … belongs to the hypostasis of the Word.'[42] This doctrine of *anhypostasia* and *enhypostasia* makes clear that, in the incarnation, 'the hypostasis [*i.e.* person] of the Word became the hypostasis [*i.e.* person] of the flesh, therefore the Word with His own flesh is the Second Person of the Trinity.'[43] That means that the faith of the Christian Church is that *one of the Trinity suffered in the flesh*. In other words, the same one person who hung on the cross and died in his own human flesh is the second person of the Triune God. The blood shed on the cross of Calvary really is God's own blood (*Acts 20:28*).

Why does it matter?

1) Jesus isn't greater or lesser than God the Son – He is God the Son. If Jesus were the sum of the divine nature of the Son plus human nature, then He would either be greater than the Son (the Son plus humanity as a positive addition) or lesser than the Son (the Son plus humanity as a negative addition). If He were lesser than the Son, then we'd constantly be searching beyond the Incarnation and the incarnate work of Christ for something better. If He were greater than the Son, then that would diminish the deity of the Son. How could a Son who could be improved upon by the addition of humanity be consubstantial with the Father?

---

[40] John of Damascus, *De Fide Orthodoxa*, iii.27
[41] John of Damascus, *De Fide Orthodoxa*, iii.9
[42] Johann Gerhard, *Loci*, Exegesis IV, §103.
[43] Johann Gerhard, *Loci*, Exegesis IV, §121.

2) Jesus doesn't mask God in the flesh – Jesus reveals God in the flesh. If Jesus were the sum of the divine nature of the Son plus human nature, then God would be hidden in Jesus. We'd never be quite sure if that was His deity or His humanity on display. And so Jesus couldn't be the express image and revelation of the Father. We'd have no certainty that our God really is the Christ-like God.

3) The Humanity of Jesus is the Humanity of God. If Jesus were the sum of the divine nature of the Son plus human nature, then not everything He did would be the act of God the Son. And that would mean that some things He did as man and some things as God. And that would mean that salvation was not of the Lord, but rather partly the work of God and partly the work of man.

A Nestorian Jesus couldn't save us. A Nestorian Christology merely points to a man joined to God and enabled by God, and so it ends up pointing to human work instead of God's work. For Nestorians, the humanity of Jesus might be very closely associated with God, but whatever it is, it is not God's own humanity. So a Nestorian Christology would mean that the one who actually died on the cross was merely a man. And that would leave us without the hope of God Himself, in His great love and mercy, taking our place to propitiate His own wrath against our sin. The good news is that the humanity of Jesus is the humanity of God, and so one of the Trinity suffered in the flesh.

4) The One who hung on the cross is the One we worship. The Christian Church lifts her voice in praise to the Crucified Saviour.

> *Thy grief and Thy compassion*
> *Were all for sinners gain;*
> *Mine, mine was the transgression,*
> *But Thine the deadly pain.*[44]
> ...
> *My sins have caused Thee, Lord, to bleed,*
> *Pointed the nail, and fixed the thorn.*[45]
> ...
> *O Love Divine! What hast Thou done?*
> *The immortal God hath died for me!*
> *The Father's co-eternal Son*

---

[44] Bernard of Clairvaux and Gerhardt, 'O Sacred Head Once Wounded', *Redemption Hymnal*, 162.

[45] Gerhardt, 'Extended On A Cursèd Tree', *Redemption Hymnal*, 166.

> *Bore all my sins upon the tree.*[46]

Yet, if it were not one of the Trinity who suffered in the flesh, our worship of the crucified would be the idolatrous worship of a man, for 'he who is not God by nature and essence must not be worshipped with divine honour nor served with divine worship.'[47] Unless the One who hung on the cross is God, He wouldn't be worthy of praise and worship. But the worship of heaven is the worship of the Crucified:

> For You were slain,
> And have redeemed us to God by Your blood …
> Worthy is the Lamb who was slain
> To receive power and riches and wisdom,
> And strength and honour and glory and blessing! (*Rev. 5:9, 12*)

For the worship of heaven is the worship of the Father and His Son, who sit together upon the throne (*Rev. 5:13*). We join with heaven in worshipping the Lamb who was slain, for He is the eternal Son and Word of the Father. The Crucified Saviour of whom we sing is one of the Trinity.

The Purpose of the Incarnation

To Die Our Death

Only the infinite God could fully pay the penalty for our sins. Only a sinless man could be our representative and die in our place. Therefore our Redeemer had to be both true God and true Man. The Mediator between God and Man must be able to represent them both; thus He must be the incarnate God.

> But the true and living God, indeed, God who is the Truth and Eternal Life, would not be able to taste death unless he himself became true man; and the same man who tasted death would not be strong enough to conquer death unless he was the true God and Eternal Life. For which man

---

[46] Charles Wesley, 'O Love Divine! What Hast Thou Done?', *Redemption Hymnal*, 173.
[47] Johann Gerhard, *Loci*, Exegesis IV, §64

will destroy death by death except that man who is a man in such a way
that he is also God?[48]

The Scriptures highlight this connection between Christ's incarnation and
His atoning death. 'He had to be made like' us in all things, sharing in our
flesh and blood, 'to make propitiation for the sins of the people' (*Heb. 2:17;
cf. v.14*). The incarnation was necessary for His atoning work of propitiation:
offering up Himself in our place as the wrath-bearing sacrifice for our sins.
As the incarnate God, He triumphed at the cross, destroying sin and death,
which are the works of the devil (*1 Jn 3:8; Heb. 2:14*).

Often, this is the first reason for the incarnation of which we
evangelicals think. However, this is not the only important reason for the
incarnation of Christ. The incarnation is much more than simply a
preparation for the cross.

To Reveal the Father

The writer to the Hebrews tells us that 'God, who at various times and in
various ways spoke in time past to the fathers by the prophets, has in these
last days spoken to us by His Son' (*Heb. 1:1-2*). The Son has always been the
Word and Revelation of the Father, and the substance of what was spoken
by the prophets (*Lk 24:27; Jn 1:18; 5:39, 46; Rev. 19:10*). Even the following
verses in Hebrews point us back to how the prophets have spoken of the
Son (*v.5, cf. Ps 2 and 2 Sam. 7:14; v.6, cf. Deut. 32:43; vv.8-9, cf. Ps 45; vv.10-12,
cf. Ps 102; v.13, cf. Ps 110*). So how has God spoken differently through His
Son now in these last days? Through the incarnation. As Calvin put it:

> Holy men of old knew God only by beholding Him in His Son as in a
> mirror. When I say this, I mean that God has never manifested Himself to
> men in any other way than through the Son, that is, His sole wisdom, light
> and truth. From this fountain Adam, Noah, Abraham, Isaac, Jacob, and
> others drank all that they had of heavenly teaching. From the same
> fountain, all the prophets have also drawn every heavenly oracle that they
> have given forth ...
> But when the Wisdom of God was at length revealed in the flesh, that
> Wisdom heartily declared to us all that can be comprehended and ought to
> be pondered concerning the Heavenly Father by the human mind. Now
> therefore, since Christ, the Sun of Righteousness, has shone, while before
> there was only a dim light, we have the perfect radiance of divine truth,

---

[48] Fulgentius, First Letter to the Scythian Monks, para. 16; cf. *Heidelberg Catechism*, Q.16 &
17.

like the wonted brilliance of midday. For truly the apostle meant to proclaim no common thing when he wrote, 'In many and various ways God spoke of old to the fathers by the prophets; but in these last days he has begun to speak to us through his beloved Son.'[49]

Jesus Himself tells us that 'he who has seen Me has seen the Father' (*Jn 14:9*). It is the incarnate Son who declares the Father to us (*Jn 1:18*). Jesus is the 'express image' of the Father (*Heb. 1:3*), and, by His incarnation, He reveals God in the flesh.

Yet, as the incarnate Christ reveals the Father to us, He is not simply giving us some information about what the Father is like. Jesus has come that we might know the Father – not just know about the Father – and that knowing the Father in the Son is eternal life (*Jn 17:3*).

> Jesus did not come to dispense arcane, previously hidden factoids about God that we are to mentally appropriate. Rather, the Son of God came to share with us his knowledge of God his Father. He came, in other words, to incorporate us into his experiential, relational knowledge of the Father through the Spirit, to share the intimacy that characterizes their knowing of one another. The knowledge of which Jesus speaks is not speculative, theoretical, or philosophical knowledge, but the intimate fellowship he has eternally enjoyed in relation to the Father and Spirit. To know God is to participate in the very life and love that the Father has for the Son by the power and presence of the Spirit (John 14:20). The Son of God has joined himself to us so that we might partake of the life-giving intimacy he has always enjoyed with his Father: 'And this is eternal life, that they know you the only true God, and Jesus Christ whom you have sent' (John 17:3).[50]

In the incarnate Christ, we glimpse the loving fellowship that eternally exists between the Father, Son, and Holy Spirit, and we are drawn into that life of love.

To Give Us His Life and His Relationship With the Father

Ultimately, in His incarnate person, and through His atoning and revealing work, the eternal Son of the Father has become flesh in order to share His life and His relationship with His Father in the Spirit with us. Paul writes to the Corinthians: 'For you know the grace of our Lord Jesus Christ, that though He was rich, yet for your sakes He became poor, that you through

---

[49] John Calvin, *Institutes of the Christian Religion*, 4.8.5 & 7.

[50] John C. Clark & Marcus Peter Johnson, *The Incarnation of God: The Mystery of the Gospel as the Foundation of Evangelical Theology* (Wheaton: Crossway, 2015), 50-51.

His poverty might become rich' (*2 Cor. 8:9*). Paul is not talking about material riches. Rather, he's telling us about a great exchange which takes place through the incarnation (including all the incarnate work) of Christ for us. For us, Christ has entered into the poverty of our situation in this fallen world, enduring all the miseries of this life, and taking upon Himself the guilt and punishment of our sins. And in exchange He shares His glorious riches with us. He has taken what was ours, and gives us what is His. Cyril put it like this:

> It follows, therefore, that He Who Is, The One Who Exists, is necessarily born of the flesh, taking all that is ours into himself so that all that is born of the flesh, that is us corruptible and perishing beings, might rest in him. In short, he took what was ours to be his very own so that we might have all that was his.[51]

Jesus shared our flesh and blood not only to 'destroy him who had the power of death, that is, the devil', but also 'release those who through fear of death were all their lifetime subject to bondage' (*Heb. 2:14-15*). As the Nicene Creed puts it, it was 'for us ... and for our salvation' that He 'came down from heaven, and was incarnate by the Holy Ghost of the Virgin Mary, and was made man.'

But what does this salvation for us, for which Christ became incarnate, look like? *Galatians 4:4-5* notes two parts to it: 'God sent forth His Son, born of a woman, born under the law, to redeem those who were under the law, that we might receive the adoption as sons.' For our redemption and our adoption: that's why Jesus came in the flesh. That's why the Incarnation happened. For us and for our salvation, through redemption and adoption. But notice this: the redemption leads on to the adoption. Christ has redeemed us in order that we might receive the adoption as sons. So often our focus is on the great Redemption we have in Jesus, and yet Paul writes that, great as our redemption is, it leads to something even greater: our adoption as sons.

Perhaps sometimes our lack of focus on the great truth of adoption is because we often reduce it to legal terms, as a mere change of status. But in *Galatians 4*, Paul makes very clear that this is no mere legal procedure. This adoption leads to us knowing (and loving) God as our Father. This adoption leads to the gift of the Holy Spirit who pours out the love of the Father in our hearts (*cf. Rom. 5:5*). Rather than a mere legal status change, this adoption is all about being received into the loving relationships of our new

---

[51] Cyril of Alexandria, *On the Unity of Christ*, 59

family – the Triune God. Cyril wrote that the incarnation of the Word was 'for this reason, that we might reap the benefit of adoption through our enriching participation in him through the Holy Spirit.'[52]

Many writers in the early church wanted to emphasise this glorious truth of being brought right into the loving fellowship of the Father, Son and Holy Spirit. Irenaeus of Lyons put it like this: 'He became what we are so that we might become what He is.'[53] Irenaeus wasn't alone here. Athanasius the Great, the champion defender of the deity of Christ against the Arians, said almost the same thing. Yet it sounds a bit odd to us today. How could we become what Jesus is? After all, Jesus is God. So were Irenaeus and Athanasius saying that we get turned into God?

Well, not really. Think of it like this: what is Jesus? He's the Son of God. And through Him we become sons of God. So we become what He is. But He is the Only-Begotten Son; we are sons by adoption and grace. Again, what it Jesus? He is the Christ, the Anointed One. And in Him we are anointed with His anointing. He is the One who has the Spirit without measure; we receive His Spirit, the Spirit of adoption, from Him, by grace.

So, when Athanasius' version of this formula of exchange is often translated 'He became man so that we might become god',[54] it's not saying we get turned into God, but rather it's echoing the language of Psalm 82 to say that, by grace, in Christ, we are made like God the Son and conformed to His image. He is divine by nature, yet by grace we are made 'partakers of the divine nature' (*2 Pet. 1:4*).

Now, maybe that sounds rather odd, maybe even alarming. But think about this: what is the divine nature? It might sound a bit abstract to talk of 'the divine nature', but it's simply the nature of God, and so that means the nature of the Triune God. And the nature of the Triune God is to always exist in the loving relationship of Father, Son and Holy Spirit. So when the Bible says we've become partakers of the divine nature, it's not saying that our humanity is somehow transformed into divinity – far from it! It's saying that we've been brought into this everlasting, loving relationship between the Father, Son and Holy Spirit. We are united to Christ, and in Him, we now share His relationship with His Father. The Father loves us with the very same love which He has for His Son. We are now sons in the Son – which was what the Bible was talking about back in Galatians where we read about how Jesus became incarnate for our adoption as sons.

---

[52] Cyril of Alexandria, *Scholia*, §25

[53] Irenaeus, *Against Heresies*, Preface to Book 5.

[54] Athanasius, *On the Incarnation*, 54.3

So Jesus became what we are, so that we might become what He is. He became man to give Himself to us and unite Himself to us in salvation. Because He shares our nature, we can be united to Him. And because the One who shares our human nature and to whom we're united enjoys the perfect love of the Father in the Spirit, we in Him enjoy that perfect love of the Trinity as well. He is the Well-Beloved Son. And through our union with the Incarnate Christ, we become well-beloved sons in the Well-Beloved Son. As the early Apostolic, William Cathcart put it: 'the crux of Christian doctrine' is that 'the Son of God is Son of Man, and the sons of men are now sons of God.'[55] Or in the words of the early church, *He became what we are so that we might become what he is.*[56]

This chapter has been long and full of the sort of details about the incarnation that might have seemed unfamiliar or required a bit more thought. But ultimately such doctrine should lead us to praise the Word who became flesh for us and for our salvation. And, as they say that Pentecostal theology is more at home, not in the *summa*, but in the song, let me leave you with some early Apostolic worship, in the form of D.P. William's English hymn on the incarnation.[57]

I cry for faith to wonder,
With the angelic throng,
Stupendous and mysterious
This sea of endless song.
Two natures in one Person
Are found complete in Him,
Infinite and Eternal
Salvation from all sin!

O Wonder of all wonders,
In Time and Heaven above,
Embracing all, and glorious,
This condescending love;
The Son of God's own bosom,
Who dwells in realms of Light,
To give Himself a ransom
Came to this world of night!

This love beyond all measure,
As high as God's own Throne,

[55] William Cathcart, *Riches of Grace*, xiii.3 (Jan. 1938), 329.
[56] We'll think about this more in chapters 23 and 30.
[57] D.P. Williams wrote hundreds of hymns in Welsh, but only a handful in English.

So broad and rich its treasure,
Unfathomable store,
Beyond all comprehension,
Yet apprehend we can
That we have found Salvation
In Him – this God and Man.
(D.P. Williams)

Chapter 12

Christ's Virgin Birth

The Nicene Creed confesses faith in the Incarnation of Christ by pointing us to the teaching of the Scriptures on the Virgin birth: 'Who for us men, and for our salvation came down from heaven, and was incarnate by the Holy Ghost of the Virgin Mary, and was made man.' Although in English we usually speak of the Virgin birth, what we're really getting at is the virginal conception of Christ. And to help us understand Christ's virginal conception, the Creed points us to two others: the Holy Spirit and the Virgin Mary.

Incarnate by the Holy Spirit

Scripture provides us with two accounts of the events surrounding the birth of Christ: one in Matthew's Gospel and one in the Gospel of Luke. Both of these accounts point us to the role of the Holy Spirit in Christ's virginal conception. Matthew is emphatic about the Holy Spirit's role in the conception of Christ, restating the fact twice in quick succession:

> Now the birth of Jesus Christ was as follows: After His mother Mary was betrothed to Joseph, before they came together, she was found with child of the Holy Spirit. Then Joseph her husband, being a just man, and not wanting to make her a public example, was minded to put her away secretly. But while he thought about these things, behold, an angel of the Lord appeared to him in a dream, saying, 'Joseph, son of David, do not be afraid to take to you Mary your wife, for that which is conceived in her is of the Holy Spirit.' (*Mt 1:18-20*)

Yet, although he places emphasis on the role of the Holy Spirit, Matthew does not explain anything further about how the Holy Spirit was involved in the incarnation of the Son.

Luke, however, does tell us a bit more, recording the angel Gabriel's words to Mary at the annunciation. When Mary asked, 'How can this be, since I do not know a man?' (*Lk 1:34*), Gabriel replied, 'The Holy Spirit will come upon you, and the power of the Highest will overshadow you; therefore, also, that Holy One who is to be born will be called the Son of God' (*Lk 1:35*). The work of the Holy Spirit is the answer to Mary's question of how a virgin could possibly have a child. In fact, Luke here presents us with a Trinitarian view of the Incarnation. The Father (Most High), Son, and Holy Spirit are all involved in the Incarnation (although it is only the Son who becomes incarnate).

Yet we must be careful with Gabriel's words here, and pay attention to exactly what he told Mary and tells us. For Gabriel did not say that the Holy Spirit would come upon the child, but upon Mary. This is very important to notice in light of what we saw about Nestorianism in the previous chapter. The Holy Spirit did not cause the incarnation by coming upon a child in Mary's womb. Rather, when the eternal Son and Word of God the Father took to himself humanity by becoming incarnate in the Virgin's womb, the Holy Spirit – who is the Son's own Spirit – came upon the Virgin, and the Son, by His own Holy Spirit, created His own humanity (of the substance of the Virgin). As Cyril put it while arguing against Nestorius' heresy:

> it is clear that the Spirit is his [the Son's], as proceeding through his ineffable nature, and is consubstantial with him. He did not need the power that is from [the Spirit] as something outside and foreign, but used him rather as his own Spirit[1]

It's not that the Holy Spirit independently acted upon the Son to unite Him to a human nature. Instead, it's that the Son acted through His own Holy Spirit to take to Himself human nature. And He created His human nature 'of the Virgin Mary.'

But Cyril of Alexandria also points us to another important reason for the Holy Spirit's role in Christ's incarnation. Cyril wants us to remember that it was for us and for our salvation that the Son became incarnate and was born of the Virgin:

> The Son came, or rather was made man, in order to reconstitute our condition within himself; first of all in his own holy, wonderful, and truly amazing birth and life. This was why he himself became the first one to be born of the Holy Spirit (I mean of course after the flesh) so that he could trace a path for grace to come to us. He wanted us to have this … regeneration and spiritual assimilation to himself, who is the true and natural Son, so that we too might be able to call God our Father, and so

---

[1] Cyril of Alexandria, *Adversus Nestorii Blasphemias*, iv.iii. (Translation from Gregory K. Hillis, 'The Natural Likeness of the Son: Cyril of Alexandria's Pneumatology' PhD dissertation, McMaster University, 2008, p.64.)

remain free of corruption as no longer owing our first father, that is Adam in whom we were corrupted. All this happened 'not from blood, not from the will of the flesh, or the will of man' (Jn 1:13) but from God through the Spirit.[2]

In other words, Jesus was born of the Holy Spirit so that we could be born of the Holy Spirit. Writing of the Incarnation, John tells us, 'But as many as received him, to them gave he power to become the sons of God, even to them that believe on his name' (*Jn 1:12* AV). Thomas Torrance wrote of this verse that, 'Just as he was born from above of the Holy Spirit, so we are born from above of the Holy Spirit through sharing in his birth.'[3] Our new birth is through the Virgin Birth of Jesus. 'Our regeneration or rebirth ... results from our sharing in the birth of Christ, from our participation in the birth of our incarnate Substitute.'[4] As Charles Wesley put it in his best-known Christmas hymn, the Incarnate Son was 'born to raise the sons of earth, born to give them second birth.'

Of the Virgin Mary

The eternal Son and Word of the Father, by His Spirit in His incarnation, created His own human nature, not *ex nihilo* ('out of nothing') like the heavens and the earth, but *ex virgine* ('out of a virgin', from her substance). Fulgentius of Ruspe put it like this:

> It was not that the Only-begotten God received an unconceived flesh, but rather, God himself was conceived in that flesh in the profoundest humility. Indeed, according to the flesh God himself was created in and from the Virgin, and in fact he who had created his own mother was created from and in that flesh.[5]

---

[2] Cyril of Alexandria, *On the Unity of Christ*, 62

[3] Thomas F. Torrance, *Incarnation* (Milton Keynes: Paternoster, 2008), 101.

[4] John C. Clark and Marcus Peter Johnson, *The Incarnation of God: The Mystery of the Gospel as the Foundation of Evangelical Theology*, 135.

[5] Fulgentius, *First Letter to the Scythian Monks*, Para. 4

The Virgin's Son

Both Matthew and Luke, in their accounts of the events surrounding Christ's birth, make clear that Mary did not conceive this baby in the normal human way, for she was a virgin. In fact, this is one of the first things that went through Mary's head when Gabriel came to her to announce Jesus' birth. When the angel told her that she would 'conceive in [her] womb and bring forth a Son' (*Lk 1:31*), Mary replied with a question: 'How can this be, since I do not know a man?' (*Lk 1:34*). Gabriel responded by pointing Mary to the powerful work of the Triune God (*Lk 1:35*). If the Lord could miraculously give a child to Mary's elderly cousin, who had been barren all her life (*Lk 1:36*), then the Lord can miraculously cause a virgin to conceive, 'For with God nothing will be impossible' (*Lk 1:37*). Humanly speaking, a virgin birth is impossible; but with the God who brought all creation into being *ex nihilo* and who gives life to the dead, a virginal conception is no difficult matter at all.

Matthew too highlights the virgin birth of Christ. Firstly, in the genealogy with which be commences his Gospel, Matthew tells us that, although Joseph was Jesus' legal, adoptive father, He was not born of Joseph, but only of Mary. 'And Jacob begot Joseph the husband of Mary, of whom was born Jesus who is called Christ' (*Mt 1:16*). Matthew then begins his account of Jesus' birth from Joseph's perspective:

> Now the birth of Jesus Christ was as follows: After His mother Mary was betrothed to Joseph, before they came together, she was found with child of the Holy Spirit. Then Joseph her husband, being a just man, and not wanting to make her a public example, was minded to put her away secretly. But while he thought about these things, behold, an angel of the Lord appeared to him in a dream, saying, 'Joseph, son of David, do not be afraid to take to you Mary your wife, for that which is conceived in her is of the Holy Spirit. And she will bring forth a Son, and you shall call His name Jesus, for He will save His people from their sins.'
>
> So all this was done that it might be fulfilled which was spoken by the Lord through the prophet, saying: 'Behold, the virgin shall be with child, and bear a Son, and they shall call His name Immanuel,' which is translated, 'God with us.'
>
> Then Joseph, being aroused from sleep, did as the angel of the Lord commanded him and took to him his wife, and did not know her till she had brought forth her firstborn Son. And he called His name JESUS. (*Mt 1:18-25*)

Matthew's account begins with Joseph discovering that Mary is pregnant, but knowing that he could not possibly be the father. Thinking that she must have betrayed him, Joseph wants to treat her kindly and bring an end to their betrothal quietly so as not to bring her into further public disgrace. But, before he can do that, the angel comes to him in a dream to tell him what has really happened. Mary has not betrayed him. Rather, it is through the Holy Spirit that Mary, a virgin, has conceived. And the child in her womb is not just any child, but the one who 'will save His people from their sins.'

So, twice here within the space of a few verses, Matthew tells us that Mary has not conceived in the normal human way, but by the Holy Spirit. First Matthew as the narrator tells us right at the beginning of the account (*Mt 1:18*) and then Matthew tells us again as the angel tells Joseph (*Mt 1:20*). But then Matthew goes on to tell us once more, by quoting Isaiah's prophecy of the virgin birth from the Old Testament (*Mt. 1:23* quoting *Isa. 7:14*).

It's upon Isaiah's words that deniers of the virgin birth frequently seize. The word which Isaiah used, they contend, does not actually technically mean 'virgin'. However, while not being the technical word referring only and specifically to someone who has never had sexual intercourse, the word Isaiah uses does imply virginity. It's the word for a young unmarried woman, and in both Isaiah's culture and the culture of Matthew, Mary and Joseph, a young unmarried woman was expected to be a virgin. The ancient Jewish translators of Old Testament into Greek (the Septuagint) certainly understood Isaiah to be speaking of a young woman who had never had sexual relations, for they translated it with the Greek word for 'virgin' (the same word Matthew uses in *Mt 1:23*), as did all Jewish translations of Isaiah until after the rise of the Christian church. Matthew clearly uses the word 'virgin', and both his wider account and that of Luke make very clear that Mary did not conceive in the normal human way, but rather, as a virgin who had not known a man.

The Seed of the Woman

In the first proclamation of the gospel after the Fall of Adam and Eve, the Lord God said to the serpent:

> And I will put enmity
> Between you and the woman,

And between your seed and her Seed;
He shall bruise your head,
And you shall bruise His heel. (*Gen. 3:15*)

The gospel promise made by the Lord in the Garden was that the Seed of the woman would crush the serpent's head. And through His virgin birth, the Lord Jesus Christ has come into this world to destroy the devil and all his works, as the Seed of the woman.

The apostle Paul points to Jesus' birth of a woman in his letter to the Galatians:

> But when the fullness of the time had come, God sent forth His Son, born of a woman, born under the law, to redeem those who were under the law, that we might receive the adoption as sons. (*Gal. 4:4-5*)

Christ did not come in a humanity created *ex nihilo*, for that would not fulfil the promise of the *protoevangelion* of *Genesis 3:15*. Instead He came 'born of a woman', *ex virgine*, as the Seed of the woman long-promised to crush the serpent's head.

In fact, Paul uses a curious word here. Although the Bible speaks in other places of people 'born of woman' or 'born of women' (*Job 14:1; Mt 11:11*), Paul does not use the same expression. Instead the word he uses for 'born' isn't the normal word for 'born', but rather the word 'become'. So, although like everyone else, Jesus was born of a woman, Paul indicates that there is a difference in Christ's birth from a woman: Jesus 'became' of a woman.

Paul uses this same word ('become') to speak of the incarnation and birth of Christ in the book of Romans, where he writes of God's 'Son Jesus Christ our Lord, who was born of the seed of David according to the flesh' (*Rom. 1:3*). Likewise in *2 Timothy 2:8*, Paul tells us that Jesus Christ was 'of the seed of David.' Just as in *Galatians 4:4*, Paul makes clear in both *Romans* and *2 Timothy* that Christ's humanity was not ex nihilo, but rather 'of the seed of David.' Christ took His humanity from the substance of His mother, whose own substance was from the line of David.[6]

---

[6] Both the word 'Seed' and Christ's descent from David are important statements about His identity, but unfortunately space doesn't permit us to look at these further here.

Of the Substance of His Mother

So, these Scriptures makes plain that Christ's humanity was created, not *ex nihilo*, but *ex virgine* – of the substance of His mother. And this distinction is of huge importance for us and for our salvation. I'll let Fulgentius of Ruspe explain why:

> If, however, God the Word had become flesh in the Virgin in such a way that he had not come from her, it is certain that God himself would not have possessed the substance of flesh from the flesh of his mother but would simply have passed through the Virgin. In such a case, he could not have accomplished the mystery of becoming the mediator for our salvation, because in that case Christ the Son of God would not have unconfusedly united true, full humanity and divine substance in himself. Therefore, the medical remedy (as it were) that divine goodness employed was that the Only-begotten God, who is in the bosom of the Father, should become man, not only in a woman but also from that woman.[7]

In other words, if Jesus didn't take His humanity from the substance of Mary, then, while He might have taken on humanity, it wouldn't be our humanity. He wouldn't be connected to us. He wouldn't be the Mediator between our nature and God. And so He wouldn't be our Saviour, for as we saw in the previous chapter, 'the unassumed is the unhealed.'

The Scriptures point us to the importance of this in the book of Hebrews:

> Inasmuch then as the children have partaken of flesh and blood, He Himself likewise shared in the same, that through death He might destroy him who had the power of death, that is, the devil, and release those who through fear of death were all their lifetime subject to bondage. For indeed He does not give aid to angels, but He does give aid to the seed of Abraham. Therefore, in all things He had to be made like His brethren, that He might be a merciful and faithful High Priest in things pertaining to God, to make propitiation for the sins of the people. (*Heb. 2:14-17*)

Here we see that Jesus 'shared in the same' flesh and blood as 'the children' whom God has given Him (see *Heb. 2:13*): the human beings He came to save. And this sharing in the same flesh and blood was necessary for the death He died to destroy the devil and his power of death: 'in all things He had to made like His brethren … to make propitiation for the sins of the people.' The atonement rests upon the incarnation of Christ, and His

---

[7] Fulgentius, *First Letter to the Scythian Monks*, para. 5

atonement is made for those whose humanity He shares. Therefore, to make atonement for us, He came to share in our humanity by taking humanity, not *ex nihilo*, but *ex virgine*.

> Therefore, the blessed Mary both conceived and bore God the Word inasmuch as he was made flesh. God the Word did not insert the flesh in which he was conceived into her womb. Nor did God Himself, who was to be conceived, take on the material of conceived or formed flesh apart from her. Instead, he assumed that flesh from her ... He received the nature of human flesh from and in the Virgin herself, and the eternal God was temporally conceived and born according to that nature ... Likewise, apart from union with the Word of God, flesh could in no way be engendered in the inmost virginal womb that had not been inseminated by intercourse with a man. Therefore, when God who was to be conceived in her arrived, at that very time, the nature of the Virgin who conceived offered this flesh from itself. Thus one must not imagine that there was any interval of time between the origin of the conceived flesh and the arrival of the Majesty who was to be conceived. Indeed, there was one conception of divinity and flesh in the womb of the Virgin Mary, and there is one Christ the Son of God, conceived in both natures.[8]

What the Incarnation of the Word in the Womb of the Virgin has to say about abortion

The doctrine of the virginal conception leads Christians to pay careful attention to unborn children. Within a few days of the annunciation, Mary arrived at her cousin Elizabeth's house. We know that Mary arrived at Elizabeth's so quickly as Elizabeth was already 6 months pregnant at the time of the annunciation (*Lk 1:36*) and Mary stayed with her for three months, and yet had left by the time of John's birth (*Lk 1:56-57*). Therefore Mary must have gone straight to Elizabeth's after Gabriel's visit. And when Mary arrived, the baby in Elizabeth's womb leapt for joy (*Lk 1:41, 44*) at the presence of 'the mother of [the] Lord' (*Lk 1:43*), and hence of the Lord whom she carried in her womb. Mary had been pregnant for probably a week at most, yet the unborn John and his mother Elizabeth recognised the presence of the person of the Son in her womb. If it was indeed within a week of the annunciation, then:

> The Christ whom the unborn John greeted was probably not even implanted in the womb. If so, the somewhat more than six month old fetus

---

[8] Fulgentius, *First Letter to the Scythian Monks*, para. 7.

to be named John responded to the arrival of a zygote not even implanted in the wall of the womb.[9]

Both the unborn John and his mother Elizabeth recognised this zygote as the Lord, and Mary as a mother: they recognised a living child in Mary's womb who was the incarnate God.

Thomas Torrance points out that we must look to Christ who became an embryo for us to understand the human personhood of embryos:

> It is surely to him who became a holy embryo in the Virgin's womb, and was born of her to be the Saviour of the world, that we must go for understanding of every human being from conception. In Christ, we see that the unborn child is as an embodied human soul, a person loved by the Lord Jesus who came to be the Saviour of the human race.[10]
>
> The virgin birth is crucial to our grasp of the nature and status in Christ's eyes of the unborn child. The Son of God became a human being for us in the womb of the Virgin Mary, bone of our bone and flesh of our flesh. He became what we are. Think of the importance of the incarnation, then, for our understanding of and regard for the unborn child. Every child in the womb has been brothered by the Lord Jesus. In becoming a human being for us, he also became an embryo for the sake of all embryos, and for our Christian understanding of the being, nature and status in God's eyes of the unborn child. So, to take no thought, or no proper thought, for the unborn child is to have no proper thought of Jesus himself as our Lord and Saviour or to appreciate his relation as the incarnate Creator to every human being.[11]

Christ became 'an embryo for the sake of all embryos', therefore Christians look at the embryo, the unborn child, as the object of Christ's great love. And so, 'from the moment of conception every human being is infinitely precious to the Lord Jesus, and is the concern of his redeeming love.'[12] With such an understanding of the human personhood of the unborn child, right from the moment of conception, resting in the cardinal doctrines of the incarnation and the virgin birth, it is no wonder that from even before the completion of the New Testament canon in the first century, Christians understood the sixth commandment to include the prohibition of abortion: 'you shall not abort a child or commit infanticide' (*Didache 2:2*).

---

[9] Graham A. D. Scott, 'Abortion and the Incarnation', *Journal of the Evangelical Theological Society*, 17 (1974), 37.

[10] Thomas Torrance, *The Being and Nature of the Unborn Child*, 3.

[11] Thomas Torrance, *The Being and Nature of the Unborn Child*, 4-5.

[12] Thomas Torrance, *The Being and Nature of the Unborn Child*, 22.

Theotokos: Mother of God

Mary is the *Theotokos* (the God-bearer or Mother of God). Often contemporary Evangelicals and Pentecostals shy away from such language, yet it is a fundamental teaching of the Christian faith. For, the fact that Mary is the Mother of God has nothing to do with the veneration of Mary, but everything to do with who Jesus is.

Mary, you see, is the mother of Jesus. But who is Jesus? Jesus is God the Son, who has taken on our flesh through His Incarnation in the womb of the Virgin Mary. Therefore Mary is the mother of God the Son. God the Son is God, so Mary is the Mother of God.

If we say that Mary is not the Mother of God, then what we end up saying is that Jesus is not God. The early church recognised this, and so when the Archbishop of Constantinople (the infamous Nestorius whom we met in the previous chapter) refused to call Mary *Theotokos* (God-bearer – the Greek equivalent of Mother of God), a major crisis broke out that led to a few major Church Councils to defend the truth that the one born of Mary is God the Son.

Cyril of Alexandria, the great defender of orthodoxy in that controversy (and one of the greatest teachers on the doctrine of the person of Christ in the history of the Church) even wrote a book *Against Those Who Are Unwilling to Confess that the Holy Virgin Is Theotokos*. Yet his book wasn't about Mary; it was all about Jesus. For Cyril, *Theotokos* (God-Bearer) or Mother of God wasn't a title on which to establish a Mariology; rather, it was an essential title for a true Christology. As Cyril wrote to the Monks of Egypt at the outset of the controversy:

> I was completely amazed that certain people should be in any doubt as to whether the holy virgin ought to be called the Mother of God or not. For if our Lord Jesus Christ is God, then how is the holy virgin who bore him not the Mother of God?[13]

But for Cyril, it wasn't only essential to agree that Mary is the Mother of God because it's a vital Christological teaching, but also because he insisted that it's the biblical thing to say. He points to three particular Scriptures: *Luke 1:41-43*; *Luke 2:11-12*; and *Isaiah 7:14* quoted in *Matthew 1:23*.

---

[13] Cyril of Alexandria, *Letter to the Monks of Egypt*, §4

In *Luke 1:41-43*, when Mary greets her cousin Elizabeth, John the Baptist leaps within Elizabeth's womb and Elizabeth, filled with the Holy Spirit, calls Mary 'the mother of my Lord' (*Lk 1:43*). Who is Elizabeth's Lord? The Lord God. If anything, Elizabeth's wording is even stronger than Mother of God, for she effectively calls Mary the Mother of YHWH.

In *Luke 2:11-12* the Angels announce the birth of Jesus to the shepherds. But who do they say is born? 'A Saviour who is Christ the Lord.' Like Elizabeth, the angels insist that the one born of Mary is the LORD himself.

Finally, in *Matthew 1:23*, Matthew quotes Isaiah, writing: '"Behold, the virgin shall be with child, and bear a Son, and they shall call His name Immanuel," which is translated, "God with us."' In his *Scholia on the Incarnation*, Cyril argues that 'God with us' 'signifies that the Word (true God of true God) came in our nature on account of flesh' and so the Son borne by Mary 'was God in the flesh, and she who gave him a fleshly birth in accordance with the flesh was truly the Mother of God.'[14] So, to say that Mary is the mother of Immanuel (as *Mt 1:23* and *Isa. 7:14* both tell us) is to say that she is the mother of God.

The Church eventually resolved the controversy The Archbishop of Constantinople in question was deposed, condemned for heresy, and anathematised. And it is the settled doctrine of the Christian Church that 'if anyone does not confess the Immanuel to be truly God, and hence the holy virgin to be Mother of God (for she gave birth in the flesh to the Word of God made flesh), let him be anathema.'[15]

So, Mary is the Mother of God. We say that because: 1) To say otherwise is to say that Jesus isn't God, 2) It is a biblical thing to say, and 3) It is the settled, orthodox doctrine of the entire Christian church.

The Theological Significance of the Virgin Birth

We have already seen that Jesus needed to be made man of the substance of His mother, in order to share in our humanity so as to be our Saviour. But why did that conception of the substance of His mother need to be a virginal conception? He would still share in our humanity if he had been conceived

---

[14] Cyril of Alexandria, *Scholia*, §27
[15] No. 1 of the Twelve Chapters of Cyril, formally accepted as the standard of orthodoxy at the Second Council of Constantinople.

of a human mother and a human father. So what is the significance of the virgin birth?

The Virgin Birth and the New Adam

The virgin birth of Jesus represents a break with the old humanity which is dead in Adam and instead provides a new creation in Christ Jesus. Paul's parallels between Adam and Christ in *Romans 5* and *1 Corinthians 15* show us that every human being has their life and destiny determined by one of these two men. Either we die in Adam or we rise with Christ (*1 Cor. 15:21-22*).

Christ is the new creation, and so He is not just connected to Adam in the same way as the rest of us. His virgin birth is the new beginning for mankind. Thus both the birth of Adam and the birth of Christ involve the creative work of God. Yet, 'whereas Adam was taken out of the ground, the new Adam is taken from the flesh of Mary and thereby incorporates within himself the fallen human narrative of sin and death in order to redeem it.'[16]

The Virgin Birth and Sola Gratia

Salvation is by grace alone (*sola gratia*), and not by human works or effort. As John tells us, our new birth is 'not of blood, nor of the will of the flesh, nor of the will of man, but of God' (*Jn 1:13*). The virgin birth demonstrates this very clearly for us, for it did not come about as the result of man's will, but God's will alone. It was not by man's works or efforts that Christ was conceived in the womb of the Virgin, but only by the grace of the Triune God. Therefore the virgin birth is a sign of divine monergism in salvation, for it declares to us that salvation is wholly of the Lord.

---

[16] Jack D. Kilcrease, *The Self-Donation of God: A Contemporary Lutheran Approach to Christ and His Benefits* (Eugene: Wipf and Stock, 2013), 140.

Chapter 13

The Sinless Life of Christ

And Born of Her, Yet Without Sin[1]

Through His incarnation, the Lord Jesus Christ, the eternal Word and Son of God, took on our humanity. Yet there was one way in which His humanity differed from ours, for while all of us since the fall live in sinful flesh, Jesus did not. For God sent 'His own Son in the likeness of sinful flesh' (*Rom. 8:3*), not in sinful flesh itself. The difference between our flesh and His is that His is not sinful. The Scriptures of both the Old and New Testaments clearly teach the sinlessness of Jesus Christ (*Isa. 53:9; Dan.9:24; Lk 1:35; Jn8:46; 2 Cor. 5:21; 1 Pet. 1:19; 2:22; Heb. 4:15; 7:26*).

Was the Humanity Christ Assumed Sinless or Fallen?

However, several highly influential 20th Century theologians such as Karl Barth and T.F. Torrance have questioned the doctrine that Christ assumed a sinless human nature. Instead, they argue that the humanity Christ assumed was a fallen human nature (but not actually sinful). Two underlying assumptions generally underpin this argument: 1) That fallenness was necessary so 'that the nature which God assumed in Christ is identical with our nature',[2] and 2) That it is possible to distinguish between fallenness and sinfulness, so that Christ's 'taking of our flesh of sin was a sinless action.'[3]

So, is fallenness needed for the human nature of Christ to be identical with our nature? It certainly isn't necessary for genuine human nature, for Adam wasn't fallen before he ate of the forbidden fruit. So Adam shows us how it is possible to be a genuine human being, sharing fully in human nature, and yet not have a fallen human nature. Therefore, if it was possible for Adam to be fully human before the Fall, then that means fallenness is not an intrinsic part of human nature. Rather fallenness is part of the

---

[1] *Westminster Shorter Catechism*, 22.

[2] Karl Barth, *Church Dogmatics*, I.2, 153.

[3] Thomas F. Torrance, *Incarnation: The Person and Life of Christ*, 63.

penalty of Adam's first sin. Therefore, to assume human nature does not mean assuming fallenness. Rather, to assume fallenness would be to assume spiritual death as the penalty of sin, and thus to require redemption from sin and its penalty.

Furthermore, it isn't possible to distinguish between fallenness and sinfulness. 'Fallen Adam is sinful Adam. Fallen nature is sinful nature, dominated by "the flesh" (in the Pauline sense) and characterized by total depravity.'[4] Fallenness cannot be ascribed to Christ, without at the same time ascribing to Him original sin. All of fallen humanity sinned in Adam and is guilty of Adam's first sin. Therefore, if Christ assumed fallen humanity, He would be guilty in Adam too, and thus could not be the sinless Saviour.

Finally, to say that Christ assumed a fallen human nature would lead us down into the error of Nestorianism. If fallenness is attributed only to Christ's human nature, then that nature has to be sharply distinguished from the One Person of Christ, who is God the Son, for God cannot be fallen.

> How can the nature be fallen without implicating the person? Only if the humanness is an agent in its own right, acting independently and autonomously: so independently, indeed, that the Son carries no responsibility for his human nature. That is absurd.[5]

Absurd indeed, for that is precisely the Nestorian error. Instead we must conclude that the Word in His incarnation assumed a sinless human nature. As the Apostolic Church confesses: 'He was sinless, guileless, holy. He was the unique exception in the history of the Race.'[6] 'Christ was made flesh, but He was not sinful flesh.'[7]

Impeccability

We have seen that the possession of a sinful nature leads to us committing sins. Utterly depraved humanity is *not able not to sin*. If Christ were merely a man who did not possess a sinful nature, He would not be a slave to sin, and thus would be *able not to sin*. Yet, the Lord Jesus Christ is much more

---

[4] Donald Macleod, *The Person of Christ*, 228.
[5] Donald Macleod, *The Person of Christ*, 228.
[6] Fundamental Truths, *Guiding Principles*, 191.
[7] *Introducing the Apostolic Church: A Manual of Belief, Practice and History*, 124.

than that; He is God incarnate, and so as God, He is *not able to sin*. The fact that Christ could not sin is referred to as His *impeccability*.

The Scriptures very clearly teach that Christ did not sin. *2 Corinthians 5:21* states that God 'made Him who knew no sin to be sin for us, that we might become the righteousness of God in Him.' Thus the atonement was possible only because Christ was Himself sinless. Only a sinless Redeemer could die in the place of sinners for their sins. The writer to the Hebrews mentions Christ's sinlessness in relation to His High-Priestly ministry: 'For we do not have a High Priest who cannot sympathize with our weaknesses, but was in all points tempted as we are, yet without sin' (*Heb. 4:15*). Peter also explicitly states that Christ 'committed no sin' (*1 Pet. 2:22*).

Yet the doctrine of impeccability goes further than stating simply that Christ did not sin. The impeccability of Christ means that it was impossible for Christ to sin. This impeccability is not due to His sinless human nature. For Adam was created with a sinless human nature and yet fell into sin. Rather, Christ's impeccability is due to the fact that His human nature has never existed as an independent person (remember the doctrines of *anhypostasia* and *enhypostasia* from chapter 11). Christ's human nature has only ever existed as the human nature of God the Son.

Therefore, those who assume that Christ could have sinned (*peccability*), divide the human nature of Christ from the one person of the Son, and undo the doctrine of the hypostatic union and the incarnation (even if they might not realise it). The only way to assume *peccability* of Christ is to adopt a Nestorian (and thus heretical) concept of who Christ is. As the Jewish convert to Christianity and Lutheran theologian Friedrich Adolf Philippi put it: 'If we granted the possibility of sinning in the case of Christ, we should be viewing Him, too abstractly, as a mere man, and we should lose the God-Man.'[8] Francis Pieper warns starkly: 'They that assume the peccability of the man Christ thereby relinquish, whether they know it or not, the incarnation of the Son of God.'[9] Jesus Christ is God the Son. Therefore, if Jesus Christ were to be able to sin, then that would mean that God would be able to sin. And God cannot sin. So the Incarnate God has to be impeccable.

But if Jesus was not able to sin, does that mean that His temptations weren't real? The Bible tells us that Jesus 'was in all points tempted as we are, yet without sin' (*Heb. 4:35; cf. Mt 4:1-11; Mk 1:12; Lk 4:1-13*). A proper understanding of the hypostatic union with its communication of attributes

---

[8] F.A. Philippi, *Glaubenslehre* IV.1, 150. Cited in Francis Pieper, *Christian Dogmatics*, 2:76.
[9] Francis Pieper, *Christian Dogmatics*, 2:76.

will help us to answer this question. In the hypostatic union, both of Christ's natures (His deity and His humanity) keep their own properties (they are not changed into something different), and the properties of each nature are now properties of the one person of Christ. That means that, as the human nature is able to suffer real temptation, Christ suffered real temptation; and as God cannot sin, Christ could not sin. Thus both can be true of Christ at once, because of the union of the two natures in one person: He could both not be able to sin and yet also genuinely suffer temptation. And this He did, not for His own sake, but for ours.

The faith of the Apostolic Church is that:

> The problem relative to the temptability yet impeccability of Christ is shrouded in the mystery of his theanthropic (God-man) person. We must declare that he was man, therefore he could be tempted; he was God, therefore he could not sin … He is not a human person with a Divine nature, but a Divine Person with a human nature, wherein the human will is always subject to the Divine.[10]

His Substitutionary Sinless Life

Christ Lived for Us

Christ did not only become our Substitute when He was nailed to the cross. Nor was it with His agony in Gethsemane. Nor even at His baptism in the Jordan. His whole incarnate life, right from the very beginning, is a gift given to us (*Isa. 9:6*). Christ's entire life was a life lived for us as our substitute. We call this the *vicarious life* of Christ. In the whole of His incarnate life, Christ did for us the things which we have not done and the things which we cannot do, as our substitute, in our place (*Isa. 59:15-16*). Paul expresses this, writing to the Galatians: 'I have been crucified with Christ; it is no longer I who live, but Christ lives in me; and the life which I now live in the flesh I live by faith in the Son of God, who loved me and gave Himself for me' (*Gal. 2:20*). Our standing before God is not grounded upon our life for Christ, but Christ's life for us. It is Christ with His

---

[10] *Introducing the Apostolic Church: A Manual of Belief, Practice and History*, 124-125.

substitutionary obedience, His pure prayers, and His perfect worship, who now lives through those who trust in Him. As Martin Luther put it:

> The chief article and foundation of the Gospel is that before you take Christ as an example, you accept and recognize him as a gift, as a present that God has given you and that is your own. This means that when you see or hear of Christ doing or suffering something, you do not doubt that Christ himself, with his deeds and suffering, belongs to you. On this you may depend as surely as if you had done it yourself; indeed as if you were Christ himself.[11]

Christ's Active Obedience

Christ's sinless life for us in our place is of the utmost importance for our salvation. As we have mentioned above, Christ had to be sinless in order for His sacrifice to be acceptable on our behalf. He could only bear our sins because He had none of His own. Indeed, we 'were not redeemed with corruptible things, like silver or gold, ... but with the precious blood of Christ, as of a lamb without blemish and without spot' (*1 Pet. 1:18-19*).

However, this is not the only significance of Christ's sinlessness for our salvation. Christ's sinless blood, shed for us, secures the forgiveness of our sins. Yet we are not only saved by Jesus' blood, but by Jesus' blood and righteousness: not just by His death at the end of a sinless life, but by the whole of His sinless life for us.

Christ, like Adam, is our covenantal representative. As such, He not only died our death, but also obeyed God fully and perfectly on our behalf. It's not only that He died for our law-breaking, but He was 'born under the law, to redeem those who were under the law' (*Gal. 4:4-5; cf. Mt 3:15; 5:17*). In other words, His whole life was lived, from Bethlehem to Calvary, under the law for our sake. We have not obeyed God's law perfectly. But Jesus has. He obeyed for us, as our Substitute in our place. This is the *active obedience* of Christ; His perfect observance of the whole of God's law in our place. His suffering in our place is known as His *passive obedience*.[12] Christ's active obedience and passive obedience cannot really be separated, as He obeyed in both ways at every moment of His earthly life, but theologians distinguish the two to remind us that we rely upon, not only Christ's death, but the whole of His life and work for us. When Christ's righteousness is

---

[11] Martin Luther, *A Brief Instruction on What to Look For and Expect in the Gospels*.

[12] Passive Obedience doesn't mean that Christ wasn't active in His sufferings; it simply comes from the Latin word for suffering.

imputed to us in justification, it is both His *active obedience* and His *passive obedience* which is credited to our account. *Romans 5:19* sums this up: 'by one Man's obedience many will be made righteous.'[13]

D.P. Williams wrote this about the Active Obedience of Christ:

> He met the demands of justice, because He met the demands of the law in full obedience, and in His pure, sinless life, He satisfied the holiness of God, and the love of God was fully pleased. And all that He met on behalf of mankind.[14]

John Calvin reminds us that we depend for our salvation upon the whole obedience of Christ – active and passive:

> Now someone asks, how has Christ abolished sin, banished the separation between us and God, and acquired righteousness to render God favourable and kindly toward us? To this we can in general reply that he has achieved this for us by the whole course of his obedience.[15]

In the dying words of one evangelical theologian, 'I'm so thankful for the active obedience of Christ. No hope without it.'[16]

Christ's Baptism for Us

Christ's Vicarious Baptism

John the Baptist baptised 'with water unto repentance' (*Mt 3:11*). Yet Jesus, as the perfect Sinless Lamb of God had no sin of which to repent. John even recognised that Jesus had no need to be baptised, and 'tried to prevent Him, saying "I need to be baptized by You, and are You coming to me?"' (*Mt 3:14*). So why did Jesus insist on being baptised by John?

The answer Jesus gives is 'to fulfil all righteousness' (*Mt 3:15*). Yet He is the righteous One, in whom there is no unrighteousness. So it wasn't for the

---

[13] We'll think about this more in chapter 24.

[14] D.P. Williams, Manuscript: 'The Shewbread', 9.

[15] John Calvin, *Institutes*, 2.16.5.

[16] J. Gresham Machen, in a telegram dictated from his deathbed to John Murray. Cited in Ned B. Stonehouse, *J. Gresham Machen: A Biographical Memoir* (Banner of Truth, 1977), 508.

sake of His own righteousness, but for ours, that Jesus was baptised. Jesus was baptised in our place, as our substitute, identifying with us in our sin. Glen Scrivener writes:

> Stunningly, while they were all confessing to their filth, the Son of God shows up. And he doesn't judge them, he joins them. He lines up with the messy people – shoulder to shoulder with all the moral failures – and he gets baptised. What is he doing? He's joining us in our failure, so we can join him in his family.[17]

Or, in the words of the Apostolic theologian, W.R. Thomas:

> At the Jordan, the great and necessary work of redemption, which He had come to accomplish, was inaugurated. Jesus had no need to be baptised, for He had no sin to confess, nor need of repentance; yet He did it to identify Himself with sinful man and to give His impeccable life as a sacrifice for sin and offer His life to God the Father to achieve and accomplish our redemption.[18]

Christ's Two-fold Baptism

Jesus was baptised for us. And He was baptised for us both in His life and in His death, for the baptism of Jesus was a two-fold baptism: in the Jordan and on Calvary (*Mt 20:22; Mk 10:38; Lk 12:50*). Jesus took our place in the waters of the Jordan and by His blood on the cross. He identified with us as our substitute and representative in both His life and in His death. In being baptised for us 'to fulfil all righteousness', Jesus entered the waters of baptism as our substitute and Head. His baptism is the real baptism. And in our baptism we're joined to Him in His double baptism – the one in the Jordan, and the one on Calvary (*Lk 12:50*).

We've already seen how Jesus' baptism is a revelation of the Triune God.[19] However, if Jesus' baptism is a two-fold baptism, in the Jordan and on the Cross, the revelation of the Jordan is also something which we should see in the cross of Calvary. The two events are so intimately connected, that what is seen and spoken at the river should be understood of Golgotha's hill. Even in the pain and suffering of the cross, even in the midst of the cry of desolation (*Mt 27:46; Mk 15:34*), we should hear the declaration of the Father's love and see the overshadowing of the Holy Spirit. And indeed,

---

[17] Glen Scrivener, *321: The Story of God, the World and You* (Leyland: Ten, 2014), 52.

[18] W.R. Thomas, *L'Emmanuele* (Naples: Edizioni Ricchezze di Grazia), 23.

[19] See above, chapter 5.

this is what the New Testament writers tell us was happening at the cross. It was 'through the eternal Spirit' (*Heb. 9:14*) that Jesus offered Himself up as the sacrifice for our sins at Calvary. And the propitiatory death of Christ upon the cross is the Father's declaration of love (*1 Jn 4:9-10*). Jesus is glorified in His death on the cross (*e.g Jn 13:31-32*), yet it is the Father who glorifies the Son (*Jn 8:54; 17:1*), and the glory with which the Father glorifies the Son is intimately associated with His love for His Son (*Jn 17:24*). In fact, Jesus explicitly told His disciples that the cross would be a revelation of His relationship with His Father (and thus of the Trinity): 'When you lift up the Son of Man, then you will know that I am He, and *that* I do nothing of Myself; but as My Father taught Me, I speak these things' (*Jn 8:28*).

The Descent of the Dove: The Incarnate Christ and the Holy Spirit

Charismatics and the Ninth Anathema

There is an increasingly popular strand of thinking among some Pentecostals and charismatics (and many other kinds of evangelicals too) that looks to Jesus as the model of a man perfectly filled with the Holy Spirit, and this idea is frequently connected to their understanding of Jesus' baptism. One Pentecostal study Bible suggests that the primary reason for Jesus' baptism by John was for 'the Holy Spirit [to] descend to empower Him for kingdom ministry' with the result that 'everything Jesus did – His healings, His suffering, His victory over sin – He did by the power of the Holy Spirit.' The writer concludes that 'Jesus could do nothing apart from the work of the Holy Spirit.'[20] William Atkinson points to the growth of this new view among Pentecostals, which focuses 'not on a Jesus able to conduct his mission by means of his innate divinity, true as that divinity is, but on a Jesus enabled to minister by means of the divine Spirit upon him.'[21] This is a change from looking to a vicarious Christ, to looking to Christ as an example.

> Prior to this change, Pentecostals read accounts of healings in the gospels and identified themselves with those coming for healing, seeing the requests of those people to Jesus as equivalent to their own prayers to God. More recently, Pentecostals reading the gospels tend rather more to

[20] *Life in the Spirit Study Bible*, comments on *Mt 3:13* and *Mt 3:16*, p.1408.
[21] William P. Atkinson, *Jesus Before Pentecost*, (Eugene, Oregon: Cascade, 2016), 120.

identify themselves with Jesus and expect the same capac.ty to heal to be evident in their lives as was evident in his.[22]

His miracles and healings are then seen, not as evidenc2 of His deity (which is very much how John present's Christ's 'Signs' in his Gospel), but as what can be done by a man perfectly filled with the Spirit. Even the descent of the Spirit upon Him at His baptism is sometimes seen as no more than a model of how we are to be filled with the Spirit. (I've even heard a few people speculate that Jesus must have spoken in tongues wher. the dove descended upon Him, even though the Bible says no such thing, for this very reason.)

Those Pentecostals and charismatics who promote this new teaching do not reject the truth that Jesus is God. Their goal was never to deny His deity, but simply to highlight His Spirit-filled humanity. Yet, this has led some to point to Jesus almost exclusively as an example that we are to follow. Somehow this focus on Jesus receiving the Spirit from outside of Himself to cast out unclean spirits and accomplish divine signs as a perfect man in the power of the Spirit has led to an almost Pelagian-like focus on what we must do to please God by following Jesus' example.

However, this is not such a surprising turn of events. It has happened before. You see, how we see Jesus – how we understand who He is – is closely tied to how we understand salvation. For Jesus is our salvation.

Cyril of Alexandria (whom we've met in our discussions of the incarnation of Christ) was someone who understood this close connection. Back in the 5th Century Cyril devoted much of the last twenty years or so of his life to defending the proper biblical understand-ng of who Jesus is, which he saw was inseparable from our understanding of salvation. One thing which Cyril wrote in the midst of the Nestorian controversy is incredibly relevant to these new ideas among Pentecostals and charismatics today. Cyril's Ninth Anathema is about the relationsh:p between Jesus and the Spirit and goes like this:

> If anyone says that the One Lord Jesus Christ was glorifi2d by the Spirit, using the power that came through him as if it were foreig⁊ to himself, and receiving from him the power to work against unclean spirits and to accomplish divine signs for men, and does not rather say that the Spirit is his very own, through whom he also worked the divine signs, let him be anathema.[23]

---

[22] Atkinson, *Jesus Before Pentecost*, 86.

[23] Cyril of Alexandria, *The Third Letter to Nestorius*. Translation in John McGuckin, *Saint Cyril of Alexandria and the Christological Controversy* (Crestwood: SVS Press, 2004), 274.

In his *Explanation of the Twelve Chapters*, Cyril explains this a bit more telling us that he's writing against those who think that Jesus 'did not make use of his own power in a God-befitting manner [to perform signs and wonders] but instead used an external power [from the Holy Spirit].' Now, Cyril wasn't denying that Jesus worked in the power of the Spirit, but what he was denying was that Jesus worked in the power of the Spirit 'as a man like any one of us, or rather like one of the saints.' Instead Cyril wants us to understand that Jesus 'had as his very own the Holy Spirit which is from him and within him essentially and so he brought about divine signs, and even when he became man he remained God and accomplished miracles in his very own power through the Spirit.'[24]

So, basically Cyril is arguing against a position very like that of those charismatics today who say that Jesus performed his miracles as a man perfectly filled with the Holy Spirit. And not only is Cyril arguing against this position, but he wants us to understand that it is an incredibly dangerous position. For Cyril it's so dangerous that he pronounces an anathema. (Cyril was the Patriarch of Alexandria, so he got to do things like that!)

Why is it so dangerous? Because it introduces a separation between the deity and humanity of Christ, and so, in some way, divides the Saviour. And if the Saviour is divided that widens the gap between us and God. How? Well, now instead of One Mediator – the God-Man – we end up with an extra level of mediation. For if there were any separation between the humanity of Christ and his deity, then we'd need the human Christ as mediator to get us to the divine Christ to be our mediator to the Father. And when we make this separation, what sort of mediation do we get from a perfect man filled with the Spirit – no more than an example to emulate to climb our way up.

So, once we start separating Jesus' humanity and His deity, we end up unravelling salvation and undoing grace. No matter how tempting it might be for us to look at Jesus in terms of a perfect example of man filled with the Spirit, that would be looking away from the gospel of the Word made flesh for us and our salvation. Cyril's *Twelve Chapters* (including the Ninth Anathema) were declared to be the faith of the Christian church at the Second Council of Constantinople (the Fifth Ecumenical Council) in AD 553.

---

[24] Cyril of Alexandria, *Explanation of the Twelve Chapters*, Explanation 9. Translation in McGuckin, 290-291.

Jesus as the Baptiser in the Holy Spirit

John the Baptist prophesied that Jesus would be the Baptiser in the Holy Spirit (*Mt 3:11; Mk 1:8; Lk 3:16; Jn 1:33; Acts 11:16*). In Jesus' own baptism, we see that the One who will pour out the Spirit is the one who is perfectly anointed with the Spirit and who lives and accomplishes His mission in perfect communion with the Spirit. The promise of Jesus as the Baptiser in the Spirit and the revelation of relationship between the Son (the Spirit Baptiser) and the Spirit at Jordan, reveal to us the deity of Christ. For it is only God who can pour out God.

Yet, John says that it is the One 'whose sandal strap I am not worthy to loose' who will baptise with the Holy Spirit (*Lk 3:16*). It is the Man Christ Jesus who was wearing sandals on His feet. Therefore the One who baptises in the Spirit is the Incarnate Christ. It is the God-Man who pours out the Holy Spirit upon the Church.

Chapter 14

The One Mediator who is our Prophet, Priest & King

'For there is one God and one Mediator between God and men, the Man Christ Jesus, who gave Himself a ransom for all' (*1 Tim. 2:5-6*). The Man Christ Jesus – God the Son Incarnate – is the only Mediator between God and humanity.

Long before the coming of Christ in the flesh, Job recognised his great need of a Mediator, lamenting that God:

> Is not a man, as I am,
> That I may answer Him,
> And that we should go to court together.
> Nor is there any mediator between us,
> Who may lay his hand on us both. (*Job 9:32-33*)

Job knew the vast difference between God and man: between the holy Creator and the sinful creature. He knew that he needed a go-between who could lay a hand on humanity and a hand on God. What Job needed, and what all sinful humanity needs, is a Mediator who is both true man and true God: the God-Man, Christ Jesus. An Apostolic catechism asks 'why did Christ take upon Himself the likeness of sinful flesh?' And the answer comes: 'That He, through His vicarious death, might be the Mediator of the Covenant of Grace to reconcile man to God.'[1] The great early Protestant theologian, Johann Gerhard agreed: 'Christ's office consists in the work of mediation between God and human beings, which is the goal or end of the incarnation.'[2] The catechism goes on to teach that our Mediator had to be God, for 'only He who was God could answer God on our behalf' and that our Mediator had to be true man, 'in order that He might die for our sins and represent us before God.' Only His mediation is acceptable, 'because being God and Man in one Person … He is able to save to the uttermost those that come to God by Him (*Heb. 7:25*).'[3]

It is the Incarnate Christ in His person and work who is the Mediator between man and God. The Mediator is the One who saves, for He is Jesus –

---

[1] *Asked and Answered: A Catechism of Apostolic Principles*, 3.a.6.

[2] Johann Gerhard, *Loci*, Exegesis IV, §320

[3] *Asked and Answered: A Catechism of Apostolic Principles*, 3.a.8-9, 11.

the LORD is salvation. The salvation of the LORD comes to us in this Man and in this Man only, for He is the God-Man: the LORD in the flesh, the only one who can both lay a hand on God and a hand on us. And so, as the God-Man, His mediation goes in both directions. He is the Mediator between God and man, and the Mediator between man and God. Athanasius put it like this: 'Our Lord, being Word and Son of God, bore a body, and became Son of Man, that, having become Mediator between God and men, He might minister the things of God to us, and ours to God.'[4] Let's have a look at how Jesus Christ ministers 'the things of God to us' and the things of man to God.

Christ the Mediator Between God and Man

As the Mediator between God and man, Christ ministers the things of God to us. How does He do that? In revelation and redemption.

Christ the Mediator of Revelation

'No one has seen God at any time. The only begotten Son, who is in the bosom of the Father, He has declared Him' (*Jn 1:18*). So Jesus, the Incarnate Son, stands as Mediator between God and Man in declaring the Father and revealing Him to us. Jesus Himself speaks about this in Matthew's Gospel:

> I thank You, Father, Lord of heaven and earth, that You have hidden these things from the wise and prudent and have revealed them to babes. Even so, Father, for so it seemed good in Your sight. All things have been delivered to Me by My Father, and no one knows the Son except the Father. Nor does anyone know the Father except the Son, and the one to whom the Son wills to reveal Him. Come to Me, all you who labour and are heavy laden, and I will give you rest. Take My yoke upon you and learn from Me, for I am gentle and lowly in heart, and you will find rest for your souls. For My yoke is easy and My burden is light. (*Mt 11:25-30; cf. Lk 10:21-24*)

The Father has delivered 'all things' to His Son, and the only way to know Him is through the revelation of the Son. Therefore, it is only in Christ that

---

[4] Athanasius, *Contra Arianos*, 4.6

we can truly know the Father, or even know what He is like. But not only that: because the Father has delivered 'all things' to His Son, the revelation of the Father mediated by the Son is a full revelation. So, as the Lord Ramsey of Canterbury expressed it, 'God is Christlike, and in Him there is no unchristlikeness at all.'[5] Or in Thomas Torrance's words: 'God is indeed really like Jesus, and … there is no unknown God behind the back of Jesus for us to fear; to see Jesus is to see the very face of God.'[6]

Jesus is the revelation of God. We see 'the light of the knowledge of the glory of God in the face of Jesus Christ' (*2 Cor. 4.6*), for Jesus is 'the brightness of His glory and the express image of His person' (*Heb. 1:3*). Therefore He reveals the Father perfectly, and whoever has seen Jesus has seen the Father whom He reveals (*Jn 14:9*). In Jesus Christ, the Mediator of God's revelation, the invisible God is visible (*Col. 1:15*).

Therefore, all our thinking about God must begin with Jesus, for there is no other God than the Father who reveals Himself in His Son in the unity of the Spirit. Glen Scrivener reminds us what this means for our theology:

> Jesus is not an optional extra in our theology – He is the foundation. He is the pole star that guides all our theological enquiries. Anything we want to know about God the Father or indeed God the Trinity, we must arrive at by thinking through 'who is Jesus?' The Father has chosen Jesus as the point of contact between Himself and us, we must always go to Jesus.[7]

Christ the Mediator of Redemption

The book of Hebrews tells us that Jesus Christ is 'the Mediator of a better covenant' (*Heb. 8:6*) or 'Mediator of the new covenant' (*Heb. 9:15; 12:24*). We will explore the redeeming work of Christ our Mediator in the next few chapters as we explore His atoning death, triumphant resurrection, ascension and abiding intercession.

---

[5] A.M. Ramsey, *God, Christ and the World: A Study in Contemporary Theology* (London: SCM Press, 1969), 99.

[6] Thomas F. Torrance, *Preaching Christ Today: The Gospel and Scientific Thinking*, 55.

[7] Glen Scrivener, 'Beginning with Jesus', *Christ the Truth*. http://christthetruth.net/2008/11/30/beginning-with-jesus/

Christ the Mediator Between Man and God

As the Mediator between man and God, Christ ministers the things of man to God. Let's have a look at what that means for worship and prayer.

Christ the Mediator of our Worship

Jesus said that 'true worshipers will worship the Father in spirit and truth' (*Jn 4:23*). Jesus also declared that He Himself is 'the Truth' (*Jn 14:6*). So, to worship the Father in truth doesn't simply mean to use true words about the Father in our worship. Rather, to worship the Father in truth means to worship the Father 'in Christ' who is the Truth. True worshippers worship the Father in the Son by the Spirit. Therefore, Jesus Christ is the Mediator of true worship. It is only through Christ that we can worship the Father in Spirit and in Truth.

It is only through Christ that we 'have access by one Spirit to the Father' (*Eph. 2:18*). It is through Him that we 'continually offer the sacrifice of praise to God, that is, the fruit of *our* lips, giving thanks to His name' (*Heb. 13:15*). In the Church, we 'as living stones, are being built up a spiritual house, a holy priesthood, to offer up spiritual sacrifices acceptable to God through Jesus Christ' (*1 Pet. 2:5*). We worship through Jesus, our only Mediator.

As our Mediator of worship, Jesus invites us into His own worship of His Father. Taking us as His brothers, Jesus says to the Father: 'I will declare Your name to My brethren; in the midst of the assembly I will sing praise to You' (*Heb. 2:12*). Not only does He declare the Father to us as the Mediator of revelation, but Jesus also leads us in singing the Father's praise. We join in Christ's song of worship, singing our praise through Him, our Mediator. As John Calvin put it, 'Christ leads our songs, and is the chief composer of our hymns.'[8] Jesus Christ is our true worship leader. James Torrance writes that Christ's worship is 'the substance of all Christian worship.'[9] Indeed,

---

[8] John Calvin, *Commentary on Hebrews*, 67.
[9] James B. Torrance, *Worship, Community, and the Triune God of Grace* (Downers Grove: IVP, 1996), 16.

'Christ's worship is our worship.'[10] The other Torrance brother explains it like this:

> Justification by Christ alone means that from first to last in the worship of God and in the ministry of the Gospel Christ himself is central, and that we draw near in worship and service only through letting Him take our place. He only is Priest. He only represents humanity. He only has an offering with which to appear before God and with which God is well-pleased. He only presents our prayers before God, and He only is our praise and thanksgiving and worship as we appear before the face of the Father. Nothing in our hands we bring—simply to His Cross we cling.[11]

Christ the Mediator of Prayer

Prayer is 'the chief exercise of faith.'[12] Prayer is not a task which we try to accomplish in the Christian life; it is the Christian's relationship with the Triune God in expression. God has given us the gift of prayer for communion with 'our Father' (*Mt 6:9*). God does not need us to tell Him anything, for He knows all things. Yet He wants us to speak to Him and tell Him things, for He wants us to communicate with Him. He wants us to come as little children before our Father, expressing our love, pouring out our cares, seeking His help, and rejoicing and giving thanks to Him.

It is because God is the Triune God that we can come to Him in prayer. The Father invites us to come to Him in prayer, and He hears us, so come to Him in faith. The Spirit enables us to pray, for it is by the Spirit that we can call God 'Father' (*Rom. 8:16*). The Spirit also prays along with us, interceding fervently and in just the right way for us (*Rom. 8:26-27*)

Yet, although the Father invites us, and the Spirit enables us, we still need a Mediator to bring us to the Father in prayer. We need the Incarnate Son, Christ our Mediator, who gives us access to the throne of grace (*Heb. 4:14-16*). It is through the blood of Jesus, shed for us, that we approach God in prayer (*Heb. 10:19-22*). So we can draw near to the Father in prayer by Christ's great sacrifice in His death on the cross. Because Christ has died for us, we can approach God with confidence (*Heb. 4:14-16; cf. 2:14-18*).

Through Christ our Mediator we come, not in our own name, but in His name: with His authority and His merit (*Jn 14:13-14; 15:16*). Calvin says

---

[10] Torrance, *Worship, Community, and the Triune God of Grace*, 17

[11] Thomas F. Torrance, *Theology in Reconstruction*, 167.

[12] Calvin, *Institutes* 3.20

it's like we're praying through Jesus' own mouth: 'we pray as it were by His mouth, since He gives us entrance and audience, and intercedes for us.'[13]

But not only does our Mediator give us access to the throne of grace and His authority and merit with which to pray, He also purifies and perfects our prayers. We'll look at this aspect of Christ's mediation more in the chapter below on His Abiding Intercession.

The Three Offices of Christ our Mediator

Both the early Protestant Reformers and the early Apostolics point us to Christ's Three Offices (theologians call this the *munus triplex*) as our Mediator. The *Catechism upon the Tenets of the Apostolic Church* teaches that the title Christ, which means Anointed, 'distinguishes our Lord in His official character of Prophet, Priest and King.'[14] John Calvin explains why:

> The title 'Christ' pertains to these three offices: for we know that under the law prophets as well as priests and kings were anointed with holy oil. Hence the illustrious name of 'Messiah' was also bestowed upon the promised Mediator.[15]

The Old Testament prophets had foretold the coming of a Prophet, a Priest, and a King. These prophecies are all fulfilled in the Lord Jesus Christ, the true Messiah and only Mediator, in His threefold office.

Christ our Prophet

From the days of Moses, the Scriptures spoke of the coming of a great prophet, greater than any other prophet. He would be a prophet like Moses, the mediator of the old covenant of Sinai. The Lord told Moses:

> I will raise up for them a Prophet like you from among their brethren, and will put My words in His mouth, and He shall speak to them all that I command Him. And it shall be that whoever will not hear My words, which He speaks in My name, I will require it of him. (*Deut. 18:18-19; cf. v.15*)

---

[13] John Calvin, *Catechism of the Church of Geneva* (1541).
[14] *Catechism upon the Tenets of the Apostolic Church*, 3.1.4
[15] Calvin, *Institutes of the Christian Religion*, ii.xv.2

This promised Prophet would speak God's own words and whoever would not receive His words would stand under God's judgment. Preaching the gospel in Solomon's portico in the Temple, after the healing of the lame man at the Beautiful Gate, Peter declares that Jesus is this Prophet (*Acts 3:20-26*; cf. Stephen in *Acts 7:37*). Jesus Christ is the Prophet like Moses, yet greater than Moses. For, unlike Moses who spoke with the God 'face to face' (*Ex. 33:11*), Jesus is the face of God, and it is in the face of Jesus, the God-Man, that we see the glory of God (*2 Cor. 4:6*).

When Jesus came into the world and revealed Himself as God in the feeding of the five thousand, those who saw the sign said, 'this is truly the Prophet who is to come into the world' (*Jn 6:14*). When men acclaimed Him as 'the Christ', they also acclaimed Him as 'the Prophet' (*Jn 7:40*).

Jesus is *the* Prophet, who is greater than all earthly prophets, and through whom all true earthly prophets speak. The Old Testament prophets spoke of Him (*Lk 24:25-27; 1 Pet. 1:11*), as do those of the new covenant, 'for the testimony of Jesus is the spirit of prophecy' (*Rev. 19.10*).

As our great Prophet, Jesus Christ reveals God to us.[16] God has spoken to us in sending His Son into the world for us (*Heb. 1:1-2*). The only-begotten Son is the one who declares God to us (*Jn 1:18*).

Why do we need Jesus as our Prophet? 'Because of the ignorance of our mind introduced through sin, we are in need of … a prophet.'[17]

Christ our Priest

In the Old Testament, priests were anointed to offer sacrifices for the people and intercede for them before God. The priests also blessed the people from God (*Num. 6:22-27*). The Old Testament prophesied the coming of an eternal Priest, 'a priest forever according to the order of Melchizedek' (*Ps 110:4*).

Jesus is that eternal priest. Again and again the book of Hebrews tells us that He is our High Priest, the one who has offered Himself as an atoning sacrifice for our sins, who intercedes for us and who brings us into the presence of God in the heavenly Holy of Holies. We will consider Christ's

---

[16] One of the earliest Apostolic Catechisms defines Christ's prophetic office as 'giving revelation of God so that men might know Him.' (Original Welsh: *Rhoddi datguddiad o Dduw, fel y byddai i ddynion Ei adnabod.*) *Holwyddoreg*, v.5. Cf. *Westminster Shorter Catechism*, Q.24: '*How doth Christ execute the office of a prophet?* Christ executeth the office of a prophet, in revealing to us, by his word and Spirit, the will of God for our salvation.'

[17] Johann Gerhard, *Loci*, Exegesis IV, §321

work as our Priest in much more detail in the chapters on the Atonement and His Abiding Intercession.

Why do we need Jesus as our Priest? 'Because of our sins and the penalties for sins, we need a priest to reconcile us to God, to make satisfaction for us, and to intercede before his judgment seat.'[18]

Christ our King

The LORD had promised to send His King, who is His Son, and all those who put their trust in Him would be blessed (*Ps 2:6-7, 12*). The LORD covenanted with David that He would establish an everlasting King with an everlasting kingdom, from David's line (*2 Sam. 7:13; 1 Chron. 17:14*). The angel Gabriel told Mary that the baby to be born from her would be this King. 'The Lord God will give Him the throne of His father David. And He will reign over the house of Jacob forever, and of His kingdom there will be no end' (*Lk 1:32-33*). When Jesus was born, and the magi came to worship 'He who has been born King of the Jews' (*Mt 2:2*), both Herod and the chief priests and scribes understood exactly what they meant by this King. They knew this King was the promised Christ (*Mt 2:5*).

At the end of His earthly ministry, the Lord Jesus demonstrated His kingship as He rode into Jerusalem on Palm Sunday, fulfilling the words of the prophet Zechariah:

> Rejoice greatly, O daughter of Zion!
> Shout, O daughter of Jerusalem!
> Behold, your King is coming to you;
> He is just and having salvation,
> Lowly and riding on a donkey,
> A colt, the foal of a donkey. (*Zech. 9:9*)

And the crowds hailed Him as the blessed 'King who comes in the name of the Lord' (*Lk 19:38*). Before Pilate, Christ confessed His kingship, saying: 'My kingdom is not of this world. If My kingdom were of this world, My servants would fight, so that I should not be delivered to the Jews; but now My kingdom is not from here' (*Jn 18:36*). When Pilate asked again, Jesus responded, 'You say rightly that I am a king' (*Jn 18:37*). On the cross, as He was crucified, Christ's kingship was mockingly, yet truthfully, proclaimed, not only in the local language, but in the languages of the world (*Lk 23:38*),

---

[18] Johann Gerhard, *Loci*, Exegesis IV, §321

for His kingship is not a local matter, but of universal scope. He is King of Kings and Lord of Lords (*Rev. 17:14; 19:16*).

How does Christ execute this office of King? He acts as our King 'in subduing us to himself, in ruling and defending us, and in restraining and conquering all his and our enemies.'[19] He is our conquering King who rescues us from the hostile kingdom of sin and death, bringing us as His subjects into His blessed kingdom, where He protects and defends us from all attacks of the enemy. And as the victorious King, He crushes the enemy beneath His feet (*Gen. 3:15; Rom. 16:20*).

Why do we need Jesus as our King? 'Because of the weakness of our will, we need a king to lead and defend us.'[20]

Christ's Humiliation and Exaltation

As the Mediator, the Lord Jesus Christ, the Incarnate God, exercises His three-fold office of Prophet, Priest and King in two estates: His estate of humiliation and His estate of exaltation. Therefore, He is our Prophet in His humiliation, and our Prophet in His exaltation. He is our Priest in His humiliation, and our Priest in His exaltation. He is our King in His humiliation, and our King in His exaltation. But what do we mean by the estates of humiliation and exaltation?

Scripture speaks of these two estates in *Philippians 2:5-11*. There Paul writes that Christ 'humbled Himself' (*v.8*) in His taking on 'the form of a bondservant' (*v.7*), and that then, after His death on the cross, God 'highly exalted Him' (*v.9*). Thus, Christ's estate of humiliation should not be confused with the incarnation. Now in His exaltation, Jesus is still incarnate. The incarnate Christ spoke of this to the disciples on the road to Emmaus on the day of His resurrection, saying: 'Ought not the Christ to have suffered these things and to enter into His glory?' (*Lk 24:26*). In His estate of exaltation, Christ 'laid aside the form of a servant. He did not lay aside His human nature, but retains it to eternity.'[21] Therefore, His humiliation was not the taking on of human flesh, but rather it consisted of His undergoing the miseries and suffering of this life for us.

[19] *Westminster Shorter Catechism*, Q.26.
[20] Johann Gerhard, *Loci*, Exegesis IV, §321
[21] *Solid Declaration of the Formula of Concord*, viii.26

The *Westminster Shorter Catechism* defines these two estates of the Incarnate Christ:

> *Wherein did Christ's humiliation consist?*
> Christ's humiliation consisted in his being born, and that in a low condition, made under the law, undergoing the miseries of this life, the wrath of God, and the cursed death of the cross; in being buried, and continuing under the power of death for a time.

> *Wherein consisteth Christ's exaltation?*
> Christ's exaltation consisteth in his rising again from the dead on the third day, in ascending up into heaven, in sitting at the right hand of God the Father, and in coming to judge the world at the last day.[22]

The same Christ who was our Prophet, Priest and King through His sinless life and atoning death, is still our Prophet, Priest and King, and our only Mediator, now in His exaltation.

---

[22] *Westminster Shorter Catechism*, Q.27-28.

Chapter 15

The Atoning Death of Christ: He Died For Us

At the centre of the Bible stands the Cross of Christ. At the centre of the Christian faith stands the Cross of Christ. At the centre of history stands the Cross of Christ. Christ's death on the Cross is not merely a detail of history or one interesting event among many; together with His ensuing resurrection and ascension, Christ's death on the Cross is the salvation of the Triune God. 'The basis of our faith is: Christ crucified.'[1]

The Lamb of God who Takes Away the Sin of the World

Standing at the centre of the Christian faith, Christ's death on the Cross is not something new which suddenly appears with the New Testament. Instead, the Cross stands from 'before the foundation of the world' (*1 Pet. 1:19-20*). It is as the Lamb slain that the Son has been set apart 'from the foundation of the world' (*Rev. 13:8*), not merely as one who would be put to death on a cross by the Romans, but as the one who would be the saving sacrifice offered up to God, 'the Lamb of God who takes away the sin of the world' (*Jn 1:29*).

The promise of the Lamb of God did not begin with the proclamation of John the Baptist. John pointed to Jesus as the Lamb of God (*Jn 1:29, 36*), yet this was not some new, enigmatic saying. The Baptist declared the arrival of the long-promised Lamb, the Lamb for whom the people of God awaited. And this wait had gone on for at least two millennia. For the first recorded prophecy of the saving Lamb of God came through the lips of Abraham.

In *Genesis 22*, 'God tested Abraham' (*Gen. 22:1*) by sending him to sacrifice his beloved son, Isaac, on a mountain top in Moriah. On the third day of their journey, Abraham and Isaac left the servants behind as the climbed to the place of sacrifice, Isaac carrying the wood for the burn offering on his back (*Gen. 22:4-6*). Yet, as they climbed, Isaac asked his

---

[1] D.P. Williams, *Riches of Grace*, xv.6 (July 1940), 62.

father, 'where is the lamb for a burnt offering?' (*Gen. 22:7*), to which Abraham replied, 'God will provide for Himself the lamb [שֶׂה, *seh*] for a burnt offering' (*Gen. 22:8*).

Later, on the mountain top, the Angel of the LORD intervened just as 'Abraham stretched out his hand and took the knife to slay his son' (*Gen. 22:10-11*). In Isaac's place, the Lord provided a substitute to be slain as a sacrifice. But it wasn't a lamb (שֶׂה, *seh*); it was a ram (אַיִל, *'ayil; Gen. 22:13*). Was Abraham mistaken about the provision of a lamb? Or are rams and lambs close enough to be interchangeable? In the later sacrificial system, rams and lambs were certainly not close enough to be interchangeable (cf. *Ex. 12:5* for a clear age-restriction on the Passover lamb). Nor did Abraham view his words as mistaken. He had not merely spoken of what he thought God might do; he had prophesied of what God was going to do. And he makes this clear in the name that he gives to the place. 'And Abraham called the name of the place, The-LORD-Will-Provide; as it is said to this day, "In the Mount of the LORD it shall be provided"' (*Gen. 22:14*). For Abraham the ram was only a temporary substitute and sacrifice; the LORD's provision of the true sacrificial Lamb was yet to come.

Some centuries later a lamb once again became of great significance as a substitutionary sacrifice for the descendants of Abraham. The children of Israel were suffering in slavery in Egypt, and the LORD God rose up to deliver them from their bondage. Yet, the mighty God, who would very soon part the waters of the Red Sea so that they could pass through on dry land, and who had just rained the plagues upon the people of Egypt, brought His salvation to the children of Israel, not through a spectacular, dramatic act, but through the death of a lamb. Each believing household (for non-Israelites were invited to believe and receive God's redemption as well) was to take a lamb (שֶׂה, *seh; Ex. 12:3*). The way of redemption from the death which the LORD would send upon the firstborn of every household in Egypt was through killing the lamb and spreading its blood on the doorposts and lintel (*Ex. 12:6-7*). In every household in the land that night there was a death; either the firstborn died, or a lamb died as his substitute, in his place.

But why a lamb? Why not a camel or a pigeon? For this particular sacrifice there could be no alternatives to a male lamb, without spot or blemish, of the first year (*Ex. 12:5*). If a lamb was too much for the household to eat, they were to get together with their neighbours to share the meal together, rather than allow any alternatives to a lamb. Why did it have to be a lamb?

Well, the promise of God's provision of a lamb as saving, substitutionary sacrifice had already been made through Abraham in *Genesis 22*. Believers in Israel were looking forward to God's provision of a lamb for Himself. Therefore, those who had heard and knew God's promise, would understand the significance of the lamb. And there could be no alternatives to the lamb, for this sacrifice was pointing them to God's promise: for it is only the sacrifice of the Lamb of God that can redeem from slavery and bondage. It is only the Lamb of God who can die as a saving substitute for sinners. Like the provision of the substitutionary ram in Moriah, and Abraham's naming of the mountain top, the Passover lamb would point God's people to the true Lamb of God who would be their true Passover, sacrificed for them (*1 Cor. 5:7*).

The Lord's promise of a substitutionary, sacrificial Lamb to come was then re-echoed through the Levitical sacrificial system He established for the children of Israel (*Lev. 1-7, 16*). The prophets looked forward to the coming of the Lamb of God as well. When David sinned with Bathsheba, he asked the LORD to cleanse him with hyssop in his great Psalm of repentance (*Ps 51:7*). David was crying out to the LORD for forgiveness for a sins (murder and adultery) for which there were no sacrifices to offer under the Levitical system. The punishment should have been death (*Num. 35; Lev. 20:10*). And so David says, 'for You do not desire sacrifice, or else I would give it' (*Ps. 51:16*). Instead He appeals for the LORD Himself to 'purge me with hyssop, and I shall be clean' (*Ps 51:7*). But why? Because hyssop points to the atoning blood of the Lamb. At Passover, hyssop was used to spread the blood upon the doorposts and lintel (*Ex. 12:22*). The blood-applying hyssop showed that a lamb had died as as a substitute instead of the firstborn son. And so David appeals to the LORD to apply the blood of the true Substitutionary Lamb as his substitute to atone for his sin. David is trusting in Abraham's prophecy, taught again and again by the sacrifices and feasts, that God would provide for Himself the Lamb.

Right from the beginning of this promise of the Lamb of God, the atonement is always associated with the shedding of the blood of the Lamb. And for Pentecostals and other evangelicals, the blood of the Lamb is right at the heart of their faith and worship. We sing that 'there is power, power, wonder-working power in the blood of the Lamb.'[2] We sing of the 'soul-cleansing blood of the Lamb,'[3] of how 'the blood has never lost its power'[4]

---

[2] *Redemption Hymnal*, 288.
[3] *Redemption Hymnal*, 309.
[4] *Redemption Hymnal*, 329.

and 'shall never lose its power,'[5] and of gaining 'an interest in the Saviour's blood.'[6]

But when we sing of the blood of the Lamb, or when the Bible speaks of Christ's blood, we are not referring to a mystical substance, but to Jesus' blood poured out in death. It is 'without *shedding* of blood [that] there is no remission' (*Heb. 9:22*). So when we speak of the blood, just like when we speak of the cross, what we are really speaking of is the work of Jesus who shed His blood upon the cross in His death for us. As Alan Stibbes concludes, the Bible uses the word 'blood' to 'express the benefits that become ours through Christ's death for us.'[7]

The blood and the cross derive their value from the person who shed His blood upon the cross. Although we frequently use both 'blood' and 'cross' as shorthand ways of referring to the atoning death of Christ (just as the Bible does), we must always remember that it is only because it is Christ's cross and Christ's blood that we are saved by His blood and cross. As Thomas Rees reminds us:

> To us the cross includes the Person of Christ, His atoning work, and His holy precious Blood … In the Redemption and salvation of humanity, we must not, we dare not separate these three: (a) His Person, (b) His Blood, (c) His Atoning work.[8]

He Died For Us

As the Lamb of God who takes away the sin of the world, Christ our Passover died for us. His death 'for us' was both for our benefit and in our place. In order not to narrow our focus to only one aspect of Christ's death for us, let's look at how He died for us as our Prophet, as our Priest, and as our King.

---

[5] *Redemption Hymnal*, 335.

[6] *Redemption Hymnal*, 324.

[7] Alan Stibbes, *His Blood Works: The Meaning of the Word 'Blood' in Scripture*, (Fearn, Ross-shire: Christian Focus, 2011), 73.

[8] Thomas Rees, *Christ Our Life* (Bradford: Puritan Press), 10 -11.

Christ Our Prophet Died For Us

Christ our Prophet reveals to us the will of God for our salvation. Nowhere can this be seen more clearly than at the cross. The Cross of Jesus Christ is the place of love, light and revelation. There on Mount Calvary, the bleeding Lamb makes known to us our Triune God. We'll look more in the next chapter at how Christ in His death on the cross reveals the attributes of God. For now we'll focus on some other aspects of His revelation as our Prophet at the cross.

Theologia Crucis

In His Cross, the Lord Jesus Christ reveals a new way – the true way – of seeing God and understanding the works of God. We call this the *theologia crucis* or *theology of the cross*. The *theology of the cross* says that we can only truly know God through the cross, and so through suffering. Martin Luther contrasted *theologians of the cross* with *theologians of glory*.

> That person does not deserve to be called a theologian who looks upon the invisible things of God as though they were clearly perceptible in those things which have ... happened. He deserves to be called a theologian, however, who comprehends the visible and manifest things of God seen through suffering and the cross. A theology of glory calls evil good and good evil. A theology of the cross calls the thing what it actually is.[9]

Luther says that 'it is not sufficient for anyone, and it does him no good to recognize God in his glory and majesty, unless he recognizes him in the humility and shame of the cross ... true theology and recognition of God are in the crucified Christ.'[10] We cannot look to the dramatic and spectacular and assume that we see the glory of God. Instead we must look to Christ Crucified. For the Lord's blessing is not found in what most impresses human beings, but rather it is found in the cross, where Christ took our curse so that we would be blessed through His suffering and death. We cannot despise the small and weak things, assuming that they are not in God's will, for 'that wisdom which sees the invisible things of God in works

---

[9] Martin Luther, *Heidelberg Disputation*, Theses 19-21.
[10] Martin Luther, *Heidelberg Disputation*, Proof 20.

as perceived by man is completely puffed up, blinded, and hardened.'[11] Instead, looking through the lenses of the cross, we can see the glory of God in suffering and the power of God in weakness. *Theologians of the cross* 'know God hidden in suffering.'[12]

Luther wasn't alone in seeing the need for us to be *theologians of the cross*, rather than *theologians of glory*. The early Apostolics saw it too. D.P. Williams taught that the Cross 'gives new meaning to a sorrowful world' and so only as *theologians of the cross*, looking through the lenses of the cross, can we properly see 'the Divine Will and Purpose.' As *theologians of the cross*, we see that 'the Way of Life is death,' and so that means the only true entrance to the glory of God is through the cross. [13] 'As we rise higher, we sink deeper into His death.'[14] The true power and glory of God are only to be found in the weakness and suffering of the cross, for 'Christ still reigns on the Tree.'[15] True glory is only found when the cross penetrates right through the soul, and true power is always 'power with Blood on it.'[16]

The *theology of the cross* shows us that God is not necessarily always like what we expect Him to be, apart from His own self-revelation in Jesus Christ and Him crucified. It is a *theology of glory* (*theologia gloriae*) which expects God to be found in shows of power and success; the theology of the cross (*theologia crucis*) knows that the foolish-looking message of the cross is really 'the power of God' (*1 Cor. 1:18*). Therefore, through His death on the cross for us, Christ our Prophet shows us the true way of seeing our God and all His works.

The Cry of Dereliction

From the cross, Christ our Prophet spoke the Word of God to us. Every word of His from the cross was the word of God (for He is God the Word). Yet, let's turn our attention to one of His seven last words from the cross where the Incarnate Word quoted the written word of Scripture. As He hung upon the tree of Golgotha, the Lord Jesus cried out, in the words of *Psalm 22:1*, 'My God, My God, why have You forsaken Me?' (*Mt 27:46; Mk 15:34*). But what does Christ our Prophet tell us in these words?

---

[11] Martin Luther, *Heidelberg Disputation*, Thesis 22.
[12] Martin Luther, *Heidelberg Disputation*, Proof 21.
[13] D.P. Williams, *Riches of Grace*, ii.8 (May 1925), 3.
[14] D.P. Williams, *Riches of Grace*, iv.2 (Nov. 1928), 30.
[15] D.P. Williams, *Riches of Grace*, iv.2 (Nov. 1928), 31.
[16] D.P. Williams, *Riches of Grace*, xi.1 (Sept. 1935), 41.

Perhaps it's easier to start with what these words don't mean. The Saviour's cry of dereliction from the cross does not mean that the Trinity was broken or that the Father rejected or completely abandoned the Son. Such ideas completely go against the very identity of God: He is the Father who loves His Son eternally in the unity of the Spirit. It would be impossible to undo the oneness of the Trinity without undoing the very being of God. Such an idea would end up leading to three Gods, and so to the heresy of Tri-theism.

Neither can it mean that the Father abandons the human nature of Christ. If it were possible for the Father to abandon the human nature of Jesus without abandoning the person of the Son, that would separate and divide between a human Christ and a divine Christ. And that is the heresy of Nestorianism.

Jesus' other words from the cross also show us that we can't interpret the cry of dereliction in those ways. He assures the repentant criminal crucified alongside Him that 'today you will be with me in Paradise' (*Lk 23:43*), and before He dies He cried out in a loud voice, 'Father, 'into Your hands I commit My spirit' (*Lk 23:46*). So in committing His spirit to the Father and in telling us that He was going to Paradise, Jesus tells us that He has not been rejected and abandoned by the Father, but is going immediately into His presence. In fact, just a short time before His arrest, Jesus warned His disciples that they were about to be scattered, but 'yet I am not alone, because the Father is with Me' (*Jn 16:32*). The Trinity was not broken on the cross and Christ was not abandoned, for both the Father (*Jn 16:32*) and the Holy Spirit (*Heb. 9:14*) were with Him in His suffering and death for us and for our salvation.

Calvin explains the cry of dereliction like this:

> We do not suggest that God was ever inimical or angry toward him. How could he be angry toward his beloved Son, 'in whom his heart reposed'? How could Christ by his intercession appease the Father toward others, if he were himself hateful to God? This is what we are saying: he bore the weight of divine severity, since he was 'stricken and afflicted' [cf. Isa. 53:5] by God's hand, and experienced all the signs of a wrathful and avenging God … Feeling himself, as it were, forsaken by God, he did not waver in the least from trust in his goodness … Even though he suffered beyond measure, he did not cease to call him his God, by whom he cried out that he had been forsaken.[17]

---

[17] John Calvin, *Institutes*, 2.16.11-12

So, Calvin argues, that it was the weight of His spiritual suffering of the wrath of God in our place, which caused the feeling of forsakenness. Yet, even in feeling forsaken, Jesus knew that He was not abandoned called upon the Father with faith in His goodness. Francis Turretin wrote that Jesus:

> was forsaken by God the Father, though not by a dissolution of the union, nor by withdrawing a participation of holiness, nor by withholding his supporting power, yet ... by suspending the joy and comfort and the sense and fruition of full felicity.[18]

Turretin reminds us that Jesus was always at the right hand of God (*Ps. 110:5*), and explains the feeling of forsakenness as 'a most oppressive sense of God's wrath resting upon him on account of our sins.'[19]

So, in His cry of dereliction, Jesus is telling us that His death is not a death like any other crucifixion. While many martyrs have gone to their death's boldly, Jesus' death is something much more fearful, causing Him to cry out of this feeling of forsakenness and to sweat drops of blood (*Lk 22:44*), all the while declaring His confidence in His God and Father, who He knew to be present with Him at all times, and especially in those moments (*Jn 16:32*).

The Declaration of His Finished Work

From the cross at the moment of His death, Jesus also cried, 'It is Finished' (*Jn 19:30*). Once again, this is not an incidental word, but rather Christ our Prophet declaring to us the salvation of our God. For not only does He declare the end of His sufferings at moment of death, but He also declares the full accomplishment of our salvation. There is nothing for us to add to what Christ has done, for He is our Saviour from first to last, and the entirety of our salvation is found in Him alone. As Calvin put it:

> Now this word, which Christ employs [i.e. 'it is finished'], well deserves our attention; for it shows that the whole accomplishment of our salvation, and all the parts of it, are contained in his death. We have already stated that his resurrection is not separated from his death, but Christ only intends to keep our faith fixed upon himself alone, and not to allow it to turn aside in any direction whatever. The meaning, therefore, is, that every thing which contributes to the salvation of men is to be found in Christ,

---

[18] Francis Turretin, *Institutes*, 2:434
[19] Francis Turretin, *Institutes*, 2:354

and ought not to be sought anywhere else; or – which amounts to the same thing – that the perfection of salvation is contained in him.[20]

That means that we should 'be satisfied with his death alone for salvation', and so Christ our prophet speaks this word to us 'chiefly for the purpose of giving peace and tranquillity to our consciences.'[21]

His Example for us

The apostle Peter tells us that, at the cross, 'Christ also suffered for us, leaving us an example' (*1 Pet. 2:21*). So, from the cross, in His death, our Prophet reveals the will of God to us by giving us His example. Now, this isn't to reduce the atoning death of Christ to a mere example. We are not saved by our attempts to follow in the footsteps of Jesus in imitation of what He did. Peter himself grounds the exemplary nature of Christ's suffering on the cross in the truth that He 'Himself bore our sins in His own body on the tree' (*1 Pet. 2:24*). Yet, without reducing His death to nothing more than an example, we can, secondarily, benefit from the example Christ showed us there (having primarily benefited from the atonement He there made for us).

Peter is not alone in pointing to the example we can receive from Christ's cross. Paul points to Christ crucified as the great model and example for how a husband is to love his wife: 'Husbands, love your wives, just as Christ also loved the church and gave Himself for her, that He might sanctify and cleanse her with the washing of water by the word' (*Eph. 5:25-26*). Writing to the Philippians, Paul points them to the model of Christ's humiliation 'to the point of death, even the death of the cross' (*Phil. 2:8*) as he instructs them to be:

> like-minded, having the same love, being of one accord, of one mind. Let nothing be done through selfish ambition or conceit, but in lowliness of mind let each esteem others better than himself. Let each of you look out not only for his own interests, but also for the interests of others. Let this mind be in you which was also in Christ Jesus (*Phil. 2:2-5*).

The writer to the Hebrews also points to the example we can take from Christ's sufferings when we become weary and discouraged in the face of temptation: 'for consider Him who endured such hostility from sinners

---

[20] John Calvin, *Commentary on the Gospel according to John*, 2:335-336.
[21] John Calvin, *Commentary on the Gospel according to John*, 2: 336.

against Himself, lest you become weary and discouraged in your souls. You have not yet resisted to bloodshed, striving against sin' (*Heb. 2:3-4*).

The Scriptures clearly point to the example we should take from Christ's sufferings in our place. However, the dangerous temptation is to look to Christ as nothing more than an example. Our temptation is to try and follow in the footsteps of the heretic Pelagius, thinking we can save ourselves by our own ability to follow Jesus as a good example. Martin Luther warned strongly against this:

> Be sure, moreover, that you do not make Christ into a Moses, as if Christ did nothing more than teach and provide examples as the other saints do, as if the Gospel were simply a textbook of teachings or laws. Therefore you should grasp Christ, his words, works, and sufferings, in a twofold manner. First as an example that is presented to you, which you should follow and imitate. As St. Peter says in 1 Peter 4, 'Christ suffered for us, thereby leaving us an example.' Thus when you see how he prays, fasts, helps people, and shows them love, so also you should do, both for yourself and for your neighbour. However this is the smallest part of the Gospel, on the basis of which it cannot yet even be called Gospel. For on this level Christ is of no more help to you than some other saint. His life remains his own and does not as yet contribute anything to you. In short this mode does not make Christians but only hypocrites. You must grasp Christ at a much higher level. Even though this higher level has for a long time been the very best, the preaching of it has been something rare. The chief article and foundation of the Gospel is that before you take Christ as an example, you accept and recognize him as a gift, as a present that God has given you and that is your own. This means that when you see or hear of Christ doing or suffering something, you do not doubt that Christ himself, with his deeds and suffering, belongs to you. On this you may depend as surely as if you had done it yourself; indeed as if you were Christ himself. See, this is what it means to have a proper grasp of the Gospel, that is, of the overwhelming goodness of God, which neither prophet, nor apostle, nor angel was ever able fully to express, and which no heart could adequately fathom or marvel at. This is the great fire of the love of God for us, whereby the heart and conscience become happy, secure, and content. This is what preaching the Christian faith means. ... Now when you have Christ as the foundation and chief blessing of your salvation, then the other part follows: that you take him as your example, giving yourself in service to your neighbour just as you see that Christ has given himself for you. See, there faith and love move forward, God's commandment is fulfilled, and a person is happy and fearless to do and to suffer all things. Therefore make note of this, that Christ as a gift nourishes your faith and makes you a Christian. But Christ as an example exercises your works. These do not make you a Christian. Actually they come forth from you because you have already been made a Christian. As widely as a gift differs from an example, so widely does faith differ from works, for faith possesses nothing of its own, only the deeds and life of Christ. Works

have something of your own in them, yet they should not belong to you but to your neighbour.[22]

We are not saved by following Christ's good example. We are saved by what He has done for us through His life, death and resurrection in our place. But once we have received Christ as a gift for salvation, then we can look to Him as our example as we love our neighbours through good works of service.

Christ Our Priest Died For Us

The Sacrificial Lamb is our Great High Priest. In the words of a 7th century hymn writer (from my own country, Northern Ireland), Christ is 'Himself the Victim and Himself the Priest.'[23] Or, as D.P. Williams put it in one of his Welsh hymns:

> Christ's our Lamb and Christ's our Altar,
> Christ's our Merit, He's our All;
> He's our Priest and King of Glory
> He's redeemed us from the Fall.[24]

Our Great High Priest offered Himself up as the atoning Lamb of God on the altar of the cross. Let's look at some of the aspects of His priestly work of dying as our atoning sacrificial Lamb.

The Lamb as Penal Substitute

Pentecostals and other Evangelicals look to Christ crucified as our *penal substitute*, which means that 'Christ in His death took our place in the bearing of the punishment for sin.'[25] Recently, three British evangelical theologians, in defending the doctrine of penal substitutionary atonement

---

[22] Martin Luther, *A Brief Instruction on What to Look For and Expect in the Gospels.*

[23] 'Draw Nigh and Take the Body of the Lord', *Hymns at the Holy Table*, 47.

[24] D.P. Williams, 'Dyma gyfoeth ddaeth i'm henaid', *Molwch Dduw*, 278. Of course, it sounds a million times better in the original Welsh.

[25] *Introducing the Apostolic Church: A Manual of Belief, Practice and History*, 129.

from attacks and caricatures, offered a carefully nuanced definition of the doctrine:

> The doctrine of penal substitution states God gave himself in the person of his Son to suffer instead of us the death, punishment and curse due to fallen humanity as the penalty for sin.[26]

The worship and preaching of the early Pentecostals were full of the doctrine of penal substitution. The Apostolic Church confessed that the Lord Jesus Christ did, 'as our Substitute, by His Atonement, make full reparation and satisfaction to God the Father for the sin of mankind,'[27] and that 'the sins of mankind [were] imputed to the Christ, as the Divine Sacrifice and Substitute for us.'[28] The early Welsh Apostolics sang of Christ on the cross as the 'offering in my place' who 'there paid all our debts in full.'[29] And they sang of how, as 'the Lamb on Calvary's hill … the weight of the faults of the world was upon Him in His agony and blood.'[30] In English, they gladly joined with their Evangelical brothers and sisters to praise our great Penal Substitute, for 'in my place condemned He stood.'[31]

But this was not some new teaching that arose with the dawn of the Pentecostal revival or the rise of the evangelical movement. Although the description of the doctrine as 'penal substitution' might have a more recent origin, the teaching itself can be found throughout the entire history of the Christian church. Sometime during the last two decades of the 1st century (possibly even before the completion of the biblical canon), Clement, an elder of the church in Rome, wrote of the substitutionary death of Christ: 'Because of the love that he had for us, Jesus Christ our Lord, in accordance with God's will, gave his blood for us, and his flesh for our flesh, and his life for our lives.'[32] The second-century *Epistle to Diognetus* speaks even more explicitly of Christ's penal substitution:

> But when our unrighteousness was fulfilled, and it had been made perfectly clear that its wages – punishment and death – were to be expected, then the season arrived during which God had decided to reveal at last his goodness and power (oh, the surpassing kindness and love of

---

[26] Steve Jeffery, Mike Ovey and Andrew Sach, *Pierced for Our Transgressions: Rediscovering the Glory of Penal Substitution*, 21.

[27] *Catechism upon the Tenets of the Apostolic Church*, 3.3.16.

[28] *Catechism upon the Tenets of the Apostolic Church*, 3.3.24.

[29] D.P. Williams, 'Ar ben Moria draw', *Molwch Dduw*, 4.

[30] D.P. Williams, 'Gwelaf Oen ar ben Calfaria', *Molwch Dduw*, 262.

[31] 'Man of Sorrows, what a Name', *Redemption Hymnal*, 170.

[32] *1 Clement* 49:6

God!) ... In his mercy he took upon himself our sins; he himself gave up his own Son as a ransom for us, the holy one for the lawless, the guiltless for the guilty, the just for the unjust, the incorruptible for the corruptible, the immortal for the mortal ... O the sweet exchange, O the incomprehensible work of God, O the unexpected blessings, that the sinfulness of many should be hidden in one righteous person, while the righteousness of one should justify many sinners![33]

In the 4th Century, the great Athanasius wrote in his book *On the Incarnation* of Christ's penal substitutionary work:

> But beyond all this, there was a debt owing which must needs be paid; for, as I said before, all men were due to die. Here, then, is the second reason why the Word dwelt among us, namely that having proved His Godhead by His works, He might offer the sacrifice on behalf of all, surrendering His own temple to death in place of all, to settle man's account with death and free him from the primal transgression ... Death there had to be, and death for all, so that the due of all might be paid. Wherefore, the Word, as I said, being Himself incapable of death, assumed a mortal body, that He might offer it as His own in place of all, and suffering for the sake of all through His union with it, 'might bring to nought him that had the power of death, that is, the devil, and might deliver them who all their lifetime were enslaved by fear of death.'[34]

> Have no fear, then. Now that the common Saviour of all has died on our behalf, we who believe in Christ no longer die, as men died aforetime, in fulfilment of the threat of the law.[35]

> He had come to bear the curse that lay on us; and how could He "become a curse" otherwise than by accepting the accursed death? And that death is the cross.[36]

Athanasius' 5th century successor, Cyril of Alexandria, taught penal substitution very clearly. Commenting on *Isaiah 53:4-6*, Cyril wrote:

> He was stricken because of our transgressions. ... For from of old we had been at enmity with God. ... It was necessary that we should be chastised for our contumacy. ... But this chastisement, which was due to fall on sinners so that they might cease warring with God, descended upon Him.

---

[33] *Diognetus* 9:2, 5

[34] Athanasius, *On the Incarnation*, 20

[35] Athanasius, *On the Incarnation*, 21

[36] Athanasius, *On the Incarnation*, 25

… God delivered Him up because of our sins so that He might release us from the penalty.[37]

In his book *On Worship in Spirit and in Truth*, Cyril explicitly wrote that the death Christ died was the punishment for our sins:

> The Only-Begotten became man … in order that, submitted to the death which threatened us as the punishment for our sins, He might thereby destroy sin and put an end to Satan's incriminations, inasmuch as in the Person of Christ we had paid the penalty owing for our sins.[38]

Cyril's 5th century explanations of penal substitutionary atonement are every bit as precise as those of 21st century evangelicals. Augustine was just as explicit, writing of Jesus 'hanging on the tree as our substitute, bearing our punishment.'[39] Augustine clearly taught that 'Christ, though guiltless, took our punishment that he might cancel our guilt, and do away with our punishment.'[40] Elsewhere he wrote of:

> the one and only Mediator between God and mankind, the man Christ Jesus, who for our sake stooped down to undergo death – that is, the penalty of sin – Himself being without sin. As He alone became the Son of Man in order that we might become through Him sons of God, so He alone, on our behalf, undertook punishment without deserving it, that we through Him might obtain grace without deserving it.[41]

So, the doctrine of penal substitutionary atonement has a long pedigree in Christian theology and worship, from the earliest days of the church to contemporary evangelicalism and Pentecostalism. But what does the Bible say about it?

Jesus on Penal Substitution

The Lord Jesus Christ presented Himself as our penal substitute. Firstly, He very clearly presented His death as substitutionary. In John's Gospel, Jesus

---

[37] Cyril of Alexandria, *In Is. 53.4-6* (ET from J.N.D Kelly, *Early Christian Doctrines*, 3rd ed., 398-9).

[38] Cyril of Alexandria, *De ador. in spir. et verit.*, 3 (ET from Kelly, *Early Christian Doctrines*, 399).

[39] Augustine, *Answer to Faustus, a Manichean*, Book 14.

[40] Augustine, *Answer to Faustus, a Manichean*, Book 14.

[41] Augustine, *Two Letters of the Pelagians*, 4.6 (ET from Michael Bird, *Evangelical Theology*, 408-409).

speaks of Himself as the Good Shepherd who 'gives His life for the sheep' (*Jn 10:11*), emphasising it again a few verses later: 'I lay down My life for the sheep' (*Jn 10:15*). The word translated 'for' in both these verses is ὑπέρ (*huper*). Unlike another New Testament word for 'for' (which we'll see below), ὑπέρ (*huper*) does not necessarily imply substitution. Instead, it often carries the more general meaning of 'on behalf of' or 'for the benefit of,' although it can, in the right context, have a substitutionary meaning: 'instead of' or 'in the place of.' So when Jesus says He lays down His life ὑπέρ (*huper*) His sheep, that could either mean that He lays down His life for their benefit or in their place. We need to look at the context to determine Jesus' meaning here. Jesus is speaking of a wolf who attacks the sheepfold. Either the wolf gets the sheep or it gets the shepherd. So the shepherd does not just lay down his life for the general benefit of his sheep, but in their place: either the sheep die or the shepherd dies. This is substitution.

Jesus makes a similar, yet more specific, statement in Matthew and Mark's Gospels. There He tells His disciples that 'the Son of Man did not come to be served, but to serve, and to give His life a ransom for many' (*Mt 20:28; Mk 10:45*). This time the word for 'for' is not ὑπέρ (*huper*) but ἀντί (*anti*), which does carry the more specific substitutionary meaning of 'instead of' or 'in the place of.' Here Jesus says He has come to give His life as a ransom price in the place of believers. He came to die in our stead and in our place. The death He came to die was a substitutionary death.

Yet here, Jesus presents His death not only as substitutionary, but also as the payment of the penalty for our sins: as a penal substitution. The ransom was the price which had to be paid to set prisoners free. The ransom Jesus pays in our place is the penalty price of sin.

The context of Jesus' 'ransom saying' makes this even clearer. Christ speaks these words as the culmination of a discussion which started with the request for James and John to sit at His right and left hands in glory (*Mt 20:20-21; Mk 35-37*). Jesus' response was to say, 'You do not know what you ask. Are you able to drink the cup that I am about to drink, and be baptized with the baptism that I am baptized with?' (*Mt. 20:22; cf. Mk 10:38*). Jesus would refer to this 'cup' again in his agonising prayer in the Garden of Gethsemane: 'Take this cup away from Me; nevertheless, not what I will, but what You will' (*Mk 14:36*). So the cup which Jesus was about to drink when He had come 'to give His life a ransom for many' was the cup of God's wrath which He bore in His death on the cross (cf. *Ps 75:8; Isa. 51:17;*

Jer. 25:15-16; Hab. 2:16). Jesus died as a ransom for many, by drinking the cup of God's wrath in our place. This is penal substitutionary atonement.[42]

Penal Substitution in the Old Testament

We've already seen the significance of the sacrificial lamb in the Old Testament. In *Genesis 22*, Abraham's trust was in the LORD's provision of a lamb as a substitute. At the Passover, the death of the lamb was very clearly a substitution for the death of the firstborn. Either a son died or a lamb died in his place. When David sinned with Bathsheba and had Uriah murdered, he cried out to the Lord for atonement through the blood of God's Lamb in His place (*Ps. 51:7*).

The Old Testament sacrificial system also teaches this truth of penal substitutionary atonement (*Lev. 1-7*). Through these sacrifices, the children of Israel offered animals as substitutes 'which [would] be judged in their place, that they might be saved.'[43] The sinner laid his hand on the head of the sacrificial animal (*Lev. 1:4; 3:2, 8, 13; 4:4, 15, 24, 29, 33; 8:14, 18, 22; 16:21*) so that it could 'be used vicariously on his behalf to secure God's approval and acceptance.'[44] Right at the centre of the theology of the book of Leviticus, the Word teaches that sinful people 'must seek atonement for sin through substitutionary sacrifice that appeases the wrath of God.'[45] However, the true atoning substitute for the sins of the children of Israel was not the animal laid upon the altar, but the coming death of the Lord Jesus (*Heb. 10:4*).

Leviticus 16 presents the rituals of the Day of Atonement. On that day, two goats were taken, and the High Priest cast lots for them: one to be 'for the LORD' and the other 'for the scapegoat' (*Lev. 16:8*). The goat 'for the LORD' was killed as a 'sin offering, which is for the people' (*Lev. 16:15*).

---

[42] Other relevant words of Christ with regard to penal substitution may include the words of institution at the Last Supper (*Mt 26:26-29; Mk 14:22-25; Lk 22:14-23; 1 Cor. 11:23-26*) and Christ's cry of dereliction from the cross (*Mt 27:46; Mk 15:34*). Michael Bird also suggests the penal substitutionary significance of *Mt 23:37/Lk 13:34*, reading the imagery as that of a hen in a farmyard fire who dies in the place of her chicks who shelter under her wings. Michael F. Bird, *Evangelical Theology* (Grand Rapids: Zondervan, 2013), 404.

[43] James M. Hamilton Jr., *God's Glory in Salvation Through Judgment: A Biblical Theology* (Wheaton: Crossway, 2010), 114.

[44] John W. Kleinig, *Leviticus*, Concordia Commentary, (St Louis: Concordia, 2003), 53.

[45] Hamilton, *God's Glory in Salvation Through Judgment*, 114.

Atonement is made through the death of the goat which stands 'for the LORD.' Glen Scrivener explains this:

> One goat is treated as a scapegoat. The other goat is treated as the LORD! And it's 'the LORD' whose blood is shed. What a fearful dramatization! These two goats will tell us of the work of the LORD Christ on the cross. On the one hand Christ is the scapegoat, taking our sins upon Himself and carrying them away. On the other hand He is the LORD sacrificed in our place. But because He is your sacrifice, therefore He can be your scapegoat.
> …
> When the LORD takes on the role of Scapegoat it's not the oppression of the weak. It's the willing sacrifice of the Strong. The LORD Almighty has *chosen* to become so meek. He stoops to identify with us on every level.[46]

All the iniquities, transgressions and sins of the children of Israel were placed upon the scapegoat (*Lev. 16:21*) who was taken out into the wilderness to die in 'a land of cutting off' (the literal meaning of the 'uninhabited land' of *verse 22*). And so the scapegoat dies, 'bear[ing] on itself all their iniquities' (*Lev. 16:22*). 'The natural reading in this case is that the animal bears the sin and guilt of the people *in their place* and they are thereby released from the burden.'[47] The scapegoat of the Day of Atonement is a penal substitute.

One of the best known, and best loved, Old Testament Scriptures which presents the penal substitutionary death of the Lord Jesus is found in *Isaiah 52:13-53:12*. Here the prophet sets forth the sufferings of the LORD's servant who 'has borne our griefs and carried our sorrows' (*Isa. 53:4*). Isaiah is explicit: 'He was bruised for our iniquities; the chastisement for our peace was upon Him, and by His stripes we are healed … the LORD has laid on Him the iniquity of us all' (*Isa. 53:5-6*). It was not for anything that He had done that He was chastised, but instead it was 'for the transgressions of My people He was stricken' (*Isa. 53:8*). The penal substitutionary language is very clear in *Isaiah 53*. But not only that, this Suffering Servant 'is the only *person* in the Old Testament who is said to "bear" the sins of others.'[48] Yet, this Suffering Servant who takes our place in dying for our sins is also the one who is 'exalted and lifted up and very high' (*Isa. 52:13*). And Isaiah has already told us exactly who that is. It is 'the Lord sitting on a throne, high and lifted up' (*Isa. 6:1*). The Suffering Servant who dies as our penal

---

[46] Glen Scrivener, *The King's English: One Year Edition*, 126. Cf. Cyril of Alexandria, *Letter 41.11-12* (pp.174-175).

[47] Jeffery, Ovey and Sach, *Pierced for Our Transgressions*, 50.

[48] David Peterson, 'Atonement in the Old Testament', *Where Wrath and Mercy Meet: Proclaiming the Atonement Today* (Milton Keynes: Paternoster, 2001), 15.

substitute in *Isaiah 53* is the Lord of Glory of *Isaiah 6*. John brings both of these Scriptures from Isaiah together, to tell us that Isaiah saw Jesus' glory and spoke of Him (*Jn 12:37-41*). Isaiah speaks to us of Jesus, the eternal Word and Son of the Father, who has taken on our humanity in order to die as our penal substitute, bearing our sin and guilt in His death in our place on the cross.

Penal Substitution in the New Testament Writers

We've already looked at what Jesus Himself had to say about penal substitution, so now let's look at what the rest of the New Testament teaches. Firstly we'll look at some passages which clearly teach the substitutionary nature of the atonement, and then we'll turn to some passages which show that this substitution is a penal substitution.

As part of Paul's summary of the gospel for the Corinthians, he tells them that 'Christ died for our sins according to the Scriptures' (*1 Cor. 15:3*). In the LXX (the Greek translation of the Old Testament, used by the earliest Christians), to die for someone's sins means to die 'in consequence of' that person's sins.[49] So if one person (Jesus) dies 'in consequence of' another person's sins (ours), that is a substitutionary death. Here in *1 Corinthians 15:3-4* we 'clearly have a statement that the gospel, consisting of Christ's substitutionary death and his resurrection is primary in Paul's proclamation.'[50]

Another Scripture from Paul's pen which very clearly teaches a substitutionary atonement is found in *Romans 5*:

> For when we were still without strength, in due time Christ died for the ungodly. For scarcely for a righteous man will one die; yet perhaps for a good man someone would even dare to die. But God demonstrates His own love toward us, in that while we were still sinners, Christ died for us. (*Rom. 5:6-8*)

The example Paul takes here is very much a death in someone's place. This death is a 'doom-averting death.'[51] This is death so that someone else won't

---

[49] Simon Gathercole, *Defending Substitution: An Essay on Atonement in Paul* (Grand Rapids: Baker, 2015), 74.

[50] Gathercole, *Defending Substitution*, 78.

[51] C. Eschner, cited in Gathercole, *Defending Substitution*, 107.

die. So this is a substitutionary death. And that, says Paul, is the type of death Christ died for us who were ungodly.

A further account of Jesus' death as substitutionary is found in John's Gospel. There Caiaphas, the High Priest, prophesied about the type of death Jesus would die, without realising that he was prophesying (*Jn 11:49-52*). Caiaphas prophesied that it was 'expedient for us that one man should die for the people, and not that the whole nation should perish' (*Jn 11:50*). John tells us that, by these words, Caiaphas 'prophesied that Jesus would die for the nation, and not for that nation only' (*Jn 11:51-52*). In the context, the chief priests have been talking about the danger of the Romans coming to 'take away both our place and our nation' (*Jn 11:48*). So when Caiphas speaks of Jesus dying 'for' the people, so that the nation wouldn't 'perish', he is talking about Jesus' destruction instead of the destruction of the nation and its people. This is a substitutionary death. Not only does Jesus die for the benefit of the people, but He dies in their place.

So far, these three Scriptures have shown us that the New Testament writers spoke of Jesus' death as substitutionary. But there are other passages which show us that this substitution is a penal substitution. Paul writes: 'For what the law could not do in that it was weak through the flesh, God did by sending His own Son in the likeness of sinful flesh, on account of sin: He condemned sin in the flesh' (*Rom. 8:3*). For N.T. Wright, this is the clearest statement of penal substitution in the New Testament:

> No clearer statement is found in Paul, or indeed anywhere else in all early Christian literature, of the early Christian belief that what happened on the cross was the judicial punishment of sin. … it is clear that Paul intends to say that in Jesus' death the damnation that sin deserved was meted out fully and finally, so that sinners over whose heads that condemnation had hung might be liberated from this threat once and for all.[52]

The reason 'there is therefore now no condemnation to those who are in Christ Jesus' (*Rom. 8:1*) is that sin has been condemned in Christ's flesh (*Rom. 8:3*) through His penal substitutionary death on the cross.

Paul tells the Galatians that 'Christ has redeemed us from the curse of the law, having become a curse for us (for it is written, "Cursed is everyone who hangs on a tree")' (*Gal. 3:13*). In the context, the curse is the punishment due to sinners for their sin (*Gal. 3:10*). Yet, Jesus sets us free from this curse by taking it upon Himself in His death on the cross. So Jesus takes the punishment we were due for our sins, and as a result we are

---

[52] N.T. Wright, 'The Letter to the Romans' in the *New Interpreters Bible*, 10:574-75.

blessed in Him. Jesus bears our curse and instead gives us His blessing. This is the great exchange of the gospel; and at its heart is penal substitution.

Peter also teaches penal substitution, writing that Jesus 'Himself bore our sins in His own body on the tree, that we, having died to sins, might live for righteousness—by whose stripes you were healed.' (*1 Pet. 2:24*). Peter is alluding back to *Isaiah 53*, where we read that 'He bore the sin of many' (*Isa. 53:12*) and 'by His stripes we are healed' (*Isa. 53:5*). The fact that it was 'on the tree' that Jesus bore our sins adds the element of bearing the curse (*cf. Gal. 3:10; Deut. 21:23*). So, Peter is here telling us that Jesus bore our sin, with its punishment and curse, by dying in our place on the cross.

In the next chapter, Peter writes that 'Christ also suffered once for sins, the just for the unjust, that He might bring us to God' (*1 Pet. 3:18*). Here we see Christ's substitutionary death in the fact that the Righteous One (Jesus) dies for the unrighteous (us). And in taking our place, He suffered for our sins. He has borne the penalty the unjust were due, in order to reconcile them to God.

In addition to these Scriptures which present Jesus' death in terms of penal substitution, another biblical concept for understanding Christ's atoning death entails a penal substitution. That concept is *propitiation*, and that's what we'll look at next.

The Lamb and Propitiation

In the parable of the Pharisee and the tax collector, the tax collector 'beat his breast, saying, "God, be merciful to me a sinner!"' (*Lk 18:13*). But his request isn't just for some sort of vague mercy. The tax collector uses the verb ἱλάσκομαι (*hilaskomai*), the verb which speaks of *propitiation*. (The only other time this verb is used in the New Testament is in *Heb. 2:17* where it speaks of Christ's work in making 'propitiation for the sins of the people.') The tax collector is calling out to God for His mercy; but even the verb he uses in asking shows that God's mercy to sinners comes in only one way: through *propitiation*.

Propitiation is not a particularly familiar word. Apart from a few occurrences in the Bible, it's not a word much used in the English language today. Yet it is very significant word, for no other single word in the English language carries the same meaning. So what does *propitiation* mean? Propitiation is a sacrifice which takes away the wrath of God.

The tax collector's prayer for God's mercy through propitiation shows us the necessity of such a sacrifice. Propitiation is necessary because it is the way God shows His mercy to sinners. God's mercy is not merely a vague niceness; it is a concrete mercy given through a sacrifice which bears God's wrath in the sinner's place.

The wrath of God is His holy reaction to sin (*e.g. 2 Thess. 1:6-10*). Ephesians tells us that while we were 'dead in trespasses and sins' (*Eph. 2:1*) we were 'children of wrath' (*Eph. 2:3*). As sinners, our fundamental problem was the wrath of God. It is from God's wrath that sinners need to be saved. Therefore, the great need of sinners is the solution to this problem of God's wrath, and propitiation is that solution. Earlier generations of believers saw this so clearly that, in the second generation of the Reformation, Martin Chemnitz could write: 'Among Christians no one doubts that by this giving of Christ's body and shedding of His blood the wrath of the Father has been satisfied and eternal redemption gained.'[53]

Nowadays, however, the Christian doctrine of propitiation is often misunderstood and confused with pagan notions. The pagan gods were seen as capricious and easily provoked, and so could burst out in vengeful anger. Humans suffering from their anger would have to find something to please the offended gods and offer it up as a sort of bribe or payment to divert their anger. So, pagan appeasement (or 'propitiation') involved man paying the price to escape the anger of the gods.

The biblical doctrine of propitiation, however, is not like that. The Triune God is not a capricious deity, lashing out for mysterious reasons. Instead, He clearly tells us in His Word that His wrath is His consistent response to sin. 'For the wrath of God is revealed from heaven against all ungodliness and unrighteousness of men' (*Rom. 1:18*). Furthermore, He is not looking for a bribe from us to distract Him from His wrath. In fact, He is not looking for us to make a propitiation at all. Completely to the contrary of the pagan idea, the Triune God of Scripture makes the propitiation Himself for us. He is not waiting for human beings to offer up a sacrifice that will take away His wrath; He has come Himself, in the person of the Son, to offer Himself up as our propitiation. It is Christ our Penal Substitute who is our Propitiation.

In fact, the Bible roots our propitiation, not in some sort of capricious anger, but in the love of God. Propitiation is the love of the Triune God in action toward us.

---

[53] Martin Chemnitz, *The Lord's Supper*, 189.

> God is love. In this the love of God was manifested toward us, that God
> has sent His only begotten Son into the world, that we might live through
> Him. In this is love, not that we loved God, but that He loved us and sent
> His Son to be the propitiation for our sins. (*1 Jn 4:8-10*)

Here John describes the overflowing, outgoing love of the Triune God. God
is love, for He is eternally the Father who loves His Son in the unity of the
Spirit. Yet this love within and among the Trinity is not an inward focused
love which keeps to itself at the exclusion of others. It is an outgoing love
which draws others into the loving relationship between the Father and His
Son in the Spirit. Therefore, the love of God has been manifested to us, so
that we might be drawn into His life of love. John tells us that this love was
manifested in the sending of the Well Beloved Son into the world for us, and
then goes on to specify that this love is found in His work as 'the
propitiation for our sins.' The love of God for us is defined in terms of
Christ's work of propitiation.

Therefore, the love of propitiation is rooted in the fact that God is love.
It is rooted in the very identity of the Triune God. Propitiation is rooted in
the eternal, loving communion of Father, Son and Holy Spirit. And seeing
this helps guard us from mistaken caricatures of the doctrines of penal
substitution and propitiation. For when we see that propitiation is rooted in
the Triune love, we see that it is neither a case of a loving Jesus intervening
for us to secure salvation from a begrudging Father, nor is it a loving Father
who forces His Son to play an unwilling role in our salvation. Quite the
contrary. As God eternally exists as Father, Son, and Holy Spirit in continual
loving fellowship, so then it's through that mutual love that our salvation is
procured.

The Father, Son and Holy Spirit are united in the loving work of
sending Jesus as the propitiation for our sins. Propitiation is not just the love
of one person of the Godhead, but the love of the entire Trinity. Therefore,
Grace of propitiation is not 'God's Riches At Christ's Expense' (as though
Jesus were merely a victim), but rather, it is the willing grace and love of
Jesus who 'has loved us and given Himself for us, an offering and sacrifice
to God for a sweet-smelling aroma' (*Eph. 5:2; cf. Jn 10:17-18*). It is not a
matter of a vicious and violent God who takes out His anger on Jesus, as an
innocent by-stander. Rather, it is rather a loving God who Himself comes
and bears His own wrath in the person of the Son. As John Stott put it: 'God
took his own loving initiative to appease His own righteous anger by

bearing it in his own self in his own Son when He took our place and died for us.'[54]

When John writes of the manifestation of the love of the Trinity, he links it with both the coming of the Son into the world (*i.e.* the Incarnation) and the propitiation of the cross. This tight connection between propitiation and incarnation is also highlighted by the writer to the Hebrews, who tells us that propitiation was the purpose of the incarnation.

> Inasmuch then as the children have partaken of flesh and blood, He Himself likewise shared in the same … Therefore, in all things He had to be made like His brethren, that He might be a merciful and faithful High Priest in things pertaining to God, to make propitiation for the sins of the people. (*Heb. 2:14, 17*)

In the context, the writer to the Hebrews tells us that the Son became incarnate to 'destroy him who had the power of death, that is the devil' (*Heb. 2:14*) and to 'release those who through fear of death were all their lifetime subject to bondage' (*Heb. 2:15*). But the word 'therefore' in *verse 17* shows us that these are not set as equal purposes of the incarnation with propitiation. Rather, the destruction of the devil and the release of those in bondage come through the propitiation rendered by Christ on the cross. Christ's work of propitiation – of offering Himself up in our place as a sacrifice to save us from the wrath of God by bearing for us – is the reason why 'in all things He had to be made like His brethren' (*Heb. 2:17*).[55] In this light, the *Heidelberg Catechism* looks to Christ's propitiatory sacrifice as the reason He must be both true man and true God:

> *Why must He be a true and righteous man?*
> Because the justice of God requires that the same human nature which has sinned should make satisfaction for sin; but one who is himself a sinner cannot satisfy for others.
>
> *Why must He also be true God?*
> That by the power of His Godhead He might bear in His manhood the burden of God's wrath, and so obtain for and restore to us righteousness and life.[56]

---

[54] John Stott, *The Cross of Christ*, 175.
[55] Cf. *Catechism upon the Tenets of the Apostolic Church*, 3.1.30.
[56] *Heidelberg Catechism*, 16-17; cf. *Catechism upon the Tenets of the Apostolic Church*, 3.6.9, and *Holwyddoreg*, viii.7 for the same teaching in Apostolic catechisms.

So this propitiatory work, for which the eternal Word and Son of the Father took to Himself our humanity in the incarnation is at the very heart of what He accomplished through His self-offering on the Cross. Paul demonstrates the centrality of propitiation to Christ's atoning work in *Romans 3*:

> being justified freely by His grace through the redemption that is in Christ Jesus, whom God set forth as a propitiation by His blood, through faith, to demonstrate His righteousness, because in His forbearance God had passed over the sins that were previously committed, to demonstrate at the present time His righteousness, that He might be just and the justifier of the one who has faith in Jesus. (*Rom. 3:24-26*)

We are justified through Christ's redemption, which is achieved through the propitiation in His blood. Our salvation rests ultimately upon Christ's work of propitiation. God is shown to be both just and the justifier of sinners through Christ's work of propitiation. This is how a just God can forgive sins justly: because He has borne the wrath for sin Himself in the person of the Son as a propitiatory sacrifice on the cross of Calvary. God's forgiveness of sin does not bypass His justice, but rather, like the tax-collector of the parable, we receive God's mercy through propitiation, and so in a just way, for Christ has taken the just punishment for sin in our place. We are justified in Christ because Christ is our propitiation. Therefore, propitiation is the very heart of Christ's atoning work in His death on the cross.[57]

This central place for propitiation in the doctrine of the atonement is very important to Apostolics. Before the English version of the Tenets, the Welsh confession of faith of the Apostolic Church spoke specifically of 'the propitiation' rather than the more general statement of 'atoning death.'[58] The earliest Welsh Apostolic confession of faith was that 'the Father, in His infinite mercy and love, has sent His Only-Begotten Son into the world to be

---

[57] The word used for propitiation in *Rom. 3:25* is the word used in the Septuagint (the Greek translation of the Old Testament used by the early Christians) for the 'mercy seat', the covering of the Ark of the Covenant. This was the place where the blood was sprinkled by the High Priest on the Day of Atonement. Therefore, Jesus is the place where propitiation happens. To borrow a phrase from Donald Fairbairn: 'Christ is the priest, the sacrifice, and the altar. He is thus the means, the content, and the locus of salvation.'

[58] In part this is due to a particularity of the English language: other languages don't have a general word equivalent to 'atonement' with which to speak of Christ's work, and so rely on more specific words which speak of what Christ accomplished in His death. So, for example, the French, Italian, and German Tenets of the Apostolic Church all rely on words related to expiation (the taking-away of sin), speaking respectively of 'mort expiatoire,' 'morte espiatoria,' and 'sühnender Tod am Kreuz.'

the Propitiation … on the altar of Calvary.'[59] The first Welsh children's catechism of the Apostolic Church asked 'What sort of death was the death of Jesus?' and the answer was 'A propitiatory death. He died for, or in the place of, mankind.'[60]

Biblically, the centrality and prominence of Christ's work of propitiation is not only for the past (when He accomplished it on Calvary), but also for the present; for His propitiation is the subject of His abiding heavenly intercession.

> My little children, these things I write to you, so that you may not sin. And if anyone sins, we have an Advocate with the Father, Jesus Christ the righteous. And He Himself is the propitiation for our sins, and not for ours only but also for the whole world. (*1 Jn 2:1-2*)

John is writing to believers here. So he is teaching us as believers that when we sin, we should come to the Lord Jesus Christ, our Advocate, and He will intercede on our behalf with His Father on the basis of His work of propitiation. When we sin, we do not have to fall back under the wrath of God, for we may confess our sins, trusting in Christ who bore the wrath for us. Jesus is, and always will be, the propitiation for our sins.

Our problem was the wrath of God. But the Father, in His great love, provided a propitiation to free us from His wrath by sending His Son to die in our place. The Son, in His great love made the propitiation for our sins in His willing self-offering on the cross for us. There He was, and now He is, and shall continue to be throughout all eternity, the Propitiation for our sins. It was through the Holy Spirit (*Heb. 9:14*), in His great love, that the Incarnate Son offered Himself up as our propitiation, and now the Holy Spirit, in His great love, applies the propitiation of Christ to us, by giving us faith and uniting us to Jesus, our Propitiation.

---

[59] *Athrawiaethau Sylfeinol*, iii. (Original Welsh: 'Y Tad, o'i anfeidrol dosturi, a'i gariad, wedi danfon Ei unig-anedig Fab i'r byd i fod yn Iawn … ar allor Calfaria.')

[60] *Holwyddoreg*, viii.1. (Original Welsh: 'Sut farwolarth oedd marwolaeth Iesu? Marwolaeth iawnol. Efe a fu farw dros, neu yn lle'r ddynoliaeth.')

The Lamb and Redemption

What does Redemption mean?

Redemption is a more familiar word than propitiation, but it is not quite as familiar for us today as would have been to people when the Bible was written. For we think of redemption as a Christian word. It's a word which we sing in church and read in the Scriptures, but it's not a word which we use much in everyday life. However, in biblical times, redemption wasn't a theological word at all. It was a word drawn from everyday life, because it was a word at home in a commercial setting. Redemption is all about paying a price to set something (or someone) free.

In the Græco-Roman world of the New Testament, there were two particularly significant and prominent situations in which redemption came into play. The first was in warfare. After a victory, the winning side would gather up the survivors from the enemy army and take them back as slaves. Yet, sometimes when they got their captives back home, they discovered that a few of them made rubbish slaves, because they'd never done any work for themselves in their lives. So they must have been rather important people back in their own homeland. So, rather than keep them around with no use, the winning side would offer them back to their own people, if they could redeem them by paying a ransom price. In British history we have an example of a similar thing. King Richard I, the Lionheart, was on his way back to England from the crusades when he was captured by the Duke of Austria and the Holy Roman Emperor and held for ransom (which is why Prince John and the Sheriff of Nottingham were able to cause so much trouble for Robin Hood). He was only set free when the ransom price was paid that the captive king was set free. He was redeemed by the payment of (a very high) price. So redemption was a way of setting captives free, by paying a ransom price.

The other prominent situation where you would find a redemption in the Græco-Roman world was the setting free of slaves. A slave could save up money to buy his freedom, and when he had enough, he would take the money to a temple where he'd pay it to the priests (who would then pay the money to the slave's master). Then it was said that whoever the god of the temple was had redeemed the slave. So redemption was a way of setting slaves free from their bondage, by paying a price.

Old Testament Redemption

Of course, the Græco-Roman world wasn't the only background to the New Testament teaching on redemption. It was already a theme in the Old Testament. Every Israelite family was familiar with redemption, because all firstborn sons in Israel had to be redeemed (*Ex. 13:11-16: Ex. 34:19-20*). Every firstborn animal was to be either killed or redeemed with a lamb offered in its place, but every firstborn son had to be redeemed. A substitute – the lamb – died in the place of the son as the price of his redemption. Every firstborn son in Israel was redeemed by the blood of a lamb.

Another way in which Israelite families would have been familiar with the concept of redemption was through the kinsman redeemer, of which we see a very clear example in the book of Ruth. Boaz was the kinsman redeemer to Naomi and Ruth. These relatives were in a bad situation and needed someone to rescue them. Boaz, as their kinsman redeemer, came to the rescue. In this case it involved both paying the price to buy their land and marrying Ruth, the widow, and allowing the first child of this marriage to be legally regarded as the son of Ruth's dead husband, to carry on his name. Although this is cultural far removed from us, the marriage and the inheritance could be regarded by Old Testament Israelites as an even greater price to pay than the money for the land: just remember the closer kinsman who would have been willing to buy the land, but wasn't willing to pay the price in terms of marriage and inheritance (*Ruth 4:1-6*). So in this case, a kinsman redeemer came to the rescue by paying a price that involved giving himself in marriage, giving over his inheritance, and paying the cost of the estate.[61]

However, the most important redemption in the Old Testament was not the redemption paid by a kinsman redeemer or the redemption of the firstborn sons. The most important redemption in the Old Testament was the LORD's redemption of His people. Throughout the Old Testament we see the LORD as the Redeemer of Israel, but the LORD's identity as Israel's Redeemer is rooted in the Passover and Exodus (*2 Sam. 7:21-24*). The LORD sent Moses to tell the Israelites, 'I am the LORD; I will bring you out from under the burdens of the Egyptians, I will rescue you from their bondage, and I will redeem you with an outstretched arm and with great judgments'

---

[61] There were other situations in which the kinsman redeemer would be required to act in different ways.

(*Ex. 6:6*). After they crossed the Red Sea on dry ground, Moses and the children of Israel sang:

> You stretched out Your right hand;
> The earth swallowed them.
> You in Your mercy have led forth
> The people whom You have redeemed;
> You have guided them in Your strength
> To Your holy habitation. (*Ex. 15:12-13*)

From then on, the Exodus becomes the great model of God's redemption, so much so that even Jesus redeeming work on the cross is spoken of by Moses and Elijah on the mount of Transfiguration as 'his exodus' (ἔξοδος; *Lk 9:31*).

And, as with all redemption, the LORD's redemption of Israel from bondage involved the payment of a price. But what was the price? The LORD did not pay money to Pharaoh to grant the freedom of his slaves. So how did He pay a price to redeem them?

The answer is that they were not merely being redeemed from slavery to Pharaoh, but redeemed from their slavery to sin. Joshua tells us that the Israelites served foreign gods in Egypt (*Josh. 24:14*). The LORD spoke of the plagues upon Egypt, especially the final plague – the death of the firstborn – as His execution of judgment 'against all the gods of Egypt' (*Ex. 12:12; cf. Num. 33:4*). The LORD poured out His judgment upon the land of Egypt on the night of the Passover and so in every household there was a death. Either the firstborn died or a lamb died in his place. This judgement upon the gods of Egypt and upon the sin of all the people who lived in the land of Egypt was the price which was paid to redeem the children of Israel, and all the mixed multitude (*Ex. 12:38*) who joined them in trusting in the blood of the lamb. As the LORD had promised, He redeemed them 'with an outstretched arm and with great judgments' (*Ex. 6:6*). For those who were redeemed, the price was paid by a substitutionary lamb in their place. But of course, 'it is not possible that the blood of bulls and goats [or lambs] could take away sins' (*Heb. 10:4*). But Jesus Christ, the Lamb of God, is the true Passover Lamb (*1 Cor. 5:7*) and so the true Redeemer of the children of Israel from their bondage and sin (*Jude 5*).

Yet even before the exodus, the Son had been redeeming individuals from evil. When Joseph brought his two sons to Jacob to receive his blessing, Jacob made the sign of the cross over them (*Gen. 48:13-14*) and said:

> God, before whom my fathers Abraham and Isaac walked,
> The God who has fed me all my life long to this day,
> The Angel who has redeemed me from all evil,
> Bless the lads. (*Gen. 48:15-16*)

It is the Angel of the LORD, the Angel who is God sent from God, who redeemed Jacob from all evil. As we have seen in chapter 2, the Angel of the LORD who is the LORD is God the Son. Therefore Jacob is looking to (the pre-incarnate) Jesus as the redeemer from all evil and the source of all blessing.

Why do we need to be redeemed?

Like the prisoners of war or the slaves of the Græco-Roman world, and like the children of Israel in Egypt, we need redemption because we are in captivity and bondage. But unlike Pharaoh's slavery or the war-winner's captivity, the bondage from which we need to be set free is not a physical one, but a spiritual bondage. For Jesus taught that the Son had come to set free those who were slaves to sin (*Jn 8:31-36*). As we have seen in chapter 8, utter depravity is this slavery to sin (*Rom. 6:20; 2 Pet. 2:19*). Born in Adam, all mankind are born dead in trespasses and sins and thus under the enslaving power of sin, without any power to set ourselves free. Instead we need someone else to pay the price for our freedom from this bondage and captivity. We need a redeemer.

How Are We Redeemed?: The Ransom Price

If to redemption is setting free through the payment of a price, then what is the price of our redemption? Jesus said that He came 'to give His life a ransom for many' (*Mt 20:28; Mk 10:45*). Jesus paid the ransom price by laying down His life in our place on the cross. Therefore, Paul tells the Ephesian elders that God has purchased the Church 'with His own blood' (*Acts 20:28*). At another time he would echo these words in writing to the Ephesians, telling them that, in Christ, 'we have redemption in His blood' (*Eph. 1:7*). The Incarnate God has paid our ransom in His own blood, which He shed for us.

How can His blood pay our ransom? It is not because His blood is a valuable object which He uses like money. Rather, it is because of what His blood means. The shedding of His blood speaks of His substitutionary death in our place. Paul tells the Romans of 'the redemption that is in Christ Jesus, whom God set forth as a propitiation by His blood' (*Rom. 3:24-25*). The ransom price of Christ's blood speaks of His work of propitiation; it is through His bearing of the wrath of God in our place that He redeems us. It is through bearing our curse that Christ 'has redeemed us from the curse of the law' (*Gal. 3:13*).

Redemption and the Christian Life

Redemption results in freedom. Those who were in slavery and bondage to sin are set free through Christ's redemptive work in shedding His blood for us on the cross. And this freedom has an impact upon the life of the redeemed. It is knowledge of the price paid for our redemption that leads to holiness in conduct (*1 Pet. 1:13-21*).

Redemption and the Future

But the ransom paid by Jesus Christ through His atoning death in our place does not only have an impact upon our lives in the here and now. Redemption is also connected to the future. Now the redeemed know freedom for lives of holiness, but then they will know the ultimate freedom of the fullness of redemption in the resurrection of the dead. Jesus associated the coming of redemption with His return 'in a cloud with power and great glory' (*Lk 21:27-28*). Paul too looks forward to Jesus' return, when we will experience 'the redemption of our body' (*Rom. 8:23*) through resurrection from the dead. Until then, the Holy Spirit seals us 'for the day of redemption' (*Eph. 4:30*). In Revelation, the heavenly host sing the praises of the Lamb who has 'redeemed us to God by [His] blood' and associates the outcome of this redemption with the saints future reign upon the earth with Christ the King. The ultimate fullness of the redemption which Christ has purchased for us with His precious blood in His death in our place upon the cross will only be realised on that last day when the dead in Christ will rise.

Reconciliation

The Scriptures tell us that believers have been 'reconciled to God through the death of His Son' (*Rom. 5:10*). Reconciliation speaks of the restoration of a good relationship. The first sin changed relationships. It changed the relationship between human beings and animals, the relationship between man and woman, and the relationship between humans and God (*Gen. 3:8-24*). As a result of their first sin, Adam and Eve were exiled from the Garden of Eden, the place of the Lord's presence and of their good relationship with Him (*Gen. 3:22-24*). Now cherubim with 'a flaming sword' were set 'to guard the way to the tree of life' (*Gen. 3:24*), demonstrating just how serious and permanent was the break in the good relationship between man and God brought about through sin.

The prophet Habakkuk tells us that God is 'of purer eyes than to behold evil, and cannot look on wickedness' (*Hab. 1:13*). Therefore it is impossible for sinners to come into God's presence. However, that doesn't mean that people want to come into God's presence but God stops them. No: sinful man does not seek God's presence (*Rom. 3:11*). Sinful man is opposed to a good relationship with God. Rather, there is enmity from man to God (*Rom. 8:7*), and both Paul and James tell us that sinful human beings are 'enemies' of God (*Rom. 5:10; Col. 1:21-22; Jas 4:4*). Sinful man is in rebellion and revolt against the Lord God.

Yet, the loving God of peace acts to put an end to this hostility. In Eden, He came to find Adam and Eve and walk with them in the Garden (*Gen. 3:8-9*). The Triune God is the God who acts to bring peace and end hostility. He acts so that we can stop being His enemies. This is reconciliation. And He has accomplished this reconciliation through the death of Jesus upon the cross.

Although reconciliation is a concept familiar to us from human relationships, there is a significant difference between the reconciliation involved in human relationships and the reconciliation of the cross. In human relationships both sides need to be involved in the work of reconciliation. However, at the cross, the Triune God has done everything for our reconciliation.

Reconciliation is Objective

Reconciliation is not something new which happens each time someone is saved. Reconciliation is something that has happened once and for all in the past. It is not a subjective change now, but rather something which God has done for us in history. And we receive what God has already accomplished for us when we receive Christ through faith.

This objective work of reconciliation was accomplished at the cross. God has reconciled us to Himself through Christ's atoning death (*Rom. 5:10-11*). So our reconciliation was accomplished 2000 years ago on hill outside Jerusalem. To the Corinthians, Paul writes:

> Now all things are of God, who has reconciled us to Himself through Jesus Christ, and has given us the ministry of reconciliation, that is, that God was in Christ reconciling the world to Himself, not imputing their trespasses to them, and has committed to us the word of reconciliation … For He made Him who knew no sin to be sin for us, that we might become the righteousness of God in Him. (*2 Cor. 5:18-19, 21*)

Reconciliation is not a mere commercial transaction which God looks upon from afar. 'God was in Christ reconciling the world to Himself.' In Jesus, God Himself has come to accomplish our reconciliation. And He does this by not imputing our sins to us, but instead by bearing them Himself in the person of the Son in His death for us. He has 'made peace through the blood of His cross' and that is the great work of reconciliation (*Col. 1:20-22; cf Eph. 2:15-16*).

These Scriptures, which show us that reconciliation is achieved at the cross, underline the fact that it is God, not us, who acts to reconcile us. And it is in Christ, through His sacrifice on the cross, that God has done this. Therefore, reconciliation is not fundamentally a change in human attitudes towards God. Rather, reconciliation is an objective event which God has accomplished for our salvation.

Reconciliation and the Love of God

The first mention of reconciliation in the New Testament shows us that reconciliation flows from the love of the Triune God. Paul writes to the Romans:

> But God demonstrates His own love toward us, in that while we were still sinners, Christ died for us. Much more then, having now been justified by His blood, we shall be saved from wrath through Him. For if when we were enemies we were reconciled to God through the death of His Son, much more, having been reconciled, we shall be saved by His life. And not only that, but we also rejoice in God through our Lord Jesus Christ, through whom we have now received the reconciliation. (*Rom. 5:8-11*)

Out of His great love, and as a demonstration of that love, the Father sent His Son to die for us and so reconcile us to Him. By His death on the cross, Jesus has removed the barrier between God and us (*i.e.* our sin and God's wrath) and so now we can enjoy a good relationship with God. That is reconciliation.

The Reconciliation Must Be Received

Yet God's loving work of reconciliation does not mean that everyone now automatically has a good relationship with God as a result of the cross. Rather, to enjoy the objective reconciliation Christ accomplished for us at the cross, we must receive the reconciliation (*Rom. 5:11*). God has objectively accomplished our reconciliation in Christ at the cross. Now we receive that (already accomplished) reconciliation through faith in Jesus Christ. We see this same pattern in *2 Corinthians*:

> God was in Christ reconciling the world to Himself, not imputing their trespasses to them, and has committed to us the word of reconciliation. Now then, we are ambassadors for Christ, as though God were pleading through us: we implore you on Christ's behalf, be reconciled to God. (*2 Cor. 5:19-20*)

The Triune God has done everything that's needed to reconcile us to Himself, and He offers this reconciliation as a gift. People are simply invited to receive this gift of reconciliation which God so freely offers. Therefore, the task of Christ's ambassadors is to tell people what God has done for them in the cross of Jesus Christ, and to invite them to receive for themselves that wonderful gift of reconciliation which flows from Christ's cross.

The Results of Reconciliation

In reconciling us to Himself, God brings an end to the state of hostility that existed between us and Him because of our sinfulness. Through the sacrificial death of Jesus Christ, our sin and God's wrath (the things which formed the barrier between us and God) have been dealt with and removed, and so now, instead of hostility, we have peace (*Rom. 5:1; Col. 1:20*).

The biblical concept of peace is much greater than our typical 21st century western idea. We tend to think of peace as the absence of war or conflict. But in the Bible it's that plus much more. The biblical idea of peace (or *shalom*) speaks not only of a ceasefire, but of the presence of the full and rich blessing of God. The biblical image of peace is not a white flag, but rather a summer's day on the terrace, where 'everyone will sit under his vine and under his fig tree, and no one shall make them afraid' (*Micah 4:4; cf. Zech. 3:10*). This is the opposite of the curse of *Genesis 3*, and indeed the Scriptures tell us that 'the God of peace will crush Satan under your feet shortly' (*Rom. 16:20*). Such peace can only be found in Jesus Christ (*Eph. 2:14*), the atoning Lamb who is our reconciliation.

So, this peace is not merely a state of mind. Rather, it's being in a good relationship with God through the blood of Jesus Christ, and enjoying the fullness of God's blessing in Jesus (*Eph. 1:3*). It is the opposite of the old hostility. Those who have received the reconciliation which is in Christ Jesus are no longer enemies of God. Now they enjoy God's favour through His grace in Jesus. By union with Christ, the reconciled enjoy communion with the Triune God, and so may enjoy His presence and His love (*Rom. 5:8*).

Christ Our King Died For Us

Christ our King rescues us from the kingdom of darkness, brings us into the kingdom of His love, and defeats all His and our enemies. And this great rescue and conquest takes place through His death on the cross.

The Victory of the Lamb (Christus Victor)

The first announcement of the gospel in the Scriptures tells us of a conqueror who would come to defeat our enemy (*Gen. 3:15*). Jesus is the mighty conqueror who destroys the dragon and crushes the serpent's head. And when Christ the King conquers, His people enter into the enjoyment of the victory He has won for them (*Rom. 16:20*; cf. how the Israelite's entered into the enjoyment of the victory one by one man – the Lord's anointed – on their behalf when David slew Goliath: *1 Sam. 17:52-54*).

'For this purpose the Son of God was manifested, that He might destroy the works of the devil' (*1 Jn 3:8*). The eternal Word and Son of the Father has come into this world and entered into our humanity in order to conquer the devil and all his works. It is for this reason that he shared in the same flesh and blood as us (*Heb. 2:14*) and made 'propitiation for the sins of the people' (*Heb. 2:17*). Therefore His victory is rooted in His work of propitiation and His substitutionary death in our place on the cross, bearing the wrath of God which was the penalty due our sin. It is because Christ is our Penal Substitute that He is our *Christus Victor*. And in 'destroy[ing] him who had the power of death, that is, the devil' (*Heb. 2:14*) Christ has 'release[d] those who through fear of death were all their lifetime subject to bondage' (*Heb. 2:15*). Through His victory He has set His people free, rescuing them from the kingdom of bondage and bringing them into the freedom of His kingdom of love. As Paul writes to the Galatians, Jesus 'gave Himself for our sins, that He might deliver us from this present evil age, according to the will of our God and Father' (*Gal. 1:4*).

This is how 'death is swallowed up in victory' (*1 Cor. 15:54*; cf. *Isa. 25:8*). Paul explains that 'the sting of death is sin, and the strength of sin is the law' (*1 Cor. 15:56*). So it is only through dealing with the demands of the law against sin that death can be swallowed up in victory. But this is exactly what Jesus has done for us in His death in our place on the cross, where He 'wiped out the handwriting of requirements that was against us, which was contrary to us. And He has taken it out of the way, having nailed it to the cross' (*Col. 2:14*). And in that act, Christ not only defeated death, but 'disarmed principalities and powers, He made a public spectacle of them, triumphing over them in it' (*Col. 2:15*). On the Cross, Christ our King conquered for us. The cross, which looked to the world like a defeat, was in reality the place of His great victory.

> By weakness and defeat,
> He won a glorious crown,
> Trod all our foes beneath His feet,
> By being trodden down.
>
> He Satan's power laid low;
> Made sin, He sin o'erthrew,
> Bowed to the grave, destroyed it so,
> And death, by dying, slew.
>
> Bless, bless the Conqueror slain,
> Slain in His victory;
> Who lived, who died, who lives again—
> For thee, His Church, for thee![62]

Through the gospel of His death and resurrection for us, 'our Saviour Jesus Christ … has abolished death and brought life and immortality to light' (*2 Tim. 1:10*). The King of Life has won the victory over death, and one day we will see the final outcome of that victory when 'there shall be no more death' (*Rev. 21:4*). Cyril of Alexandria wrote:

> When He shed His blood for us, Jesus Christ destroyed death and corruptibility. … For if He had not died for us, we should not have been saved; and if He had not gone down among the dead, death's cruel empire would never have been shattered.[63]

Or, in the words of Martin Luther, sung with such joy each Easter all over the world:

> It was a strange and dreadful strife
> When Life and death contended;
> The victory remained with Life,
> The reign of death was ended.
> Holy Scripture plainly saith
> That death is swallowed up by death,
> Is sting is lost forever. Alleluia![64]

---

[62] Samuel L. Gandy, 'His be the Victor's Name.'
[63] Cyril of Alexandria, *Glaph. In Exod.* 2 – (ET in Kelly, Early Christian Doctrines, 397-8).
[64] Martin Luther, 'Christ Jesus Lay in Death's Strong Bands'.

The Lamb at the Centre of the Throne

Not only has Christ our King been crucified for us, concuering death by His death, but now the crucified Lamb sits enthroned above. Twice in Revelation we are told that the Lamb who was slain is in the centre of the throne (*Rev. 5:6; 7:17*). Not only is our crucified, victorious King seated upon the throne of heaven, but it is precisely as the slain lamb – as our sacrifice – that He reigns. At the very centre of God's rule and authority, there is the slain Lamb who lives. And so, all the rule and power of God are exercised through the crucified One who sits at His right hand (the place of God's power and glory). The slain Lamb at the centre of the throne shows us that the sovereign rule and reign of the Triune God is cruciform. We cannot look to earthly ideas of power, kingship and authority and assume that we can reason up from them to the nature of God's kingship and authority, as if it were merely quantatively greater. The Lamb at the centre of the throne demonstrates that God's kingship and authority are of a qualitatively different form than those of earthly powers. Rather, the God of heaven and earth exercises His power and authority in a cross-shaped way. The royal glory of the High King of Heaven is revealed (and exercised) through the bleeding sacrificial Lamb of God who takes away the sins of the world.

Chapter 16

The Atoning Death of Christ: We Died In Him

At the cross, one of the Trinity suffered in the flesh. Jesus Christ, our incarnate God, died for us. But not only did Jesus die for us, we died in Him.

> Christ did not bear our sins in his body to simply settle a score in our stead any more than we die to sin by merely emulating his example of self-mortification. Our incarnate Saviour did not suffer a death that has no intrinsic relation to us or bearing upon us. Rather, he died for us to mediate the saving benefits of his death to us as we share in his vicarious humanity. Christ did not die to exempt sinners from dying themselves; his death saves us from sin precisely because it kills our sinful self![1]

Paul ties together Christ's death for us with our death in Him in an inseparable way, writing to the Corinthians that 'if One died for all, then all died' (2 Cor. 5:14).

> There [i.e. 2 Cor. 5:14] the apostle, it is obvious, uses these two expressions interchangeably: He died for all, and all died in Him. He describes the same thing from two different points of view. The first of the two describes the vicarious death of Christ as an objective fact; the second sets forth the same great transaction, in terms which intimate that we too are said to have done it. Thus we may either say, Christ died for us; or say, we died in Him. We may equally affirm He was crucified for us, or we were co-crucified with Him. This alternating phraseology, duly observed, makes all plain. But it must be fully apprehended that we have not two acts presented to us by the expression, — one on Christ's side, and another on ours, that is, an experience on our side parallel to His. We have but one public representative, corporate act performed by the Son of God, in which we share as truly as if we had accomplished that atonement ourselves.[2]

Our death in Him is not some later experience in the Christian life, to be added on to what we have received through His death for us. All those who are trusting in Christ's substitutionary death in their place have also died in

---

[1] John C. Clark & Marcus Peter Johnson, *The Incarnation of God: The Mystery of the Gospel as the Foundation of Evangelical Theology*, (Wheaton: Crossway, 2015), 147.

[2] George Smeaton, *The Apostles' Doctrine of the Atonement* (Edinburgh: Banner of Truth, 1991; originally published 1870), 162.

Him. This is how Jesus saves: by taking us safely through death and out the other side into resurrection life. In the words of Cyril of Alexandria, 'He who did not know death descended into death alongside us through his own flesh so that we too might rise up with him to life.'[3]

Representation and Substitution

Christ is our Substitute: the one who died in our place. So, if Jesus died instead of us, how can we have died in Him? How could Jesus both die instead of us and with us? Think of Adam. When Adam sinned in the Garden, He sinned in our place. In one sense, Adam was our sinning substitute: because He sinned in our place, we are born sinful and under the judgment of death. Yet, Adam was our substitute because he was our head. We sinned in Adam, because he was our federal (covenant) head, who represented us before God; and we sinned in Adam, because he was our natural head: all of his descendants were unitedly present in him when he sinned.[4] So, Adam, the head of the old humanity, sinned both as our substitute, and as our representative at the same time. He sinned for us, and we sinned in him.

And the Scriptures love to show us the parallel between the first and last Adams. Just as Adam's sin is the source of our sin and death, Christ's life and death is the source of our forgiveness and life (*Rom. 5:12-21*). Just as Adam could not only sin in our place, but we could also sin in him, so too with Christ and His death. Christ died in our place, and we died in Him. Christ our Head is both our Substitute and our Representative. His is an inclusive place-taking: He takes our place, yet we are included in what He does.[5]

This inclusive place-taking is significant for the doctrine of penal substitution; for it means that the imputation of our sin to Christ rests upon His union with us. Critics of penal substitution object to the transfer of guilt and sin from one person to another. However, if we are united to Christ in His substitutionary death, then He bears our sin and guilt, because of our

---

[3] Cyril of Alexandria, *To the Monks of Egypt*.

[4] On federalism, realism, and the transmission of sin, see chapter 8.

[5] D.P. Williams wrote of this inclusive place-taking as 'our death … with Him as Substitute.' *Riches of Grace*, xv.6 (July 1940), 61.

union, and so it is not an arbitrary transfer. The great Oxford Puritan, John Owen, explained it like this:

> When he is punished, they [those who are saved] also are punished [in Him]: for in this point of view the ... head and those represented by him are not considered as distinct, but as one; for although they are not one in respect of personal unity, they are, however, one, – that is, one body in mystical union, yea, *one mystical Christ*; – namely, the surety is the head, those represented by him the members; and when the head is punished, the members also are punished.[6]

The Head and the members are so united that when the Head is punished, the members are punished in Him. So, believers are united to Christ in such a way, that when Christ died for our sins on the cross, we died in Him.

The Scriptures on Our Death in Christ

It is particularly in the epistles of Paul that we find the Scriptural teaching on our death in Christ. Perhaps the best known passage on the theme is found in *Romans 6*.

> What shall we say then? Shall we continue in sin that grace may abound? Certainly not! How shall we who died to sin live any longer in it? Or do you not know that as many of us as were baptized into Christ Jesus were baptized into His death? Therefore we were buried with Him through baptism into death, that just as Christ was raised from the dead by the glory of the Father, even so we also should walk in newness of life. For if we have been united together in the likeness of His death, certainly we also shall be in the likeness of His resurrection, knowing this, that our old man was crucified with Him, that the body of sin might be done away with, that we should no longer be slaves of sin. For he who has died has been freed from sin. (*Rom. 6:1-7; cf. Col. 2:11-12*)

Here Paul shows us the connection between our baptism and our union with Christ in His death. We are 'baptized into His death' and 'united together in the likeness of His death', not as something new now, but rather because 'our old man was crucified with Him.' 'We share the grave of our

---

[6] John Owen, *A Dissertation on Divine Justice, Works of John Owen*, 10:598.

incarnate Substitute because we participate in his death.'[7] It is through this co-crucifixion with Christ that we are freed from sin and its slavery. Christ's work of propitiation as our penal substitute has freed us from the penalty of sin, for He bore it in our place, but through our death in Him (our co-crucifixion with Him) we are also freed from the power of sin. Because we have died with Christ, 'the sin that still dwells in the flesh, is mortified and deprived of its vigour.'[8] Paul doesn't mean that believers no longer commit sinful deeds (*cf. 1 Jn 1:8*), but rather our relationship to sin has changed.

> Formerly, death reigned (5:17) and sin reigned in death (5:21). But when 'we were baptized into Christ Jesus' (... 6:3), our relationship to sin was thereby altered. We are now no longer slaves to sin. As a result of this liberation from the mastery of sin, we are enabled to battle what once enslaved us.[9]

Paul goes on to tell us that the declaration that we have died in Christ is powerful for the ongoing Christian life. 'Likewise you also, reckon yourselves to be dead indeed to sin, but alive to God in Christ Jesus our Lord. Therefore do not let sin reign in your mortal body, that you should obey it in its lusts' (*Rom. 6:11-12*). The 'therefore' connects our reckoning of ourselves as dead to sin (through co-crucifixion with Christ) with our not letting sin reign in our bodies. Because we know that in dying in Christ we have died to sin, we need not cede to sin's attempts to ensnare us once again under its slavery. Gerhard put it like this:

> Since you are dead to sin, therefore you should not permit sin to have dominion. Just as natural death does not have dominion over Christ, so also the spiritual death of sin should not have dominion over you.[10]

In the next chapter, Paul shows that, through our death in Christ, we have not only died to sin, but died to the law (*Rom. 7:1-6*). Our union with Christ in His death and resurrection has changed our relationship to the law of God. While once the law aroused our sinful passions (*Rom. 7:5*) and thus stood over us to accuse and reveal our guilt, now through our death in Christ, we have died to the mastery of the law. No longer do its accusations determine our lives; instead our lives are determined by the Lord in whom

---

[7] Clark and Johnson, *The Incarnation of God*, 147.

[8] Johann Gerhard, *Annotations on the First Six Chapters of St Paul's Epistle to the Romans* (Jena: Steinmann, 1645; English Translation: Malone: Repristination Press, 2014), 257.

[9] Michael P. Middendorf, *Romans 1-8*, Concordia Commentary (St Louis: CPH, 2013), 464.

[10] Gerhard, *Annotations on the First Six Chapters of St Paul's Epistle to the Romans*, 262.

we have died and whom we now serve in the freedom of the Spirit (*Rom. 7:6*).

Again in Galatians, Paul makes a connection between our death in Christ and the law:

> For I through the law died to the law that I might live to God. I have been crucified with Christ; it is no longer I who live, but Christ lives in me; and the life which I now live in the flesh I live by faith in the Son of God, who loved me and gave Himself for me. (*Gal. 2:19-20*)

It is in our co-crucifixion with Christ that we have died to the law. As Calvin explains, 'the law carries within itself the curse which slays us. Hence it follows, that the death which is brought on by the law is truly deadly.'[11] Yet, by death-union with Christ, we have died to the law and hence to its stinging curse.

> Ingrafted into the death of Christ, we derive from it a secret energy, as the twig does from the root ... Being then crucified with him, we are freed from all the curse and guilt of the law. He who endeavours to set aside that deliverance makes void the cross of Christ. But let us remember, that we are delivered from the yoke of the law, only by becoming one with Christ, as the twig draws its sap from the root, only by growing into one nature.[12]

Not only have we died to the law in Christ's death, but also we have died to ourselves. For 'it is no longer I who live, but Christ lives in me' (*Gal. 2:20*). Luther writes that this means:

> We must look away from our own person. Christ and my conscience must become one, so that I can see nothing else but Christ crucified and raised from the dead for me. If I keep on looking at myself, I am gone. If we lose sight of Christ and begin to consider our past, we simply go to pieces. We must turn our eyes to the brazen serpent, Christ crucified, and believe with all our heart that He is our righteousness and our life. For Christ, on whom our eyes are fixed, in whom we live, who lives in us, is Lord over Law, sin, death, and all evil ... Since Christ is now living in me, He abolishes the Law, condemns sin, and destroys death in me. These foes vanish in His presence. Christ abiding in me drives out every evil. This union with Christ delivers ... and separates me from my sinful self. As long as I abide in Christ, nothing can hurt me ... Faith connects you so intimately with Christ, that He and you become as it were one person. As such you may

---

[11] John Calvin, *Commentaries on the Epistle to the Galatians*, 73.
[12] John Calvin, *Commentaries on the Epistle to the Galatians*, 74.

boldly say: 'I am now one with Christ. Therefore Christ's righteousness, victory, and life are mine.'[13]

Calvin agrees with Luther, writing that, the Christian who has died in Christ:

> Does not live by his own life, but is animated by the secret power of Christ; so that Christ may be said to live and grow in him; for, as the soul enlivens the body, so Christ imparts life to his members. It is a remarkable sentiment, that believers live out of themselves, that is, they live in Christ; which can only be accomplished by holding real and actual communication with him.[14]

Therefore, as we have died in Christ and it is He who now lives in us, the Apostolics taught that 'at the Cross we find the death and end of the old nature, not only of its bad qualities, but of its supposed good qualities also.'[15] Our crucifixion with Christ means that we cannot rely on ourselves for anything good, 'for [we] died, and [our] life is hidden with Christ in God' (*Col. 3:3*). But hidden in Christ, through 'the death of the Cross, we are transformed to the life of the Spirit and brought into unity with God.'[16] Through our co-crucifixion, 'God can deal with us internally, namely with the old Adamic nature, and bring us into vital union with the Risen Christ, who is the Life Eternal.'[17]

Through our union with Him in His death, 'those who are Christ's have crucified the flesh with its passions and desires' (*Gal. 5:24*). The mortification of sin in our lives is not our independent work, but flows from our co-crucifixion with Jesus. Therefore, Christ's cross is our only boast, for 'in the cross of our Lord Jesus Christ … the world has been crucified to me, and I to the world' (*Gal. 6:14; cf. Col. 2:20*).

> As little as a crucified person receives the world and the world in turn receives him, so little do I care for what the world holds in high regard, for I have died to the world. That which the world loves is a cross and an opponent to me, as, for example, the lust of the flesh, the lust of the eyes, pride-filled living. That which the world regards as a cross is dear to me, as, for example, persecution and adversity and the like.[18]

---

[13] Martin Luther, *Commentary on Galatians* (Grand Rapids: Zondervan, 1939), 77.
[14] John Calvin, *Commentaries on the Epistle to the Galatians*, 74.
[15] D.P. Williams, *Riches of Grace*, i.11 (Dec. 1920), 27.
[16] D.P. Williams, *Riches of Grace*, i.11 (Dec. 1920), 28.
[17] D.P. Williams, *Riches of Grace*, i.11 (Dec. 1920), 27.
[18] Johann Gerhard, *Schola Pietatis*, 1:73-74.

Recapitulation

Adam, the natural and covenant head of the human race, sinned for us and we sinned in him. But Jesus Christ has come as a second Adam and a new head. And that was always the plan: the first Adam was always intended to point us to the last Adam. The first Adam was created in the Image, as the image of the Image, a sketch to be filled out by the coming of the true Image Himself. Through His incarnation and atonement, Jesus takes us out from under Adam's headship, and unites us instead to Himself as our heavenly Head. He takes on Adam's fate, and gives us a new destiny in our new Head. And so, 'as in Adam all die, even so in Christ all shall be made alive' (*1 Cor. 15:22*). The early church had a word for this. They called it a re-heading-up, or *recapitulation*. Where Adam our head failed, Christ came to undo his failure and give a new beginning to a new humanity under His headship. The word *recapitulation* is usually associated with Irenaeus, but the teaching wasn't just limited to one man. In fact, the Greek word is even found in the New Testament in describing the eternal purpose of the Triune God 'that in the dispensation of the fullness of the times He might gather together in one all things in Christ, both which are in heaven and which are on earth — in Him' (*Eph. 1:10*). Let's have a quick look at what Irenaeus and some later teachers of recapitulation, Athanasius and Cyril of Alexandria, had to say about our death in Christ which takes us out of Adam's headship, and brings us under the headship of Jesus.

For Irenaeus this re-heading-up of humanity in the Incarnate Son was essential so that He could 'kill sin and destroy death and give life to humankind,' with the result that 'sin would be put to death by humanity, and humanity would escape from death.'[19] This was why He became incarnate, so that 'He recapitulated in Himself His own handiwork.'[20]

> He has therefore, in His work of recapitulation, summed up all things ... in order that, as our species went down to death through a vanquished man, so we may ascend to life through a victorious one; and as through a man death received the palm [of victory] against us, so again by a man we may receive the palm against death.[21]

---

[19] Irenaeus, *Against Heresies*, 3.18.7

[20] Irenaeus, *Against Heresies*, 3.22.1

[21] Irenaeus, *Against Heresies*, 5.21.1

Our first head, Adam, had taken us down into his sin and death, and so in His recapitulation, Jesus lifts us up to life by taking us down into His own death and then up into His victorious resurrection. In His recapitulation, we have died and risen in Him. As Athanasius explained:

> He surrendered His body to death in place of all, and offered it to the Father. This He did out of sheer love for us, so that in His death all might die, and the law of death thereby be abolished.[22]

Because our head has died in our place, Athanasius says, we have died in His death, and therefore we are free from the power of death through the death of our Living Head. Cyril of Alexandria puts it like this:

> Now, however, the one who was pictured dimly long ago, the true lamb, the spotless sacrifice, is led to the slaughter for all, to drive away the sin of the world, to overturn the destroyer of the world, to abolish death by dying for all, to undo the curse that is against us … The lamb is to become the second Adam, not from the earth, but from heaven, and to become the source of all good for human nature, the deliverance from imported corruption, the bestower of eternal life, the basis for [theosis], the source of all piety and righteousness and the road to the kingdom of heaven. For one lamb 'died for all,' rescuing the entire flock on earth for God the Father – one for all, that he might subject all to God, one for all, that he might gain all … When we were in many sins and therefore deserved death and decay, the Father gave his Son as a ransom for us, one for all, since all are in him, and he is greater than all. One died that all may live in him. Death swallowed up the lamb for all and vomited forth all in him and with him since we were all in Christ who died and was raised for us and on our behalf.[23]

Christ died for us and rescued us, says Cyril, because we all died in Him. As Cyril understands the Scriptures, you can't separate Christ's death for us from our death in Him. Our Substitute's place-taking is an inclusive place-taking. And so penal substitution and recapitulation can sit comfortably together as complementary ways of speaking of the atoning work of Christ. Christ was able to re-head us up in Him by bearing the wrath of God for us in our place.

---

[22] Athanasius, *On the Incarnation*, 8
[23] Cyril of Alexandria, *In Io.*, 2.Intro. (ET 1:76; comments on *Jn 1:29*).

Salvation Through Judgment

The salvation of the Triune God is not a salvation that avoids judgment, but rather a salvation through judgment. How were Noah and his family saved? Not by being zapped to a tropical island while the rest of the world was judged, but by being carried safely through the judgment in the Ark, and out the other side into a new and abundant life. How were the Israelites saved from slavery in Egypt? Not by being zapped into the Promised Land and suddenly finding themselves each under his own vine and under his own fig tree, but by being safely sheltered under the blood through the judgment of the death of the firstborn, and then carried safely through the Red Sea, where Pharaoh's armies were judged, and the conquest of Canaan, where God's judgment fell upon the peoples of the land. And so it has always been; the true and living God saves by carrying His people safely through the judgment and out on the other side into newness of life.

And that is exactly what has taken place at the cross. On Calvary's tree, Jesus bore the judgment in our place. Yet, He didn't bear it independently of us, at a distance from us. No; we died in Him. So in Him, we have passed safely through God's judgment. And in Him we are raised up to newness of life on the other side. He is our Ark and our Lamb in whom we shelter from the cup of God's wrath; and yet, hidden in Him, we have drunk it to the dregs (*Mk 10:39*).

Sin entails the judgment of death (*Gen. 2:17*). And because God is both just and loving, He cannot withhold the judgment for sin. However, as Thomas Torrance writes, in Christ 'God actually takes upon himself the sentence of rejection and bears it instead of mankind,' yet this:

> Does not mean in the slightest degree a mitigation of divine judgment, but the very reverse, the complete and entire fulfilment of the divine judgment – and therefore the vicarious act of God in the life and death of Christ is man's complete and total exposure as guilty and a complete and total judgement. The cross is the utter condemnation of men and women. But when God took that condemnation upon himself, then his action was entirely the positive action of his mercy and will to be on humanity's side, a positive action to accept humanity.[24]

---

[24] Thomas F. Torrance, *Atonement*, 155-156.

In other words, the fullness of God's judgment has been poured out upon us in our death with Christ, and yet, because we are sheltered in Him, we experience that outpouring of judgment as pure mercy and acceptance. We have died in Him, and in that death He has carried us safely down through the judgment and up again into resurrection life.

Peter writes that 'the time has come for judgment to begin at the house of God; and if it begins with us first, what will be the end of those who do not obey the gospel of God?' (*1 Pet. 4:17*). God's judgment does not skip His people, but begins first in His Temple. Christ is the true Temple of God (*Jn 2:21*), and we are God's Temple in Christ and filled with His Spirit (*Eph. 2:21-22*). The judgment has begun in God's Temple, by being poured out upon Christ in His atoning death. And united to Christ we are the house of God in Him and have died with Him in His death. In Him, the judgment has begun with us first. But blessed are those who have passed through the judgment in Him, as the House of God, sheltered in His death. We need not wait in fear for the judgment to come, for we have already gone through it in its fullness in our co-crucifixion with Christ. 'The way to the Life Eternal is the way of death' but those who have died with Him, have already passed through death in Him, and so 'with Him we shall live.'[25]

We Live Through Death in Him

God's 'basic principle' is 'life out of death.' And so 'it is a matter of impossibility to be begotten into Eternal Life without being buried into His death, and it must be *His* death … For in our union with Him in His death, the fulness of His Life will work in us and manifest itself through us.'[26] Therefore, 'the roots of the Church must be deep in His death.'[27]

Back in the fourth century, Gregory of Nazianzus expressed this truth:

> We needed an Incarnate God, a God put to death, that we might live. We were put to death together with Him, that we might be cleansed; we rose

---

[25] D.P. Williams, *Riches of Grace*, i.11 (Dec. 1920), 29.
[26] D.P. Williams, *Riches of Grace*, xi.4 (March 1936), 307-308.
[27] D.P. Williams, *Riches of Grace*, xi.4 (March 1936), 309.

again with Him because we were put to death with Him; we were glorified with Him, because we rose again with Him.[28]

Over twelve-hundred years later, the same truth would come from the pen of Richard Sibbes, writing that the:

> Whole Christ mystical was crucified, and whole Christ mystical is risen again, even though the crucifying was confined to Christ the head, not the members ... this crucifying belonged to the head, and the head rose. Yet all believers – whole Christ – as soon as they are one with Christ by reason of the mystical union, are dead and crucified in Christ their head, and they are risen and sit in heavenly places, in Christ their head. So a true believer, when he is made one with Christ, reasons: 'My corruption of nature, this natural pride of heart and enmity of goodness, is crucified, and I in my head am now risen and sit in heaven ... And because the members must conform to the head, I must die to sin more and more, be crucified to sin, and rise by the Spirit of Christ and ascend with him. The more I know and meditate upon this, the more I am transformed into the likeness of his death and resurrection.'[29]

At the same time, in Germany, Johann Gerhard was writing:

> The reason Christ allowed Himself to be crucified was so that our old man (our sinful flesh) would be crucified with Him at the same time ... Christ wanted to be buried so that we might, in a spiritual manner, be buried with Him ... Consequently, see to it that you do not again try to search [the old man] out and violate the status of Christ's grave and rip it open again.[30]

Our salvation, our life, and our victory over sin all flow from our co-crucifixion with Christ. It is because we have died in Him that we shall live.

---

[28] Gregory of Nazianzus, *Oration 45.28*
[29] Richard Sibbes, *Glorious Freedom*, 116-117.
[30] Johann Gerhard, *Schola Pietatis*, 73; cf. 69.

Chapter 17

The Resurrection

Gospel & History

When Paul sums up the gospel in *1 Corinthians 15*, He does not stop with Christ's atoning death. Rather, the apostle's summary of the gospel, the message which he taught as of first importance, is 'that Christ died for our sins according to the Scriptures, and that He was buried, and that He rose again the third day according to the Scriptures' (*1 Cor 15:3-4*). Christ's triumphant resurrection from the dead is of central importance to the gospel message and thus to the Christian faith.

The Resurrection and the Historical Grounding of the Christian Faith

Christianity is a faith grounded in history. And the resurrection of Jesus Christ is the key historical event on which our faith stands. For the earliest Christian preachers in the Acts of the Apostles, the resurrection of Jesus Christ is the chief apologetic of the gospel. Christianity is not a philosophy or way of life that makes sense apart from its historical claims, for, as the apostle Paul tells us, 'if Christ is not risen, your faith is futile; you are still in your sins' (*1 Cor. 15:17*). Thomas Torrance writes:

> If the resurrection is not an event in history, a happening within the same order of reality as we belong to, then atonement and redemption are empty vanities, for they achieve nothing for historical men and women in this world. Unless the atonement through the resurrection breaks into and is real in our historical and physical existence, and continues to be valid as saving power in our earthly and temporal being, it is ultimately a mockery … [and] quite irrelevant to men and women of flesh and blood and [has] no message to offer them in their actual existence … the denial of a genuine resurrection is meaningless and without relevance to the ongoing

life of the world. Everything depends on the resurrection of the body, otherwise all we have is a ghost for a saviour.[1]

We are not saved by a timeless principle; we are saved by the historical Saviour, the Incarnate God and His historical work for us in His life, death and resurrection. Christian salvation rests on historical events in Nazareth, Bethlehem, Galilee, Judea and Jerusalem.

The Empty Cross and the Empty Tomb Belong Together

The Risen Lord is the Lamb who was slain (*Rev. 5:6*). The triumphant resurrection of Jesus Christ cannot by separated from His atoning death on the cross, for it is precisely 'from the dead' that He has risen (*Mt 28:7; Rom. 1:4; 1 Cor. 15:20; 1 Pet. 1:3*). Without His death there could be no resurrection. And without His resurrection, His death would give us no hope. 'If Christ is not risen, then our preaching is empty and your faith is also empty … if Christ is not risen your faith is futile; you are still in your sins!' (*1 Cor. 15:14, 17*). The death and resurrection of Christ go together, and cannot be separated. As Calvin put it:

> Whenever mention is made of his death alone, we are to understand at the same time what belongs to his resurrection. Also, the same … applies to the word 'resurrection': whenever it is mentioned separately from death, we are to understand it as including what has to do especially with his death.[2]

What Happened when Christ was Raised?

Each of the four Gospels records the fact that Jesus rose from the dead after His death on the cross. None of the Gospels records the resurrection itself; rather, like the disciples, we discover the fact of Christ's resurrection through first encountering the empty tomb (*Mt 28:6; Mk 16:6; Lk 24:3; Jn 20:1-8*) and then the Risen Lord. The Lord Jesus Christ, who had been crucified, who had been dead and buried, was no longer in the grave; He is alive.

---

[1] T.F. Torrance, *Atonement*, 244-245.
[2] John Calvin, *Institutes of the Christian Religion*, 2.16.13

Paul writes that Christ is the 'firstfruits' of the dead (*Rom. 5:20, 23*). Yet, in the Bible, we have accounts of people miraculously coming back to life before the resurrection of Christ. Jesus Himself raised three people from the dead (*Lk 7:11-17; Mt 9:18-26; Mk 5:22-24, 35-43; Lk 8:40-42, 49-56; Jn 11*), as had Elijah (*1 Kgs 17:17-24*) and Elisha (*2 Kgs 4:18-37*; and even Elisha's dead bones in *2 Kgs 13:21*). So if Christ was not the first person to come back to life, how could He be the firstfruits? The answer is that there was a difference between Christ's resurrection and these previous restorations to life. Lazarus, the widow of Nain's son, Jairus' daughter, and the others were restored to life, only eventually to die again someday. However, 'Christ, having been raised from the dead, dies no more. Death no longer has dominion over Him' (*Rom. 6:9*). Thus, Christ's resurrection was much more than simply a temporary restoration to life.[3]

Who Raised Jesus from the Dead?

The Bible tells us that God the Father raised Jesus from the dead. Paul writes that 'Christ was raised from the dead by the glory of the Father' (*Rom. 6:4*; see also *1 Cor 6:14; Gal 1:1; Eph 1:20*). On the day of Pentecost, Peter preached of Christ 'whom God raised up, having loosed the pains of death, because it was not possible that He should be held by it' (*Acts 2:24*).

Yet the Bible also clearly tells us that Jesus participated in His own resurrection. Jesus Himself declared:

> Therefore My Father loves Me, because I lay down My life that I may take it again. No one takes it from Me, but I lay it down of Myself. I have power to lay it down, and I have power to take it again. This command I have received from My Father. (*Jn 10:17-18*)

Similarly, after having cleansed the Temple, He said 'Destroy this temple, and in three days I will raise it up... But He was speaking of the temple of His body' (*Jn 2:19, 21*). In both of these instances, Christ clearly points to His own role in His resurrection.

Although it is not explicitly stated that the Holy Spirit was involved in Christ's resurrection, we do find a strong hint of the Spirit's role in *Romans 8:11*: 'But if the Spirit of Him who raised Jesus from the dead dwells in you, He who raised Christ from the dead will also give life to your mortal bodies

---

[3] This is not to deny the incredibly miraculous nature of the raising of Lazarus & co. I simply wish to emphasize that Christ's resurrection was even more incredible and miraculous.

through His Spirit who dwells in you.' Furthermore, in His resurrection, Christ was 'justified in the Spirit' (*1 Tim. 3:16*). Just as we see the action of each of the three persons of the Trinity in other great works of God (e.g. Creation, Atonement, Salvation, Baptism in the Holy Spirit, the Body of Christ), the Father, Son and Holy Spirit were all involved in Christ's Resurrection, for the external works of the Trinity are undivided.[4]

The Nature of Christ's Resurrection Body

Two facts emerge very clearly from the Gospel accounts of Christ's resurrection appearances. Firstly, there was a clear continuity between Christ's body before His death and His body after His resurrection. Secondly, His body was not exactly the same after His resurrection as it had been before His death.

We know that there was continuity between the body that hung on the Cross and Christ's resurrection body, as the tomb was empty after the resurrection. Not only that, but Jesus could show the marks in His hands and side from the nails and the spear (*Jn 20:20*). Thus Christ's resurrection was a physical, bodily resurrection. After all, He had 'flesh and bones' (*Lk 24:39*) and when the disciples 'gave Him a piece of a broiled fish and some honeycomb ... He took it and ate in their presence' (*Lk 24:42-43*).

Yet we also see in the Gospel accounts some degree of difference between Christ's body before and after His resurrection. People did not always recognise Him, so it would seem that His appearance was not exactly the same as it had been before His death. Evidently His appearance had not completely changed, for people did recognize Him at other times. Some people have tried to explain this by saying that, in His resurrection body, He could change appearance, but this is mere conjecture; it is not the clear teaching of Scripture. When the two disciples recognized Jesus in Emmaus, we are told that it was because 'their eyes were opened' (*Lk 24:31*), not because Jesus changed appearance. A more preferable solution, based on the biblical evidence, is that Christ's body had changed appearance at the resurrection, because His body was transformed to a state of perfection. Thus the effects of hardship and suffering on His body would have been eliminated, changing His appearance somewhat. The Bible does indeed teach us that our resurrection bodies (of which Christ is the firstfruits) will

---

[4] *Opera trinitatis ad extra indivsa sunt.* See above, chapter 5.

be 'incorruptible' (*1 Cor. 15:52*). This means that weakness, sickness, and suffering will no longer be possible (not to mention death).

According to the Scriptures: The Old Testament and Christ's Resurrection

When Paul summarises the gospel for the Corinthians, he writes that Jesus' resurrection from the dead on the third day was 'according to the Scriptures' (*1 Cor. 15:4*). Jesus, likewise, on the day of His resurrection, told the two disciples on the road to Emmaus that 'the prophets have spoken' concerning how He would 'suffer these things and … enter into His glory' (*Lk 24:25-27*). The resurrection of Jesus Christ, therefore, was not a New Testament surprise, but rather, it was deeply rooted in the Old Testament Scriptures. Let's briefly examine some of the Old Testament teaching on Jesus' resurrection.

'That He Rose Again … According to the Scriptures'

Both Peter (*Acts 2:25-38*) and Paul (*Acts 13:34-37*) refer to *Psalm 16* in their preaching on the resurrection of Christ.

> I have set the Lord always before me;
> Because He is at my right hand I shall not be moved.
> Therefore my heart is glad, and my glory rejoices;
> My flesh also will rest in hope.
> For You will not leave my soul in Sheol,
> Nor will You allow Your Holy One to see corruption.
> You will show me the path of life;
> In Your presence is fullness of joy;
> At Your right hand are pleasures forevermore. (*Ps 16:8-11*)

On the Day of Pentecost, Peter explained that David could not be referring to himself in this Psalm as 'he is both dead and buried, and his tomb is with us to this day' (*Acts 2:29*). Instead, David was prophesying of Jesus, and so 'spoke concerning the resurrection of the Christ, that His soul was not left in Hades, nor did His flesh see corruption' (*Acts 2:31*). Likewise, Paul preached that 'David, after he had served his own generation by the will of God, fell asleep, was buried with his fathers, and saw corruption; but He whom God raised up saw no corruption' (*Acts 13:36-37*). The Bible emphatically tells us, therefore, that *Psalm 16* speaks of the resurrection of Jesus Christ. So, a thousand years before it happened, David sang of Christ's rising from the dead.

The prophet Isaiah also spoke of Christ's resurrection. In the middle of one of the most outstanding Old Testament prophecies of the atoning death of Christ, Isaiah tell us:

> Yet it pleased the Lord to bruise Him;
> He has put Him to grief.
> When You make His soul an offering for sin,
> He shall see His seed, He shall prolong His days,
> And the pleasure of the Lord shall prosper in His hand. (*Isa. 53:10*)

The expression 'to prolong one's days' occurs quite frequently in the Old Testament and refers to the extension of earthly life. But here it refers to the Suffering Servant who has died. It is the one was has been bruised, put to grief, made an offering for sin; the one who has been 'smitten by God, and afflicted' (*Isa. 53:4*), 'led like a lamb to the slaughter' (*Isa. 53:7*), 'cut off from the land of the living' (*Isa. 53:8*). The one who will prolong His days is the one for whom 'they made His grave with the wicked – but with the rich at His death' (*Isa. 53:9*). So the one of whom Isaiah speaks in *Isaiah 53:10* is one who has very definitely died, but now, after death, His earthly life will be prolonged and 'He shall see His seed.' This is resurrection from the dead. Over 700 years before the birth of Jesus, the prophet Isaiah wrote of His resurrection from the dead.

'The Third Day according to the Scriptures'

Yet Paul specifies that it was on 'the third day' that Christ rose 'according to the Scriptures.' Where in the Old Testament do we find the connection between the resurrection of Jesus Christ and the third day?

We're introduced to the significance of the third day in the very first chapter of the Bible. In the description of the six days of creation in Genesis 1, more attention is given over to the third day (*Gen. 1:9-13*) than any other day apart from the sixth, the day that mankind was created. And why does the third day get so much attention in *Genesis 1*? Because of seeds. Jesus would later draw our attention to how seeds have been created to give us a demonstration of death and resurrection: 'Most assuredly, I say to you, unless a grain of wheat falls into the ground and dies, it remains alone; but if it dies, it produces much grain' (*Jn 12:24*). So the third day is the day of seeds, which go through death and out the other side into life in anticipation of the death and resurrection of Jesus Christ, and the abundant fruit which comes from His resurrection life. Michael Reeves sums it up like this:

> There on the third day of Genesis 1 we see the first fruits of creation (as Christ, raised on the third day, would be the first fruits of the *new* creation, of resurrection from the dead). These first fruits each reproduce 'according to their kinds' because they have seed – the next generation – *within* them. Thus *what happens to the fruit happens to the seed*. So it is, says Paul, with Adam and Christ. They are the firstfruits of two very different crops: one of death, the other of life. All others are but seed in one of those fruits.[5]

The third day is a day of seeds, with their death and resurrection, and of firstfruits, with their crop that will ultimately follow on.

When He formed the children of Israel into His covenant people, the Lord showed them that the third day was a day of the appearing of the Lord to declare His salvation. On the 'third day' He appeared to the people on Mount Sinai:

> Then the Lord said to Moses, 'Go to the people and consecrate them today and tomorrow, and let them wash their clothes. And let them be ready for the third day. For on the third day the Lord will come down upon Mount Sinai in the sight of all the people … Then it came to pass on the third day, in the morning, that there were thunderings and lightnings, and a thick cloud on the mountain; and the sound of the trumpet was very loud, so that all the people who were in the camp trembled. And Moses brought the people out of the camp to meet with God, and they stood at the foot of the mountain. Now Mount Sinai was completely in smoke, because the Lord descended upon it in fire. Its smoke ascended like the smoke of a furnace, and the whole mountain quaked greatly. And when the blast of the trumpet sounded long and became louder and louder, Moses spoke, and God answered him by voice. Then the Lord came down upon Mount Sinai, on the top of the mountain. And the Lord called Moses to the top of the mountain, and Moses went up.' (*Ex. 19:10-11, 16-20*)

It was on this third day that the LORD God appeared in His glory to His people on the mountain, and spoke to them concerning the salvation He had wrought for them: 'I am the LORD your God, who brought you out of the land of Egypt, out of the house of bondage' (*Ex. 20:2*). Likewise, Jesus appeared in the glory of the resurrection from the dead on the third day and

---

[5] Michael Reeves, *Christ Our Life* (Milton Keynes: Paternoster, 2014), 29.

by His resurrection appearing declares to us that He is the LORD our God who has brought us out of the land of bondage of sin and death.

The prophet Hosea spoke of the salvation that would come through a third day resurrection:

> Come, and let us return to the LORD;
> For He has torn, but He will heal us;
> He has stricken, but He will bind us up.
> After two days He will revive us;
> On the third day He will raise us up,
> That we may live in His sight.
> Let us know,
> Let us pursue the knowledge of the Lord.
> His going forth is established as the morning;
> He will come to us like the rain,
> Like the latter and former rain to the earth. (*Hos. 6:1-3*)

The binding up and healing of those who are stricken and torn will occur 'on the third day'. It is this third day on which the Lord gives the reviving of new life. And He does it by raising us up: by resurrection.

But this life-giving resurrection of His people is not something that the Lord does from afar. It's connected to the Lord's own coming. 'His going forth is established … He will come to us.' So life-giving resurrection 'on the third day' is through the coming of the Lord Himself to the earth for our salvation. It is the incarnate God who will raise us up on the third day. And from the rest of the Scriptures we know that that is through His own resurrection on the third day.

When Christ Himself pointed to an Old Testament prophecy of the third day resurrection, it was to the life of the prophet Jonah that He pointed. In response the requests for a sign from the scribes and Pharisees, and later from the Pharisees and Sadducees, Jesus promised the sign of the prophet Jonah:

> Then some of the scribes and Pharisees answered, saying, 'Teacher, we want to see a sign from You.' But He answered and said to them, 'An evil and adulterous generation seeks after a sign, and no sign will be given to it except the sign of the prophet Jonah. For as Jonah was three days and three nights in the belly of the great fish, so will the Son of Man be three days and three nights in the heart of the earth. The men of Nineveh will rise up in the judgment with this generation and condemn it, because they repented at the preaching of Jonah; and indeed a greater than Jonah is here.' (*Mt 12:38-41*)

> Then the Pharisees and Sadducees came, and testing Him asked that He would show them a sign from heaven. He answered and said to them … 'A wicked and adulterous generation seeks after a sign, and no sign shall be given to it except the sign of the prophet Jonah.' And He left them and departed. (*Mt 16:1-2, 4*)

On both occasions Jesus refers back to *Jonah 1:17*, where, having been cast to his death in the sea, God saved Jonah through being 'buried' for three days and three nights in the belly of the great fish. Jesus tells the Pharisees that this was a sign of his own burial in the tomb, only to rise from the grave on the third day.

One more 'third day' in the Old Testament has a significant connection with resurrection. In *Genesis 22*, Abraham took Isaac up the mountain to offer him on the altar 'on the third day' (*Gen. 22:4*). This Scripture has a particularly strong connection with the atoning death of Christ, as it is the beginning of the promise of the Lamb of God, yet the New Testament also connects it with resurrection.

> By faith Abraham, when he was tested, offered up Isaac, and he who had received the promises offered up his only begotten son, of whom it was said, 'In Isaac your seed shall be called,' concluding that God was able to raise him up, even from the dead, from which he also received him in a figurative sense. (*Heb. 11:17-19*)

According to the writer to the Hebrews, that 'third day' on Moriah was a day of resurrection faith, and a day of pre-figuration of the resurrection. Abraham's faith was in the God who raises the dead. And Isaac's safe return from the altar to his father was a shadow anticipating the resurrection of Jesus Christ from the dead very nearby on another third day.

The Overall Old Testament Pattern of God's Salvation: Through Death and Out into Life

The LORD saved Noah and his family and brought them into a new and fruitful life by carrying them upon the very floodwaters that brought death and destruction as His judgment upon the earth (*Gen. 6-8*). He delivered Joseph and all his family from the famine by the attempt of Joseph's brothers to kill him (*Gen. 45:4-8*). The LORD God brought the children of Israel out of their bondage in Egypt through the death of either the firstborn or the substitutionary lamb, into their new life as a free people in covenant relationship with Him (*Ex. 12:29-42*). He saved Jonah by having him cast out of the boat to his death in the stormy sea, only to preserve him alive through three days and nights buried in the belly of the great fish (*Jonah 1:4-17*). Again and again throughout the Old Testament we see this pattern, that God saves through His judgement (e.g. *Isa. 34-35; Jer. 23:1-8; 29:1-14; Ezek. 37; Hos. 2:2-23*). God saves by carrying His people through death and out the other side into life; He saves by resurrection from the dead.

Christ's Resurrection and Ours

Christ has triumphed over the grave, rising from the dead as the Firstfruits of the dead:

> But now Christ is risen from the dead, and has become the firstfruits of those who have fallen asleep. For since by man came death, by Man also came the resurrection of the dead. For as in Adam all die, even so in Christ all shall be made alive. But each one in his own order: Christ the firstfruits, afterward those who are Christ's at His coming. (*1 Cor. 15:20-23*)

As the Firstfruits, the Lord Jesus is not the only one who will be resurrected, for 'He who raised up the Lord Jesus will also raise us up with Jesus' (*2 Cor. 4:14*). Scripture attaches the promise of our resurrection to the resurrection of Jesus Christ: 'And God both raised up the Lord and will also raise us up by His power' (*1 Cor. 6:14*).

Christ's resurrection has achieved our resurrection (*1 Cor. 15:21*) and also serves as the guarantee and pledge of our future resurrection (*2 Cor. 4:14*). All believers will be raised 'in Christ.' This will not merely be a resuscitation, like that of Jairus' daughter or Lazarus who were raised to die again, but a true resurrection, no more to die, like that of Jesus Himself. For our resurrection is in Him, and thus it is a sharing in Christ's resurrection. In Christ, and like Christ, we will be raised with glorified bodies, never to die again. For the Lord Jesus Christ 'will transform our lowly body that it may be conformed to His glorious body' (*Phil. 3:21*). As Martin Chemnitz put it:

> The substance and nature of our body will remain also in the state of glorification, but in gifts it will be like His glorious body, and it will be

found in fashion as the body of Christ in glory … He was made in fashion like us in His humiliation. But we will be in fashion like He is in glory.[6]

Paul gives a detailed description of the connection between our resurrection and the resurrection of Christ in *1 Corinthians 15:12-58*. Firstly, he shows us that Jesus' resurrection is so tightly linked to our resurrection that you can't have one without the other: to deny the resurrection of believers is to deny the resurrection of Christ. 'If there is no resurrection of the dead, then Christ is not risen … for if the dead do not rise, then Christ is not risen' (*1 Cor. 15:13, 16*). This means that Christ's resurrection is the great proof and guarantee of our future resurrection. Because Christ the Firstfruits has been raised, all those who are Christ's will be raised to life with Him at His return (*1 Cor. 15:22-23*).

Yet Christ's resurrection is not only proof of the fact of the future resurrection of believers in Christ, but also the proof and guarantee of the nature of our resurrection. Like Christ in His resurrection, our bodies will be transformed in the resurrection of the dead. In death, our bodies are sown in the ground like seeds, but in the resurrection they will be raised up into glorious plants (*1 Cor. 15:35-44*).

> The body is sown in corruption, it is raised in incorruption. It is sown in dishonour, it is raised in glory. It is sown in weakness, it is raised in power. It is sown a natural body, it is raised a spiritual body. (*1 Cor. 15:42-44*)

Believers' bodies will be raised 'incorruptible', no longer subject to weakness, sickness, suffering or death.

When He raised Lazarus from the dead, Jesus spoke of the connection between our resurrection and His. 'I am the resurrection and the life. He who believes in Me, though he may die, he shall live. And whoever lives and believes in Me shall never die' (*Jn 11:25-26*). It is because Jesus is Himself the Resurrection and the Life that believers will live again, by being raised from the dead, through Jesus' resurrection from the dead. By partaking of Him who is the resurrection, though we may die, we shall live again. And so Jesus told His disciples on the night of His betrayal, 'Because I live, you will live also' (*Jn 14:19*).

---

[6] Chemnitz, *Loci*, 1:171

Raised to New Life

The Scripture grounds our salvation by God's grace alone in the resurrection of Jesus Christ. In salvation, God has 'made us alive together with Christ (by grace you have been saved), and raised us up together' (*Eph. 2:5-6*). Those who were dead in sin need a new life. So God lifts us out of death into life, by making us alive together with Christ, which is salvation by grace. Our new life is the life of His resurrection; we have been raised up together with Him.

Jesus proclaimed this new life through His resurrection when He raised Lazarus from the dead: 'I am the resurrection and the life. He who believes in Me, though he may die, he shall live. And whoever lives and believes in Me shall never die' (*Jn 11:25-26*). As we've seen above, Jesus here clearly links the resurrection of believers with His own resurrection. Yet He also links His life with our new spiritual life. Because He is the life, 'whoever lives and believes in [Him] shall never die.' Here the life comes before death and brings freedom from spiritual and eternal death. Thus the one who is the Resurrection and the Life is the source of our new life. Our regeneration is through the resurrection life of Jesus.

Peter teaches the same thing in his first epistle:

> Blessed be the God and Father of our Lord Jesus Christ, who according to His abundant mercy has begotten us again to a living hope through the resurrection of Jesus Christ from the dead (*1 Pet. 1:3*)

We are born again through the resurrection of Jesus Christ. So if our regeneration means being raised with Him by His resurrection, then where should we look for assurance of our new birth? Not to our experience, for the new birth does not come from within us, and our feelings fluctuate. Rather than bringing assurance, looking within can lead us into either despair or hypocrisy, for by looking within we see the greatness of our sin. True assurance of a new birth which comes from above (not from within) can only be found by looking to the way we have been born again: 'through the resurrection of Jesus Christ from the dead.' It's by looking out to Jesus who was raised from the dead for us that we find true assurance of our regeneration.

Raised for our Justification

The Scriptures also ground our justification in the resurrection of Jesus Christ. In fact, the Bible speaks of the resurrection as Jesus' justification:

> And without controversy great is the mystery of godliness: God was manifested in the flesh, justified in the Spirit, seen by angels, preached among the Gentiles, believed on in the world, received up in glory. (*1 Tim. 3:16*)

Jesus was 'justified in the Spirit' when He was raised from the dead. The resurrection was God's declaration of 'righteous' over Christ. (He had no sin to be forgiven, and needed no imputation of righteousness from another, but He was declared to be righteous by the resurrection, because He is righteous.) In the resurrection, the Father in the Spirit vindicated Christ, declaring to all that Jesus had no sin to hold Him in the grave, and so His resurrection is His justification.

Through raising Jesus from the dead, the Father affirmed His acceptance of the Incarnate Son's atoning sacrifice. In the words of an Apostolic missionary writer, the resurrection 'sealed the Atonement and bore testimony to its adequacy and certainty for men's salvation.' Yet, 'it was even more than the pledge and seal of His acceptance with His Father.'[7] The resurrection is Christ's vindication and justification. It declares and shows Him to be righteous: that He had no sin to hold Him in the grave. As D.P. Williams put it, in the resurrection of Jesus Christ 'His Father vindicated His life and death.'[8]

And His vindication is our justification. The Lord Jesus Christ was 'delivered up for our trespasses and raised for our justification' (*Rom. 4:25 ESV*). He is declared righteous, because He is righteous. Yet, as He is declared righteous, we are declared righteous in Him, with His righteousness, because we are united to Him in His resurrection. When we are united to Christ in faith, we are united to Him in His resurrection-justification.

This connection between our justification and the resurrection of Jesus Christ can also be seen through the link between the resurrection and the forgiveness of sins (which is an aspect of justification). Paul proclaimed in

---

[7] Stephen H. Brooks, *The Resurrection of Jesus Christ*, (Bradford: Puritan Press, n.d.), 25, 22.
[8] D.P. Williams, *The Trinity*, 2:34.

Pisidian Antioch that forgiveness of sins is preached through the Man whom 'God raised up [who] saw no corruption' (*Acts 13:37-38*). Writing to the Corinthians, Paul warned them that 'if Christ is not risen, your faith is futile; you are still in your sins' (*1 Cor. 15:17*), again making the connection between the resurrection and forgiveness. Therefore, we can join our voices with the early Apostolics in answering the question from their earliest catechism: 'What is revealed to us in His resurrection? It is revealed to us, through His resurrection, that sinners have been justified before God.'[9]

The Resurrection of Christ and the Resurrection of the Heavens and the Earth

All of God's work of salvation comes through the resurrection of the crucified Christ. Therefore the Bible does not limit the results of Jesus' resurrection to human beings, but extends His resurrection power to all of creation.

> And He is the head of the body, the church, who is the beginning, the firstborn from the dead, that in all things He may have the preeminence. For it pleased the Father that in Him all the fullness should dwell, and by Him to reconcile all things to Himself, by Him, whether things on earth or things in heaven, having made peace through the blood of His cross. (*Col. 1:18-20*)

Jesus, 'the firstborn from the dead' is the one who reconciles all things on earth and in heaven to God. But what are these 'all things' which Jesus reconciles? Within the context, the expression 'all things' has already been used four times in the previous verses. There we read:

> For by Him *all things* were created that are in heaven and that are on earth, visible and invisible, whether thrones or dominions or principalities or powers. *All things* were created through Him and for Him. And He is before *all things*, and in Him *all things* consist. (*Col. 1:16-17*)

---

[9] *Holwyddoreg*, ix.5. Original Welsh: *Beth ddatguddir i ni yn Ei adgyfodiad? Datguddir i ni, trwy Ei adgyfodiad, fod pechadur wedi ei gyfiawnhau ger bron Duw.*

So 'all things', in this context, refers to all of creation, both the visible creation and the invisible creation, including angelic powers. Therefore, in light of this context, when Paul writes in *verse 20* that all things have been reconciled by the Firstborn from the dead, he is telling us that Christ reconciles the whole of creation, both in heaven and on earth, visible and invisible. Christ's work of reconciliation is not limited to human beings, but takes in the whole of created reality. Here we see a cosmic renewal: 'God's work in Christ has in view a reclamation of the entire universe, tainted as it is by human sin.'[10] This is brought about by Jesus' death ('through the blood of His cross') and resurrection ('firstborn from the dead'). This includes the heavens and the earth themselves. So the resurrection of the crucified Christ is what ultimately ushers in the new heavens and the new earth.[11]

---

[10] Douglas J. Moo, *The Letters to the Colossians and to Philemon*, Pillar New Testament Commentary (Grand Rapids: Eerdmans, 2008), 137.

[11] Gregory Beale also demonstrates that *Rev. 3:14*, in comparison with *Isa. 65:16-17* and *Rev. 1:5*, also points to the inauguration of the new heavens and new earth through the resurrection of Jesus Christ. See G.K. Beale, *The Book of Revelation*, New International Greek Testament Commentary, 297-301.

Chapter 18

The Ascension

Forty days after His Resurrection, Jesus left the earth and was taken up into heaven in the presence of His disciples. This is what we mean by the Ascension of Christ.

The Nature of Christ's Ascension

Luke considered the Ascension important enough to record it twice: once in Luke's Gospel and once in Acts. Here are the two descriptions which he records: 'And He led them out as far as Bethany, and He lifted up His hands and blessed them. Now it came to pass, while He blessed them, that He was parted from them and carried up into heaven' (*Lk 24:50-51*) 'Now when He had spoken these things, while they watched, He was taken up, and a cloud received Him out of their sight' (*Acts 1:9*).

Christ Ascended Bodily

From both of Luke's accounts we can see that Christ ascended bodily into heaven. For forty days Jesus had been appearing to His followers on earth in His resurrection body. At the moment of the Ascension the disciples saw Christ in His resurrection body being taken up into heaven. He did not leave His body behind on earth. This means that at the Ascension, the Incarnate Christ, the God-Man, was taken up into heaven. The Ascension was not therefore the end of Christ's incarnation. Rather, now in heaven there is 'one Mediator between God and men, the Man Christ Jesus' (*1 Tim. 2:5*).

Christ Ascended into Heaven

Luke 24:51 specifies that Christ was 'carried up into heaven'. *Mark 16:19* agrees that 'He was received up into heaven'. When the two angels spoke to the disciples immediately after the Ascension, they confirmed that the disciples had seen 'Him go into heaven' (*Acts 1:11*). Thus at the Ascension, Christ did not simply leave the earth; the Ascension does not only mark the end of His earthly ministry, but the beginning of the ministry of the God-Man in heaven.

Christ was Highly Exalted

The Ascension was more than simply a change of location. On the day of Pentecost, Peter spoke of the Ascension in terms of Jesus being 'exalted to the right hand of God' (*Acts 2:33*). Paul writes of the Ascension as Christ being 'received up in glory' (*1 Tim. 3:16*). Thus, at the Ascension, Christ not only went up from earth to heaven, but He also arrived in heaven in a state of exaltation and glory. As God, Christ had enjoyed glory and exaltation with the Father even 'before the world was' (*Jn 17:5*), but then He had not been the God-Man. The Ascension involved the exaltation of Christ Incarnate.

Christ Sat Down at the Right Hand of God

In Mark's account of the Ascension he tells us that Jesus 'was received up into heaven, and sat down at the right hand of God' (*Mark 16:19*). We call this sitting down of Christ at the right hand of God Christ's *Session*. Peter tells us that Christ 'has gone into heaven and is at the right hand of God' (*1 Pet. 3:22*). Thus Christ is there now; this is His current position. The writer of Hebrews links Christ's session with His atoning death: 'when He had by Himself purged our sins, [He] sat down at the right hand of the Majesty on high' (*Heb. 1:3*). Christ's ascension is the commencement of His session. (We'll return to the subject of Christ's session in the next chapter.)

The Culmination of the Cross

Christ's Ascension, like His Resurrection, is not simply a fact of history. It is also an event of great theological and practical importance. Christ's ascension to the right hand of the Father was the culmination of the work of the Cross. But how can that be? Didn't Jesus cry 'it is finished' at Calvary (*Jn 19:30*)? Indeed; but the ascension of Christ is not a separate work from His Cross. The crucifixion on Mount Calvary and the ascension from the Mount of Olives must be kept together. It's not the ascension is something else more important than the Cross; it's that the Cross finds its culmination in the ascension.

We can see this very clearly in the great Old Testament ascension passage: *Leviticus 16*. There Moses presents us with the ritual for the Day of Atonement, where we see a sacrifice leading to entry into the Holy of Holies. The sacrifice and the entrance into the presence of the Lord go together; they can't be separated. The High Priest could not enter into the Holy of Holies without the blood of the sacrifice. And the reason the sacrifice has been made is so that the blood can be presented in the Holy of Holies.

> And Aaron shall bring the bull of the sin offering, which is for himself, and make atonement for himself and for his house, and shall kill the bull as the sin offering which is for himself. Then he shall take a censer full of burning coals of fire from the altar before the Lord, with his hands full of sweet incense beaten fine, and bring it inside the veil. And he shall put the incense on the fire before the Lord, that the cloud of incense may cover the mercy seat that is on the Testimony, lest he die. He shall take some of the blood of the bull and sprinkle it with his finger on the mercy seat on the east side; and before the mercy seat he shall sprinkle some of the blood with his finger seven times. Then he shall kill the goat of the sin offering, which is for the people, bring its blood inside the veil, do with that blood as he did with the blood of the bull, and sprinkle it on the mercy seat and before the mercy seat. So he shall make atonement for the Holy Place, because of the uncleanness of the children of Israel, and because of their transgressions, for all their sins; and so he shall do for the tabernacle of meeting which remains among them in the midst of their uncleanness. There shall be no man in the tabernacle of meeting when he goes in to make atonement in the Holy Place, until he comes out, that he may make atonement for himself, for his household, and for all the assembly of Israel.

(*Lev. 16:11-17*)

Presenting the blood of the sacrifice in the presence of God was the culmination of the sacrifice of the Day of Atonement. And while the High Priest was presenting the blood, the Tabernacle was to be empty (*Lev. 16:17*). The only other people who could have entered the Tabernacle at any time would have been other priests. So, in other words, while the High Priest was presenting the blood of the atoning sacrifice before the presence of God, there were to be no other priests making any other offerings. For, if other priests were making other offerings, that would mean that people weren't trusting in the blood being presented to God by the High Priest.

Each year on the Day of Atonement, the High Priest offered a sacrifice and then presented its blood in the presence of the Lord in the Holy of Holies as a picture of the great High Priestly work of the Lord Jesus Christ who would offer His own blood once for all and then enter into the presence of God in the heavenly Holy of Holies (*Heb. 7:26-27; 8:1-2*). The writer to the Hebrews tells us that the earthly Tabernacle with its ceremonies and rituals was only 'symbolic for the present time' (*Heb. 9:9*) of the true, heavenly Tabernacle. Explicitly, Hebrews tells us that the ritual of the Day of Atonement pointed to, and was fulfilled by Christ in his death and ascension:

> But Christ came as High Priest of the good things to come, with the greater and more perfect tabernacle not made with hands, that is, not of this creation. Not with the blood of goats and calves, but with His own blood He entered the Most Holy Place once for all, having obtained eternal redemption … For Christ has not entered the holy places made with hands, which are copies of the true, but into heaven itself, now to appear in the presence of God for us; not that He should offer Himself often, as the high priest enters the Most Holy Place every year with blood of another — He then would have had to suffer often since the foundation of the world; but now, once at the end of the ages, He has appeared to put away sin by the sacrifice of Himself. (*Heb. 9:11-12, 24-26*)

Once and for all, Christ our Great High Priest has entered into heaven itself with His own blood as the culmination of the work of the Cross, in fulfilment of *Leviticus 16*.

Christ Ascended for us

Why did the High Priest enter into the Holy of Holies each year with the blood of the sacrifice on the Day of Atonement? He went in for the people of God, as their representative. The normal uniform of the High Priest was a demonstration to everyone that he carried out his ministry as the representative of the children of the Israel.

The garments of the High Priest are carefully described in *Exodus 28*. There we read that on the shoulders of his ephod were two engraved stones:

> Then you shall take two onyx stones and engrave on them the names of the sons of Israel: six of their names on one stone and six names on the other stone, in order of their birth. With the work of an engraver in stone, like the engravings of a signet, you shall engrave the two stones with the names of the sons of Israel. You shall set them in settings of gold. And you shall put the two stones on the shoulders of the ephod as memorial stones for the sons of Israel. So Aaron shall bear their names before the Lord on his two shoulders as a memorial. (*Ex. 28:9-11*)

Likewise, the High Priest's breastplate was to be covered with engraved precious stones:

> And you shall put settings of stones in it, four rows of stones: The first row shall be a sardius, a topaz, and an emerald; this shall be the first row; the second row shall be a turquoise, a sapphire, and a diamond; the third row, a jacinth, an agate, and an amethyst; and the fourth row, a beryl, an onyx, and a jasper. They shall be set in gold settings. And the stones shall have the names of the sons of Israel, twelve according to their names, like the engravings of a signet, each one with its own name; they shall be according to the twelve tribes … So Aaron shall bear the names of the sons of Israel on the breastplate of judgment over his heart, when he goes into the holy place, as a memorial before the Lord continually. And you shall put in the breastplate of judgment the Urim and the Thummim, and they shall be over Aaron's heart when he goes in before the Lord. So Aaron shall bear the judgment of the children of Israel over his heart before the Lord continually. (*Ex. 28:17-21, 29-30*)

So, the High Priest's normal uniform was covered with the names of the twelve tribes of Israel to show that he was set apart as their representative to bear their names before the Lord. And when he carried out his work, he did so for the people, as their representative before God. When he entered into the Holy of Holies with the blood on the Day of Atonement, he did so 'that he may make atonement for himself, for his household, and for all the assembly of Israel' (*Lev. 16:17*). The High Priest was the representative of God's people who entered into the Holy of Holies on their behalf. The High Priest entered into the presence of God for them. And their atonement was only complete when their High Priest entered into God's presence for them.

The Lord Jesus is our Great High Priest who has ascended into God's presence for us, on our behalf, as our representative (*Heb. 9:11-12*). Like the High Priests of the Old Testament, Jesus our Great High Priest carries His people upon His shoulders (*Lk 15:4-6*) into the presence of God the Father in the heavenly Holy of Holies. Like the High Priests of old, Jesus our Great High Priest 'bear[s] the judgment of the children … over his heart before the Lord continually' (*Ex. 28:30*).

> Before the throne of God above
> I have a strong and perfect plea
> A great High Priest whose name is love
> Who ever lives and pleads for me
> My name is graven on His hands
> My name is written on His heart
> I know that while in heav'n He stands
> No tongue can bid me thence depart[1]

The Lord Jesus Christ, our Great Heavenly High Priest, is our Man in heaven. There in the heavenly Holy of Holies He represents us. Our Great High Priest, the Sacrificed Lamb, sits in heaven on our behalf. And so our salvation rests on His once for all sacrifice and entrance into the presence of the Father.

We Ascend in Christ

Leviticus 16 is not the only Old Testament passage which teaches us of the meaning of Christ's ascension. David also sings of Christ's ascension in the Psalms.

Psalm 24 is a psalm of the ascension. David asks, 'Who may ascend to the hill of the LORD? Or who may stand in His holy place? (*Ps 24:3*). The hill of the LORD is Jerusalem, where the Temple was, because that was where the dwelling place of God was to be found, in the Holy of Holies, enthroned between the cherubim. But, just as we've seen with the Tabernacle, the earthly Temple was only a shadow of the true heavenly Temple. David is not just singing in *Psalm 24* of who can go into the Jerusalem temple. For, after all, only the High Priest could enter earthly Holy of Holies, and only in very specific circumstances, as we've seen above. Therefore David cannot be talking about the earthly Holy of Holies.

---

[1] Charitie Lees Bancroft (1841-1892)

In fact, David makes that clear as the Psalm goes on, and he sings of the 'everlasting doors' (*Ps 24:7, 9*). These doors are the way into God's Holy of Holies, but the doors of the Jerusalem temple had a beginning and an end, so certainly were not everlasting doors. So *Psalm 24* is not talking about ascending to the Temple in Jerusalem, but ascending into the very presence of God in His true heavenly Holy of Holies.

And this ascending matters, because it is not so much a going up as a being welcomed up (*Ps 24:5-6*). So this ascending means being welcomed into the presence of God. This welcome from God is seen in receiving 'blessing from the LORD and righteousness from the God of his salvation' (*Ps 24:5*). The one who ascends is the one who is blessed, so blessing from God isn't primarily about God sending good things down to us, but about God lifting us up into His presence to enjoy fellowship with Him. Righteousness is provided by the God who saves, so once again we see that salvation is of the Lord.

Yet, there is a problem with this ascending. For the answer to David's question of who may ascend is 'He who has clean hands and a pure heart, who has not lifted up his soul to an idol, nor sworn deceitfully' (*Ps 24:4*). This ascent calls for purity, both within ('pure heart') and without ('clean hands'). Yet unclean hands flow out from the sinful hearts of mankind. 'Who can say, "I have made my heart clean, I am pure from my sin?"' (*Prov. 20:9*): the answer, as we have seen in the chapter on sin, is no one. David tells us that this blessed ascent is for 'the generation of those who seek Him, who seek Your face' (*Ps 24:6*); yet Paul tells us, 'there is none who seeks after God' (*Rom. 3:11*).

So does that mean that there is no one who ascends? The book of Hebrews tells us that, though we cannot cleanse our own hearts and hands, our hearts and hands can be cleansed through the blood of Jesus, allowing us to enter into the heavenly Holy of Holies:

> Therefore, brethren, having boldness to enter the Holiest by the blood of Jesus, by a new and living way which He consecrated for us, through the veil, that is, His flesh, and having a High Priest over the house of God, let us draw near with a true heart in full assurance of faith, having our hearts sprinkled from an evil conscience and our bodies washed with pure water. (*Heb. 10:19-22*)

It is only through the shed blood of our Great High Priest that our hearts and hands can be cleansed so that we can 'enter the Holiest' and 'draw near.' He has taken all our uncleanness and impurity on Him and dealt with it once and for all through His death in our place on the Cross. And He gives us His righteousness – His purity – to take the place of our unclean hands and impure heart.

But *Psalm 24* also shows us that Jesus, our Great High Priest, is the one who ascends. He is 'the King of Glory' who enters in (*Ps 24:7-10; cf. Jn 17:5*). He is the LORD of Victory, having won the victory of the ages through His death on the cross and resurrection from the dead.

Yet why the question, 'who is this King of Glory?' God the Son, the Eternal Word, has shared in the Father's glory for all eternity. But now something is different, which prompts the question: He ascends as Man. This is the Incarnate God who ascends. And so there is a Man in heaven upon the throne of God. By His ascension, Jesus has taken our humanity to the very centre of God's throne. A member of the human race is a member of the Trinity. And His people are members of Him.

Therefore, Christ does not ascend alone. He hasn't just taken our humanity to heaven; He's taken us to heaven, for we're united to Him. So, 'who may ascend to the hill of the LORD?' Only Christ, the only man with clean hands and a pure heart. Yet, united to Christ and clothed with Him for righteousness, we ascend in Him.

David sings of our ascension in Christ in another Psalm:

> The chariots of God are twenty thousand,
> Even thousands of thousands;
> The Lord is among them as in Sinai, in the Holy Place.
> You have ascended on high,
> You have led captivity captive;
> You have received gifts among men,
> Even from the rebellious,
> That the Lord God might dwell there…
> They have seen Your procession, O God,
> The procession of my God, my King, into the sanctuary.
> The singers went before, the players on instruments followed after;
> Among them were the maidens playing timbrels.   (*Ps 68:17-18, 24-25*)

Paul tells us in *Ephesians 4* that this Psalm is speaking of Christ's ascension (*Eph. 4:8-10*). David sings here of the mighty, triumphant, victorious King who returns from His Conquest leading captives in His train. The image is that of a triumphal procession, where the conquering king would lead his captured enemies behind his chariot in a victory parade. Yet here they start off captive and rebellious, but end up rejoicing as singers and players of instruments. When Christ the victorious king leads His captured enemies behind Him in His ascension, He transforms them into joyful worshippers.

Paul explains this in *Ephesians 2*:

> But God, who is rich in mercy, because of His great love with which He
> loved us, even when we were dead in trespasses, made us alive together
> with Christ (by grace you have been saved), and raised us up together, and
> made us sit together in the heavenly places in Christ Jesus (*Eph. 2:4-6*)

Believers look forward to the day when our bodies will be raised from the
grave and will be forever with the Lord physically. Yet already we are
raised, ascended, and seated with Him spiritually in the heavenly realms.
Believers really are united to Christ. As W.R. Thomas put it, 'the ascension
is not the elevation of one isolated individual, but the elevation of the Head
of the Body, which is the Church; and this Head cannot be separated from
His members.'[2]

Our Ascension in Christ and the Christian Life and Worship

In fact, it's our ascension in Christ, so that we are seated now in the
heavenly realms in Him, that makes the Christian life possible. The
Christian life is an ascended life. Our prayer takes place in heaven: we
boldly approach the throne of grace through Jesus Christ to whom we're
united and in whom we've ascended (*Heb. 4:16*).

Our worship takes place in heaven too. The first thing Christ's disciples
did when He ascended into heaven was that 'they worshipped Him' (*Lk
24:52*). Their worship flowed out of the Ascension of Christ. And worship
still flows out of Christ's Ascension today. The Ascension enables us to
worship. We're raised up in Christ's ascension and seated with Him in the
heavenly realms. That means that, in Jesus, we've been taken into the true
Holy of Holies. We've been taken right in to the very presence of the Father.
We've been taken right to His Throne.

So, in our worship, we're not simply making a loud noise from far
away, hoping God will hear and be pleased. We must never think of
Christian worship like that. That is the worship of Baal (*1 Kgs 18:26-29*), not
the worship of the Triune God. For Christian worship is not something we
do to get God's attention. Rather, worship is what happens when God has
got our attention. You see, worship isn't really about our singing and our
actions. (Those are simply ways we express our worship.) Worship is really
about our hearts being captivated by the beauty of Christ our Saviour.

---

[2] W.R. Thomas, *L'Emmanuele* (Naples: Edizioni Ricchezze di Grazia), 44.

Worship is really about delighting in our Triune God – Father, Son and Holy Spirit.

So, the Ascension lifts us up to the Throne of God, where we sit with Jesus, giving glory and honour to the Father through Him: rejoicing in the loving fellowship of the Father, Son and Holy Spirit, through the blood of Jesus. By the Ascension, we're brought right into the heavenly Throne room to worship in the very presence of our God.

The writer to the Hebrews tells us that in Christian worship we join with the angels and the whole company of Christ's Church, in the presence of God and of Jesus our Mediator.

> But you have come to Mount Zion and to the city of the living God, the heavenly Jerusalem, to an innumerable company of angels, to the general assembly and church of the firstborn who are registered in heaven, to God the Judge of all, to the spirits of just men made perfect, to Jesus the Mediator of the new covenant, and to the blood of sprinkling that speaks better things than that of Abel. (*Heb. 12:22-24*)

There in heaven, Jesus is our true λειτουργός (*leitourgos*), our true worship leader (*Heb. 8:2*) who draws us into the eternal loving communion of the Triune God.

And Christ our λειτουργός (*leitourgos*), through His ascension, gives us every cause to worship the Triune God. For in the Ascension we see that our salvation is completed. The blood has been presented before the Father in Heaven, once and for all. So our salvation is settled. Jesus has paid the full price and it has been accepted by the Father for us. By His ascension we have assurance that we are free from striving and works, through resting in the Finished Work of Jesus; and we can give Him all the glory, thanks and praise.

Because we have ascended in Christ, the minds of believers are to be set on the things above:

> If then you were raised with Christ, seek those things which are above, where Christ is, sitting at the right hand of God. Set your mind on things above, not on things on the earth. For you died, and your life is hidden with Christ in God. (*Col. 3:1-3*)

The ascension of Christ our Saviour lifts our eyes and minds from the things of this world to our glorious Saviour who reigns far above all the heavens, and so we are filled with His comfort and built up in Him as we look to our ascended Head.

Christ's Ascension and the Life of the Church

What was Jesus doing when He ascended? He didn't stop everything, tell them he was about to ascend, and then give a countdown. Quite the contrary; Luke tells us He was in the middle of something when He ascended. 'He lifted up His hands and blessed them. Now it came to pass, while He blessed them, that He was parted from them and carried up into heaven' (*Lk 24:50-51*). As the Lord Jesus Christ ascended into heaven, He was in the middle of blessing His disciples. He didn't finish blessing them and then ascend, but rather continued blessing them as He ascended. And having ascended, He continues still to bless His people. His ascension to the Father's right hand doesn't mean an end to His blessing. Instead, His ascension is the guarantee of His blessing upon all those who trust in Him.

> See! He lifts His hands above;
> See! He shows the prints of love;
> Hark! His gracious lips bestow
> Blessings on His Church below.[3]

What hands are those that are raised in blessing? The nail-scarred hands. The hands that were nailed to the Cross. For the Cross and the ascension cannot be separated. Christ's ascension, as we have seen, is the completion and culmination of the work of the Cross. The two belong together as part of that one, once and for all, saving work. Jesus, the Crucified, now stands in heaven as our Surety, our Acceptance, our Guarantee, our Security, and it is from Him that all blessing flows to His Church below.

The Baptism in the Holy Spirit flows from the Ascension of Christ

During the Old Testament, no one was baptized in the Holy Spirit. Even during Jesus' earthly ministry the Holy Spirit was not poured out on His disciples. It was only after the Ascension that Christ baptized the believers in the Holy Spirit. John explains this, telling us that, during Christ's earthly ministry, 'Holy Spirit was not yet given, because Jesus was not yet glorified'

---

[3] From Charles Wesley's great ascension hymn, 'Hail the Day that Sees Him Rise'. *Redemption Hymnal*, 188.

(*Jn 7:39*).   When Jesus did ascend, 'being exalted to the right hand of God, and having received from the Father the promise of the Holy Spirit, He poured out' the Spirit on the disciples (*Acts 2:33*).   Thus we can only receive the Baptism in the Holy Spirit because Jesus has ascended.

Christ's Headship of His Church flows from His Ascension

The apostle Paul connects Christ's Ascension with His Headship of the Church (*Eph. 1:20-23*).   Thus the Ascension is of immense benefit to the Church here on earth, for through it we have the Lord Jesus Christ for our Head. We shall examine the doctrine of Christ's Headship in chapter 29.

Christ's Gift of Men to the Church flows from His Ascension

The Ascended Head of the Church gives gifts of men to His Church as ministers:

> When He ascended on high,
> He led captivity captive,
> And gave gifts to men.
> (Now this, "He ascended"—what does it mean but that He also first descended into the lower parts of the earth? He who descended is also the One who ascended far above all the heavens, that He might fill all things.) And He Himself gave some to be apostles, some prophets, some evangelists, and some pastors and teachers, for the equipping of the saints for the work of ministry, for the edifying of the body of Christ (*Eph 4:8-12*).

Thus we see another great benefit to the Church from the ascension of Christ: the ascended Christ gives ministry gifts to His Body. We'll look at this below in chapters 36-38.

Christ's Ascension and the Future

The Ascension Assures Us of Christ's Return

When Jesus ascended, the angels spoke to His disciples, saying: 'Men of Galilee, why do you stand gazing up into heaven? This same Jesus, who was taken up from you into heaven, will so come in like manner as you saw Him go into heaven' (*Acts 1:11*). So the ascension is a guarantee of Christ's return in the same way as He went. He ascended from the earth, and He will return to the earth. He ascended in the flesh, and He will return in the flesh. He ascended with all authority in heaven and on earth (*Mt. 28:18*), and He will return with all authority in heaven and on earth. And as He ascended in the presence of His people, He will return still to be with us forever.

The Ascension Assures Us of Our Future Ascension

We don't normally talk about the ascension of believers, yet the Bible does teach that, at the return of Christ, living believers 'shall be caught up … in the clouds to meet the Lord in the air. And thus we shall always be with the Lord' (*1 Thess. 4:17*). Normally we call this the Rapture. Jesus Himself linked His ascension with His coming again to catch up believers to Himself, saying 'if I go and prepare a place for you, I will come again and receive you to Myself; that where I am, there you may be also' (*Jn 14:3*). Because Christ has been taken up into heaven, we know that it is possible for us to be taken up into heaven. Thanks to Christ's promise, we have the assurance that because He has ascended into heaven, He will return to take us up too.

The Ascension Assures Us of Our Future Home in Heaven

Jesus' promise that He would come again for His people also included the promise of a future home for believers with Him in heaven.

> In My Father's house are many mansions; if it were not so, I would have told you. I go to prepare a place for you. And if I go and prepare a place for

you, I will come again and receive you to Myself; that where I am, there you may be also. (*Jn 14:2-3*)

Part of the purpose of Christ's Ascension was to prepare a place for believers, thus the Ascension is a pledge and guarantee of our future home in heaven with Christ.

The Ascended Presence of Christ

Before His ascension, the Lord Jesus promised His presence. On the night of His betrayal He had told His disciples that He would not leave them orphans, but would come to them (*Jn 14:18*). Earlier, He had promised His presence on earth in the Church after His ascension: 'for where two or three are gathered together in My name, I am there in the midst of them' (*Mt 18:20*). The last words of the resurrected Christ which Matthew records in His Gospel are 'lo, I am with you always, even to the end of the age' (*Mt 28:20*). When Paul writes of Christ's ascension, he too tells us of Christ's presence. Jesus 'ascended far above all the heavens, that He might fill all things' (*Eph. 4:10*). So the ascension of Christ does not speak to us of Christ's absence. Rather, through His ascension, Christ is present in a different way than during His earthly ministry or at His return. The faith of the Apostolic Church is that 'the ascension also secures the universal presence of Christ, for it means he is no longer "here" or "there" but "everywhere" (*cf. Matt 28:20; John 11:15, 21*).'[4]   Mark tells us after the ascension that Jesus was 'working with [His disciples] and confirming the word' (*Mk 16:20*). Cyril of Alexandria puts it like this:

> Just as he is the Lord of Glory and then abases himself into the low status of the slave's form, so he asks to take up his eternally inherent glory again, and he does this in a way that befits a man. Since he is eternally God he ascends from the limitations of our condition to the pre-eminence and glory of his own Godhead so that every knee should bend before the one

---

[4] *Introducing the Apostolic Church: A Manual of Belief, History and Practice*, 134. Cf. W.R. Thomas (former president of both the Italian and UK Apostolic Churches) who writes that the ascension results in 'the universality of [Christ's] personal presence' and that this is 'because of the Hypostatic Union.' W.R. Thomas, *L'Emmanuele* (Naples: Edizioni Ricchezze di Grazia) 47, 50.

true and natural Son, albeit as I have said, one who is made flesh and has become as we are.[5]

How is this so? Because Jesus, in His ascension, has taken His humanity to the right hand of God.

Where is the Right Hand of God?

When Christ ascended to the right hand of God, it was not merely an assumption into heaven like that of Enoch or Elijah. Unlike them, Jesus 'has become higher than the heavens' (*Heb. 7:26*), for He 'ascended far above all the heavens, that He might fill all things' (*Eph. 4:10*). As the Word and Son of the Father, He was already above the highest heavens and already filled all things from all eternity. At His ascension, it is now as the Word Incarnate – as the God-Man – that He fills all things. So the right hand of God, where Christ sits, must be 'higher than the heavens' and must 'fill all things.' Indeed, the Lord says, 'My right hand has stretched out the heavens' (*Isa. 43:13*), so His right hand is greater than and encompasses the whole of creation. As John of Damascus asks, 'how would He who is uncircumscribed have a physical right hand?'[6] Even when Christ returns in glory to the earth, He will not be leaving the Father's right hand, but rather He will be both 'sitting at the right hand of the power, and coming on the clouds of heaven' at the same time (*Mt 26:64*). Johann Gerhard concludes: 'Therefore the right hand of God is not a finite, circumscribed place in heaven.'[7] Or, as Luther famously (and bluntly) put it: 'the right hand of God is everywhere.'[8]

In His ascension, Christ has not disappeared, far away, to a location, which is not here, called 'the right hand of God.' Rather, He has 'ascended far above all the heavens, that He might fill all things' (*Eph. 4:10*). After the Reformation, the Reformed objected to this doctrine, arguing that 'it is repugnant to the nature of the body, which is circumscribed and finite, has parts outside parts and ought to be of itself visible and palpable.'[9] Instead they maintained that Christ was present on earth only in His divine nature

---

[5] Cyril of Alexandria, *On the Unity of Christ*, 123-24.

[6] John of Damascus, *De Fide Orthodoxa*, iv.2 (ET p.336).

[7] Johann Gerhard, *Loci*, Exegesis IV, §220

[8] Martin Luther, 'Confession Concerning Christ's Supper'.

[9] Francis Turretin, *Institutes of Elenctic Theology*, 2:327

after the ascension. But the Lutherans, seeing the Scriptures we've looked at above concerning Christ's post-ascension presence, replied:

> Since the promises of the presence of Christ in the church speak of His whole and entire person, which consists of two natures and exists in two natures, why should we then exclude and allow to be taken from us the presence of the one nature through which Christ is our Brother and regards us in love as His own flesh? For where Scripture does not restrict us, we ought not limit the promises of Christ to only His divine nature.[10]

To separate the divine nature of Christ (saying it can be present now in the Church and fill all things) from the human nature of Christ (saying that it is confined in one location in heaven and does not fill all things) does not find any justification in Scripture. For Paul tells us it is the Christ who 'descended into the lower parts of the earth' (*Eph. 4:9*), and so the incarnate Christ, who ascended to fill all things.

But not only does this separation of Christ's humanity and divinity conflict with the Scriptures which speak of His post-ascension presence, but also such a separation begins to open the door towards a Nestorian[11] concept of Christ at odds with the faith of the Christian Church that He is:

> One and the Same Christ, Son, Lord, Only-begotten; acknowledged in Two Natures unconfusedly, unchangeably, indivisibly, inseparably … not as though He were parted or divided into Two Persons, but One and the Self-same Son and Only-begotten God, Word, Lord, Jesus Christ.[12]

Apostolic theologians stood strongly opposed to the Reformed allowance of a separation between Christ's human and divine natures: 'It undermines the unity of His Divine Person. It was not the human at one time, nor the Divine nature at another time, that were in operation, but His complete Person, the God-Man.'[13]

---

[10] Martin Chemnitz, *The Two Natures In Christ*, 451.

[11] The prominent Reformed theologian, Bruce McCormack, admits that 'Cyril's theology … triumphed at Chalcedon … But here's the thing: classical Reformed theology clearly stood on the [other] side,' i.e., that it 'grants a certain [as in a degree of] victory to Nestorius,' that Chalcedonian Christological orthodoxy, by itself, is 'not Reformed,' and that classical Reformed Christology is Chalcedonian Christology reconstructed. Bruce McCormack, 'Reformed Christology and the Westminster HTFC Report: A Critical Comment'.

[12] *The Definition of Chalcedon.*

[13] D.P. Williams, *The Trinity*, 2:28. Cf. W.R. Thomas: 'Christ's person was Divine – He was, is, and will eternally be God, blessèd and glorious. Therefore His humanity, which He assumed in the incarnation for man's redemption … had to be exalted above all the heavens with Him who had united it to Himself.' W.R. Thomas, *L'Emmanuele*, 51.

The Significance of the Ascension Presence of the Incarnate Christ

Why does it matter so much that the presence of Christ in the Church now in this age is the presence of the God-Man and not only His divine nature? It matters greatly, because it means that we have no access to God apart from through the incarnate Christ who lived, died and rose for us. The danger of Reformed division of the human and divine natures is seen in many emphases within current Christian worship songs. The problem here is when our songs point us, not to God in the flesh, our one and only Mediator, but instead send our attention away from the Incarnation of Christ to look for a God other than the One who has come in the flesh. The Incarnation gets swallowed up by a mere spiritual coming down and rising up of God. God's decisive action in the world through the Incarnation of Christ gets pushed into the background by a calling upon God to act outside of the Incarnation here and now.

This can be a significant problem for 21st century Pentecostal and charismatic worship. So much of our contemporary concept of worship is allergic to the Incarnation. For 'worship' has too often become about how we feel in the here and now, rather than about what God has done for us in Christ two thousand years ago in Nazareth, Bethlehem and Calvary.

The gospel is the good news of the God who took on flesh for us and for our salvation. Jesus Christ our Saviour, the Son and Word of God the Father, is and ever will be the Incarnate Christ. He has so joined our humanity to Himself that He will never abandon it (which assures us that He will never abandon us!). That means the only Saviour of whom we can sing is the Incarnate Saviour. The only salvation of which we can sing is the salvation found in the Word made flesh. The only Spirit on whom we can rely is the Spirit poured out by the Incarnate Christ and who glorifies the Incarnate Christ. The only Christ whom we can encounter is the Christ who has come in the flesh.

When we know that the Christ who is present 'where two or three are gathered together in [His] name' is the Incarnate Christ, the eternal Word and Son of the Father with His own humanity in which He suffered for us and for our salvation, then we will not succumb to a temptation to seek the glory, majesty, and power of God apart from Jesus Christ who died for us and lives.

Chapter 19

Christ's Heavenly Session & Abiding Intercession

Christ's Heavenly Session

When He ascended up on high, the Lord Jesus Christ sat down at the right hand of God the Father. He has sat down in heaven because His sacrificial work is finished (*Heb. 1:3; 10:12*). Christ's 'session' is the word we use for this 'sitting-down' of Jesus. And this session of Christ is much more significant than merely a change of position: it is an enthronement. In His session, the Incarnate Christ, our Mediator, is enthroned as our Prophet, our Priest and our King.

Christ is Seated as Our King

The present session of the Lord Jesus Christ means that 'there is a glorified man on the throne of deity.'[1] David prophesied the enthronement of Christ as King at God's right hand in *Psalm 110*:

> The LORD said to my Lord,
> 'Sit at My right hand,
> Till I make Your enemies Your footstool.'
> The Lord shall send the rod of Your strength out of Zion.
> Rule in the midst of Your enemies! (*Ps 110:1-2*)

The frequent references to this Psalm by Christ and His apostles (*Mt. 22:41-46; 26:64; Mk 12:35-37; 14:62; 16:19; Lk 20:41-44; 22:69; Acts 2:34-36; Rom. 8:34; 1 Cor. 15:25; Eph. 1:20; Col. 3:1; Heb. 1:3, 13; 5:6; 7:17, 21; 8:1; 10:12-13; 12:2*) make clear that David is speaking about the Lord Jesus here. As Peter put it, 'David did not ascend into the heavens,' but rather, he was writing about Jesus (*Acts 2:34*). The New Testament associates this enthronement of Christ in *Psalm 110* both with His present session, now that He has ascended (*Acts*

---

[1] *Introducing the Apostolic Church: A Manuel of Belief, Practice and History*, 134.

2:34), and with His future millennial reign (*1 Cor. 15:25*). David tells us here that Christ is enthroned as his Lord (cf. *Mt. 22:41-46*). Therefore in His session, Jesus sits enthroned as King over the greatest of all kings of Israel. In His present session, Jesus, the God-Man, is enthroned as King of Kings and Lord of Lords.

Paul writes of this enthronement in *Ephesians 1:19-23*. There we read that the Father:

> raised [Jesus] from the dead and seated Him at His right hand in the heavenly places, far above all principality and power and might and dominion, and every name that is named, not only in this age but also in that which is to come. And He put all things under His feet. (*Eph. 1:20-22*)

The Kingship and reign in which Christ now sits is higher than any other kingship, not only now in heaven and earth, but also over any other kingship 'not only in this age, but also in that which is to come' (*v. 21*). As Peter tells us, in His session at the right hand of God, even 'angels and authorities and powers hav[e] been made subject to' the God-Man (*1 Pet. 3:22*). And this kingly session of Christ is for the benefit of the Church which is His Body (*Eph. 1:22-23*).

Christ's session at the Father's right hand flows from His victorious conquest at the cross. In the book of Revelation, Jesus says, 'I also overcame and sat down with My Father on His throne' (*Rev. 3:21*). The conquering King has ascended to the throne in triumph, and now His victory is displayed in His exalted glory. Therefore, in the centre of God's throne there is the Lamb who was slain (*Rev. 5:6; 7:17*). Jesus reigns as exalted King, not in spite of His sufferings and death, but precisely as the One who suffered and died for us. The cross is not exchanged for the crown. Rather, as D.P. Williams put it, 'Christ still reigns on the Tree.'[2]

Christ is Seated as Our Prophet

Christ is not only enthroned as King, but also as Prophet. His prophetical office was not limited to His estate of humiliation; He is still our Prophet now in His estate of exaltation. Mark emphasises Christ's session as our Prophet in His account of the ascension of Christ and the post-ascension ministry of the Church:

---

[2] D.P. Williams, *Riches of Grace*, iv.2 (Nov. 1928), 31.

> So then, after the Lord had spoken to them, He was received up into heaven, and sat down at the right hand of God. And they went out and preached everywhere, the Lord working with them and confirming the word through the accompanying signs. Amen. (*Mark 16:19-20*)

The Lord who ascended and 'sat down at the right hand of God' is the Lord who confirmed the word. In His session at the right hand of the Father, the Lord Jesus, as our Prophet, works through and with His servants to proclaim the Word of God, and to confirm the Gospel Word with accompanying signs.

The Lord Jesus continues to carry out His ministry as our Prophet who declares to us the Word of God through the ministers He gives to His Church. It is from His seat at the Father's right hand, 'far above all the heavens,' that Christ the Head gives gifts of men to His Church as apostles, prophets, evangelists, pastors and teachers (*Eph. 4:8-11*). And it is Christ, being seated as our great Prophet, who ministers the word through His ministers, as they carry out their ministries only in union with Him. He is the true Prophet, who speaks through the prophets, and the living Word, who ministers the Word through each of the five ministries.

Yet, it is not only through the ministers of the Church that our enthroned Prophet speaks the Word. On the Day of Pentecost, Peter explained that:

> This Jesus God has raised up, of which we are all witnesses. Therefore being exalted to the right hand of God, and having received from the Father the promise of the Holy Spirit, He poured out this which you now see and hear. (*Acts 2:32-33*)

What did they now see and hear? They saw and heard the results of the outpouring of the Holy Spirit to baptise the Church. They saw and heard people speaking, in languages they had never learnt, 'the wonderful works of God' (*Acts 2:11*), 'as the Spirit gave them utterance' (*Acts 2:4*). Christ, our Prophet, poured out the Spirit upon His people, who 'gave them utterance' to speak the Word: to proclaim Christ. When we are involved in evangelism, as we speak to others about Jesus and what he has done, Christ our Prophet is speaking His Word through us. In this way, 'the Church is to be a community of prophets'[3] in and through the present heavenly ministry of Christ our Prophet.

---

[3] Roger Stronstad, *The Prophethood of All Believers: A Study in Luke's Charismatic Theology*, Journal of Pentecostal Theology Supplement Series 16 (Sheffield: Sheffield Academic Press, 1999), 123.

Christ is Seated as Our Priest

David's prophecy of Christ's session doesn't only speak of His session as King, but also of His session as Priest:

> The LORD said to my Lord,
> 'Sit at My right hand,
> Till I make Your enemies Your footstool.' ...
> The LORD has sworn
> And will not relent,
> 'You are a priest forever
> According to the order of Melchizedek.' (*Ps 110:1, 4*)

The enthroned King is to have an everlasting priesthood, standing before God on the part of His people, and bringing God's blessing to His people. Like Melchizedek (*Gen. 14:18-20; Heb. 5:5-11; 6:19-7:28*), He is a King-Priest, and through His priestly ministry He brings kingly righteousness and peace to His people, and blesses them in bread and wine. As our priest who presents the blood of His sacrifice in the heavenly Holy of Holies, Christ is the giver of repentance and the forgiveness of sins (*Acts 5:29-31*).

The book of Hebrews places a special emphasis on Christ's present session as our Great High Priest. It was 'when He had by Himself purged our sins' that Jesus 'sat down at the right hand of the Majesty on high' (*Heb. 1:3*). As we have seen in the last chapter, the Ascension of Christ is His entrance into the heavenly Holy of Holies, there to present His blood in the presence of the Father (*Heb. 9:12*). Thus, as His priesthood in the estate of humiliation was His once-for-all self-offering on the altar of the cross, so His priesthood in the estate of exaltation consists of the priestly ministry within the veil: presenting His blood for us and offering up prayer to the Father on behalf of His people (*Heb. 6:19-20; 8:1-7*). His on-going priestly ministry does not add anything to His completed sacrifice. That is why He has sat down (*Heb. 10:11-14*). Instead His on-going priestly ministry in heaven rests upon and flows from that one finished sacrifice accomplished on the cross of Calvary. We'll look in Jesus' ongoing priestly session now as we consider His abiding intercession.

Christ's Abiding Intercession

The Scriptures speak of Christ's present ministry in heaven as an abiding intercession. This focuses our attention on His exalted priesthood which consists of a double intercession: Jesus intercedes for us by presenting His blood for us, and Jesus intercedes for us by praying for us.

Christ Intercedes for His People

Christ's intercession, as with the rest of His priesthood, was foretold in the Old Testament. Isaiah prophesied of the Suffering Servant:

> Therefore I will divide Him a portion with the great,
> And He shall divide the spoil with the strong,
> Because He poured out His soul unto death,
> And He was numbered with the transgressors,
> And He bore the sin of many,
> And made intercession for the transgressors. (*Isa. 53:12*)

Not only would He die as the sin-bearer, but the Suffering Servant would also make 'intercession for the transgressors.' The parallelism in *Isaiah 53:12* sets the transgressors for whom He would make intercession alongside those with whom He was numbered and those whose sin He bore. Therefore, the transgressors for whom Jesus would make intercession are the same transgressors for whom He died. Christ's intercession cannot be separated from His atoning death.

In the New Testament we read that this work of intercession is the focus of Christ's present ministry. Jesus is 'able to save to the uttermost those who come to God through Him, since He always lives to make intercession for them' (*Heb. 7:25*). The Christ who died and rose again is now at the right hand of the Father where He 'makes intercession for us' (*Rom. 8:34*). Not only do these verses from Hebrews and Romans tell us that this is what Jesus is now doing, but they also tell us for whom He is interceding. He intercedes for 'those who come to God through Him' (*Heb. 7:25*) and 'for us' (*Rom. 8:34*), which, in the context, refers to those who are justified (*Rom. 8:33*) and have received 'the love of God which is in Christ Jesus our Lord' (*Rom. 8:39*). It is believers who 'have an Advocate with the Father' in Jesus Christ our righteous Intercessor (*1 Jn 2:1*).

We can see this reflected in Jesus' High Priestly Prayer, which He prayed on the night He was betrayed. There Jesus said to His Father:

> I pray for them. I do not pray for the world but for those whom You have given Me, for they are yours. And all Mine are Yours, and Yours are Mine … I do not pray for these alone, but also for all those who will believe in Me through their word. (*Jn 17:9-10, 20*)

As High Priest on the night of His arrest He interceded for believers. And now as our Great High Priest seated at the right hand of the Father, He continues to intercede for His people. Jesus is praying for us now, and His ministry of intercession will continue perpetually until His return.

The Old Testament shows us this too in type and shadow. The Israelite high priest bore the names of the twelves tribes of Israel, engraved on precious stones, on his shoulders and over his breast (*Ex 28:12; 39:6-7*). The Scripture says he was to bear their names 'before the LORD' (*Ex. 28:12*). Thus, as he carried out his priestly ministry in the presence of the LORD, the high priest carried the people of Israel with him on his person. He stood before the LORD in their name and for them. As he entered into the Holy of Holies on the Day of Atonement with blood and incense, the high priest carried out the ministry of intercession for his people, the people of the LORD God. And Jesus does the same for us. 'My name is graven on His hands. My name is written on His heart.'[4]

Christ's Intercession is an Abiding Intercession

The Lord Jesus 'always lives to make intercession' for us (*Heb. 7:25*). Just as His life cannot end, neither can His intercession. His intercession consists not only of His words spoken in prayer, but of the very presence of His person.

> For Christ has not entered the holy places made with hands, *which are* copies of the true, but into heaven itself, now to appear in the presence of God for us; not that He should offer Himself often, as the high priest enters the Most Holy Place every year with blood of another — He then would have had to suffer often since the foundation of the world; but now, once at the end of the ages, He has appeared to put away sin by the sacrifice of Himself. (*Heb. 9:24-26*)

---

[4] Charitie Lees Bancroft, 'Before the Throne of God Above'.

Therefore, as long as His person endures, so shall His intercession. 'I know that while in heav'n He stands, no tongue can bid me thence depart.'[5]

Christ's Intercession is an Effective Intercession

Not only does Christ's intercession abide forever, but it abides effectively forever. At Lazarus' graveside, Jesus prayed to His Father, saying, 'I know that You always hear Me, but because of the people who are standing by I said this, that they may believe that You sent Me' (*Jn 11:42*). The Father always hears the Son's prayers. This doesn't just mean that He happens to hear the words that the Son pronounces. When the Bible says God 'hears' prayer, it is talking about how He answers prayer. So if the Father always hears the Son's prayer, then the Son's prayer is always effective. With Charles Wesley we sing this truth:

> The Father hears Him pray,
> His dear Anointed One;
> He cannot turn away
> The presence of His Son.[6]

Yet, in the same hymn, Wesley also shows us that the efficacy of Christ's High Priestly intercession for us now in heaven is directly tied to the great value of His atoning death on Calvary:

> Five bleeding wounds He bears,
> Received on Calvary;
> They pour effectual prayers,
> They strongly plead for me;
> 'Forgive him, oh forgive,' they cry,
> 'Nor let that ransomed sinner die.'[7]

As the Puritan theologian Stephen Charnock taught, 'the efficacy of his plea depends on the value and purity of his sacrifice.'[8]

---

[5] Bancroft, 'Before the Throne of God Above'.

[6] Charles Wesley, 'Arise, My Soul Arise', *Redemption Hymnal*, 200.

[7] Wesley, 'Arise, My Soul Arise.'

[8] Stephen Charnock, 'Christ's Intercession,' *The Complete Works of Stephen Charnock*, (Edinburgh: James Nichol, 1866), 5:102.

Christ's Ministry as Intercessor For His People

Christ appears before God on behalf of His People

Just as the Old Testament high priest appeared before God on behalf of the people (*Ex 28:29*), so too Jesus our great heavenly High Priest appears in the presence of God, not for His own sake, but on our behalf. Our High Priest has entered 'into heaven itself, now to appear in the presence of God for us' (*Heb. 9:24*). This appearance before God on our behalf is (as we have seen in the previous chapter on the Ascension) the culmination of Christ's saving work of the cross. It is by His appearance in the presence of God in intercession for us that He 'save[s] to the uttermost those who come to God through Him' (*Heb. 7:25*). D.P. Williams said, 'Christ is the author of our eternal salvation, and is making our salvation effectual within us by His continual ministry on our behalf before the Father.'[9]

Paul connects the intercession of Christ with the believer's security in *Romans 8:31-39*. 'Who is he who condemns? It is Christ who died, and furthermore is also risen, who is even at the right hand of God, who also makes intercession for us' (*v.34*). Because the ascended Christ makes intercession for us, we have no need to fear 'tribulation, or distress, or persecution, or famine, or nakedness, or peril, or sword' (*v.35*), for, in the face of Christ's effectual intercession, nothing can 'separate us from the love of God which is in Christ Jesus our Lord' (*v.39*).

Christ's appearance for us in heaven is, in itself, an intercession, for His blood speaks (*Heb. 12:24*). 'His presence, therefore, in our humanity at the right hand of God, with the signs of His sacrifice, is sufficient for our justification and absolution. At the sight of His wounds, the charges brought by the infamous accuser are dismissed.'[10]

In Him we enter the Holy of Holies by His Blood

Just as the Old Testament high priest entered into the Holy of Holies in the tabernacle and temple by the blood of the sacrifice on the Day of Atonement (*Lev. 16:3*), so, as we have seen, Jesus has entered into the true heavenly Holy of Holies by His blood at His ascension. But now that our great

---

[9] D.P. Williams, *Herald of Grace*, 2.4 (June 1942), 48.
[10] W.R. Thomas, *L'Emmanuele* (Naples: Edizioni Ricchezze di Grazia), 60.

heavenly High Priest sits within the veil, we too have 'boldness to enter the Holiest by the blood of Jesus, by a new and living way which He consecrated for us, through the veil, that is, His flesh' (*Heb. 10:19-20*). By our great Intercessor in the heavenly Holy of Holies, we can 'come boldly to the throne of grace, that we may obtain mercy and find grace to help in time of need' (*Heb. 4:16*). So Jesus, by His intercession, brings us in so that we can pray and intercede, not shouting our requests from a distance and hoping they will be heard, but right into the presence of God at His throne of grace.

The prayers and intercessions of Christians are not works which we accomplish for God or to try to merit His favour. Rather, Christians pray and intercede in their union with Christ. 'The true saints on earth, from their union with Christ, the Great High Priest, are themselves made intercessors' and so can pray with confidence, relying on Him to whom they are united.[11]

He offers up the Incense of Prayer Before God

When the Old Testament high priest entered the Holiest place on the Day of Atonement, he entered with incense (*Lev. 16:12-13*). The New Testament teaches us the significance of the offering of incense up to God: 'bowls full of incense, which are the prayers of the saints' (*Rev. 5:8*). Even in Old Testament times, the Psalmist had drawn a connection between incense and prayer (*Ps 141:2*).

So, as the high priest of the Old Covenant entered with incense, so the High Priest of the New Covenant enters with prayer. He is seated in heaven as the one who intercedes for us (*Rom. 8:34; Heb. 7:25*), and although He intercedes even without words, by presenting Himself as the Lamb once slain for us, this doesn't mean that His intercession doesn't also include praying for us (for the word Greek word for *intercede* means 'to bring requests'), just as He did for His people on the night of His betrayal (*Jn 17*).

When Paul tells us that there is 'one Mediator between God and men, the Man Christ Jesus' (*1 Tim. 2:5*), it is in the context of writing to Timothy about prayer (*1 Tim. 2:1-8*). Therefore Christ our Intercessor is the Mediator of our prayers. The one who prays for us is the one who presents our prayers as sweet-smelling incense to the Father.

Following in rich line of Welsh exegetical tradition, the early Apostolics understood the incense offering Angel of *Revelation 8* to be Christ our Intercessor:

---

[11] W.R. Thomas, *L'Emmanuele* (Naples: Edizioni Ricchezze di Grazia), 61.

> Then another angel, having a golden censer, came and stood at the altar.
> He was given much incense, that he should offer it with the prayers of all
> the saints upon the golden altar which was before the throne. And the
> smoke of the incense, with the prayers of the saints, ascended before God
> from the angel's hand. (*Rev. 8:3-4*)

On these verses, D.P. Williams commented that 'there is much incense
needed even to purify our prayer.'[12] This incense is:

> the fragrance of Him who died, giving His life on the altar of the Cross,
> and going through the fire of God's judgment, which fills the heavens with
> a cloud of incense as a testimony that keeps us alive when we draw nigh.[13]

Jesus Christ, our Mediator and Intercessor in prayer, takes our prayers with
all their weaknesses, and purifies them, presenting them perfect to His
Father. The eighteenth century theologian, George Lewis, in the first ever
systematic theology written in the Welsh language, pointed out what an
encouragement this truth is to us when we find prayer difficult: 'When they
experience lots of stagnation of spirit in prayer, they are cheered as they
consider that their Great High Priest offers lots of incense to sweeten their
imperfect supplications (*Rev. 8:3*).'[14]

He bears the iniquity of the Holy Things

Over his forehead, the Old Testament high priest wore the inscription
'Holiness to the LORD' (*Ex. 28:36*). The reason given for this is:

> so it shall be on Aaron's forehead, that Aaron may bear the iniquity of the
> holy things which the children of Israel hallow in all their holy gifts; and it
> shall always be on his forehead, that they may be accepted before the Lord'
> (*Ex. 28:38*)

The high priest, through his work of sacrifice and intercession on behalf of
the people, bore the iniquity of the holy things. In other words, the sin and
impurity in the people's offerings was purified through Aaron's priestly
work for them.

Yet Jesus is a much greater High Priest than Aaron. Today the people
of God do not offer blood sacrifices, thanks to the once-for-all sacrifice of

---

[12] D.P. Williams, *Herald of Grace*, 1.11 (Nov. 1941), 162.

[13] D.P. Williams, *Herald of Grace*, 2.5 (July 1942), 60.

[14] George Lewis, *Drych Ysgrythyrol*, 176.

Christ upon the altar of Calvary. However, we come into the presence of the Lord with the sacrifice of praise (*Heb. 13:15*) and the sacrifice of service (*Rom. 12:1*).[15] And yet, like the children of Israel, our 'holy things' are touched by our sins, and need to be purified. So Jesus, our High Priest, Intercessor, and Mediator, takes our praise, our worship, and our service, and purifies it all, presenting it perfect to His Father.

Drawing on *Hebrews 9:23-24*, D.P. Williams writes:

> Let us not forget that it has to do with God's people, that the heavenly things themselves be purified; the thought is that all our life's activities, our acts of devotion, our services, even our worship, our praying, our preaching, and our praise are not pure in His sight. ... He discerns the feelings, the motives, the spiritual pride, the lack of love, the ignorance, the irreverence of His people concerning the things that are divine. All things done in His church are done in His presence, defiling the very courts of heaven itself, though we may be unconscious of those defilements and uncleanness. He has appeared before God for us; our access is sure; His blood speaks for us and purifies our service from the defilement of the flesh; and this work is continually going on for us in the heavens.[16]

He Puts an End to Matters of Controversy

Under the old covenant, when difficult controversies arose, they were to be brought to 'the priest who stands to minister ... before the LORD your God' (*Deut. 17:8-12*). Similarly today, when controversies and contentions arise in Christ's church, we can come in prayer to our Intercessor, who constantly prays for the unity of His Body (*Jn 17:21-23*). D.P. Williams says:

> In our assemblies if any matter of difference was dealt with, as it should be, in the presence of our High Priest, bickering and devouring words would soon disappear in the realisation that the High Priest's presence would bring swift satisfaction, and settlement would be realized. Self-exhibition and self-defence remain silent in the realisation that He is there.[17]

---

[15] These are not atoning sacrifices and add nothing to the once-for-all sacrifice of Christ.
[16] D.P. Williams, *Herald of Grace*, 1.11 (Nov. 1941), 162.
[17] D.P. Williams, *Herald of Grace*, 2.5 (July 1942), 60.

He blesses His People

When Jesus, our High Priest, ascended to the heavenly Holy of Holies to carry out His ministry of intercession, He was in the middle of blessing His disciples. 'While He blessed them … He was parted from them and carried up into heaven' (*Lk 24:51*). That blessing has not ended, but continues. Through the intercession of our High Priest, the Father blesses us still.

The LORD gave the Aaronic high priest a special form of blessing with which to bless the people.

> Speak to Aaron and his sons, saying, 'This is the way you shall bless the children of Israel. Say to them:
>> The Lord bless you and keep you;
>> The Lord make His face shine upon you,
>> And be gracious to you;
>> The Lord lift up His countenance upon you,
>> And give you peace.'
> So they shall put My name on the children of Israel, and I will bless them.
> (*Num. 6:23-27*)

Throughout the history of the Christian church, Christians have looked to this three-fold blessing as a Trinitarian blessing.[18] In the words of D.P. Williams:

> Thus we find the triple blessing of the Triune God as a benediction upon them; the Father (the Source), the Son (the Channel), and the Holy Spirit (the Imparter of the fulness of God's blessing). How much more is that blessing, now that our Lord has now taken His place within the heavenly sanctuary, to our enrichment with the fulness of blessings through His Priesthood.[19]

This blessing from the heavenly sanctuary includes 'every spiritual blessing in the heavenly places in Christ' (*Eph. 1:3*). This includes the blessing of feeding upon Christ at His Table. Just as Melchizedek blessed Abraham with bread and wine (*Gen. 14:18*), so too our true Melchizedek blesses us with His body and blood in bread and wine in the sacrament of the Breaking of Bread. The early Apostolics taught that Christ 'the Priest … ministers to the redeemed … [in the] Breaking of Bread and drinking of the

---

[18] See e.g. Johann Gerhard, *Loci*, Exegesis III, §152
[19] D.P. Williams, *Herald of Grace*, 2.5 (July 1942), 60.

cup, as we gather around the Table of the Lord, deriving from Him the blessings of our redemption.'[20]

Christ our Intercessor continually ministers for and to His people as their Great High Priest. His intercession is 'His perpetual ministry for the perfection of His people.'[21]

---

[20] D.P. Williams, *Herald of Grace*, 2.4 (June 1942), 47-48.
[21] D.P. Williams, *Herald of Grace*, 2.4 (June 1942), 48.

Chapter 20

Christ's Second Coming & Millennial Reign

When Christ ascended into heaven, His disciples 'looked steadfastly toward heaven as He went up' (*Acts 1:10*). While their gaze was fixed on heaven, even after they could no longer see Jesus, two angels appeared beside them and asked: 'Men of Galilee, why do you stand gazing up into heaven? This same Jesus, who was taken up from you into heaven, will so come in like manner as you saw Him go into heaven' (*Acts 1:11*). The angels brought the disciples a timely reminder that Christ would return. Jesus had already spoken of this to His disciples during His earthly ministry. For example, in *John 14:3* Jesus promised them that He would return: 'if I go and prepare a place for you, I will come again and receive you to Myself; that where I am, there you may be also.' Christ also spoke of His return in his eschatological discourses (e.g. *Lk 21:27; Mk 13:26; Mt 24:30*) as well as in several parables (e.g. the parable of the wise and foolish virgins, *Mt 25:1-13*). Thus the fact that Jesus would return was not a new teaching brought by the angels, rather it was a reminder to the disciples of what Jesus Himself had already taught them. These words of the angels continue to function as a reminder to us that *Jesus Christ will return again to earth*.

The Return of Christ

Christ promised that He will return. The angels proclaimed the truth of Christ's second coming. And throughout the New Testament the apostles declared this promise of Christ: that He will return. However, the Scriptures not only tell us that Christ will return, they also tell us a few things about His return.

A Physical, Bodily Return

The angels announced to the disciples on the day of the ascension that 'This same Jesus, who was taken up from you into heaven, will so come in like manner as you saw Him go into heaven' (*Acts 1:11*). His return will be in the same way as His ascension. Just as He ascended in a physical body, so He will return in a physical body. It must be remembered that the Incarnation was not a temporary event; Christ is still incarnate. He did not lose His human nature (and body) when He ascended to heaven. Rather He continues as God Incarnate, the God-Man. As such, He still has a human body, and so must still have His body when He returns to earth. In fact, Christ's bodily return was also taught in the Old Testament. *Zechariah 14:4* teaches us that 'in that day His feet will stand on the Mount of Olives.' For His feet to stand in a particular place, it is necessary for Him to return bodily.

An Imminent Return

The Scriptures do not tell us when Christ will return; however, they do warn us that His return will be unexpected. In the context of writing about Christ's second coming, Peter states that 'the day of the Lord will come as a thief in the night' (*2 Pet. 3:10*)[1], and calls those who are not living in expectancy of Christ's return 'scoffers' (*2 Pet. 3:3-4*). Paul also writes of the unexpected timing of Christ's return in *1 Thessalonians 5:2*, stating 'that the day of the Lord so comes as a thief in the night.'

A related theme to the unexpected timing of Christ's return is, paradoxically, that Christians should always be expecting His return. Paul writes of 'heaven, from which we also eagerly wait for the Saviour, the Lord Jesus Christ' (*Phil. 3:20*).   Likewise he gave thanks to God for the Thessalonians who were waiting for the Son of God to come back from heaven (*1 Thess. 1:10*). Scripture does not speak of Christians awaiting signs that must come to pass before Christ's return; rather it speaks of Christians

---

[1] This verse goes on to mention the passing away of heaven and earth and their replacement by the new heaven and the new earth. Yet this statement would appear to refer to both aspects: thus 'the day of the Lord' would include both Christ's return and the coming of the new heaven and new earth.

at all times expecting the return of Christ. In order to have a real present expectancy of Christ's return, that return must be possible at any moment.

James tells us that 'the coming of the Lord is at hand' (*Jas 5:8*). Thus it is not something we should think of as far away in the distant future; rather, He could return at any moment. Christ Himself speaks of the imminence of His Coming at the end of the book of Revelation, saying 'surely I am coming quickly' (*Rev. 22:20*).

Christ's Return For His Saints

In *John 14:3*, Jesus spoke of returning *for* believers: 'if I go and prepare a place for you, I will come again and receive you to Myself; that where I am, there you may be also.' Christ was speaking about coming to get His people and take them to be with Him in heaven. Paul also writes about this return *for* believers in *1 Thessalonians 4:16-17*:

> For the Lord Himself will descend from heaven with a shout, with the voice of an archangel, and with the trumpet of God. And the dead in Christ will rise first. Then we who are alive and remain shall be caught up together with them in the clouds to meet the Lord in the air. And thus we shall always be with the Lord.

In this passage we learn that (i) the Lord will come down from heaven, (ii) His people, both living and dead (then raised to life), will be gathered to meet Him in the air, and (iii) they will then always remain with the Lord. Thus Christ returns *for* His people, in order to take them to be with Him.

The Dead in Christ

In *1 Thessalonians 4*, Paul is writing to comfort the Thessalonian Christians concerning fellow-believers who had died (*1 Thess. 4:13*). Thus he explains what will happen to Christians who have died when Christ returns. Verse 16 tells us that 'the dead in Christ will rise', so all believers who have died before Christ's return will be resurrected on that day, and will then be caught up together with living believers to meet Christ in the air (*1 Thess.*

4:17). This will be the fulfilment of the promise that 'He who raised up the Lord Jesus will also raise us up with Jesus' (*2 Cor. 4:14*).

The doctrine of the resurrection of the dead is of great importance to the Christian faith. Unlike many other belief systems, Christianity does not know any dualism in which the physical (including the body) is viewed as negative and the spiritual (including the soul) is viewed as positive. On the contrary, the biblical faith teaches that God considered His physical creation 'very good' (*Gen. 1:31*). As a result, it is not beneficial for the soul to leave the body; it is not moving to a higher sphere of existence. Rather, the separation of body and soul at death is only temporary as we await the resurrection of the dead. After all, Christ did not only die to save our souls, but to save us as whole people. As Paul writes to the Romans, we are currently 'eagerly waiting for … the redemption of our body' (*Rom. 8:23*). Furthermore he explains that 'we were saved in this hope' (*Rom. 8:24*); thus the hope of the redemption of the body (the hope of the resurrection of the dead) is part of the experience of salvation. The resurrection, or *glorification*, is the future aspect of our salvation.

The bodies with which the souls of the dead in Christ will be reunited at the resurrection are the very same bodies which were laid in the grave. We have already seen that this was the case at Jesus' resurrection.[2] In the Old Testament, the prophet Daniel declared that 'many of those who sleep in the dust of the earth shall awake, some to everlasting life, some to shame and everlasting contempt' (*Dan. 12:2*). The reference to sleeping in the dust of the earth makes clear that Daniel is referring to bodily resurrection. Jesus Himself spoke of the time when those 'who are in the graves will hear His voice and come forth' (*Jn 5:28-29*).

Moreover, the believer's resurrection body will be like Christ's resurrection body. Scripture teaches that Christ 'will transform our lowly body that it may be conformed to His glorious body' (*Phil. 3:21*) and likewise that 'when He is revealed, we shall be like Him' (*1 Jn 3:2*). When Jesus rose from the dead, He demonstrated very clearly that it was with the same body which had been crucified and buried. His resurrection body was still a body of 'flesh and bones' (*Lk 24:39*). Thus one of the ways in which the believer's resurrection body will be like that of Christ, is that the believer will be raised with the body which was buried, a body of 'flesh and bones'.

Yet, in other ways this resurrection body will be different from that which was laid in the grave, just as was Christ's resurrection body. Again *Philippians 3:21* is particularly relevant: '[Christ] will transform our lowly

---

[2] See Chapter 17.

body that it may be conformed to His glorious body.' The emphasis in this verse is actually on the change that will take place in our bodies at the resurrection. Like Christ's resurrection body, the believer's resurrection body will be perfected. That is why the Bible speaks of this change as *glorification*. As we read in 1 *Corinthians 15:52*, our resurrection bodies will be 'incorruptible'.

Those who are alive and remain

Not all Christians will die before Christ returns; He is not waiting for the last believer to die off before He can come back. This means that there will be living Christians who cannot be resurrected at Christ's coming (not having been dead in the first place). So what will happen to them? Do they miss out on the blessings of the resurrection just because they have not died?

Paul also deals with this question. To the Corinthians he writes:

> Behold, I tell you a mystery: We shall not all sleep, but we shall all be changed—in a moment, in the twinkling of an eye, at the last trumpet. For the trumpet will sound, and the dead will be raised incorruptible, and we shall be changed. For this corruptible must put on incorruption, and this mortal must put on immortality. So when this corruptible has put on incorruption, and this mortal has put on immortality, then shall be brought to pass the saying that is written:
> 'Death is swallowed up in victory.'
> 'O Death, where is your sting? O Hades, where is your victory?'
> (1 *Cor. 15:51-55*)

Thus, even those believers who have not died will be glorified; their bodies will be transformed (and can be spoken of as resurrection bodies) even though they have not technically been resurrected themselves (although they will share in Christ's resurrection). *Verse 51* tells us that 'we shall all be changed' whether or not we 'sleep'. Thus there is no difference in what happens to those who have died and those who are still alive.

The Rapture

Paul explains to the Thessalonians that 'the dead in Christ will rise first. Then we who are alive and remain shall be caught up together with them in the clouds to meet the Lord in the air. And thus we shall always be with the

Lord' (*1 Thess. 4:16-17*). Thus when the dead in Christ are resurrected and the living in Christ glorified, they are also 'caught up … in the clouds to meet the Lord in the air.' This catching-up is referred to as the *rapture*.[3] The result of the rapture in *verse 17* is that 'thus we shall always be with the Lord.' From that moment on, believers will be where the Incarnate Christ is.

Christ's Return With His Saints

Scripture does not only teach that Christ will return *for* believers to take them to be with Him. He will not simply take His saints out of the world and then leave the unbelieving world to carry on as normal. Rather Scripture teaches that, after[4] Christ has returned for his saints, He will return with His saints.[5] Jude, the Lord's brother, records Enoch's prophecy of Christ's return, declaring: 'Behold, the Lord comes with ten thousands of His saints' (*Jude 14*). In the book of Revelation a description is given of Christ's return to earth, which includes the fact that 'the armies in heaven, clothed in fine linen, white and clean, followed Him' (*Rev. 19:14*). Earlier in the same chapter we read that it was the Bride of the Lamb to whom 'it was granted to be arrayed in fine linen, clean and bright, for the fine linen is the righteous acts of the saints' (*Rev. 19:8*). Thus the heavenly armies clothed in fine linen are none other than the members of Christ's Bride, namely His saints. How can believers return with Christ? Simply because Christ has already returned for them and 'thus [they] shall always be with the Lord.'

---

[3] The word rapture simply comes from the Latin verb, used in the Latin translation of this passage, meaning 'to catch up'.

[4] Theologians vary in their views as to whether this is immediately after or after a certain period of time. Space will not allow us to enter into discussion of the events which some interpreters understand to intervene on earth between the rapture and Christ's return with His Saints to commence His millennial reign (notably the *Tribulation*). Rather, this chapter, like our Tenet, will keep its focus on Christ's action.

[5] Saints are not a special type of Christian; rather the Bible calls all true believers saints.

Christ's Millennial Reign Upon the Earth

Millennial Views

The book of Revelation speaks of a thousand-year reign of Christ upon the earth. Among evangelical Christians, there are three main views of this thousand-year reign, or millennium.

Amillennialism

Amillennialism literally means no-millennium, but it's not that amillennialists don't believe in any Millennium at all. Rather, Amillennialism is the view that the thousand years of *Revelation 20* should be interpreted symbolically of the kingdom of God present on earth throughout the whole period between the first and second comings of Christ. Those who follow this eschatological view 'hold that the promises made to Israel, David, and Abraham in the Old Testament are fulfilled by Jesus Christ and his church during this present age.'[6] They understand the binding of Satan for a thousand years to represent the victory over Satan and the powers of evil won by Christ through His death and resurrection. Amillennialism rose to prominence at the time of Augustine (AD 354-430) who was the first to give systematic expression to the amillennial system.

Postmillennialism

Postmillennialism is the view that Christ will return after the end of the Millennium. Postmillennialists expect the church age to transition into the Millennium. Classical Postmillennialism is very similar to Amillennialism, except that it expects worldwide revival to take place before the return of Christ, with the conversion of all nations. As more and more people are saved, there will be peace on earth, and this peaceful period of world-wide revival is what Classical Postmillennialism calls the Millennium. Like

---

[6] Kim Riddelbarger, *A Case for Amillennialism: Understanding the End Times* (Grand Rapids: Baker, 2003), 31.

Amillennialism, Postmillennialism does not see this as a literal thousand years; unlike Amillennialism, Postmillennialism does not see this as the entire church age. This millennial period will begin gradually and end with the return of Christ. A more recent form of Postmillennialism gained a certain degree of popularity among charismatics, where it was known as 'Kingdom Now' or 'dominion theology.'

Premillennialism

Premillennialism is the view that Christ will return before the Millennium begins. When Christ returns He will usher in His thousand-year long reign upon the earth. This was the earliest understanding of the Millennium in the history of the church, being held by such early Fathers as Papias, Justin Martyr, Irenaeus, and Tertullian.[7] This is significant as Papias was born about 30 years before the completion of the New Testament and was a disciple of John, and Irenaeus was a disciple of John's disciple Polycarp. Thus, if John, the seer of the vision of the Millennium in *Revelation 20*, was opposed to a premillennial understanding of his words, it's likely that Papias and Irenaeus would have known. Yet Papias taught 'that after the resurrection of the dead there will be a period of a thousand years when the kingdom of Christ will be set up in material form on this earth.'[8] In the middle of the second century, Justin Martyr would write:

> I, and all other wholeheartedly orthodox Christians, feel certain that there will be a resurrection of the flesh, followed by a thousand years in the rebuilt, embellished, and enlarged city of Jerusalem, as was announced by the prophets Ezekiel, Isaiah, and the others.[9]

As this is the doctrine expressed in the Tenets of the Apostolic Church, we shall examine in more detail the case for Premillennialism below.

---

[7] Although, it should be noted that not all modern forms of Premillennialism correspond the ancient Premillennialism of the Irenaeus and Justin. In the Ancient Church Premillennialism was called *Chiliasm* (from the Greek word for one thousand).

[8] *Fragments of Papias*, 3.12

[9] Justin Martyr, *Dialogue with Trypho*, 80.5

Premillennialism: The Apostolic Doctrine

The Premillennial view of the Millennium is that when Christ returns with His saints, He will remain on the earth to reign as King for a thousand years. We call this Christ's *Millennial Reign*. The key passage in Scripture for this doctrine of Christ's reign on the earth for a thousand years after His return is *Revelation 20*. There we read that, after Jesus comes back with His saints, Satan will be bound in the bottomless pit for a thousand years, 'so that he should deceive the nations no more till the thousand years were finished' (*Rev. 20:2-3*).

John then goes on to describe what will happen on earth during those thousand years:

> And I saw thrones, and they sat on them, and judgment was committed to them. Then I saw the souls of those who had been beheaded for their witness to Jesus and for the word of God, who had not worshiped the beast or his image, and had not received his mark on their foreheads or on their hands. And they lived and reigned with Christ for a thousand years. But the rest of the dead did not live again until the thousand years were finished. This is the first resurrection. Blessed and holy is he who has part in the first resurrection. Over such the second death has no power, but they shall be priests of God and of Christ, and shall reign with Him a thousand years. (*Rev. 20:4-6*)

This passage teaches that Christ will reign upon the earth for a thousand years with His glorified saints.[10] Thus, during Christ's Millennial Reign, (i) Satan will be bound for a thousand years, (ii) Christ will reign upon the earth, and (iii) His saints will reign with Him.[11]

---

[10] For those who see a time interval between the rapture and the beginning of the Millennium this would include both those who have been raptured and have now returned along with Christ (the 'they' who sit on the thrones in *verse 4* are the returning saints of chapter 19:14), and those who have come to faith since the rapture (these are the 'those who had been beheaded' of *verse 4*).

[11] The Millennial Reign will also be an important period for fulfilment of promises made by God to Israel. As this is not a work on eschatology *per se*, space will not permit a discussion of these aspects of Christ's Millennial Reign, nor of how the Millennial Reign will come to its end. The promises yet to be fulfilled to Israel are also a further proof that Christ will indeed reign upon the earth after His return.

Premillennialism in Revelation 20

John is at pains to emphasise the 'thousand years' in *Revelation 20*: six times within the space of six verses he uses the expression 'thousand years' (*Rev. 20:2-7*). The Millennium, then, is not a minor detail of the text, but John's great point of emphasis here. This 'thousand years' begins after Christ's return (*Rev. 19:11-16*), with the binding of Satan in the bottomless pit (*Rev. 20:2-3*).

Yet, the six-fold repetition of 'thousand years' after the account of the return of Christ isn't the only aspect of *Revelation 20* that points us to Premillennialism. In *verses 4-5* we also see the resurrection occurring in two parts, on either side of the thousand years. At the beginning of the thousand years 'the souls of those who had been beheaded for their witness to Jesus and for the word of God' are resurrected and they live and reign with Christ for the Millennium. 'But the rest of the dead did not live again until the thousand years were finished' (*Rev. 20:5*). If Christ does not return before the Millennium, then how can the martyrs be resurrected before the Millennium without being resurrected long before the return of Christ?

Not only are the saints resurrected at Christ's return and before the Millennium, but John also tells us that they 'reigned with Christ for a thousand years' (*Rev. 20:4;* see also *verse 6*). The saints are to reign with Christ after His return and their resurrection, so this necessitates a period of time (the 'thousand years') in which they will reign with Him.

Believers' Future Reign with Christ

So the fact of believers' future reign with Christ points us to a premillennial understanding of Christ's return. Yet *Revelation 20* isn't the only Scripture which speaks of the saints' future reign with Jesus. Earlier in Revelation the redeemed sing the praise of the Lamb:

> For You were slain,
> And have redeemed us to God by Your blood
> Out of every tribe and tongue and people and nation,
> And have made us kings and priests to our God;
> And we shall reign on the earth. (*Rev. 5:9-10*)

The letter to the church at Thyatira also speaks of such a reign; when Christ comes He will give the overcomers 'power over the nations' (*Rev. 2:25-27*). Similarly, Paul writes, 'If we endure, we shall also reign with Him' (*2 Tim. 2:12*). Jesus had even promised the twelve apostles 'that in the regeneration, when the Son of Man sits on the throne of His glory, you who have followed Me will also sit on twelve thrones, judging the twelve tribes of Israel' (*Mt 19:28*).

Christ's Reign from His Coming to the End of Time

Paul writes to the Corinthians of Christ's handing over of the Kingdom to the Father 'after' (εἶτα) His coming (*1 Cor. 15:23-25*). It is 'when he shall have put down all rule and all authority and power' (*v.24 AV*) that Christ will then deliver His Kingdom to the Father. So the sequence here is, first the resurrection of Christ, then the resurrection of those who belong to Christ at the moment of His return, and after that He puts down all rule and authority and the Kingdom comes to its end. So, although Paul does not speak of a thousand years, he does here indicate some interval between Christ's return and 'the end', during which Christ will reign.

The Millennial Reign in the Old Testament

As well as the explicit teaching of *Revelation 20* and the consistent New Testament teaching of a future reign of believers with Christ upon the earth, we also find the concept of the millennium in the Old Testament Scriptures. A number of Old Testament prophecies speak of a time which neither fits the conditions we know on earth now, and yet which do not speak of the conditions in the new heavens and the new earth either. Isaiah spoke of a such a time:

> It shall come to pass in that day
> That the LORD will punish on high the host of exalted ones,
> And on the earth the kings of the earth.
> They will be gathered together,
> As prisoners are gathered in the pit,
> And will be shut up in the prison;
> After many days they will be punished.
> Then the moon will be disgraced
> And the sun ashamed;
> For the LORD of hosts will reign

> On Mount Zion and in Jerusalem
> And before His elders, gloriously. (*Isa. 24:21-23*)

While the LORD of Hosts reigns in Jerusalem, the kings of the earth and the host of exalted beings are gathered together as prisoners awaiting punishment. So at the same time as the Lord is reigning gloriously on the earth, prisoners are awaiting a coming day of judgment. Therefore, this cannot be the new earth. The judgement upon these kings is in two phases: first they will be 'gathered in the pit' and then 'after many days they will be punished.' This points to an intermediate kingdom, between Christ's return and the final judgment and eternal state.[12]

Earlier in *Isaiah 11:6-11*, the prophet spoke of a time when predators and prey would dwell in peace together, and when the children of women would fear nothing from serpents (*cf. Gen. 3:15*). It would be a time when the whole earth would 'be full of the knowledge of the LORD as the waters cover the sea' (*v.9*). The promised Root of Jesse (the Messiah) will be there, and the nations will gather to Him (*v.10*). Yet, the Messianic King will still, 'in that day,' be recovering 'the remnant of His people' (*v.11*), and, still 'in that day' there will be Gentiles who will seek Him for salvation (*v.10*). So, despite the glory of this 'resting place' of the Rod of Jesse, this cannot be the new earth. Rather, Isaiah points us to a time after Christ's return, when He will reign in glory and peace upon the earth.

Towards the end of his prophecy, Isaiah speaks of the age to come. Here Isaiah prophesies two things in quick succession: the eternal state of the 'new heavens and a new earth' (*Isa. 65:17-18b*), followed immediately by a prophecy of the millennial kingdom (*Isa. 65:18c-25*). The repeated expression 'for behold, I create' (*vv. 17-18*) introduces each of these successive prophecies.[13] Like *Isaiah 11*, the millennial prophecy here in *Isaiah 65* speaks of a time when 'the wolf and the lamb shall feed together' (*v.25*). However, this is clearly not the eternal state, for, there will still be death and sin (*v.20*). This is a kingdom where the Lord Himself will bring great comfort and blessing to His people, far greater than they know in this present age; yet it is not the new earth.

It is not only Isaiah who speaks of this intermediate kingdom between the return of Christ and the eternal state. Both Solomon and Zechariah also speak of it in *Psalm 72:8-14, Zechariah 8* and *Zechariah 14:5-17*. *Isaiah 2:2-4* and *Micah 4:1-5* may also refer to the millennial kingdom.

---

[12] Note also the strong parallels between *Isa. 24:21-23* and *Rev. 19-20*.

[13] For further details on this division of these oracles, see J. Alec Motyer, *The Prophecy of Isaiah: An Introduction and Commentary*, (Downers Grove: IVP, 1993), 529.

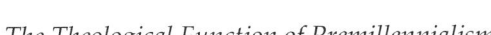

The Theological Function of Premillennialism

Those who reject the doctrine of a future millennial kingdom after the return of Christ often question its theological function.[14] In the early church, premillennialism was seen by theologians such as Irenaeus as a major bulwark against the gnostic heretics who saw created reality as evil and unredeemable. Against the Gnostics, premillennialism pointed to the goodness of God's creation, as it looked, not just to a future for our souls in heaven, but a bodily future here, upon this very same earth. The doctrine of Christ's future millennial kingdom points to a time when *this* earth (as opposed to the new earth) 'shall be full of the knowledge of the LORD as the waters cover the sea' (*Isa. 11:9*). This earth has not been written off and abandoned to sin and the devil; rather, it will be the site of Christ's future glorious reign.[15]

Premillennialism also underscores the doctrine of *Solus Christus* (*Christ Alone*). It is not the human beings, whether society by its cultural advances or even the church by her missionary endeavours, who set up Christ's Kingdom upon this earth, but Christ Himself, and Christ alone. As Daniel told Nebuchadnezzar: 'the God of heaven will set up a kingdom which shall never be destroyed' (*Dan. 2:44*). Christ is the rock which struck the image in Nebuchadnezzar's dream and which 'became a great mountain and filled the whole earth' (*Dan. 2:35*). The great Apostolic missionary apostle, E.H. Williams, warned against the creeping influence of Postmillennialism among charismatics and Pentecostals, with its concept of the church's role in 'the establishment of an earthly political kingdom at this time and in this Age.' Instead, it is 'the Lord [who] is destined to establish His earthly kingdom, and to rule and reign here on earth for a thousand years.'[16] The contemporary 'Kingdom Now' variety of Postmillennialism tends to take

[14] E.g. Richard Bauckham, 'Must Christian Eschatology be Millenarian?: A Response to Jürgen Moltmann,' in K. E. Brower and M. W. Elliott ed., *'The reader must understand': Eschatology in Bible and Theology* (Leicester: Apollos, 1997) 263-277.

[15] For further details on the function of premillennialism in the theology of the early church, see Donald Fairbairn, 'Contemporary Millennial/Tribulational Debates: Whose Side was the Early Church On?', in Craig L. Blomberg and Sung Wook Chung ed., *A Case for Historic Premillennialism: An Alternative to 'Left Behind' Eschatology* (Grand Rapids: Baker, 2009), 105-131.

[16] E.H. Williams, *End-Time Living: 1994 Penygroes Convention Bible Readings* (Penygroes: ACTS, 1994), 20. Williams particularly notes how the Postmillennial 'Kingdom Now' emphasis has subtly crept into confessionally Premillennial Pentecostal churches through the songs which we sing.

the focus from Christ, to the church's role in the establishment of the kingdom. Premillennialism, on the other hand, guards the *Sola Christus*.

The doctrine of the imminence of Christ's return is also an important aspect of premillennial hope. Post-millennialism (and often amillennialism too) pushes the expectancy of Christ's return into the distance. Premillennialism, however, is not waiting for a golden age of the church on earth before Christ's coming. Instead, it looks with fervent hope and expectation to the coming of the Lord, that He might soon set up His millennial kingdom upon the earth.

Finally, sometimes the question is asked of whether all these hopes could not simply be met by the eternal state beginning immediately upon Christ's return. Such a beginning to the new heavens and new earth could be imminent, would guard the *Solus Christus*, and would witness to the goodness of the physical creation and the redemption of the body in the resurrection. However, a move directly to the new heavens and the new earth would not involve the redemption of this present form of the heavens and the earth. In our salvation, we are not immediately glorified and given resurrection bodies, but rather, these bodies in their current form are saved, all the while looking forward to the day of the resurrection of the body. The millennial kingdom will see the redemption of this earth (in its current form), all the while in anticipation of its resurrection (along with the heavens) after the Millennium, into the new heavens and the new earth.

'Christ has died. Christ is risen. Christ will come again.' At the centre of the doctrine of the return of Christ and His millennial Kingdom, is Christ the soon-coming-King. We must not allow ourselves to be distracted from Him by speculations over details of events surrounding His return. Jesus is the Coming One. Jesus is the King. It is to Him that 'the Spirit and the Bride say, "Come!"' (*Rev. 22:17*).

Chapter 21

We shall see Him as He is: The New Heavens, the New Earth & the Beatific Vision

The End

The millennial kingdom is not the end. Rather, the end will come after the Millennium, when all things are under the feet of Christ the King.

> Then comes the end, when He delivers the kingdom to God the Father, when He puts an end to all rule and all authority and power. For He must reign till He has put all enemies under His feet. The last enemy that will be destroyed is death. For 'He has put all things under His feet.' But when He says 'all things are put under Him,' it is evident that He who put all things under Him is excepted. Now when all things are made subject to Him, then the Son Himself will also be subject to Him who put all things under Him, that God may be all in all. (*1 Cor. 15:24-28*)

D.P. Williams expounded these verses, writing:

> the great effect and the wonderful outcome of Calvary being accomplished, when at the end of the Millennium He will return everything back to God the Father. He will give back the Creation to God, perfected through the redeeming work on Calvary … He will give back the waters and the air, the material and vegetable kingdoms, animal and man, redeemed in the Person of the Lord Jesus Christ. … And [the Father] will have joy throughout Eternity to His Infinite Heart because He is satisfied in His own Son.[1]

The New Heavens and the New Earth

After the Millennium and the final judgment, John 'saw a new heaven and a new earth, for the first heaven and the first earth had passed away' (*Rev.*

---

[1] D.P. Williams, *Riches of Grace*, i.11 (Dec. 1920), 7. For further explanation of these verses, see Augustine, *The Trinity*, 1.3.16.

21:1). But why will the heavens and the earth pass away and why will they become new? The answer to this lies in Adam's sin. The Lord put a curse upon all of nature because of man's sin. 'Cursed is the ground for your sake' (*Gen. 3:17*), He told Adam. Paul explains this a bit more in Romans:

> For the creation was subjected to futility, not willingly, but because of Him who subjected it in hope; because the creation itself also will be delivered from the bondage of corruption into the glorious liberty of the children of God. For we know that the whole creation groans and labours with birth pangs together until now. (*Rom. 8:20-22*)

Just as all mankind has fallen into bondage through Adam's first sin, so too all of creation lies in bondage because of that same first sin. And so all of creation 'eagerly waits' for the resurrection of the dead and its own 'resurrection' to newness (*Rom. 8:19*). Then the heavens and the earth will be set free from the curse and 'delivered from the bondage of corruption' (*Rom. 8:21*).

But how will this deliverance of the creation happen? The answer the Scriptures give is, by fire.

> By the word of God the heavens were of old, and the earth standing out of water and in the water, by which the world that then existed perished, being flooded with water. But the heavens and the earth which are now preserved by the same word, are reserved for fire until the day of judgment and perdition of ungodly men. ... But the day of the Lord will come as a thief in the night, in which the heavens will pass away with a great noise, and the elements will melt with fervent heat; both the earth and the works that are in it will be burned up. Therefore, since all these things will be dissolved, what manner of persons ought you to be in holy conduct and godliness, looking for and hastening the coming of the day of God, because of which the heavens will be dissolved, being on fire, and the elements will melt with fervent heat? Nevertheless we, according to His promise, look for new heavens and a new earth in which righteousness dwells. (*2 Pet. 3:5-7, 10-13*)

Just as the world before the flood was washed away by the waters, so too the present world will be burnt away in the fire. But does that mean the present creation is destroyed? Or does it mean that the present creation is renewed?

View 1: A Brand New Heaven and Earth (Annihilation of the Old Heaven and Earth)

Some theologians[2] believe that the fire will annihilate the old heaven and earth and God will create a brand new heaven and earth out of nothing (*ex nihilo*). They base this on Jesus statement that 'heaven and earth will pass away, but My words will by no means pass away' *(Lk 21:33)*, as well as the use of the word 'perish' in *Hebrews 1:11* and the word 'create' in *Isaiah 65:17*.

However, none of these words necessitate annihilation and a new creation *ex nihilo*. The same word for 'create' *(Isa. 65:17)* is used of God's creation of man *(Gen. 1:27)* and yet man was created from the dust of the earth *(Gen. 2:7)*. The Greek word for 'perish' *(Heb. 1:11)* is used a hundred times in the New Testament and can be used of things that can't function the way they were intended anymore (like wineskins with holes in them) or things that have got lost. It's also the word used for people perishing in hell, which (as we have seen in chapter 10) is not an annihilation.

View 2: Resurrection of Heaven and Earth

Other theologians believe that the fire will purify and renovate heaven and earth so that they will become new. Augustine wrote:

> The judgment having been finished this heaven and this earth will cease to be when a new heaven and a new earth will begin to be. For by a change of things, not by an entire destruction, will this world pass away.[3]

Paul writes to the Corinthians that 'the form of this world is passing away' *(1 Cor. 7:31)*. As when we die, the form of our bodies decays in the ground, yet this does not mean that our substance ceases to exist, and so God can resurrect our bodies on the last day. Therefore the fiery destruction of the heavens and the earth is like death, through which 'the form of this world' passes away; but the God who created the heavens and the earth by His Word and Spirit is the God who raises the dead. And so the new heavens and new earth are the resurrected heavens and resurrected earth.

---

[2] Including the great Johann Gerhard.
[3] Augustine, *City of God*, 20.14

This is always God's way of redemption: through death and out the other side into resurrection life. And redemption is exactly what is happening with the coming of the new heavens and new earth: 'the creation itself also will be delivered from the bondage of corruption into the glorious liberty of the children of God' (*Rom. 8:21*).

Peter's teaching on the burning up and melting of the heavens and earth in the fire (*2 Pet. 3:5-7, 10-13*) also points to this being a resurrection. Peter compares this destruction of the world to the destruction of the world by water in the flood of Noah's day (*v.6*). Yet the earth which 'perished' in the flood wasn't annihilated. It was the same earth which had a new life as it was once again filled with plants, animals and human beings after the flood. The watery judgment of the flood brought cleansing and a new beginning to the earth; and that, says Peter, is what the fire will do at the end of the age. Francis Turretin explained it like this:

> What fire melts and burns up is not usually annihilated; yea, they are only purged of dross and impurities, as in the metallic kingdom the metal is not annihilated but purged, and comes forth purer after being subjected to fire.[4]

On that last day, the Lord will bring the heavens and the earth safe through the fiery judgment and purification, and safely out the other side into resurrection life.

Life in the New Heavens and the New Earth

The first generation Apostolic writer, Thomas Napier Turnbull, wrote that this life of the redeemed in the new heavens and the new earth 'will be a most blessed and glorious life, a permanent life of good things, and above all, a life of fellowship with the Father, Son, and Holy Spirit, and with the saints of God of all ages.'[5] We will see God (we'll think about this more below), and from Him flows all the blessedness of that life of the age to come.

John describes life in the New Heavens and New Earth in *Revelation 21:1-22:5*. There we read of the blessed life of the redeemed in the presence of the Triune God, where all the evil effects of sin will be banished. The saints will know the perfect comfort of God, and 'there shall be no more

---

[4] Francis Turretin, *Institutes*, 3:591
[5] T.N. Turnbull, *Tenet Booklet 3.3*, 19.

death, nor sorrow, nor crying. There shall be no more pain, for the former things have passed away' (*Rev. 21:4; cf. Rev. 7:15-16*). In this eternal state, 'there shall be no more curse' (*Rev. 22:3*); rather, because the sin and all its results will be no more, we will once again have free access to 'the tree of life' (*Rev. 22:2*). As a result of the Triune God's perfect presence, comfort and care, the redeemed will enjoy unspeakable bliss in the glory of God (*Ps 16:11; Jn 17:24*), of which we can only know a foretaste now in this age through the eschatological in-breaking of the Holy Spirit's filling (*1 Pet. 1:8*).

Even our glorified resurrection bodies will be transformed by the sight and presence of the Lord, so that, as Jesus shone in the radiance of His glory at His transfiguration, so 'the righteous will shine forth as the sun in the kingdom of their Father' (*Mt. 13:43*). The in-breaking of the glory of this glory in the Transfiguration of Christ also points to the fellowship the saints will enjoy with one another, through their mutual fellowship with the Father and His Son in the Spirit, in the eternal state. We will know one another, just as the disciples knew Moses and Elijah, despite never having met in this earthly life (*Mt 17:3-4*).

The New Jerusalem: Heaven Meets Earth

When John sees the new heaven and new earth, he also sees 'the holy city, New Jerusalem, coming down out of heaven from God, prepared as a bride adorned for her husband' (*Rev. 21:2*). In this city, the Lord dwells with His people (*Rev. 21:3*). Yet, John is not the first to have a vision of this heavenly city. The prophet Ezekiel saw it, telling us that the name of the city is 'the LORD is there' (*Ezek. 48:35*). Ezekiel looks forward to a time when the presence of the LORD will not be hidden behind closed doors in the Holy of Holies. Instead it will fill the entire city, to the extent that it will be called 'the LORD is there.'

Ezekiel's description of the glorious city of the presence of God with His people (*Ezek. 48:30-35*) corresponds to John's description of the New Jerusalem (*Rev. 21:9-14*). However, this city is not just a very nice place to live. John tells us:

> But I saw no temple in it, for the Lord God Almighty and the Lamb are its temple. The city had no need of the sun or of the moon to shine in it, for the glory of God illuminated it. The Lamb is its light. (*Rev. 21:22-23*)

There is no temple in the city, because the Triune God Himself is there. The city itself is God's Holy of Holies. 'Behold, the tabernacle of God is with men, and He will dwell with them, and they shall be His people. God Himself will be with them and be their God' (*Rev. 21:3*). This is the life of the New Jerusalem: the Triune God dwelling with His people, they in Him and He in them as His Holy of Holies. For the city itself is 'the Bride, the Lamb's wife' (*Rev. 21:9*). This is the eternal future of the Church, which is the Body of Christ. The Church is to be called 'the LORD is there.'

This has been the plan of God for humanity from the beginning. When God had created man, He set him in the Garden of Eden (*Gen. 2:15*). Yet Eden was not only a garden, but a temple. We are told that the LORD God placed the man in the garden 'to tend and keep it' (*Gen. 2:15*). Yet this combination of words ('tend and keep') is only used elsewhere of the service of the Levites in the tabernacle and temple. Eden is also the place where 'the Voice of the LORD God' walked with man (*Gen. 3:8*), just as He would later in the tabernacle and temple (*cf. Lev. 26:11-12*). So, Eden was the place of meeting with the presence of God, and where Adam served and worshipped Him.

Thus, Eden was a Garden-Temple.[6] But the New Jerusalem will also be a Garden-Temple. In it 'a pure river of water of life, clear as crystal' flows from the Lord's throne, 'and on either side of the river, … the tree of life, which bore twelve fruits' (*Rev. 22:1-2*). This Temple-City is a garden filled with fruits and leaves and pure water. It is a new Eden greater than Eden. For while in the old Eden, the Word of the LORD walked with man and met with man, in this new Eden, the Word of the LORD, with His Father and His Spirit, will dwell continually with man. Adam was banished from God's temple through his sin at the tree. Yet the second Adam came, and by His death on the Tree, has restored His people to God's Temple by making them God's Temple. This is the glory of the heaven on earth of the New Jerusalem.

---

[6] Even the decorations of the temple/tabernacle remind us of Eden (gold and onyx; trees and fruit; cherubim).

The Beatific Vision

In the New Jerusalem, we 'shall see His face' (*Rev. 22:4*).[7] And the face of the Lord is the place of 'fullness of joy' (*Ps 16:11*). The blessings and joy of life in the eternal state flow from the God who will there dwell with His people. We will see Him, and seeing Him we will know the fullness of blessing and bliss in Him. 'All joy, all blessing, all goodness in eternal life emanate from seeing Him.'[8] This is the great blessing which Jesus promised to the 'pure in heart' (and only those who clothed with Christ's righteousness could be described as 'pure in heart'): 'Blessed are the pure in heart, for they shall see God' (*Mt 5:28*). Like John in Revelation, David in the Psalms tells us that this seeing of God's face will be in the eschatological future, when the Lord has raised us from the dead (*Ps 17:15*).

The Beatific Vision is the fulfilment of eternal life, for in seeing His face, we will know the Father and the Son in the Spirit in the fullest way possible to human beings (*cf. Jn 17:3*). Even the most glorious glimpse we have of God in this life is but a dim reflection compared to that day. For then, finally, we shall see Him 'face to face' (*1 Cor. 13:12*). And when we do, then 'we shall be like Him, for we shall see Him as He is' (*1 Jn 3:2*). The Beatific Vision will transform us, and this sight of the face of the Lord will be of such beauty that there will no longer be any turning away.

Thomas Aquinas wrote of the Beatific Vision, saying: 'thus, when we arrive at our last end, what was formerly *believed* about God will be *seen*, and what was *hoped for* as absent will be closely *embraced* as present.' He goes on, telling us that he who:

> Sees God must rejoice in the vision of Him ... Thus, in the vision of God, who is goodness and truth itself, there must be love or joyous fruition, no less than comprehension. This accords with Isaiah 66:14: 'You shall see and your heart shall rejoice.'[9]

After the Reformation, Protestant theologians agreed. Turretin writes that this 'vision begets love. God cannot be seen without being loved; love

---

[7] The early Apostolic writer Thomas Rees comments on this verse that this is 'an actual, visible presence of the Lord, and an eternal consciousness of it.' Thomas Rees, *Christ Our Life*, 38.

[8] Johann Gerhard, *Schola Pietatis*, 1:320

[9] Thomas Aquinas, *Compendium of Theology* (*Shorter Summa*), 164-165.

draws joy after it because he cannot be possessed without filling with joy.'[10]
Turretin also points out how the Beatific Vision is the exact opposite of hell:

> Vision is opposed to the banishing of the damned from his face and to the most dense darkness of ignorance in which they lie; love to the most furious hatred which they cherish towards him; joy to the dreadful despair and wailing which will arise from the multiplicity and continuity of the torments they will feel.[11]

Turretin and Aquinas both argued that, as God is invisible (*Col. 1:15; 1 Tim. 1:17; 6:16; Heb. 11:27; Ex 33:20*), this must be an intellectual vision (as opposed to a vision with our eyes). However, Job looked forward to the day of his resurrection, when he would see the Lord with his own eyes:

> For I know that my Redeemer lives,
> And He shall stand at last on the earth;
> And after my skin is destroyed, this I know,
> That in my flesh I shall see God,
> Whom I shall see for myself,
> And my eyes shall behold, and not another.
> How my heart yearns within me! (*Job 19:25-27*)

The New Testament teaching that we shall see Him 'face to face' (*1 Cor. 13:12*) and 'as He is' (*1 Jn 3:2*), would appear to agree with Job's assessment that our 'eyes shall behold' Him. Against those who argue that God's invisibility would prevent us from seeing Him with our eyes, Francis Pieper simply reminds us, 'how this is possible can hardly be a problem for a Christian.'[12] After all, the Christian sees 'the glory of God in the face of Jesus Christ' (*2 Cor. 4:6*) and Jesus Christ is the visible 'image of the invisible God' (*Col. 1:15*). Therefore, John Owen defines the Beatific Vision as 'such a … sight of God and his glory, especially as manifested in Christ, as will make us blessed unto eternity.'[13]

One of the most beautiful hymns in the English language expresses this glorious truth that 'the King there in His beauty, without a veil is seen':

> The Bride eyes not her garment,
> But her dear Bridegroom's face;
> I will not gaze at glory,
> But on My King of grace;

---

[10] Francis Turretin, *Institutes*, 3:609
[11] Francis Turretin, *Institutes*, 3:609
[12] Francis Pieper, *Christian Dogmatics*, 3:551
[13] John Owen, *Works*, 1:240.

> Not at the crown He gifteth,
> But on His piercèd hand;
> The Lamb is all the glory
> Of Immanuel's land.[14]

The Welsh Apostolics sang of it equally beautifully in D.P. Williams' Welsh hymns (of which my English translation will do no justice to the beauty):

> There at last I'll see my Bridegroom,
> Gaze upon His beauteous face,
> Rest upon His Cross and Cov'nant,
> For He suffered my disgrace:
> Head of Calvary!
> We shall ever sing His grace.[15]

Our chief end is 'to enjoy His face,'[16] writes D.P. Williams, and 'we [shall] be entranced by the vision of His beauty and glorious excellences.'[17] As Thomas Rees put it, 'there is that Glory awaiting us, but our Glory will be lost in His Glory.'[18]

The great theologian of the British North American colonies, Jonathan Edwards, drew out the connection between the Beatific Vision and theosis (which we shall look at in chapter 23). Edwards points out that as we gaze upon Jesus in joy and bliss, we do so still united to Jesus. So we enjoy the Beatific Vision as sons in the Son, sharing in Jesus' relationship with His Father. 'The saints shall enjoy God as partaking with Christ of His enjoyment of God, for they are united to him and are glorified and made happy in the enjoyment of God as his members.' He goes on:

> They being in Christ shall partake of the love God the Father [has] to Christ, and as the Son knows the Father so they shall partake with him in his sight of God, as being as it were parts of him as he is in the bosom of the Father.[19]

---

[14] A.R. Cousin (constructed from the letters of Samuel Rutherford), 'The Sands of Time are Sinking', *Redemption Hymnal*, 87.

[15] D.P. Williams, 'Tiroedd hyfryd yr addewid', *Molwch Dduw*, 327 verse 4. See also 'Mae rhyw ddyheadau cryfion', *Molwch Dduw*, 315.

[16] D.P. Williams, 'Mae rhyw ddyheadau cryfion', *Molwch Dduw*, 315.

[17] D.P. Williams, *Herald of Grace*, 5.11 (Nov. 1945), 219.

[18] Thomas Rees, *Christ Our Life*, 39.

[19] Jonathan Edwards, 'Manuscript Sermon on Rom. 2:10 (1735)' L.44v-L.45r., transcribed by Kyle Stobel in 'A Spiritual Sight of Love: Constructing a Doctrine of the Beatific Vision', *Union Theology*.

In the meantime, we join with David in longing for the day of this Beatific Vision when we shall see Him as He is.

> One thing I have desired of the LORD,
> That will I seek:
> That I may dwell in the house of the LORD
> All the days of my life,
> To behold the beauty of the LORD. (*Ps 27:4*)

In the words of another Apostolic hymn-writer:

> Fain would I see Thee, fairest Lord:
> My love is not content
> To find Thee only in Thy Word
> Or in the Sacrament.
>
> If thus to meet Thee in a Book
> Begets a bright surprise;
> If thus on Bread and Wine to look
> With rapture melts my eyes –
>
> What will it be, O God of grace,
> Thy very self to view,
> Conversing with Thee face to face,
> As Moses used to do?

As the hymn concludes, this Beatific Vision – seeing the Lord face to face – is 'the only heaven … the heart will wish to know.'[20]

---

[20] *Alone with God: A Primer on Prayer* (Apostolic Witnesses 1962-1963), 51. Compare Ian Macpherson's (past principal of the Apostolic Church Bible College, Penygroes) most famous hymn, 'If I but knew Thee as Thou art', *Redemption Hymnal*, 78.

Tenet 4

Justification & Sanctification
of the believer
through
the finished work of Christ.

Chapter 22

Grace & Union with Christ

Grace is not a Thing

The heart of the Reformation was the nature of grace, because the nature of grace is at the heart of the gospel. Both the Reformers and their opponents believed in salvation by grace. However, each side understood grace in a different way. Still today, the question of the nature of grace is the big dividing issue between Roman Catholic and Reformation Protestant theologies.

For the Roman Catholic Church, grace is understood as a thing. The old Roman Catholic *Penny Catechism* teaches that 'grace is a supernatural gift of God, freely bestowed upon us for our sanctification and salvation' and that man obtains this gift 'chiefly by prayer and the holy Sacraments.'[1] The newer *Catechism of the Catholic Church* teaches that 'grace is the help God gives us to respond to our vocation of becoming his adopted sons,'[2] and that it is 'infused by the Holy Spirit into our soul to heal it of sin' as 'a habitual gift.'[3] The medieval Catholic teaching on grace, which the Reformation rejected, can be traced back to the concept of *habitual grace* drawn up by Thomas Aquinas. For Aquinas, *habitual grace* was a created substance in the soul. It is 'something bestowed on man by God.'[4]

The Reformation rejected these ideas of grace as a substance poured into us, or as a help sent from God. For, if grace were either of those things, it would require something in us, and make salvation in some way dependent upon us. If grace were a substance poured out into us, our salvation would depend in part on how good we were at getting and holding onto this substance. If grace were a help sent from God, then our salvation would depend in part on how good we were at cooperating with

---

[1] *A Catechism of Christian Doctrine* (*The Penny Catechism*), 139-140
[2] *Catechism of the Catholic Church*, 2021.
[3] *Catechism of the Catholic Church*, 1999-2000.
[4] Thomas Aquinas, *Summa Theologicae*, II-I, 110, 1.

God's help. So salvation would not be by grace alone (*sola gratia*) and in Christ alone (*solus Christus*).

However, Protestant ideas about grace can also lead to misunderstandings. Liberal Protestant equations between grace and niceness may simply eliminate any place for the incarnation or cross. Evangelical Protestants often rely on definitions of grace as 'God's unmerited favour.' Yet, even here a problem can arise; we can end up thinking of grace as little more than a principle. So how does the Bible present God's grace?

Grace is Christ and Him Crucified

The Scriptures tell us that 'the grace of God that brings salvation has appeared to all men' (*Titus 2:11*). So, grace is not a thing or a principle, but rather grace has made an appearance. Grace was visible. But when did grace appear? Paul tells us when he writes that God:

> has saved us and called us with a holy calling, not according to our works, but according to His own purpose and grace which was given to us in Christ Jesus before time began, but has now been revealed by the appearing of our Saviour Jesus Christ, who has abolished death and brought life and immortality to light through the gospel (*2 Tim. 1:9-10*).

The grace by which we are saved was revealed by the appearing of Christ and through the cross of Christ. This is the same grace which was given to us 'before time began.' But even then it was given to us 'in Christ.' Notice that Paul does not say that grace is given by Christ, but that grace is given to us 'in Christ.' It is not that Christ's teaching and example lead to grace, but rather that grace has appeared in His person and His work: in His incarnation and His atonement. Therefore, it is not simply that Jesus came and died and rose because of a principle called grace. No; Jesus came and lived for us, obeyed for us, died for us, triumphed for us, rose for us, *and that is grace*.

The most well-known Scripture telling us that we are saved by grace also tells us what this grace is:

> But God, who is rich in mercy, because of His great love with which He loved us, even when we were dead in trespasses, made us alive together

> with Christ (by grace you have been saved), and raised us up together, and
> made us sit together in the heavenly places in Christ Jesus. (*Eph. 2:4-6*)

Paul's famous words 'by grace you have been saved' are actually a little aside, explaining what it is to be made 'alive together with Christ.' So, being saved by grace means being alive in Christ. Getting grace means getting Jesus the Risen Saviour. The grace of God is found only in Jesus Christ.

John tells us this too. At the beginning of his gospel, he writes that:

> the Word became flesh and dwelt among us, and we beheld His glory, the
> glory as of the only begotten of the Father, full of grace and truth ... And of
> His fullness we have all received, and grace for grace.[5] (*Jn 1:14, 16*)

Grace and truth are not substances of which Jesus is full. Rather, Jesus is full of truth because He is 'the Truth' (*Jn 14:6*). So, just in the same way, Jesus is full of grace, because He is the Grace of God. Jesus is the fullness of grace. 'God himself is the content of his saving grace in Jesus Christ.'[6] Grace is Jesus Christ and Him crucified.

Therefore, to be saved by grace alone means to be saved by Christ alone. Or, in the words of the Apostolic tenet, to be saved 'through the finished work of Christ.' In fact, it was in this way that many of the Reformers preferred to speak of *salvation by grace alone*. The Scottish Reformer, John Knox, preferred to speak of 'justification through the blood of Christ.'[7] Why? Because he didn't want people to think that grace and faith were 'things' which saved. Salvation is found in Christ alone.

Union with Christ

We've seen who Jesus is and what He has done for our salvation. But how does this salvation get from Jesus to us?

---

[5] Or, as the ESV translates this, 'received grace upon grace.'

[6] Thomas F. Torrance, *The Trinitarian Faith*, 138.

[7] T.F. Torrance, 'From John Knox to John McLeod Campbell: A Reading of Scottish Theology', in David F. Wright & Gary D. Badcock, ed., *Disruption to Diversity: Edinburgh Divinity 1846-1996* (Edinburgh: T & T Clark, 1996), 3.

> First, we must understand that as long as Christ remains outside of us, and
> we are separated from him, all that he has suffered and done for the
> salvation of the human race remains useless and of no value to us.
> Therefore, to share in what he has received from the Father, he had to
> become ours and dwell within us … for, as I have said, all that he
> possesses is nothing to us until we grow into one body with him.[8]

What Christ has accomplished for us becomes ours as we are united to Him.
By what He has done *for us*, Christ has fully accomplished our salvation. But
now this salvation becomes ours through Christ *in us*, as we are united to
Him by faith.

Marriage Union

Throughout the Bible, the relationship between Christ and His people is
described as a marriage. In fact, Paul tells us that human marriage points to
the true marriage between Christ and His Church: 'This is a great mystery,
but I speak concerning Christ and the church' (*Eph. 5:32*). So, by thinking in
terms of marriage, we can begin to understand what is involved in our
union with Christ.

In a marriage, a husband gives himself and all that he has to his wife,
and a wife gives herself and all that she has to her husband. They promise
one another, 'all that I am I give to you, and all that I have I share with you.'
So, in marriage union with Christ, He gives us all that He is and shares with
us all that He has. All His is ours and all ours is His. The Song of Solomon
puts it like this: 'I am my beloved's and my beloved is mine' (*Cant. 6:3*).

Of course, in our marriage union to Christ, this is not a marriage of
equals. He is the King of Kings and Lord of Lords, and in comparison we,
the bride, are like a poor peasant with great debts. But, in a marriage what's
his is hers and what's hers is his. So He takes all her debt, and in return she
shares in all His riches. So, in union with Christ, He takes all our sin, guilt,
shame and death, and in return He gives us His righteousness, His honour,
His glory, and His life. Martin Luther wrote that:

> Faith … unites the soul to Christ, as the wife to the husband, by which
> mystery, as the Apostle teaches, Christ and the soul are made one flesh.
> Now if they are one flesh, and if a true marriage – nay, by far the most
> perfect of all marriages – is accomplished between them (for human
> marriages are but feeble types of this one great marriage), then it follows

---

[8] John Calvin, *Institutes of the Christian Religion*, 3.1.1

that all they have becomes theirs in common, as well good things as evil things; so that whatsoever Christ possesses, that the believing soul may take to itself and boast of as its own, and whatever belongs to the soul, that Christ claims as His.

If we compare these possessions, we shall see how inestimable is the gain. Christ is full of grace, life, and salvation; the soul is full of sin, death, and condemnation. Let faith step in, and then sin, death, and hell will belong to Christ, and grace, life, and salvation to the soul For, if He is a Husband, He must needs take to Himself that which is His wife's, and at the same time, impart to His wife that which is His. For, in giving her His own body and Himself, how can He but give her all that is His? And, in taking to Himself the body of His wife, how can He but take to Himself all that is hers?[9]

Rather than comparing us to an indebted peasant, Luther says it would be more fitting to compare the bride in this marriage to 'a needy and impious harlot':

Who then can value highly enough these royal nuptials? Who can comprehend the riches of the glory of this grace? Christ, that rich and pious Husband, takes as a wife a needy and impious harlot, redeeming her from all her evils and supplying her with all His good things. It is impossible now that her sins should destroy her, since they have been laid upon Christ and swallowed up in Him, and since she has in her Husband Christ a righteousness which she may claim as her own, and which she can set up with confidence against all her sins, against death and hell, saying, 'If I have sinned, my Christ, in whom I believe, has not sinned; all mine is His, and all His is mine,' as it is written, 'My beloved is mine, and I am His' (Cant. ii. 16).[10]

What's ours is His and what's His is ours. All ours is His and all His is ours. That is grace, and that is what it is to be united to Christ. Through our union with Him, He has taken our death and we share in His life. He takes our sin, because He is united to us, and we're clothed in His righteousness, because we're united to Him.

Paul tells us that 'the God and Father of our Lord Jesus Christ … has blessed us with every spiritual blessing in the heavenly places in Christ' (*Eph. 1:3*). So every blessing that we have, we have 'in Christ' – in union with Him. He is the well beloved Son of God, and we are well beloved sons in the Well-Beloved Son (*Eph. 1:5-6*). He has been declared righteous through His resurrection, and we are declared righteous (justified) in Him (*1 Cor. 1:30*). He is the Father's heir, and we have an inheritance in Him

---

[9] Martin Luther, *The Freedom of a Christian.*
[10] Martin Luther, *The Freedom of a Christian.*

(*Acts 26:18; Eph. 1:11*). He is the One upon whom God has set His seal (*Jn 6:27*), and in Him we too are sealed with the Spirit (*Eph. 1:13*).

Therefore, Jesus Christ, who died for our sins and rose again for our justification, is not only for the beginning of our salvation. Jesus is not only the entry way into the possibility of getting blessings from God. Every spiritual blessing is found in Christ and only in Christ. There is nothing to be added to Jesus. And so we trust in Him, knowing that He is all we need, that He has done all that needs to be done, and that we have been blessed with every spiritual blessing in Him.

When Are We Blessed In Christ?

Ephesians 1:3 tells us that God '*has blessed* us with every spiritual blessing in the heavenly places in Christ.' It is not that He might bless us, or even that He's going to bless us some time in the future. The Scripture tells us here that He has already blessed us in Christ. When did this happen? We were blessed with every spiritual blessing in Christ when we were united to Christ through faith.

So does that mean that there is nothing more to the Christian life than conversion? Certainly not. Just think of the example of our resurrection bodies. It is 'in Christ' that we shall be raised incorruptible (*1 Thess. 4:16; 1 Cor. 15:21-22, 42-45, 50-54*). So our glorified, incorruptible, immortal, resurrection bodies are a blessing which is ours 'in Christ.' However, we do not live in these resurrection bodies yet. Paul tells us that we have already been blessed with every spiritual blessing in Christ. Yet he also tells us that we await the day of resurrection to receive this blessing which is ours in Christ. So, our resurrection bodies are guaranteed by our union with Christ, but our experience of them is delayed until the resurrection of the dead. Objectively, they are ours already in Christ; but they are not yet ours in experience.

Therefore, in the Christian life, conversion is not the end. We are to grow in grace. We are to be filled with the Spirit. We are to be raised with an incorruptible body. We are to know an eternal inheritance in the love and fellowship of the Triune God, where we shall see Him face to face. All these things are ours in Christ. Yet we do not experience them all at conversion.

However, if they are all already ours in Christ, that means we do not need anything else to rely on in order to receive these blessings. We grow in grace, not by relying on our efforts to please God, but by relying on Christ, to whom we are united. In Him we have died to sin and live to righteousness. We grow in grace by living out the reality of who we are in Christ. Likewise, we are filled with the Spirit, not by relying on our obedience, our tarrying, or our spirituality; but by relying on Christ to whom we are united. He has been anointed without measure with the Spirit, and He is the One who pours out the Spirit upon His people. So we look to Him expectantly and trust in Him to pour out what He has promised.

How Are We United to Christ?

By the Holy Spirit

It is the Holy Spirit who unites believers to Christ (*1 Cor. 6:17*). In the words of D.P. Williams, 'the Holy Spirit is the … union between the Son and the sons.'[11] The Spirit is never alone, for He is the Spirit of the Father and the Son, who by perichoresis indwells and is indwelt by the Father and the Son.[12] *In John 14:15-23* we see that Jesus comes to us through the Holy Spirit (*Jn 14:18*). And when the Son comes to us by the Spirit to make His home with us, He is not alone. For He is the Son eternally begotten of His Father, who is never apart from the Father with whom He is one. Therefore, when the Son comes to make His home with us by the Spirit, the Father comes to make His home with us in the Son by the Spirit, with whom He is one (*Jn 14:23*).

Through Faith

Faith is God's gift (*Eph. 2:8; Phil. 1:29; 2 Pet. 1:1*). God gives this gift of faith through the hearing of His Word (*Rom. 10:17*) and this gift of faith is ours 'through the Spirit' (*Gal. 5:5*). As the Westminster Shorter Catechism puts it, 'the Spirit applieth to us the redemption purchased by Christ, by working

---

[11] D.P. Williams, 'Sonship', Unpublished Manuscript.
[12] For perichoresis, see chapter 5.

faith in us, and thereby uniting us to Christ.'[13] Faith is resting and relying upon Christ who is freely given to us in His gospel Word. And to rest and rely on Christ is to be united to Him.

What this Union with Christ Involves

'The God and Father of our Lord Jesus Christ ... has blessed us with every spiritual blessing in the heavenly places in Christ' (*Eph. 1:3*). This is how God blesses His children: by giving us to Christ and Christ to us. So there is no other way of receiving any spiritual blessing apart from being united to Christ. In the rest of *Ephesians 1*, Paul outlines just what these spiritual blessings include, with which we are blessed through union with Christ (*Eph. 1:3-14*). There he lists our election (*v.4*), our sanctification (*v.4*), our adoption (*v.5*), our justification (*v.6*: 'accepted in the Beloved'), our redemption (*v.7*), our forgiveness (*v.7*), our wisdom and understanding (*v.8*), our inheritance (*v.11*), and our sealing with the Holy Spirit (*v.11*). All of these blessings are received 'according to the riches of His grace' (*v.7*) and 'in Christ.' After all, the grace of God is found only in Jesus Christ.

Paul wants to make very clear here in *Ephesians 1* that every aspect of our salvation, from first to last, is 'in Christ.' Every blessing which we have from God is ours 'in Christ.' Jesus Christ is the one Mediator between God and man (*1 Tim. 2:5-6*). Therefore, it is Christ our Mediator who mediates to us every one of God's blessings. There is no blessing from God apart from Jesus Christ. Any purported blessing which is found apart from Christ is no blessing at all.[14]

---

[13] *Westminster Shorter Catechism*, 30.

[14] Certainly no spiritual or heavenly blessing is found outside of Christ (*Eph. 1:3*). But what of temporal blessings? Doesn't Jesus say that God makes the rain to fall on the just and the unjust, and the sun to rise on the evil and the good? (*Mt 5:45*). Indeed; but the context in which He says it is in encouraging believers to pray for the unjust (*Mt 5:44*). Just as we pray for the unjust through the Son, so too God bestows His temporal blessings upon them through the Son. Granted, these are not spiritual blessings in union with Christ. However *opera trinitatis ad extra indivsa sunt*; therefore the Father never bestows any blessing apart from through the Son and by the Spirit. When Paul writes of Christ as the 'one Mediator between God and men' in 1 Tim 2:5 it is also in the context of praying for those outside the church (*1 Tim. 2:1-4*).

Four Aspects of Union with Christ

Union with Christ in Election

Paul writes that we have been chosen in Christ 'before the foundation of the world' (*Eph. 1:4*). Thus, the Father's love to us in the Son comes first. Before we even existed, and so long before we have the chance to do anything good or anything bad, the Father chose us in union with Christ the Son. Therefore, neither our election nor our union with Christ can in any way depend upon our own merit, for our union with Christ in election precedes our existence and hence any possibility of merit. Rather, our union with Christ in election can only depend upon the good pleasure of the will of Triune God and His grace toward us in Jesus (*Eph. 1.5-6*), the Lamb who was slain from the foundation of the world (*Rev. 13:8*).

As election occurs in union with Christ, it is not a speculative doctrine. Rather it is all about Jesus, and cannot be considered apart from Him. In the Bible, the doctrine of election is set forth to demonstrate the depth of God's love toward us in Christ, showing us that it is the Triune God in His loving-kindness who takes the initiative in our salvation.

Union with Christ in the Incarnation

In His incarnation, Christ entered into union with our humanity. God was, in the incarnation, 'by the very act, raising human nature into union with Himself in the person of Jesus Christ.'[15] And this hypostatic union is what makes possible our union with Christ (and through our union with Christ, our participation in the divine nature[16]). 'While the Son of God takes up from man his human nature … the Son enables man to participate in His own Divine Nature'[17]

Yet, not only does the Son's assumption of our humanity into the hypostatic union make possible our union with Him in our actual experience, and our partaking of the divine nature (*2 Pet. 1:4*), but it also

---

[15] D.P. Williams, 'The Unique Child', *Riches of Grace*, 12.12 (Dec. 1959), 370.

[16] See chapter 23 (on Sonship/Theosis).

[17] W.R. Thomas, *On Ephesians*, 21-22.

means that He has joined Himself to us for our salvation in such a way that His death is our death, and His resurrection is our resurrection; that we have died and risen in Him. In His incarnation, God the Son has united Himself to us:

> In order that he might sanctify and justify our flesh in his birth, life, death, and resurrection, bringing us into his filial relation with the Father. All that Christ did in union with our flesh, in other words, was done vicariously for us.[18]

Union with Christ in Actual Experience

For we who trust in Christ, our actual experience of union with Him begins when the Holy Spirit unites us to Christ by faith in our conversion. In baptism we are baptised into His death (*Rom. 6:4; Col. 2:12*), demonstrating that this union with Him in our actual experience is not a separate union, but rather the fruition of our union with Him in election and in His incarnation. It is by this union with Christ in our actual experience that we receive Christ as our salvation and live in Him. This is the union of which Calvin speaks when he says that 'to share in what he has received from the Father, he had to become ours and dwell within us.'[19] We'll consider this union in actual experience further in the next few chapters as we look at sonship, justification, and sanctification.

Union with Christ in the Consummation

The final and full manifestation of our union with Christ is still yet to come. When Christ returns and we are raised and glorified in Him, then we will know the consummation of our union with Him in our eternal home where we will never be parted from the One to whom we are united.

---

[18] Marcus Peter Johnson, *One with Christ*, 37.
[19] John Calvin, *Institutes of the Christian Religion*, 3.1.1

Double Grace in Jesus

Grace is Jesus. To be saved by grace alone is to be saved in Christ alone, united to the One who loved us and gave Himself for us. Calvin pointed out that, in union with Christ, we receive a double grace:

> Christ was given to us by God's generosity, to be grasped and possessed by us in faith. By partaking of him, we principally receive a double grace: namely, that being reconciled to God through Christ's blamelessness [justification], we may have in heaven instead of a Judge a gracious Father; and secondly, that sanctified by Christ's spirit we may cultivate blamelessness and purity of life.[20]

Through the One Gift that is Christ and Him Crucified, we receive double grace: justification and sanctification in the Beloved. Therefore, if we partake of Christ and His finished work, we partake of both justification and sanctification. There is a distinction between the two (which we'll look at in the coming chapters): justification is not sanctification and sanctification is not justification. Yet, justification and sanctification cannot be separated, because we receive both by partaking of Christ and Him crucified. Christ is our justification and Christ is our sanctification; therefore, united to Christ we partake of both. And that means we can't be sanctified without being justified, and if we're justified, we will certainly be sanctified; for both aspects of this double grace are ours in Christ Jesus.

By faith we are united to Christ. Therefore, we don't just get righteousness from Jesus and holiness from Jesus. Rather, in Christ, we have Christ for righteousness and Christ for holiness. 'I have been crucified with Christ; it is no longer I who live, but Christ lives in me, and the life which I now live in the flesh I live by faith in the Son of God, who loved me and gave Himself for me' (*Gal. 2:20*). Through our union with Him, He has taken our death and we have been given His life. He has taken our sin, because He is united to us. And we are clothed in Him for righteousness, because we're united to Him.

Grace is Jesus: Jesus given for us (in His finished work) and Jesus given to us (in our union with Him). And seeing what grace truly is – Christ and Him Crucified – we see that grace is not a means to an end. Rather, throughout eternity we will enjoy the riches of God's grace in Jesus (*Eph.*

---

[20] Calvin, *Inst.* 3.11.1

2:7). This is God's plan for us for the ages to come: to give us grace by giving us Christ.

Chapter 23

Sons in the Son: Theosis & Adoption

In salvation, God does not only forgive our sins and accept us as righteous in His sight, but He also welcomes us into His family as well-beloved sons in the Well-Beloved Son. On the night of His arrest, Jesus told His disciples, 'I will not leave you orphans' (*Jn 14:18*). The Son of God does not leave us outside of the family. In Him we are children of His heavenly Father. This is why the eternal Son took on our humanity and came into the world, so that 'as many as received Him, to them He gave the right to become children of God, to those who believe in His name' (*Jn 1:12*), so that 'He might be the firstborn among many brethren' (*Rom. 8:29*). As Fulgentius of Ruspe put it:

> Therefore, in order for men to become sons of God, they receive the only Son of God by faith, and when he gives power, they receive this power both to believe in him and to belong to the number of the sons of God.[1]

In more recent times, J.I. Packer has written that this sonship is 'the highest privilege that the gospel offers: higher even than justification … Adoption is higher because of the richer relationship with God that it involves.'[2] The early Apostolic, William Cathcart, put it like this:

> There could be no greater greatness in [God's] sight than to be made a son; therefore, He conferred the greatest thing possible to give … True Christianity is primarily a matter, then, of our relationship to God, which was lost in Adam and restored in Christ.[3]

Theologians have not always used the same terminology to speak of this relationship of sonship which we receive by grace in the true Son. Sometimes it is called *adoption*, as that is the terminology used by the apostle Paul. However, some theologians think of adoption in purely legal terms as giving us only a new status, and don't include the relational elements of sonship.[4] And, as adoption is a Pauline expression, limiting our

---

[1] Fulgentius, *First Letter to the Scythian Monks*, para. 51.

[2] J.I. Packer, *Knowing God*, 228.

[3] William Cathcart, *Riches of Grace*, xiii.5 (May 1938), 410.

[4] Welsh theology tended to speak of this sonship in terms of both adoption and regeneration. But by this they didn't mean the same thing as we've seen in the doctrine of

consideration of this relational sonship to passages which speak of adoption would mean ignoring what Biblical writers other than Paul have to say about it. What Paul spoke of in terms of being adopted as sons, John often wrote of in terms of being children born of God. As the early church recognised, with their concept of *theosis*, the emphasis was not on the procedure of how we become God's children, but rather on the fact that we are His children by His work of grace (not naturally). Jesus alone is the true and natural Son of the Father, but through union with Christ, 'by participation and grace we have ourselves become sons through him in the Spirit.'[5]

Sons in the Son

Jesus is the Son of God by nature. Believers in Christ are sons of God by adoption and grace. In Christ we receive 'adoption as sons … according to the good pleasure of [God's] will, to the praise of the glory of His grace' (*Eph. 1:5-6*). This adoption flows solely from the grace of God in Christ Jesus. It is not because of anything we have done to merit a place in God's family. We were 'children of wrath' (*Eph. 2:3*) and 'sons of disobedience' (*Eph. 2:2*). But now, through God's grace in Jesus, through the finished work of Jesus for us, we have been graciously adopted into the family as sons and daughters of the living God. Cyril of Alexandria wrote about our sonship by adoption and grace:

> We receive from His mercy a grace which has given us the rank of sons of God, with an extrinsic dignity added to us, adoptive sons modelled after the true Son and called to the glory of the Son by nature.[6]
>
> He is the true Son existing from the Father, but we are adopted because of his love for humanity … We who are made sons too are compared with

---

regeneration above (chapter 9), which they referred to technically as 'effectual calling.' See *The Welsh Calvinistic Methodist Confession of Faith of 1823*, Articles 22 & 25-26. As many of the early Apostolics were brought up in this Welsh theological environment, they sometimes speak of this sonship in terms of regeneration or the New Birth (in addition to using that terminology for the doctrine of regeneration proper in other contexts).

  [5] Cyril of Alexandria, *De Incar. Unigen.* 254-6. Translation from Donald Fairbairn, *Grace and Christology in the Early Church*, 100.

  [6] Cyril of Alexandria, *Dial. Trin.* ii.439.d (SC edition 1:290).

him. We enjoy the good that comes by grace rather than the honours that come by nature.[7]

Through Jesus who is the true Son by nature, we are made sons by adoption and grace.

Why Sons?

Before we go any further, we should just clear up an issue about the language of sonship. For many of the adopted sons of God are daughters. So, why does the Bible, and why do we, following the biblical language, speak of the 'sons' of God, rather than something more gender neutral like 'children'?

Well, at times the Bible does speak about us as the 'children of God' (*1 Jn 3:1*), so it's perfectly biblical to speak of our adoption as children of God. Yet the Bible also uses the language of sonship (for both sons and daughters) because it tells us something else beyond the language of being a child of God. In the Græco-Roman world of the New Testament, daughters didn't have inheritance rights: only sons did. So, when Paul writes of the adoption of all believers, whether male or female, as 'sons', what he's telling us is that there is no distinction among the children of God. The salvation which is ours as sons in the Son does not differ depending on our sex, race, class, culture, or any other human social division. All the children of God are made 'sons' with a full inheritance. In other words, by calling all believers, whether male or female, 'sons', the Bible is telling us that there are no second class children of God.

That explains the biblical language of sonship. But why do we keep that language today in a society where sons and daughters have equal inheritance rights? We don't have to keep exclusively to the language of sonship. We convey the same biblical truth by speaking of 'sons and daughters' of God or 'children' of God. But, there is still a good reason not to always abandon the language of sonship, for our sonship is found in Christ the Son. So the language of sonship shows the connection between our sonship and Jesus. When we say that we are sons in the Son, we can immediately see that it is in Christ alone that we have this new relationship with the Father.

---

[7] Cyril, *In Io.* on 1:12 (ET 1:60).

Adoption Through Christ

It is because Jesus, the Son of God by nature, took on our nature and suffered and died in our place, that we can receive the adoption of sons. It is through Christ's incarnation and propitiation that He brings 'many sons to glory' (*Heb. 2:10-18*). Paul tells us that our adoption was the reason for Christ's incarnation and His redeeming work:

> But when the fullness of the time had come, God sent forth His Son, born of a woman, born under the law, to redeem those who were under the law, that we might receive the adoption as sons. (*Gal. 4:4-5*)

Therefore, our sonship flows from the cross of Calvary. It is because Christ, the natural Son, has taken our nature and died in our place, that we are adopted as sons of the living God.

Adoption in Christ

But it is not only through the work of Christ that we are received into the family of God as His children, but also in union with Christ. In Christ, we are well-beloved sons in the Well-Beloved Son. As Martin Luther preached:

> Christ is the child of God; therefore, he who clothes himself in Christ, God's son, must be the child of God. He is clothed with divine adoption, which unquestionably must constitute him a child of God.[8]

It is those who have received Christ who have been given 'the right to become children of God' (*Jn 1:12*). It is those who 'have put on Christ' who are 'sons of God through faith in Christ Jesus' (*Gal. 3:26-27*). Thus, our sonship is not only a result of Christ's saving work, but also a blessing which we have received in union with Christ, the true Son. As the early Apostolics put it, in our union with Christ, 'He imparts all that He is unto us.'[9] United to the Son, we are adopted as sons. He is the well-beloved Son of the Father, and in our union with Him, we are well-beloved sons in the well-beloved Son.

---

[8] *Sermons of Martin Luther*, ed. John Nicholas Lenker, vol. 6, *Sermons on Epistle Texts for Advent and Christmas* (Grand Rapids, 1988), 287. This sermon is on *Gal. 3:23-29*.

[9] W.J. Williams, *Riches of Grace*, i.9 (1920), 32.

The Formula of Exchange

The early church saw believers' sonship in the Son as the great purpose of Christ's incarnation and saving work, and summed this up with something which has come to be known as *the formula of exchange*. Over the centuries the formula of exchange has been stated in different words, but the basic idea has been Irenaeus' statement that 'He became what we are so that we might become what He is,'[10] which we looked at above in the chapter on the Incarnation.[11] Augustine's version of the exchange formula highlights how our adoption as sons is at the centre of this 'becoming what He is': 'The Son of God became the Son of Man that he might make the sons of men sons of God.'[12]

Like the early church fathers, the early Apostolics saw this as exchange as the heart of the salvation which we have in Christ. The Scottish apostle, and missionary to Australia, William Cathcart, put the formula of exchange like this: 'The Son of God is Son of Man, and the sons of men are now sons of God. This is the fruit of His Mediatorship to God and to men … the very crux of Christian Doctrine.'[13]

Adopted into Christ's Sonship with the Father

When we are united to Christ as sons in the Son, we are adopted into Christ's sonship with the Father. As William Cathcart put it, 'being placed as sons we are given capacity to enjoy and inherit that unique relationship that the Son had with the Father.'[14]

His Father is now our Father

On the morning that Jesus rose from the dead, He spoke to Mary Magdalene, telling her to go and tell His brethren 'I am ascending to My Father and your Father, and to My God and your God' (*Jn 20:17*). As a result

---

[10] Irenaeus, *Against Heresies*, Preface to Book 5.

[11] Chapter 11. See the section on 'To Give Us His Life and His Relationship With the Father'.

[12] Augustine, *Mainz Sermons*, 13.1

[13] William Cathcart, *Riches of Grace*, xiii.3 (Jan 1938), 329.

[14] William Cathcart, *Riches of Grace*, xiii.5 (May 1938), 410.

of the death and resurrection of the Incarnate Son, believers now share His Father as their own Father. Commenting on this verse, the great Cambridge Puritan, Richard Sibbes, wrote: 'We have a common Father and a common God with Christ … Christ is the first Son, and in him, and for his sake, we are sons.'[15]

Because believers share with Christ, our Lord, His Father, we can pray to His Father as our Father, and especially in the prayer to 'our Father' given as a gift to us to pray by our Lord (*Mt 6:9*). As we pray the Lord's Prayer, we are confessing our faith that we are sons in the Son, adopted in grace into His relationship with His Father. As D.P. Williams put it, 'we find Him "our Father" in the fullest sense by the Spirit of adoption.'[16] Our heavenly Father, 'has brought us into intimate relationship with Himself through our Lord Jesus Christ and the effectual working of the Holy Ghost; into intimacy of fellowship and communion with Him.'[17] Therefore, as we call upon Him as 'our Father', 'it implies that God has imparted unto us His own quality of life; His Image; yea, that we are partakers of the divine nature.'[18] Sharing in the Son's relationship with His Father, and so having His Father as our Father, the saints are 'restor[ed] to the position of true sonship in His Family.'[19] Jonathan Edwards put it like this:

> For being members of God's own natural Son, they are in a sort partakers of his relation to the Father: they are not only sons of God by regeneration, but by a kind of communion in the sonship of the eternal Son.[20]

His Inheritance is now our Inheritance

The adopted children of God are 'heirs of God and joint heirs with Christ' (*Rom. 8:17; cf. Gal. 4:7*). If we are sons in the Son, sharing in Christ's relationship with His Father, then we also share in Christ's inheritance, as His co-heirs. Our inheritance is found in Christ, through our union with Him (*Eph. 1:11; cf. Eph. 3:6*) and the seal of the Holy Spirit 'is the guarantee of our inheritance until the redemption of the purchased possession' (*Eph. 1:13-14*).

[15] Richard Sibbes, *A Heavenly Conference* (Edinburgh: Banner of Truth, 2016), 80, 91.
[16] D.P. Williams, *Morning Meditations on the Lord's Prayer*, 18.
[17] D.P. Williams, *Morning Meditations on the Lord's Prayer*, 18.
[18] D.P. Williams, *Morning Meditations on the Lord's Prayer*, 14.
[19] D.P. Williams, *Riches of Grace*, xiv.5 (May 1939), 390.
[20] Jonathan Edwards, 'The Excellency of Christ', *Works*, 19:593.

If our inheritance is found in Christ Himself, then it is much greater than simply a home in heaven. As William Cathcart put it:

> This, then, is our inheritance who are sons, that we should not merely get to Heaven, but should inherit His Character, and thus be related to the Father through the Son, not merely as possessors of the uncreated Life, but possessors of the inimitable Character of Christ.[21]

Our inheritance in Christ is Christ Himself and every spiritual blessing which is found in Him. D.P. Williams wrote:

> This is the wealth of Christ's inheritance, the riches of His glory, forgiveness through the blood of His cross, justification, sanctification and all spiritual blessings … baptism, gifts, patience, grace, love. joy and peace, these are the wealth of the blessings in heavenly places … [for] the honourable position that is awaiting us.[22]

Loved with the same love the Father has for the Son

John points us to the wonder of the great love that the Father has for us in calling us His children: 'Behold what manner of love the Father has bestowed on us, that we should be called children of God!' (*1 Jn 3:1*). Yet, this love is not just a great love, but the very love with which the Father loves His eternal Son. Jesus reveals this to us in His great high priestly prayer on the night of His arrest. In this prayer, Jesus prays for all those who will believe in Him (*Jn 17:20*), and tells us that the Father has 'loved them as You have loved Me' (*Jn 17:23*), and asks that 'the love with which You loved me may be in them, and I in them (*Jn 17:26*). Here, Jesus reveals that the Father loves those who are united to Christ through faith in the same way and with the same love with which He loves Jesus. The Father loves us in the same way He loves His Son. God the Father loves His adopted sons by grace with the same love with which He loves His eternal Son. Therefore, we are as loved as the Son.

> So nigh, so very nigh to God,
> I cannot nearer be;
> For in the person of His Son
> I am as near as He.

---

21 William Cathcart, *Riches of Grace*, xiii.5 (May 1938), 411.
22 D.P. Williams, *All Sovereignty is His*, 75.

> So dear, so very dear to God,
> More dear I cannot be;
> The love wherewith He loves the Son —
> Such is His love to me![23]

Richard Sibbes put it like this:

> There is a firm foundation when God loveth us in his Son, and we are
> children in his natural Son, in whom we are adopted. Then our state is
> firm. Our first state in the first Adam was not firm, but now our nature is
> taken into the unity of the second person, it is firm. So that the love and
> care and fatherly disposition of God towards us, it is sweet to us, because it
> is tender to his Son. It is eternal to us, because it is eternal to him. He can as
> soon cease to love his Son, as cease to love us. For with the same love he
> loveth all Christ mystical, head and members. There is not the least finger
> of Christ, the least despised member of Christ, but God looketh on him
> with that sweet eternal tenderness with which he looketh upon his Son,
> preserving the prerogative of the head.[24]

There was not a time when the Father 'commenced to love the Son, because
there was no commencement to it. Therefore, there is no commencement to
His Love towards His Church', this Body of well-beloved sons in the Well-
Beloved Son, chosen and predestined to sonship in union with Christ from
all eternity.[25] And in the same way, just as there was no beginning to the
Father's love for His Son, so too there will be no end to this love, and,
therefore, no end to His love for His sons by adoption and grace.

That we share in the very love that the Father has for Jesus, His Son,
means that our adoption is not just a legal status. Adoption is not merely a
forensic matter. Instead, in adoption, believers participate in the loving
fellowship between the Father and the Son in the Spirit. This is 'a very
intimate relationship and fellowship with God'[26] and the greatest privilege
which God could possibly give to His Church, for sharing in this love
between the Father, Son and Holy Spirit, the Church partakes of the divine
nature (*2 Pet. 1:4*).

Cyril of Alexandria said that this love was why the Son took on our
flesh. 'He ... became human, for this reason: in order to make that which
was hated in ancient times, because of the transgression in the beginning

---

[23] Catesby Paget, 'A Mind at Perfect Peace with God', *Redemption Hymnal*, 386.
[24] Richard Sibbes, *A Heavenly Conference*, 106.
[25] D.P. Williams, *Riches of Grace*, xii.1 (Sept. 1936), 14.
[26] W.J. Williams, *Riches of Grace*, i.9 (1920), 32.

and the sin that had crept in, to be loved by God.'[27] Christ has come to 'openly grant such love to you as [He Himself has] from the Father.'[28]

The Spirit and Sonship

Writing to the Romans, Paul tells us that our adoption to sonship in the Son is effected by the Holy Spirit, who is the Spirit of Adoption:

> For as many as are led by the Spirit of God, these are sons of God. For you did not receive the spirit of bondage again to fear, but you received the Spirit of adoption by whom we cry out, 'Abba, Father.' The Spirit Himself bears witness with our spirit that we are children of God, and if children, then heirs—heirs of God and joint heirs with Christ, if indeed we suffer with Him, that we may also be glorified together. (*Rom. 8:14-17*)

The Holy Spirit unites believers to Christ, and so it is through the Holy Spirit that we enter into the love and fellowship shared between the Father and the Son. As D.P. Williams put it, 'the Holy Spirit is the … union between the Son and the sons.'[29] Therefore, our sonship is a participation in the love and fellowship of the Trinity.

The Spirit who is the Spirit of Adoption, is the same Spirit who is the Spirit of the Father and the Spirit of the Son (*Rom. 8:9*: 'the Spirit of God … the Spirit of Christ'). This is the Holy Spirit who unites us to Christ (*Rom. 8:9-10*). So the Spirit of Adoption shares with believers the things of the Father and the Son (whose Spirit He is), by bringing them into that participation in the loving communion of the Trinity. Without the Spirit we have nothing to do with Christ (*Rom. 8:9*). However, with the Spirit, we are united to Christ in such a way that when the Spirit lives in us, Christ lives in us. It is the Spirit who places us 'in Christ' so that we become sons in the Son as we are adopted by the Father in Christ through the Spirit.

---

[27] Cyril of Alexandria, *In Io.*, on Jn 15:9-10 (ET 2:227-228).

[28] Cyril of Alexandria, *In Io.*, on Jn 15:9-10 (ET 2:228).

[29] D.P. Williams, 'Sonship', Unpublished Manuscript. The Puritan, Richard Sibbes wrote that it is 'by the Spirit of the Father and the Son, by the Holy Ghost,' that believers 'are ingrafted into Christ by a spirit of adoption, and have the stamp of the Father upon them.' (Sibbes, *A Heavenly Conference*, 90.) The twentieth century Scottish charismatic theologian, Thomas Smail, wrote that the Spirit 'catches us up into that relationship that Christ has with His Father.' (Thomas Smail, *Reflected Glory*, 55.)

Yet, the Holy Spirit is not only involved in our adoption by uniting us to the Son. The Spirit also makes sure that we know that we are well-beloved children in this new family. The Father's love is poured out in our hearts by the Spirit (*Rom. 5:5*), and so the Holy Spirit shows us and gives us to experience the love of the Triune God for us. 'The Spirit Himself bears witness with our spirit that we are children of God' (*Rom. 8:16*). He makes us aware of our sonship by making us aware of the Father's love for us in Christ through the Spirit. The Holy Spirit lets us know that we are as loved as the Son.

And so, in the Spirit, we cry out 'Abba, Father' (*Rom. 8:15*). It is not just that the Holy Spirit teaches us that we should call God 'Father'. Rather, as the Holy Spirit fills our hearts with God's love, we respond, overwhelmed by love and joy, crying out to 'Abba, Father.' The Holy Spirit opens our eyes to see the Lord as He truly is, and so we can't help but cry out in joy to our loving Father.

Therefore, our inheritance from God and with Christ is a happy and joyful inheritance. Those who have been adopted as sons in the Son through the Spirit are now 'heirs of God and joint heirs with Christ' (*Rom. 8:17*), sharing in the rights and privileges of the Firstborn Son. This great inheritance which we now possess from God and with Christ is the Father's great love and our joyful, loving fellowship with the Father, Son and Holy Spirit for all eternity. The Father is always overflowing with love for His Son, and the Spirit brings us into that same loving relationship through union with the Son. Thus, we who abide in Christ will always be as loved as the Son.

In *Galatians*, Paul connects our adoption as sons with the outpouring of the Holy Spirit in our hearts. 'And because you are sons, God has sent forth the Spirit of His Son into your hearts, crying out, "Abba, Father!"' (*Gal. 4:6*). As a result of our sonship, the Holy Spirit is poured out in a way that assures us of our sonship.[30]

By uniting us to Christ as sons in the Son, the Holy Spirit of adoption brings us into the loving fellowship of the Triune God. 'It is to this end that the Holy Spirit has been sent, in order to qualify many sons for Glory, and to restore the fallen sons of Adam to be the sons of the Living God on the image of the Son of His Love.'[31]

---

[30] We'll look at this more in chapter 26 on the baptism of the Holy Spirit.
[31] D.P. Williams, *Riches of Grace*, xiv.5 (May 1939), 393.

Partakers of the Divine Nature: The Doctrine of Theosis

This truth that believers are adopted into the Christ's sonship with the Father is the central theme of the doctrine of *theosis*.[32] *Theosis* is the name given to the doctrine which expresses partaking of the divine nature (*cf. 2 Pet. 1:4*). In theosis 'we share by grace in the same fellowship or love that the persons of the Trinity share by nature.'[33]

> What many (perhaps most) within the early church meant by the disconcerting word theosis, or deification, was believers' sharing in the warm fellowship that has existed from all eternity between the persons of the Trinity.[34]

By participation in the Son's own relationship with His Father, through the Spirit, the life of believers is, by grace, a life in the Trinity, or *theosis*. One early Apostolic writer summed up this theosis, writing that, 'in the mystery of the Holiest Trinity and the Incarnation, the Paternity of God to His only Son reaches us in a real and effective way; redeemed by the blood of Christ and members of His Body.'[35] This is the Triune God's purpose for the Church: to be 'a Body of people wonderfully united to the Trinity,' partaking of the divine nature (*2 Pet. 1:4*) and of 'the life of God.'[36] Theosis means 'oneness with the Trinity' by sharing through the Spirit in the Son's

---

[32] There is a different doctrine of theosis held by the Eastern Orthodox which arose with Palamite theology in the 14th Century (drawing on mystical themes found in some of the church fathers). The doctrine of theosis centred in our adoption into Christ's sonship with the Father, as expressed by the early Apostolics, continues in a line of theological heritage which can be seen in the writings of early fathers such as Irenaeus, Athanasius and Cyril of Alexandria. For more on this distinction, see Donald Fairbairn, 'Patristic Soteriology: Three Trajectories', *Journal of the Evangelical Theological Society*, 50.2 (June 2007). For more on theosis in early Apostolic theology, see Jonathan Black, 'The Church in the Eternal Purpose of the Triune God: Toward a Pentecostal Trinitarian Ecclesiology of Theosis drawing on the early theology of the Apostolic Church in the United Kingdom', PhD dissertation, University of Chester, 2016. For a straightforward, biblical introduction to the doctrine of theosis, see Donald Fairbairn, *Life in the Trinity* (Downers Grove: IVP, 2009).

[33] Fairbairn, *Life in the Trinity*, 36.

[34] Fairbairn, *Life in the Trinity*, 10-11.

[35] W.R. Thomas, *The Paraclete*, xxix.

[36] D.P. Williams, *Riches of Grace*, vii.1 (Sept. 1931), 16.

relationship with His Father.[37] And this is 'the ultimate purpose of the work of the Trinity in the Redemptive Plan … through the Blood.'[38]

This is what Jesus prayed for on the night of His arrest. Our Saviour lifted His voice to the Father, praying for all those who would believe in Him, and asking:

> that they all may be one, as You, Father, are in Me, and I in You; that they also may be one in Us … that they may be one just as We are one: I in them, and You in Me; that they may be made perfect in one. (*Jn 17:21-23*)

Christ's prayer for the unity of His Church is a prayer for the Church's unity in the Father and the Son. This is not merely a unity of purpose or mission, but a unity of loving fellowship as exists from all eternity between the Father, Son and Holy Spirit. The Church is to find its life and unity in the loving communion of the Triune God. This is theosis.

As people can sometimes be confused or put off by the language of theosis or oneness with the Trinity, it's important to explain what this doesn't mean. Theosis does not mean that we stop being human beings and are turned into gods. We are not absorbed into deity so that we would 'lose self-consciousness and self-identity and individuality,' but rather 'we shall be ourselves eternally.'[39] We do not become sons of God in the same way that Jesus is the Son of God: He is the Son by nature, we are sons by adoption and grace.

In theosis we partake of the divine nature (*2 Pet. 1:4*). But what is the divine nature? The divine nature of the Triune God is to live in perfect loving communion. The Father has always loved His Son in the joy of the Spirit, and in theosis we are brought into that loving communion which is the nature of the Triune God. The Church participates in the divine nature by participating in the life of love and fellowship of the Trinity into which it is immersed.

And as a result, through our union with Christ the true Son, we share in His immortality, incorruption and godliness (*2 Pet. 1:3-7*). 'The attributes of His Person [are] so communicated to us … that we are transformed by them.'[40] This transformation flows from our fellowship with Christ. So theosis consists primarily in participation in the intimate loving communion

---

[37] D.P. Williams, *The Trinity*, 1:56.

[38] D.P. Williams, *The Trinity*, 1:58.

[39] Thomas Rees, *The Divine Masterpiece* (Penygroes: Apostolic Publications, 1943), 10.

[40] D.P. Williams, 'From Glory to Glory', *The Glorious Gospel* (Penygroes: Apostolic Publications, 1940), 45.

of the Father, Son and Holy Spirit, yet this results in a participation in incorruption as the church participates in Christ himself. As Irenaeus put it, 'by communion with Him we ... receive participation in incorruptibility.'[41] Therefore, the early Apostolics prayed:

> Our Father, O Holy God, work Your nature in our nature so that we will be steadfast in Your nature, because You share with us Your perfections and we partake of Your divine nature and are one with You to all eternity. We ask You through grace to set this life and faith in the depths of our nature for the sake of Your Holy Name. Amen.[42]

And all the while they could sing:

> I shall be one
> With the Father and the Son
> In the place prepared for me
> And taste the delight
> Of the Heavenly country bright
> By free grace from Calvary.[43]

This theosis, or union with the Triune God, is the reason for Christ's incarnation and atonement. In the words of Richard Sibbes:

> The great and glorious union of Christ to our natures is that he may take us into his mystical body, and so make us one with himself, and one with the Father ... The sweet union of the two natures of Christ is to confirm union between the Father and us, and Christ and us.[44]

---

[41] Irenaeus, *On the Apostolic Preaching*, (Crestwood: SVS, 1997), 40 (p.65).

[42] D.P. Williams, 'Gweddi' (Welsh Prayer), Cyfarfod y Diaconiaid Cyffredinol, Abertawe, 31st January, 1922. *Transactions of the Apostolic Church for the Year 1922*, p.14a.

[43] Free verse translation from D.P. Williams' Welsh hymn 'Mae'm golwg ar y Wlad', *Molwch Dduw*, 19.

[44] Richard Sibbes, *A Heavenly Conference*, 107.

Chapter 24

Justification

The Doctrine Upon Which the Church Stands or Falls

Suddenly, in the 16th century, the printing presses and taverns of Europe were filled with the good news of Jesus Christ. The Reformation, and with it revival, had come. And at the heart of the Reformation was the gospel of free justification in Christ. During the Reformation, this doctrine of justification by faith alone changed the world, and still today it is at the very heart of the gospel message. In fact, Paul told the Galatians that to deny justification by faith alone was to deny the gospel; to preach another message was to preach a false gospel (*Gal. 1:6-9; cf. Gal. 3:1-9*). Those who abandon the doctrine of justification by faith alone 'have fallen from grace' (*Gal. 5:4*). It is no wonder then that Calvin declared that justification by faith alone is 'the main hinge on which religion turns'[1] or that it has so often been called the doctrine 'upon which the church stands or falls.'[2] It really is that important. True Christianity depends upon this doctrine. Our salvation rests upon this doctrine. In the words of Luther, 'if this doctrine of justification is lost, the whole Christian doctrine is lost.'[3] Therefore, it is very important that we understand the doctrine of justification by faith alone.

In Germany, in the year 1519, Martin Luther's Reformation breakthrough came from *Romans 1:17*: 'For in it the righteousness of God is revealed from faith to faith; as it is written, "The just shall live by faith."' Luther himself explains what happened:

> Though I lived as a monk without reproach, I felt that I was a sinner before
> God with an extremely disturbed conscience. I could not believe that he

---

[1] John Calvin, *Institutes of the Christian Religion*, 3.11.1

[2] This famous saying can be traced back to the early 17th Century theologian Johann Heinrich Alsted.

[3] Martin Luther, *Latin Exegetical Works*, Erlangen Edition, 21,2C; translation from Robert Preus, *Justification and Rome: An Evaluation of Recent Dialogues* (St Louis: Concordia, 1997).

was placated by my satisfaction. I did not love, yes, I hated the righteous God who punishes sinners, and secretly, if not blasphemously, certainly murmuring greatly, I was angry with God, and said, 'As if, indeed, it is not enough, that miserable sinners, eternally lost through original sin, are crushed by every kind of calamity by the law of the decalogue [the Ten Commandments], without having God add pain to pain by the gospel and also by the gospel threatening us with his righteousness and wrath!' Thus I raged with a fierce and troubled conscience. Nevertheless, I beat importunately upon Paul at that place, most ardently desiring to know what St Paul wanted.

At last, by the mercy of God, meditating day and night, I gave heed to the context of the words, namely, 'In it the righteousness of God is revealed, as it is written, "He who through faith is righteous shall live."' There I began to understand that the righteousness of God is that by which the righteous lives by a gift of God, namely by faith. And this is the meaning: the righteousness of God is revealed by the gospel, namely, the passive righteousness with which merciful God justifies us by faith, as it is written, 'He who through faith is righteous shall live.' Here I felt that I was altogether born again and had entered paradise itself through open gates.[4]

Reading Romans, Luther discovered the good news that the God of grace offers to sinners the gift of His righteousness as He justifies us through faith.

In France, another book of the Bible inspired gospel-Reformation. In 1534 a placard was nailed to the door of the king's bedroom, denouncing 'the huge, horrible, and unbearable abuses of the papal mass.' The biblical text to which the placards pointed was from the book of Hebrews: '[Christ] does not need daily, as those high priests, to offer up sacrifices, first for His own sins and then for the people's, for this He did once for all when He offered up Himself' (*Heb. 7:27*).

If, in Germany, Romans 1:17 was the spark that had ignited the Reformation, in France, this was it. If Christ's sacrifice for sin on the cross was a complete work, and thus neither need be nor can be repeated, then all our attempts to atone for sin must be both unnecessary and insulting to Christ, in that they suggest his work is not sufficient. If Christ's sacrifice was indeed 'once for all', then there can be no need for other priests or high priests to offer up more. With that, the Mass, the priests who offered it, and all other acts of atonement for sin were shown to be useless. The only recourse was simple trust in Christ and his complete work.[5]

---

[4] Martin Luther, *Preface to the Complete Edition of Luther's Latin Writings, Luther's Works*, 34:336-337.

[5] Michael Reeves, *The Unquenchable Flame: Introducing the Reformation* (Nottingham: IVP, 2009), 92.

These two key Reformation Scriptures, which sparked the revival in Germany and France, show us that at the heart of the Reformation and its doctrine of justification stand Christ's finished work and God's free gift of righteousness through faith.

What is Justification?

Declared Righteous

The Scriptural term 'to justify' does not mean 'to make righteous', but rather 'to declare righteous.' It was in this distinction that the difference between the Reformers and Rome was found. For Rome, justification was (and still is) considered as a process. Gradually, throughout the whole length of their lives, believers are made righteous, and this, in Roman Catholic theology, is called justification. According to Rome, 'Justification is not only the remission of sins, but also the sanctification and renewal of the interior man.'[6]

The Reformers, on the other hand, saw that, in Scripture, justification is not a process, but a declaration. That the Reformers had the correct biblical understanding of the term can be seen in three ways. 1.) The opposite of *justification* is *condemnation* (*e.g. Rom. 8:33-34*). As James Buchanan explains: 'the justification of the one no more signifies the infusion of righteousness, than the condemnation of the other signifies the infusion of wickedness.'[7] Just as condemnation is a legal declaration of guilt, so its opposite, justification, is a legal declaration of righteousness. 2.) Correlative terms. The other terms with which justification is associated refer to legal judgement. Turretin puts it like this:

> A judicial process is set forth and mention is made of an accusing 'law', of 'accused persons' who are guilty (*hypodikoi*, Rom. 3:19), of a 'hand-writing' contrary to us (Col. 2:14), of divine 'justice' demanding punishment (Rom.

---

[6] Council of Trent, cited in *Catechism of the Catholic Church*, 1989; cf. *Catechism of the Catholic Church*, 2019.

[7] James Buchanan, *The Doctrine of Justification: An Outline of Its History in the Church and of its Exposition from Scripture* (Birmingham, Alabama: Solid Ground Classic Reprints, 2006; originally published in Edinburgh, 1867), 229-230.

3:24, 26), of an 'advocate' pleading the cause (1 Jn 2:1), of 'satisfaction' and imputed righteousness (Rom. 4 and 5), of a 'throne of grace' before which we are absolved (Heb. 4:16), of a 'judge' pronouncing sentence (Rom. 3:20) and absolving sinners (Rom. 4:5).[8]

3.) The equivalent expressions to justification are judicial. Those who are justified do 'not come into judgment' (*Jn 5:24*) and are 'not condemned' (*Jn 3:18*), but rather, they are 'accepted in the Beloved' (*Eph. 1:5-6*). They have righteousness imputed to them and sin not imputed (*Rom. 4:3, 6-8*), and are reconciled to God (*2 Cor. 5:19, 21*).

Therefore, justification is a legal declaration. It does not mean that God makes us righteous; rather it means that He declares us to be righteous. God the Judge pronounces a verdict upon us, but instead of pronouncing a verdict of *guilty*, He pronounces a verdict of *righteous* (we'll look at how He can do this below). Justification is different from regeneration and sanctification in that it doesn't involve any change inside of us. Rather, justification is something that God does for us, outside of us; it is an objective declaration which gives us a new status as righteous.

The fact that justification is a legal declaration means that it is not an on-going process (unlike sanctification). Rather it is instantaneous. All those who have faith in Christ have been justified already; it is not something for which we have to wait or strive. For Rome, justification depends on sanctification. But in the biblical doctrine of the Protestant Reformation, justification does not depend on our sanctification (yet all who are justified will be sanctified).

The Forgiveness of Sins

In Justification, God declares us to be righteous in His sight. However this declaration rests on two other aspects of justification. The first of these is that God forgives our sins. In *Romans 4* we read:

> But to him who does not work but believes on Him who justifies the ungodly, his faith is accounted for righteousness, just as David also describes the blessedness of the man to whom God imputes righteousness apart from works: 'Blessed are those whose lawless deeds are forgiven, and whose sins are covered; Blessed is the man to whom the LORD shall not impute sin.' (*Rom. 4:5-8*)

---

[8] Francis Turretin, *Institutes of Elenctic Theology*, 2:634-635.

Paul is arguing here that those who have faith, and thus are justified, are the ones being described by David in the verses he quotes from *Psalm 32*. Therefore, if you have been justified, your 'lawless deeds are forgiven' (which is a way of speaking about sin, according to *1 Jn 3:4*), your 'sins are covered' and God does 'not impute sin' to you (He doesn't reckon sin to your account). This is a wonderful truth; in justifying us, God forgives our sins.

However, sometimes this is all people think of when it comes to justification. Often people sum it up as being 'just as if I'd never sinned.' Yet, that diminishes the reality of what God has done for us in justification. If justification were no more than being 'just as if I'd never sinned', then we would merely be declared 'not guilty.' But justification is much, much more and much, much greater than 'just as if I'd never sinned.' And also, if justification were only about being 'just as if I'd never sinned', what about the guilt of original sin? We are all born guilty in Adam, and so not only must justification deal with the problem of our actual sins, but also with the guilt of Adam's first sin. Justification is even more than the forgiveness of sins, as marvellous as that is, for this is only the negative aspect of justification.[9] There is also a positive side.

The Imputation of Christ's Righteousness

In the positive side of justification, God gives us something. More specifically He imputes something to us. We have already seen this word above in *Romans 4*, where God does not impute sin to those who are justified. To *impute* means to *reckon*, or to *credit*. If God imputes something to us, He credits it to our account. So if God doesn't impute our sins to us, that means He doesn't credit them against us; He doesn't reckon them to our account, which is very good news for us.

Yet in justification there is something which God does impute to us. This was the truth which sparked Martin Luther's Reformation in Germany, that the righteousness of God is a gift which He gives to us (*Rom. 1:17*). In justification, the Lord imputes righteousness to believers. And this righteousness is the Lord's own righteousness (*Rom. 3:21-22*).

---

[9] Not negative in the sense of bad, but negative in the sense of taking something away.

Alien Righteousness

The righteousness with which God justifies the ungodly is not their own, but His. This is why theologians say that Christians possess an *alien* righteousness; it is alien because it is not our own and does not come from us, but rather it is something completely external to us. It is Christ's righteousness, which God imputes to us by faith alone. This is not something which we have in ourselves, but instead something with which God clothes us from the outside. To be justified is to be 'clothed in righteousness divine.'[10]

This doctrine of alien righteousness once again highlights the difference between the teaching of Rome and the Reformers: between being made righteous and being declared righteous. The Roman Catholics thought that God poured out righteousness into our hearts so that it became ours and our hearts were progressively made righteous. This wasn't an alien righteousness, but rather a righteousness that became the Christian's own. In that scheme, salvation depends on one becoming righteous. Without an alien righteousness, salvation would depend on me changing: on me getting better.

But, in the biblical doctrine of the Reformers, salvation does not depend on my righteousness, but on God clothing me with an alien righteousness. Right from the very beginning of the Scriptures this is the pattern we see in salvation. Even in the immediate aftermath of Adam and Eve's first sin, we are given a powerful image of this as the LORD God clothes our first parents with the sacrificial victim (*Gen. 3:21*). Paul tells us that God 'imputes righteousness apart from works' (*Rom. 4:6*), and so this righteousness does not come from good works done by the one justified, but rather, it is an *alien* righteousness. Paul goes on to call this 'the gift of righteousness' (*Rom. 5:17*). Again it is not one's own righteousness, but an *alien* righteousness, for it comes as a gift from outside of us.

Imputation

This alien righteousness is imputed to believers (*Rom. 4:3-4, 6; Gal. 3:6*). If righteousness is imputed to us, it is accounted to us, or reckoned to our

---

[10] Charles Wesley, 'Tis Finished, the Messiah Dies', *Redemption Hymnal*, 167; 'And Can it Be', *Redemption Hymnal*, 324.

account. This doctrine of imputation is not something confined to the New Testament; in fact, the New Testament writers look to the Old Testament to teach the truth of justification through imputation. It is Abraham, the great father of Israel and model of faith, to whom the Scriptures point us as the great example of justification through imputation. In *Genesis 15*, the Word of the LORD appeared to Abraham, and Abraham 'believed in the LORD, and He accounted it to him for righteousness' (*Gen. 15:6*). Abraham was saved through imputed righteousness. And all the true children of Abraham by faith are saved in the same way.

The Lord does 'not impute sin' to those whom He blesses with salvation in Christ (*Rom. 4:8*). This is how the Lord justifies us from the guilt of Adam's first sin. The guilt with which we were clothed through our union with Adam is no longer reckoned to us when we are justified in Christ. Instead of imputing Adam's guilt to us, 'God imputes righteousness apart from works' (*Rom. 4:6*). We are justified, not by the righteousness of our works, but by an alien righteousness which is imputed to us.

In *Romans 4*, Paul sets out a parallel between the non-imputation of sin and the imputation of righteousness. Then, in *Romans 5*, Paul goes on to set out his great parallel between being 'in Adam' and being 'in Christ.' Putting this all together, what we see is that sin is imputed in Adam, and righteousness is imputed in Christ. The sin belongs to Adam, but we are subject to its guilt through our union with Adam; and the righteousness belongs to Christ, yet believers are counted righteous with His righteousness through their union with Christ. That which belongs to the head to whom we're united is imputed to us, whether that be guilt in Adam or righteousness in Christ.

The Righteousness of Christ

This *alien* righteousness which is imputed to believers in union with Christ is Christ's righteousness. In his parallel between Adam and Christ in *Romans 5*, Paul demonstrates that the righteousness in which all those united to Christ share is Christ's own righteousness:

> Therefore, as through one man's offense judgment came to all men, resulting in condemnation, even so through one Man's righteous act the free gift came to all men, resulting in justification of life. For as by one man's disobedience many were made sinners, so also by one Man's obedience many will be made righteous. (*Rom. 5:18-19*)

It is not by their own righteous acts or their own obedience that believers are justified, but rather by the righteous act and obedience of the One Man, Jesus Christ our heavenly Head. The righteousness belongs to Him.

Paul writes to the Philippians concerning this righteousness which He has in Christ:

> Yet indeed I also count all things loss for the excellence of the knowledge of Christ Jesus my Lord, for whom I have suffered the loss of all things, and count them as rubbish, that I may gain Christ and be found in Him, not having my own righteousness, which is from the law, but that which is through faith in Christ, the righteousness which is from God by faith. (*Phil. 3:8-9*)

The righteousness upon which Paul relies is not his own righteousness, but rather an alien righteousness 'which is from God.' This is the righteousness which God imputes to believers. It is not something which comes 'from the law', through our works and obedience, but rather, it is a gift which is received 'through faith in Christ.' Those who are found in Christ, united to Him, share in this righteousness, which comes from God and is received by faith. So this is an alien, imputed righteousness which is found only in Christ. And this righteousness 'is to be sought nowhere else than in Christ, who is Jehovah our righteousness, and who of God is made unto us righteousness.'[11]

Writing to the Corinthians, Paul tells us that Jesus Christ 'became for us … righteousness' (*1 Cor. 1:30*). In his next epistle to Corinth, Paul tells us that God 'made Him who knew no sin to be sin for us, that we might become the righteousness of God in Him' (*2 Cor. 5:21*). We become the righteousness of God in Christ in the same way in which He was made to be sin for us, which was by imputation. Christ was not turned into sin; the sin was never His own, but was always ours. Yet, through our union with Him, it was imputed to Him so that He paid the full penalty for our sin through His death in our place on the cross. In the same way, through our union with Him, His righteousness is imputed to us, so that we enjoy its full benefit. Martin Luther called this 'the great exchange': Christ took our sin and, in return, we receive the imputation of His righteousness. United to Christ, believers are clothed with Him for righteousness.

Paul tells the Romans that 'the end of the law is Christ for righteousness to everyone who believes' (*Rom. 10:4*, literal translation). 'Christ for righteousness' is set out as the opposite of 'being ignorant of

---

[11] Turretin, *Institutes of Elenctic Theology*, 2:652.

God's righteousness' and of 'seeking to establish [one's] own righteousness' (*Rom. 10:3*). The goal of the law is not for us to attempt to establish our own righteousness through the works of the law, but rather to look to Christ for His righteousness. 'He becomes righteousness for us when we believe on him.'[12] The righteousness with which we are justified is the righteousness of Christ imputed to us.

In the Old Testament, the prophet Isaiah uses the imagery of being clothed with righteousness:

> I will greatly rejoice in the LORD,
> My soul shall be joyful in my God;
> For He has clothed me with the garments of salvation,
> He has covered me with the robe of righteousness. (*Isa. 61:10*)

At first glance, this might look like a verse speaking of the imputation of an alien righteousness to believers. However, it is not a believer who is speaking in this Scripture: it is Jesus who is speaking. It is the LORD who will rejoice in the LORD His God (*Isa. 61:10; cf. v.8*). The robe of righteousness and the garments of salvation belong to Christ; but all those who take refuge in Him – all those who are united to Him in faith – are clothed with Him, and therefore clothed with His royal robe of righteousness. United to Him, His righteousness is ours. As Calvin wrote, 'You see that our righteousness is not in us but in Christ, that we possess it only because we are partakers in Christ; indeed, with him we possess all its riches.'[13]

Calvin draws on an ancient illustration of this from Ambrose:

> For this reason, it seems to me that Ambrose beautifully stated an example of this righteousness in the blessing of Jacob: noting that, as he did not of himself deserve the right of the firstborn, concealed in his brother's clothing and wearing his brother's coat, which gave out an agreeable odour [Gen. 27:27], he ingratiated himself with his father, so that to his own benefit he received the blessing while impersonating another. And we in like manner hide under the precious purity of our first-born brother, Christ, so that we may be attested righteous in God's sight ... In order that we may appear before God's face unto salvation we must smell sweetly with his odour, and our vices must be covered and buried by his perfection.[14]

---

[12] John Piper, *Counted Righteous in Christ* (Leicester: IVP, 2002), 89.
[13] Calvin, *Institutes*, iii.xi.23
[14] Calvin, *Institutes*, iii.xi.23

A bit more succinctly, Luther put it like this: 'through faith ... Christ's righteousness becomes our righteousness and all that he has becomes ours, rather he himself becomes ours.'[15] The doctrine of justification through the imputation of Christ's righteousness means that united to Christ, believers have Christ for righteousness. Therefore, our righteousness does not depend on us; it cannot fluctuate as a result of what we do. Those who are clothed with Christ for righteousness cannot be more justified or less justified. 'Righteous in Christ' is the status of all believers.

Simil iustus et peccator

The righteousness of Christ, in whom we are clothed, is His righteousness and is found in Him alone. It is an alien righteousness: not a change inside of us, but something external to us.[16] And so, although we are righteous by status in God's eyes, for we are clothed with the perfect righteousness of Jesus, our hearts are still sinful (*Rom. 7:7-25*). We are, at the same time, both righteous and sinners: *simil iustus et peccator*. As Luther explains: 'In myself outside of Christ, I am a sinner; in Christ outside of myself, I am not a sinner.'[17]

> Believers inwardly are always sinners; therefore they are always justified from without. The hypocrites, on the other hand, are always righteous inwardly; therefore they are always sinners from without. By 'inwardly' I mean, as we appear before judgment and opinion; by from 'without,' as we appear before God and His judgment. We are righteous 'outside ourselves' when our righteousness does not flow from our works; but is ours alone by divine imputation. Such imputation, however, is not merited by us, nor does it lie with our power, as the prophet says in Hosea 13:9: 'O Israel, thou hast destroyed thyself; but in me is thine help.' Of ourselves we are always wicked, as the Psalmist says in Psalm 51:3 'My sin is ever before me.' But the hypocrites, say: 'My righteousness is ever before me, and blessed are they who do works of righteousness.'
>
> The text says: 'Blessed are they whose iniquities are forgiven'; that is to say: Blessed are they who by grace are freed from the burden of iniquity, namely, of the actual sins which they have committed. That, however, is not sufficient, unless also their 'sins are covered,' that is unless the radical evil (original sin) which is in them is not charged to them as sin. That is

---

[15] Martin Luther, *Two Kinds of Righteousness, Luther's Works*, 31:298.

[16] Cf. *The Apostolic Church: Its Principles and Practices*, 195. This is fundamental to the distinction between justification and sanctification.

[17] Martin Luther, WA 38:205. Translation from Paul Althaus, *The Theology of Martin Luther*, 243.

covered when, though still existing, it is not regarded, considered and imputed by God; as we read: 'Blessed is the man to whom the Lord will not impute sin.'[18]

This truth is a great comfort to believers when we are confronted with our own sin. Because we, though sinful, have in 'Christ a righteousness which [we] may claim as [our] own', when we face the accusations of the enemy of our souls, we have confidence in Him to say, 'If I have sinned, my Christ, in whom I believe, has not sinned; all mine is His, and all His is mine.'[19] As the hymn-writer put it:

> What though the vile accuser roar
> Of sins that I have done;
> I know them well, and thousands more;
> My God, He knoweth none.[20]

The imputation of Christ's righteousness is a wonderful truth. That we sinful humans should have the righteousness of our Lord Jesus Christ credited to our account, is gloriously incredible yet splendidly true. This means that God does not only see us as forgiven (thus not negatively sinful), but as righteous (positively with the perfect righteousness of Christ). As a result, 'there is therefore now no condemnation to those who are in Christ Jesus' (*Rom. 8:1*).

> The Father embraces us in Christ when he clothes us with the innocence of Christ and accepts it as ours that by the benefit of it he may hold us as holy, pure, and innocent. For Christ's righteousness, which as it alone is perfect alone can bear the sight of God, must appear in court on our behalf, and stand surety in judgment. Furnished with this righteousness, we obtain continual forgiveness of sins in faith. Covered with this purity, the sordidness and uncleanness of our imperfections are not ascribed to us but are hidden as if buried that they may not come into God's judgment, until the hour arrives when, the old man slain and clearly destroyed in us, the divine goodness will receive us into blessed peace with the new Adam. There let us await the Day of the Lord in which, having received incorruptible bodies, we will be carried into the glory of the Heavenly Kingdom.[21]

---

[18] Martin Luther, *Commentary on Romans*, (Grand Rapids: Kregel, 1976), 83.
[19] Martin Luther, *The Freedom of a Christian*.
[20] Samuel Gandy, alt. Zac Hicks.
[21] Calvin, *Institutes*, iii.xiv.12

How are we Justified?

Justified By His Blood

How can God be just if He justifies sinners? Paul addresses this question in his epistle to the Romans, writing:

> But now the righteousness of God apart from the law is revealed, being witnessed by the Law and the Prophets, even the righteousness of God, through faith in Jesus Christ, to all and on all who believe. For there is no difference; for all have sinned and fall short of the glory of God, being justified freely by His grace through the redemption that is in Christ Jesus, whom God set forth as a propitiation by His blood, through faith, to demonstrate His righteousness, because in His forbearance God had passed over the sins that were previously committed, to demonstrate at the present time His righteousness, that He might be just and the justifier of the one who has faith in Jesus. (*Rom. 3:21-26*)

Here we see that, firstly, God only justifies one type of person, namely 'the one who has faith in Jesus' (*Rom. 3:26*). Secondly, it is God's own righteousness that makes our justification possible (*vv. 21-22*); it is 'the righteousness of God' that is 'to all and on all who believe.' This is what we've seen as we've been considering the imputation of Christ's righteousness. Thirdly, we are 'justified freely by His grace through the redemption that is in Christ Jesus' (*v.24*). Here justification is specifically linked with redemption and 'propitiation by His blood'. Redemption, propitiation and the blood of Christ all speak to us of the Atonement. Thus it is only through Christ's atoning death that we are justified.

This is why Jesus had to die. God couldn't just forgive and forget, for if He did, He would be unjust. When God revealed Himself to Moses, He made clear that He would 'by no means clear... the guilty' (*Ex 34:7*). He is a God of justice; therefore guilt must be punished. The Scriptures tell us clearly that 'He who justifies the wicked, and he who condemns the just, both of them alike are an abomination to the LORD' (*Prov. 17:15*).

And so Jesus died for our sin. If our sin were simply left unpunished, that would be the situation described in *Proverbs 17:15*. Instead, Christ bore the punishment for our sins on the cross. That's why Paul refers to *propitiation* in *Romans 3:25*. As the propitiation for our sins, Christ bore the wrath of God, the punishment for sin, in our place. God 'made Him who knew no sin to be sin for us, that we might become the righteousness of God in Him' (*2 Cor. 5:21*). Jesus Christ took our sin upon Him and bore its punishment. As it was our sin, it was we who deserved the punishment; but God in His love and His grace provided forgiveness for us. God the Son willingly took our flesh upon Him and came into this world to bear the wrath which we deserved, by offering up His life as the propitiation for our sins.

Thus, we are justified through Christ's death on the cross in our place;[22] we are 'justified by His blood' (*Rom. 5:9*). Justification and atonement go together; without the atonement there could be no justification. By His atoning death, Christ has taken the punishment for our sin, and therefore God is both 'just and the justifier of the one who has faith in Jesus' (*Rom. 3:26*).

Justified by His Resurrection

Yet, it is not only the righteousness and blood of Christ which are connected in Scripture with our justification. Christ 'was delivered up for our trespasses and raised for our justification' (*Rom. 4:25 ESV*). But what is the connection between Jesus' resurrection and our justification?

At the cross, the wrath of God had been poured out upon the sinless Saviour for our sin. But on the third day the Saviour was declared righteous by His resurrection from the dead. As Paul puts it, Jesus was 'justified in the Spirit' (*1 Tim. 3:16*). Through the Triune work of the resurrection of Jesus Christ from the dead, the Father declared in His Son by the Spirit that the Incarnate Son was indeed righteous. The incarnate Son had no sin to hold Him in the grave, and the resurrection demonstrated that. The resurrection is the vindication and justification of Jesus Christ.[23]

Christ's resurrection is the Father's declaration that He is righteous. And united to Christ in His resurrection, we receive the same verdict. Thus, He was 'raised for our justification' (*Rom. 4:25*).

> Our justification is a participation in Christ's own resurrection-justification, in which he was released from the verdict of condemnation and his

---

[22] D.P. Williams, *Justification*, 5.
[23] Jesus is not justified through the imputation of an alien righteous like we are; He is declared righteous because He is righteous.

righteous obedience was supremely vindicated. In our union with the resurrected Jesus, we share in the vindication and affirmation of Christ's life and death.[24]

Justified By Grace Alone (Sola Gratia)

Christ's work – His active and passive obedience,[25] His sinless life, atoning death, and triumphant resurrection – is the basis for our justification. But how do we benefit from what Christ has done? Do we have to do something good to attract God's attention or gain His favour? Certainly not! For a start, we have already seen that that would be impossible. Being utterly depraved, we cannot do anything good to earn God's favour; 'all our righteousnesses are like filthy rags' (*Isa. 64:6*). So there is no way we can merit our justification.

How then can we be justified? The answer of the Scriptures is that we are 'justified freely by His grace' (*Rom. 3:24*). Justification comes by God's grace, not our merit. It's all about what God has done for us in Christ, not what we do. Grace has nothing to do with what we deserve and everything to do with what Christ has done. We cannot do anything to win, merit or deserve grace. God gives His grace freely in Jesus, who was given for us and is offered to us in the gospel.

Justification is a gift of God. As Paul emphasises, it is 'by grace you have been saved … by grace you have been saved through faith, and that not of yourselves; it is the gift of God, not of works, lest anyone should boast' (*Eph. 2:5, 8-9*).

There's no room for confusion here. We are justified solely by the grace of God. Hence we speak about justification by grace *alone*. It is not grace plus something else that justifies us: not grace plus works, not grace plus our cooperation. This was what the Reformation was about. The Roman Catholic Church did not deny that we needed God's grace to be justified, but it insisted that it was grace plus something else. The Reformers responded with the cry of *Sola Gratia* ('by grace alone'). In response to the Reformation, the Roman Catholic Church codified its official teaching that we must 'cooperate with God … to prepare and dispose [ourselves] for the attainment of justification'[26]; in other words people have to do something

---

[24] Marcus Peter Johnson, *One With Christ: An Evangelical Theology of Salvation* (Wheaton: Crossway, 2013), 107.

[25] See chapter 13.

[26] Council of Trent, Sixth Session, Canon IV

first in order to be able to be justified. But that's an outright denial that justification is by grace alone. That's saying that justification comes by grace plus our works, which are thought to prepare us to receive God's grace. However, this is not the Scriptural teaching; rather the Bible makes clear that we are 'justified freely by His grace' (*Rom. 3:24*).

As we have seen in the last chapter, grace is Christ and Him crucified for us. Therefore to be justified by grace alone means to be justified in Christ alone (*Solus Christus*). We come to Jesus and rely wholly upon Him, and find ourselves clothed in Christ alone for righteousness.

> Nothing in my hand I bring,
> Simply to Thy cross I cling;
> Naked, come to Thee for dress;
> Helpless, look to Thee for grace:
> Foul, I to the fountain fly;
> Wash me, Saviour, or I die.[27]

Justified Through Faith Alone (Sola Fide)

God justifies sinners by His grace in Jesus. But how do we receive this justification? As we have seen above, we cannot do anything to prepare ourselves to receive it; so how can we be justified? Paul gives us the answer: we are 'justified by faith' (*Rom. 5:1*). God is 'the justifier of the one who has faith in Jesus' (*Rom. 3:26*). For, it is 'by grace you have been saved through faith, and that not of yourselves; it is the gift of God' (*Eph. 2:8*).

The Scriptures frequently contrast faith and works with regard to justification:

> knowing that a man is not justified by the works of the law but by faith in Jesus Christ, even we have believed in Christ Jesus, that we might be justified by faith in Christ and not by the works of the law; for by the works of the law no flesh shall be justified. (*Gal. 2:16*)

Here we see that it is impossible to be justified by our efforts to please God; yet justification comes by faith in Jesus Christ. Our works will never save us. Only Christ, who died and rose for us, can save, and we receive that salvation through faith in Him. Not faith plus works, but through faith alone.

---

[27] Augustus Montague Toplady, 'Rock of Ages', *Redemption Hymnal*, 341.

But what is the difference between faith and works? Are they not both ways of having some sort of merit before God? Not at all! Significantly, the Bible never says that we are justified *on the basis of* our faith, but rather it is always 'by faith' or 'through faith'.

> For, as regards justification, faith is something merely passive, bringing nothing of ours to the recovering of God's favour but receiving from Christ that which we lack.[28]

Christ's work alone is the basis of our justification (both His sinless life and His atoning death). Faith is simply 'personal reliance on the Person and work of Christ alone… It is self-despairing trust in the Lord Jesus Christ our only Saviour.'[29]

What is Faith?

The *Heidelberg Catechism* provides us with a thorough, yet glorious, definition of true faith:

> True faith is not only a certain knowledge whereby I hold for truth all that God has revealed to us in His Word; but also a hearty trust, which the Holy Spirit works in me by the Gospel, that not only to others, but to me also, forgiveness of sins, everlasting righteousness and salvation are freely given by God, merely of grace, only for the sake of Christ's merits.[30]

As the catechism shows us, there are two elements to true faith which go together: (i) intellectual assent to the truth, and (ii) personal trust.

Intellectual Assent. This means knowing the facts of the gospel and believing that they are true. In order to have faith in Christ and His redemptive work we need to know the facts about who He is and what He has done (*i.e.* the gospel). We need to know that Jesus is God the Son who has taken on our humanity to live for us, obey for us, die for us, and rise for us. Not only do we need to know these facts, but we also need to accept that they are true. Yet true biblical faith is more than mental assent to the facts of the gospel. Thus there is a second essential element to true saving faith.

---

[28] Calvin, *Institutes*, iii.xiii.5

[29] Philip H. Eveson, *The Great Exchange: Justification by Faith Alone in the Light of Recent Thought* (Leominster: Day One, 1996), 198-199.

[30] *Heidelberg Catechism*, Q.21

Personal Trust. This is the realisation that Jesus didn't just die for people in general, or for other people, but for *me*. This is when, in the realisation that my soul is guilty and defiled by sin, I look to Christ for the forgiveness which comes only through His atoning work. In other words, this is trusting Christ for salvation, what the *Heidelberg Catechism* refers to as 'a hearty trust … that not only to others, but to me also, forgiveness of sins, everlasting righteousness and salvation are freely given by God, merely of grace, only for the sake of Christ's merits.'[31] Faith is flying to the Son of God for refuge (*Ps 2:12; 34:22*).

The Object of Faith

As we've just seen, true faith has for its object Christ and His saving work. As Paul told the Philippian gaoler, 'Believe on the Lord Jesus Christ, and you will be saved' (*Acts 16:31*). We are justified 'by faith in Jesus Christ' (*Gal. 2:16; cf. Rom. 3:26*). The Lord Jesus Christ, God the Son who took on human flesh and died for our sin, rising again on the third day, is the object of our faith. We believe in Him 'who became for us wisdom from God — and righteousness and sanctification and redemption' (*1 Cor. 1:30*).

Justification and the Christian Life

As we have seen, justification is an instantaneous declaration; it is not an on-going process. It happens the moment we trust in Jesus for salvation, not gradually throughout our Christian life. Yet this glorious declaration should have a major impact on our Christian lives. If '*there is* therefore now no condemnation to those who are in Christ Jesus' (*Rom. 8:1*), then that will have some implications in life.

In justification Christ's righteousness is imputed to us, our sins are forgiven, and God declares us to be righteous in His sight. That means that we now have the standing of righteous. If we are in Christ, then we are

---

[31] *Heidelberg Catechism*, Q.21

righteous with His righteousness. This is important for when we sin, for, as *1 John 1:8* tells us, 'if we say that we have no sin, we deceive ourselves, and the truth is not in us.' Christians still sin; but the doctrine of justification by the imputation of Christ's righteousness assures us of the forgiveness of our sins. Justification does not only deal with sins before conversion, but sins we commit as Christians as well. Instead of imputing our sins to us, God looks on the righteousness of Christ.

This is not to say that sin doesn't matter if we are saved. Far from it! John is writing to Christians when he says 'if we confess our sins, He is faithful and just to forgive us our sins and to cleanse us from all unrighteousness' (*1 Jn 1:9*). Paul's opponents accused him of teaching that sin didn't matter if you were a Christian because of His doctrine of justification by the imputation of Christ's righteousness. These opponents argued that, if we are justified by grace alone, then it would even be a good thing to continue sinning, as that would allow for more of God's grace. Paul responded by writing: 'What shall we say then? Shall we continue in sin that grace may abound? Certainly not! How shall we who died to sin live any longer in it?' (*Rom. 6:1*). Yes, our sins, past, present and future, are forgiven, but that is no reason to continue in the sin from which Christ has set us free.

Because we are clothed with the spotless robe of Christ for righteousness, we don't lose our salvation every time we sin. For our justification is not based on our works or merits, but on Christ's sinless life, atoning death, and triumphant resurrection. If we cannot merit justification by the good things we do, we cannot lose it by doing something sinful.[32] Justification is based solely on what Christ has done; never on what we do. Therefore we have the assurance of forgiveness when we confess our sins to God; for our standing before God relies not on our feelings or actions, but solely on Christ.

Sometimes, when we sin, we don't feel good enough or worthy enough to approach the Father in prayer, to tell others of Jesus, or to spend time in fellowship with the Lord in His Word. It's true, we *are* unworthy because of our sin (that's a fact); but Christ is worthy, and we stand before God with Christ's righteousness, not our filthy rags. Rather than looking to our sin and unworthiness, we should look to Jesus 'who was delivered up for our trespasses and raised for our justification' (*Rom. 4:25* ESV), entrusting ourselves to His blood and righteousness.

---

[32] We'll look at the possibility of falling from grace in chapter 39.

This spotless robe the same appears
When ruined nature sinks in years;
No age can change its glorious hue,
The robe of Christ is ever new.[33]

There is 'now no condemnation to those who are in Christ Jesus' (*Rom. 8:1*).

So Christians are both justified and sinners. Even the apostle Paul was both justified and a sinner (see *Romans 7*). We must not forget that we are *sinners saved by grace*. The sin in our life is serious and must lead us to repentance, but it does not negate our justification. God has accepted us as righteous while we are still sinful; in the words of the Reformers, we are *simil iustus et peccator* – justified and sinful at the same time. Our salvation does not begin by grace and then continue by our own works or merits. The presence of sin in our lives should always remind us that we do not deserve the salvation that God has freely given us by His love and grace in Jesus, and drive us back to the Cross and humble reliance on Christ crucified, our only Saviour.

Justification and Works

Yet, if we are not justified by our good works, and we do not keep our justification by our good works, what is the relationship between good works and justification? Does James not say 'that a man is justified by works, and not by faith only' (*Jas 2:24*)? Indeed, James does say this, but we need to look a bit more carefully at what else James says in the context.

> What does it profit, my brethren, if someone says he has faith but does not have works? Can faith save him? … Thus also faith by itself, if it does not have works, is dead. But someone will say, 'You have faith, and I have works.' Show me your faith without your works, and I will show you my faith by my works. You believe that there is one God. You do well. Even the demons believe—and tremble! But do you want to know, O foolish man, that faith without works is dead? Was not Abraham our father justified by works when he offered Isaac his son on the altar? Do you see

---

[33] Zinzendorf, tr. John Wesley, 'Jesus Thy Blood and Righteousness', *Redemption Hymnal*, 366.

that faith was working together with his works, and by works faith was made perfect? And the Scripture was fulfilled which says, 'Abraham believed God, and it was accounted to him for righteousness.' And he was called the friend of God. You see then that a man is justified by works, and not by faith only. Likewise, was not Rahab the harlot also justified by works when she received the messengers and sent them out another way? For as the body without the spirit is dead, so faith without works is dead also. (*Jas 2:14-26*)

Some people have tried to use this passage to say that James and Paul disagree about how we are justified; but that is simply not the case. It is the same Holy Spirit who inspired James and Paul to write Scripture, thus there cannot be any disagreement in what they teach.

James himself states clearly here that Abraham was justified by faith, citing *Genesis 15:6* (*Jas 2:23*). So James is not denying the doctrine of justification by faith alone. Rather, his focus is on something else. In *James 2:14-26* the focus is not so much on justification as it is on the true nature of saving faith. James is contrasting true saving faith with another type of 'faith' which does not save; he is contrasting saving faith with 'dead faith'. Thus, James' argument in this passage is that the way in which we can distinguish between true faith and 'dead faith' is by looking at the works which result from that faith. Works are the fruit of true saving faith (*verses 18-19*). Faith without works is a 'dead faith'; it is akin to what the demons have – an intellectual assent without entrusting oneself to Christ and His saving work. True saving faith and regeneration go together. Thus, if we are regenerate (born again), we have received a new life; we are 'a new creation' (*2 Cor. 5:17*). This means we have been transformed by God's grace and will seek to serve Him by works of thankfulness. This is not the basis of justification, but it will always accompany justification.

Yet, James still says 'that a man is justified by works, and not by faith only' (*Jas 2:24*). So what does he mean? In the context, the 'faith only' would appear to refer to this 'dead faith' which James is combatting. But what about the statement 'that a man is justified by works'? In order to understand James here, we need to think about the Greek word he uses. In English *justification* is a theological word with a very precise meaning. However, the Greek word which we translate as *to justify* can sometimes have a different meaning. Sometimes instead of referring to a legal declaration, the verb can mean *to show that someone is righteous*. An example of this meaning can be found in *Luke 16:15*: 'And He said to them, "You are those who justify yourselves before men, but God knows your hearts."' Here Jesus is speaking to the Pharisees, but He is not saying that they declare themselves to be righteous; rather He is saying that they try to show other people how righteous they are. Another example is found in *Romans 3:4* (which quotes *Ps 51:4*): 'That You may be justified in Your words, and may overcome when You are judged.' The very next verse (*Rom. 3:5*) explains that this is referring to the fact that 'our unrighteousness demonstrates the righteousness of God'. Thus *justified* here refers to a *demonstration* of righteousness, not a *declaration*.

This is also the way in which James is using the word in *James 2:24*. James knows that we are declared righteous by God at conversion, by grace alone, through faith alone, on the basis of the work of Christ alone. (After all, he quotes *Gen. 15:6* which tells us about Abraham's justification by faith, many years before he offered Isaac on the altar.) What James is referring to here is the demonstration that the believer is righteous. By faith we are declared righteous, and the works which flow from that faith demonstrate that righteousness. This demonstration of righteousness of which James speaks, is 'the mere evidence, manifestation, or proof of' God's declaration of righteousness through faith in Jesus Christ.[34] This is the relationship between faith and works. Our works are not the basis of our justification, but rather they are the result of our faith and show that we have been justified. By faith Christ's righteousness is imputed to us and by our works we are shown to be righteous.

Justification and the Trinity

In recent years, some Pentecostals have complained that the Reformation doctrine of justification isn't Trinitarian enough, and have instead gone off in search of something new.[35] However, Herman Bavinck reminds us just how Trinitarian the true Reformation doctrine of justification really is:

> It is he [God] and he alone who for his own sake blots out our transgressions and no longer remembers our sins (Isa. 43:25). We are

---

[34] Buchanan, *The Doctrine of Justification*, 244.

[35] Veli-Matti Kärkkäinen, *Spirit and Salvation*, A Constructive Christian Theology for the Pluralistic World, Vol. 4 (Grand Rapids: Eerdmans, 2016), 344; Frank D. Macchia, *Justified in the Spirit: Creation, Redemption and the Triune God*, (Grand Rapids: Eerdmans, 2010), 39.

justified by his grace as a gift (Rom. 3:24; Gal. 3:18; Eph. 2:8; Titus 3:5–7).
More specifically, it is the Father from whom this benefit proceeds, for he
is the lawgiver and judge (James 4:12), but also the merciful God, who
abounds in steadfast love, and blots out transgressions for his name's sake
(Num. 14:18; Pss. 32:2; 103:3; 130:4; Isa. 43:25; Rom. 3:24; 4:6; 8:33; 2 Cor.
5:19). He himself paved a way in Christ to distribute this benefit, so that
Christ, too, possessed the power to forgive sins (Matt. 9:2–6; John 5:22, 27),
and himself sent the Holy Spirit to apply this benefit to the hearts of his
children (John 14:26; Rom. 8:15–16; 1 Cor. 6:11). In the past, Reformed
theologians put it as follows: The Father justifies effectively; the Son,
meritoriously; the Holy Spirit, applicationally. And to complete the picture
at once, let us add: faith apprehends, the sacraments seal, and works
declare.[36]

The God who justifies the ungodly, by grace alone, through faith alone, in
Christ alone, is the Triune God.

The Five Solas

The doctrine of the Reformation is often summed up with five Latin
expressions: the five *solas* of the Reformation. These five solas remind us
that we are saved by God's free grace alone (*sola gratia*). And if salvation is
by grace alone, that means it is not found in anything in us, or in other
people, or churches, but is found in Christ alone (*solus Christus*). If salvation
is outside of us, and found only in Christ, then the only way we can receive
this great salvation is by faith alone (*sola fide*). This gracious salvation in
Christ is not something we have discovered for ourselves, but something
which God has revealed to us in His Word, and so by the Scriptures alone
(*sola Scriptura*). And if all that is case, then the Triune God has done
everything for our salvation; sinful human beings have contributed nothing
to save themselves, but cast themselves wholly upon the saving work of the
Triune God in Christ Jesus. Therefore, all the glory goes to God alone (*soli
Deo gloria*).

Justification by grace alone, through faith alone – justification through
the finished work of Christ – leads us to cry *soli Deo gloria*. The Lord has

---

[36] Herman Bavinck, *Reformed Dogmatics*, 4:205.

done it all. He is our salvation, from beginning to end. And as it leads us to give all glory to the Triune God alone, 'justification by faith ... is the sum of all piety.'[37]

This is the doctrine upon which the church stands or falls. So let us heed Luther's words:

> This doctrine can never be urged and taught enough. If this doctrine is overthrown or disappears, then all knowledge of the truth is lost at the same time. If this doctrine flourishes, then all good things flourish: religion, true worship, the glory of God, the right knowledge of all conditions of life and of all things.[38]

---

[37] Calvin, *Inst.*, iii.xv.7

[38] Luther, *Latin Exegetical Works*, Erlangen Edition 21,12. Translation from Preus, *Justification and Rome.*

Chapter 25

Sanctification

The Lord Jesus Christ offered Himself up as the atoning sacrifice for sin on the cross of Calvary 'that He might sanctify the people' (*Heb. 13:12*). Throughout the Scriptures the Lord makes known that this is His desire for His people: 'You shall be holy, for I the LORD your God am holy' (*Lev. 19:2*). Peter takes up this call in the New Testament, writing, 'as He who called you is holy, you also be holy in all your conduct, because it is written, "Be holy, for I am holy"' (*1 Pet. 1:15-16*). The Triune God's desire for His people is that they should be holy like Him. *Sanctification* is how we become holy like our holy God, and sanctification is the will of the God of holiness for His people (*1 Thess. 4:3*).

Holy in Jesus

What do *holiness* and *sanctification* mean? Although the two words look very different in English, in actual fact they are very closely related concepts. The verb *to sanctify* simply means *to make holy*. Thus *sanctification* is the process of being made holy. In the Old Testament the Hebrew words used for sanctification and holiness originally referred to the idea of separation. However, as the words are used in context in the Old Testament we can see that they took on a more important theological meaning. Thus sanctification referred to being set apart for God's service. When applied to God's people sanctification also took on the additional idea of separation from whatever is displeasing to God. The same idea is seen in the New Testament where sanctification refers to separation to God and separation from sinful practices. And as we are separated to God and from sin, we become like Him, being 'conformed to the image of His Son' (*Rom. 8:29*).

Thus sanctification refers to being set apart for God and being separated from all that is sinful. And God does this in Christ and through the Holy Spirit. Jesus is our sanctification. 'Sanctification is a Person; it is absolutely, wholly and utterly the glorious Person of Christ. Christ is as much the totality of our sanctification as He is of our justification.'[1] To be sanctified is to be holy in Jesus. And so sanctification is 'God forging us into the likeness of Christ through our participation in his death and resurrection.'[2]

Definitive Sanctification: The Instantaneous Act

Definitive Sanctification is the aspect of sanctification that happens when we become Christians. This is why the Bible sometimes speaks of sanctification in the past tense. Hence Paul writes to the Corinthians as 'those sanctified in Christ Jesus' (*1 Cor. 1:2* ESV; *cf. 1 Cor. 6:11*). Paul also describes this as having died to sin. In Romans 6, he explains that Christians have 'died to sin' (*Rom. 6:2*), that 'our old man was crucified with Him, that the body of sin might be done away with, that we should no longer be slaves of sin' (*Rom. 6:6*). This is something that has occurred once (hence the term *definitive* sanctification) and is applied to us when we are united with Christ. Therefore all Christians have been sanctified in that they have died to sin through their union with Christ in His death. Definitive sanctification is the application of redemption to the believer. In redemption, Christ set us free from the power of sin by paying the price of His death on the Cross. When we come to faith in Christ this freedom from sin's power is applied to our lives in definitive sanctification. As a result then of definitive sanctification, we are no longer slaves to sin. Instead we are new creations in Christ Jesus, for 'old things have passed away; behold, all things have become new.' (*2 Cor. 5:17*).

Progressive Sanctification: The Continual Process

Although the Bible speaks of Christians as having been sanctified, it also speaks of them as being sanctified. This sanctification in the present is what we refer to as *Progressive Sanctification*.

---

[1] W.A.C. Rowe, *One Lord, One Faith*, 95.
[2] Johnson, *One with Christ*, 118.

Despite our definitive sanctification, Christians still sin. James writes that 'we all stumble in many things' (*Jas 3:2*) and John writes (to Christians) that 'if we say that we have no sin, we deceive ourselves, and the truth is not in us' (*1 Jn 1:8*). Thus the Scriptures teach that Christians are not sinless. Rather, Christians are *simil iustus et peccator* – justified and sinful at the same time.[3] Therefore sin is still something that must be dealt with throughout this life. This is where progressive sanctification comes in. Through redemption we are set free from slavery to sin; through definitive sanctification this freedom from sin's power is applied to us; and through progressive sanctification the results of this freedom are worked out in our lives day by day.

Whereas definitive sanctification is a one-time event, progressive sanctification, as the name suggests, is something continuous. It begins with definitive sanctification (at the time of salvation) and continues until the end of our earthly life. It will never be complete in this life, but only when we will 'see Him as He is', for then 'we shall be like Him' (*1 Jn 3:2*).

Sanctification and Justification

In sanctification we are conformed to the image of Christ (*Rom. 8:29*). The same Christ who is our holiness and sanctification, is also our righteousness, in whom we are justified (*1 Cor. 1:30*). As Calvin put it, 'he cannot be divided into pieces.'[4] United to Christ as well-beloved sons in the Well-Beloved Son, we have Christ Himself as our double grace of justification and sanctification. United to the righteous one, we are righteous in Him. United to the holy one, we are holy in Him. Calvin explains:

> Why, then, are we justified by faith? Because by faith we grasp Christ's righteousness, by which alone we are reconciled to God. Yet you could not grasp this without at the same time grasping sanctification also. For he 'is given unto us for righteousness, wisdom, sanctification, and redemption' [1 Cor. 1:30]. Therefore Christ justifies no one whom he does not at the same time sanctify. These benefits are joined together by an everlasting and indissoluble bond, so that those whom he illumines by his wisdom, he redeems; those whom he redeems, he justifies; those whom he justifies, he sanctifies.
>
> But, since the question concerns only justification and sanctification, let us dwell upon these. Although we may distinguish them, Christ

---

[3] See chapter 24.
[4] John Calvin, *Institutes of the Christian Religion*, 3.16.1

contains both of them inseparably in himself ... Since, therefore, it is solely by expending himself that the Lord gives us these benefits to enjoy, he bestows both of them at the same time, the one never without the other. Thus it is clear how true it is that we are justified not without works yet not through works, since in our sharing in Christ, which justifies us, sanctification is just as much included as righteousness.[5]

United to Christ, we are blessed with every spiritual blessing in Him (*Eph. 1:3*), and so in Him we are clothed with His righteousness and share in His holiness. United to Christ, the holiness of the believer is always Christ's holiness: it is always His holy life bearing fruit in us. As Luther wrote:

My holiness, righteousness and purity do not stem from me, nor do they depend on me. They come solely from Christ and are based only in Him, in whom I am rooted by faith, just as sap flows from the stalk into the branches. Now I am like Him and of His kind. Both He and I are of one nature and essence, and I bear fruit in Him and through Him. The fruit is not mine; it is the Vine's.[6]

Trinitarian Holiness

Sanctification is God's work. It is 'God breaking into our nature with a sin-consuming and soul-keeping energy.'[7] And God does this sanctifying work in us 'in our Redeemer', by 'the indwelling life of Christ.'[8] And this sanctifying union with Christ our Redeemer comes as we participate in Him by the Holy Spirit.[9] So sanctification is a Trinitarian work. The Father sanctifies us in the Son by the Holy Spirit.

And this is exactly what we find in the Scriptures. Jude writes that we are 'sanctified by God the Father' (*Jude 1*) and Paul writes that sanctification is the Father's will (*1 Thess. 4:3*). As W.A.C. Rowe writes, 'it is from the Father's glorious holiness that true sanctification and righteousness proceed.'[10]

This holiness which proceeds from the Father is found in the Son. Christ Himself is our sanctification (*1 Cor. 1:30*). Christ gave Himself for His

---

[5] Calvin, *Institutes*, 3.16.1

[6] Martin Luther, 'Sermon on the Gospel of St John 15:5', *Luther's Works*, 24:226.

[7] D.P. Williams, *Riches of Grace*, x.2 (Nov. 1934), 55.

[8] D.P. Williams, *Riches of Grace*, x.2 (Nov. 1934), 50.

[9] D.P. Williams, *Riches of Grace*, x.5 (May 1935), 170.

[10] W.A.C. Rowe, *One Lord, One Faith*, 101.

Church, 'that He might sanctify and cleanse her' (*Eph. 5:25-26; cf. Heb. 13:12*). We are holy in Him (*1 Cor. 1:2; Eph. 1:1; Col. 1:2; 2 Cor. 5:17*), for sanctification is found in oneness with the crucified Saviour (Heb. 2:11). And it is the Holy Spirit who makes us one with Christ, and so applies to us the holiness of Christ, by uniting us to Christ so that we partake of Him for holiness. The Spirit's work of sanctification is 'in the name of the Lord Jesus' (*1 Cor. 6:11; cf. 1 Pet. 1:2*).

Sanctified By His Blood

The sanctification, which is ours in Christ, is ours only through the finished work of Christ. Our sanctification is only through His blood (*Heb. 10:29; 13:12*). This holiness is not something we merit or achieve for ourselves. We cannot climb up to Christ to lay hold of His holiness. He must come down to us; and He has come down to us through His incarnation and His cross. As D.P. Williams wrote, 'to be like Christ … is not possible to the natural man, born in sin. He must be new-created from above.'[11] And this new creation from above comes only through the death and resurrection of Jesus Christ, 'our Redeemer, who has made such rich provision whereby we may enjoy this blessed … sanctification.'[12] Sanctification is always and only 'by His own blood.'[13] In the words of another older Apostolic theologian, 'Christ and the cross are the only and sufficient grounds for sanctification.'[14]

Sanctified in the Crucified and Risen Saviour

Christ, the Incarnate Son of God, who died and rose again for us, is our holiness. So we are sanctified in union with the one who died and rose again. Our holiness is found in union with Him in His death and

---

[11] D.P. Williams, *Riches of Grace*, x.2 (Nov. 1934), 49.

[12] D.P. Williams, *Riches of Grace*, x.2 (Nov. 1934), 50.

[13] D.P. Williams, *Riches of Grace*, x.2 (Nov. 1934), 55, cf. 53.

[14] W.A.C. Rowe, *One Lord, One Faith*, 102.

resurrection. United to Christ in His death, the power of sin is overcome in us through our death to sin in Him. United to Christ in His resurrection, we live unto righteousness through our being raised to newness of life in Him. We call these two sides of sanctification *mortification* and *vivification*.

> Both things [mortification of the flesh and vivification of the spirit] happen to us by participation in Christ. For if we truly partake in his death, 'our old man is crucified by his power, and the body of sin perishes,' that the corruption of original nature may no longer thrive. If we share in his resurrection, through it we are raised up into newness of life to correspond with the righteousness of God.[15]

Mortification: United to Christ in His Death

Mortification means the *putting to death* of sin. Paul warns the Romans that 'if you live according to the flesh you will die; but if by the Spirit you put to death the deeds of the body, you will live' (*Rom. 8:13*). In *Colossians* he relates this putting to death to specific sinful practices: 'Therefore put to death your members which are on the earth: fornication, uncleanness, passion, evil desire, and covetousness, which is idolatry' (*Col. 3:5*). The Scriptures also state the same truth in more general terms: 'Therefore do not let sin reign in your mortal body, that you should obey it in its lusts' (*Rom. 6:12*). This mortification may be 'a painful process' for it is 'a process of severing, of cutting out, and this entails suffering.'[16] Mortification may mean 'the plucking out of the eye [*Mt 5:29; 18:9; Mk 9:47*], the cutting off of the right hand [*Mt 5:30*], the offering up of Isaac [*Gen. 22*], the loss of all things, the counting of all things as dung [*Phil. 3:8*].'[17] However, as the great Puritan, John Owen, pointed out from *Romans 8:13*, 'The vigour, and power, and comfort of our spiritual life depends on the mortification of the deeds of the flesh ... Be killing sin or it will be killing you.'[18]

Yet this mortification is not something which we do by ourselves, through our own efforts or by our own strength. It is only because 'our old man was crucified with Him, that the body of sin might be done away with, that we should no longer be slaves of sin' (*Rom. 6:6*). The true putting to

---

[15] Calvin, *Institutes*, 3.3.9

[16] D.P. Williams, *Riches of Grace*, x.2 (Nov. 1934), 51.

[17] D.P. Williams, *Riches of Grace*, x.2 (Nov. 1934), 51-52.

[18] John Owen, *Of the Mortification of Sin in Believers*, 49, 50.

death of sin occurs only through our death in union with Christ. 'The mortification of the flesh is the effect of the cross of Christ.'[19]

Jesus said, 'If anyone desires to come after Me, let him deny himself, and take up his cross daily, and follow Me' (*Lk 9:23; cf. Mt 10:38-39; Mk 8:34*). Likewise, He told them:

> Unless a grain of wheat falls into the ground and dies, it remains alone; but if it dies, it produces much grain. He who loves his life will lose it, and he who hates his life in this world will keep it for eternal life. If anyone serves Me, let him follow Me; and where I am, there My servant will be also. If anyone serves Me, him My Father will honour. (*Jn 12:24-26*)

We take up our cross daily, not independently of Christ's cross, nor merely in imitation, but in following after Him by falling into the ground in union with His death. True holiness in Christ is found through dying in Christ's death. On the night of His arrest, Jesus prayed to His Father, saying 'for their sakes I sanctify Myself, that they also may be sanctified' (*Jn 17:19*). Christ sanctified Himself in His death that we might be sanctified in death-union with Him. In mortification we live out of our death-union with Christ by taking up our cross daily to follow Him (*Lk 9:23*), knowing that 'I have been crucified with Christ; it is no longer I who live, but Christ lives in me; and the life which I now live in the flesh I live by faith in the Son of God, who loved me and gave Himself for me' (*Gal. 2:20*).

> His dying crimson, like a robe
> Spreads o'er His body on the tree;
> Then am I dead to all the globe,
> And all the globe is dead to me.[20]

We have died to sin in Him. And now, through our death-union with Him, by His Spirit we put to death the deeds of the flesh. That is mortification.

Vivification: United to Christ in His Resurrection

Yet the goal in sanctification isn't just for us to mortify sin. Rather, the goal of the Triune God in our sanctification is to conform us to the image of Christ (*Rom. 8:29*). *Vivification* (or *quickening*) means living to righteousness in Christ Jesus (*1 Pet. 2:24; Eph. 4:24*). By His resurrection, we are raised to

---

[19] John Calvin, *Commentary on Galatians*, 169.
[20] Isaac Watts, 'When I Survey the Wondrous Cross', *New Redemption Hymnal*, 227.

newness and holiness of life in Him. United to Christ in His resurrection, we 'have entered into the life of the Spirit of Life and Righteousness, energised by the Holy Ghost.'[21]

> And if Christ is in you, the body is dead because of sin, but the Spirit is life because of righteousness. But if the Spirit of Him who raised Jesus from the dead dwells in you, He who raised Christ from the dead will also give life to your mortal bodies through His Spirit who dwells in you. Therefore, brethren, we are debtors—not to the flesh, to live according to the flesh. For if you live according to the flesh you will die; but if by the Spirit you put to death the deeds of the body, you will live. For as many as are led by the Spirit of God, these are sons of God. (*Rom. 8:10-14*)

Mortification and vivification are inseparable, for they both take place in the indivisible Christ. Having died with Christ, we are raised in Him. And through the resurrection of Christ we live a new life of holiness in the Spirit, which empowers us to mortify the sinful deeds of the flesh. Mortification leads to vivification (*Rom. 6:4*). And vivification leads to mortification (*Rom. 8:11-13; Col. 3:1-5; Phil. 3:10*). The two are so tightly inter-connected that they can't be unravelled. For the two are found in union with the one Christ who died and rose for us.

Partakers of the (Holy) Divine Nature

United to Christ as well-beloved sons in the Well-Beloved Son, we share in His relationship with the Father; and so our life is found in the loving fellowship of the Triune God and we are made 'partakers of the divine nature' (*2 Pet. 1:4*). We've already seen this when we looked at theosis.[22]

Partaking of the divine nature, 'His divine power has given to us all things that pertain to life and godliness' (*2 Pet. 1:3*), and so we partake of the holiness, godliness, and incorruption of the Son to whom we are united. And so we are transformed in Him. On the last day, 'when He is revealed, we shall be like Him, for we shall see Him as He is' (*1 Jn 3:2*), and so we shall be fully conformed to the image of the Son (*Rom. 8:29*). Yet, even now

---

[21] D.P. Williams, *Riches of Grace*, x.3 (Jan. 1935), 92.
[22] See Chapter 23.

already, we are being transformed and conformed more and more to His image as we behold Him.

> But we all, with unveiled face, beholding as in a mirror the glory of the Lord, are being transformed into the same image from glory to glory, just as by the Spirit of the Lord ... For it is the God who commanded light to shine out of darkness, who has shone in our hearts to give the light of the knowledge of the glory of God in the face of Jesus Christ' (*2 Cor. 3:18; 4:6*).

The Father shines forth His glory in the Son that through the glory of the Son the Spirit might transform us into to the image of the Son. And the Spirit transforms from glory to glory, by taking of what is the Son's, and communicating it to us (*Jn 16:14*). In other words, the Father has sent the Spirit to sweep us up into the Father's love for His Son and so through the Spirit we participate in the Son, and all that is His. Our sanctification flows from our theosis:[23] it is because we are sons in the Son by the Spirit, and so partakers of the divine nature, that we are holy in Jesus.

Sanctified By Faith

It is by faith that we partake of Christ and all His benefits, and so by faith that we partake of holiness in Him. The Lord Jesus commissioned Paul to preach the gospel to the Gentiles 'that they may receive forgiveness of sins and an inheritance among those who are sanctified by faith in Me' (*Acts 26:18*). True faith works through love (*Gal. 5:6*), for 'faith without works is dead' (*Jas 2:26*).

Sanctification is not something we do for ourselves through our works and efforts in order to please God. Rather, it is God's work in us through faith and flows from the gospel of free grace in Jesus. The faith by which we are sanctified is faith in Jesus Christ, the crucified and risen Son of God (*Acts 26:18*). Therefore, we are sanctified by faith in Christ and His finished work. We are sanctified by faith in Jesus, because faith lays hold of Jesus so that He:

> Is not outside us but dwells within us. Not only does he cleave to us by an indivisible bond of fellowship, but with a wonderful communion, day by

---

[23] See chapter 23.

day, he grows more and more into one body with us, until he becomes
completely one with us.[24]

Not only the beginning of our Christian life, but every moment of our
Christian walk, is lived by faith in Jesus Christ and Him crucified. 'As you
therefore have received Christ Jesus the Lord, so walk in Him, rooted and
built up in Him and established in the faith, as you have been taught,
abounding in it with thanksgiving' (*Col. 2:6-7*). Remember, sin is unfaith; so,
if sanctification includes the mortification of sin, that must involve putting
unbelief to death, which can only be through faith in Jesus. And, as 'faith
comes by hearing, and hearing by the word of God' (*Rom. 10:17*), Christians
need the Word for holiness. The Church must hear the proclamation of the
gospel if she is to be sanctified by faith.

Sanctified through the Word

Faith comes by hearing and hearing by the Word of Christ (*Rom. 10:17*). So,
if we are sanctified by faith, then we are sanctified by the Word. In His great
High-Priestly prayer, Jesus prayed for our sanctification. 'Sanctify them by
Your truth. Your word is truth … And for their sakes I sanctify Myself, that
they also may be sanctified by the truth' (*Jn 17:17, 19*). Jesus is the Truth (*Jn
14:6*) and the Word (*Jn 1:1*), and in the written and spoken Word we
encounter Jesus, the living Word and Truth of God. The truth we have
heard and been taught in the Word 'is in Jesus' (*Eph. 4:21*). So to be
sanctified by the Truth is to be sanctified by Christ in His Word. In the
Gospel Word 'the treasures of grace are opened to us' and so in the Word
we meet Christ 'clothed with His gospel.'[25] As we read and hear the Word of
Christ, it elevates 'the soul to a delight in Him and Him alone.'[26] And so we
'set [our] mind on things above, not on things on the earth. For [we] died,
and [our] life is hidden with Christ in God' (*Col. 3:2-3*), and as a result we
'therefore put to death [our] members which are on the earth' (*Col. 3:5*).

  If it is Christ the Word who sanctifies us by His Word, and if
mortification and vivification occur only in union with Christ in His death
and resurrection, then the Word which we need for our sanctification is His
Gospel Word: the Word of the Incarnate Son who died and rose for us, and

---

[24] Calvin, *Institutes*, 3.2.24
[25] Calvin, *Institutes*, 3.2.6
[26] D.P. Williams, *Riches of Grace*, x.5 (May 1935), 170.

in whom we have died and risen. The law shows us our desperate need of holiness, but only the gospel has the power to sanctify.

> The glorious experience of regeneration from the guilt of sin has enraptured the soul right into the joy and peace of the new life. But this experience is soon followed by the thunderclaps of the Law, by the which God lays bare the old nature. It shows how exceeding sinful that nature is, and the enmity that is inherent in the fallen human nature towards God.[27]

But the 'remedy' to the blow of the Law is the message of the Cross: the Gospel Word of Christ and Him crucified, and us crucified in Him.[28] As John Owen explained:

> Christ is not in the law; he is not proposed in it, not communicated by it, – we are not made partakers of him thereby. This is the work of grace, of the gospel. In it is Christ revealed, by it he is proposed and exhibited unto us; thereby are we made partakers of him and all the benefits of his mediation. And he it is alone who came to, and can, destroy this work of the devil … This 'the Son of God was manifested to destroy.' He alone ruins the kingdom of Satan, whose power is acted in the rule of sin. Wherefore, hereunto our assurance of this comfortable truth is principally resolved. And what Christ hath done, and doth, for this end, is a great part of the subject of gospel revelation.[29]

> It is that which the law and all the duties of it cannot procure. The law and its duties, as we have declared, can never destroy the dominion of sin. [30]

God's word of Law kills, as it reveals our sin. But His Gospel Word, the Word of Christ and Him crucified and risen for us and our salvation, gives life and holiness as Christ comes to us and gives Himself to us in His Word. Then, empowered by Christ in His Word, we long to be like Him, and, as the law shows us what He is like, it serves us as a guide. And so 'all Scripture … is profitable for doctrine, for reproof, for correction, for instruction in righteousness, that the man of God may be complete, thoroughly equipped for every good work' (*2 Tim. 3:16-17*). As D.P. Williams reminds us, 'The ministry of the Word … works on the hearts of the saints.'[31]

---

[27] D.P. Williams, *Riches of Grace*, x.3 (Jan. 1935), 91.

[28] D.P. Williams, *Riches of Grace*, x.3 (Jan. 1935), 92.

[29] John Owen, *A Treatise of the Dominion of Sin and Grace*, chapter 5.

[30] John Owen, *A Treatise of the Dominion of Sin and Grace*, chapter 6.

[31] D.P. Williams, *Apostolic Church 1928 Council Minutes*, 142.

Sanctified through the Breaking of Bread

In the Holy Supper, the bread which we break and the cup which we bless are a participation in the most holy body and blood of our holy Saviour (*1 Cor. 10:16*). In the Breaking of Bread 'we are partaking of the very life and everything that is in Christ.'[32] As we feed upon His most holy body and blood, we partake of Christ and all His benefits, and so we participate in His holiness. Therefore the holy sacrament of the Breaking of Bread is for our sanctification.[33] The Lord's Supper is 'a special means of grace.'[34]

The crucified and risen Christ, with all His holiness, indwells His Church in two ways: through the Holy Spirit who unites us to Christ by faith, and bodily 'as we continually eat his body and blood through the Eucharist.'[35] As Cyril of Alexandria puts it:

> The one who receives the flesh of our Saviour Christ and drinks his precious blood, as he himself says, is found to be one with him, mixed together, as it were, and mingled with him through participation so that they are found in Christ, and Christ in them.[36]

In D.P. Williams' words, Christ's body and blood in the sacrament are our 'sustenance for the spiritual life.'[37] The Breaking of Bread is 'the means of expression and participation of the New Life through His Death.'[38] As we 'drink His Blood' and 'eat His Flesh' we 'derive the properties of God' from Christ the Incarnate Son, and so we are transformed and sanctified by Him.[39] Therefore 'repeated, lifelong participation in the Lord's Supper is central to one's growing relationship to the Trinity, just as lifelong devotion to God's Word, to prayer and to the indwelling of the Holy Spirit are central.'[40] For the Breaking of Bread is 'a remedy which God has given us to

---

[32] *Apostolic Church 1928 Council Minutes*, 141.

[33] *1928 Council Minutes*, 95.

[34] *1928 Council Minutes*, 141.

[35] Donald Fairbairn, *Life in the Trinity*, 216.

[36] Cyril of Alexandria, *In Io.* 4.2 (on Jn 6:56; ET 1:239).

[37] D.P. Williams, *Athrawieathau Sylfeinol*, 10.

[38] D.P. Williams, 'The Ministry of the Word', *The Enduring Word* (Penygroes: Apostolic Publications, 1944), 171.

[39] D.P. Williams, *Riches of Grace*, xi.1 (Sept. 1935), 205.

[40] Donald Fairbairn, *Life in the Trinity*, 216.

help our weakness, strengthen our faith, increase our charity [love], and advance us in all holiness of life.'[41]

> The sacrament of the Lord's Supper is as a spiritual feast to nourish our faith, and to strengthen us to walk in all holiness by Christ living and working in us … Its end is not only that we may remember Christ's death in history, but in the mystery of it … that so we may receive and enjoy all the promises of the new covenant.[42]

Holiness Under the Cross

Our holiness is found in union with the Crucified Christ, and so we are sanctified in the holy Incarnate Son, who humbled Himself to enter into all the sufferings and miseries of this life for us.

> But we see Jesus, who was made a little lower than the angels, for the suffering of death crowned with glory and honour, that He, by the grace of God, might taste death for everyone. For it was fitting for Him, for whom are all things and by whom are all things, in bringing many sons to glory, to make the captain of their salvation perfect through sufferings. For both He who sanctifies and those who are being sanctified are all of one, for which reason He is not ashamed to call them brethren. (*Heb. 2:9-11*).

The one who sanctifies us is the one who suffered for us, even unto death. The one in whom we are sanctified is the one to whom we have been united in His suffering and death. And because of this union, we should not be surprised by our sufferings. Rather, Peter encourages us

> Beloved, do not think it strange concerning the fiery trial which is to try you, as though some strange thing happened to you; but rejoice to the extent that you partake of Christ's sufferings, that when His glory is revealed, you may also be glad with exceeding joy. (*1 Pet. 4:12-13*)

As Jesus Himself warned His disciples, because He was hated by the world, those who are united to Him will also be hated by the world (*Jn 15:18-19; cf. Acts 14:22*). Yet, 'as the sufferings of Christ abound in us, so our consolation

---

[41] John Calvin, *Short Treatise on the Supper of Our Lord*, 28.
[42] Walter Marshall, *The Gospel-Mystery of Sanctification*, (London & Edinburgh: Oliphants, 1954; originally published 1692), 197.

also abounds through Christ' (*2 Cor. 1:5; cf. Phil. 1:29-30*). These sufferings with Christ which abound in us are part of our union with Christ in His death, and are used by God to mortify our sinful flesh.

> We are hard-pressed on every side, yet not crushed; we are perplexed, but not in despair; persecuted, but not forsaken; struck down, but not destroyed — always carrying about in the body the dying of the Lord Jesus, that the life of Jesus also may be manifested in our body. For we who live are always delivered to death for Jesus' sake, that the life of Jesus also may be manifested in our mortal flesh. (*2 Cor. 4:8-11*)

We suffer in death-union with Christ that the life of Christ might be manifest in us; for, the One to whom we are united and in whose holiness we share, is not only the One who suffered and died, but also the one who triumphed and rose. Just as at the cross of Jesus, God brought life through death, so too in the Christian's cross – our union with Christ in His cross – the Triune God brings life through death, and glory through suffering. It is in 'the fellowship of His sufferings, being conformed to His death' that we know 'the power of His resurrection' (*Phil. 3:10-11*). The Christian life is a cross-shaped life. Luther put it like this:

> The holy Christian people are externally recognized by the holy possession of the sacred cross. They must endure every misfortune and persecution, all kinds of trials and evil from the devil, the world, and the flesh … by inward sadness, timidity, fear, outward poverty, contempt, illness, and weakness, in order to become like their head, Christ.[43]

Holiness is being conformed to the image of Christ, and the only true Christ there is, is the Crucified Christ. So holiness means sharing in 'the fellowship of His sufferings, being conformed to His death' (*Phil. 3:10*). True holiness is found only through the cross. Therefore the Christian rejoices in suffering, because in our suffering we partake of Christ's sufferings, experience the sanctifying power of His death and resurrection, and know close fellowship with Him (*Rom. 5:3-5; 8:16-17; Jas 1:2-4*). The holy Christian glories not in his holiness, but in the cross. For true holiness is found in the Christ of the cross, comes to us through His death on the cross, and is manifest in us as we live under the cross.

---

[43] Luther, *On the Councils and the Churches, Luther's Works*, LW41:164.

Tenet 5

The Baptism of the Holy Ghost
for believers,
with signs following.

Chapter 26

The Baptism of the Holy Spirit

The Apostolic Church began with the Baptism in the Holy Spirit. One evening in the village of Penygroes the Holy Spirit fell on three groups of believers gathered for different reasons in three different places in the village. Some had just got saved; others had been Christians for years. Yet the Holy Spirit fell on them all alike that night, and with such significance that the early leaders of the movement all considered that night's outpouring of the Holy Spirit to be the true beginning of the Apostolic Church.

Pentecostals agree that the Baptism of the Holy Spirit is of great significance. It is, after all, 'the crown jewel of Pentecostal distinctives.'[1] Yet the Baptism of the Spirit did not begin in the Welsh Revival or in Azusa Street or Topeka. The New Testament Church began with the Baptism of the Holy Spirit. But just what is the Baptism in the Holy Spirit and what is its great significance?

The Bible and the Baptism of the Holy Spirit

When we think of the Baptism of the Spirit in biblical terms, our attention is particularly drawn to the Day of Pentecost and subsequent outpourings in the Acts of the Apostles. However, the biblical witness is not confined to one book alone, or even to one Testament alone.

---

[1] Frank Macchia, *Baptized in the Spirit: A Global Pentecostal Theology* (Grand Rapids: Zondervan, 2006), 20.

Terminology

The Bible uses more than one fixed expression to speak of what we call the Baptism of the Holy Spirit. When our Lord spoke of the Baptism of the Holy Spirit to His disciples before ascending to the Father's right hand, He referred to it not only as being *'baptized with the Holy Spirit'* (*Acts 1:5*), but also as *'the Promise of the Father'* (*Acts 1:4*) and the Holy Spirit *coming upon* believers (*Acts 1:8*). When the experience is described for the first time in the next chapter, it is called being *'filled with the Holy Spirit'* (*Acts 2:4*). In Peter's explanation of what has happened, he speaks again of *'the promise'* (*Acts 2:33, 39*) and also adds the description of it as the Holy Spirit being *'poured out'* (*Acts 2:17, 33*) and as *'the gift of the Holy Spirit'* (*Acts 2:28*). So, even within the book of Acts, there are multiple ways of referring to the Baptism of the Holy Spirit.

Identifying these various expressions in the accounts surrounding the Day of Pentecost enables us to identify further instances of the Baptism in the Holy Spirit later in Acts. The expression *'baptized with the Holy Spirit'* only occurs once more in Acts after the Day of Pentecost, in *Acts 11:16* where Peter is describing what happened in Cornelius' house. Here Peter ties together Jesus' promise of His disciples being *'baptized with the Holy Spirit'* with *'the same gift'* (*Acts 11:17*) given to both Cornelius and his household and Peter and the rest of the 120 on the Day of Pentecost, for 'the Holy Spirit *fell upon* them, as upon us at the beginning' (*Acts 11:15; cf. 10:44*). Here the Baptism of the Holy Spirit is referred to both as the *'gift'* (a description already found in *Acts 2*) and as the Holy Spirit *falling upon* believers (an expression not used in *Acts 2*, but shown here in *Acts 11* to carry the same meaning). Peter uses one further expression in Cornelius' house just after the Holy Spirit has fallen on the household, declaring that they 'have *received the Holy Spirit* just as we have' (*Acts 10:47*).

From the events surrounding the Day of Pentecost and Peter's visit to Cornelius, therefore, we can identify eight biblical expressions which refer to the Baptism in the Holy Spirit:

1. Baptised with/in the Holy Spirit
2. Being filled with the Holy Spirit
3. The Holy Spirit falling on believers
4. The Holy Spirit coming upon believers
5. The Holy Spirit being poured out on believers

6. Receiving the Holy Spirit
7. Receiving the Promise
8. The Gift of the Holy Spirit

These expressions then allow us to identify other occurrences of the Baptism in the Holy Spirit in Acts where the specific term *baptised* is not used. Furthermore, this variety of terminology helps to take us beyond the book of Acts to see what the rest of the Scriptures have to say about the Baptism of the Holy Spirit.

The Baptism of the Holy Spirit in the Old Testament

Jesus calls the Baptism of the Holy Spirit 'the Promise of the Father' (*Acts 1:4*), indicating that this promise was not only revealed during Jesus' earthly ministry, but had already been made in the Old Testament. Although it would not be explicitly stated until later by the prophets, the first indication of this Promise of the Spirit is found in Genesis at the Creation of man, when 'the LORD God formed man of the dust of the ground, and breathed into his nostrils the breath of life; and man became a living being' (*Gen. 2:7*). While most modern commentators have followed Augustine in seeing this as the creation of the soul, an older interpretation, well represented by Cyril of Alexandria, reads this in rather a different way, and a way which bears directly upon the Promise of the Baptism in the Holy Spirit.[2] This interpretation sees here the Lord Jesus – the eternal Word of the Father – breathing the Holy Spirit into Adam. That means man was created, at the very beginning, filled with the Spirit. And so that means human beings were created to be filled with the Spirit.

This Promise becomes explicit with the prophets. In fact, the prophets speak of two types of promise of the Holy Spirit: the promise of the Holy Spirit *within us* and the promise of the Holy Spirit *upon us*. These promises indicate two different types of things which the Father was going to send the Holy Spirit to do. The promise that the LORD would put His Spirit within us is connected to a new heart, and thus to regeneration, whilst the promises that the LORD would pour out His Spirit upon us are the promises associated with the Baptism in the Holy Spirit.

Perhaps the most obvious place to start looking at this promise of the Holy Spirit being poured out upon us is *Joel 2:28-29*, the passage to which

---

[2] See chapter 7.

Peter turns to explain what's happening on the Day of Pentecost. For Joel, the promise is the Spirit poured out on all God's people. This outpouring is not reserved for a particular class or group such as the priesthood or the prophets, but rather is for sons and daughters, old and young, children and servants. Thus the Lord's outpouring of the Holy Spirit is not confined within any human distinctions or limitations, whether they be of sex, age or social status (a promise on which Peter picks up on the Day of Pentecost in *Acts 2:39*, declaring that 'the promise is to you and to your children, and to all who are afar off, as many as the Lord our God will call').

Furthermore, Joel tells us that this promise of the outpouring of the Spirit brings with it revelation. When the Spirit is poured out, people prophesy, dream dreams and see visions. Thus in the outpouring of the Spirit, the Lord reveals Himself to His people. As we have already seen at the start of this book, Jesus is the revelation of God, and Jesus Himself teaches that the Holy Spirit's role in the lives of the people of God is to glorify Jesus and to take of what is Christ's and make it known (*Jn. 16:14*). Therefore, this is not a revelation independent of Christ, but rather as Christ pours out the Spirit (*Acts 2:33*), the Spirit glorifies Christ and points to Him, and thus we receive a revelation of God in Christ through the outpouring of the Spirit. As John declares in *Revelation 19:10*, 'the testimony of Jesus is the spirit of prophecy.'

However, *Joel 2* is not the first place that we find the Promise of the Father stated. Moses was the first prophet of God to speak of this outpouring of the Spirit. When the LORD poured out His Spirit on the elders of Israel and they prophesied, two of the elders had not gathered with the others, and yet the Spirit was poured out upon them too, and they prophesied out in the camp. Joshua was worried that this wasn't right, so he wanted them to stop, but Moses wouldn't let Joshua stop them. Instead he declared: 'Oh, that all the Lord's people were prophets and that the Lord would put His Spirit upon them!' (*Num. 11:29*). For Moses, it was no bad thing to see more people filled with the Spirit and prophesying. Rather this was his desire, and as the prophet of the LORD he saw that ultimately this was God's desire: to fill all His people with the Holy Spirit and to give them all such revelation of Himself.

The prophet Isaiah contributes significantly to our understanding of the outpouring of the Holy Spirit. In *Isaiah 32*, he prophesies about barrenness, dryness and abandonment, 'until the Spirit is poured upon us from on high' (*Isa. 32:15*). Then, when the Spirit is poured out, things change. For when the Spirit is poured out, 'the wilderness becomes a fruitful field, and the fruitful field is counted a forest.' When the Spirit replaces the wilderness with fruitfulness, He doesn't just give a few tufts of grass. Rather, this fruitful field is so full of vegetation that it is called a forest. Thus, by the outpouring of His Spirit, the Lord utterly transforms the barren place to make it a place of abundant life.

This transformation occurs as the Lord's justice turns the wilderness into a fruitful field that knows His righteousness (*Isa. 32:16*). This points us to the Cross of Christ, for it is there that we see God's righteousness in a barren place, the place of death, bringing righteousness and fruitfulness. There is God's justice and all our righteousness: there in Christ and Him crucified for us. As the Holy Spirit is poured out, He glorifies Jesus and points us to Christ the Lord our Righteousness, pointing us away from any attempts at finding merit in ourselves, and out to Jesus who has done everything for us. Thus, as the Spirit is poured out upon us, He assures us that, indeed, in Jesus, God's justice has been satisfied and, in Jesus, we are clothed with righteousness divine. So this revelatory encounter with the Holy Spirit is an encounter in which He assures us of the great salvation which we have in Christ. The Holy Spirit opens our eyes to see afresh the righteousness of Christ for us. As a result, we know 'peace' and 'quietness', and can 'dwell in a peaceful habitation … and in quiet resting places' (*Isa. 32:17-18*), assured of the safety and security we have in Christ.

This association between the outpouring of the Holy Spirit and assurance is seen even more clearly in *Isaiah 44:1-8*. Again, there is assurance of righteousness. The Lord calls the deceiver (Jacob) upright (Jeshurun) (*Isa. 44:2*); He calls the sinful righteous. This is what the Lord has done for us in justification. Yet Isaiah links this gracious declaration of righteousness with the outpouring of the Spirit. Jacob and Jeshurun have no need to fear, 'for' the Lord will pour out His Spirit (*Isa. 44:3*). The declaration of 'upright' or 'righteous' has already been made, but now through the outpouring of His Spirit, the Lord assures His people that they are indeed upright and righteous in His sight. Thus the baptism in the Holy Spirit brings with it an assurance of justification.

Yet not only does the Lord assure us of imputed righteousness, He also assures us that we are His. This is not merely a legal assurance of status, but a loving assurance of relationship. Verse 5 shows that the result of this outpouring of the Spirit is that:

> One will say, 'I am the Lord's';
> Another will call himself by the name of Jacob;

Another will write with his hand, 'The Lord's,'
And name himself by the name of Israel.

Although they already belonged to the Lord, now they recognise this afresh in a new way. Suddenly, they have this confidence in identifying themselves as the Lord's people. They speak with the assurance that they belong to Him. They write His name upon themselves and identify themselves with the name of the Lord's people. What's happening is that, as the Lord pours out His Spirit upon them, He's assuring them that they really are His (cf. *Rom. 5:5; Gal. 4:6*). The result of such assurance from the Lord through the outpouring of the Spirit is strength and stability. 'They will spring up among the grass like willows by the watercourses' (*Isa. 44:4*).

Later Isaiah shows the close connection between the outpouring of the Spirit and the Word of God (*Isa. 59:20-21*). Not only does the Lord pour out His Spirit upon His people, but also, He puts His words in their mouths. We have already noted the connection between the Baptism of the Spirit and revelation and prophecy in the Old Testament. So, when the Holy Spirit is poured out, He empowers us to speak of Christ, the Living Word of God.

Ezekiel also prophesied of the outpouring of the Holy Spirit. In *Ezekiel 39:29* the Scripture speaks of the coming restoration of God's people, beyond the Exile; yet, in doing so, it connects outpouring of the Holy Spirit with God's face no longer being hidden. In the Exile, God had hidden His face from Israel in punishment for sin, because they were unfaithful to Him (*Ezek. 39:23-24; cf. Deut. 31:16-18; 32:19-20*). This meant death (*Ezek. 29:23*), for to turn away from the Lord is to turn away from Life (*cf. John 17:3*).

Yet, when God shows His face, the opposite is the case. When He shows His face, He brings rescue from judgement (*Ezek. 39:25, 28*) and the Lord is hallowed in His people (*Ezek. 39:27*). Where God's face is shown, there is salvation. This has been the case right from the beginning, for it was the Face of the Lord who came to enjoy fellowship with Adam and Eve in the Garden (*Gen. 3:8* – 'presence of the LORD God' is literally 'face of the LORD God'). There the Face of the LORD God is also called the Voice of the LORD God:[3] this is Jesus, the living Word of God.

So salvation is found in the Face of God, because salvation is found in Jesus, and Jesus is the Face of God. But what is the connection between this and the Baptism of the Holy Spirit? God's face shines upon us in Jesus, and so the face of God is known to all those who trust in Christ for salvation.

---

[3] Although many Bible translations render this 'sound of the LORD God', the word used for sound is literally 'Voice'.

Yet, this does not mean that believers always feel the smile of God's face. Although his face is not hidden from us in Christ, sometimes believers feel as though His face is hidden. An example of this can be found in *Psalm 143* where David, though trusting in the LORD and sheltering in Him (*Ps 143:8-10*), prays to the LORD, 'Do not hide Your face from me' (*Ps 143:7*). Although He knows the face of the Lord in salvation, yet He cries out for the experience of what is already his in Christ.

The same dynamic is at work in Ezekiel's promise. In the very act of saving His people, God reveals His face. His face is no longer hidden, but is shining upon them in Jesus. Objectively, God shows His face in Jesus. Yet subjectively, we may still feel like He's far away. However, God deals with this feeling of hiddenness when He pours out His Spirit. As He pours out His Spirit into our hearts, the Spirit assures us that God's face isn't hidden from us, but rather is shining upon us in Jesus.

The Baptism of the Holy Spirit in the New Testament

John the Baptist's Prophecy of the Baptism in the Holy Spirit

The Promise of the Baptism of the Holy Spirit was not only made by the Old Testament Prophets, but also during the earthly life of Christ by another prophet: John the Baptist. John points to Jesus as the One who 'will baptize you with the Holy Spirit' (*Mk 1:8*). In Luke's gospel, John the Baptist speaks of the baptism of the Spirit to answer the questions of the people as to whether or not he was the Messiah (*Lk 3:15-17*). John is not the Messiah, for he only baptises with water, but the coming Messiah will baptise with the Spirit: it is the One who is anointed beyond measure with the Spirit who can pour out the Spirit (*Jn 1:33*). It is only the Son of God who can pour out God the Holy Spirit (*Jn 1:34*).

In Matthew's gospel, John the Baptist speaks of the baptism of the Spirit to the Pharisees and Sadducees:

> I indeed baptize you with water unto repentance, but He who is coming after me is mightier than I, whose sandals I am not worthy to carry. He will baptize you with the Holy Spirit and fire. His winnowing fan is in His hand, and He will thoroughly clean out His threshing floor, and gather His wheat into the barn; but He will burn up the chaff with unquenchable fire. (*Mt 3:13-14*)

In the context, John is speaking of God's judgment upon the unrepentant, and He points to Jesus, the Spirit-Baptiser, as the one who will bring this divine judgment. John doesn't suggest that the baptism of the Holy Spirit is only for some believers here. Rather, he points to a universal outpouring. The only possible outcomes are baptism in the Spirit or baptism in fire. There isn't a third option of non-baptism. So John the Baptist looks forward to a day when, ultimately, all Christians will partake of the baptism of the Holy Spirit. John the Baptist is pointing to an eschatological dimension of the baptism in the Holy Spirit. Just as it is in the last day that the fiery baptism of God's judgement will be experienced by the finally impenitent, so too it's in the last day that the all Christians will partake of the fullness of the baptism of the Holy Spirit. We'll look more at this eschatological dimension of baptism in the Spirit below.

Jesus' Teaching on the Baptism of the Holy Spirit

When Jesus speaks to His disciples of 'the Promise of the Father', He does not only point them to the Old Testament prophets and John the Baptist to find the content of this promise. Rather, He told them 'to wait for the Promise of the Father, "which," He said, "you have heard from Me"' (*Acts 1:4*). Here He reminds His disciples that He had already spoken to them about this promise. But what had Jesus told them about it?

It is Luke who records these words of Jesus at the beginning of Acts, so Luke's Gospel is the closest context where we can examine Jesus speaking of this promise to His disciples, which He does in *Luke 11:9-13*. There Jesus speaks of our 'heavenly Father' giving a gift, and tells us that the content of this gift is the Holy Spirit (*Lk 11:13*).

As a good gift (cf. *Mt 7:11*), the Father's outpouring of the Spirit is not something earned or merited. Rather, the Heavenly Father freely gives to His children out of His great love for them. And Jesus encourages us to ask for this gift. We are to pray for the outpouring of the Spirit, trusting that our heavenly Father will answer.

Jesus also taught concerning this gift on the night of His betrayal and arrest in *John 14-16*. Let's work backwards through Jesus' teaching on the outpouring of the Holy Spirit in those chapters.

In *John 16:7*, Jesus tells us that it is to our advantage that He go away and send the Spirit. Christ is preparing His disciples for the fact that He's about to be arrested and crucified, and then rise from the dead and ascend into heaven. So, when He says that it's to our advantage that He go away, He is not only speaking of His death on the Cross, but rather, primarily here, of His ascension to the right hand of the Father. The ascension is to our advantage because it leads to the sending of the Holy Spirit.

Why is it to our advantage that Christ ascend and send the Spirit? It is to our advantage because of the work the Spirit will do when He comes. Christ sends the Spirit with a mission. The Holy Spirit comes to bring conviction so that people will come to Jesus for salvation (*Jn 16:8-11*). The Holy Spirit 'will convict the world of sin' (*Jn 16:8*), and this conviction of sin is 'because they do not believe in' Jesus (*Jn 16:9*; cf. what we have said above in chapter 8 on sin as unbelief). This conviction is a gracious work of the Holy Spirit which brings people to see their need of Christ.

Yet the Spirit does not only convict of sin; He also 'guide[s] … into all truth' (*Jn 16:13*). He led the New Testament writers into all truth as they wrote the New Testament Scriptures under His inspiration, as He took of what is Christ's and declared it through them (*Jn 16:14*). And today He still declares the truth of Christ as He illumines the Scriptures to us, enabling us to understand and feed upon the Word of God as we see Christ in all the Scriptures.

And in all that He does, the Holy Spirit glorifies Christ (*Jn 16:14*). As people come under the conviction of the Holy Spirit and are saved, they and we see how glorious Jesus is. As the Spirit leads us into the Scriptural Truth of Jesus, we see more and more how glorious Jesus is. As the gifts of the Spirit point us to Jesus we see more and more how glorious Jesus is. When the Holy Spirit is truly moving, Jesus Christ will be glorified.

As the Holy Spirit is poured out, glorifying Christ, the Spirit brings joy (*Jn 16:19-24*). Jesus' disciples are going to go from having hearts filled with sorrow to having hearts filled with joy. And what's the thing that's going to change to bring that about? Jesus is going to send the Spirit.

Jesus is going away, and the disciples are going to have sorrow, but they'll rejoice when He sees them again, not when they see Him (*Jn 16:22*). So He is not talking to them about His resurrection appearances, when they see Him, but instead when He sees them. As we have seen above, Ezekiel prophesied of the connection between the LORD's face shining upon us and the outpouring of the Holy Spirit (*Ezek. 39:29*). When the Spirit is poured out we know that our God's face is smiling upon us in Jesus, and that fills our hearts with heavenly joy. We know that Jesus sees us when He pours out the Spirit.

Therefore, the baptism of the Holy Spirit brings us assurance. For God's face smiles on us in Jesus in salvation, but we have a wonderful experience of that love, which gives us assurance, in the outpouring of the Spirit. As the Spirit is poured out upon us, we rejoice because we know the great love of our God for us.

So what is the thing the disciples will ask for in that day – *i.e.* when Jesus has gone away – the thing which the Father will give them (*Jn 16:23-24*)? What is the thing they are going to ask for and receive which will make their joy full? The outpouring of the Holy Spirit. They will ask for and receive the Spirit who comes in Jesus' Name, the Promise for which they wait in Jerusalem after Christ's ascension. This is a request that Jesus says the Father will give, and this is a prayer that leads to fullness of joy.

Earlier in the discourse, Jesus had declared that 'when the Helper comes, whom I shall send to you from the Father, the Spirit of truth who proceeds from the Father, He will testify of Me' (*Jn 15:26*). It is Christ Himself who would send the Holy Spirit from the Father. Just as John the Baptist prophesied, Jesus is the One who baptises in the Holy Spirit. And, when Christ pours out the Spirit, the Spirit testifies to Christ. The Spirit comes to empower us for evangelism; not just to give us a bit of help or a bit of motivation, but to Himself bear witness to Jesus through us. The Holy Spirit is at work as we share the Gospel, and the Holy Spirit is at work in the lives of the people to whom we talk about Jesus. We tell people of Jesus and of His death for our sins and His rising again to give us new life, and we call people to turn from their sins and trust in Jesus (*Jn 15:27*). But it's the Holy Spirit who convicts people of sin and of their need of Jesus. It's the Holy Spirit who draws people to Jesus for salvation. It's the Holy Spirit who creates faith in people through the Word and gives them new life. And He does all that as we tell people the Gospel, for 'faith comes from hearing, and hearing through the word of Christ' (*Rom. 10:17 ESV*).

Christ calls us to be witnesses to Him. A witness is someone who tells the truth, so we're called to tell people the truth about who Jesus is and what He's done for us. Here Jesus points out to His disciples that they were to be witnesses because they were there (*Jn 15:27*); they saw His life, death and resurrection. Yet, we weren't there, but are still called to be witnesses to Christ. How is that possible? Because Jesus pours out His Holy Spirit on us, and the Holy Spirit is the true Witness (*Jn 15:26*). And that true witness witnesses through us as we tell people about Jesus.

The first major portion of teaching on the Holy Spirit in the Upper Room discourse is found in *John 14:15-28*. Here Jesus promises that the

Father would send the Holy Spirit after Jesus departs (*Jn 14:25-26*). The Spirit is already with them, but will come to them in a new way (*Jn 14:17*). As Augustine wrote:

> Already, therefore, had the disciples that Holy Spirit whom the Lord promised, for without Him they could not call Him Lord; but they had Him not as yet in the way promised by the Lord … they had Him not as yet to the same extent as He was afterwards to be possessed [4]

This is the same before a believer is baptised in the Holy Spirit. All Christians have the Holy Spirit, for otherwise they wouldn't be Christians (*Rom. 8:9*). But, when we're baptised in the Holy Spirit, then we have Him in this great abundant way promised by the Lord.

Christ teaches that the Spirit cannot be received by the world (*Jn 14:17*). Only Christians can receive the Spirit like this. The world doesn't see the Holy Spirit or know Him, but when we trust in Jesus, then our eyes are opened up to the reality of the Holy Spirit. We see how the Holy Spirit has shown us our sin and drawn us to the Saviour, and we see the joy He gives in Jesus. And Christians know Him, for to be a Christian is to know the Father, Son and Holy Spirit.

When Christ pours out the Holy Spirit on believers, then we know that we are not orphans. Jesus says, 'I will not leave you orphans; I will come to you … If anyone loves Me, he will keep My word; and My Father will love him, and We will come to him and make Our home with him' (*Jn 14:18, 23*). So, when the Holy Spirit is poured out upon us, the Father and the Son come to make their home with us too. Therefore we know we're not orphans, because we know we're part of the family. The baptism of the Holy Spirit assures us that we've been adopted as sons and daughters of the living God, for in the baptism of the Holy Spirit the love of our heavenly Father is poured out in our hearts (*Rom. 5:5*). In being filled with the Spirit, we experience what it is to live in the warm loving fellowship between the Father, Son and Holy Spirit. We experience what it is to share in the love the Father has for Jesus, His Well-Beloved Son.

Associated with the outpouring of the Spirit, Christ promises His disciples a double peace: 'Peace I leave with you, My peace I give to you; not as the world gives do I give to you' (*Jn 14:27*). By this immersion in the love of the Trinity when the Spirit is poured out, the Triune God brings us peace. We already have peace with God through Jesus Christ and what He has done for us in offering Himself up in our place in His death on the

---

[4] Augustine, *Tractates on the Gospel of St John*, Tractate 74.

Cross. Yet here Christ speaks of a double peace: He both leaves peace and gives peace.

He's been talking about when He would ascend to the Father. So, when He ascends, He leaves behind His peace: the peace of the Cross, where He bore the wrath of God in our place, the peace of the Resurrection, where we have been raised to new life through His justification, and the peace of the Ascension, whereby Jesus ever lives to intercede for us at the Father's Right Hand on High. This is the peace of Christ's finished work, 'for He Himself is our peace' (*Eph. 2:14*).

Yet, secondly, Christ tells us that He also gives peace. This is not an addition to the finished work of the Cross, but rather, having left us His peace objectively through His saving work, Jesus also wants to pour out His Spirit who'll give us a subjective experience of the peace that's already ours through Jesus' blood. Jesus has made peace for us, but He also wants to assure us of that peace by giving us a great experience of it through the Holy Spirit. As we're baptised in the Holy Spirit, we experience the great peace that is already ours in Jesus. As we're immersed in the love of the Trinity, we're overwhelmed by the God of Peace.

Earlier in John's Gospel, Jesus spoke of the outpouring of the Holy Spirit on a feast day in Jerusalem:

> On the last day, that great day of the feast, Jesus stood and cried out, saying, 'If anyone thirsts, let him come to Me and drink. He who believes in Me, as the Scripture has said, out of his heart will flow rivers of living water.' But this He spoke concerning the Spirit, whom those believing in Him would receive; for the Holy Spirit was not yet given, because Jesus was not yet glorified. (*Jn 7:37-39*)

Here we see that Jesus is the source of the outpouring of the Spirit. If you want to know this fullness of the Spirit, then you must come to Jesus. Furthermore, the Spirit is given after Jesus is glorified. So that's now – as a result of His Cross, His Resurrection and His Ascension. This is a gift won for us at the Cross which Jesus now pours out from the Throne. The gift of the Holy Spirit cannot be separated from Christ and His Cross. The Holy Spirit is the Spirit who flows from the Cross and who glorifies the Christ of the Cross. So now anyone who thirsts can come to Jesus and drink. How is one to drink? By 'believing in Him' (*Jn 7:39*). Come trusting in Jesus and the Promise He gives. Come with your thirst and ask Him to graciously pour out His Spirit upon you.

Then, as a result of Christ's outpouring of the Spirit, 'rivers of living water' will flow out of the hearts of believers filled with the Holy Spirit. Cyril of Alexandria explains that like this:

> [They] will revel in the richest graces from God. They will be so full of gifts from the Spirit that not only is their own mind made fat, but they can now overflow into the hearts of others, gushing forth God's good gifts like a flowing river to their neighbour too.[5]

It is not believers in themselves who come up with living water for people. We can't actually save anyone. But the Triune God fills us, and floods us, and fills us to overflowing. Only God can give 'living water.' But as He fills us He overflows from us to sweep those around us – those whom we tell about Jesus – into His river of life.

The Baptism of the Holy Spirit in the Acts of the Apostles

Particularly among Pentecostals, the most well-known Scriptures pertaining to the Baptism of the Holy Spirit tend to be those from the book of Acts. This is understandable, for in Acts we are not only told about the Baptism of the Spirit, but actually read accounts of this now happening to people in the New Testament Church.

'When the Day of Pentecost had fully come' (*Acts 2:1*) the Promise of the Father was poured out by Christ the Head upon His Church. The Day of Pentecost is both unique (with its sound from heaven and tongues of fire) and yet also in continuity with later experiences of the Baptism of the Holy Spirit (*Acts 11:15, 17*). Christ the crucified, risen and exalted Head of the Church (*Acts 2:23, 32-33*) poured out the Holy Spirit from the Father 'and they were all filled with the Holy Spirit and began to speak with other tongues, as the Spirit gave them utterance' (*Acts 2:4*). The immediate result was a proclamation of 'the wonderful works of God' (*Acts 2:11*) in the languages of the people who had gathered in Jerusalem for the feast from all over the known-world, and Peter's bold proclamation of the gospel. The Baptism in the Spirit resulted in revelation through both the Pentecostal tongues and the Petrine preaching.

Following on from the Day of Pentecost, Luke presents four more instances of the Baptism in the Holy Spirit throughout the book of Acts: the reception of the Holy Spirit by the Samaritan believers (*Acts 8:14-19*), Paul's

---

[5] Cyril of Alexandria, *In Io.* (on *Jn 7:38*; ET 1:307).

filling with the Holy Spirit (*Acts 9:17-18*), the Holy Spirit falling upon Cornelius and his household (*Acts 10:44-48; 11:15-18*), and the coming of the Holy Spirit upon the disciples at Ephesus (*Acts 19:1-7*). There is also one account in Acts of the whole church being filled with the Holy Spirit which involves many who had already been baptised in the Spirit (*Acts 4:31*). We shall return to these accounts later when we look at issues such as subsequence and tongues.

The Baptism of the Holy Spirit in the Epistles

While Acts provides us with descriptions of the Baptism in the Spirit, the epistles provide us with some more teaching on the experience. In Galatians, Paul connects the reception of the Spirit with 'the hearing of faith' (*Gal. 3:2, 5*), and with experiential assurance of adoption as the sons of God (*Gal. 4:6*). In Ephesians, he writes of how we have been 'sealed with the Holy Spirit of promise, who is the guarantee of our inheritance until the redemption of the purchased possession' (*Eph. 1:13-14*). In Romans, we read of how 'the love of God has been poured out in our hearts by the Holy Spirit who was given to us' (*Rom. 5:5*). Again, we'll encounter these texts later in this chapter.

The Meaning of the Baptism of the Holy Spirit

The baptism of the Holy Spirit is not an invisible experience. Unlike justification, which we cannot see, the baptism of the Spirit is experiential in nature. On the Day of Pentecost, the disciples themselves, and then the crowds outside, saw what had happened when Jesus poured out the Holy Spirit. Not only do we read of the sound 'of a rushing mighty wind' (*Acts 2:2*), the tongues of fire (*Acts 2:3*) and the speaking in unlearnt languages (*Acts 2:4*), but Peter also speaks later in his sermon of 'this which you now see and hear' (*Acts 2:33*).

But the tangible, experiential nature of the baptism of the Holy Spirit was not confined only to that first occasion on the Day of Pentecost. When the Samaritan believers were baptised in the Spirit, Simon the Sorcerer 'saw that through the laying on of the apostles' hands the Holy Spirit was given' and so 'offered them money' to try to buy this power (*Acts 8:18*). Something visible happened which Simon saw as the Spirit was poured out: something so tangible that he wanted to try to buy the ability to show others.

Paul takes up the experiential nature of baptism in the Holy Spirit in *Galatians 3* to give a tangible demonstration that God works among people through faith in His Word and not due to human merit. He asks the Galatians:

> This only I want to learn from you: Did you receive the Spirit by the works of the law or by the hearing of faith? … Therefore He who supplies the Spirit to you and works miracles among you, does He do it by the works of the law, or by the hearing of faith? (*Gal. 3:2, 5*)

In the context, it is clear that the answer is 'by the hearing of faith.' Yet, the very question itself points to the experiential nature of their reception of the Holy Spirit. Gordon Fee writes:

> The entire argument comes aground if this appeal is not also to a reception of the Spirit that was dramatically experienced … Here is the demonstration that the experience of the Spirit in the Pauline churches was very much like that described and understood by Luke – as visibly and experientially accompanied by phenomena that gave certain evidence of the presence of the Spirit of God … God is present among them by his Spirit, and the fresh supply of the Spirit finds expression in miraculous deeds of various kinds.[6]

The Baptism of the Holy Spirit is tangible and experiential; people will know that something has happened when they have been baptised in the Spirit.

The Baptism of the Holy Spirit and Union with Christ

The Scriptures describe the Baptism of the Holy Spirit as a 'promise' (*Acts 1:4; 2:33*) and a 'gift' (*Acts 10:45-46*). But what is the content of the promise and the gift? The Father's promise (*Acts 1:4*) is 'the promise of the Holy Spirit' (*Acts 2:33*) or 'the gift of the Holy Spirit' (*Acts 2:38*). So the content of this promise and gift is the Holy Spirit Himself.

---

[6] Gordon D. Fee, *Galatians: Pentecostal Commentary* (Blandford Forum: Deo, 2007), 106-107, 111.

This is not to say that believers only suddenly encounter the Holy Spirit in the baptism of the Spirit. It is the Holy Spirit who convicts of sin, righteousness and judgment (*Jn 16:8*). He shows us the reality of our sin before God. He shows us the righteousness of Jesus, which He freely offers to us in the gospel. And He shows us the victorious judgment of the ruler of this world through Christ's victorious cross and resurrection. In other words, the Spirit opens up our eyes to our condition and need and to the beauty and salvation of Christ and His finished work. And as He does, the Spirit works faith in us and unites us to Christ. So, without the Holy Spirit we could not be Christians (*Rom. 8:9-11*).

So then, if we've already got the Holy Spirit, what do we mean that the baptism of the Holy Spirit is the gift of the Spirit Himself? Now, traditionally, Pentecostals quite often turn to the concept of *'power for evangelism'* at this point. The argument is that the baptism of the Spirit is described with a different purpose than salvation, so it is not a different Spirit, but a different goal.

In a sense, this is right, yet it also rather limits the nature of this gift. Yes the Holy Spirit is doing something different in the baptism of the Spirit than what He does in regeneration and conversion. However, we must not lose sight of the fact that He is not only giving power; He is giving Himself, though in a different way.

It can be thought of like this. Regeneration/conversion is an upward movement: the Holy Spirit lifts us up out of the grave, unites us to Christ and seats us with Him in the heavenlies. All that is incredibly glorious and objectively true, but we cannot see it. It is also full salvation (and this is very important, for nothing needs to be added to it). Through that upward sweep of the Spirit, the Father 'has blessed us with every spiritual blessing in the heavenly places in Christ' (*Eph. 1:3*). And so, united to Christ, we already have every spiritual blessing in Him. (Therefore, it is wrong to speak of the baptism in the Holy Spirit as a *'second blessing'* – all blessings are contained in the 'first' blessing.)

Who is it to whom we are united and in whom we are blessed? It is the Christ: the Anointed One. And so 'in Him' we partake of His anointing, His Spirit. The Spirit unites us to Christ and in Christ we partake of His Spirit. All of this is objectively true, but we can't see it.

So where does the baptism in the Holy Spirit come in? The baptism of the Holy Spirit, as we have seen, is a tangible experience; it can be 'seen' (*cf. Acts 8:18*). So, if we think of regeneration/conversion as the upward sweep of the Spirit, we can think of the baptism of the Holy Spirit as the downward sweep. First He sweeps us up into union with Christ in the heavenly places where we are blessed with every blessing in Christ, and then He sweeps down upon us bringing us a tangible experience of the blessing of the heavenly places here on earth.

Thus the baptism of the Holy Spirit is a wonderful *experience* of what is already true. It is not the beginning of being loved by God. God already loves us, as He has shown clearly and powerfully through the atoning death of Jesus on the cross. It is not the beginning of being the children of God. We are already His well-beloved children. Through our adoption in union with Christ, we are already well-beloved sons in the Well-Beloved Son. Yet, in the baptism of the Holy Spirit, what is already true is authenticated and assured by the sealing of the Spirit (*Eph. 1:13*).

We might know that we are God's beloved children, and believe that we are God's beloved children, yet we might not know that experience of the love of God. But as God pours out His love in our hearts through the baptism of the Holy Spirit (*Rom. 5:5*), He assures us of what is already true.

The Outward Flow of the Spirit

However, the baptism of the Holy Spirit is not only a coming upon; it is also a filling. In the baptism, the Holy Spirit does not merely sweep over us and then go on beyond us. Rather, He fills us and sweeps us outward into His mission in the world. This is where the power for evangelism comes in. In the book of Acts, the result of being filled with the Holy Spirit is speaking the Word with boldness. It is not simply that the Holy Spirit gives us some power. The Holy Spirit Himself is the power, and He carries us out in mission, filled with Him as our power. His is the mission. He is the power. And He is the true witness to Christ (*Acts 5:32; 1 Jn 5:8-9*). Yet, filled with Him, we have the privilege of taking part in His mission as He makes us powerful witnesses (*Lk 24:49; Acts 1:8; 5:32*).

This outward flow doesn't find its end in 'evangelism' but in salvation. We evangelise, but through this outward flow of the Spirit in us in mission, the Triune God saves. The Spirit flows outward in mission in order to sweep others upward as He gives them new life and unites them to Christ.

From Jesus, To Jesus

It is Jesus who baptises in the Holy Spirit (*Mt 3:11; Mk 1:8; Lk 3:16; 24:49 Jn 1:33; Acts 2:33*). As Peter explained on the Day of Pentecost: 'Therefore being exalted to the right hand of God, and having received from the Father the promise of the Holy Spirit, He poured out this which you now see and hear' (*Acts 2:33*). And the Spirit's role and delight is to glorify Jesus (*Jn 16:14*). Therefore, the baptism of the Holy Spirit comes from Jesus and leads back to Jesus.

Already, we have seen this in the outward flow of the Spirit in mission; but that is not the only way this is true. The foremost question about any experience purporting to be the baptism of the Spirit (or another filling of the Spirit) is '*does it glorify Jesus?*' Any experience that leads away from love for and delight in Christ cannot be the genuine work of the Holy Spirit. Any experience that distracts from Christ does exactly the opposite of what the Holy Spirit does.

So, the fullness of the Spirit is seen in a life that looks to Christ, glories in Christ, and gives glory to Christ. This is exactly what we find described in Ephesians:

> And do not be drunk with wine, in which is dissipation; but be filled with the Spirit, speaking to one another in psalms and hymns and spiritual songs, singing and making melody in your heart to the Lord, giving thanks always for all things to God the Father in the name of our Lord Jesus Christ, submitting to one another in the fear of God. (*Eph. 5:18-21*)

Here Paul notes several signs of the Spirit's fullness in believers: they speak to one another about Christ and what He has done (*v.19*), they sing praise to Christ (*v.19*), they thank God for Christ and all things through Him (*v.20*), and they respect and honour one another for Christ's sake (*v.21*). Each of these four signs of the fullness of the Spirit is concerned with Christ: they demonstrate a life where what we say, how we act, and why we do what we do is all centred on Christ. A Spirit-filled life is a life in which everything is about Christ, to Christ, through Christ and for Christ. In short, a life full of the Holy Spirit is a life that glorifies Jesus Christ. After all, that is the role of the Holy Spirit (*Jn 16:14*).

The Baptism of the Spirit and Eschatology

The writer to the Hebrews describes receiving the Spirit as tasting 'the powers of the age to come' (*Heb. 6:4-5*). As we have seen, we already have every spiritual blessing in Christ (*Eph. 1:3*), so the baptism in the Holy Spirit is not a new and separate blessing. Rather, it is an in-breaking now of the future age when, 'in the ages to come [God will] show the exceeding riches of His grace in His kindness toward us in Christ Jesus' (*Eph. 2:7*). In the future ages it won't be a different grace – God's grace is always 'in Christ Jesus' – but we will experience His grace in a new way. Revelation describes this as the city which is the Lamb's wife (that's us – the Church), yet this city had no temple 'for the Lord God Almighty and the Lamb are its temple' (*Rev. 21:22*). This is the most intimate picture of fellowship with God, where the whole City has become His Holy of Holies and we live there in the enjoyment of the presence and fellowship of the Trinity forever.

And yet, already the Bible tells us that we 'are being built together for a dwelling place of God in the Spirit' (*Eph. 2:22*). The Spirit brings something of the future age into the present. Then we will know life in the Holy of Holies of the Triune God's love and fellowship in its fullness, but now already the Spirit brings us something of the experience of that love and fellowship in part. And this is the love and fellowship, the power and mission, and ultimately the glory of the Triune God.

The Baptism of the Holy Spirit and the Trinity

The Baptism of the Holy Spirit is not just about the Holy Spirit. The Father gives the Promise to the Son who pours out the Spirit. The outpoured Spirit glorifies Christ (*Jn 16:14*), who glorifies the Father in and through the Church (*Eph. 3:20-21*).

The night before the Cross, Jesus told His disciples, 'I will not leave you orphans; I will come to you' (*Jn 14:18*). But how would He come? In the context He's talking about the coming of the Holy Spirit; so through filling us with His Holy Spirit, Christ fills us with Himself. which is the very purpose of His Ascension (*Eph. 4:10*).

What's more, Jesus doesn't only talk about His coming, but the Father's as well (*Jn 14:23*). So in the filling of the Holy Spirit, the Father and the Son come and fill us too. The Spirit brings the Father and the Son who indwell

Him with Him, and so, as we are filled with the Spirit, we are filled with Christ and filled with the Father. Therefore, the baptism in the Holy Spirit is an immersion in the Triune God. So, we can define the baptism of the Holy Spirit as *a Trinitarian encounter in which Jesus fills us with Himself and with the Father through filling us with the Spirit.*

The Relational Nature of the Baptism of the Holy Spirit

The facts that the gift is the Spirit Himself, that there is a Trinitarian purpose to the baptism of the Spirit, and that it is an in-breaking of the love and fellowship we will one day enjoy in full with the Triune God, all demonstrate that this baptism is something relational. Paul writes of this relational nature of the outpouring of the Holy Spirit in his letter to the Romans: 'the love of God has been poured out in our hearts by the Holy Spirit who was given to us' (*Rom. 5:5*). As we have already seen, this outpouring of the Holy Spirit is experiential, so this is not merely a mental idea of the love of God. Rather, through the outpouring of the Spirit in our hearts, we experience the love of the Father for His well-beloved children.

In the context in Romans, Paul is writing of the love of God that carries us through tribulations to produce perseverance, character and hope. This is not just a vague idea that God is a loving God, but a true experience of knowing God's love in the heart. It is not just knowing that God is love, but that He loves *me* as His child; He accepts *me* and delights in *me*. And as He fills our hearts with His love, our hearts are filled with love for Him in return.

We have already seen this promised in *Isaiah 44:3-5* and *Ezekiel 39:29*. God the Holy Spirit Himself comes to bring us this assurance of the love of God for us and our place in His family. We are already well beloved sons in the Well Beloved Son by grace and adoption in union with Christ. Now the baptism in the Holy Spirit is an enjoyment of the relational experience of that adoption, so that we not only know about the Father's love for us, but have it poured out in our hearts by the Spirit (*Rom. 5:5*).

The Spirit of Sonship

Early Pentecostals often looked to the Spirit's descent upon Jesus at His baptism as in some way paradigmatic to our reception of the baptism of the

Holy Spirit.[7] There, as the dove descended, the Father spoke, declaring 'This is my beloved Son, in whom I am well pleased' (*Mt 3:17*). The outpouring of the Spirit is associated with the Father's declaration of sonship, acceptance, and fatherly love.

Paul makes a similar connection between the outpouring of the Spirit and sonship: 'because you are sons, God has sent forth the Spirit of His Son into your hearts, crying out, "Abba, Father!"' (*Gal. 4:6*). As the Spirit is poured out into the hearts of believers – the sons of God – he causes them to recognise and respond to this sonship and the Father's great love for His adopted children. The Spirit who 'catches us up into that relationship that Christ has with his Father'[8] brings us into the experience of that relationship of sonship which has already been objectively established. In Christ, we are 'sons in the Son', and the baptism of the Holy Spirit is an experience of this loving relationship of sonship. The outpouring of the Spirit thus provides the church with an experiential assurance of sonship. The baptism of the Spirit is a revelatory experience in which the Father acknowledges us as his children (*Acts 15:8*). 'We are caught up in the love of Christ and filled with joy as we begin to glimpse the significance of our divine adoption.'[9] This is what is meant by the seal of the Spirit (*Eph. 1:13*).

What About Power?

But if Jesus talked about the baptism of the Spirit in terms of receiving power (*Acts 1:8*), how does that fit together with this experience of sonship? Firstly, according to Christ, power in itself is useless (*Mt 7:22-23*). So any concept of the baptism of the Spirit as raw spiritual power stands in complete contradiction to being 'known' by Christ (cf. *Mt 7:23*: 'I never knew you'); yet knowing and being known by the Father and the Son is the essence of eternal life (*Jn 17:3; 10:27*). Therefore, any power associated with the baptism in the Spirit must be power-in-relationship. It is not a power that somehow associates itself with Christ (cf. *Acts 19:13-17*), nor a power for

---

[7] Although, as E.H. Williams reminds us, we cannot draw a direct parallel as 'this is not really an example of the "baptism"'. Ernest H. Williams, *The Gift and Gifts of the Spirit* (Penygroes: Apostolic Church Training School, 1990), 16. See above, chapter 13 (Charismatics and the Ninth Anathema) for further discussion of related issues.

[8] Thomas Smail, *Reflected Glory: The Spirit in Christ and Christians* (London: Hodder and Stoughton, 1975), 55.

[9] Robert P. Menzies, *Speaking in Tongues: Jesus and the Apostolic Church as Models for the Church Today* (Cleveland, Tennessee: CPT Press, 2016), 163.

the sake of Christ, which we can wield as our own work to gain divine favour (cf. the reliance on what they have done in Christ's name in *Mt 7:22-23*). Rather it is the power of Christ himself as he comes to his church through his Spirit (*Mt 28:20; Mk 16:20; Jn 14:23*). This is the power which the Body experiences as the outpouring of the Spirit gives it that experiential assurance of its union with Christ the Head. It is as the outpouring of the Spirit reveals to us experientially the reality of the fellowship which we share with Christ and his Church that we are empowered, in fellowship with the Triune God, as Christ's witnesses. The baptism of the Spirit reveals this fellowship and that revelation gives power-in-fellowship: the power of the Spirit Himself, in fellowship with the Father and the Son.

Christ's promise is not so much about *having* power as it is about *being* witnesses (*Acts 1:8*). Thus it is as the Spirit experientially carries us into transformative fellowship with Christ in his resurrection life that 'believers are released from the fear of death into a self-transcending freedom which enables them to place themselves at God's complete disposal.'[10] The power flows from experiencing through the Spirit the fellowship the Body has with the Head, and so the empowering Pentecostal experience is revelatory encounter with the Trinity. So the power of the Pentecostal baptism flows from the assurance of God's love. It is because we hear, in the baptism of the Spirit, the Father's declaration that we are beloved sons in the Son, with whom he is well pleased, that we are empowered as gospel witnesses.

The Spirit of Love

If the baptism of the Spirit is to be understood in terms of an experience of the Father's great love for his adopted children, then love must be a fundamental category for understanding this doctrine. Paul connects the outpouring of the Spirit with the outpouring of God's love: 'the love of God has been poured out in our hearts by the Holy Spirit who was given to us' (*Rom. 5:5*). This is how the early Apostolics understood the baptism of the Spirit: as an immersion in the love which flows from the cross.[11]

---

[10] Simon Chan, *Pentecostal Theology and the Christian Spiritual Tradition*, 55.

[11] E.g. the writings of D.P. Williams and Frank Hodges. See, Jonathan Black, 'The Church in the Eternal Purpose of the Triune God: Toward a Pentecostal Trinitarian Theology of Theosis drawing on the early theology of the Apostolic Church in the United Kingdom', PhD diss., University of Chester, 2016.

Yet the love which the Spirit pours out in our hearts is not merely a love from God; it is an experiential participation in the divine love itself, the loving fellowship of the Father, Son and Holy Spirit. Therefore, to be baptised in the Spirit is to be immersed in the Trinity.[12]

The Baptism of the Spirit as an Experience of Theosis

As an immersion in the Triune God, in the baptism of the Holy Spirit 'the soul is enraptured in fellowship with the Father and the Son.'[13] This baptism brings the church 'into the very heart of God.'[14] So through the baptism in the Holy Spirit 'the Trinity ... is united to the Church.'[15] This is an experience of theosis.[16]

The baptism of the Spirit is not theosis itself, but rather an experience of theosis: the believer has already been brought into this participation in the divine life through union with Christ and now in the baptism receives an experiential foretaste of the full enjoyment of that participation in the age to come. So the baptism of the Holy Spirit is both an eschatological in-breaking and an experience of what is already ours in Christ. As Martyn Lloyd Jones put it:

> There is no experience possible to the Christian in this world than this experience of the baptism with the Spirit. There is only one thing beyond this and that is the glory itself. As Peter puts it there in 1 Peter 1:8, 'rejoice with a joy unspeakable and full of glory.' It is a touch of the glory everlasting and there is nothing that brings a man nearer to that than this, the baptism with the Spirit.[17]

---

[12] Frank Hodges used almost identical language in *Floods Upon the Dry Ground* (Penygroes: Apostolic Publications, 1939), 135.

[13] D.P. Williams, *Riches of Grace*, xiii.3 (Jan. 1938), 308.

[14] Frank Hodges, *Riches of Grace*, iii.5&6 (Jan. & Mar. 1928), 246.

[15] W.R. Thomas, *The Paraclete*, xv.

[16] See Chapters 23 (on Sonship) and 30 (the Eternal Purpose).

[17] Martyn Lloyd Jones, *Joy Unspeakable: The Baptism and Gifts of the Holy Spirit* (Eastbourne: Kingsway, 2008), 384.

The Baptism in the Holy Spirit and Suffering (Theologia Crucis)

In the Baptism in the Holy Spirit we are immersed in the God of the Cross. Yet the Cross is not only the place of the revelation of the love of the Triune God, but also the place where 'one of the Trinity suffered in the flesh.' Therefore, if the Baptism in the Holy Spirit is truly a baptism in the Cruciform God, then it must take account of suffering.

D.P. Williams strongly associated the Baptism of the Holy Spirit with *the theology of the cross (theologia crucis)*,[18] seeing the connection between the two in *2 Corinthians 5:5* where the Baptism of the Holy Spirit is spoken of as the 'guarantee' of the 'exceeding and eternal weight of glory' as we pass through the afflictions of this life (*2 Cor. 4:17*). He wrote that 'it is when actually bearing His death in us that we find Life flooding, streaming, running through us.'[19] The true Christian life involves a dying to self and to one's own powers, strength and even moral ability. 'As we rise higher, we sink deeper to His death.'[20] So, in order to bring the light of Christ to others, we must know the fellowship of His sufferings, for 'the Spirit is working out the Throne-life through death.'[21] Thus, the power for evangelism which the Spirit gives is not a raw power displayed when we are strong, but rather the power of Christ's death which shines forth in the midst of all our weaknesses and suffering. True Pentecostal power is always 'power with Blood on it'[22], and so faithful church will find that 'Pentecost will always lead to suffering.'[23] So, through being filled with the Spirit, 'we may know the ministry of mutual fellowship in suffering with Christ, and with every member of the Body; the ministry of compassion and weeping.'[24] When we abandon this call to a cross-shaped life in the Spirit for a theology of glory, we turn aside from the deep things of God and His eternal purpose in Christ for the superficialities of religion, like children playing with sandcastles, afraid to face 'the rough seas and the strong winds of persecution.'[25]

---

[18] For an overview of *theologia crucis*, see above, chapter 15.

[19] D.P. Williams, 'The Transformed Life and Its Imparting Power', *Riches of Grace*, xv.10 (Nov. 1940), 110.

[20] D.P. Williams, 'Editorial', *Riches of Grace*, iv.2 (Nov. 1928), 30.

[21] D.P. Williams, 'The Transformed Life and Its Imparting Power', *Riches of Grace*, xv.10 (Nov. 1940), 111.

[22] D.P. Williams, 'Exposition', *Riches of Grace*, xi.1 (Sept. 1935), 42.

[23] D.P. Williams, 'Exposition', *Riches of Grace*, i.9 (1920), 5.

[24] D.P. Williams, 'Exposition', *Riches of Grace*, iii.1 (March 1927), 45.

[25] D.P. Williams, 'Exposition', *Riches of Grace*, i.9 (1920), 5.

Christ has warned His people that, 'in the world you will have tribulations' (*Jn 16:33*). Paul exhorted the disciples in the assemblies he planted to continue in the faith, warning them that 'we must through many tribulations enter the kingdom of God' (*Acts 14:22*). As D.P. Williams teaches, the Baptism in the Holy Spirit is not an escape from such tribulations, but rather through it Christ strengthens us in our weaknesses and troubles, as we know the fellowship of His sufferings. We can 'rejoice in hope of the glory of God' even in tribulations, 'because the love of God has been poured out in our hearts by the Holy Spirit who was given to us' (*Rom. 5:2-5*).

Pentecostal Issues and the Baptism of the Spirit

The Doctrine of Subsequence

When are Christians baptized in the Holy Spirit? Is it something that happens automatically at the same time as regeneration, or does it come later? Pentecostals say that, according to the New Testament, the Baptism in the Holy Spirit does not occur automatically at the same time as conversion. In fact we see in the Scriptural examples that it was something that normally happened to Christians after being saved. This is what we call the doctrine of *subsequence*: the fact that the Baptism in the Holy Spirit is subsequent to salvation. This subsequence is a logical subsequence (rather than a strictly temporal subsequence), because the two can happen at the same time chronologically, as in the case of Cornelius and his household in *Acts 10:44-48*.

The General Pattern of Subsequence in the Acts of the Apostles

In *Acts 2*, with the day of Pentecost, it is very clear that the disciples were baptized in the Holy Spirit some time after being saved (*Acts 2:1-4*). Most of these people had been followers of Jesus for quite some time before His crucifixion. They knew that Jesus had died on the Cross and risen again. In fact they had probably all seen Him after His resurrection. So, in addition to the fact that they were already Jesus' followers, we have good evidence that they believed the gospel: that Jesus had died for their sins and risen again. Thus these people were saved. Their obedience to Jesus' command in staying in the city and waiting for the Baptism in the Holy Spirit (*cf. Lk 24:49*) is further proof of their faith. Yet they had to wait ten days after Jesus ascended before receiving the promised Baptism in the Holy Spirit. So it is very clear that there was a time gap between their salvation and their Baptism in the Holy Spirit.

However we must admit that this is an unusual case. This was the first time that anyone was baptized in the Holy Spirit. In fact the Bible states explicitly that people could not receive the Holy Spirit until Christ was glorified (*Jn 7:39*). Therefore, by itself, the Day of Pentecost does not provide us with sufficient grounds for a doctrine of subsequence.

The Samaritan believers' baptism in the Spirit (*Acts 8:5-25*), however, provides a much firmer footing. Philip preached the gospel in Samaria and multitudes were saved. Yet they were not baptized in the Holy Spirit until later, when Peter and John came down from Jerusalem and prayed for them. Luke records what took place:

> Now when the apostles who were at Jerusalem heard that Samaria had received the word of God, they sent Peter and John to them, who, when they had come down, prayed for them that they might receive the Holy Spirit. For as yet He had fallen upon none of them. They had only been baptized in the name of the Lord Jesus. Then they laid hands on them, and they received the Holy Spirit. (*Acts 8:14-17*)

These Samaritans had 'received the word of God' and been baptized, yet they still hadn't been baptized in the Holy Spirit. In fact there was time for word of their faith to reach the apostles in Jerusalem and for them to send Peter and John in between the salvation of the Samaritans and their Baptism in the Holy Spirit. Thus we have a very clear example of subsequence.

In *Acts 9* we encounter the apostle Paul's own baptism in the Holy Spirit. Paul (at that time known as Saul) was converted on the road to Damascus when He saw the Lord (*Acts 9:3-6*). Three days later (*Acts 9:9*) Ananias came to see Paul, saying 'Brother Saul, the Lord Jesus, who appeared to you on the road as you came, has sent me that you may receive your sight and be filled with the Holy Spirit' (*Acts 9:17*). Although Luke does not actually record the moment when Saul was baptized in the Holy Spirit, Ananias' words make it clear that it was subsequent to his conversion.

In *Acts 19:1-7* we have another clear example of subsequence. When Paul encountered some disciples in Ephesus, his first question to them was 'Did you receive the Holy Spirit when you believed?' (*Acts 19:2*) (or, in the words of the Authorized Version, 'Have ye received the Holy Ghost since ye believed?').[26] The very fact that Paul could ask such a question shows that he considered the Baptism in the Holy Spirit to be something distinct from conversion, for if all Christians were automatically baptized in the Holy Spirit at the moment of conversion, this question wouldn't make any sense. So this question shows that it is possible to believe (and thus become a Christian) without being baptized in the Holy Spirit.

Indeed, this is what we see when these disciples are baptized in the Holy Spirit. Although not all theologians agree as to when exactly these disciples were saved,[27] what is clear to everyone is that they were baptized in water before being baptized in the Spirit. As baptism is for those who already believe, this shows that they were saved before being baptized in the Holy Spirit.

Cornelius and his household (*Acts 10:1-11:18*) appear to have been saved and baptized in the Holy Spirit during the same sermon. Chronologically, there is no distinction here; however, that does not rule out a logical distinction (that regeneration and baptism in the Spirit are two distinct events, even though they may happen on the same occasion), nor a logical subsequence. Cornelius and his household neither prove nor disprove the doctrine of subsequence. So we cannot use this one example to contradict all the other clear examples of subsequence which we have seen. In this case it seems that Baptism in the Holy Spirit immediately followed salvation. Therefore, although we should not forget the unique circumstances in this event, it would appear that such a close proximity in time between the two is possible. In fact, from all the examples we have seen in Acts, it would be fair to say that it is desirable to be baptized in the Holy Spirit as soon after conversion as possible. It is not something to put off until one has been a Christian for many years.

---

[26] Either translation is possible. The Greek includes neither the word 'when' nor the word 'since', but would literally be translated 'having believed'. Ultimately, the mere fact that Paul asked the question is significant enough without debating how to translate the question.

[27] Some think it was before Paul came. Others think it was after Paul spoke to them, but before they were baptised.

Jesus' Teaching on Praying for the Holy Spirit

During His earthly ministry, Jesus taught His disciples about praying to receive the good gift of the Holy Spirit (*Lk 11:9-13; cf. Mt 7:7-11*). The context shows us that Jesus was talking to believers. As the Spirit 'was not yet given' (*Jn 7:39*) and, as the tense of *ask* gives it a repetitive character, this teaching must be applied post-Pentecost. So Jesus here shows us that believers are to pray for the Father's gift of the Spirit. The very fact that we are encouraged to *ask* demonstrates the subsequence of this experience, for if it were something that happened automatically at conversion, believers wouldn't have to ask for it.

Paul on Subsequence

Two texts in Paul's epistles also point to the baptism of the Holy Spirit as an experience subsequent to conversion. To the Ephesians, Paul writes: 'in whom also, having believed, you were sealed with the Holy Spirit of promise, who is the guarantee of our inheritance until the redemption of the purchased possession' (*Eph. 1:13-14*). When does this sealing of the Spirit take place? Although some English translations say 'when you believed', making this sound like something that takes place at the same time as conversion, the Greek literally says 'having believed'.[28] These people have believed. Only those who have believed can receive the seal of the Holy Spirit. This accords well with the meaning of the seal. A seal authenticates. So the seal of the Spirit authenticates our identity as God's well-beloved children and heirs (*cf. vv.4-5, 11; Acts 15:8*). If the seal is to authenticate God's children, then you have to be among the children of God to be authenticated. Ephesians 1:13 might not point to a long delay between salvation and the baptism of the Spirit, but it does indicate logical subsequence.

Paul gives another indication of subsequence, by telling the Galatians something very similar: 'And because you are sons, God has sent forth the Spirit of His Son into your hearts, crying out, "Abba, Father!"' (*Gal. 4:6*). It is because we are already sons that God pours out the Spirit of His Son upon us, so that we might have this experiential assurance of His fatherly love

---

[28] Hence the Authorised Version's translation 'after that ye believed.'

toward us. First we are adopted into God's family as sons in the Son. Then the Spirit is poured out upon us as the seal of our sonship.

Throughout the New Testament, then, not only in the examples of the baptism in the Spirit in the book of Acts, but also in Paul's letters and Christ's teaching, we find a distinction between the baptism of the Holy Spirit and conversion. In fact, this distinction between the two goes all the way back into the Old Testament with the prophets' distinction between the promise of the Holy Spirit *within us* and the promise of the Holy Spirit *upon us*. This distinction between the two promises is the heart of the theology of subsequence. For the doctrine of subsequence tells us that the baptism of the Spirit is not the same thing as getting saved, but rather a promise which is given to those who have received salvation in Christ.[29]

Signs Following: Is Speaking in Tongues the Evidence of Baptism in the Spirit?

From the earliest days of the Pentecostal revivals, Pentecostals have seen a strong connection between the baptism in the Holy Spirit and speaking in other tongues. Some Pentecostal denominations hold strongly to a doctrine of tongues as the initial physical evidence of the baptism in the Spirit (e.g. the Assemblies of God), while others, in their confessions of faith, speak somewhat less dogmatically of 'signs following' the baptism in the Holy Spirit (e.g. the Apostolic Church and the Elim Pentecostal Church).[30] But

---

[29] For more detailed works on the Pentecostal doctrine of subsequence, interacting at length with the major opponents of the doctrine, see, e.g.: Roger Stronstad, *The Charismatic Theology of St Luke* (Peabody, Massachusetts: Hendrickson, 1984); Robert P. Menzies, *Empowered for Witness: The Spirit in Luke-Acts* (London: T&T Clark, 1994, 2004); William W. Menzies & Robert P. Menzies, *Spirit and Power: Foundations of Pentecostal Experience* (Grand Rapids: Zondervan, 2000); William P. Atkinson, *Baptism in the Spirit: Luke-Acts and the Dunn Debate* (Eugene, Oregon: Pickwick, 2011).

[30] North American Pentecostal writers often assert that 'Classical Pentecostals hold that the initial physical evidence … of Spirit-baptism is speaking in tongues (if there is no manifestation of tongues, then there has been no Spirit-baptism).' (Douglas A. Oss, 'A Pentecostal/Charismatic View', in Wayne Grudem, ed., *Are Miraculous Gifts For Today?: Four Views*, 260.) However, although this may be the common view among Pentecostals in North America, it is not necessarily so in other parts of the world. As noted above, only one of the three indigenous British Pentecostal denominations holds strictly to the American understanding of initial physical evidence. This has been a difference between European and North American Pentecostal theology from the very beginning of the movement. Early European Pentecostal leaders, including George Jeffreys (Elim, UK), T.B. Barratt (Norway), and

what are these signs following? Do they consist of speaking in tongues? And does that mean that speaking in tongues is the initial physical evidence of the baptism in the Holy Spirit (such that no tongues would mean no baptism)?

The Connection between Tongues and the Baptism of the Spirit: Arguments for Initial Physical Evidence

The traditional Pentecostal argument for tongues as the initial physical evidence of the baptism in the Holy Spirit is based on *historical precedent in the book of Acts*. On the day of Pentecost, there were three things which happened when the disciples were baptized in the Holy Spirit: 'there came a sound from heaven as of a rushing mighty wind' (*Acts 2:2*), 'there appeared to them divided tongues, as of fire' (*Acts 2:3*) and 'began to speak with other tongues, as the Spirit gave them utterance' (*Acts 2:4*). Only one of these was repeated again on other occasions when people were baptized in the Holy Spirit: speaking in tongues.

In *Acts 10*, how did Peter and his companions know that Cornelius and his household had been baptized in the Holy Spirit? Luke answers this question for us:

> Those of the circumcision who believed were astonished, as many as came with Peter, because the gift of the Holy Spirit had been poured out on the Gentiles also. For they heard them speak with tongues and magnify God. (*Acts 10:45-46*)

They knew the Gentiles had received the gift (the Baptism in the Holy Spirit) because they heard them speak in tongues. Thus for Peter and his companions, speaking in tongues functioned as some sort of evidence that these people had been baptized in the Holy Spirit. In *Acts 11:15* Peter compares the Baptism in the Holy Spirit of Cornelius and his household with that of the disciples on the day of Pentecost. The outward similarity between these two events was that they both involved speaking in tongues.

The disciples at Ephesus (*Acts 19:1-7*) showed the same evidence of their Baptism in the Holy Spirit as those in Jerusalem and Caesarea: 'the Holy Spirit came upon them, and they spoke with tongues and prophesied'

Jonathan Paul (Germany), did not hold to the North American 'no tongues, no baptism' understanding of initial physical evidence. See, Keith Warrington, *Pentecostal Theology: A Theology of Encounter* (London: T&T Clark, 2008), 121.

(*Acts 19:6*). Here prophecy is also mentioned, but the evidence which is shared with the other accounts is speaking in tongues.

In the case of the Samaritan believers (*Acts 8:5-25*), the evidence of their Baptism in the Spirit is not explicitly mentioned. However, what is clear is that there is some sort of evidence. *Acts 8:18-19* records the reaction of Simon the Sorcerer when he saw people being baptized in the Holy Spirit through the laying on of the apostles' hands: 'when Simon saw that through the laying on of the apostles' hands the Holy Spirit was given, he offered them money, saying, "Give me this power also, that anyone on whom I lay hands may receive the Holy Spirit"' (*Acts 8:18-19*). Simon *saw* something that he thought would make a good magic trick. He seems to have been equating receiving the Holy Spirit with the evidence he saw, and so he wanted to buy the ability to lay hands on people and cause the evidence to be seen.

Although this passage does not specifically mention speaking in tongues, speaking in tongues could fit in very well as the evidence which Simon saw.

In the case of the apostle Paul (*Acts 9:17*) we do not actually have a description of his Baptism in the Holy Spirit, thus we don't have the opportunity to hear about the evidence in his case. However, we do know that Paul spoke in tongues. He wrote to the Corinthians, saying 'I thank my God I speak with tongues more than you all' (*1 Cor. 14:18*). Thus it is not impossible that he spoke in tongues when he was baptized in the Spirit.

A more recent Pentecostal argument for the doctrine of initial physical evidence takes a redemptive-historical approach. Douglas Oss summarises this approach:

> Simply stated, in the Old Testament when the Spirit came upon the prophets, prophetic speech always accompanied the Spirit's anointing. Likewise in Acts, when the Spirit comes upon an individual for the first time, Spirit-prompted speech occurs, except that in Acts the utterance is in tongues. Another dimension of this redemptive-historical development pertains specifically to Acts 10:44-46, where tongues is more than evidence of an individual experience (although it is that). There glossolalia [speaking in tongues] also functions as evidence of the inclusion of Gentiles in the Spirit's anointing. Stated in principle, it is evidence that the Spirit's power is for *all* who come into the kingdom.[31]

---

[31] Douglas A. Oss, 'A Pentecostal/Charismatic View', in Wayne Grudem, ed., *Are Miraculous Gifts For Today?: Four Views*, 262-263.

The redemptive-historical approach, then, does not rely on an imitation of incidents from the book of Acts, but rather, looks to the whole of Scripture to see a connection between the coming of the Holy Spirit and inspired speech.

Signs Following: An Alternative to Initial Physical Evidence

The arguments put forward for the doctrine of initial physical evidence are the same arguments on which Elim and the Apostolics rely for their doctrine of 'signs following'. For 'signs following' still sees a very close connection between speaking in tongues and the baptism of the Holy Spirit.[32] Speaking in tongues is still held to be 'the Scriptural evidence of the baptism'[33] or 'the God-witness of the Baptism of the Spirit,'[34] and so the 'signs following' are expected to include speaking in tongues. The difference between 'signs following' and 'initial physical evidence' is not the connection between the baptism in the Holy Spirit and speaking in tongues, but rather a rejection of the American 'initial physical evidence' position that 'if there is no manifestation of tongues, then there has been no Spirit-baptism.'[35] Instead, the Apostolic position is that speaking in tongues is considered to be 'the overflowing sign' of the baptism in the Holy Spirit.[36] We are not just to assume that we have received in faith without any tangible experience.[37] The experiential nature of the baptism means that there will be signs following.

> Undoubtedly it is true that there is a possibility for you to have real fullness of the Holy Ghost, and that fullness not rightly directed to utterance of tongues ... it has not come out in tongues, but the fullness has

---

[32] In fact, 'initial physical evidence' could be regarded as a subset of 'signs following'. In the year 2000, 68% of British Apostolic ministers, and 42% of British Elim pastors believed that 'speaking in tongues is necessary as initial evidence of the baptism in the Holy Spirit.' The same survey showed that 37% of Apostolic ministers and 72% of Elim pastors believed that the 'baptism in the Spirit can occur without speaking in tongues.' See William K. Kay, *Pentecostals in Britain* (Carlisle: Paternoster, 2000), 74. North American Pentecostals quite often mistakenly assume that 'signs following' diminishes the place of speaking in tongues.

[33] *The Apostolic Church: Its Principles and Practices*, 199.

[34] *Minutes of the International Council Meeting (Apostles and Prophets), Great Horton Church, Bradford, Tues. 19th Jan 1932- Mon 25th Jan. 1932*, p.13.

[35] Douglas A. Oss, 'A Pentecostal/Charismatic View', 260.

[36] *Minutes of the International Council Meeting, Jan. 1932*, p.28.

[37] See T.V. Lewis, 'What is the Sign of the Baptism of the Holy Spirit?, *Herald of Grace (Official Organ of the Apostolic Church in New Zealand and Australia)* 12.3 (Nov. 1952), 54-56.

come in ... Our teaching is that they should expect speaking in tongues; but the Holy Ghost may work in another way.[38]

Thus, the difference between the 'initial physical evidence' position and the 'signs following' position, is in the necessary timing of speaking in tongues. Those who advocate 'initial physical evidence' say speaking in tongues must happen at the same moment as the baptism in the Spirit, while those who advocate 'signs following' say that speaking in tongues is the normal overflowing sign of the Spirit's fullness, but this might not be at exactly the same time, and the tongues may follow later. This position avoids the danger of confusing the baptism of the Spirit with nothing other than the ability to speak in tongues.

The Significance of the Sign of Tongues

Why is speaking in tongues the overflowing sign of the fullness of the Spirit? The early Apostolic theologian, T.N. Turnbull's answer was because, in the baptism of the Spirit, you are filled with a Person, and He is 'one who speaks. The Holy Spirit is a Person and not an influence, and when He comes He speaks through us.'[39] When Jesus baptises in the Holy Spirit, He fills us with the Spirit who speaks, and so speech inspired by the Spirit – speaking in tongues – is the overflowing sign of that fullness. This is also why the baptism of the Holy Spirit empowers us for evangelism: because, being filled with the Spirit who speaks, He speaks through us to 'enable us to testify of Christ, and empower us to confess Him before men.'[40]

More recently, Robert Menzies, a Pentecostal theologian, has pointed to six ways in which speaking in tongues is a valuable sign:

1. Tongues are a sign of our connection to the calling and power of the [1st Century] apostolic church.
2. Tongues also signify who we are: the end-time prophets that Joel anticipated.
3. The diversity of tongues reminds us of the scope and nature of our mission.
4. The intimacy of tongues reminds us that God is with us.

---

[38] *Minutes of the International Council Meeting, Jan. 1932*, p.14.
[39] T.N. Turnbull, *Riches of Grace*, xv.9 (Oct. 1940), 104.
[40] T.N. Turnbull, *Riches of Grace*, 14.7 (July 1961), 218.

5. The strangeness of tongues reminds us of our need to rely on the
   Holy Spirit.

6. The drama of tongues reminds us that a transcendent God delights to
   communicate with us.[41]

Receiving the Baptism of the Holy Spirit

On the Day of Pentecost, Peter encouraged the crowd to respond to the
Word, saying:

> Repent, and let every one of you be baptized in the name of Jesus Christ
> for the remission of sins; and you shall receive the gift of the Holy Spirit.
> For the promise is to you and to your children, and to all who are afar off,
> as many as the Lord our God will call. (*Acts 2:38-39*)

Here we see two things about receiving the baptism of the Holy Spirit:
firstly, the baptism of the Spirit is for those who have repented and had
their sins forgiven. So this promise is for Christians. Secondly, the promise
of the baptism in the Holy Spirit is for all Christians ('as many as the Lord
our God will call'). So, if you are a Christian, you can have the assurance
that this promise is for you. The question though is how to receive what
God has promised.

Receiving the Baptism of the Holy Spirit by Faith

We should remember that Christ pours out the Spirit on His people as a
result of the Cross. Thus it is a gift of His grace. That means that we don't
have to (in fact, we cannot) work to earn the baptism in the Holy Spirit; it
cannot be merited, only received through God's grace which flows from the
Cross. So we do not need to wait until we are 'good enough'; we can never
make ourselves 'good enough' to receive the third person of the Trinity. We
can only be baptized in the Holy Spirit because God has imputed to us the

---

[41] Robert P. Menzies, *Speaking in Tongues: Jesus and the Apostolic Church as Models for the
Church Today* (Cleveland, Tennessee: CPT Press, 2016), 157-165.

righteousness of Christ. So it is Christ's merit, not our own, upon which we rely to receive the baptism of the Holy Spirit.

Paul ties the baptism of the Spirit very closely to the cross of Christ, telling us that, one of the reasons for which Christ bore our curse upon the cross, was so 'that we might receive the promise of the Spirit through faith' (*Gal. 3:13-14*). Thus the baptism of the Spirit flows from the cross of Christ (*cf. Acts 2:23-24, 32-33*), and therefore, this baptism is a gift of God's grace. But Paul also tells us here how we receive this gift: 'that we might receive the promise of the Spirit through faith' (*Gal. 3:14*). The baptism of the Holy Spirit (or sealing of the Spirit in *Eph. 1:13*) is one of the blessings with which we are blessed in Christ (*Eph. 1:3*) through His death and resurrection for us, and therefore, like all the blessings of the cross, we receive it through faith in Jesus.

Earlier in the same chapter, Paul asks two questions showing that we cannot work to merit the baptism of the Holy Spirit. 'Did you receive the Spirit by the works of the law, or by the hearing of faith? … Therefore He who supplies the Spirit to you and works miracles among you, does He do it by the works of the law, or by the hearing of faith?' (*Gal. 3:2,5*). In the context it is clear that the answer to both questions is 'by the hearing of faith.' By grace God promises us the Baptism in the Holy Spirit, and it is by faith that we receive that promise.

But what about *Acts 5:32*, where Peter says that God has given the Holy Spirit 'to those who obey Him'? Does this not suggest that our own good works or merits have a role to play in receiving the baptism of the Holy Spirit? In light of what Peter had already taught on the Day of Pentecost (*Acts 2:23-24, 32-33, 38-39*), that would seem a rather unlikely interpretation. Furthermore, it contradicts completely what Paul teaches in Galatians and would raise significant problems for our understanding of what happened to Cornelius and his household. Cornelius was saved and baptised in the Spirit at the same time, so if his baptism in the Spirit was down to his own good works and obedience, that would appear to attribute his salvation to his own good works and obedience as well.

So then, what does Peter mean by speaking of 'the Holy Spirit whom God has given to those who obey Him' (*Acts 5:32*)? For a start, this is not a statement of condition. Peter does not say, if you obey, you will receive the Holy Spirit.

> The text does *not* say either that the Holy Spirit *will* be given to those who shall obey him, or that the Holy Spirit *was* given to those who previously obeyed him, but, interestingly and suggestively, that the Holy Spirit was

given in the past to those who are *now* obeying him. The text reads literally: 'and so is the Holy Spirit whom God gave [past] to those who are [present] obeying him.' One meaning of the text is at least this: obedience is the present *result* of the *prior* gift of the Spirit.[42]

We also need to take account of the ways in which the New Testament speaks of obedience. The same Greek word πειθαρχέω (*peitharcheo*) is used in *Acts 27:21*, where it has to be translated 'listened' rather than obeyed, because the Greek word has a wider meaning than the English word 'obey' and so includes the idea of listening. The same is true of another Greek word for obey ὑπακούω (*hypakouo*), which can be used of 'obeying' the faith (*Acts 6:7*), 'obeying' doctrine (*Rom. 6:17*) or 'obeying' the gospel (*Rom. 10:16; 2 Thess. 1:8*). Christ is 'the author of eternal salvation to all who obey Him' (*Heb. 5:9*). These Greek concepts of 'obedience,' then, have a wider meaning than what we think of as obedience in English. Instead, they can include the idea of hearing, believing and responding appropriately. 'At times this involves action, but, in other contexts, it simply means to accept and trust what was heard.'[43]

Therefore, *Acts 5:32* does not teach that the baptism of the Holy Spirit is merited by our works of obedience. Rather, Peter here speaks of the hearing of faith, and of the obedience which flows from walking in the Spirit. Those who obey God in this context are not those who perform the works of the law (like the chief priests to whom Peter was speaking), but rather, those who trust in the gospel of Jesus Christ.

The Baptism of the Holy Spirit and Prayer

In Luke's Gospel, Jesus spoke of prayer to receive the Holy Spirit:

> So I say to you, ask, and it will be given to you; seek, and you will find; knock, and it will be opened to you. For everyone who asks receives, and he who seeks finds, and to him who knocks it will be opened. If a son asks for bread from any father among you, will he give him a stone? Or if he asks for a fish, will he give him a serpent instead of a fish? Or if he asks for an egg, will he offer him a scorpion? If you then, being evil, know how to give good gifts to your children, how much more will your heavenly Father give the Holy Spirit to those who ask Him. (*Lk 11:9-13*)

---

[42] Frederick Dale Brunner, *A Theology of the Holy Spirit: The Pentecostal Experience and the New Testament Witness*, (London: Hodder & Stoughton, 1970), 172.

[43] Michael P. Middendorf, *Romans 1-8*, Concordia Commentary (St Louis: Concordia, 2013), 60.

Here, Jesus teaches us to come to a loving Father in prayer to ask for the gift of the Holy Spirit. Prayer is 'chief exercise of faith',[44] and so by asking in prayer for the baptism of the Spirit, we are expressing our faith in the One who baptises in the Spirit and relying, not on ourselves, but on Him.

The Baptism of the Holy Spirit and Water Baptism

There is a frequent connection between baptism in the Spirit and water baptism in the Acts of the Apostles. Both Paul (*Acts 9:17-18*) and the Ephesian disciples (*Acts 19:5-6*) appear to have been baptised with the Spirit on the same occasion as their water baptism. Yet, this was not an automatic result of water baptism. The Ephesian disciples were first baptised in water, and then, after having been baptised, the Holy Spirit came upon them through the laying of the apostle's hands. The baptism in water and baptism in the Spirit were two distinct events, even though they both occurred on the same occasion. We can see this from the other examples of baptism in the Spirit in Acts as well. The Samaritans were baptised in the Spirit some time after their water baptism, but Cornelius and his household were first baptised in the Spirit and then baptised in water. Although the two can occur on the same occasion, they are not the same thing, nor does water baptism automatically produce baptism in the Spirit.

The Baptism of the Holy Spirit and Laying On of Hands

Several times in Acts we see a connection between the laying on of hands and the baptism in the Holy Spirit. It was 'through the laying on of the apostles' hands' that the believers in Samaria received the baptism of the Spirit (*Acts 8:17-18*). It was through the laying on of an apostle's hands that the Ephesian disciples were filled with the Holy Spirit (*Acts 19:6*). And, it would appear that, an ordinary believer, directed by the Lord, laid hands on Paul for him to be baptised in the Holy Spirit (*Acts 9:12, 17-18*). The Presbyterian charismatic theologian, J. Rodman Williams, concludes that 'the laying on of hands is thus the means of grace whereby the Holy Spirit may be received.'[45] The original statement of faith of the Elim Pentecostal

---

[44] Calvin, *Institutes*, 3.20
[45] J. Rodman Williams, *Renewal Theology* (Grand Rapids: Zondervan, 1996), 2:289.

Church included the laying on of hands (for the baptism of the Holy Spirit) as an 'ordinance' on a par with water baptism and the breaking of bread.[46]

Apostolic theology has refrained from going so far as to see the laying on of hands as a means of grace, for God has not bound Himself to work in this way. Neither the first disciples (*Acts 2:4*) nor Cornelius and his household (*Acts 10:44*) had hands laid on them, and yet there was no doubt as to their receiving of the baptism in the Holy Spirit. Although not seeing this as a means of grace, Apostolic theologians did recognise the importance of the biblical precedent, and particularly of the connection with the ministry of apostles. T.N. Turnbull wrote that apostles have authority 'to lay hands on the converts that they might receive the Holy Spirit' and sees this as 'one of the features which distinguishes the apostle from the evangelist.' He concludes: 'Certainly when apostles can be present they should lay on hands for the Baptism of the Spirit, but when this is not possible, God will use others, as in the case when Ananias laid hands on Saul.'[47]

In summary then, the baptism of the Holy Spirit is poured out by the Lord Jesus Christ, the Head of the Church, as a result of His life, death, resurrection and ascension for us (*Acts 2:23-33*). It is received through the merits of the atoning work of Christ, not through any merit of our own (*Gal. 3:13-14*). Therefore, believers are baptised in the Holy Spirit by grace alone, through faith alone, in Christ alone (*Gal. 3:2, 5; Eph. 1:3*). The Lord Jesus Himself encourages believers to express their faith in prayer for this good gift (*Lk 11:13*). So we should pray in faith to for the outpouring of the Spirit, relying wholly upon Jesus Christ and His work for us.

---

[46] For the original *Declaration of Faith of the Elim Pentecostal Churches*, see Walter J. Hollenweger, *The Pentecostals* (London: SCM, 1972), 519. Elim also added 'the anointing of the sick with oil' as a fourth 'ordinance.' That their ordinance of 'the laying on of hands' was for the baptism in the Spirit, see Richard Bicknell, 'The Ordinances: The Marginalised Aspects of Pentecostalism', in Keith Warrington, ed., *Pentecostal Perspectives* (Carlisle: Paternoster, 1998), 210-211.

[47] T.N. Turnbull, *What God Hath Wrought*, (Bradford: Puritan Press, 1959), 172.

Concluding Theses on the Baptism of the Holy Spirit

1. The baptism in the Holy Spirit flows from the grace of Christ's Cross (*Acts 2:22-33*).

2. The baptism in the Holy Spirit is ours 'in Christ' and thus is not a 'second blessing' (*Eph. 1:3*).

3. The baptism in the Holy Spirit is distinct from and theologically subsequent to the Holy Spirit's regenerating work (*Acts 8:14-17; Acts 19:1-7*).

4. The baptism in the Holy Spirit is only received by those who have been saved, and thus is dependent upon the Holy Spirit's prior work of regeneration (*Acts 19:2; Acts 10:44-48*).

5. The baptism in the Holy Spirit is a tangible experience (*Acts 8:18*).

6. The baptism in the Holy Spirit is received by grace alone through faith alone (*Gal. 3:2,5*).

7. The baptism in the Holy Spirit is dependent upon God's prior work of justification by the blood of Christ (*Gal. 3:13-14*).

8. The baptism in the Holy Spirit carries us outward on the Spirit's mission of witness to Christ.

9. The baptism in the Holy Spirit means that the Holy Spirit through us is the true witness to Jesus Christ.

10. God has redeemed and justified us in Christ in order to fill us with His Holy Spirit (*Gal. 3:13-14*).

11. In filling us with His Spirit, Christ fills us with Himself.

12. As Christ fills us with Himself through the baptism in the Holy Spirit, this then is the goal of His descent and ascension (*Eph. 4:10*).

13. Through the mutual indwelling (perichoresis) of the Father, Son and Holy Spirit, the baptism in the Holy Spirit is an immersion in the Trinity.

14. The baptism in the Holy Spirit is an eschatological in-breaking which gives a foretaste of the life of the age to come.

15. The baptism in the Holy Spirit carries us into the tangible experience of theosis.

16. The baptism in the Holy Spirit carries us into the experience of the eschatological reality of the Church.

17. The baptism in the Holy Spirit not only flows from the grace of Christ's Cross, but it carries us and others back to the grace of Christ's Cross.

Tenet 6

The nine gifts of the Holy Ghost
for the edification,
exhortation & comfort
of the Church,
which is the body of Christ.

Chapter 27

The Gifts of the Holy Spirit

Pentecostals believe in the gifts of the Holy Spirit. In fact, all Christians believe in spiritual gifts; what sets Pentecostals and charismatics apart from other evangelicals when it comes to the gifts is the belief that specifically the nine gifts listed in *1 Corinthians 12:8-10* all continue to be given by the Triune God in the church today. As the great Apostolic missionary apostle, E.H. Williams, put it:

> Most of us will readily admit that this aspect of our Christian heritage has for centuries been rarely discussed, if indeed such gifts have been manifest to any appreciable extent in the church during those years. In a very general way the church has believed that the Spirit has been moving in the church and that as he is a God who never changes, he must have been gifting his church as was originally intended. However, there has not been a distinct acknowledgement and public recognition of such manifestations, and when they have appeared they have [often] been credited more to the man involved than to the Spirit who gave them.[1]

What are the Gifts of the Spirit?

Pneumatikon: Spiritual Things

The expressions 'gifts of the Spirit' or 'spiritual gifts' which are familiar to us today, are not precisely biblical expressions. The Scriptures use a variety of words for these gifts to highlight different aspects of their nature.

When Paul writes to the Corinthians telling them that 'concerning spiritual gifts, brethren, I do not want you to be ignorant' (*1 Cor. 12:1*), the word 'gift' isn't part of the Greek original. (It's been added by the translators to make the sentence readable in English.) Literally, Paul writes of πνευματικῶν (*pneumatikon*): 'spirituals' or 'spiritual things.' This is

---

[1] Ernest H. Williams, *Our Apostolic Heritage* (Bognor Regis: Anchor, 1985), 31.

probably the word which the Corinthians used for the gifts when writing to Paul.

Now, if the gifts of the Spirit are 'spiritual things', we need to understand in what way they are spiritual (and in what way they aren't). Firstly, how are the gifts *not* spiritual things? They are not spiritual in the sense of being a marker of the spirituality of those who are used in the gifts. (What we learn about the Corinthian assembly in Paul's letters to them should make that clear.) These 'spiritual things' are not evidence of spiritual maturity. They are not given because of how 'spiritual' we are.

So how are the gifts 'spiritual things'? The gifts are spiritual in the sense of being the work of the Spirit. The writer to the Hebrews highlights this true spiritual nature of the gifts:

> How shall we escape if we neglect so great a salvation, which at the first began to be spoken by the Lord, and was confirmed to us by those who heard Him, God also bearing witness both with signs and wonders, with various miracles, and gifts of the Holy Spirit, according to His own will? (*Heb. 2:3-4*)

The 'gifts of the Holy Spirit'[2] are spiritual here in three ways. Firstly, they come from the Holy Spirit. Secondly, they are used by God in His evangelistic mission in which the Holy Spirit is calling people to repentance and faith in Christ. And thirdly, they are part of the Holy Spirit's work of pointing people to Jesus and thus glorifying Him (*Jn 16:14*). So, the gifts of the Spirit are 'spiritual', not because of any 'spirituality' in us; but because they come from the Spirit, to be used in the work of the Spirit, in mission and bringing glory to Jesus.

Charismata: Gifts of Grace

By far the most familiar biblical word for the gifts of the Spirit is χαρίσματα (*charismata*) or χάρισμα (*charisma*) in the singular. This word emphasises the grace of God in the gifts of the Spirit. In fact, it is not a special word for the spiritual gifts. Paul also uses this word to refer to eternal life (*Rom. 6:23*), justification (*Rom. 5:15-16*), marriage and celibacy (*1 Cor. 7:7*), and being saved from death (*2 Cor. 1:10-11*). So the word χαρίσματα (*charismata*) doesn't so much tell us about the nature of the gifts

---

[2] Literally the writer to the Hebrews calls them 'distributions of the Holy Spirit' (πνεύματος ἁγίου μερισμοῖς).

as it tells us about their origin. The gifts of the Spirit find their origin in the grace of the Triune God. Paul starts *1 Corinthians 12* with the word πνευματικῶν (*pneumatikon*), but switches in *verse 4* to χαρίσματα (*charismata*), emphasising even more that these gifts are not spiritual because of anything in us. The gifts are not received by the church because of our merits, but only flowing from the merit of Christ, as outpourings of God's gracious love. As gifts of grace, the gifts come from Christ and flow from His cross. And as 'spiritual' gifts, the gifts lead back to Christ, to bring Him glory and witness to Him. In the words of an interpretation of tongues which were so influential to the theology of the Scottish charismatic theologian Thomas Smail, 'the Spirit comes from the cross.'[3]

Diakonia: Ways of Service

After calling them gifts of grace (*1 Cor. 12:4*), Paul immediately goes on to call the gifts διακονία (*diakonia*): 'service.' He tells the Corinthians that 'there are differences of ministries [διακονία (*diakonia*)], but the same Lord' (*1 Cor. 12:5*). As ways of service, the gifts of the Spirit are not given to an individual for personal benefit. Rather, the gifts of the Holy Spirit are given 'for the profit of all' (*1 Cor. 12:7*). Therefore, there is a responsibility involved in being used in the gifts of the Holy Spirit:

> As each one has received a gift, minister it to one another, as good stewards of the manifold grace of God. If anyone speaks, let him speak as the oracles of God. If anyone ministers, let him do it as with the ability which God supplies, that in all things God may be glorified through Jesus Christ, to whom belong the glory and the dominion forever and ever. Amen. (*1 Pet. 4:10-11*)

The gifts of the Holy Spirit are distributed for the benefit of the church. Therefore, those who are used in the various gifts must be 'good stewards' so that the whole church may benefit and the Triune God may be glorified.

---

[3] Tom Smail, 'The Cross and the Spirit: Towards a Theology of Renewal', in Tom Smail, Andrew Walker, & Nigel Wright, *Charismatic Renewal: The Search For a Theology* (London: SPCK, 1993), 55. Smail comments, 'That, in a sentence, has been at the centre of my own thinking about Christian renewal ever since.'

Phanerosis: The Manifestation of the Holy Spirit

It is the φανέρωσις (*phanerosis*) or manifestation of the Spirit which benefits the whole church (*1 Cor. 12:7*). So, when the gifts of the Spirit are in operation, the Holy Spirit manifests Himself in the assembly. The presence of the Lord is known in the gifts.

The Holy Spirit is already present in the assembly before He manifests His presence in the gifts. The church is 'a dwelling place of God in the Spirit' (*Eph. 2:22*). So, the gifts come from the Spirit who fills the Body, and who fills its members. These manifestations of the Spirit are outward displays of the Holy Spirit who is already at work within us. Therefore, there is no access to the gifts apart from the presence of the Holy Spirit Himself in the life of believers and filling the church. The gifts cannot be sought or received apart from the Holy Spirit's filling. In the book of Acts, several times we see the expressions 'filled with the Holy Spirit' or 'full of the Holy Spirit' at the very moment of someone being used in a gift of the Spirit (Peter in *Acts 4:8*; the Christians in *Acts 4:31*; Stephen in *Acts 7:55*; Paul in *Acts 13:9-12*; cf. also the Holy Spirit's personal working of the miracle involving Philip in *Acts 8:39*). It is impossible to bypass the Holy Spirit to get to His gifts. Any ability resides in the Spirit Himself, not in the believer used in the gift.

Energema: Effective Activities

A final name used by Paul for the Gifts of the Spirit in *1 Corinthians 12* is ἐνέργημα (*energema*): activities or works, but with an emphasis on the fact that they produce effects. The Holy Spirit's gifts are not just for show. They are not just powerful displays or glorious signs. The gifts of the Spirit produce effects. The Triune God works effectively through the various gifts.

What do the Gifts Do?

Edification, Exhortation and Comfort

Paul writes to the Corinthians of the effect of one of the gifts of the spirit in particular: 'he who prophesies speaks edification and exhortation and comfort to men' (*1 Cor. 14:3*). Paul is contrasting prophecy with uninterpreted tongues (*1 Cor. 14:1-5*). In fact, he's contrasting gifts used properly with gifts used improperly (tongues being used improperly when they are not accompanied by interpretation). So the right use of the gifts leads to edification, exhortation and comfort. The Tenets of the Apostolic Church look to these three, not only as the goal of prophecy and interpreted tongues, but of all the gifts.

The church services of the early Christians demonstrate the role of edification in all the gifts. Paul writes to the Corinthians, that 'whenever you come together, each of you has a psalm, has a teaching, has a tongue, has a revelation, has an interpretation. Let all things be done for edification' (*1 Cor. 14:26*). Every contribution made by an individual in Christian worship should edify the church, whether it be by the ordinary means of grace (here *teaching*), the charismatic gifts of the Holy Spirit (a *tongue*, a *revelation*, or an *interpretation*), or even in the songs we sing (a *psalm*; cf. *Eph. 5:19; Col. 3:16*). Such edification, or building up, is the calling of believers towards one another, and ultimately finds its origin in Christ the Head (*Eph. 4:16*). So it is the Lord Jesus Christ, the Head and Builder of the Church (*Mt 16:18*) who builds up His Church through the individual members as they, relying on Him, edify one another in love. And so, through the Spirit, the Head of the Church provides the gifts to contribute to this edification.

But not only do the gifts edify, they also exhort and comfort. The word for exhortation in *1 Corinthians 14:3* is παράκλησις (*paraklesis*), which is related to the word *Paraclete* (Greek: παράκλητος, *parakletos*), the word which Jesus used for the Holy Spirit as He taught His disciples on the night of His betrayal (*Jn 14:16, 26; 15:26; 16:7*). But not only that, the Holy Spirit is 'another' *Paraclete* (*Jn 14:16*), so Jesus Himself is the first *Paraclete* (as John calls Him in *1 Jn 2:1*). A *paraclete* is one who comes alongside to encourage, exhort, support, comfort and counsel. So in the gifts of the Spirit, Christ the Head of the Church, comes alongside us as our *Paraclete*, through the Holy Spirit, to encourage, comfort and counsel His Bride. In the gifts, the Builder of the Church (*Mt 16:18*) walks alongside as our Encourager and our Comforter.

Direction in Mission

The gifts can also give guidance and direction in mission. In *Acts 16*, Paul and his travelling companions were planning to evangelise in Asia; however, the Holy Spirit worked through the gifts to send them to Europe instead.

> Now when they had gone through Phrygia and the region of Galatia, they were forbidden by the Holy Spirit to preach the word in Asia. After they had come to Mysia, they tried to go into Bithynia, but the Spirit did not permit them. So passing by Mysia, they came down to Troas. And a vision appeared to Paul in the night. A man of Macedonia stood and pleaded with him, saying, 'Come over to Macedonia and help us.' Now after he had seen the vision, immediately we sought to go to Macedonia, concluding that the Lord had called us to preach the gospel to them. (*Acts 16:6-10*)

Twice, the Holy Spirit forbids or does not permit them to go where they had planned. This was probably through prophecy, but the text does not specify precisely how. The emphasis is on the Spirit's leading, not on the precise form of the gift.[4] The way the Holy Spirit leads them to the right place is through Paul's vision. So, through a combination of gifts of the Spirit, perhaps through a combination of different people, the Holy Spirit led them to the place He wanted them to continue their evangelistic work. At times the Lord directs our mission and evangelism through the gifts of the Spirit.

Open Doors for the Gospel

The Lord also uses gifts of the Spirit to open doors for the proclamation of the gospel. In *Acts 3*, Peter and John were going up to the Temple to pray. On the way, they met a lame man asking for alms at the Beautiful Gate. Famously, Peter told the man, 'Silver and gold I do not have, but what I do

---

[4] Some Apostolic interpreters would see here the prerogative of the office of the prophet, as Silas (a prophet according to *Acts 15:32*) was travelling with Paul. However, although this is likely the speech of the Holy Spirit through the prophet, the text does not specify that. And so we cannot use it to make a hard and fast distinction between the roles of the gift of prophecy and the office of the prophet.

have I give you: In the name of Jesus Christ of Nazareth, rise up and walk' (*Acts 3:6*). And the man did rise up and walk (*Acts 3:7-8*). But that was not the end of it, for this miracle drew a crowd of people who 'were filled with wonder and amazement at what had happened' (*Acts 3:10*), and 'when Peter saw it, he responded to the people' (*Acts 3:12*) by preaching the gospel of Jesus Christ to them (*Acts 3:12-26*). And this led to preaching Christ to the high priest and the Sanhedrin (*Acts 4:1-12*). The miracle had opened up the door to tell this great crowd of people of Jesus and what He has done. The gift of the Spirit opened up the door for the proclamation of the gospel.

The gifts open up opportunities to proclaim the gospel. And the gifts also witness to and confirm the preaching of the gospel (*Heb. 2:3-4*). As Mark tells us, after the ascension, the disciples 'went out and preached everywhere, the Lord working with them and confirming the word through the accompanying signs' (*Mk 16:20*).

The Gifts and the Trinity

The gifts of the Holy Spirit are the work of the Triune God (*1 Cor. 12:4-6*). The gifts are distributed by the Holy Spirit (*1 Cor. 12:4, 7-11*), for Christ's service (*1 Cor. 12:5*). And God the Father is at work to produce fruit through all these gifts (*1 Cor. 12:6*). These Trinitarian gifts 'derive from the Spirit of God in and from Christ.'[5] It is the same Triune God who ministers to His church in each of the gifts (*1 Cor. 12:4-6*).

> In this spiritual ministry therefore we stand closely related to the entire Trinity. They are gifts freely given by the Holy Spirit. They are manifestations administered under the acknowledged Headship of Jesus Christ, our Sovereign Lord. They are operations of God the Father.[6]

Therefore, in every true spiritual gift, the Holy Trinity is at work. And thus, the gifts aren't all about us, but all about the Triune God who is their Giver, and who manifests Himself in the gifts. This means that the gifts of the Spirit should point to Christ, the One whom they serve, rather than to those being used in the gifts.

---

[5] Amos Yong, *Renewing Christian Theology: Systematics for a Global Christianity* (Waco: Baylor University Press, 2014), 74.

[6] D.T. Rennie, *The Gifts of the Holy Spirit* (Bradford: Puritan Press 1967), 39.

In *Matthew* 7, Jesus speaks of some people who have great confidence in their spiritual gifts:

> Not everyone who says to Me, 'Lord, Lord,' shall enter the kingdom of heaven, but he who does the will of My Father in heaven. Many will say to Me in that day, 'Lord, Lord, have we not prophesied in Your name, cast out demons in Your name, and done many wonders in Your name?' And then I will declare to them, 'I never knew you; depart from Me, you who practice lawlessness! (*Mt 7:21-23*)

When confronted with the Saviour, these people point to their prophecies, their casting out of demons, and the many wonders they have performed. Their confidence is in their gifts, and not in the saving work of the Triune God through the cross of Christ. If we see the gifts as pointing to ourselves, they are of no use to us. The most important thing is not the working of miracles, but knowing Christ and being known by Him: knowing the Father through the Son in the Spirit, for this is eternal life (*Jn 17:3*).

The Gifts and the Gospel

The Spirit who distributes these Trinitarian gifts 'remains the Spirit whom the Father gave to us through the Son who was to die and rise again. That is why the Spirit can so often be seen to be working within the rhythm of Christ's cross and resurrection.'[7] The gifts should not lead us to place confidence in ourselves and what we have received, but should point us always beyond ourselves to the grace of God in Jesus Christ. These are gifts of grace, pointing us always to our dependence upon the God of grace.

Signs and wonders are never enough in and of themselves. Instead we must see the One to whom these signs point and trust in Him alone (*Jn 6:26*). The signs attest the Word, not the preacher (*Mt 7:21-23*). For the Triune God gives these spiritual gifts to bear witness to the Word of grace, which is the gospel of our salvation (*Heb. 2:3-4; Acts 14:3*).

The power displayed in the true gifts of the Spirit is the power of the cross: the power of the Lord who died and rose again. And this cruciform

---

[7] Thomas Smail, 'The Cross and the Spirit: Towards a Theology of Renewal', in Smail, Walker and Wright, ed., *Charismatic Renewal: The Search for a Theology* (London: SPCK, 1993), 70.

power is not just power which 'takes people out of trouble', but the power of 'a saving God who can use their trouble for their remaking, just as he used the awful suffering of Jesus for the remaking of the world.'[8]

> Far from advancing beyond the cross when we are renewed in the Spirit, needing to return to it only when we sin and need pardon ... the more we are filled with the Spirit, the more we shall share in both cross and resurrection, again and again. The triumphalistic expectations of uninterrupted release and constant victory which the more naïve part of the charismatic constituency has sometimes cherished and even taught are contradicted by both Scripture and experience alike.[9]

Therefore, seen in such a crucicentric perspective, the gifts of the Spirit should point us to 'a charismatic theology of the cross' where:

> The spiritual gifts are not to be elevated as signs of the divine glory. Instead they ought to be seen as invitations to bear witness ... perhaps even to the point of martyrdom (Acts 1:8) and death, in ways that turn this world upside down (17:6). Recipients of the charismata, in other words, become servants who build up, edify, and encourage others, even if that involves their own self-diminishment ... The people of God are most authentically the body of Christ if they follow in the footsteps of Christ's weakness, living not in human strength but in the power of the Spirit of the crucified Lord.[10]

The Gifts and the Worship of the Church

For the early Apostolics, and many other Pentecostals, two verses stood at the heart of their understanding of the liturgy and the worship of the church: *Acts 2:42* and *1 Corinthians: 14:26*.[11]

> And they continued steadfastly in the apostles' doctrine and fellowship, in the breaking of bread, and in prayers. (*Acts 2:42*)

---

[8] Smail, 'The Cross and the Spirit: Towards a Theology of Renewal', 68.

[9] Smail, 'The Cross and the Spirit: Towards a Theology of Renewal', 68.

[10] Yong, *Renewing Christian Theology*, 73-74. For more on the *theologia crucis* (theology of the cross) see chapter 15 above.

[11] See e.g. D. Kongo Jones, 'The Apostolic Form of Christian Worship', *Riches of Grace*, iii.1 (1926), 48-51.

> How is it then, brethren? Whenever you come together, each of you has a
> psalm, has a teaching, has a tongue, has a revelation, has an interpretation.
> Let all things be done for edification. (*1 Cor. 14:26*)

While the former of these Scriptures highlights the formal and liturgical life
of the assembly, the latter points to the variety involved in Christian
worship through the gifts of the Spirit, and the role of every member of the
Body in edifying one another in love. One early Apostolic writer drew on *1
Corinthians 14:26* to write that here:

> We have a glimpse of the Apostolic form of Christian worship. The New
> Testament writers know nothing at all of an individualistic conception of
> Christianity. It is perfectly true that the salvation of the soul must, of
> necessity, be an individual experience. But the believer, who has been
> saved through faith in Jesus, seeks the fellowship of his Christian brother.
> No man can grow into spiritual perfection by himself. This is why the
> Apostles of the Lord Jesus insisted upon the assembling together of the
> saints ... These people had gathered together to worship God ... all the
> members present alive, and submissive to the promptings of the Holy
> Spirit; and every one moved to action, through the divine inspiration of
> God ... There is nothing monotonous about this service, but every member
> contributing his share as led by the Spirit ... It is so simple, so spiritual, so
> divine, plenty of variety, yet perfect unity, leading to oneness of mind,
> humbleness of spirit, and purity of heart.[12]

There was general agreement on this among the various Pentecostal
movements in the United Kingdom. Harold Horton, of the Assemblies of
God, insisted that anyone who had been to a Pentecostal Breaking of Bread
service could not 'imagine anything more like this Scriptural pattern than
one of those services,'[13] considering *1 Corinthians 14:26* to 'give instructions
for the conduct of the ... Meeting with the definite inclusion of Spiritual
gifts.'[14] Donald Gee wrote of this early Christian pattern of worship:

> Meetings would present a constant spiritual freshness and power of grip
> and attraction without any shallow striving after novelties just for their
> own sake. That the meetings were 'open' in the sense of possessing a
> general liberty for all to take part as the Spirit moved upon members of the
> congregation seems beyond question ... It is a fallacy, however, to think
> that we can achieve a scriptural New Testament assembly by simply
> throwing our meetings open for all to take part as they will ... The open
> ministry of the early churches was for spiritual gifts, not for natural

---

[12] D. Kongo Jones, 'The Apostolic Form of Christian Worship', 48-50.

[13] Harold Horton, *The Gifts of the Spirit*, (Nottingham: AoG Publishing House, 1934; U.S.
Edition, Springfield: GPH, 1975), 177.

[14] Horton, *The Gifts of the Spirit*, 189.

activity … Actually speaking, there was the highest order permeating and safeguarding the liberty of the early Christian congregations.[15]

Beyond the world of early British Pentecostalism, the more recent American Pentecostal exegete, Gordon Fee, writes that *1 Corinthians 14:26* 'offers a description of what should be happening at their gatherings … that each one has opportunity to participate in the corporate ministry of the body.'[16] Both the openness to the Holy Spirit's distribution of gifts, and the order laid down in Scripture for the use of those gifts (*1 Cor. 14:6-39*) and for the governing of the assembly are necessary for the full flourishing of Pentecostal worship. In the next chapter we'll consider each of the nine gifts of the Spirit listed in *1 Corinthians 12:8-10*.

---

[15] Donald Gee, *Concerning Spiritual Gifts*, (Springfield: GPH, U.S. ed. 1937; rev. 1980), 16.

[16] Gordon Fee, *The First Epistle to the Corinthians*, New International Commentary on the New Testament (Grand Rapids: Eerdmans, 1987), 690.

Chapter 28

The Nine Gifts

The Word of Wisdom and the Word of Knowledge

Although Pentecostals are well-known for their belief in that the Holy Spirit continues to distribute the nine gifts listed in *1 Corinthians 12:8-10* in the church today, what is perhaps not quite so well known is that Pentecostals have not always agreed on the nature of some of these gifts. This is particularly true of the gifts of the word of wisdom and the word of knowledge. Two early British Pentecostals, through their writings, greatly influenced world-wide Pentecostalism with two quite different ideas of these gifts. Harold Horton saw these as divinely-given fragments of wisdom or knowledge.[1] For Horton, 'word' was a reference to the fragmentary nature of such revelation, and did not in any way indicate that these were vocal gifts.

Donald Gee, on the other hand, while agreeing with Horton that these gifts are supernatural, insisted that 'word' indicates 'a spoken utterance through a direct operation of the Holy Spirit at a given moment.'[2] The source of the wisdom and knowledge which are spoken in these gifts is always in Christ Himself, 'in whom are hidden all the treasures of wisdom and knowledge' (*Col. 2:3*). Gee particularly taught that the word of knowledge was 'a teaching gift in the church,'[3] and connected it particularly with the office of the teacher.[4]

The Apostolics agreed with Donald Gee that 'word' means that these gifts are spoken, defining them as 'wisdom expressed in words' and 'knowledge expressed in words.'[5] Although they recognised that this gift 'is

---

[1] Harold Horton, *The Gifts of the Spirit* (Nottingham: AoG Publishing House, 1934; U.S. Edition, Springfield: GPH, 1975), 40, 56.

[2] Donald Gee, *Concerning Spiritual Gifts* (Springfield: GPH, U.S. ed. 1937; rev. 1980), 39.

[3] Gee, *Concerning Spiritual Gifts*, 134.

[4] Gee, *Concerning Spiritual Gifts*, 136.

[5] *The Apostolic Church: Its Principles and Practices*, 204.

of special value in dealing with individuals in search of truth and in the realm of teaching and preaching,'⁶ they disagreed, however, with Gee's insistence on tying the word of knowledge to the office of the teacher. The Apostolics have always seen a connection between the 'word' of wisdom and knowledge and Jesus, the 'Word', 'in whom are hidden all the treasures of wisdom and knowledge' (*Col. 2:3*):

> The Logos of John 1:1 denotes Christ as the One in whom has been hid from eternity all God has to say to man; the One who faithfully and completely brings that to light, being both its representative and expression. So we read in John 1:18: 'He hath *declared* Him' – made the Father known by expressing and expounding. Jesus Christ – God manifest in flesh – is *the* Logos, *the word* in whom and by whom God's mind and purpose toward humanity find their true and complete and perfect expression … As the Living Word reveals the invisible God, so this spoken word [of wisdom] reveals His otherwise unknowable thought.⁷

Thus, the word of knowledge and the word of wisdom cannot be separated from Christ the Living Word who is the revelation of God.

Both knowledge and wisdom were big issues for the Corinthians. Some people in the assembly had got the wrong idea about knowledge and wisdom, thinking they needed some secret 'knowledge' and 'wisdom' as the key to true spirituality. And so, in the name of 'wisdom', people were putting influence on them to reject Paul and the gospel he preached.

The first three chapters of *1 Corinthians* are dominated by discussion of wisdom. This is the same book in which we find the word of wisdom listed as a gift of the Spirit, and therefore it is important to examine this context to see how the same author uses the same word in the same letter.

> For Jews request a sign, and Greeks seek after wisdom; but we preach Christ crucified, to the Jews a stumbling block and to the Greeks foolishness, but to those who are called, both Jews and Greeks, Christ the power of God and the wisdom of God. (*1 Cor. 1:22-24*)

> But of Him you are in Christ Jesus, who became for us wisdom from God — and righteousness and sanctification and redemption. (*1 Cor. 1:30*)

> However, we speak wisdom among those who are mature, yet not the wisdom of this age, nor of the rulers of this age, who are coming to nothing. But we speak the wisdom of God in a mystery, the hidden wisdom which God ordained before the ages for our glory, which none of

---

⁶ *The Apostolic Church: Its Principles and Practices*, 204.
⁷⁷ David T. Rennie, *The Gifts of the Holy Spirit* (Bradford: Puritan Press, 1967), 45-46.

the rulers of this age knew; for had they known, they would not have crucified the Lord of glory. But as it is written:

'Eye has not seen, nor ear heard,

Nor have entered into the heart of man

The things which God has prepared for those who love Him.'

But God has revealed them to us through His Spirit. For the Spirit searches all things, yes, the deep things of God. (*1 Cor. 2:6-10*)

When Paul writes about wisdom to the Corinthians, he's writing about Christ and His saving work. God's wisdom is His purpose in redeeming His church through the death of Jesus on the cross. Therefore, to speak a word of wisdom is to speak concerning Christ and His cross. Thus the gift of the word of wisdom would appear from the context in *1 Corinthians* to be a gift of speaking under the inspiration of the Holy Spirit concerning the gospel of Jesus Christ and Him crucified.

When we look at how Paul writes of knowledge in his letters we see a similar pattern (*1 Cor. 8:6-7; 2 Cor. 2:14-15; 4:6; Eph. 1:17*). Rather than some sort of secret knowledge known only to a special few, Paul is writing of a knowledge which has been openly declared: the knowledge of God in Christ.

Therefore, the word of wisdom and the word of knowledge, although they are supernatural gifts, they might not always be obviously supernatural to those who hear. For by these gifts the same open wisdom and knowledge is spoken which is always to be declared in the church's proclamation and in our evangelism and building one another up in love: the wisdom of Christ and His Cross, and the knowledge of God in Christ.

> In addition to making known the otherwise unknowable facts relative to persons, places and particular circumstances, the word of knowledge can and does shed illumination upon and provide inspiration regarding revealed truth. Indeed this would appear to have been its major function in the experience of Paul … The word of knowledge does not add to the Bible. But it can and does provide inspiring light upon the sacred page and this aspect of the gift finds utterance through the ministry of the Spirit-filled Teacher.[8]

These are supernatural gifts, and so the word of wisdom and word of knowledge are not the same as normal preaching and evangelism. Rather, these are gifts of revelation by which we speak in situations where, otherwise, we would not have the gospel-focused knowledge and wisdom needed for that moment. This may take place in preaching and teaching, in

---

[8] David T. Rennie, *The Gifts of the Holy Spirit*, 59-60.

the convening of a service, in a presbytery discussion, in witnessing one to one, in discipleship settings, or in the cure of souls.[9]

The Gift of Faith

The spiritual gift of faith (*1 Cor. 12:9*) is not to be confused with the saving gift of faith (*Eph. 2:8*). 'Saving faith is a gift from God given gratuitously; the gift of faith is a spiritual impartation for effective service.'[10] In the ancient church, Cyril of Jerusalem described this gift as 'that faith which works things above man' (i.e. beyond man's power and ability),[11] and John Chrysostom wrote that Paul was:

> Not meaning by this faith the faith of doctrines, but the faith of miracles; concerning which Christ says, 'If you have faith as a grain of mustard-seed, you shall say to this mountain, Remove, and it shall remove.' (Mt 17:20) And the Apostles too concerning this besought Him, saying, Increase our faith (Lk 17:5): for this is the mother of the miracles.[12]

In the Apostolic Church, D.T. Rennie described this gift of faith as 'miraculously-given miracle-producing faith.'[13] The Canadian evangelical exegete, D.A. Carson, calls this 'special faith' which 'enables a believer to trust God to bring about certain things for which he or she cannot claim some divine promise recorded in Scripture, or some state of affairs grounded in the gospel.'[14]

What do the Scriptures tell us of this gift? In the immediate context of *1 Corinthians*, Paul connects the gift of faith with faith to 'remove mountains' (*1 Cor. 13:2*), which is the faith of which Jesus spoke in the Gospels (*Mt 17:20; 21:21; Mk 11:22-23; cf. Lk 17:6*). In the context of speaking of this mountain-removing faith, Jesus told His disciples, 'whatever things you ask in prayer, believing, you will receive' (*Mt 21:22; cf. Mk 11:24*). To pray

---

[9] *i.e.* Pastoral care and counsel.

[10] David T. Rennie, *The Gifts of the Holy Spirit*, 66.

[11] Cyril of Jerusalem, *Catechetical Lectures*, 5.11

[12] John Chrysostom, *Homilies on 1 Corinthians*, Homily 29.

[13] David T. Rennie, *The Gifts of the Holy Spirit*, 61.

[14] D.A. Carson, *Showing the Spirit: A Theological Exposition of 1 Corinthians 12-14* (Milton Keynes: Authentic, 2010), 29-30.

believing is to pray in faith, which is the type of prayer James writes of which heals the sick:

> Is anyone among you sick? Let him call for the elders of the church, and let them pray over him, anointing him with oil in the name of the Lord. And the prayer of faith will save the sick, and the Lord will raise him up. And if he has committed sins, he will be forgiven. Confess your trespasses to one another, and pray for one another, that you may be healed. The effective, fervent prayer of a righteous man avails much. Elijah was a man with a nature like ours, and he prayed earnestly that it would not rain; and it did not rain on the land for three years and six months. And he prayed again, and the heaven gave rain, and the earth produced its fruit. (*Jas 5:14-18*)

The prayer of faith prayed by the elders for healing is compared to the prayer of Elijah in *1 Kings 18:42*. But this prayer of Elijah was not simply fervent prayer, but prayer rooted in the faith which came through the Word of the LORD. The LORD had spoken and said that He would 'send rain on the earth' (*1 Kgs 18:1*), and so Elijah could pray the prayer of faith, resting upon God's revealed word.

> There is reason to think that 'the prayer of faith' is not simply the fervent prayer of the faithful, but a prayer informed by a charismatic insight into God's specific will and timing, such as Elijah's prayer, given as an example ([Jas] 5:17,18). It is thus possible James allows there may be times when the elders are not given this faith.[15]

Both through James' teaching on the presbytery's prayer of faith and the position of this gift in the list in *1 Corinthians 12*, there would appear to be a strong connection between the gift of faith and the gifts of healings and workings of miracles.

> Although it is listed separately, as given 'to another,' there is a sense in which this and the following two items belong together – and indeed would at times seem not quite possible to differentiate. Faith that 'moved a mountain' could also rightly be called the working of a miracle.[16]

The healing of the lame man at the Beautiful Gate may be an example of a healing which came about as a result of the gift of faith (*Acts 3:16*). The Apostolic Church has summed up the gift of faith as 'a special endowment

---

[15] Max Turner, *The Holy Spirit and Spiritual Gifts: Then and Now* (Carlisle: Paternoster, 1996), 253-254.
[16] Gordon Fee, *The First Epistle to the Corinthians*, New International Commentary on the New Testament (Grand Rapids: Eerdmans, 1987), 593-594.

of faith by the Spirit and is of special value in connection with evangelisation, forward moves, healings and miracles.'[17]

Gifts of Healings

Throughout the Scriptures, the Lord reveals Himself to be a healing God (*Ex 15:26; Acts 10:38; Jas 5:13-16*). During His earthly ministry, the Lord Jesus, in His great compassion, healed many who were sick, and sent his disciples to do the same. Now in the church, the Lord has promised gifts of healings (*1 Cor. 12:9*) and instructed Christians in what to do when they are sick (*Jas. 5:14*).

> Jesus, Paul, and the rest of the early church lived in regular expectation that God would heal people's physical bodies … Only among the intellectuals and in a 'scientific age' is it thought to be too hard for God to heal the sick.[18]

When the Triune God created the world, He saw that 'it was very good' (*Gen. 1:31*). The deterioration and decay of illness was not part of His good creation as it was created to be. Rather, sickness and disease are part of the curse upon the world as the result of the Fall into sin. As the early British Pentecostal leader, George Jeffreys, put it:

> Sin, sickness, death, mortality, the curse upon the earth and the bondage of corruption from which the animal creation suffers came into the world as a result of the first Adam's disobedience.[19]

In general, sickness is the result of Adam's first sin. Although there are times when the Scriptures connect sickness with particular sins, or with the sins of individuals (*e.g. 1 Cor. 11:27-30; 2 Chron. 26:16-19; Ps 38:3; 107:17; Jn 5:14; Jas 5:15*), the Lord makes very clear to His disciples that this is not a general rule. When His disciples see a man born blind, they ask Him: 'who sinned, this man or his parents, that he was born blind?' (*Jn 9:2*). Yet Jesus'

---

[17] *The Apostolic Church: Its Principles and Practices*, 205.

[18] Fee, *The First Epistle to the Corinthians*, 594.

[19] George Jeffreys, *Healing Rays* (London: Elim, 1932), 37. George Jeffreys was the founder of the Elim Pentecostal Church, the largest Pentecostal denomination in the United Kingdom.

reply banishes the notion that any assumed link could be made between sickness or disability and particular, individual sins: 'Neither this man nor his parents sinned, but that the works of God should be revealed in him' (*Jn 9:3*). Thus, sickness, ill-health, and disability, are the results of sin in the world in general; they are results of the curse upon the world for Adam's first sin. As an early Apostolic put it: 'it was not always personal sin which was the cause of sickness. Therefore, we must not judge one another when we [suffer from] sickness of any kind.'[20] Another early British Pentecostal, Donald Gee of the Assemblies of God, warned the movement that:

> Part of the unfortunate manner in which faith in Divine Healing sometimes has been sincerely promulgated … is this continual suggestion that failure to get healed is rooted in some deep spiritual failure in the one who is sick. This attitude has added mental suffering to physical suffering, and in extreme cases turned belief in Divine Healing into a scourge rather than a privilege, and a burden rather than a relief.[21]

For any teaching on divine healing to be biblical, it must take account of the biblical example of faithful saints who were left sick (and the corresponding pastoral reality). The Scriptures show us not only great healings, but also believers who were not healed. Even the apostle Paul could not heal Trophimus, but left him sick in Miletus (*2 Tim. 4:20*). As Donald Gee reminded British Pentecostals of an earlier generation, this text cannot be ignored or explained away, as if there was something lacking in the faith of Trophimus:

> Those who want, somehow or other, to fit this verse about the illness of Trophimus with their own doctrine of divine healing are tempted to assert that he must have failed somewhere. But that is the worst possible way of interpreting the Scriptures. There is nothing whatever, in the statement, or in its context, to suggest anything spiritually or morally wrong about Trophimus.[22]

And Trophimus was not alone. Epaphroditus was sick nearly to the point of death (*Phil. 2:25-30*). And Paul himself suffered sickness in Galatia (*Gal. 4:13*). He also encouraged Timothy to use medical remedies for illness (*1 Tim. 5:23*). The biblical truth that the Triune God is a healing God and that He gives gifts of healings to His people does not cancel out the equally biblical truths that Christians may suffer illness, that God works through

---

[20] Frank Hodges, *Divine Healing* (Penygroes: The Apostolic Church, 1929), 7.

[21] Donald Gee, *Trophimus I Left Sick* (London: Elim, 1952), 12.

[22] Gee, *Trophimus I Left Sick*, 12.

sickness, and that medical treatment is to be received as a good gift from God.[23] Such Scriptures remind us that 'healing, like other spiritual gifts, is as the Spirit himself determines (*1 Cor. 12:8-11*).'[24]

The erroneous and damaging notion that lack of healing is to be attributed to lack of faith misunderstands the nature of biblical faith. Faith is not a power of the believer, but a resting and relying on Christ. Faith is the empty hand which lays hold of Jesus, and so faith's power is in its object: the living Saviour. Contemporary Elim theologian, Keith Warrington, highlights two reasons why 'the suggestion that an insufficient amount of faith could restrict Jesus is wrong.'[25]

> First, the teaching of Jesus concerning faith is related to its existence, not its quantity. The person who came to Jesus for help had already expressed faith. Secondly, the belief that a person's faith can be developed to achieve a greater level of success is a distortion of the NT teaching concerning faith. It undermines the majesty and love of Jesus, making him a servant of a 'faith' by which he may be coerced or enabled to function. The encouragement by some today that Christians should develop greater faith in order that healing might occur causes heartache for those who remain unhealed. It also reflects a fundamental misunderstanding of the concept of faith as recorded in the Gospels.[26]

It is vital that such errors are avoided and repudiated when it comes to teaching on divine healing. Yet, the reason we so strongly reject such errors, is so that false teaching doesn't close people's eyes and ears to the biblical truth that the Triune God is a healing God, and that He truly gives gifts of healings in His church.

The Holy Spirit does not only distribute a single gift of healing, but rather gifts of healings in the plural. Therefore, the Lord is not bound always to heal in the same way, but rather, just as there are a variety of gifts,

---

[23] Biblical Pentecostals have always acknowledged that God can, and does, use sickness and suffering for our good. In the early days of Pentecostalism, Frank Hodges wrote that Job's 'sufferings were allowed of God for the perfecting of his character, the trial of his faith, and to demonstrate the power of God to sustain and carry through trials of the fiercest nature.' Hodges, *Divine Healing*, 8. A more recent British Pentecostal writer on divine healing notes that, 'God sometimes withholds healing when he knows that physical sickness will be for our spiritual good.' David Petts, *Body Builders*, 167. Petts looks to the example of Job, along with *Heb. 12:10-11*; *Gen. 32:22-32*; and *2 Cor. 12:1-10* for support.

[24] David Petts, *Just A Taste of Heaven: A Biblical and Balanced Approach to God's Healing Power* (Mattersey: Mattersey Hall, 2006), 180.

[25] Keith Warrington, *Pentecostal Theology: A Theology of Encounter* (London: T&T Clark, 2008), 286.

[26] Warrington, *Pentecostal Theology*, 286-287.

healing from the Lord may come in a variety of forms. And that is just what we see in the descriptions of the ministry of healing in Scripture. A sick Christian is to 'call for the elders of the church, and let them pray over him, anointing him with oil in the name of the Lord. And the prayer of faith will save the sick, and the Lord will raise him up' (*Jas 5:14-15*). In evangelistic situations, on the other hand, not only the elders, but all sorts of Christians, filled with the Spirit, 'will lay hands on the sick, and they will recover' (*Mk 16:18*) as a sign accompanying the preaching of the gospel.

The Lord also gives gifts of healing at the Table. Frank Hodges, the pioneer apostle of the Apostolic Church in the midlands of England, highlighted that, during Christ's earthly ministry, people were often healed 'by touching Christ, or Christ touching them.' And today, we know that same 'nearness of the Person of Christ' as we touch Him and He touches us, as we partake of His body and blood in the Breaking of Bread, and so, in the sacrament, 'faith appropriates of health to spirit, soul, and body.'[27] Early British Pentecostals recorded many testimonies of such healing at the Table.[28]

No matter the situation, it must always be remembered that these healings are gifts of grace. Therefore, healing does not depend on our worthiness or our efforts, but solely upon the compassion of our Saviour, Jesus Christ. Both Gee for the Assemblies of God, and Rowe for the Apostolic Church, stressed that healing flows from the very life of the Son:

> They [i.e. the gifts of healing] are the very life of the great Head of the Church, flowing by the Holy Ghost through the members of His body.[29]

> Divine healing comes from the stream of the life of God in the Incarnate Christ which flows through the cross.[30]

The healing which God gives is not merely a gift He gives as a result of what Jesus has done (although, as with all gifts of grace, it does flow from the cross); but rather, it is the very divine life of the Incarnate Son Himself,

---

[27] Frank Hodges, *Divine Healing*, 19-20.

[28] See e.g. David Allen, *Neglected Feast: Rescuing the Breaking of Bread* (Nottingham: Expression, 2007), 72 for a testimony from W.F.P. Burton, British Pentecostal pioneer missionary to the Congo. NB Burton states that the miraculous healing occurred 'while feasting on the Lord Jesus' in the Breaking of Bread, thus demonstrating that the high view of Christ's presence in the sacrament was not limited to the Apostolics, for Burton was a leading figure in the British Assemblies of God, and the healing he reports was in an AoG church in Lancashire.

[29] Donald Gee, *Concerning Spiritual Gifts*, 53.

[30] W.A.C. Rowe, *One Lord, One Faith*, 347.

to whom believers are united by the Holy Spirit, flowing from the Head to His Body. Gifts of healings, then, flow from theosis: partaking of the divine nature as well-beloved sons in the Well-Beloved Son, we share in His immortality and incorruption (*2 Pet. 1:3-7*). So, 'by communion with Him we … receive participation in incorruptibility.'[31] We will only experience the fullness of this participation in the resurrection, but already, by gifts of healings, we can experience it now in part.

It is the Spirit of the age to come (*Heb. 6:4-5*) who distributes these gifts of healings; and so the fullness of the gift of healing is not found in this life, but in the life of the world to come, through the resurrection and glorification of the body.

> Sickness in the world is a result of Adam's sin. Christ's death on the cross dealt with Adam's sin. Therefore, Christ's death has dealt with the cause of sickness. Accordingly Christians may expect healing today. But the final outworking of Christ's victory at Calvary will not be consummated until he comes again. Therefore some Christians may not be healed until Christ returns. Healings experienced today must be seen as the work of the Spirit who gives foretastes of the age to come.[32]

If the fullness of the gifts of healings were to be found in this life, that would mean Christians who never die. All the gifts of healings received in this life, no matter how miraculous and glorious they may be, are only partial, in that one day we will die. But in the resurrection we will know the fullness of God's healing, so that 'there shall be no more pain, for the former things have passed away' (*Rev. 21:4*).

> For the trumpet will sound, and the dead will be raised incorruptible, and we shall be changed. For this corruptible must put on incorruption, and this mortal must put on immortality. So when this corruptible has put on incorruption, and this mortal has put on immortality, then shall be brought to pass the saying that is written: 'Death is swallowed up in victory.' (*1 Cor. 15:52-54*)

The resurrection of the body is the ultimate healing. But now in His great love and compassion, the Lord gives blessed foretastes of that ultimate healing through the gifts of healings He distributes in His church by the Holy Spirit, who breaks into this age with the powers of the age to come. The full healing of the resurrection is guaranteed for us in Christ (*Eph. 1:3; Phil. 3:20-21*) and by the sealing of the Holy Spirit (*Eph. 1:13-14; Rom. 8:23*).

---

[31] Irenaeus, *On the Apostolic Preaching*, (Crestwood: SVS, 1997), 40 (p.65).

[32] Petts, *Just A Taste of Heaven*, 113.

In sum, the witness of the New Testament writers is that God will indeed grant miraculous gifts of healing, and that these are joyful experiences of, and pointers to, the holistic nature of God's eschatological salvation, the first fruits of the consummation to come.[33]

The Working of Miracles

Biblical miracles are not merely spectacular displays of power. Rather they are signs which point to the glory of the Triune God. 'The Gift of the Working of Miracles is essentially a gift which manifests supernatural power at the same time as it reveals the good purposes of God and glorifies Him.'[34]

The book of Acts gives us many examples of such miracles in the life of the early church. Philip the evangelist was caught away by the Spirit of the Lord and transported to another place (*Acts 8:39-40*). Dorcas was raised to life from the dead (*Acts 9:41*). Elymas was struck blind in God's judgment (*Acts 13:9-11*). In Philippi, an earthquake hit, opening all the prison doors and loosing all the prisoners chains, and yet no one was hurt and none of the prisoners ran away (*Acts 16:25-28*). On Malta, Paul was bitten by a poisonous viper, and yet came to no harm whatsoever (*Acts 28:1-6*). And the Triune God still gives miraculous signs today 'as He wills,' 'by the same Spirit' and 'for the profit of all' (*1 Cor. 12:7, 10-11*). And as the Lord works such miracles today through His people, He bears witness to the great salvation found in Jesus, and confirms the preaching of the gospel (*Heb. 2:3-4*).

---

[33] Turner, *The Holy Spirit and Spiritual Gifts: Then and Now*, 260.
[34] *The Apostolic Church: Its Principles and Practices*, 205.

Prophecy

The Nature of Prophecy

Prophecy is not something that comes from man, but from God. Through the prophet Jeremiah, the LORD warned His people:

> Do not listen to the words of the prophets who prophesy to you.
> They make you worthless;
> They speak a vision of their own heart,
> Not from the mouth of the Lord. (*Jer. 23:16*)

Similarly, Ezekiel warns against 'prophets who follow their own spirit and have seen nothing' (*Ezek. 13:3*), and in the New Testament, Peter reminds us that 'prophecy never came by the will of man, but holy men of God spoke as they were moved by the Holy Spirit' (*2 Pet. 1:22*). Therefore, prophecy is not a skill which lies within man, which people can develop. It is not something which can be learnt. The origin of prophecy is not in us, but outside of us, in the Triune God. Thus, the type of statements that are often heard today, such as 'prophesy growth over your church' or 'prophesy health over your family' do not reflect the biblical nature of prophecy.[35] We cannot decide what to prophesy, for prophecy does not come from within us. It is a word that comes from outside of us, by which the Triune God addresses His people, not with their thoughts and desires, but with His.

The realisation that prophecy is an external Word of God may tempt us to confuse prophecy with biblical preaching. Yet, although preaching may involve an element of prophecy, the two are not the same and shouldn't be equated. The Bible uses different words for *preaching* and *prophesying*, and the Lord gives different gifts of *teachers* and *prophets*. Both preaching and prophesying, teachers and prophets proclaim the Word of the Lord, but in different ways.

Nor should prophecy be confused with predicting the future. God may speak about the future in prophesy (*e.g. Acts 21:4, 11*), but most prophecy in the Bible is not about future events. In *1 Corinthians 14:24-25* we see prophecy that speaks to unbelievers about the past or the present, rather than a prediction of the future. Furthermore, when God speaks about the

---

[35] This reflects more the prophecies of the prophets of Baal (*1 Kgs 18:29*) than true prophecy from the Triune God.

future through prophecy, it is not a 'prediction.' Predictions (like the weather forecast) aren't certain. They may be contingent on other events. But, when God speaks about the future, it is certain.

What about Jonah's prophecy to Nineveh? 'Yet forty days, and Nineveh shall be overthrown' was his message (*Jonah 3:4*), and yet, Nineveh was not overthrown. Does that mean that God's word is not certain? Certainly not. When God speaks of the future, it may, as in the case of Nineveh, be a warning and a call to repentance. If things had continued as they were, the Lord would have overthrown the city. But the people of Nineveh repented, and so the Lord rescinded the sentence in His mercy and grace.

Prophecy should never be treated like a Christian horoscope. Prophecy is not a thing to be toyed with, because we have a fascination with knowing the unknown future. Rather, God chooses what to reveal of the future and when. We are simply called to trust in the God who holds the future in His hands, whether He reveals to us what it entails or not.

Prophecy involves speech. It is not just a feeling or impression. Wayne Grudem has defined prophecy as 'speaking merely human words to report something God brings to mind.'[36] But this doesn't take account of the close connection established in the Scriptures between prophecy and speech. The prophet Agabus spoke 'by the Spirit', not merely by his own words (*Acts 11:28*). Later, in Caesarea, when Agabus prophesied, he began by establishing whose words these were: 'Thus says the Holy Spirit' (*Acts 21:11*). The prophecy by which Paul and Barnabas were called and set apart to their apostolic ministries was delivered in the first person, and so not as human words, but as divine words (*Acts 13:2*). When Paul prophesied to Elymas the sorcerer, it was 'filled with the Holy Spirit' that he spoke (*Acts 13:9-11*). In *2 Corinthians 12:9*, Paul records words spoken by the Lord and addressed to him in the first person, which are not a quotation of Scripture, and so he seems to be quoting a first person prophecy. Even the very purpose of prophecy shows that speaking is an intrinsic part of the gift: 'he who prophesies speaks edification and exhortation and comfort to men' (*1 Cor. 14:3*).[37]

---

[36] Wayne Grudem, *The Gift of Prophecy* (3rd ed., Eastbourne, 2000), 51, 71.

[37] All these examples are from the New Testament simply because Grudem bases his argument on seeing New Testament prophecy as something different from Old Testament prophecy. I am not conceding his division of the Testaments, but simply demonstrating that even from just the New Testament, his argument that prophecy consists merely of human words does not hold.

God can use feelings and impressions, but this is not the same as prophecy proper. Thomas Aquinas warns that there must be certainty that the prophetic word is God's word, or 'else, were he not certain about this, the faith which relies on the utterances of the prophet would not be certain.' Aquinas points out that the certainty of God's prophetic revelation is seen in that Abraham was willing to sacrifice Isaac on the altar 'which he nowise would have done had he not been most certain of the Divine revelation.'[38] Thomas is clear that God does speak prophetically through forms which are not spoken with 'prophetic certitude', but this is not the same as the gift of prophecy:

> Again, sometimes the prophet's mind is moved to speak something, so that he understands what the Holy Ghost means by the words he utters; like David who said (2 Samuel 23:2): 'The Spirit of the Lord hath spoken by me'; while, on the other hand, sometimes the person whose mind is moved to utter certain words knows not what the Holy Ghost means by them, as was the case with Caiaphas (John 11:51). Again, when the Holy Ghost moves a man's mind to do something, sometimes the latter understands the meaning of it, like Jeremias who hid his loin-cloth in the Euphrates (Jeremiah 13:1-11); while sometimes he does not understand it – thus the soldiers, who divided Christ's garments, understood not the meaning of what they did. Accordingly, when a man knows that he is being moved by the Holy Ghost to think something, or signify something by word or deed, this belongs properly to prophecy; whereas when he is moved, without his knowing it, this is not perfect prophecy, but a prophetic instinct. Nevertheless it must be observed that since the prophet's mind is a defective instrument, as stated above, even true prophets know not all that the Holy Ghost means by the things they see, or speak, or even do.[39]

So, now we've eliminated a number of ideas of what prophecy is not, what is prophecy? D.P. Williams defined prophecy as 'a Divinely generated utterance through human lips by the indwelling Spirit of God',[40] or 'the Voice of God as heard through the lips of men.'[41] Other Apostolic writers agreed. The early Apostolic prophet, T.N. Turnbull defined prophecy as 'The Holy Spirit speaking through the mouths of men',[42] and W.A.C. Rowe wrote that 'true prophecy is the Word of God.'[43] But this is not a uniquely Apostolic understanding of the biblical presentation of prophecy. New

[38] Thomas Aquinas, *Summa Theologicae,* II-II, 171, 5.
[39] Aquinas, *Summa Theologicae,* II-II, 173, 4.
[40] D.P. Williams, *The Prophetical Ministry in the Church*, 7.
[41] D.P. Williams, *The Prophetical Ministry in the Church*, 15.
[42] T.N. Turnbull, *Prophecy in the Church Age*, 32.
[43] W.A.C. Rowe, *One Lord, One Faith*, 265.

Testament scholar David Aune writes that 'the distinctive feature of prophetic speech was not so much its content or form, but its supernatural origin. Christian prophetic speech, then, is Christian discourse presented with divine legitimation.'[44] Thomas Aquinas defines this gift, writing:

> Prophecy first and chiefly consists in knowledge, because … prophets know things that are far removed from man's knowledge. … Prophecy consists secondarily in speech, in so far as the prophets declare for the instruction of others, the things they know through being taught of God. … Now those things above human ken which are revealed by God cannot be confirmed by human reason.[45]

> All those things that are the matter of prophecy have the common aspect of being unknowable to man except by Divine revelation.[46]

> The end of prophecy is the manifestation of a truth that surpasses the faculty of man.[47]

What do these definitions from early British Pentecostals, a prominent New Testament scholar with expertise in early Christian prophecy, and a medieval theologian have in common? Two things: 1) *Supernatural origin:* prophecy comes from God, not from us; and 2) *Making God's revelation known:* prophecy involves speech.

So, in prophecy, God speaks. But it is not a distant God who speaks in prophecy. Christians who prophesy are united to Christ and filled with the Holy Spirit. As well-beloved sons in the Well-Beloved Son, they are partakers of the divine nature. Christians live within the loving communication between the Father, Son, and Holy Spirit, and are filled with the Spirit who speaks.[48] So that's why Paul can say, 'you can all prophesy' (*1 Cor. 14:31*); not because of any ability innate in us, but because, in Christ, we share in the Son's relationship with His Father, and are anointed with His Spirit of anointing.

By contrast, in other religions, the prophetic revelation claimed from their non-trinitarian god is often indirect, and only to one prophet (or a very small number of prophets). In Mormonism, the revelation Joseph Smith supposedly received involved the mediation of the angel Mornoi, the golden tablets, and the stones in his hat. In Islam, the Quran is said to have

---

[44] David E. Aune, *Prophecy in Early Christianity*, 338.

[45] Aquinas, *Summa Theologicae*, II-II, 171, 1.

[46] Aquinas, *Summa Theologicae*, II-II, 171, 3, ad. 2.

[47] Aquinas, *Summa Theologicae*, II-II, 174, 2.

[48] T.N. Turnbull, *Riches of Grace*, xv.9 (Oct. 1940), 104.

been mediated to Muhammad through the angel Gabriel. Christian prophecy, by contrast, is (usually) direct, and has no need of any other mediation. Nor does it need to be limited to a small number of prophets. For Christians are united to Christ, the Living Word, who then fills them with His Spirit who distributes the gift of prophecy.

Furthermore, in Christian prophecy, the Lord is present in His Word. We'll look at the concept of the three-fold word in chapter 35, but for now we can look back to *1 Corinthians 12:7* and remember that prophecy is a *manifestation* of God by the Spirit.

Prophecy and the Trinity

Prophecy, as with all the gifts of the Spirit, finds its origin in the Triune God (*1 Cor. 12:4-6*). We see this in practice in the letter to the church in Thyatira (*Rev. 2:18-29*), a prophecy recorded in Scripture which is explicitly said to be both the words of Christ and what the Holy Spirit says to the churches. The prophetic letter to Thyatira begins, 'these things says the Son of God' (*Rev. 2:18*), yet ends 'He who has an ear, let him hear what the Spirit says to the churches' (*Rev. 2:29*). Both the Son and the Spirit are speaking in the prophecy. And not only in this one, but the same pattern is repeated throughout the prophetic letters to the seven churches of Asia (*Rev. 2:1, 7; 2:8, 11; 2:12, 17; 3:1, 6; 3:7, 13; 3:14, 22*). In fact, John's prophetic vision in the book of Revelation began when he 'was in the Spirit on the Lord's Day', but 'in the Spirit' it was the Son whom He heard and saw (*Rev. 1:10-11*).

The Spirit dwells in the Son and the Son dwells in the Spirit. And the Spirit and the Son dwell in the Father, and the Father dwells in the Spirit and the Son. This is the perichoresis of the three persons of the Trinity.[49] So where the Spirit is, there too are the Father and the Son. And when the Spirit moves in prophecy, it is an operation of the Triune God. For the external works of the Trinity are indivisible.[50] Therefore, it is the Triune God who speaks in prophecy, as the Father reveals Himself in the Son by the Spirit.

And not only is prophecy an indivisible operation of the Triune God, but prophecy is also the result of the Triune pentecostal outpouring. In *Acts 1*, Jesus spoke to His disciples of the promise of the Father (*Acts 1:4*), which was the outpouring of the Spirit (*Acts 1:5*), which would make them witnesses to the Son (*Acts 1:8; cf. Rev. 19:10*). Then in *Acts 2*, Peter declares

---

[49] See chapter 5.
[50] *Opera Trinitatis ad extra indivsa sunt*; see chapter 5.

that the exalted Son poured out from the Father 'what you now see and hear' (*Acts 2:33*). What did they now see and hear as a result of this Trinitarian outpouring? They saw and heard men and women prophesying in the languages of all the visitors to the city (*Acts 2:4-12*), and Peter's prophetic proclamation of Christ (*Acts 2:14*).

Prophecy and the Gospel

True prophecy points us to Jesus Christ, for 'the testimony of Jesus is the spirit of prophecy' (*Rev. 19:10*). The spoken Word in prophecy must be full of the living Word, and the gifts of the Spirit must always contribute to the Spirit's work of glorifying Christ (*Jn 16:14*). Jesus promised that the outpoured Holy Spirit would glorify Him 'for He will take of what is Mine and declare it to you' (*Jn 16:14*), and that is exactly what happens in prophecy, as by the Spirit, the Son speaks in His church (*Rev. 2:18, 29*). And prophecy brings the church 'edification and exhortation [*paraklesis*] and comfort' (*1 Cor. 14:3*). True building up, *paraklesis* and comfort are found only in Jesus, the Builder of His Church (*Mt 16:18*) and the first Paraclete (*Jn 14:16*). Thus true prophecy lifts the eyes of the church to Him who is the Good News.

And true prophecy also confirms the preaching of the gospel, just like the other signs and wonders and gifts of the Holy Spirit (*Heb. 2:3-4; Acts 14:3*). Paul writes to the Corinthians that:

> If all prophesy, and an unbeliever or an uninformed person comes in, he is convinced by all, he is convicted by all. And thus the secrets of his heart are revealed; and so, falling down on his face, he will worship God and report that God is truly among you. (*1 Cor. 14:24-25*)

The Lord can use prophecy to bring conviction of sin and of the truth of the gospel of Jesus Christ, and so prophecy can powerfully confirm the preaching of the cross. For signs like prophecy point, not to themselves, but to Jesus (*cf. Jn 6:26*).

Therefore, Jesus is the test of true prophecy, as true prophecy points to the true Jesus. 'No one speaking by the Spirit of God calls Jesus accursed, and no one can say that Jesus is Lord except by the Holy Spirit' (*1 Cor. 12:3*). The Holy Spirit always glorifies the Lord Jesus, and so any Spirit-inspired speech must glorify Him. John tells His readers that the Incarnate Christ is the test of true prophecy from the Spirit of God:

> Beloved, do not believe every spirit, but test the spirits, whether they are of God; because many false prophets have gone out into the world. By this you know the Spirit of God: Every spirit that confesses that Jesus Christ has come in the flesh is of God, and every spirit that does not confess that Jesus Christ has come in the flesh is not of God. And this is the spirit of the Antichrist, which you have heard was coming, and is now already in the world. (*1 Jn 4:1-3*)

It is not simply the right language, but that right Jesus who is glorified in prophecy (*cf. 2 Cor. 11:4*): God the Son who has taken on our humanity to live, suffer, die and rise again for us and for our salvation.

Prophecy is of no worth without the Love of God, which is Jesus (*1 Cor. 12:31-13:3; 14:1*). Every spiritual blessing that we have (including gifts like prophecy) is ours in (and only in) Christ (*Eph. 1:3*). Therefore, the gift of prophecy depends on our union with Christ, which is union with Him in His death and resurrection. For prophecy flows from the cross of Christ (*Acts 2:23-24, 32-33*). In prophecy we hear the words of 'the First and the Last, who was dead, and came to life' (*Rev. 2:8*). Thus, prophecy depends on the cross and resurrection of Jesus. It is a gift which depends on what Christ has done, not on what we have done, for it is a gift of God's grace.

Prophecy and the Authority of Scripture

In prophecy, the Lord speaks; but prophecy is not Scripture. Rather, prophecy must always be subject to the authority of Scripture. The Scriptures teach that prophecy is to be weighed (*1 Cor. 14:29; 1 Thess. 5:19-22; 1 Jn 4:1*). One of the primary tests for weighing prophecy is to judge it against Scripture, for the Holy Spirit who inspired the Scriptures cannot contradict Himself. If any supposed prophecy is contrary to Scripture, it is not the word of God, and therefore it is false prophecy. As the Apostolic Church has always insisted, 'The Word [the Bible] is the standard of teaching and not experience ... We stand not on experience and manifestation but on what the Word teaches.'[51] For prophecy to be accepted as true prophecy, it must be 'in perfect accord with the written Word of God.'[52]

---

[51] *Minutes of the Convocation of Apostles and Prophets, Bradford, January 1932*, p.14.

[52] *The Apostolic Church: Its Principles and Practices* (Rev. Ed., Penygroes: Apostolic Publications, 1961), 131.

The Discerning of Spirits

There may be some connection between the discerning of spirits and the weighing of prophecy. Both Paul and John write of discerning prophecies in relation to the Spirit (although they use a different Greek word for discerning from the one used of this gift). 'Do not quench the Spirit. Do not despise prophecies. Test [discern] all things; hold fast what is good' (*1 Thess. 5:19-21*). 'Beloved, do not believe every spirit, but test [discern] the spirits, whether they are of God; because many false prophets have gone out into the world' (*1 Jn 4:1*). Furthermore, within the immediate context of the list of the gifts, Paul uses the same word as the gift for discerning in relation to the judging of prophecies (*1 Cor. 14:29*). Certainly discernment is called for in the judging of prophecies, and the gift of discerning of spirits may well be of great value there; however, prophecies are to be judged whether or not any of the other gifts (including discerning of spirits) are in operation. So, it would seem overly restrictive to limit this gift only to the weighing of prophecy.

Some examples in the book of Acts may help us to discern the nature of this gift. A clear example is found in *Acts 5*, where Peter discerns that it was Satan who filled the heart of Ananias 'to lie to the Holy Spirit' (*Acts 5:3*). In Paphos, Paul, 'filled with the Holy Spirit,' discerned that Elymas was 'full of all deceit and all fraud, ... [a] son of the devil, ...[an] enemy of all righteousness, [who would] not cease perverting the straight ways of the Lord' (*Acts 13:9-10*).

In *Acts 8*, Simon the Sorcerer tries to buy the power to lay hands on people to receive the baptism of the Holy Spirit. Peter reacts, saying:

> Your money perish with you, because you thought that the gift of God could be purchased with money! You have neither part nor portion in this matter, for your heart is not right in the sight of God. Repent therefore of this your wickedness, and pray God if perhaps the thought of your heart may be forgiven you. For I see that you are poisoned by bitterness and bound by iniquity. (*Acts 8:20-23*)

Although the first part of Peter's statement could come simply from Simon's expressed desire, Peter goes on to speak of what he sees in Simon's heart, particularly in *verse 23*, where Simon's bitterness does not appear to be outwardly visible in his words and actions. Thus it appears that this is something which has been supernaturally revealed to Peter, and so this may well be an example of the gift of discerning of spirits.

Another likely occurred in Philippi, where 'a certain slave girl possessed with a spirit of divination' followed Paul and Silas around, shouting out, 'these men are the servants of the Most High God, who proclaim to us the way of salvation.' (*Acts 16:16-18*). The words she spoke were true, and yet Paul recognised that it was by an evil spirit that she was speaking, and so cast it out. Paul discerned that it was not the Holy Spirit, but an evil spirit which had prompted the girl to speak. As Don Carson puts it: 'There is ever a need to distinguish demonic forces from the Holy Spirit. This gift is apparently designed to meet that need.'[53] Or, in the words of a former President of the General Council of the Apostolic Church:

> This gift is the divinely-imparted power to distinguish the deceptive imitations of infernal inspiration and action from the genuine inspired ministry of the Holy Spirit … The gift of discernment of spirits does not contain the power of exorcism. But this power does abide within the church awaiting the command of faith (Mark 16:17).[54]

Tongues and Interpretation

The gift of tongues first appeared on the Day of Pentecost with the outpouring of the Holy Spirit. The disciples, upon whom the Spirit fell, 'began to speak with other tongues, as the Spirit gave them utterance' (*Acts 2:4*). Leaving the upper room, they moved out into the crowd that filled the city for the feast, 'speaking in [their] own tongues the wonderful works of God' (*Acts 2:11*). So, the gift of tongues means speaking the things of God in another language which the speaker has not studied and learnt. At times these may be other recognisable human languages (as on the day of Pentecost).[55] Yet, the Scriptures do not suggest that this is always, or even

---

[53] Carson, *Showing the Spirit*, 31.

[54] Rennie, *The Gifts of the Holy Spirit*, 99, 102.

[55] Pentecostals have many such testimonies of someone hearing their native language spoken in tongues in a meeting. In the early years of the Apostolic Church, Welsh-speaking pastors often heard English people, or people on the mission field who had never heard the Welsh language suddenly praise God in Welsh. E.g. Frank Hodges (an Englishman), pioneer of the Apostolic Church in the English Midlands, spoke in Welsh when he was baptised in the

normally the case. Paul's instructions to the Corinthian assembly concerning the gift of tongues and the need for interpretation show us that, normally in the life of the church, there is no one present who understands the language spoken in tongues, and so the complementary gift of interpretation is needed so that the church may benefit (*1 Cor. 14:6-28*).

Paul's famous words in *1 Corinthians 13*, that 'though I speak with the tongues of men and of angels, but have not love, I have become a sounding brass or a clanging cymbal' (*1 Cor. 13:1*), raise the possibility that tongues may sometimes be human languages and sometimes angelic languages. Although many commentators have suggested that 'tongues of angels' is hyperbole, this doesn't fit so well in the context, where Paul is specifically writing about spiritual gifts, including the gift of tongues.

> On its own this could mean nothing more than 'speak eloquently,' as some have argued and as it is popularly understood. But since it is not on its own, but follows directly from 12:28-30 and anticipates 14:1-25, most likely this is either Paul's or their understanding (or both) of 'speaking in tongues.' 'Tongues of men' would then refer to human speech, inspired by the Spirit but unknown to the speaker; 'tongues of angels' would reflect an understanding that the tongues-speaker was communicating in the dialect(s) of heaven.[56]

This may account for why Paul does not generally expect tongues to be understood by anyone present in the assembly.

The Scriptures give clear, and strict, instructions for the use of the gifts of tongues and interpretation in the church. The main principle is that everything in the assembly must 'be done for edification' (*1 Cor. 14:26*). Uninterpreted, and thus unintelligible, tongues do not edify the Body (*1 Cor. 14:6*; although, Paul tells us, they do edify the individual: *1 Cor. 14:4*), and so tongues should not be spoken aloud publicly without an interpretation (*1 Cor. 14:27-28*). Uninterpreted tongues in the assembly bring confusion rather than edification:

> Therefore if the whole church comes together in one place, and all speak with tongues, and there come in those who are uninformed or unbelievers, will they not say that you are out of your mind? (*1 Cor. 14:23*)

Holy Spirit; see James Worsfold, *Origins of the Apostolic Church in Great Britain*, 201. For an example from the British Assemblies of God of a student from Burkina Faso hearing tongues given in his native language, Moré, and confirming the subsequent interpretation, see Petts, *Body Builders*, 134-135. A similar occurrence happened in my old assembly in Brussels, but there the language was Arabic.

[56] Fee, *The First Epistle to the Corinthians*, 630.

Does this mean that there is never a place for corporate tongues? Not necessarily; the answer would appear to depend upon the context. In the public service of the church, where unbelievers may be present or where there is the possibility of confusion and disorder, tongues are always to be interpreted (*1 Cor. 14:13-19, 26-28*) and must be strictly limited to 'two or at the most three' speakers, 'each in turn' (*1 Cor. 14:27*). However, there are other occasions in Scripture where groups of people speak in tongues together and without interpretation (*Acts 2:4, 11; 10:46; 19:6*). Each of these, however, is associated with people receiving the baptism in the Holy Spirit, and not a description of the regular public worship of the church. God can, and does act in such a way, filling groups of people with the Spirit at the same time, and giving them the accompanying sign of tongues, but when it comes to the public worship of the church, we have the responsibility to ensure that everything is 'done decently and in order' (*1 Cor. 14:40*). Tongues are not to be forbidden (*1 Cor. 14:39*), yet they are to be kept within the guidelines which the Lord has given in His Word. When someone speaks in tongues, they are not in an ecstatic state, and so they have control over whether to speak or not to speak (*cf. 1 Cor. 14:30-32*). So, the speaker in tongues can keep to the order set down by Paul in the Scriptures, for the Holy Spirit who gives the gift of tongues is the same Holy Spirit who inspired Paul to write Scripture. The Holy Spirit does not contradict Himself. And so the order He has inspired is always to be maintained, 'for God is not the author of confusion but of peace, as in all the churches of the saints' (*1 Cor. 14:33*).

What is the content of speaking in tongues and to whom are tongues addressed? The crowds on the Day of Pentecost heard the disciples 'speaking in our own tongues the wonderful works of God' (*Acts 2:11*). When Cornelius and his household were baptised in the Holy Spirit, Peter and his companions 'heard them speak with tongues and magnify God' (*Acts 10:46*). Paul tells us that prayer in tongues involves the 'giving of thanks' (*1 Cor. 14:16-17*) and intercession (*Rom. 8:26*). Thus, the focus of the content of tongues-speech is upon the Triune God. Tongues declare His wonderful works, magnify Him, thank Him, and intercede with Him. But, although we see the God-ward focus of tongues in these Scriptures, we also see that tongues can be addressed in two directions: sometimes tongues are addressed to God (in prayer, intercession, thanksgiving, and worship), and sometimes they are addressed to human beings, declaring the wondrous works of the saving God, and edifying the Body of Christ.

In addition to this function of speaking in tongues as charismatic prayer, Paul envisions tongues as blessing the church in another way. Paul declares that speaking in tongues, when exercised in concert with the gift of interpretation, can be the vehicle through which the Holy Spirit speaks to the larger church body. In this way tongues with interpretation functions very much like prophecy. The difference, however, is that in this instance, the message to the church is issued first through an inspired, unintelligible utterance in tongues. This 'message in tongues' is then followed by a Spirit-inspired interpretation of this utterance that is proclaimed in the vernacular of those present and thus understood by all.[57]

The Triune God distributes gifts in His church by the Holy Spirit, flowing purely from His grace in Jesus Christ. And through these gracious gifts, Christ the Head builds up the church which is His Body, as He edifies, exhorts, and comforts her by His Spirit.

---

[57] Robert P. Menzies, *Speaking in Tongues: Jesus and the Apostolic Church as Models for the Church Today* (Cleveland, TN: CPT Press, 2016), 146.

Chapter 29

The Church which is the Body of Christ

'There is nothing higher nor nearer the Heart of our Glorified Lord than His Church.'[1] And if the Church is indeed so important to Christ, then it certainly deserves our attention. The Bible tells us that Christ 'loved the church and gave Himself for her' (*Eph. 5:25*) and the Incarnate God 'purchased' the Church 'with His own blood' (*Acts 20:28*). The Church is not simply something quite important to Christ; rather, Scripture clearly teaches that Christ *died* for His Church. This places a far greater importance on the Church than anything else ever possibly could.

According to these Scriptures, the Incarnate Son did not simply die for individuals, but also for His Church. The Church is an actual object which Jesus loves and for which He died; it is not merely a word used to describe the group of all Christians.[2]

The Being of the Church

What the Church is Not

In order to examine the doctrine of the Church, let's first look at what the Church is not. In everyday language we use the word *church* in a variety of ways. But, we have to be careful as these are not always the same ways in which the Bible uses the word. As a result, it is easy to get confused about what the church actually is.

---

[1] D.P. Williams, in the Foreword to Thomas Rees, *The Divine Masterpiece: Bible Readings upon 'The Church which is His Body'* (Penygroes: Apostolic Publications, 1943), 2. (D.P. Williams was the founding apostle of the Apostolic Church.)

[2] In theological language, we would say that the Church is an *ontological reality*.

Firstly, the church is not a building. Although we often use the word *church* to refer to the buildings where we meet, this is not the biblical meaning of the word. In fact, the earliest Christians (those who lived in New Testament times) did not even have special buildings in which to meet.

Secondly, the church is not a meeting. Often we talk about 'going to church' on a Sunday or for a meeting during the week, yet this is really just a form of shorthand to say that we are going to a meeting of the church. The church itself continues to exist in-between meetings.

Thirdly, the church is not a denomination. When Christ died for His Church, it was not just one particular denomination for which He died. The biblical concept of *church* transcends these three ways in which we commonly use the word. Christ's Church is not confined to a building, a meeting, or a denomination, but is something much greater.

There is also another concept of *church* of which we must rid ourselves at this point; namely the idea that the Church is a voluntary association or group of people. This idea seems more attractive as it goes beyond the limitations of buildings, meetings and denominations; but it doesn't go far enough. While it is true that the Church is made up of people, rather than bricks, the Church is more than merely a group of people. As we have already seen, the fact that Christ loves and died for His Church indicates that it is much more than simply a convenient name for a group of people. Further, seeing the Church as a voluntary association places the emphasis on human works rather than Christ's work. If the church is a voluntary association of people, then that would mean that I belong to the church as a result of my voluntary decision to join and to stay a member; the emphasis is placed on what I do. However, Scripture teaches that it is Christ who is building His Church (*Mt 16:18*) and that it is He who adds members to it (*Acts 2:47*). Our belonging to the Church of Jesus Christ is by grace alone (*sola gratia*), not by our works; it depends wholly on Christ, the Head and Builder of the Church, not on anything we do.

Singaporean Pentecostal theologian Simon Chan points out two negative consequences of seeing the Church simply as a voluntary association or group of people. Firstly, he notes that this idea contributes to an individualism which sees the church 'as essentially a service provider catering to the needs of individual Christians'.[3] Here, the danger is that we think of the church as existing for our own individual benefit. Secondly, Chan notes that such a view of the church sees it as something 'brought

---

[3] Simon Chan, 'Mother Church: Toward a Pentecostal Ecclesiology', *Pneuma*, 22.2 (Autumn, 2000), 178.

about by people united for a common purpose'[4], rather than remembering that it is Christ who builds His Church (*Mt 16:18*).

What the Church Is

Now that we have considered what the Church is not, we must turn to consider what it is. The Tenets of the Apostolic Church define it as 'the church which is the body of Christ' (see *Eph. 1:22-23; Col. 1:24*). Yet, what do we mean by the Body of Christ?

Firstly, the Body of Christ clearly belongs to Christ; it is Christ's possession and only exists in relation to Him. We have already noted that it is Christ who builds the Church; yet it is not just any church that He builds, but rather 'My Church' (*Mt 16:18*). The Church belongs to Christ and cannot exist apart from Him.

Secondly, it is His Body, singular. There is only one Body. Thus the Church is a unity. As a result, there is no room for division, enmity and strife in the Church. One church does not exist to compete with another.

Thirdly, the Body of Christ is a living organism. In the words of D.P. Williams, the Church is 'a Spiritual Organism … not a gathering of individuals merely, but every individual possesses Eternal Life in oneness and mystical union organised into a corporate unity for the purpose of being effective in service'.[5] D.P. Williams is underlining here the fact that the Church is not just a group of people, but rather a living Body united to Christ its Head and indwelt by His eternal life. Elsewhere D.P. Williams wrote that the Body of Christ is 'a Divine structure in which the Life of Christ indwells.'[6] So the Church is both a living organism filled with the life of Christ and a structure (or organization). The two (organism and organization) are not in opposition to one another, but, rather, are complementary characteristics of the Body of Christ.

Paul describes the functioning of the Body of Christ, underlining that it is both an organism and an organization or structure, just like the human body (*1 Cor. 12:12-31*). He stresses both the fact that the Church is a living organism (the Body), but also the importance of structure or organization. Each part needs to play its own role and do its own job, thus there is need of

---

[4] Chan, 'Mother Church', 179.

[5] D.P. Williams, 'Grace and Apostleship', *Riches of Grace*, xv 9 (October 1940), 98.

[6] D.P. Williams, 'The Ministry of the Word', in *The Enduring Word* (Penygroes: Apostolic Publications, 1944), 174.

structure and organization in the Body. Each member must know his role and place and fulfil it. We should neither be jealous of the roles of other members of the Body nor think of our own role as unnecessary (*1 Cor. 12:15-19*). On the other hand, we should not think of ourselves as indispensable, or more important than others (*1 Cor. 12:21-22*). All the members of the Body are necessary and important.[7]

So, we have seen that the Body of Christ (i) belongs to Christ and cannot exist without Him, (ii) is one (a unity), and (iii) is an organized and structured living organism. Yet, what are the implications of this for the nature of the Church?

The One, Holy, Catholic and Apostolic Church

The One Church

Jesus declared that there would be 'one fold and one shepherd' (*Jn 10:16 AV*).[8] The Scriptures are clear: there is 'one body' (*Rom. 12:5; 1 Cor. 10:17; 12:12-13, 20; Eph. 4:4*). This is the great prayer of Jesus, that those who believe in Him would be 'made perfect in one' (*Jn 17:23*) and all 'be one' as the Father is in the Son and the Son in the Father (*Jn 17:21*).

In the New Testament, the emphasis on the oneness of the Body is often focused on the unity of Jews and Gentiles in the Body of Christ. In Ephesians, Paul writes of the mystery of the Church:

> which in other ages was not made known to the sons of men, as it has now been revealed by the Spirit to His holy apostles and prophets: that the Gentiles should be fellow heirs, of the same body, and partakers of His promise in Christ through the gospel (*Eph. 3:5-6*).

In the Church there is no Jew or Gentile; we are all one in Christ. Yet this isn't limited to the unity of Jews and Gentiles. If such a significant social barrier has no place in the Church, then neither do any other social barriers. There should be no place for distinctions in Christ's Church based on race,

---

[7] We'll think more about the structure of the Church in chapters 36-38.

[8] I've cited this verse in the Authorised Version, simply because that's the wording that's familiar to generations of Apostolics around the world as the motto of the Apostolic Church.

culture, age, or any other social groupings. In Christ we are all one. This means that the local assembly, the local expression of the Body of Christ should not be defined in terms of race, culture or age.[9] Rather it should be a place where genuine relationships are formed across racial, cultural and age lines, on the basis of our common fellowship with Christ and fellow membership of His Body.

How does the unity of the Body of Christ come about? Firstly, this unity comes about on the basis of Christ's atoning work. All the members of Christ's Body share in the benefits of the Cross. As Paul writes:

> For He Himself is our peace, who has made both one, and has broken down the middle wall of separation, having abolished in His flesh the enmity, that is, the law of commandments contained in ordinances, so as to create in Himself one new man from the two, thus making peace, and that He might reconcile them both to God in one body through the cross, thereby putting to death the enmity. And He came and preached peace to you who were afar off and to those who were near. For through Him we both have access by one Spirit to the Father. (*Eph. 2:14-18*)

Paul was writing to the Ephesians about Jews and Gentiles. The Gentiles were those 'who were afar off' and the Jews were 'those who were near' (*Eph. 2:17*). Yet Christ has reconciled these two groups 'to God in one body through the cross' (*Eph 2:16*). The cross is the only true basis for unity in the Church. We are not united by common interests or goals, but by Christ's atoning work at the Cross. This means that the unity of the Body of Christ is not something we bring about; it is not a human work. Rather, it is a work of God; Christ Himself unites the members of His Church into One Body through His Cross. John points to the incarnate Christ and His shed blood as the ground of all true Christian fellowship. Christians have fellowship with one another, because we have fellowship with the incarnate and crucified Christ, for 'truly our fellowship is with the Father and with His Son Jesus

---

[9] Of course, some localities are only home to one race or culture, in which case the local assembly will be reflective of that reality. However, in multiracial or multicultural environments the assembly should not limit itself to one race or culture. The only biblically legitimate social boundary on the assembly is that of language, for *1 Corinthians 14:13-19* stresses the importance of everyone in the assembly understanding what is said, in order that all may be edified.

As for age, I cannot imagine a locality that has residents of only one age, thus there would not seem to be any normal circumstances which would allow for an assembly composed only of one age-group. (The exception to this may be in the beginning stages of the planting of a new assembly, but even then this should not be encouraged to last long.) This means that each age-group needs to be considerate of the others.

Christ' and in our loving fellowship with the Father and the Son in the Spirit, through our union with Christ, 'we have fellowship with one another, and the blood of Jesus Christ [God's] Son cleanses us from all sin' *(1 Jn 1:3, 7)*. Through the blood of Jesus, we are brought into the loving fellowship of the Triune God as well-beloved sons in the well-beloved Son, and in that fellowship we are one Body with all those who share in the same loving fellowship of the Trinity.

The basis for our unity is the Cross, but the means by which it is achieved is by the agency of the Holy Spirit *(Eph. 2:18)*. In *1 Corinthians 12:13* we read that 'by one Spirit we were all baptized into one body – whether Jews or Greeks, whether slaves or free – and have all been made to drink into one Spirit.' The role of the Holy Spirit is essential in the formation and unity of the Body of Christ. As W.H. Lewis wrote, 'the Holy Spirit is not here to create individual units, independent of others, but rather that all should participate in the blessings, privileges, and responsibilities of the Body.'[10]

The Baptism of the Holy Spirit and the One Church

But what is the place of the baptism of the Holy Spirit in relation to membership of the Body of Christ? *1 Corinthians 12:13* has often been used as a proof-text by those who would seek to deny a Pentecostal understanding of the baptism. The argument runs, that Paul here says that you become a member of the Body of Christ through the baptism of the Spirit, therefore every Christian must be baptised in the Spirit at conversion, as every Christian is part of the one Body of Christ. However, this would sweep away all the biblical teaching we have seen in *chapter 26* on the subsequence of the baptism of the Spirit to regeneration on the basis of a particular understanding of one proof-text. Often Pentecostals, in return, have responded with an exegetically untenable distinction between baptism by the Spirit into the Body (at conversion) and a baptism by Christ in the Spirit (subsequent to conversion). On both sides, these arguments are weak, but they do serve to draw our attention to this verse and the connection it highlights between the baptism of the Holy Spirit and the Church which is the Body of Christ.

---

[10] W.H. Lewis, 'The Relationships of the Body of Christ', *Riches of Grace*, vii 6, (July 1932), 240.

There is no explicit language about becoming a Christian in *1 Corinthians 12:13*. Gordon Fee points out that 'Paul's present concern is not to delineate how an individual becomes a believer, but to explain how the many of them, diverse as they are, are in fact one body.'[11] The theme is the unity of the Body, not joining the Body. So how does the baptism of the Spirit relate to the unity of the Body of Christ?

The Baptism of the Holy Spirit is poured out by the exalted Christ as a gift of His ascension (*Acts 2:33*). Jesus has ascended and been seated in glory as Head of the Church (*Eph. 1:20-23*) and from that position of ascension glory, the Head baptises His Body in the Spirit (*Eph. 1:13-14*). It is in union with the ascended Head that the Church receives this blessed outpouring (*Eph. 1:3, 13-14*). The Church has been 'raised … up together, and made [to] sit together in the heavenly places in Christ Jesus' (*Eph. 2:6*). In Christ's ascension, the Church ascends. Seated in the heavenly realms with Jesus, He pours out His Holy Spirit upon His Church.

The Holy Spirit brings the heavenly places to us. Those who 'have become partakers of the Holy Spirit … have tasted … the powers of the age to come', and have 'tasted the heavenly gift' (*Heb. 6:4-5*). In the heavenly places the Church is blessed with every spiritual blessing in Christ, including the baptism of the Holy Spirit (*Eph. 1:3*). In the age to come, the Church will be filled with all the fullness of the Holy Spirit (*Mt 3:11; Lk 3:16; Gal. 3:13-14; 1 Cor. 15:44*) as she knows the fullness of immersion in the Triune God. But now, through our personal baptism with the Spirit, we have a foretaste of that fullness of the age to come. As Simon Chan puts it, 'Spirit baptism is the personal appropriation of an eschatological reality.'[12]

Eschatologically, the Church is united as one through the eschatological fullness of the baptism of the Holy Spirit, which is the immersion in the love of the Triune God and the ultimate experience of theosis.[13] That blessed unity is already objectively ours now through our union with Christ (*Eph. 1:3*). The present-day experience of baptism in the Holy Spirit brings the experience of that ultimate eschatological reality into the present in a dynamic way. So the baptism in the Holy Spirit brings us a foretaste of heaven on earth: of the age to come in the present age. And this means that the baptism in the Holy Spirit has an ecclesial focus now in this age. The baptism of the Holy Spirit should lead us deeper into 'our

---

[11] Gordon D. Fee, *God's Empowering Presence: The Holy Spirit in the Letters of Paul* (Peabody: Hendrickson, 1994), 178.

[12] Simon Chan, *Pentecostal Ecclesiology*, 96.

[13] See chapters 24 and 26.

communal life or our fellowship with Christ.'[14] So in one Spirit we are all baptised into one Body, for the eschatological fullness of the baptism of the Spirit constitutes us as one Church, and now in this age, all those who trust in Christ, live in the light of that reality in the heavenly places which we will experience in fullness in the age to come.[15]

The Sin of Schism

Because Christ is the Head of one Body, the One Shepherd of the one fold, to divide the Body of Christ or separate oneself from it is no light matter at all. A church split is not only unfortunate, but a serious sin: the sin of *schism*.

Paul was greatly concerned about the emerging divisions in the church in Corinth, and urged the assembly not to rend themselves in schisms. 'Now I plead with you, brethren, by the name of our Lord Jesus Christ, that you all speak the same thing, and that there be no divisions among you, but that you be perfectly joined together in the same mind and in the same judgment' (*1 Cor. 1:10*). The church is to be united, not divided, and this is such a serious matter that Paul addresses them solemnly in the name of the Lord. 'There should be no schism in the body, but ... the members should have the same care for one another' (*1 Cor. 12:25*; see also *3:3; 11:18*).

To the Romans, Paul gives a warning against those who cause schism and divide the Church:

> Now I urge you, brethren, note those who cause divisions and offenses, contrary to the doctrine which you learned, and avoid them. For those who are such do not serve our Lord Jesus Christ, but their own belly, and by smooth and flattering speech deceive the hearts of the simple. (*Rom. 16:17-18*)

Here Paul shows us the connection between schism and heresy. The schisms against which he warns the Romans are 'contrary to the doctrine which [they] learned.' So these divisions are being brought about through false teaching. Not every schism is caused by heresy, but every heresy is a

---

[14] Chan, 'Mother Church', 181.

[15] For a much more detailed look at these issues, see Jonathan Black, 'The Church in the Eternal Purpose of the Triune God: Toward a Pentecostal Trinitarian Ecclesiology of Theosis drawing on the early theology of the Apostolic Church in the United Kingdom' (PhD dissertation, University of Chester, 2016), 6.3.4.3.

schism.[16] Furthermore, those who divide the Body of Christ and rend it in schism, are not servants of Jesus Christ, irrespective of their title or position. Similarly, Jude tells us that those who cause such divisions do not have the Holy Spirit (*Jude 19;* cf. also the sin of Diotrephes in *3 Jr. 9-10*). Believers are to note and avoid these dangerous schismatics, for, whether by heresy or simply by division, they lead people away from Christ.

And it's not only those who cause schisms who are in danger. The writer to the Hebrews also warns Christians not to simply drift off into schism by 'forsaking the assembling of ourselves together, as is the manner of some' (*Heb. 10:25*). When Christians stop meeting with the church, whether through conscious decision or through neglect, they divide themselves from the one body, and so commit the sin of schism.[17]

The ancient church took the sin of schism very seriously indeed. Cyprian of Carthage wrote:

> Whoever dissociates himself from the Church is joined to a counterfeit paramour, he is cut off from the promises of Christ, and neither will he who abandons Christ's Church attain to Christ's rewards. He is a foreigner, he is deconsecrated, and he is an enemy. He cannot have God as his Father who does not have the Church as his Mother.[18]

It's not that church membership or attendance is a work which must be performed to attain salvation; it's that when we cut ourselves off from the church, we cut ourselves off from hearing the promises of Christ proclaimed in His Word and displayed at His Table. When we cut ourselves off from the church, we are withdrawing ourselves from the Head who is one with His Body. As we keep ourselves away from the means of grace in the gathering of the assembly, we are in great danger of falling from grace (it's no accident that *Heb. 10:25* comes just before *Heb. 10:26-31*). Therefore, in

---

[16] This is how the Reformation defended itself against the charge of schism, arguing that it was the Papacy which was in schism, not the Reformation, because it had fallen into heresy, and so 'it behooved us to withdraw from them that we might come to Christ.' John Calvin, *Institutes,* iv.ii.6. (Calvin points to *Jn 16:2*.) Essentially the same argument was used by the early Apostolics for the emergence of their denomination in the aftermath of the Welsh Revival of 1904-1905. E.g. T.N. Turnbull, *What God Hath Wrought,* 15. *Souvenir Exhibiting the Movements of God in the Apostolic Church,* 10; *Minutes of the International Council of Apostles and Prophets of the Apostolic Church, March 1928,* 22.

[17] Some will try to justify their churchless schism by saying they are part of the invisible church, and so not cut off from the Body; however, the Scripture also ties our participation in the one Body to participation in the local assembly. 'For we, though many, are one bread and one body; for we all partake of that one bread' (*1 Cor. 10:17*).

[18] Cyprian of Carthage, *De Unitate,* 6

forsaking the church as our mother, we are running from Christ our great elder Brother, rather than abiding in Him (cf. *Jn 15:6*). And cut off from Christ, we would no longer be sons in the Son, and so no longer have God for our Father.

But this analogy of the church as our mother also works the other way round, as a very positive thing indeed. Calvin speaks of this as a great privilege: 'For those to whom [God] is Father, the church may also be mother.'[19] When we have the church for mother, we are fed, protected, taught, and disciplined by her, to the glory of our heavenly Father.

Schism is never a good thing. Churchlessness is never a good thing. 'It is always disastrous to leave the church.'[20]

> The Lord warns with the words: 'He who is not with me is against me, and he who does not gather with me scatters' (Mt 12:30) … He who ruptures Christ's peace and concord acts against Christ. He who gathers elsewhere than in the Church scatters Christ's Church.[21]

We are not to split ourselves off from the assembly and set up our own meetings instead (that's gathering elsewhere than in the Church), for that is the great sin of schism. And those who cause schisms and divisions are not servants of Christ (*Rom. 16:17-18*).

Concerning the unity of the Body and the evil of trying to divide it, Cyprian has a glorious insight connected with Christ's seamless robe and how the soldiers cast lots for it rather than divide it. His interest isn't in the fulfilment of prophecy in the seamless robe, but instead Cyprian sees the robe itself as prophetic and pointing forward to an immensely important truth for Christians. For Cyprian, this isn't merely a garment for someone to wear; this is the robe of Christ and so just as Christ's actions were significant and teach us, so was His robe. For Christians, you see, are clothed with the robe of Christ. (After all, don't we sing of 'this spotless robe', of our 'beauteous dress', and of being 'clothed with righteousness divine'?) And so it seems that Cyprian reckons that, if we are clothed with Christ's robe, then we can learn something about our clothing from the description of that robe which He wore on earth.

And what do we learn from the description of that robe? That it was seamless and even the soldiers didn't divide it. So here's what Cyprian had to say:

---

19 John Calvin, *Institutes*, iv.i.1
20 John Calvin, *Institutes*, iv.i.4
21 Cyprian of Carthage, *De Unitate*, 6

> When someone would be clothed with Christ, he receives a perfect suit of clothing, and an undamaged tunic. But what comes into his possession is common property... Christ was wearing the unity that proceeds 'from the upper part' (that means 'proceeding from heaven and from the Father'), which could never at all be torn apart by him who receives and possesses it, but rather with it secures for himself something that has a firm integrity. He who rends and splits Christ's Church cannot possess Christ's robe ... So truly because Christ's people cannot be torn apart, his tunic, 'woven without seam,' and holding fast together, has not become divided amongst its owners. The description 'unable to be split (united, linked together),' reveals the concord that holds together the unity of our people who have put on Christ. By the sign and seal of the tunic Christ has declared the unity of his Church.[22]

See what Cyprian's saying. Christ's robe cannot be divided. When we're saved, we're clothed in His robe of righteousness. But there is only one robe – not one for each of us. We all share in the one robe of Christ. And therefore the indivisibility of the robe points to the indivisibility of the Church, for the whole Church is clothed together in this single robe of Christ's righteousness.

Now, Cyprian's not just making stuff up off the top of his head. Already there you can see that his thought is steeped in the biblical language of being clothed with righteousness and salvation (e.g. *Isa. 61:10*). But he also looks back to the Old Testament to see the prophetic significance of the dividing of a garment, when the prophet Ahijah tore his robe in 12 pieces before Jeroboam to signify the division of the kingdom (*1 Kgs 11:29-39*). These might not be the first passages of Scripture our minds would jump to when we read of the soldiers casting lots for Christ's robe so as not to divide it, but they certainly show us that Cyprian's thinking is deeply saturated with Scripture here.

This is glorious, Christ exalting truth, which Cyprian sees in some soldiers casting lots for a robe. And it reminds us that the unity of the Church isn't found in us – it's not something for us to try to create. No, the unity of the Church is found in Christ and His righteousness with which we are all together clothed.

Our unity is found in the righteousness of Christ – which is the work of Christ for us in His sinless life and atoning death. Through His saving work, we are brought together and united in one Body, as one Church. (And so the sin of schism is a sin against the righteousness and saving work of Christ.)

---

[22] Cyprian of Carthage, *De Unitate*, 7

The One Church is Holy

The Church of the Christian faith is not only one, but 'one holy catholic and apostolic Church.'[23] Just as her unity is found through being clothed in Christ for righteousness, so too that royal robe, which is the Head of the Church Himself, is her holiness. Holy mother Church is holy only in the Holy One. Christ prayed on the night of His arrest, not only for the unity of His Church, but for her sanctification:

> Sanctify them by Your truth. Your word is truth. As You sent Me into the world, I also have sent them into the world. And for their sakes I sanctify Myself, that they also may be sanctified by the truth. (*Jn 17:17-19*)

In *Ephesians 5*, we see that the holiness of the Church is included in the reason for which Christ died for her:

> Christ also loved the church and gave Himself for her, that He might sanctify and cleanse her with the washing of water by the word, that He might present her to Himself a glorious church, not having spot or wrinkle or any such thing, but that she should be holy and without blemish. (*Eph. 5:25-27*)

The holiness of the Church flows from the Holy One who offered Himself up on the Cross so she might be holy in Him. The holiness of the Church flows from the cross of Christ.

The Holy God dwells in the Church as His temple. 'Do you not know that you are the temple of God and that the Spirit of God dwells in you? If anyone defiles the temple of God, God will destroy him. For the temple of God is holy, which temple you are' (*1 Cor. 3:16-17*). Through the blood of Jesus, her union with Christ her Head, and the indwelling of the Holy Spirit who is mutually indwelt[24] by the Father and the Son, the Church which is the Body of Christ is a holy temple in the Lord, and a communion of saints.

Sancta Sanctis: Holy Things to the Holy

The holiness of the Church is both expressed and outworked through the holy sacraments. From early in the church's history, and still in many parts

---

[23] *Nicene Creed*
[24] See chapter 5 for discussion of the doctrine of perichoresis.

of the world today, the cry *sancta sanctis* ('holy things to the holy', sometimes paraphrased in English liturgies as 'God's Holy Gifts for God's Holy People') rang out from the Lord's Table as His people gathered to the sacrament. In the Apostolic Church, although those words have probably not often, if ever, been proclaimed aloud from the Table, the same proclamation has been made at the Table in another way. Our tradition was for the words 'Holiness unto the Lord' to be engraved upon the chalice and paten, and embroidered on the table linen and veil. Often these were even carved into the communion table itself, and, in at least a few assemblies, they were painted on an archway over the table.[25] Visibly, through the engraving and embroidering of the words 'Holiness unto the Lord', the Lord's holiness is proclaimed in His gift of the body and blood of Christ in the sacrament. The sacrament is holy, declares the holiness of the Lord, and builds up the Church in holiness. The Breaking of Bread is for sanctification.[26] The sacraments are holy things for holy people: *sancta sancti*.

And these holy things for the holy have been entrusted by the Head to His Church. They are the Church's sacraments; they do not belong to individuals. For someone to be baptised, they need someone else to do the baptising. Therefore baptism can never be an individual act, but is always a sacrament of the Church. The same should be true of the Lord's Supper. It is not an individual, private act of devotion, but the communal event at the very heart of the being of the assembly (*i.e.* the local church). We do not take to ourselves a holiness through an individualist and private imitation of the sacraments, but rather we share in the one holiness, which is the holiness of Christ our Head, as we come together to break bread.

The One Church is Catholic

The one Church is the holy catholic church.[27] The word catholic comes from a Greek expression meaning 'with the whole'. Ignatius of Antioch, writing

---

[25] On Good Friday the assemblies in my Area meet together for the Breaking of Bread, and we use the original chalice of the Bradford assembly, mother church of the Apostolic assemblies in the north of England. And prominently engraved upon it are the words, 'Holiness unto the Lord.' So this practice dates right back to the beginning of the Apostolic Church.

[26] *Minutes of the International Council of Apostles and Prophets of the Apostolic Church, March 1928*, 95.

[27] Catholic is not the name of a denomination. The Reformers and all orthodox protestants throughout the centuries have been happily catholic without being Roman

during the reign of the emperor Trajan (AD 98-117), declared: 'Wherever Jesus Christ is, there is the catholic church.'[28] The wholeness of the church is found only in Christ. It is not something which we can create for ourselves, but must receive it from the Head.

How does catholicity differ from unity? The unity of the Church speaks of the fact that there is only one Church. However, the catholicity of the Church speaks of the fact that this one church encompasses the whole: it encompasses every language, culture, age, and class, not only throughout the world, but throughout history as well. It is a universal church, geographically, socially, and continuously. And a catholic church cannot cut itself off from the whole. A catholic church cannot be limited in its mission field, in its doctrine, or in its worship.[29]

The Church is one, because we are clothed with Christ. And, when we have put on Christ, 'there is neither Jew nor Greek, there is neither slave nor free, there is neither male nor female; for you are all one in Christ Jesus' (*Gal. 3:27-28*). In the one Body of Jesus Christ, 'there is neither Greek nor Jew, circumcised nor uncircumcised, barbarian, Scythian, slave nor free, but Christ is all and in all' (*Col. 3:11*). That is what it means for the one church to be the catholic church.

The church triumphant in heaven (with whom we are united in the one church of Jesus Christ) is a catholic church. There in the heavenly holy of holies, the church sings to her head in praise:

> For You were slain,
> And have redeemed us to God by Your blood
> Our of every tribe and tongue and people and nation,
> And have made us kings and priests to our God. (*Rev. 5:9-10*)

The heavenly multitude whom John saw, were a catholic church:

Catholics. Just as when we say that the one Church is the apostolic church, we are not using the word apostolic as the name of a denomination. The Apostolic Church denomination is not the one true church, but the one true church is apostolic. Likewise, the Roman Catholic Church is not the one true church, but the one true church is catholic.

[28] Ignatius, *Smyrnaeans* 8:2

[29] It is well worth considering the implications of the increasing disposability of the songs we sing, and the noticeable downplaying of public prayer and the sacraments among some charismatics and evangelicals, and asking what this says about the catholicity (or lack thereof) of our worship. If a Christian from 1st century Ephesus, 5th century Alexandria, 16th century Wittenberg, or a 21st century village in the Malawian bush were transported into one of our services, despite the differences in culture, language and style, would they be able to recognise that this was the church of Jesus Christ at worship? (I'm not saying the answer is no; I'm simply saying that this is a question we should regularly ask ourselves.)

> After these things I looked, and behold, a great multitude which no one
> could number, of all nations, tribes, peoples, and tongues, standing before
> the throne and before the Lamb, clothed with white robes, with palm
> branches in their hands, and crying out with a loud voice, saying,
> 'Salvation belongs to our God who sits on the throne, and to the Lamb!'
> (*Rev. 7:9-10*)

The one church of all ages, of every nation, tribe, language and people, are
united as one in their adoration of their one Saviour. And the church
militant on earth, which is united to the church triumphant in heaven, is
also to be such a catholic church of unity in diversity, encompassing the
whole. And this is not just true in a global sense, but in the local assembly as
well. The local assembly is the local manifestation of the one Body of Christ.
Therefore, if the one Body is catholic, its local expression can only be
catholic. The assembly should know no social limits or distinctions, for we
are all one in Christ, bought with the same blood, and united to the same
Head. In the one holy catholic church:

> All national, social, intellectual, and religious barriers are eliminated ...
> Calvary banishes all elements that feed national pride and that foster racial
> distinctions. The Cross embraces all nations, likewise the Body or the
> Church of Christ. The ambassador of Christ knows no boundaries except
> the essential and irreconcilable gulf between life and death, sin and
> holiness, light and darkness, love and hate, and heaven and hell. Here
> alone we believe that the marvellous High Priestly Prayer of our blessed
> Lord, 'that they all may be one' (Jn 17:21) will be ultimately answered and
> will become an accomplished fact.[30]

The doctrine of the church is also to be catholic, encompassing the
whole. 'No prophecy of Scripture is of any private interpretation' (*2 Pet.
1:20*). We do not determine doctrine as individuals, by private
interpretation. Each local church does not simply determine its own local
doctrine.[31] Rather, Christ the Head has given gifts of apostles, prophets,
evangelists, pastors, and teachers to His Body:

> till we all come to the unity of the faith and of the knowledge of the Son of
> God, to a perfect man, to the measure of the stature of the fullness of
> Christ; that we should no longer be children, tossed to and fro and carried
> about with every wind of doctrine, by the trickery of men, in the cunning
> craftiness of deceitful plotting, but, speaking the truth in love, may grow
> up in all things into Him who is the head—Christ. (*Eph. 4:13-15*)

---

[30] W.H. Lewis, *The Body of Christ*, Tenets of the Apostolic Church, Vol. 6.2 (The Apostolic
Church: Penygroes, 1954), 14.

[31] If it did, that would be schism.

For there is 'one faith' (*Eph. 4:5*), which is the faith of the whole church – the church catholic. And the whole church must 'contend earnestly' for this one faith 'which was once for all delivered to the saints' (*Jude 3*). This one faith is the truth of the Triune God revealed in Jesus Christ and proclaimed in His Church in the power of His Spirit. The truth comes from above; it is not discovered from below. And so the Christian faith is not determined by each individual believer, nor by each local assembly or group of assemblies. Rather, the faith is one, and all believers and all assemblies are called to unity in that one faith which is revealed in the Word. The assembly does not determine the truth; the assembly submits herself, honourably and faithfully, to the Truth which the Church proclaims in her preaching.[32]

> Since all Truth is one [for Christ is one], it must be incorporated in One Body, a Body prepared for the Truth which has been predestinated to be [manifested] in that Body of Spirit-baptized believers ... There can be no conflict between Divine truths, in themselves, but only in our imperfect co-operation.[33]

But how does the one church guard this unity of the faith? Vincent of Lérins famously provided the answer back in the 5th century:

> In the catholic church itself, all possible care must be taken, that we hold that faith which has been believed everywhere, always, by all. For that is truly and in the strictest sense 'catholic,' which, as the name itself and the reason of the thing declare, comprehends all universally.[34]

If we find that our teaching goes against that which has been believed everywhere, always, by all, then we are in danger of departing from the catholic faith. This is not to downplay in any way the authority of Scripture. To test our interpretations against that which has been believed everywhere, always, by all, does not mean that we are placing church history, creeds and councils on a higher level of authority than the word of God. Rather, it means we are placing the creeds and councils, the careful dogmatic deliberations of the apostles, prophets, evangelists, pastors and teachers with which the living Christ has graciously gifted His Church in the past, in their submission to the Scriptures, on a higher level of authority than our own individual reasoning. Rather than say, 'I think it means', we say, 'the

---

[32] D.P. Williams, *Riches of Grace*, x.1 (Sept. 1934), 7.

[33] D.P. Williams, *Riches of Grace*, x.1 (Sept. 1934), 7. The unity of the faith has been a very important theme in Apostolic thought. See e.g. W.A.C. Rowe, *One Lord, One Faith*, 298-310.

[34] Vincent of Lérins, *Commonitoria*, 6.2

Christian church has thought long and hard about this, with mu
and searching of the Scriptures, and as a result of that, this
understanding of the Scriptures that has been universally accepted.'

That's what we're doing when we confess a Creed, or subscribe to
confession of faith, or the tenets of a church. But what about the
Reformation or rise of Pentecostalism? Didn't they change doctrine from
what had been believed always, everywhere by all. No, they didn't. At the
time of the Reformation, there was no doctrine held always, everywhere, by
all concerning justification. At the time of the rise of Pentecostalism, there
was no doctrine held always, everywhere, by all concerning the baptism in
the Holy Spirit. Doctrine can be clarified, but settled doctrine which has
been believed always, everywhere, by all should not be rejected. As Martin
Luther, the great Reformer put it:

> A Council has no power to establish new articles of faith, even though the
> Holy Spirit is present ... [However] a Council has the power – and is also
> duty bound to exercise it – to suppress and condemn new articles of faith,
> in accordance with Scripture and the ancient faith.[35]

In the Apostolic Church in the UK, this is reflected in how doctrinal
decisions are made, and what doctrinal decisions can be made. The Tenets
of the Apostolic Church are our settled doctrine, believed and accepted by
all Apostolics, and so 'these Tenets shall forever be the doctrinal standard of
The Apostolic Church and shall not be subject to change in any way
whatsoever.'[36] Yet, within the scope of the tenets, decisions may be made by
the apostles in Council which clarify (rather than depart from) the church's
doctrine.[37] However, to maintain the catholicity of the church, 'no change in
connection with doctrinal matters shall be made without consultation with
every Apostles' Council throughout the world.'[38] Thus, at least within this
one Pentecostal denomination and the world-wide fellowship of which we
are a part, we strive to uphold something of the catholicity of the church's
faith.

---

[35] Martin Luther, 'On the Councils and the Church (1539)', *Luther's Works*, 41:123.
[36] *Constitution of the Apostolic Church*, 2.
[37] *Constitution of the Apostolic Church*, 7.4.2.3
[38] *Minutes of the Annual General Council of the Apostolic Church, 1951*, 23.a.iii.A.

ırch is apostolic. Right from the initial outpouring ...upon the Church on the Day of Pentecost, she has ...ued steadfastly in the apostles' doctrine and fellowship' (*Acts 2:42*). And continuing in both the doctrine of the apostles and the fellowship of the apostles, the one Church is apostolic.[39] Jesus Christ, the Head of the Church, is 'the apostle ... of our confession' (*Heb. 3:1*). Whoever receives His apostles, receives Christ the Chief Apostle (*Mt 10:40; Jn 13:20*). The Church is 'built on the foundation of the apostles and prophets, Jesus Christ Himself being the chief cornerstone' (*Eph. 2:20*). And so the Body of Christ continues steadfastly in fellowship with the apostles whom He has gifted to His Church.

In fellowship with the apostles, the Church continues at the same time in the apostles' doctrine. In the Bible, fellowship and doctrine cannot be separated. We have fellowship with one another as the Church because 'our fellowship is with the Father and with His Son Jesus Christ' (*1 Jn 1:3*), yet that fellowship depends on doctrine; for to have fellowship with the Father and the Son, we must know the Father and the Son (*Jn 17:3; cf. Rom. 6:17; 1 Tim. 6:1; 2 Jn 9*). The unity and fellowship of the Church rests upon the true doctrine of the God of our salvation. This is the doctrine preached and taught by the first apostles, and which the true apostles of Jesus Christ continue to proclaim and guard today. And so the true church of Jesus Christ continues steadfastly in the apostles' fellowship only when also continuing steadfastly in the apostles' doctrine.

Recognising a True Church

In a world where anyone can put a sign above the door saying 'church', how do we recognise a true one? During the Reformation, this was a question that had to be faced by the Protestant Reformers. John Calvin concluded:

---

[39] Some ecclesial traditions (such as the Anglicans, Eastern Orthodox, and Roman Catholics) prefer to emphasise a continuity in the apostles' fellowship (through their bishops, whom they see as successors to the apostles), while other ecclesial traditions (free-church traditions) prefer to emphasise a continuity with the apostles' doctrine. The Apostolic Church finds her apostolicity in both.

> From this the face of the church comes forth and becomes visible to ou.
> eyes. Wherever we see the Word of God purely preached and heard, and
> the sacraments administered according to Christ's institution, there, it is
> not to be doubted, a church of God exists. For his promise cannot fail:
> 'Wherever two or three are gathered in my name, there I am in the midst of
> them … If it has the ministry of the Word and honours it, if it has the
> administration of the sacraments, it deserves without doubt to be held and
> considered a church. For it is certain that such things are not without
> fruit.[40]

Similarly, the Lutherans confessed that the church 'is the assembly of all believers among whom the Gospel is preached in its purity and the holy sacraments are administered according to the Gospel.'[41] Standing in the heritage of the Protestant Reformation, the Apostolic Church is in full agreement.

However, the Apostolics also point to another necessity in the visible church, in service to the Word and sacraments: the ordained ministry.[42] One Apostolic catechism asks: 'How is the Church on earth known?' The answer points to *Acts 2:42*: 'And they continued steadfastly in the apostles' doctrine and fellowship, in the breaking of bread, and in prayers.'[43] By continuing steadfastly in the apostles' doctrine, the church holds fast to the preaching of the pure gospel Word. By continuing steadfastly in the Breaking of Bread, the church holds fast to the true sacraments.[44] By continuing steadfastly in prayer, the church holds fast to faith in the One proclaimed in the Word and sacraments. But to continue steadfastly in the apostles' fellowship shows the church's need of the ordained ministry.

The visible church should be made up of those who are in communion (*fellowship*) with the apostles. Apostleship is 'a foundational office in the church'[45] and thus a necessary office: 'The Headship of the glorified Christ *must* find expression among the members of His Body, and Apostleship

---

[40] Calvin, *Institutes*, iv.i.9

[41] *Augsburg Confession*, 7

[42] In this, the Apostolics are in accord with the great majority of the church throughout history. Cf. Article 19 of the *39 Articles of Religion* of the Church of England which echoes the definitions of Calvin and the Lutherans, but also notes the need for 'all those things that of necessity are requisite to the same', thus including the necessity of the ordained ministry in the basic definition of the church by word and sacrament.

[43] *Asked and Answered: A Catechism of Apostolic Principles* (Bradford: Puritan Press, 1953), p.24, Q.6.

[44] NB Baptism precedes the Lord's Supper, therefore to continue in the latter implies the former as well.

[45] *Fundamentals*, 25; cf. *Eph. 2:20*.

'*ogy*

. authority, dignity and humility.'[46] If the Church
.iowship, then the apostleship itself is a necessity, for
_ missionary to China pointed out, 'the Apostleship is
.nsable to the Body's perfecting, without which the Body
.d incomplete.'[47] E.H. Williams notes that apostles (and
.ld a *vital* place in the Body of Christ'[48], and W.H. Lewis
.hat they (along with the other four Ascension ministries) are
.ly essential' and, without them, 'the Church will never be able fully
.resent her exalted Head.'[49] In fact, Lewis goes so far as to argue that,
. cannot explain away the necessity of the gifts and ministries and offices
.f the New Testament, and yet still claim with any Biblical authority to be
the Body of Christ.'[50] In the Apostolic Church's earliest confessional
document, D.P. Williams writes:

> We believe that the assembly of people is not a true church according to
> the New Testament depiction unless it has chosen ones, who are elect[51] to
> serve and minister the Word, as shepherds and elders to care for the flock
> … One of the first things the apostles did in establishing the early church
> was to set it in the care of such ministers, that there might be order and
> unity.[52]

Eighteen centuries earlier, Ignatius had made the point much more forcibly:
'apart from [the ordained ministry] no group can be called a church.'[53]

But, remember the catechism question we started with: 'How is the
Church on earth known?' Not what is the church, but how do we recognise
it? The answer from *Acts 2:42* of fellowship with the apostles (as well as
word and sacrament) is a tool which aids us in the discernment of the true
church. So, this doesn't un-church all those gospel preaching churches who
trust in the Word and rightly administer the sacraments, but belong to
communions which do not recognise apostles. The true church may be
present, but not yet fully seen.[54]

---

[46] *Fundamentals*, 25 (emphasis mine).

[47] C.C. Ireson, *Riches of Grace*, 12.1 (January 1959), 22.

[48] E.H. Williams, *Riches of Grace*, 12.7 (July 1959), 215. Emphasis mine.

[49] W.H. Lewis, *Riches of Grace*, 12.7 (July 1959), 222.

[50] W.H. Lewis, *Riches of Grace*, 12.7 (July 1959), 222.

[51] Elect of God, not elected by the assembly.

[52] *Athrawiaethau Sylfeinol*, ix.

[53] Ignatius, *Trallians*, 3:1. We'll look more at the Apostolic understanding of the ordained ministry in chapters 36-37.

[54] In theological language, the apostleship is of the *plene esse* (or fullness of being) of the church.

The Headship of Christ

The Father gave Christ 'to be head over all things to the church, which is His body, the fullness of Him who fills all in all' (*Eph. 1:22-23*). Not only is the Church the Body of Christ, but also Christ is the Head of the Church. The Scriptures tell us again in *Ephesians 5:23* that 'Christ is head of the church' and in *Colossians 1:18* that 'He is the head of the body, the church'. Christ's Headship of the Church is an important biblical truth which Paul heavily underscores in his epistles to the Ephesians and Colossians.

In New Testament Greek the word *head* (κεφαλή, *kephalē*) carries not only the meaning of the physical body part, but also the meaning of *authority over*. Therefore Christ's Headship of the Church points to His authority over the Church. As the Head of the Church, Christ is the supreme authority in the Church and it is His role to control and direct His Body. This means that Christ should also have the pre-eminence in His Church. It is God the Father who has given Christ to the Church as Head (*Eph. 1:22-23*). Thus Christ's Headship is a gift from God to the Church.

Greek writers in New Testament times considered the head to be both the ruling part of the body and also its supply centre.[55] The Bible teaches that this is indeed the case with the Church; the Body of Christ is both ruled over by her heavenly Head and is supplied by Him with life and power. Paul writes that Christ supplies the Church with gifts of men, in order that the Church:

> may grow up in all things into Him who is the head – Christ – from whom the whole body, joined and knit together by what every joint supplies, according to the effective working by which every part does its share, causes growth of the body for the edifying of itself in love. (*Eph. 4:15-16*)

It is Christ the Head who supplies His Body with all that it needs, that it might be built up and edified.

---

[55] I note this as there has been some controversy over the meaning of the word κεφαλή in recent years. Although it can carry the meaning of supply centre of the body, this meaning is always linked to that of the authority of the head over the body. We cannot simply chose the subordinate meaning regarding supplying the body and ignore the primary meaning of *authority over*. This discussion is of particular importance with regard to gender roles.

Christ equips and supplies His Body through the Holy Spirit. In the words of contemporary Pentecostal theologian, Frank Macchia, 'in Christ, the Spirit-baptized church draws from his fullness as his body, drinking together from the Spirit in him.'[56] As *1 Corinthians 12:13* teaches, 'by one Spirit we were all baptized into one body – whether Jews or Greeks, whether slaves or free – and have all been made to drink into one Spirit.' Not only does the Holy Spirit incorporate us into the Body of Christ, but also, as members of that Body, we drink into Him, and thus receive from Him the supply and nourishment that comes from Christ our Head. As W.H. Lewis notes, Christ 'is the life of the members. From the living Head life streams through the Body.'[57]

The Church, then, is built up as the ministers and members give expression to this life of Christ in the Body. As we have read in *Ephesians 4:15-16*, the Body is built up by what every member supplies and when every member 'does its share'. However, those same verses also teach that what every member does should find its source in Christ the Head. Ultimately it is He who builds up and edifies the Body through the ministers and members.[58] After all, Christ did promise that He Himself would build His Church (*Mt 16:18*).

The Totus Christus: The Vision Glorious

Christ's Headship of the Church also means that, not only is there a unity within the Body of Christ, but there is also a unity between the Church and her heavenly Head. When Christ appeared to Saul on the road to Damascus, He asked, 'why are you persecuting me?' (*Acts 9:4*), not 'why are you persecuting the church?' He revealed His identity by saying, 'I am Jesus, whom you are persecuting' (*Acts 9:5*). At this time Christ had already ascended to heaven, so Saul could not physically persecute Him. Rather, Saul was persecuting the members of Christ's Body. Yet Christ considered the persecution of the members of His Body to be persecution of Himself. There is such a unity between Christ the Head and His Body that to persecute the Church is to persecute Christ. Some years later, Paul would

---

[56] Frank D. Macchia, *Baptized in the Spirit: A Global Pentecostal Theology* (Grand Rapids: Zondervan, 2006), 203.

[57] W.H. Lewis, *The Body of Christ* (Bradford: Puritan Press, 1954), 17.

[58] We will discuss the expression of Christ's Headship through the ministers He has given to the Church in chapter 36.

write, 'For as the body is one and has many members, but all the members of that one body, being many, are one body, so also is Christ' (*1 Cor. 12:12*). Notice carefully what Paul does here: he calls the one body made up of many members Christ. The Body and the Head together are called Christ. There is such a oneness between Christ the Head and the Church which is His Body that the Body and Head together are the *totus Christus*.[59]

The life of the church is not her own, but the life of her Risen Head: the resurrection life of Christ which flows from the Head to the body. It's for this reason that the church is Christ's Body: not merely because the Body belongs to him, but because the life of the Body is Christ's own resurrection life. And so the Body can even be called 'Christ' (*1 Cor. 12:12*), because 'He is one with the members.'[60]

This unity between Christ the Head and the Church which is His Body, stands at the heart of what the early Apostolics called 'the Apostolic vision', or 'the vision glorious'. D.P. Williams called this the 'comprehensive vision' which 'absorbed' the apostle Paul:

> Redemption to him was a principle of reconciliation of things in Heaven and things in earth, a 'gathering' of all things together in Christ Jesus, under one Central Head, in one harmonious whole, (*Eph. 1:10; Col.1*), of which the organism of the Church is only the commencement, to compare with the consummation of redemption ... their crowning end in a glorious state whereby Christ in and through His redemptive excellences will express Himself through an infinite variety in Heaven and earth.[61]

Therefore, the Church can never rightly be considered in isolation from Christ her Head in whom she partakes in the Totus Christus.

> The Great Mystery, therefore, consists in two parts: Christ and the Church, the Head and the Body ... these are two parts of the eternal plan of God, the two members of the mystical Christ. These two are one: a New Man.[62]

This glorious vision of Christ and His Church is at the heart of the eternal purpose, the centrepiece of Apostolic theology. In the *totus Christus* –

---

[59] Theologians have taken this Latin expression from the writings of Augustine: *Totus Christus caput et membra* ('the whole Christ, Head and members'); earlier Apostolics often referred to this as *the Christ mystical*, in continuity with the way the Puritans in Britain (e.g. Richard Sibbes) spoke of the Totus Christus.

[60] D.P. Williams, *Riches of Grace*, xiii.5 (May 1938), 393.

[61] D.P. Williams, *Riches of Grace*, xv.8 (Sept. 1940), 98; See also, Williams, *Trinity*, 2:53-54.

[62] W.R. Thomas, *On Ephesians*, 161.

as one Body *in* Christ – the Church exists within the love of the Father for His Son.

> The Paternity of God to His Son, in the mystery of the Holy Trinity and of the Incarnation, really and effectively reaches us – the members of His Body … by grace we have become partakers of the Divine Nature, and constituted a new creation in Christ … It is the Holy Spirit that presents to us the reality of the Fatherhood or Paternity of God; 'in Jesus' we see the Father (John 14:9), and 'by' the Spirit we embrace the Father.[63]

So it is as the Body of Christ, united to her Head as one – the *totus Christus* – that we partake of theosis as a Body of sons in the Son, with Christ's Father as our Father.[64]

The fullness of Him who fills all in all

The Body, to which Christ is united as Head, is 'the fullness of Him who fills all in all' (*Eph. 1:23*). So, not only is the Church united to Christ, but the Church is also filled by Christ.[65] The first generation Apostolic apostle, Thomas Rees, points out:

> In Christ dwelleth the fulness of the Godhead bodily [Col. 2:9]. Likewise in the Body of Christ dwelleth His fulness. Christ is the express image of God; so the Body of Christ is, in some degree, bearing His own image.[66]

It is through being filled with the Holy Spirit that the fullness of God in Christ fills the Church which is His Body, as the Father, Son and Holy Spirit mutually indwell one another in perichoresis (*cf. Jn 14:16-23*). As Christ fills us with the Spirit, He fills us with Himself, and in the fullness of the Son by the Spirit, the Father comes and fills the Church (*Eph. 2:21-22; 1 Cor. 3:17*). So the Church is filled with the fullness of the Triune God.

> While the Father is the source and centre of all fullness, the Son is the sum and substance of all fullness, the Church is the sphere and recipient of all fullness, the Holy Spirit is the One dispensing all the fullness.[67]

---

[63] W.R. Thomas, *On Ephesians*, 214-215.

[64] We'll come back to this Eternal Purpose in chapter 30.

[65] For detailed exegetical discussion of this verse see Harold W. Hoehner, *Ephesians: An Exegetical Commentary* (Grand Rapids: Baker, 2002), 296-301.

[66] Thomas Rees, *The Divine Masterpiece: Bible Readings upon 'The Church which is His Body'* (Penygroes: Apostolic Publications, 1943), 10.

This fullness in the Church means the theosis of the Church. The Church participates in the divine nature by participating in the life of loving fellowship of the Trinity into whom she is immersed in all the fullness of Christ. This fullness is the goal of Christ's death, resurrection and ascension (*Eph. 4:10*) and the goal of the growth of the Church (*Eph. 4:13*).

From Genesis to Revelation: The Temple and the Bride

The Church is the Temple of the Holy Spirit

The Church is the Temple of the Holy Spirit. 'Do you not know that you are the temple of God and that the Spirit of God dwells in you?' (*1 Cor. 3:16*).[68] This Temple is built from 'living stones' – the members of the Church – who are 'a holy priesthood, to offer up spiritual sacrifices acceptable to God through Jesus Christ' (*1 Pet. 2:5*). And so this temple is both the house built by God (*Heb. 3:3-6*), as Christ builds His Church (*Mt 16:18*), and the house indwelt by God, as Christ pours out His Spirit.

> Now, therefore, you are no longer strangers and foreigners, but fellow citizens with the saints and members of the household of God, having been built on the foundation of the apostles and prophets, Jesus Christ Himself being the chief cornerstone, in whom the whole building, being fitted together, grows into a holy temple in the Lord, in whom you also are being built together for a dwelling place of God in the Spirit. (*Eph. 2:19-22*)

Seeing the Church as the Temple of the Holy Spirit isn't an alternative to the truth that the Church is the Body of Christ. The context in *Ephesians 2* shows us that this Temple is brought about through Christ's cross (*Eph. 2:13*) and Christ's pouring out of the Holy Spirit (*Eph. 2:18*). The Church is built by Christ, into Christ, and filled by Christ with His Spirit, so that it is a dwelling place for the true and living God.

---

[67] W.R. Thomas, *On Ephesians*, 138. Notice how this is tied to the monarchy of the Father and the Trinitarian *taxis*. (For more on those doctrines see above, chapters 3 and 5.)

[68] 'You' is plural in this verse, referring to the Church.

The Church is God's Temple. Yet Christ Himself is God's Temple (*Jn* 2:18-22). Therefore, it is only in Christ and filled with Christ that His Body, the Church, is the Temple. It is only as the Totus Christus that the Church is the true dwelling place of God. The Body cannot be separated from her Head. It is only abiding in Christ that God dwells in the Church by His Spirit.

Yet, this Temple is the goal of creation. The Garden of Eden was a Garden Temple – the dwelling place of God with man. Adam was created by the eternal Son and Word of the Father stooping down to the dust to form the man and breath into Him the Holy Spirit (*Gen. 2:7*).[69] He was created in the image of God, filled with the Spirit of God, to walk in the Garden Temple in communion with the Son of God (*Gen. 3:8*). The Triune God's purpose for humanity is seen in the way Adam was created: to dwell in the presence of the Lord, in His holy temple.

And at the end of the story we see another temple. The New Jerusalem descends from heaven: a city with no temple, for 'the Lord God Almighty and the Lamb are its temple' (*Rev. 21:22*). This city is a perfect cube in which dwells the Triune God, shining in the light of His glory; the whole city is a Holy of Holies. But it is a Holy of Holies in which the Church dwells, in and with the Triune God. History is moving from a temple to a temple: from Eden to the New Jerusalem.

Already now we experience a foretaste of that glorious future in the outpouring of the Spirit in the Church. For already, the Church is 'a holy temple in the Lord' and 'a dwelling place of God in the Spirit.' Yet one day we will know this presence and loving fellowship of the Triune God in all fullness.

The Church is the Bride of Christ

Back in the Garden of Eden, the Lord God made a bride for the first Adam. Eve was taken out of Adam's wounded side while he slept a deep, death-like sleep (*Gen. 2:21-22*). This wound in Adam's side was pierced with a death-like wound to give life to his bride.

The Second Adam also has a Bride, and her life too comes from her Bridegroom's wounded side. While the first Adam slept a death-like sleep, the Second Adam slept the sleep of death for His Bride. For, through Christ's death and resurrection – from His pierced side – Christ's Bride, the

---

[69] See the discussion of this in chapter 7.

Church, is given life. The bride taken out of the man's wounded side in his death-like sleep was the pinnacle of creation (*Gen. 2:23-24*). And this movement towards the bride in the creation week points us to God's goal for the whole of creation. Just as the sixth day culminated with a bride taken out of the first man's side, so too the goal of all creation is for a Bride to be brought out of the side of the Last Man, the Second Adam, the Lord Jesus.

In Revelation, the New Jerusalem (which is the Church) is 'the Bride, the Lamb's wife' (*Rev. 21:9*). There we see the 'consummation of the Divine Union.'[70] Marriage points us to the 'great mystery … concerning Christ and the Church' (*Eph. 5:32*). The Church on earth now is destined for 'the marriage Supper of the Lamb' (*Rev. 19:9*), where she will eat and drink in the presence of God in an even fuller way than Moses, Aaron, Nadab, Abihu, and the seventy elders of Israel (*Ex 24:9-11*). In the words of one Apostolic hymn-writer, the Bride of the Lamb will experience 'heaven one long Eucharist.'[71] And so, the image of the Church as the Bride of Christ points us to the reality of the union and intimate loving fellowship between Christ and His Church. As D.P. Williams put it, the Church is 'the Bride in the sense that Christ, the Bridegroom, holds affectionate relationship with the redeemed as the object of His love.'[72]

As His Bride, 'Christ also loved the church and gave Himself for her' (*Eph. 5:25*). Thomas Rees was moved to wonder at these words of the apostle Paul:

> In these … words there are depths that are fathomless, heights that are measureless, and riches that are unsearchable and boundless. Can human reason and logic solve this mystery divine? Why should Christ seek a Church, a Bride from fallen humanity to share His wealth, His riches, His inheritance, and His glory? There is no human philosophy that can unravel this glorious and soul-stirring divine revelation.[73]

This great exchange and marriage union is for believers together as one Body in Christ: the Church. And as the Church is brought into this deep and intimate communion with Christ, her Head and heavenly Bridegroom, we see once again this theme of the theosis of the Church. 'The Bridegroom King and His chosen Bride [are] joined together in an indissoluble union of

---

[70] Thomas Rees, *The Divine Masterpiece*, 62.

[71] Ian Macpherson, *Hymns at the Holy Table*, 52.

[72] *Minutes of the International Council of Apostles and Prophets of the Apostolic Church, March 1928*, 153.

[73] Thomas Rees, *The Divine Masterpiece*, 52.

love.'[74] Sharing in the love of her Bridegroom, she shares in the love between the Father and the Son (*Jn 15:9; 16:27; 17:23, 26*). 'It was [the Son's] love that bought her; His love sought her; and His love brought her to His side. He has infused her with His love. His glory is her glory; and her glory is His glory – the glory of love.'[75]

Why is the Church So Important?

The incarnate Son and Word of the Father 'loved the church and gave Himself for her' (*Eph. 5:25*), purchasing her 'with His own blood' (*Acts 20:28*). Therefore, 'there is nothing higher nor nearer the Heart of our Glorified Lord than His Church.'[76] The Church is the object of Christ's love and for which He died.

Yet why did Christ die for the Church? Clearly it was not because of any merit in the Church, for that would render superfluous God's grace in the Cross. Moreover, the Bible teaches that Christ 'loved the church and gave Himself for her, that He might sanctify and cleanse her with the washing of water by the word' (*Eph. 5:25-26*). That the Church needs to be sanctified and cleansed demonstrates that she did not deserve or merit Christ's love. Rather, the Lord Jesus came in grace and died for her in order to save and sanctify her. Christ died for the Church because of her sin, not her merit.

So, if the importance of the Church does not lie in her own merit, why is she so important? The Bible answers this question by showing that the Church is involved in God's *eternal purpose*. 'The manifold wisdom of God [is] made known by the church to the principalities and powers in the heavenly places, according to the eternal purpose which He accomplished in Christ Jesus our Lord' (*Eph. 3:10-11*). The centre of God's eternal purpose is in Christ, yet the Church is also involved. The fact that this is an *eternal* purpose shows us that the Church does not just exist temporarily; the Church will continue to exist after Christ's return. The same chapter of

---

[74] Thomas Rees, *The Divine Masterpiece*, 54.

[75] Thomas Rees, *The Divine Masterpiece*, 60.

[76] D.P. Williams, in the Foreword to Thomas Rees, *The Divine Masterpiece*, 2.

Ephesians ends: 'Unto him be glory in the church by Christ Jesus throughout all ages, world without end. Amen.' (*Eph. 3:21* AV). The Church is to continue to bring glory to Christ throughout all eternity. This is indeed a high calling.

How does the Church bring glory to God? The Bible tells us that the Church brings glory to God as the expression of His grace. Christ saved us and 'raised us up together, and made us sit together in the heavenly places in Christ Jesus, that in the ages to come He might show the exceeding riches of His grace in His kindness toward us in Christ Jesus' (*Eph. 2:6-7*). The Church will show God's grace, not only now on earth, but also 'in the ages to come.' For all eternity God's grace will be seen in the Church and thus God will be glorified in the Church through Christ Jesus. This is the eternal destiny of the Church according to God's eternal purpose, which He purposed in Christ.

This place of the Church in God's eternal purpose demonstrates her importance. So 'it is the Church which gives the real reason and purpose of [Christ's] Incarnation and Atonement.'[77] The salvation of individuals is a means to an end: that end being our building up together into one Body in Christ, united to Him and filled with His fullness: His Church. We are saved in order to be part of the Body of Christ. The idea of an individual Christian who keeps apart from the Church is not at all biblical (*NB Heb. 10:25*). In Scripture we find Christians together in assemblies, the local expressions of the Body of Christ.

---

[77] D.P. Williams, *The Trinity*, 2:36.

Chapter 30

The Eternal Purpose of the Triune God

The Father has 'an Eternal Purpose of all things in His Son and for His Son.'[1] And the Church, which is the Body of Christ, exists for this eternal purpose of the Triune God. 'The manifold wisdom of God [is] made known by the church to the principalities and powers in the heavenly places, according to the eternal purpose which He accomplished in Christ Jesus our Lord' (*Eph. 3:10-11*). The centre of the Father's eternal purpose is in His Son, the Lord Jesus Christ. 'All the purposes of God are bound up in His Son.'[2] Yet the Father has chosen the Church in Christ and united her to Him, so that the Church is one Body with the Incarnate Son as the *Totus Christus* (*Rom. 12:5; 1 Cor. 12:12*). Therefore the eternal purpose of the Triune God for the Son is also an eternal purpose for the Church. Christ and His Body are so intimately linked that 'the Church is called the Eternal Purpose of God (*Eph. 1:22-23; 3:1-6*).'[3]

This eternal purpose is the heart of Apostolic theology and the 'most distinctive feature of Apostolic faith and purpose.'[4] As W.A.C. Rowe explains:

> The Apostolic Church is a Messenger Church. It was specially called into being to bear a message. That message is the Eternal Purpose of God (Ephesians 3:11). Some people think erroneously that our main objective is to declare that there are Apostles and Prophets for today. That is not the Apostolic Vision: that is incidental, though important … The Eternal Purpose is the goal.[5]

The Eternal Purpose is 'the heavenly vision'[6] which stands at the centre of Apostolic thought: the Apostolic Vision, or 'the vision glorious'.

---

[1] D.P. Williams, *All Sovereignty is His*, 73.

[2] D.P. Williams, 'The Ministry of the Word', *The Enduring Word: Incarnate, Written, Spoken* (Penygroes: Apostolic Publications, 1944), 178.

[3] Jacob Purnell, *Riches of Grace*, v.5 (May 1930), 209.

[4] W.A.C. Rowe, *One Lord, One Faith*, 81.

[5] W.A.C. Rowe, *One Lord, One Faith*, 81.

[6] Welsh: '*Weledigaeth Nefol*': D.P. Williams, *Athrawiaethau Sylfeinol*, 4.

All Things Gathered Under Christ as Head

The Eternal Purpose of the Triune God is for all things to be gathered together under Christ as Head (*Eph. 1:7-12*). This includes 'all things … both which are on heaven and which are on earth' (*Eph. 1:10*). Ultimately this purpose includes both the redeemed, resurrected believers and the holy angels. Ultimately this purpose includes both the new heaven and the new earth. This is the radical redemption and renewal of creation, 'because the creation itself also will be delivered from the bondage of corruption into the glorious liberty of the children of God' (*Rom. 8:21*). Under Christ's eternal Headship, all the effects of sin and the curse will be undone, and the heavens and the earth will finally become what they were created to be.

God's Eternal Purpose is not a plan to save our souls out of the world. Nor is it a plan to give us the things of this fallen world. Rather, the Eternal Purpose of the Triune God is a plan to redeem and renew the whole of creation in Christ as Head (*Eph. 1:10*). All things will be gathered together 'in Christ' under Christ as Head.

But when will this be? 'In the dispensation of the fullness of times' (*Eph. 1:10*). Our temptation may be not to think too much about these verses because they sound like they're just talking about something very far away in eternity future. However, 'the fullness of times' is not quite as far away as we might assume. To the Galatians, Paul writes that, 'when the fullness of the time had come, God sent forth His Son, born of a woman, born under the law, to redeem those who were under the law, that we might receive the adoption as sons' (*Gal. 4:4-5*). The fullness of time has already begun in the incarnation of Christ. Those who live between Christ's ascension and His return are those 'upon whom the fulfilment of the ages has come' (*1 Cor. 10:11*). Therefore, God is already putting His eternal purpose into effect now (*Eph. 3:10*). When we become Christians, the Holy Spirit unites us to Christ. And the Holy Spirit also unites us to One another in One Body in Christ, and unites us to Christ as Head of the One Body. So, this gathering together under Christ as Head has already begun. We don't yet see the final result (and we won't see it until after Christ's return). But we already see the beginnings.

So why does the Triune God include us in His Eternal Purpose? The reason is because of 'His good pleasure' (*Eph. 1:9*). His purpose does not depend on us. It is not rooted in how good we are, or how bad we are. God was not waiting around to see how we would turn out before coming up with a plan for us. Rather, the Triune God had included us in His eternal purpose even 'before the foundation of the world' (*Eph. 1:4*). Before we could ever have managed to do anything good or anything bad, the Father chose us in Christ (*Eph. 1:4*). Therefore our inclusion in God's eternal purpose does not depend on our efforts, our works, our abilities, or our goodness. The plan of God rests solely on 'His good pleasure.'

And so He includes us because He wants to. He is not obligated to choose us because of anything in us or anything we've done. Ephesians is very clear about this: we were 'dead in trespasses and sins' (*Eph. 2:1*), 'sons of disobedience' (*Eph. 2:2*), and 'children of wrath' (*Eph. 2:3*). There wasn't something brilliant about us that made God have to include us in His plan. 'But God, who is rich in mercy, because of His great love with which He loved us, even when we were dead in trespasses, made us alive together with Christ (by grace you have been saved)' (*Eph. 2:4-5*). God saves us and includes us in His plan because of His great love for us and His magnificent grace. That is His good pleasure: His love and His grace.

Our place in the eternal purpose of the Triune God comes through 'the riches of His grace' (*Eph. 1:7*). And God has made this grace 'abound toward us' (*Eph. 1:8*). Here we must be careful not to accidentally end up thinking of God's grace as a substance of which He gives us lots. As we have seen, grace is Christ and Him crucified.[7] So here we read of God in His great love reaching out to us in Christ. This is overflowing grace: God overflowing in love towards us in Christ (*cf. Eph. 2:7; 1:3*).

The Triune God is a fountain of overflowing love. From all eternity the Father has been overflowing with love for His Son in the Spirit. And His great love is so boundless that He does not want it to remain only among the Father, Son and Holy Spirit. Rather, He overflows in love toward us. That is the reason for the creation of the world and for our salvation: that we would be caught up in His overflowing love in Christ by the Spirit. The first chapter of *Ephesians* gives us a wonderful expression of Triune love, as the Father, Son and Holy Spirit together lavish upon us the grace that is Jesus Christ given for us. God's eternal purpose for the church in Christ is the outward expression of the loving essence of the Triune God.

And this overflowing love of the Triune God toward us in Christ finds its focus at the cross. The love of God is not vague niceness, but rather is found in 'redemption through His blood' (*Eph. 1:7*). The third chapter of

---

[7] See chapter 22.

Ephesians tells us that this eternal purpose has been 'accomplished in Christ Jesus our Lord' (*Eph. 3:11*). How did Christ accomplish the eternal purpose of God? Through His incarnation and atonement. The eternal purpose has been accomplished through the incarnate God dying on the cross: through one of the Trinity suffering in the flesh.

So, what is this eternal purpose accomplished through Christ's incarnation and atonement? Through His cross, resurrection, and ascension, the Lord Jesus Christ, the Incarnate Word and Son of the Father, has been highly exalted and given as Head over all things to the Church, which is His Body (*Eph. 1:20-23*). The Body is united to the Head in the closest possible way, so that together they are one: the *Totus Christus*.[8] And Christ the Head fills His Body with all His fullness, and through His Body, He will fill all things (*Eph. 4:7-10; Eph. 1:7-12*). The eternal purpose of the Triune God is the theosis of the Body of Christ; that we might eternally dwell in our glorious and highly exalted Saviour and Head, and He in us, and so through this union with the Head, the Body partakes of the divine nature, sharing in the loving communion between the Father, Son and Holy Spirit.

Three Things Before the Foundation of the World

The Eternal Purpose of the Triune God looks forward to eternity future, when all things will be gathered together under Christ's Headship (*Eph. 1:10*) and the Church will know 'the exceeding riches of His grace in His kindness toward us in Christ Jesus' (*Eph. 2:7*). Yet, this Eternal Purpose also stretches back to eternity past.

The Father's Eternal Love for His Son

The Scriptures speak of three things 'before the foundation of the world.'[9] The first of these is found in Jesus' High-Priestly prayer on the night of His

---

[8] See chapter 29.

[9] These three things before the foundation of the world have been a major theme of Apostolic theology from its earliest days. They feature prominently in the writings of all the

betrayal. There the Lord Jesus, the eternal Word and Son of the Father, gives us a glimpse of the relationship He has shared with His Father from before the foundation of the world. That night, Jesus prayed, 'O Father, glorify Me together with Yourself, with the glory which I had with You before the world was' (*Jn 17:5*). Later in the same prayer, He speaks of the eternal love of the Father for the Son: 'You have loved me … You loved me before the foundation of the world' (*Jn 17:23-24*). Before the foundation of the world, the Father loved His Son in the joy of the Holy Spirit, and this perfect loving fellowship was the glory of the Triune God from all eternity.

The Foreordination of the Son as the Atoning Lamb of God

However, the Father, Son and Holy Spirit did not keep their love to themselves, but instead chose to share the goodness of their love through the Son.

> Knowing that you were not redeemed with corruptible things, like silver or gold, from your aimless conduct received by tradition from your fathers, but with the precious blood of Christ, as of a lamb without blemish and without spot. He indeed was foreordained before the foundation of the world, but was manifest in these last times for you who through Him believe in God, who raised Him from the dead and gave Him glory, so that your faith and hope are in God. (*1 Pet. 1:18-21*)

The Son was foreordained as the atoning Lamb before the foundation of the world. Therefore, Christ's incarnation and atoning work have been planned for all eternity. The Father foreordained the Son as the Lamb, sanctifying Him (setting Him apart) and sending Him into the world (*Jn 10:36*). This is God's 'own purpose and grace which was given to us in Christ Jesus before time began' (*2 Tim. 1:9*).

Thus, from all eternity, the Father has set apart His Son as the atoning Lamb, in order to send Him into the world by becoming incarnate for us and for our salvation. This foreordination of the Son stands at the heart of the internal work of the Triune God (*opera ad intra*) which governs and directs His external works (*opera ad extra*). We refer to this internal arrangement within the Trinity, in which the Son is foreordained as our Lamb, as the *Pactum Salutis* or Covenant of Redemption. The *Pactum Salutis*

---

most significant early Apostolic theologians: D.P. Williams, W.H. Lewis, Thomas Rees, and W.R. Thomas.

is 'the eternal self-determination of the blessed Trinity, who wills to communicate the bliss of his triune life to elect sinners through the mediation of Jesus Christ, for the glory of Jesus Christ.'[10] It is through this Covenant of Redemption that the Triune God directs all things to Christ and for Christ, that all things may ultimately be gathered together under Christ as Head (*Eph. 1:10-12; Col. 1:18*).

The Election of the Church in the Son

God's election of the Church is rooted in His grace in Jesus Christ (*Eph. 1:4-6*), and should always and only be thought of in relation to Christ and God's grace in Him (*cf. Rom. 11:5*: 'the election of grace'). Election is not an obscure biblical teaching, but is taught repeatedly and explicitly in the Scriptures. So, all evangelicals hold to the doctrine of election in some form. Let's just look at a few key passages which not only point to the fact of election, but also show us something of the nature of that election.

When *Ephesians 1* enumerates the spiritual blessings with which we are blessed in Christ, it starts off with our election:

> He chose us in Him before the foundation of the world, that we should be holy and without blame before Him in love, having predestined us to adoption as sons by Jesus Christ to Himself, according to the good pleasure of His will, to the praise of the glory of His grace. (*Eph. 1:4-6*)

Here we learn that:

1) Election is something that God did before creation.
2) In Election we are chosen 'in Christ'.
3) Election has a goal – we are to be holy, we are to be adopted as sons of God.
4) The reason for election is the good pleasure of God's will.

This shows us that it is only the goal or result of election which will be seen in us. Both the timing of election and the reason for our election are outside of us. Being elected before creation means that we didn't exist to do anything to get elected, and this is further clarified by the fact that the only reason stated for why we are elected is God's will, not anything in us. That

---

[10] Scott R. Swain, 'The Covenant of Redemption', in Michael Allen and Scott R. Swain, *Christian Dogmatics: Reformed Theology for the Church Catholic* (Grand Rapids: Baker, 2016), 109.

means that this is indeed an election of grace. It's not a reward that we have earned, but rather, something which God does for us in Christ, even though we don't deserve it.

The grace of election is also highlighted in *2 Timothy 1:9-10*:

> [God] has saved us and called us with a holy calling, not according to our works, but according to His own purpose and grace which was given to us in Christ Jesus before time began, but has now been revealed by the appearing of our Saviour Jesus Christ, who has abolished death and brought life and immortality to light through the gospel.

Here we learn that God gave us His grace in Christ before time began. How did God give us grace in Christ before time began? Well, *Ephesians 1:4* has just told us: in election. Here in *2 Timothy 1:9* Paul is explaining just what that election is: election is God giving us His grace before time began. So this passage teaches us the following about election:

1) Election is God's grace given to us before time began.
2) Election is God's grace given to us in Christ Jesus.
3) Election leads to a holy calling.
4) The reason for election is not our works, but God's purpose and grace.

In effect, these two passages teach us the same things about election, and both very clearly attribute election, not to something in us, but to God Himself. He elects us because of His grace, His purpose, His good pleasure, His will. In fact, not only does He elect us because of His grace, but His election of us is His grace given to us before time began.

Theologians call this doctrine *Unconditional Election* (i.e. we don't have to do anything to meet any conditions to get elected). Some Pentecostals and evangelicals, however, hold to a different doctrine of election, known as *Conditional Election*.[11] As the name implies, this view does not see election based solely in God's sovereign good pleasure and grace, but rather sees some condition which man must meet in order to be elected. That condition is foreseen faith. The idea is that God knows in advance who will believe and so elects them. This, however, means that the ultimate reason why someone is elect lies within that person himself, rather than in God and His

---

[11] One later Apostolic theologian, writing in the 1980s, after his retirement, did advocate conditional election in view of faith, but he stands alone against the entire Apostolic theological tradition before him. All the early Apostolic theologians not only taught unconditional election, but also viewed it as one of the central features of their system of theology.

grace. James Arminius defined conditional election as 'the decree of God, by which, of Himself, from eternity, He decreed to justify in (or through) Christ, believers, and to accept them unto eternal life, to the praise of His glorious grace.'[12]

But what about *Romans 8:29*? Doesn't it teach this form of conditional election? 'For whom He foreknew, He also predestined to be conformed to the image of His Son, that He might be the firstborn among many brethren' (*Rom. 8:29*). Here Paul does indeed write of predestination of those whom God foreknew, but this is a foreknowledge of people, not of facts. Although many people read this verse as if it were to say 'whom he knew in advance would believe', that isn't what it actually says. Paul is writing here about how God knows individuals in advance, not just information about individuals.

This verb 'foreknow' is used 5 times in the New Testament (*Acts 26:5; Rom. 8:29; 11:2; 1 Pet. 1:20; 2 Pet. 3:17*) and the corresponding noun ('foreknowledge') is used twice (*Acts 2:23; 1 Pet. 1:2*), allowing us to see how it is used in context. Like the verb 'to know' in the Bible, 'to foreknow' appears to have a much stronger meaning than mere intellectual cognition. Rather, it seems to imply 'a peculiar interest, delight, affection, and action'[13]. To foreknow means to forelove. 'That God foreknew us is but another way of saying that he set his gracious and merciful regard upon us, that he knew us from eternity past with a sovereign and distinguishing delight. God's foreknowledge is an active, creative work of divine love.'[14] As the early Apostolics put it, God's foreknowledge 'is something more than foresight,' but includes God's provision of 'divine grace … to wean and draw us to Himself.'[15] God's foreknowledge of the Church is His love for the Church from before the creation of the world.[16]

Some people object that a belief in unconditional election is detrimental to evangelism. However, in the New Testament, God's Sovereign election is a motivation to evangelism. In *Acts 18:9-10*, God encourages Paul in his evangelism in Corinth by telling him, 'Do not be afraid, but speak, and do not keep silent; for I am with you, and no one will attack you to hurt you; for I have many people in this city.' God encourages Paul to continue evangelism because He has His elect in that place and they need to hear the

---

[12] James Arminius, *Works*, 3:311.
[13] John Murray, *The Epistle to the Romans*, 1:317.
[14] Sam Storms, *Chosen for Life: The Case for Divine Election* (Wheaton: Crossway, 2007), 103
[15] Thomas Rees, *Riches of Grace*, ii.9 (Aug. 1925), 111.
[16] D.P. Williams, *Riches of Grace*, iii.1 (March 1927), 30.

gospel. As a result, Paul stays in Corinth for a year and six months (*Acts 18:11*).

In *2 Timothy 2:10* Paul writes, 'therefore I endure all things for the sake of the elect, that they also may obtain the salvation which is in Christ Jesus with eternal glory.' He is willing to go through many hardships to preach the gospel, because of the elect. The doctrine of election is the guarantee that there will be those who respond to the gospel in faith.

The Triune God does not act 'according to the will of man but by the will of God [in] Divine Election.'[17] This unconditional election is 'the very hub of God's eternal purpose.'[18] In the words of an early Apostolic prophecy:

> Chosen and predestined are some, according to mine eternal purposes, unconditionally, according to the Divine decree that has found its essence in the Eternal One… For I definitely tell you that anyone that declares that I have not the right, according to mine own will and purposes, to choose unconditionally, I say unto you that you will find that I am Sovereign, that I have the authority thus to do and have done from the beginning, and it shall be done even to the end … And in the mystery of this declaration, I forbid the right even of my creation to ask me, 'Why is it so?' for it has pleased the Lord your God thus to choose, to purpose, to pre-ordain, and it shall be done according to the purposes of that which has been woven in the garment of the Eternal purposes throughout the ages, saith the Lord.[19]

This unconditional election is not an arbitrary act, but rather an expression of God's Fatherly love. The Church is elect of God the Father (*Eph. 1:3-4; 1 Pet. 1:2*) in predestination to sonship (*Eph. 1:5*). So, in His Fatherly love, the Father has chosen the Church to be brought into the Fatherly love which He has for His Son (*cf. Jn 17:23*). God's election is not merely a matter of sovereignty and providence, but rather it is for the goal of theosis in His eternal purpose. Thus, the Welsh Apostolics rejoiced to sing:

> O the depths of God's riches of grace
> O the heights of His wisdom sublime
> He elected us!

---

[17] W.J. Williams, *Riches of Grace*, i.9 (1920), 30.

[18] D.P. Williams, *Riches of Grace*, xi.1 (Sept. 1935), 204. Williams specifically writes that 'there are saints elected unconditionally in the heart of God in the eternity' (p.203). He also uses the Welsh word *diamodol* (unconditional) to speak of election.

[19] 'The Eternal Security of God's Elect: The Word of the Lord through the Prophet W.J. Williams', *Riches of Grace*, x. 5 (May 1935), 210-211. The prophecy was given in Bradford on 9th Dec., 1933.

...
In the counsel of the Three-in-One
In the love of the predestined Son,
He elected us![20]

So, it is in His great love for His Son, that the Father has appointed the Son as Redeemer, and elected the Church to sonship in Him. Therefore, because 'there was no commencement to' the love of the Father for His Son, that means 'there is no commencement to His love towards His Church in the Eternal Plan of God.'[21]

> Before the foundation of the world, God loved His Son, and in loving Him in eternity He ordained Him to be our Saviour, and in that Divine Ordination ... He found His Church and we are in the bosom of the Triune God, redeemed![22]

Thus, from all eternity, the Triune God has purposed the incarnation and atoning work of Christ (*1 Pet. 1:18-21; Rev. 13:8*), our unconditional election in Christ, with our names written in the Lamb's Book of Life (*Eph. 1:4; Rev. 17:8*), and our inheritance to share in the Son's relationship with His Father (*Jn 17:5, 23-24; Mt 25:34*).

Through Jesus and For Jesus

The Lord Jesus Christ stands at the centre of everything, from eternity past to eternity future. It is Jesus who is the reason for the creation of the heavens and the earth, and He will be the glory of the new heavens and the new earth. 'All things were created through Him and for Him' (*Col. 1:16*). Not only is He the agent and mediator of creation, through whom all things were made (*Jn 1:3*), but He is also the purpose of all creation. All things were made *for* Him.

This means that the coming of the eternal Word and Son of the Father into our world through the incarnation was not an afterthought. The work of the Incarnate Son was not an emergency backup plan. Rather:

---

[20] D.P. Williams, 'Etholedigaeth Gras', *Molwch Dduw*, 139 / *Cyfoeth Gras* ii.1 (July 1921), 40.

[21] D.P. Williams, *Riches of Grace* xii.1 (Sept. 1936), 14.

[22] D.P. Williams, *Riches of Grace* xii.1 (Sept. 1936), 17.

> Well before sin entered into creation, before the rebellion of Satan, and before the fall of man, there in the bosom of the Father, in the mystery of His will, in the womb of eternity - there was the Cross. The Death of our Lord on the Cross of Calvary was not an afterthought, but an essential part of that original plan and resolve of the Trinity.[23]

Creation exists for Christ. And, as the eternal purpose of the Triune God for Christ also involves His Body, that means that creation exists for Christ and His Church. 'The Body of Christ is the reason for the creation of the universe … In Creation we have the platform erected by God for the realization of the Eternal plan.'[24]

Therefore, the Church takes precedence over both creation and the kingdom, as the eternal purpose of God. The world was created for the outworking of the Father's election concerning the Church, and the kingdom exists for the building of the Body. God's purpose for the Church is 'not something that came into being since the Fall,' but rather, D.P. Williams wrote, 'the Cross was in the Heart of the Godhead in Eternity.'[25] This means that the incarnation and the cross were not a new plan to repair humanity's sudden predicament. The incarnation and cross of Christ were not simply a way to restore fallen creation or an emergency reaction to human sin. Christ's incarnation and cross are the very purpose of creation, so that through the incarnation and cross of Christ, God may accomplish His eternal purpose to have a Church united in the loving fellowship of the Triune God.[26]

If Christ's incarnation and cross are the reason for the creation of the heavens and the earth and everything in them, then the cross is 'the centre of time and eternity.'[27] As the early Apostolic thinker, W.H. Lewis, expressed it:

> Calvary is the basis and ground of human hope and Divine purpose. It is the axle of the whole universe. Not only is Calvary the centre of the created universe, but Calvary is the centre of the Divine Nature. Calvary is tabernacled in the heart of God. Calvary is older than the universe; before the mountains were brought forth, before the stars were rolled into their wondrous paths; before the first ray of light shot through the gloom, God had fore-ordained the Lamb in the Eternal counsels of Eternity. In other

---

[23] W.R. Thomas, *On Ephesians*, 68; cf. W.H. Lewis, *Riches of Grace*, vii.4 (March 1932), 124.

[24] W.R. Thomas, *On Ephesians*, 65.

[25] D.P. Williams, *Riches of Grace*, v.3 (Jan. 1930), 98.

[26] See e.g. D.P. Williams, *Riches of Grace*, vii.1 (Sept. 1931), 15. In theological language, Apostolic theology has advocated a particular form of *supralapsarianism*.

[27] W.H. Lewis, *Riches of Grace*, vii.4 (March 1932), 125.

words, the idea of sacrifice stretches forth from eternity to eternity. It is not an after-thought of God because of the calamity of sin. Calvary is older than everything else. Calvary is not built on Leviticus; rather, Leviticus is built on Calvary. During the forty days Moses was on the Mount, God revealed to him the Eternal Reality and Substance; He revealed Calvary and all that it meant. Then as he came down and built the tabernacle, and established the priesthood, all was the outward expression of the Eternal Realities. Calvary was older than Leviticus, older than the Mosaic Law. It is embedded in the very depths of the Godhead.[28]

The outcome of this eternal purpose, foreordained before the foundation of the world, and accomplished through the cross of Christ, is 'the Church in unity with the Trinity ... [and] the Trinity in unity with the Church.'[29]

Life in the Trinity

So the end goal of the eternal purpose of the Triune God is the theosis of the Church: to have the Body of Christ, united to the Son and filled with His fullness, and so, in the Son, living in the unity of the Trinity, dwelling in the loving communion of the Triune God. Already, in Christ, the Church is 'being built together for a dwelling place of God in the Spirit' (*Eph. 2:22*). The Church is the Body of Christ, filled with all the fullness of God (*Eph. 1:22-23*). United to the Son, who is her Head, indwelt by the Holy Spirit, and filled with all the fullness of God, already now (*Eph. 3:10-11*) the Church enjoys the beginning of sharing in the loving communion of the Triune God. Already, the Church is a body of well-beloved sons in the Well-Beloved Son, and so shares in the love of the Father for His eternal Son, and in the Son's relationship with His Father.

'The basic doctrine of the Christian faith' is, as D.P. Williams summarised it, 'that God is the Father, and that He has a Son within His essence eternally.'[30] So the Father-Son relationship is the very heart of the Christian faith.

And the calling of the Church is to enjoy life in knowing the Father and the Son (*Jn 17:3*). We know the Father by sharing in the Son's relationship

---

[28] W.H. Lewis, *Riches of Grace*, xi.1 (Sept. 1935), 57.
[29] W.H. Lewis, *Riches of Grace*, x.1 (Sept. 1934), 25, 31.
[30] D.P Williams, *The Trinity*, 1:77.

with His Father through the Spirit. The Lord Jesus Christ, the Head of the Church, is the Son of the Father by nature; yet in Him, united to Him as our Head, we are sons by grace.

Partakers of the Divine Nature

As a body of well-beloved sons in the Well-Beloved Son, the Church partakes of the divine nature (2 *Pet. 1:4*). This does not mean that we stop being human and start being God. Rather, the divine nature of the Triune God is to live in perfect, loving relationships; the Father always perfectly loves His Son in the joy of the Holy Spirit. This is an outgoing, loving fellowship. And through Jesus Christ – through His life, death, and resurrection, His incarnation and atonement – we are brought into that outgoing, loving fellowship. Through Jesus Christ, who became incarnate for us and for our salvation, the Church is brought into the loving fellowship of the Father, Son, and Holy Spirit. In the eternal purpose of the Triune God, the Church is to 'be made perfect in one' by sharing in the very love which the Father has for His Son (*Jn 17:23, 26*). By grace, the Church shares in the Son's own relationship with the Father, and so, in Jesus, we are as loved as Him.

The election of the Church 'has its origin in the love of the Father and will have its consummation in His perfect love in us.'[31] The life of the Church is found in her 'participation in that divine love,'[32] and so the Church lives in the love shared between the Father, Son and Holy Spirit. The members of the Body of Christ share in the Father's love as His sons by grace. So God the Father is, by His grace, 'the Father of the Church', because:

> The Paternity of God to His Son, in the mystery of the Holy Trinity and of the Incarnation, really and effectively reaches us – the members of His Body ... by grace we have become partakers of the Divine Nature, and constituted a new creation in Christ ... It is the Holy Spirit that presents to us the reality of the Fatherhood or Paternity of God; 'in Jesus' we see the Father (John 14:9), and 'by' the Spirit we embrace the Father.[33]

---

[31] W.R. Thomas, *On Ephesians*, 66.

[32] W.R. Thomas, *On Ephesians*, 66.

[33] W.R. Thomas, *On Ephesians*, 214-215.

Through her union with Christ her heavenly Head, the Church is a Body of well-beloved sons in the Well-Beloved Son, and so she shares in the love between the Father and the Son in the Spirit. Thus the Church participates in the love of the Triune God: we are loved with the very love which the Father has for His Son (*Jn 17:23*).

At the same time, the Church is the fullness of Christ (*Eph. 1:23*). As the Church is filled with the Holy Spirit, by perichoresis she is filled with the Father and the Son, and so filled with the fullness of the Triune God. So, both by participation in Christ and by this filling through the Spirit, the Church shares in the loving communion of the Trinity.

The only existence the Church has, is an existence as the Body which is united to Christ the Head. So Christ is the life of the Church. The life of Christ is the life of God the Son, which He shares with the Father and the Holy Spirit. And so the Church lives in the life of the Holy and Consubstantial Trinity.

Tenet 7

**The Sacraments
of Baptism
by immersion
and of
the Lord's Supper.**

Chapter 31

Baptism

The Sacraments

It was Jesus Himself who told His disciples to baptise and to celebrate the Lord's Supper. As children we often learn the rhyme that a sacrament is 'an outward seal and sign of an inward work divine' instituted by Christ.[1] The *Heidelberg Catechism* explains this a bit more:

> The Sacraments are visible holy signs and seals appointed of God for this end, that by the use thereof He may the more fully declare and seal to us the promise of the Gospel: namely, that of free grace, He grants us the forgiveness of sins and everlasting life for the sake of the one sacrifice of Christ accomplished on the cross.[2]

So of what are the sacraments signs and seals? They're signs and seals of the gospel. They signify and seal to us the promises of the gospel and direct us to the gospel. Therefore baptism and the Lord's Supper are true means of grace to us as they point us to the gospel, for through them God strengthens and grows our faith, and we grow in our communion with Christ. And that means that these sacraments are very important for our Christian growth.

A sacrament is not only a sign instituted by the Lord, but one which is accompanied by His Gospel Word. Luther says that 'in every sacrament there is a word of divine promise, to be believed by whoever receives the sign, and that the sign alone cannot be a sacrament.'[3] Augustine's rule reminds us that 'when the Word is added to the element it becomes a sacrament.'[4] Thus the Church possesses only two sacraments, baptism in

---

[1] See *Asked and Answered: A Catechism of Apostolic Principles*, 7.1.

[2] *Heidelberg Catechism*, 66.

[3] Martin Luther, *Luther's Works*, 36:92.

[4] *Accedat verbum ad elementum et fit sacramentum*. Augustine, *Tractates in John*, 80.3.

water and the Lord's Supper, for it is only in these two rites that we have the sign instituted by Christ attached to His Gospel Word.[5]

The power of the sacraments is not found in the external elements of water, bread and wine, but in the Word of God to which they are attached. In his *Small Catechism*, Luther explains:

> It is not the water indeed that does [such great things] but the Word of God, which is in and with the water, and faith, which trusts this Word of God in the water.
> It is not the eating and drinking, indeed, that does them, but the words, which are given here, 'Given and shed for you, for the forgiveness of sins.'[6]

Without the Word, we would have only washing, eating and drinking. But, attached to Christ's Word, these become powerful gospel sacraments.

The Means of Grace

The sacraments are, along with the proclamation of the Word, *means of grace*. The means of grace are the ways in which God has promised by His Spirit to deliver Christ and all His benefits to us. In other words, God acts by His Word and sacraments to show us His grace by giving us Jesus and building us up in our union with Him. Through the means of grace, God embraces us with the reality of Christ's death and resurrection for us. Through the means of grace God is at work to save sinners and sanctify saints. In the means of grace, the Triune God works powerfully through the ordinary, tangible, means of human words, water, bread and wine. As Luther put it:

> You cannot give me a single example of a person who was made a Christian or received the Holy Spirit apart from something external. Where did these Christians get the information that Christ is their Saviour? Was it not from reading or from hearing? It did not drop down from heaven. It came from Scripture and the Word … [God] always grasps something physical as a means by which he deals with you, something that is beneficial.[7]

---

[5] For the Apostolic Church, cf. *Athrawiaethau Sylfeinol*, vii.

[6] Martin Luther, *Small Catechism*, iv & vi.

[7] Martin Luther, 'Sermon on Luke 18, 1528', *WA* 27:60.20-23. Translation from Robert Kolb and Charles P. Arand, *The Genius of Luther's Theology* (Grand Rapids: Baker, 2008), 177.

Elsewhere Luther wrote: 'God grants His Spirit or grace to no one, except through or with the preceding outward Word.'[8] That outward Word by which the Spirit comes to us and delivers to us God's grace in Jesus is the Word set forth in proclamation and the sacraments.[9]

Visible Words

The sacraments are 'visible words' which present the gospel of Jesus Christ and His saving work for us to us in a way we can see, touch, and taste.

> The Christ who is offered and received in the 'audible' gospel is also offered and received in the 'visible' gospel – always and only through faith and by the power of the Holy Spirit. God's Word, whether audible or visible, whether inscripturated or incarnate, is never devoid of his real presence.[10]

Calvin calls the sacraments 'mirrors in which we may contemplate the riches of God's grace, which he lavishes upon us.'[11] These visible words:

> Make us more certain of the trustworthiness of God's Word. And because we are of flesh, they are shown to us under things of flesh, to instruct us according to our dull capacity, and to lead us by the hand as tutors lead children. Augustine calls a sacrament 'a visible word' for the reason that it represents God's promises as painted in a picture and sets them before our sight, portrayed graphically and in the manner of images.[12]

What Happens in a Baptism?

Baptism is the sacrament of the beginning of the Christian life. In Baptism a new believer is immersed in water 'in the name of the Father and of the Son and of the Holy Spirit' (*Mt 28:19*).

---

[8] Martin Luther, *Smalcald Articles*, iii.viii.

[9] The proclamation of the Word includes preaching, the reading of the Scriptures, and prophecy.

[10] Johnson, *One with Christ*, 226.

[11] Calvin, *Institutes*, 4.16.6

[12] Calvin, *Institutes*, 4.16.6

Baptism by Immersion

The Greek word translated *to baptise* literally means *to immerse* or *to dip*. So to baptise someone is to put them completely under the water and then to bring them back up out again. After Jesus' baptism, 'he came up out of the water' (*Mk 1:10*; ESV). This further reinforces the concept of baptism by immersion. When Philip baptised the Ethiopian eunuch, 'both Philip and the eunuch went down into the water, and he baptized him [and] they came up out of the water' (*Acts 8:38-39*). For such a journey across the desert, there would have been plenty of drinking water in the chariot. Yet the drinking water they had available was not enough for a baptism. Instead they had to wait until 'as they went down the road, they came to some water' (*Acts 8:36*) and then they had to go down into that water. Thus sprinkling could not have been an option; immersion was required for baptism.

The reason why immersion is a necessary aspect of Baptism is due to the meaning of the sacrament. *Colossians 2:12* tells us that we were 'buried with Him in baptism, in which you also were raised with Him through faith in the working of God, who raised Him from the dead.' Similarly, Paul writes to the Romans:

> Or do you not know that as many of us as were baptized into Christ Jesus were baptized into His death? Therefore we were buried with Him through baptism into death, that just as Christ was raised from the dead by the glory of the Father, even so we also should walk in newness of life. (*Rom. 6:3-4*)

Therefore baptism is a sign of our union with Christ in His death, burial and resurrection. And so being 'buried' under the water demonstrates our death and burial in union with Christ. Coming up out of the water is the powerful image of our being raised with Christ to newness of life.

On Baptism by Affusion or Aspersion

Many church traditions practice a different form of baptism than immersion: baptism by either *affusion* or *aspersion*. Instead of the person baptised being put under the water and brought back up out again, some water is poured (*affusion*) or sprinkled (*aspersion*) on the candidate's head.

Historically, it seems likely that affusion and aspersion arose from practical considerations.[13] However, a theological justification later emerged, connecting the pouring of the water with the outpouring of the Holy Spirit.[14]

However, as we have seen in chapter 26, the baptism of the Holy Spirit is not the same as baptism in water. Therefore, it is a confusion of categories to apply the imagery of baptism in the Spirit to the sacrament of water baptism. Instead, the Scriptures tell us that what is signified in the sacrament is not the outpouring of the Spirit, but our union with Christ in His death and resurrection (*Col. 2:12; Rom. 6:3-4*). Therefore, *aspersion* and *affusion* signify the wrong thing in baptism. The textual, theological, and historical data all point to baptism by immersion.

Immersion of a Believer

From the meaning of the sacrament of baptism we can see that only those who have been united to Christ in His death and resurrection are eligible. This means that Baptism is only for believers, for it is in salvation that we are united to Christ, and it is only those who believe who are saved. Paul specifically links baptism with faith when writing to the Colossians, telling them that, 'in [baptism] you also were raised with Him through faith in the working of God, who raised Him from the dead' (*Col. 2:12*).

The book of Acts records many baptisms, and so there we can see the type of people who were baptised in the early church. On the Day of Pentecost, Peter preached and 'then those who gladly received his word were baptized' (*Acts 2:41*). So on the Day of Pentecost, the 3000 people who were baptised were those who responded with faith to the preaching of the Gospel. In *Acts 8*, both the Samaritans (*Acts 8:14, 16*) and the Ethiopian eunuch (*Acts 8:36-38*) received the Word with faith before being baptised. The faith of Cornelius and his household was attested by their baptism in the Holy Spirit before they were baptised in water (*Acts 10:44-48*). These are just a few of the examples of baptisms in the book of Acts, yet they serve to establish the fact that it was those who had received the Gospel in faith who were baptised in the early Church. Thus, it is believers, and believers alone, who should be baptised.

---

[13] *Didache* 7

[14] E.g. Louis Berkhof, *Systematic Theology* (Edinburgh: Banner of Truth, 1958), 631.

On Infant Baptism

If the Scriptures point us to the baptism of believers, why do so many churches practice infant baptism? Each tradition which practices infant baptism does so with a different rationale. Lutherans see baptism as the way in which the Lord grants faith to children. Roman Catholics tie baptism to salvation, and so argue that 'the Church and parents would deny a child the precious gift of becoming a child of God were they not to confer Baptism shortly after birth.'[15] Many Wesleyans view infant baptism as the way in which God grants prevenient grace so that these children might later repent and believe the gospel. Presbyterians argue that baptism is the sign and seal of membership of the New Covenant, and that Covenant membership rightly belongs to believers and their children.

Among evangelical advocates of infant baptism, one of the most frequently advanced justifications is the description of household baptisms in the New Testament.[16] Cornelius was baptised along with his whole household (*Acts 10:48; cf. 11:14*). The same happened with Lydia and her household (*Acts 16:15*), and then the Philippian jailer with his (*Acts 16:31-33*). In the epistles, we read of Paul's baptism of the household of Stephanas (*1 Cor. 1:16*). Another example in Corinth may be Crispus and his household (*Acts 18:8*).

However, we read specifically that the household of Cornelius who were baptised were 'those who heard the word' (*Acts 10:44*), and that Crispus 'believed on the Lord with all his household' (*Acts 18:8*). Paul and Silas 'spoke the word of the Lord' not only to the Philippian jailer, but 'to all who were in his house' (*Acts 16:32*). While in the case of Lydia and Stephanas, all we know is that the household was baptised, in the other three cases where we have a description of not only the baptism, but also the evangelism, we find that in each case, the whole household who were baptised also heard and believed the gospel. As Beasley-Murray sums it up:

> Luke, in writing these narratives, does not have in view infant members of the families. His language cannot be pressed to extend to them. He has in

---

[15] *Catechism of the Catholic Church*, 1250.

[16] Michael Horton, *The Christian Faith: A Systematic Theology for Pilgrims on the Way* (Grand Rapids: Zondervan, 2011), 795; Edward W.A. Koehler, *A Summary of Christian Doctrine* (St Louis: Concordia, 2006), 274.

mind ordinary believers and uses language applicable only to them. Abuse of it leads to degradation of the Scripture.[17]

Crispus and Cornelius did not believe for their households, but with them. And this is the same pattern we should understand of the other household baptisms in the New Testament. These are not examples of infant baptism, but rather examples of whole families coming to faith in Jesus and being baptised together as believers in Christ the Saviour.

Immersion in the Name of the Father, Son and Holy Spirit

A sacrament, to be a sacrament, cannot simply be a bare sign, but needs the Word of God. The Word which is joined to the immersion of a believer in water in the sacrament of baptism are the words which Christ used when He instituted the sacrament, namely 'in the name of the Father and of the Son and of the Holy Spirit' (*Mt 28:19*).[18] Through these words in baptism, we are acknowledged as members of the family of the Triune God, having been received as sons and daughters of God the Father through the saving work of His only-begotten Son. And submitting to baptism in this name, we confess our faith in the Triune God. As T.N. Turnbull put it:

> The converts not only believe with the heart, but openly confess their belief in the three persons of the Godhead. Our belief in the Trinity constitutes the basis for our beliefs. It is the foundation of our faith.[19]

Each of the Sacraments must be accompanied by the Word of God, as they are a visible representation of the truth that is conveyed to us by the Word. This means that not only do we use the words of institution at the moment of Baptism, but that the Baptism will take place during a service at which the Word is read and preached, and the sacrament thus explained. The sacraments are not magical rites and must be explained by the Word.

---

[17] G.R. Beasley-Murray, *Baptism in the New Testament* (Eerdmans, 1962), 315.

[18] These words are also referred to as the Baptismal Formula.

[19] T.N. Turnbull, *The Full Gospel*, 15.

Baptism is God's Work

Baptised into the Trinity

Baptism doesn't only involve an action, but also the Word. As we have just seen, baptism differs from simply being dunked under water because of the word that goes with it: 'in the name of the Father and of the Son and of the Holy Spirit' (*Mt 28:19*). So, in baptism our acceptance and welcome by the Triune God is proclaimed. Through our union with Christ in His death and resurrection, we have been welcomed into the family of God as sons in the Son, and brought into the blessings of fellowship and communion with the Holy Trinity. In baptism a new name is declared over us – the name of our new, heavenly family.

God's Word to Us

Sometimes we're tempted to think of baptism as our word to God – as us showing Him our commitment. But that's not really what it's about at all. Quite the contrary, baptism is God's Word to us. In baptism God is speaking to us about Christ's death and resurrection for us, and about our union with Him. And that means we don't have to wait until we think we're good enough. Not at all! For it's not our testimony to God, but His testimony to us. Baptism is His word to us about how He's saved us from judgement and brought us to life in the death and resurrection of Jesus. And so through God's Word to us in baptism the Holy Spirit strengthens our faith through the clear representation of our union with Christ in death and resurrection and strengthens us for our walk in newness of life.

God's Word to the World

Have you ever noticed how a baptismal service is often also such a great evangelistic occasion? Non-Christians come along and they see a powerful picture of the gospel of Jesus Christ and hear the gospel proclaimed as well. You see, God isn't only speaking to the person being baptised, but also to all who witness the baptism. For the Christians who witness a baptism, it reminds us that God has done the same thing for us, uniting us to Christ in His death and resurrection, and so further strengthens our faith. For the non-Christians who witness a baptism, they hear the gospel in the preaching and see the gospel demonstrated in the baptism. And to everyone, baptism speaks a word about a new reality: in baptism everyone sees that the one baptised no longer belongs to the old life in this world, but is now a member of the family of the Triune God.

The Meaning of Baptism

Jesus' Baptism is the Real Baptism

As we've already noticed several times throughout this book, Jesus' baptism is a moment where we catch a glimpse of the life of the Trinity. Here we see something of the eternal love and fellowship of the Father, Son, and Holy Spirit. Here we see their unity of will and purpose.

When it comes to the sacrament of baptism, Jesus' baptism is of course very significant for us. But we must be careful not to limit Jesus' baptism to a mere example for us. What if Jesus' baptism is much more than an example? And what if our baptism isn't so much our action of obedience, but God's action? In fact, there are no 'what ifs' about it – that's exactly what we see in the Bible. Jesus isn't baptised to remind us to get baptised sometime, but 'to fulfil all righteousness' (*Mt 3:15*). The baptism of Jesus Christ is not just a motivating example to guide us towards an act of obedience in our own baptism. Far from it! Jesus' baptism is the real baptism. Jesus entered the waters of baptism as our substitute and Head. His baptism is the real baptism.

But if His baptism is the real baptism, what about our baptism? Well, our baptism is a baptism in union with Christ. We are baptised into His baptism. United to Christ, we are buried with Him (*Col. 2:12*), we pass safely through the waters of judgement in Him, and then we are raised with Him. United to Him we enter the water 'in Him', and just as surely as we feel the waters envelop us, we know that we are washed in His blood, we know the bond of the Spirit who unites us to Christ, as well beloved sons in the well beloved Son, and we know the Father's declaration of love for us in Jesus. Just as surely as we are embraced by the waters of baptism, so we are embraced by the overflowing love of Father, Son and Holy Spirit.

It's not that Jesus' baptism is merely an example for us to follow. Nor did Jesus in His baptism hallow the waters so that they'd be a blessing to us. No. It's that Jesus' Baptism is the real baptism, and in our baptism we're joined to Him in His double baptism – the one in the Jordan, and the one on Calvary (*Lk 12:50*). Remember *Ephesians 4:5*: there is 'one Lord, one faith, one baptism'. Jesus' baptism is the real baptism.

Union with Christ in His Death and Resurrection

As we've already seen, the action involved in baptism – going down under the water and coming back up – points us to the truth that in baptism, God speaks to us of our union with Christ in His death and resurrection (*Rom. 6:3-4; Col. 2:12*). And the language Scripture uses to connect baptism with this union to Christ in His death and resurrection is strong language; baptism isn't just a weak reminder of this union. God is at work in our union with Christ when we pass through the waters of baptism. 'For as many of you as were baptized into Christ have put on Christ' (*Gal. 3:27*). As Calvin explains:

> Just as the twig draws substance and nourishment from the root to which it is grafted, so those who receive baptism with right faith truly feel the effective working of Christ's death in the mortification of their flesh, together with the working of his resurrection in the vivification of the Spirit … Our faith receives from baptism the advantage of its sure testimony to us that we are not only engrafted into the death and life of Christ, but so united to Christ himself that we become sharers in all his blessings.[20]

Why Water?

The sacrament of baptism involves immersion in water. Just as in the other sacrament there is a significance to the elements of bread and wine, so too

---

[20] Calvin, *Institutes*, 4.15.5-6

there is a significance to the element used in baptism. So why does baptism occur in water?

Water and Judgment

The fact that this immersion takes place in water means that the symbolism is even greater than simply that of the grave. Water speaks to us of God's judgement (*see Ex 14:26-29; Jonah 1:7-16 and Gen. 7:6-24; cf. 1 Pet. 3:21*). Therefore the waters of baptism speak to us of the death and judgement we deserve from God for our sin, and coming up out of the water signifies that, only through Christ's merits and our union with Him in His death and resurrection, we have passed safely through God's judgement.

Water and Cleansing

The Scriptures also connect baptism with forgiveness and cleansing. On the Day of Pentecost, Peter called upon those who were responding to the gospel to 'be baptized in the name of Jesus Christ for the remission of sins' (*Acts 2:38*). As Calvin points out, the Scriptures:

> did not mean to signify that our cleansing and salvation are accomplished by water, or that water contains in itself the power to cleanse, regenerate, and renew; nor that here is the cause of salvation, but only that in this sacrament are received the knowledge and certainty of such gifts … Indeed, baptism promises us no other purification than through the sprinkling of Christ's blood, which is represented by means of water from the resemblance to cleansing and washing.[21]

Water and Life

The Bible also closely associates water with new life in Christ. Those who are born again are 'born of water and the Spirit' (*Jn 3:5*). Whoever drinks of the water Christ gives 'will never thirst. But the water that I shall give him will become in him a fountain of water springing up into everlasting life' (*Jn 4:14; cf. Isa. 55:1*). And in the age to come, He who is the Alpha and the Omega, the Beginning and the End 'will give of the fountain of

---

[21] Calvin, *Institutes*, 4.15.2

the water of life freely to him who thirsts' (*Rev. 21:6; cf. 22:1, 17*). Thus, baptism by immersion in water points us to the new life which is ours through our union to Christ who carries us safely through God's judgment in His death and resurrection, and who cleanses us from all sin by His precious blood. Baptism is 'a seal of the life in Him.'[22]

The Benefit of Baptism

If Baptism is a means of grace, then that means that it is used by the Holy Spirit to bless believers in union with Christ. Thus it is not just a symbol. If it is a sacrament, then there must be both a sign and a thing signified, which is communicated to us by the Holy Spirit. The thing signified in Baptism, as we have seen, is our passing through death and judgement and rising again to newness of life through our union with Christ in His death and resurrection. Thus, in baptism the Holy Spirit strengthens our faith through the clear representation of our union with Christ in death and resurrection and strengthens us for our walk in newness of life. Baptism should not only strengthen the faith of those being baptised, but also of all believers who witness a Baptism.

Peter tells us that baptism 'now saves us' (*1 Pet. 3:21*). But why does he say that? Well, remember, this is the Word of the LORD. It's not just Peter's idea – these are God's very words. So it's definitely true what he says. Therefore, what exactly does Peter say now saves us?

> There is also an antitype which now saves us—baptism (not the removal of the filth of the flesh, but the answer of a good conscience toward God), through the resurrection of Jesus Christ, who has gone into heaven and is at the right hand of God, angels and authorities and powers having been made subject to Him. (*1 Pet. 3:21-22*)

Baptism, he says, saves 'through the resurrection of Jesus Christ'. So, it's not some magic power in the water or the baptistry or in the minister. No, the power that saves is Jesus, in His mighty, victorious, resurrection power. So,

---

[22] D.P. Williams, *Riches of Grace*, vii.3 (Jan. 1932), 82.

it's not about what we do, but all about what Jesus has done – dying and rising for us.

And, Peter clarifies, it's 'not the removal of the filth of the flesh, but the answer of a good conscience toward God' that he's talking about when he's talking about baptism. So it's not a ritual that saves us. Rather it's the appeal to God through baptism. (The word that gets translated 'answer' really means an earnest request; so it's an appeal for something you intensely desire.) In other words, it's calling out to God with faith in Jesus. And this faith in Christ means a 'good conscience', for those who trust in Him are fully forgiven in Jesus and clothed with Him for righteousness.

The Bible is very clear that it's only 'by grace you have been saved through faith, and that not of yourselves; it is the gift of God, not of works, lest anyone should boast' (*Eph. 2:8-9*). So baptism is not a work by which we earn our salvation. No, baptism is the expression of that faith in Jesus by which we are saved.

Baptism is the New Testament way – the biblical way – to respond in faith to the gospel of salvation in Jesus Christ. So often today we've replaced baptism with raising a hand or filling in a card and then put off baptism for ages. But God says Baptism is the way we respond in faith to the gospel appeal. 'New Testament conversions always include water baptism.'[23] We're saved by faith in Jesus, but we see that we're saved – and everyone else sees that we're saved – as that faith is expressed in baptism. (And that's why the Lord's Supper is for those who have been baptised.[24])

Peter says that the type, of which baptism which now saves us is the antitype, is Noah's Ark (*1 Pet. 3:20-21*). But what's baptism got to do with Noah's Ark? Isn't Jesus the true Ark, not baptism? Yes, Jesus is the true Ark. And Jesus' baptism – His double baptism, the one in the Jordan and the one on the Cross – that's the true baptism. In our baptism we're united to Jesus in His baptism. We're united to Him in the waters of the Jordan hearing the Father's declaration of love. And we're united to Him in His death and resurrection. So in baptism, we're baptised in Jesus – the true Ark. And in Jesus we pass safely through the waters of God's judgement and come out

---

[23] D.T. Rennie, *Riches of Grace*, 13.5 (May 1960), 145. Cf. T.N. Turnbull: 'The time when the convert ought to go through the waters of baptism is the first opportunity after a person has become a Christian. The early Christians, as soon as they believed, were straightway baptised … We are to baptise them the moment they are regenerated.' Turnbull, *The Full Gospel*, 14. NB Turnbull: 'If we claim that baptism is not essential, we are guilty of making ourselves wiser than God.' Turnbull, *The Full Gospel*, 13.

[24] *Apostolic Presbytery Reports for 1920*, 65.

safely on the other side. So baptism is a wonderful gospel picture of that great gospel truth. Baptism is a visible Gospel Word.

Chapter 32

The Breaking of Bread:
This Do In Remembrance of Me

The Heart of Christian Worship

From the night of Christ's betrayal, down to today, and onward to the end of the world, the Breaking of Bread has stood and always will stand at the very heart of Christian worship. This is how Christ, the Head the Church, Himself has taught us to worship; and this is where Christ promises to meet with His Church, as He, the host of the feast, at His Table feeds us with His own body and blood.

Throughout her history, the Christian church has recognised the Lord's Supper as the Sacrament of Sacraments. Yet, unlike the waters of baptism through which we pass only once, the Lord receives and feeds us at His Table over and over again. And so we come week after week, Lord's Day after Lord's Day, to gather as Christ's church around Christ's Table in worship.

Like the earliest Christians, the purpose of our gathering together on the Lord's Day is 'to break bread.' The apostle Paul was in Troas for one Sunday only, and yet the Scripture tells us that the purpose of the Christians' coming together on the 'first day of the week' was not primarily to hear Paul preach (which they did), but 'to break bread' (*Acts 20:7*). For the Christians of Troas, top billing did not go to the guest speaker, but to the Breaking of Bread. The great excitement for the Christians of Troas was not about the dynamic preaching, the powerful gifts of the Spirit, or lively new songs, but about the Lord's Supper. And so, like the earliest Christians, we meet in our assemblies around the world on the first day of the week (and every first day of the week) to break bread.

Yet, while we are in Troas, we should learn a few more lessons from the church there about the sacrament. For, while it was not the preacher but the sacrament which was at the centre of the life of the church in Troas, that did not mean that there was no preaching. Rather, Paul preached a very long sermon (*Acts 20:7-11*), for Word and Sacrament go together. True preaching does not take anything away from the Breaking of Bread. In fact, the Table needs the Word to accompany it.

During Paul's long sermon, the young Eutychus fell asleep and plunged to his death from the third story window, and as we think on these events, it is probably the raising of Eutychus from the dead which we find the most remarkable. Yet, what is perhaps more remarkable than this mighty miracle, is the reaction of the church. For while the death and raising to life of Eutychus could interrupt the preaching of the Word, it did not in any way interrupt the chief purpose of the gathering of the assembly: the Breaking of Bread (*Acts 20:11*). If it had been us today, we might well have forgotten all about the sacrament in the midst of the excitement, the testimony and the praise in the aftermath of such a miracle, but not so in Troas. While there was certainly rejoicing and praise for the raising of Eutychus (captured by Luke's understated 'and they were not a little comforted' – *Acts 20:12*), this didn't interrupt or detract in any way from the Lord's Supper. And so we see that, in Scripture and the early church, the sacrament towers over testimony, praise, miracles and gifts of the Spirit in its centrality and importance. No matter what great thing God had done in their midst, even raising the dead in the middle of the sermon, it could not compete with what God would do in their midst in the Breaking of Bread.

Someone came back from the dead, and yet the Breaking of Bread wasn't abandoned, for the Breaking of Bread is a matter of life and death: in it we feed upon the Bread of Life. The Breaking of Bread is so important that, in the words of D.P. Williams, 'to neglect and disregard the Holy Sacrament is to disregard the very Covenant itself.'[1]

This Do

What is the Breaking of Bread? What makes the sacrament? Here we must be very careful to take our instruction from the Lord Jesus Himself rather than either the traditions we have inherited or the traditions of others

---

[1] D.P Williams, *Riches of Grace*, iii.7 (May 1928), 275.

around us in the Christian world today. For our Lord has laid out for us in His Word exactly what we must do at His Table.

Just as water in church is not enough for the sacrament of Baptism, so too bread and wine in church are not enough for the sacrament of the Lord's Supper. So what actually is necessary? The Scriptures set it out for us in *1 Corinthians 11:23-26*:

> For I received from the Lord that which I also delivered to you: that the Lord Jesus on the same night in which He was betrayed took bread; and when He had given thanks, He broke it and said, 'Take, eat; this is My body which is broken for you; do this in remembrance of Me.' In the same manner He also took the cup after supper, saying, 'This cup is the new covenant in My blood. This do, as often as you drink it, in remembrance of Me.' For as often as you eat this bread and drink this cup, you proclaim the Lord's death till He comes.

Those words are probably very familiar, for we hear them every Sunday morning at the Table. Jesus does not merely tell us to use or even eat and drink bread and wine, but rather tells us what we are to do when we eat and drink ('This do, as often as you drink it'). In this passage we are told what Jesus did and what He commands us to do in the Breaking of Bread, which we can set out in eight points as follows:

1. Take Bread
2. Give Thanks
3. Break Bread
4. Proclamation of the Word: *'This is My body which is broken for you.'*
5. Eat
6. Take the Cup
7. Proclamation of the Word: *'This cup is the new covenant in My blood.'*
8. Drink of the Cup

So in this list we can see that, boiled down to its bare basics, the Breaking of Bread involves eight things. This is not a particular liturgy or order of service that can be adapted from time to time; this is just the very bare bones of what makes the Lord's Supper. As Cyprian of Carthage pointed out in the first treatise on the doctrine of the Lord's Supper in the history of the Christian Church:

> If this is commanded by the Lord, and confirmed and handed on by his apostle, we should do that which the Lord also did as often as we will

drink in remembrance of the Lord. We find that what he has commanded is only observed by us if we do expressly those things that the Lord did.[2]

We shall briefly look at each of these things (combining the bread and the cup in our brief examination).

Taking Bread and Wine (The Emblems)

Our Lord Jesus Christ Himself has specified what we should use in the Breaking of Bread. Thus, just as we cannot substitute any other element for water in baptism, we cannot substitute any other elements than bread and wine in the Lord's Supper.

On the Bread: Leavened or Unleavened?

One of the issues which sparked the Great Schism between the Eastern and Western churches in AD 1054 was the type of bread used for the sacrament. The western churches used unleavened bread; the eastern churches insisted on leavened bread.[3] At the Reformation, the Lutherans favoured unleavened bread and the Reformed favoured leavened bread, but this time neither side condemned the other for their choice of bread.

For the Reformed, Francis Turretin argued that although 'the bread [Christ] used was unleavened; [this was] not from the necessity of the thing, but from an accidental circumstance of time, on account of the feast of Passover.'[4] The Scriptural text of the passages concerning the sacrament does not use the Greek word for unleavened bread, but simply the normal word for bread. Thus, according to Turretin's argument, Christ simply used the bread that was to hand. On that day it happened to be unleavened bread, but the bread we normally have to hand is leavened. The Lutherans agreed that there is 'no divine command in existence as to what kind of

---

[2] Cyprian of Carthage, *The Nature of Holy Communion*, 10.2

[3] Granted, there were other, weightier issues at stake, but the question of unleavened bread was one of the sparks which lit the fuse. The year before the mutual excommunications, a Byzantine archbishop, at the Patriarch's behest, wrote a letter to all the bishops of the western church condemning the use of unleavened bread. There was no going back after that.

[4] Francis Turretin, *Institutes*, 3:430.

bread,' and so argued for their liberty to use unleavened bread because 'it is all left up to Christian freedom.'[5]

The agreement of the two camps in the Reformation over the lack of explicit Scriptural teaching on the type of bread, and the principle of Christian freedom should govern our discussions over leavened or unleavened bread. In various countries, the practice in the Apostolic Church differs. So, in Belgium, for example, leavened bread is used in the Supper; while in the United Kingdom we traditionally use unleavened bread.[6]

The reason British Apostolics have traditionally used unleavened bread is two-fold. Firstly, the Apostolic desire to conform to the pattern of the early church leads us to look to what would have been used at the Last Supper, and therefore to unleavened bread. W.A.C. Rowe writes: 'To be as near to the original pattern as possible, undoubtedly the use of unleavened bread is best.'[7] Secondly, leaven involves corruption, and is, at times, used as a symbol of sin in Scripture. Therefore, the Apostolics have seen unleavened bread, which represents 'no corruption', as setting forth 'more faithfully the *sinless* Saviour.'[8] The breaking of unleavened bread points to the Righteous One, who knew no sin, yet was broken for our sins.

The Cup of Wine

The colour of the wine is not mentioned in the Scriptures, and is irrelevant to the sacrament. We don't know what colour of wine was used at the Last Supper. White was the preference in the Roman Empire, but we do know from archaeological inscriptions that there was red wine produced in that period in the Holy Land. So either red or white wine could have been used

---

[5] Johann Gerhard, *A Comprehensive Explanation of Holy Baptism and the Lord's Supper*, 230.

[6] Formerly, the doctrine of the Apostolic Church was that unleavened bread was to be used. However this was revised in 1985 so that the rule is now simply 'bread'. At the same time the requirement for 'unfermented wine' was removed and replaced with 'wine'. *The Constitution of the Apostolic Church, Third Revision*, (Penygroes: The Apostolic Church, 1985), 5.6.i (p. 25). The unleavened bread rule dates back to at least the Council of 1929 (*1929 Council Minutes*, p.162), and in the Council of 1932 it was noted that this was a matter which 'has been decided before and an International Letter sent out all around the churches that it was unleavened bread that should be used where possible.' (*1932 Council Minutes*, p.8)

[7] W.A.C. Rowe, *One Lord, One Faith*, 208. Unfortunately Pastor Rowe was mistaken in his next statement, for he uses the same argument for unfermented wine. However, the wine at the Last Supper – and in every Lord's Supper around the world for the entirety of church history before the year 1869 – was certainly true (*i.e.* fermented) wine.

[8] Rowe, *One Lord, One Faith*, 208.

by Jesus. Historically, the western church assumed it was white, and generally used white wine. The eastern church used red wine, but didn't base its use of red in the historical circumstances of the Last Supper.[9] At the Reformation, both the Reformed and the Lutherans agreed that either colour was acceptable. For the Reformed, Turretin wrote, 'Common "wine" is instituted, of indifferent colour, undiluted with water because it is called simply the "fruit of the vine" (*Mt. 26:29; Mk 14:25*).'[10] On the part of the Lutherans, Gerhard again argued that this was a matter of 'Christian freedom,'[11] for in Scripture 'nothing is directed whether ... the wine be red or white; just so long as it obviously is ... wine.'[12] It is only in more recent years, with the rise of Zwinglian memorialism, that the colour of wine has become an issue.

The Biblical significance of the cup of wine is not found in its colour, but elsewhere. There is a significance to the wine, and a significance to the cup. In the Scriptures, wine is viewed as a good gift of God 'that makes glad the heart of man' (*Ps 104:15*). Wine was one of the images used by the Lord to speak to Israel of the blessing of the Promised Land (*Deut. 7:13; 11:14; 33:28*), and of the blessing of the life of the age to come (*Isa. 25:6-8; Amos 9:13*). Christ Himself promises that He will drink wine with His people in the coming Kingdom (*Mt 26:29; cf. Mk 14:25; Lk 22:18*). Scripturally, wine points us to the great and joyful blessings of the salvation of the Lord (*Isa. 62:8-9; Jn 2:1-10*). So the wine at the Breaking of Bread is significant, not because of its colour, but because of what it represents in Scripture: the rich blessing of the Saviour which gladdens our hearts.[13]

Furthermore, Jesus is the True Vine (*Jn 15:1*), and He specifically calls the wine we drink in the sacrament 'the fruit of the vine' (*Mt 26:29; Mk 14:25; Lk 22:18*). The wine of the Supper points us to the source of our 'true drink' (*cf. Jn 6:55*), for it is the blood of the True Vine.[14]

But not only is the wine significant, the cup is significant too. In the Garden of Gethsemane, Jesus connects His impending death as our propitiation with a cup: 'O My Father, if it is possible, let this cup pass from Me; nevertheless, not as I will, but as You will ... O My Father, if this cup

---

[9] Cf. the eastern insistence on leavened bread contrary to the usage at the Last Supper.

[10] Turretin, *Institutes*, 3:431

[11] Gerhard, *Comprehensive Explanation*, 230.

[12] Gerhard, *Comprehensive Explanation*, 230-231.

[13] Cf. D.P. Williams, 'Shewbread' MSS, p.10.

[14] NB The Apostolic Church's insistence that the wine used in the sacrament must 'come from the grape' (*1932 Council Minutes*, p.8). Therefore Ribena or any substance made from any other fruit is in no way appropriate for the sacrament of the Lord's Supper.

cannot pass away from Me unless I drink it, Your will be done' (*Mt 26:39, 42; cf. Mk 14:26; Lk 22:42; Jn 18:11*). Earlier, He had used the same image when talking to His disciples (*Mt 20:23*). But this is not a new image; it is one rooted in the Old Testament Scriptures. The prophet Jeremiah spoke of the 'wine cup of fury from [the LORD's] hand' (*Jer. 25:15; cf. 49:12*; cf., in the New Testament, *Rev. 14:10; 16:19*). To drink the wine of this cup is to suffer the wrath of God. And that's what Jesus is praying about in the Garden of Gethsemane; the cup of which He speaks to His Father is the cup of God's wrath, which Christ has drunk to the dregs for us through His atoning death in our place on the cross. Christ has drunk the cup of God's wrath, so that we may instead drink of the cup of His blessing (*1 Cor. 10:16*). Therefore the cup of wine speaks to us of Christ's propitiation and the great exchange which took place at Calvary.

Giving Thanks

The bread and wine are not our offering to God. Rather than offering them up to Him as a sacrifice with supplication, we receive them from Him with thanksgiving. Yet this is not the normal thanksgiving before a meal, for we are not thanking God for a meal of bread and wine, but for the true food with which He feeds us in the Supper: the body of Christ broken for us and the blood of Christ shed for us. So we give thanks to the Father for His sending of His Son, our Lord Jesus Christ, to take on our humanity and live and die in our place. We give thanks for Christ's 'one ... full, perfect, and sufficient sacrifice, oblation and satisfaction, for the sins of the whole world'[15] upon the Cross of Calvary.[16]

Thus, as we give thanks for Christ's once and for all sacrifice at the Table, we see that the Eucharist[17] is not in any way a reoffering of Christ's sacrifice, but rather looks back in thanksgiving to His finished work.

---

[15] From Cranmer's Prayer of Consecration, in 'The Order for the Administration of the Lord's Supper or Holy Communion', *Book of Common Prayer*.

[16] In the British Apostolic Church, although we consecrate the bread and wine separately, we typically only have one joint thanksgiving before the consecration of the bread. In the Belgian Church there are two separate thanksgivings: one over the bread and one over the cup. It seems this diversity of practice was present in the early days of the Apostolic Church. Andrew Turnbull speaks of two thanksgivings in Scotland: 'one gives thanks for the bread and another gives thanks for the wine.' (*1928 Council Minutes*, p.136.)

[17] This name for the sacrament comes from the Greek for 'to give thanks.'

For the Protestant Reformers, this was the key to the difference between a biblical Lord's Supper and the Roman sacrifice of the Mass, arguing that 'the Mass at bottom is nothing else but a denial of the one sacrifice and passion of Jesus Christ, and an accursed idolatry.'[18]

> The papalist Mass … militates against the one propitiatory sacrifice of Christ in many ways and is an affront to it. For there is only one propitiatory sacrifice that expiates and renders satisfaction for sins – the offering of Christ made on the cross (*Heb. 7:27; 9:12, 26; 10:12*) … Therefore, it is a detestable affront against the sacrifice of Christ to invent another propitiatory sacrifice for sins. Neither does it relieve the situation for the papalists that they say they do not offer another but the same sacrifice which was offered on the cross, repeated more frequently, and indeed daily for sins. For the epistle to the Hebrews says clearly and expressly and repeats a number of times that Christ offered Himself once for sins in such a way that He might not have need to offer daily for sins, and that He would not offer Himself repeatedly, as the Levitical priest entered into the holy place every year.[19]

The Words of Institution (The Verba)

The Sacrament needs the Word to make it powerful and effective. The sacrament isn't a sacrament without the Word, but joined to the Word it is an effective means of grace. The Words of Christ Himself – *'This is My Body…. This is My Blood…'* – have an essential place at the very centre of the sacrament of Holy Communion. Without them there is no sacrament and we end up merely having something to eat and drink together. As Martin Luther put it, 'The words are the first thing; for without the word the cup and the bread would be nothing.'[20] Elsewhere he writes, 'all Christians are bound by the institution and command of Christ to speak these words (scil. "This is my body") in the Lord's Supper. I even think the enthusiasts would not dare to omit them with good conscience.'[21]

---

[18] *Heidelberg Catechism*, 80.
[19] Chemnitz, *Examination of the Council of Trent*, 2:494-495
[20] Martin Luther, *Confession Concerning Christ's Supper*, LW 37:338.
[21] Luther, *Confession Concerning Christ's Supper*, WA 26, 283, 35 ff.

Consecration by the Words of Institution

It is Christ's Words of Institution which consecrate (or bless) the bread and wine and through which the elements are sacramentally united to His body and blood. Paul writes that it is the 'cup of blessing which we bless' by which we partake of the blood of Christ (*1 Cor. 10:16*), and Mark tells us that when Jesus took the bread, He 'blessed and broke it,' saying 'this is My body' (*Mk 14:22*). There is a blessing which is to accompany the Breaking of Bread, and Mark shows us that this blessing is Christ's own declaration of promise: 'This is my Body ... This is my Blood' (*Mk 14:22, 24*). We give thanks for the sacrament (*1 Cor. 11:24*), yet Christ blesses the bread and wine, and thus consecrates them as His body and blood.

Yet, doesn't Paul say that we bless this cup of blessing (*1 Cor. 10:16*)? Indeed; Christ speaks His blessing over the bread and cup through His ministers. Therefore, the apostles and elders consecrate the sacrament, and yet the blessing which they speak is never their own, for it is Christ's own words which they repeat, and which He speaks through them. As Bugenhagen, the Reformer, put it:

> It would be folly to omit these words of institution, and a sin not to trust in them. For without these [words], I ask, what would we look for in the bread and the cup? The minister of our church publicly recites these words of the sacred institution over the bread and the cup which have been placed upon the [Lord's Table] ... since he knows that nothing can take place through his own power but that all takes place by the power and institution of Christ.[22]

D.P. Williams reminds us that these words are not the minister's own blessing, but 'the blessing of Christ', through which 'the effectiveness of the Finished Work on Man's behalf is spiritually experienced and appropriated' by those who partake of Christ's body and blood in the Breaking of Bread.[23] In the words of Luther, 'We ... do not breathe or whisper over the bread but do speak the divine, almighty, heavenly, and holy words which Christ Himself spoke at the Supper with His holy lips and commanded us to speak.'[24]

---

[22] HS 127f: cited in Bjarne Wollan Teigen, *The Lord's Supper in the Theology of Martin Chemnitz* (Brewster, Mass.: Trinity Lutheran Press, 1986), 79.

[23] D.P. Williams, *Riches of Grace*, iii.7 (May 1928), 276.

[24] Martin Luther, *LW* 40:211-212

The bread and cup must be blessed with the Verba, for this is Christ's command (*1 Cor. 11:24-25*), and this is what makes of the bread and wine a sacrament (for the Word must be added to the element). Furthermore, God's Word accomplishes what it says. Therefore, as Christ declares, 'this is my body ... this is my blood', we have His true body and His true blood in the sacrament. Therefore:

> The Words of Institution are spoken in our Lord's Supper, not merely for the sake of history, but to show to the church that Christ Himself, through His Word, according to His command and promise is present in the action of the Supper and by the power of this Word offers the body and blood to those who eat. For it is He who distributes, though it be through the minister; it is He who says; 'This is my body.' It is He who is efficacious through His Word, so that the bread is His body and the wine His blood.[25]

The Words are Christ's, spoken in His person and in His name. Christ speaks through His ministers, and works powerfully and graciously by His Word.

As Christ's proclamation to His church, the Words of Institution should not be hidden in a Eucharistic Prayer. The Verba are to be set apart as the Words of Christ, and not hidden amongst mere human words in a prayer. They are a Gospel proclamation from God to us, not merely a narrative account of which we remind God in prayer. Therefore in Apostolic practice, as it is Christ's Words which effect the consecration, they follow the prayer, immediately before partaking of the communion. As Chemnitz argued back in the days of the Reformation:

> He acts wickedly who takes away the consecration of the Eucharist from the words of divine institution and transfers it to the prayers ... [for] the Eucharist is sanctified or consecrated, not by the prayer of man, but by the word of institution; and that the institution is not to be mutilated but is to be used in its entirety for the blessing of the Eucharist and for its administration.[26]

The Bible, the Ordained Ministry, and the Consecration and Administration of the Lord's Supper

When the apostle visits Troas, he takes the Table (*Acts 20:11*). Those who partake of the sacrament of the Breaking of Bread do so in fellowship with

---

[25] Martin Chemnitz, *Examination of the Council of Trent*, 2:229
[26] Chemnitz, *Examination of the Council of Trent*, 2:226, 228.

the apostles (*Acts 2:42*) to whom the Lord entrusted the administration of the sacrament, by commissioning them, 'This Do' (*1 Cor. 11:24-25*).[27] While the apostle could take the Table on his visit to Troas or other assemblies, he was not there every Lord's Day, and so this was one of the reasons that the church needed ordained 'elders in every city' (*Titus 1:5*). One of the significant roles of the ordained ministry[28] is responsibility for the Lord's Table and who communes there.

According to *1 Corinthians 4:1*, the ordained ministers are 'servants of Christ and stewards of the mysteries of God.' (In the context, this particularly refers back to Paul, Apollos and Cephas, in *1 Cor. 3:22*. While Paul and Cephas were apostles, the evidence is not quite so clear in the case of Apollos.[29] Certainly they were all ordained ascension ministers/elders.) The word 'mysteries' here in *1 Corinthians 4:1* is ultimately where we get our word sacrament,[30] and so sometimes older translations will render this 'stewards of God's sacraments.' However, the technical meaning of *mysterion* (sacrament) probably arose later, and so God's mysteries should be given a wider meaning in *1 Corinthians 4:1*, connected to revelation of the gospel, and encompassing both the proclamation of the Word and the administration of the sacraments. Christ's servants – His apostles, prophets, evangelists, pastors (and elders) and teachers – serve Him in their stewardship of the gospel proclamation of Word and Sacrament. This stewardship is not entrusted to each individual Christian on his own behalf, but to the ordained ministry for the benefit of the church. In other words, the presbytery does have a responsibility for who does and does not take Communion (just as they have a responsibility over who is or is not baptised).

In *John 20*, on the evening of His Resurrection, Jesus 'breathed on [the apostles] and said to them, "Receive the Holy Spirit. If you forgive the sins

---

[27] In Matthew, where the emphasis is on the partaking, the 12 are called 'disciples', as representatives of the Church (*Mt 26:26*). In Luke, where the emphasis is on repeating with the 'do this', the 12 are called 'apostles', as representatives of the ordained ministry (*Lk 22:14, 19*). The distinction in emphasis between Matthew/Mark (reception of the sacrament) and Luke/1 Corinthians ('do this') is well established among biblical scholars.

[28] By 'ordained ministry' we are referring here to ascension ministers/elders. Neither Scripture nor church history gives this role to deacons. E.g. One of the oldest Council decrees in the history of the Christian church is one which tells off deacons for trying to take the Table, something that it says they've never been able to do; Council of Nicea, Canon 18.

[29] Although Andrew Wilson makes a strong case that Apollos was indeed an apostle. See Andrew Wilson, 'Apostle Apollos?' *Journal of the Evangelical Theological Society*, 56.2 (2013), 325-335.

[30] *Sacramentum* being the Latin translation of *mysterion*.

of any, they are forgiven them; if you retain the sins of any, they are retained' (*Jn 20:22-23*). This reception of the Spirit is clearly rather different from that of the day of Pentecost in *Acts 2*. Here it is only to His apostles that Christ gives the Spirit and for a specific role, namely authority to dispense God's forgiveness of sins.[31] Although that might sound rather odd to us, it is explicitly stated in the biblical text. So how do the apostles (and other ordained ascension ministers) exercise this authority to dispense God's forgiveness? At least in part, this is by offering or withholding the cup of the blood 'shed for many for the remission of sins' (*Mt 26:28*).[32] This is not an arbitrary withholding, but rather is a result of unrepentant sin. So, the ministers of the church, in their responsibility to proclaim God's forgiveness or point out to Christians their unrepentant sin, have a responsibility for who does or does not take Communion.

Finally, the presbytery have a responsibility of care for the flock (*Acts 20:28; 1 Pet. 5:1-5; Heb. 13:17*). To allow members of the flock to continue living in openly unrepentant sin without alerting them to the danger would not be to care for the flock.

The Apostolic Church, the Ordained Ministry and the Lord's Supper

In Apostolic theology, the ministry of the Sacrament has been confided to the apostleship and through ordination is conferred from the apostleship to the presbytery in the local assemblies.[33] Thus 'the administration of the Lord's table should be in the hands of the Apostles, Pastors ... or Elders, the highest office always taking the actual administration.'[34]

---

[31] These same apostles would receive the Holy Spirit with a different purpose on the Day of Pentecost along with the other believers.

[32] This authority is known as the office of the keys (*Matt. 16:19*) and includes the proclamation of the gospel, declaration of God's forgiveness (after the self-examination at the Table), taking the Table, and the authority to excommunicate.

[33] E.g. D.P. Williams, 'Divine Order in the Assembly of the Saints', *Riches of Grace* ii.5 (Dec. 1923), 6-11; D.P. Williams, 'Apostleship', *Riches of Grace*, ii.7 (November 1924), 5-11; D.P. Williams, *The Work of an Evangelist*, 111; D.P. Williams, *The Prophetical Ministry*, 78-87. This understanding is reflected in *Athrawiaethau Sylfeinol*, 10,13; *Fundamental Truths Believed by the Apostolic Church*, ix; *The Apostolic Church: Its Principles and Practices*, 176-179,215,250. Cf. *Apostolic Church Presbytery Reports* 1920 pp.62-63; *1928 Council Minutes*, p.27.

[34] *Guiding Principles*, 215; 1961 ed., 125. Although they do also make room for 'from time to time giv[ing] place to one another in love and esteem' and for 'readily respond[ing] to the Word of the Lord, should direction be given by Him to make an exception in any particular instance', *Guiding Principles*, 178-179. Cf. *Minutes 1920*, p.65.

The earliest official statement of the Apostolic Church's doctrine makes clear that the ministers of the church are to admit to the sacrament those who, as far as is possible to discern, show evidence of having been 'born again and converted by the grace of God from death to life, from darkness to light, from the domain of Satan to God.'[35] On the other hand, the presbytery is to refuse the sacrament to those who fall under Paul's ban in *1 Corinthians 5:6-11* or who are unrepentant of the sins listed in *1 Corinthians 6:9-10*.[36] The *Fundamental Truths Believed By the Apostolic Church* reiterates this position, and further adds that for the presbytery 'to be remiss in this watchfulness as regards the meetness of those who would partake of the Lord's Table, is to bring death to those who, because of want of spiritual oversight by the servants of God, are so allowed to approach the Table of the Lord.'[37]

Why is the consecration to be carried out by ordained apostles or presbyters? Firstly, this is Christ's institution. D.P. Williams points out that this is 'derived from … definite Scriptures' including *Luke 22* and *1 Corinthians 11*.[38] It is the apostleship and eldership who have been entrusted by the Head of the Church with the responsibility for the authoritative proclamation of the Word and for the feeding and guarding of the flock, and both of these responsibilities coincide at the Table.

Furthermore, the apostles and presbyters minister through union with Christ. He is the true apostle and true presbyter. He is the one who truly speaks the Words of Institution at His Table. And so He speaks His words through those whom He has given as gifts to His church, through whom to exercise His Headship ministries in the Body. The apostles and elders do not consecrate the Supper in their own right or authority, but only in Christ's name and stead, as Christ's representatives standing *in persona Christi*.[39]

---

[35] *Athrawiaethau Sylfeinol*, 10

[36] Ibid. The *Athrawiaethau Sylfeinol* also points to *Ezekiel 44:4-9*, where 'the prophet was set as a watchman in the gate to see who was coming in and out, that not one uncircumcised of flesh nor uncircumcised of heart should desecrate His sanctuary, by abomination, in offering bread, the fat, and the blood.'

[37] *Fundamental Truths Believed by the Apostolic Church*, vii.a

[38] D.P. Williams, *Riches of Grace*, ii.7 (Nov. 1924), 9.

[39] D.P. Williams, *Riches of Grace*, ii.7 (Nov. 1924), 5-6, 9-10; D.P. Williams, *The Prophetical Ministry in the Church*, 78-79.

The Fraction (Breaking the Bread)

The breaking of the bread is part of the Lord's Supper. The Head of the Church does not call us to pray over pre-broken bread, but to take a loaf, give thanks, and break it. This might seem like a mere matter of detail, but important theological (and biblical) points are at stake here.

The Church Partakes of One Christ

There is only one Christ who has given Himself for the sins of His people. Each member of His Church does not have his or her own personal saviour, but all share together in the one Christ, the one and only Saviour of mankind. Therefore we don't eat separate, individual pieces of bread (which would point to separate, individual saviours), but instead eat bread broken from the one loaf, which displays the one Christ of whom we all partake.

His Body Broken for Our Sake

The Lord's Table proclaims, not simply the body of Christ, but His body which was broken for us. It is not only His Incarnation which is displayed, but His atoning death. The fraction sets forth this gospel clearly, that Christ's body was broken for us on the Cross of Calvary. We remember and proclaim not only His life, but above all, His death in our place. We gather round the Table not merely to encounter divine life and power, but to feed on the broken body and shed blood of the Crucified God Incarnate.

The Church is One Body

'For we, though many, are one bread and one body; for we all partake of that one bread.' (*1 Cor. 10:17*) The Scripture teaches that the unity of the church flows from the unity of the one bread of which we partake in the Supper. Ultimately this unity flows from the fact that we all feed on the one Christ, the Living Bread of Heaven, at His Table, yet this is displayed as we break one loaf together.

The Lutheran-Reformed Dispute over the Fraction

Lutherans see the fraction as a Reformed demonstration of their denial of the real presence. As a result, they have historically preferred to use, what Gerhard called, 'little round breads.'[40] The Reformed, on the other hand viewed the fraction as essential to the nature of the sacrament. Turretin explained that 'it is not an accidental and indifferent ceremony, but according to the institution of Christ, no less necessary than taking it in hand, delivering, and communing.'[41] Therefore, those who lack the fraction 'cannot be said to have the Supper entire as to all its parts, but defective and mutilated – if not as to the symbols, at least as to the rites instituted and commanded by Christ.'[42]

The Apostolic Position on the Fraction

The Apostolics have never shared the Lutheran aversion to the fraction. Quite the contrary, they join with Turretin in arguing that the fraction has been instituted by Christ and so is a necessary part of the sacrament of the Breaking of Bread. It is not a denial of the presence of Christ, for it is His command. In the Apostolic Church, the bread is to 'be put on the plate in one whole piece' and broken at the consecration, due to the importance of the 'one loaf' in Scripture (*1 Cor. 10:17*).[43]

Eating and Drinking

Of Both Kinds

At the Lord's Supper we both eat and drink. It is not a choice between one or the other; both are essential to the sacrament. In the Medieval church, it had become the common practice to give only the bread to communicants, and to withhold the cup from the laity, reserving it only for the priest.[44] Yet,

---

[40] Gerhard, *Comprehensive Explanation*, 232; *i.e.* individual communion wafers.

[41] Turretin, *Institutes*, 3:443

[42] Turretin, *Institutes*, 3:446

[43] *Apostolic Church 1932 Council Minutes*, 8-9.

[44] This continued in Roman Catholicism until the Second Vatican Council in the 1960s when a compromise was made: 'communion under both kinds may be granted when the bishops think fit, not only to clerics and religious, but also to the laity, in cases to be determined

at the institution of the Lord's Supper, Christ said both 'take, eat' and 'drink' (*1 Cor. 11:24-25*). And He specifically pointed out that we should 'all' drink from the cup: 'Drink from it, all of you' (*Mt 26:27*). Martin Luther fought for an end to the withholding of the cup, so that all Christians could receive the sacrament in both kinds:

> Matthew, Mark, and Luke agree that Christ gave the whole sacrament to all the disciples, and it is certain that Paul delivered both kinds ... Both Matthew and Mark attach the note of universality to the cup, not the bread – as though the Spirit saw this schism coming, by which some would be forbidden to partake of the cup, which Christ desired should be common to all.[45]

Not only was the withholding of the cup contrary to Christ's instructions and the apostles' practice, and so contrary to the Scriptures, but it also hid the Gospel Word which the sacrament is to proclaim visibly.

> This mutilation of the sacrament impugns the twofold end on account of which the sacrament was instituted: that it may be a commemoration of the death of Christ, which cannot be done under one kind, but necessarily demands two, the one of which is separated from the other to designate the separation of the body from the blood.[46]

Without partaking of the bread and wine, we don't receive the benefit of the sacrament. Someone else can't benefit us by receiving it on our behalf. And so it's not enough for the priest or the pastor to drink from the cup; we all need the cup.

> Just as one cannot be baptized for someone else, that is, if it is going to do some good for the other person, so also no one else can receive the blessing of Christ's body and blood in the holy Supper on behalf of someone else; rather, one must in true faith individually come forward and participate in this heavenly mealtime.[47]

---

by the Apostolic See, as for instance, to the newly ordained in the Mass of their sacred ordination, to the newly professed in the Mass of their religious profession, and to the newly baptized in the Mass which follows their baptism' (*Sacrosanctum Concilium*, 55). Communion under both kinds still requires the special permission of the bishop, although now, in some countries, the Roman Catholic bishops have given a blanket permission.

[45] Martin Luther, *On the Babylonian Captivity of the Church*.

[46] Turretin, *Institutes*, 3:454

[47] Gerhard, *Comprehensive Explanation*, 327-328

As the English Reformation summed it up in the Thirty Nine Articles: 'The Cup of the Lord is not to be denied to the Lay-people: for both the parts of the Lord's Supper, by Christ's ordinance and commandment, ought to be ministered to all Christian men alike.'[48]

One Cup

At the Last Supper, although there would have been plenty of cups on the table for the meal, in the sacrament Christ and His apostles shared in one cup together. The practice of the Apostolic Church from its earliest days was to reject the common free-church practice of each communicant drinking from an individual cup, and to maintain instead a strong stand for the necessity of sharing together in the common chalice.[49] But this was not just a traditional practice: for the Apostolics, this was a significant biblical and theological matter.

The Exegetical Reason for the Chalice

The reason we use a chalice - a common cup - is because that's part of the biblical sacrament of the Lord's Supper. On the night of the last supper, Jesus 'took *the* cup' (*1 Cor. 11:25*). Throughout that passage, and likewise in *Matthew 26*, *Mark 14* and *Luke 22*, the cup is always referred to in the

---

[48] *The Thirty Nine Articles of Religion*, Article 30: 'Of Both Kinds'

[49] In recent years, under the influence of the common practice in contemporary evangelicalism, assemblies in some areas have moved away from the traditional Apostolic use of the chalice. I suspect that in large part this has been for pragmatic reasons, and often without realising that our use of the common chalice was not merely a tradition or an accident of history, but a principled doctrinal position. Among the other British Pentecostals, Elim widely used little individual cups from its earliest days, while the Assemblies of God generally favoured the common chalice until the late 1960s and early 1970s. In 1969 significant concerns were raised among the British Assemblies of God about the widespread abandonment of the chalice for little glasses (Malcolm Clive Dyer, 'An Examination of the Theology and Practice of the Lord's Supper in British Pentecostalism', MPhil Dissertation, King's College, London, 2004, p.115).

For those who recoil from the common chalice on the grounds of hygiene, scientific studies have shown that there are significantly more germs on the rims of little individual communion cups than on the rim of the chalice. This is because the individual cups are so small that other people's fingers will have had to touch their rims, whereas no one's fingers touch the rim of the chalice, and it is wiped with a purificator after it has left the lips of each communicant.

singular. So the Bible specifies that Jesus took one cup and that the disciples all drank from one cup. And along with that Jesus said, 'This do, as often as you drink it, in remembrance of Me' (*1 Cor. 11:25*). We are to do what He does there with His disciples, which is to share one cup together. That's the exegetical reason we use one cup, but that goes together with the theological reason.

The Theological Reason for the Chalice

Why did Jesus give them one cup to share? After all, they would all have had their own cup in front of them as part of the meal. Why didn't he bless all the individual cups and tell them all to drink from their own cups? The answer is found in the very nature of what the sacrament is.

The Breaking of Bread is a participation in the body and blood of our Lord Jesus Christ (*1 Cor. 10:16*). As we share together in bread and wine, we all feed on the same Saviour. It is the same Jesus who strengthens and sustains each of us. It is the same Jesus to whom we are all united by faith and in whom we grow. And the Breaking of Bread is also a remembrance of the great once-and-for-all sacrifice of Jesus in our place. It's the same Jesus who shed His blood for each of us, and through His death for us, we each partake of the same blessings in Him.

So at the Lord's Table, we see that we all share in the same blessings, the same salvation, because we all share in the same Saviour. There isn't one Jesus with one set of blessings for me and another Jesus with a different set of blessings for you. No. The same blood flowed for us, and so we partake together of the same blood.

The Breaking of Bread isn't a celebration of an individualistic salvation, but of the common Saviour in whom we share. It's a meal of the Church, where we come together as one Body, not because of anything we have done, but all because of our Heavenly Head – the Lord Jesus – and what He has accomplished for us. *1 Corinthians 10:17* stresses the close connection between the unity of the Body and the sacrament: 'For we, though many, are one bread and one body; for we all partake of that one bread.' So 'there is to be one cup, just as there is one loaf. The church is one body, for Christ is not divided into one hundred or more fragments.'[50] At the Table, we have communion together in the One Christ, and that's why it's important that

---

[50] Robert Letham, *The Lord's Supper: Eternal Word in Broken Bread* (Philipsburg: P&R, 2001), 42.

we share together in one bread and one cup. 'As we share the same cup, we realise that we have an equal share, a common interest in the same Saviour. We realise that we are all on the same level – just sinners saved by grace.'[51]

What about Intinction?

Now in the 21st century, little cups have already gone out of fashion somewhat. The chalice has made something of a come-back.[52] However, the fashion for the re-emergence of the chalice has tended to go in the direction of a third alternative: neither drinking together from one cup, nor drinking separately from individual cups, but rather not drinking at all. *Intinction* (dipping the bread in the cup) became popular during the swine flu epidemic a few years ago, and appears to have grown in its popularity ever since.

So is intinction the way forward? After all, for many churches it's a return to the one cup: an end to the individualism of the little cups. So couldn't we all find unity in intinction?

Well, although it might seem to have a lot going for it, intinction also has one major lack: no one drinks. Christ's command was 'This do, as often as you drink it' (*1 Cor. 11:25*). Our proclamation of the Lord's death is 'as often as [we] ... drink this cup' (*1 Cor. 11:26*). And the following verses on examining ourselves before coming to the Table speak repeatedly of drinking (*1 Cor. 11:27-29*). Christ's detailed instructions for the sacrament of the Lord's Supper involve both eating bread and drinking of the cup, and so intinction, in which no one drinks, is contrary to the instructions for the sacrament.

And this isn't a new or novel argument. In fact, the very first mention of intinction in history was a rejection of the practice as inconsistent with the Scriptural instructions:

> But their practice of giving the people intincted Eucharist for the fulfillment of communion is not received from the gospel witness, where,

---

[51] Edwin Williams, *Riches of Grace*, vii 5 (May 1932), 214.

[52] Although the majority of all evangelical churches in the United Kingdom have always continued to use the chalice, as Anglicans make up the majority of evangelicals, and Anglicans, by law, must use a chalice.

when he gave the apostles his body and blood, giving the bread separately and the chalice separately is recorded.[53]

Yet this isn't the only problem with intinction, for it also joins the body and blood, which are set forth in the sacrament separately. In other words, in the Lord's Supper we first eat bread, as Christ's body broken for us, and then drink of the cup, as His blood shed for us, and this proclaims His death – for it is by death that the blood was separated from the body. But by soaking the bread in the wine, we set forth instead the blood in the body, rather than poured out from it in death. So intinction is both contrary to Christ's instructions in Scripture for the sacrament and also fails to set forth clearly the Lord's death.

For as often as you eat this bread and drink this cup: On the Frequency of the Breaking of Bread

From the outset, the weekly gathering around the Lord's Table for the Breaking of Bread has been the very heart of worship in the Apostolic Church, for this is what we have understood to be the New Testament pattern. Thomas Turnbull characterised the faith and worship of the Apostolic Church by writing that we 'joyfully dare to stand for first-century Christianity, its faith, its practices and its government.'[54] The Apostolic Vision involves 'the establishing of the New Testament teachings, doctrines and practices in every country of the world.'[55] The Church's 'expansion and development should be according to the pattern revealed in the New Testament … a Church which is in every respect a continuation of the New Testament Church.'[56]

The New Testament Pattern of Weekly Communion

This New Testament pattern of worship is seen in the book of Acts. In *Acts 2:42* we read that the church 'continued steadfastly in 'in the apostles' doctrine and fellowship, in the breaking of bread, and in prayers.' The early church was united in fellowship with the apostles, receiving their Gospel-

---

[53] Julius I, AD 340
[54] T.N. Turnbull, *What God Hath Wrought*, 11.
[55] Turnbull, *What God Hath Wrought*, 11.
[56] Turnbull, *What God Hath Wrought*, 12.

teaching, sharing in the sacrament together, and praying together as a church in worship.[57] Gathering together as the church to hear the Word, partake of the sacrament, and respond with prayers of praise and thanksgiving, then, is the pattern of Christian worship right from the very beginning. In those early days of revival in Jerusalem, the Breaking of Bread was not only a weekly, but a daily event (*Acts 2:46*).

In more ordinary times in the life of the church, the Breaking of Bread was not celebrated daily, but still held at least once a week. But, even more importantly than that, the Breaking of Bread was the main purpose of the gathering together of the church on the first day of the week. *Acts 20* states the reason for which the disciples came together on Sundays in Troas: it was 'to break bread' (*Acts 20:7*). This is particularly of significance given that the apostle Paul was briefly visiting Troas on the particular Sunday dealt with in *Acts 20*. Even though the great apostle was visiting and preaching, the church gathered, not to hear Paul, but to break bread.

Perhaps even more interestingly, nothing could distract the church in Troas from the Breaking of Bread. As we've already noted, even though Eutychus died and was raised to life, such a great miracle did not send the church immediately out to the streets to speak about what had happened, but rather they went back to the upper room for Word and Sacrament. The Gospel of Jesus Christ who died for the forgiveness of our sins as set forth in the preached Word and in the bread and wine of the Lord's Table, is a much greater miracle and infinitely better good news than even a young man being raised from the dead! What we might have been tempted to view as a fantastic 'missional opportunity', for the apostle Paul and the early church was something of less significance than the Breaking of Bread.

Paul also wrote to the Corinthians about the Breaking of Bread as the purpose of the church's meeting together. In *1 Corinthians 11:20* he laments that when they all 'come together in one place, it is not to eat the Lord's Supper.' The implication here is that it should be to eat the Lord's Supper.[58]

---

[57] The reference to 'the' prayers in *Acts 2:42* is to corporate, liturgical prayer, and thus to the worship of the Church.

[58] Gordon Fee, *The First Epistle to the Corinthians*, The New International Commentary on the New Testament (Grand Rapids: Eerdmans, 1987), 540; Howard Marshall, 'The Biblical Basis of Communion', *Interchange* 40:54; Robert Letham, *The Lord's Supper: Eternal Word in Broken Bread* (Phillipsburg: P&R, 2001), 57; Francis Turretin, *Institutes of Elenctic Theology*, Vol. 3, 445; Anthony C. Thiselton, *1 Corinthians: A Shorter Exegetical and Pastoral Commentary* (Grand Rapids: Eerdmans, 2006), 182-183; Anthony C. Thiselton, *The First Epistle to the Corinthians*, New International Greek Testament Commentary (Carlisle: Paternoster, 2000), 862-863; Hughes Oliphant Old, *Worship: Reformed According to Scripture* (Louisville: Westminster John Know, 2002), 115.

That is what the Corinthians think they are doing when they come together, and that is what Paul wishes they were doing when they come together, but, due to the abuses of the sacrament in the Corinthian assembly, it's not really what they are doing. Paul does not try to fix the situation by telling them to Break Bread less often (even temporarily until the abuses are corrected). He fully agrees with the Corinthians that the purpose of the church meeting together is to Break Bread.

As Paul recounts the Words of Institution to the Corinthians, he repeats Jesus' instruction, 'This Do' (*1 Cor. 24-25*). Thus the Supper is a command of Christ for the worship of the church. As Johann Gerhard put it, 'Christ our Lord has not given us the freedom to use the holy Supper or not use it; rather, He has expressly set down the command: Do such to my remembrance, which command all obedient disciples of Christ, as His servants, should justly follow.'[59] Why should the gathering of the church include things every Sunday (as an apparent necessity for worship) that Christ hasn't commanded, but exclude those things which He has expressly commanded for Christian worship?

Furthermore, in *1 Corinthians 1:26* Paul tells us that the frequency of proclaiming Christ's death goes along with the frequency of the Supper! 'For as often as you eat this bread and drink this cup, you proclaim the Lord's death until He comes.' These are not merely liturgical words, but rather also an argument from the apostle to maintain the frequency of their participation in the sacrament. The word $\gamma\grave{\alpha}\rho$ ('*for*') links this verse back to 'do this' of *verse 24* and the 'this do, as often as you drink it' of *verse 25*. The reason the purpose of the church's meeting together is to Break Bread is because the sacrament and the proclamation of the Christ's death go together. The sacrament is abused and is no sacrament at all without the proclamation, and the proclamation finds its completion in the sacrament.

The Book of Revelation presents the worship of heaven. There we see the multitude gathered around the throne giving glory to the Lamb who was slain and lives (*Rev. 5*). It is the sacrificed Lamb who is at the centre of heaven's worship. And this worship culminates in the Marriage Supper of the Lamb (*Rev. 19:6-9*). In reflection of the worship of the heavenly Holy of Holies, the church on earth gathers around the Lamb who was slain and lives as we gather around His Table in worship. Significantly, John received this vision of the heavenly worship, centred on the Lamb who was

---

[59] Johann Gerhard, *A Comprehensive Explanation of Holy Baptism and the Lord's Supper* (English Translation, Malone: Repristination Press, 2014; original text, 1610), 453

sacrificed for our sin, when he 'was in the Spirit on the Lord's Day' (*Rev. 1:10*).

It's on the Lord's Day that the Church keeps the fourth Commandment: 'remember the Sabbath day, to keep it holy' (*Ex. 20:8*).[60] This day on which we Break Bread week after week is a day set apart (holy) to the Lord, for His worship and use, and as British Assemblies of God theologian David Allen points out, the Breaking of Bread is 'when all is said and done, the only act of corporate worship that Jesus commands us to continue till the end of the present age.'[61] The day on which the Lord Jesus rose triumphant from the tomb is the day on which we gather to meet with the living Lord at His Table. So it is only appropriate that 'in the church of the New Testament there was no Lord's Day without the Lord's Supper.'[62]

The Testimony of Church History to Weekly Communion

The testimony of church history is important, not because we should blindly follow older traditions, but because we are not the first people to read and interpret the Scriptures, so we should learn from those who have read and applied the Word of God before us.

The earliest non-biblical sources we have for the history of the early church confirm that weekly Breaking of Bread on the Lord's Day was indeed the practice of the Christian church from the very beginning. The *Didache* is a manual of pastoral instruction and guidelines for worship which dates to between AD 60 and AD 100. So it was composed at the same time as the New Testament texts and gives us an historical glimpse of church life in the New Testament period.[63] Didache 14:1 gives the clear instruction: 'On the Lord's own day gather together and break bread and give thanks [Gk. *eucharistesate*], having first confessed your sins.'

The earliest description of Christian Worship we have from outside the New Testament comes from the pen of Justin Martyr about 50 years after

---

[60] 'It is expected that all members will observe the sanctity of the Lord's Day, namely Sunday, the first day of the week.' *Introducing the Apostolic Church: A Manual of Belief, Practice and History* (Penygroes: Apostolic Church, 1988), 29.

[61] David Allen, *Neglected Feast: Rescuing the Breaking of Bread* (Nottingham: Expression, 2007), 85.

[62] Hermann Sasse, 'The Lord's Supper', *We Confess the Sacraments*, 99.

[63] The aspect of the *Didache* which has usually been of most interest to Apostolics is its references to apostles and prophets.

the completion of the New Testament. Justin describes the weekly Breaking of Bread:

> And on the day called Sunday, all who live in cities or in the country gather together to one place, and the memoirs of the apostles or the writings of the prophets are read, as long as time permits; then, when the reader has finished, the ruler in a discourse instructs and exhorts to the imitation of these good things. Then we all stand up together and pray, and, as we said before, when our prayer is ended, bread and wine and water are brought, and the ruler likewise offers up prayers and thanksgivings, to the best of his ability, and the people assent, saying Amen; and there is a distribution to each, and a participation of that over which thanks have been given.[64]

Justin Martyr's description of Christian worship fits well with what we see in *Acts 2:42* and *Acts 20.*[65]

The vast majority of churches around the world have practiced weekly communion (at minimum) throughout the church's entire history. For at least the first 1500 years of church history this was the practice of every church in the world. Although some Protestant churches moved away from weekly communion after the Reformation, in each case this was due, not to Protestant teaching, but to the interference of the secular authorities. The consensus voice of the Protestant Reformers was in favour of weekly communion. Luther and Cranmer were able to achieve this; Calvin was thwarted by the city council in Geneva (and it is from this particular interference of a city council in the affairs of a church that the practice of some Protestants celebrating the sacrament with less frequency has arisen. Calvin made very clear that such a reduction was unbiblical and insisted that the Lord's Table be set even on the Sundays on which he was not allowed to administer the sacrament as a reminder that, biblically, it should be there.)[66]

From the very beginning of the Pentecostal movement in the United Kingdom, Breaking of Bread each and every Lord's Day was the centrepiece

---

[64] Justin Martyr, *The First Apology*, 67

[65] It's also remarkably similar to an old-fashioned, traditional Apostolic Breaking of Bread Service, with a 'time around the Word'/'time of sharing' of Bible readings, followed by a time of open worship and prayer, and all culminating in the sacrament and then ending (as Justin Martyr goes on to explain) with the bringing of tithes and offerings.

[66] Calvin argued that infrequent Communion was 'a veritable invention of the devil, whoever was instrumental in introducing it.' Calvin, *Institutes*, 4.17.46

of Pentecostal worship.[67] All three British Pentecostal denominations (the Apostolic Church, Elim, and the Assemblies of God) were in agreement on this weekly pattern of Communion and its centrality as the most important service.[68] So central and important was the Breaking of Bread to Pentecostal identity that it was often pointed to by Pentecostals as their greatest distinctive: 'The manner in which the Lord's Supper is celebrated in the Pentecostal movement is perhaps its most valuable distinctive feature and should be cherished for the precious heritage that it is.'[69] The contemporary American Pentecostal theologian, Chris Green, calls the Breaking of Bread 'the heart of the Christian life and so ... the very centre of Pentecostal worship.'[70] As the great academic observer of Pentecostalism Walther Hollenweger put it, 'the service of the Lord's Supper is the central point of Pentecostal worship. It is as it were the holy of holies.'[71]

Weekly Communion in the Practice and Theology of the Apostolic Church

Weekly Breaking of Bread has been the practice and teaching of the Apostolic Church for the (over) 100 years of its existence. As W.A.C. Rowe noted, the Breaking of Bread 'is the *centre* of the greatest and most important expression of Church activity. The Lord's Supper takes an absolutely *central place* in congregational worship.'[72] In the worship of an Apostolic assembly:

> The actual participation in the Breaking of Bread should take the main place of honour. This vital part should not be pushed into some odd corner of the time available and be gone through in a hurried or perfunctory manner, as if it were merely a duty to be accomplished. Given the climactic place of importance, all else should flow toward it, or if experienced earlier in the gathering everything that ensues should flow from it.[73]

---

[67] Malcolm Clive Dyer, 'An Examination of the Theology and Practice of the Lord's Supper in British Pentecostalism' (MPhil diss., King's College, London, 2004), 167.

[68] Dyer, 'An Examination of the Theology and Practice of the Lord's Supper in British Pentecostalism', 103; Richard Bicknell, 'In Memory of Christ's Sacrifice: Roots and Shoots of Elim's Eucharistic Expression', *Journal of the European Pentecostal Theological Association*, 17 (1997), 76-78.

[69] W.H. Urch, 'The Worship of the Church,' *Elim Evangel*, 21.7.47, 419.

[70] Chris E.W. Green, *Toward a Pentecostal Theology of the Lord's Supper: Foretasting the Kingdom* (Cleveland TN: CPT Press, 2012), 316.

[71] Walther Hollenweger, *The Pentecostals* (London: SCM, 1972), 385.

[72] W.A.C. Rowe, *One Lord, One Faith*, 201 (emphasis original).

[73] Rowe, *One Lord, One Faith*, 213-214.

This is the position taken too by our current 'manual of belief and practice': 'the Breaking of Bread service is not an appendage.' Rather, it is 'fundamental to Christian life and blessing and is a vitalising force in true worship.'[74]

D.P. Williams looked to Christ's Words of Institution, particularly the word over the cup, as the reason for weekly Communion. 'The Cup is the New Testament, the new covenant made with Blood – the Blood of the Slain Lamb. To neglect and disregard the Holy Sacrament is to disregard the very Covenant itself.'[75] Pastor Dan likened the Breaking of Bread to the Church's wedding ring: 'No true wife will disparage her marriage ring.'[76] He also connects the weekly celebration of the Supper with the frequency of proclamation of the Lord's Death in *1 Corinthians 11:26*:

> It is the time when the saints are together unveiling, exhibiting the Person, His deeds, sufferings and victory, His constant priesthood, and His glorious soon-coming. It is a sign of the Treaty of Peace made on the Cross, and, now that all enmity has been slain, declaring to all the unsaved world their belief in the Saviour, their satisfaction in the salvation wrought, and their deliverance from sin, the world, and the tyranny of the Enemy; also exhibiting before the principalities of all the higher realms the utter victory of Christ over all the hosts of Darkness, regaining for lost men all the rights stolen by Satan, and putting his legions to open shame by the Cross. That ere long He will come to 'divide the spoil,' giving to every one his portion, place and position, when the Enemy will ... be allocated to the domain of despair.[77]

In other words, by gathering at the Lord's Table, the Church proclaims (to one another, to the world, and to the principalities and powers) the Lord's death until He comes. The Proclamation of the Gospel Good News of Christ Crucified goes together with the Breaking of Bread.

During the war, there were some in the church who were neglecting the weekly celebration of the sacrament. As a result, the Lord spoke in prophecy at the Penygroes Convention of 1943:

> I will mention the Breaking of Bread ... 'This do in remembrance of Me,' saith the Word; the disciples regularly came the first day of the week to My house. Do you love Me so much that you will remember my death until I come? This is not of Man's appointment; it is of divine appointment. If it

---

[74] *Introducing the Apostolic Church: A Manual of Belief, Practice and History* (Penygroes: The Apostolic Church, 1988), 42.

[75] D.P. Williams, 'Editorial Note: The Lord's Table', *Riches of Grace*, iii.2 (May 1928), 275.

[76] D.P. Williams, *Riches of Grace*, iii.2 (May 1928), 275.

[77] D.P. Williams, *Riches of Grace*, iii.2 (May 1928), 275.

> was man that had ordained it, then there would be reason for you not to
> come, but when your Master, before He left the earth, gave commandment
> unto you, 'This do in remembrance of Me,' then there is need for you to
> come as often as you can, until I come … to remember My death.[78]

The prophecy continued by stating that the reason for some not communing
weekly was 'because they have left their first love.' Yet the antidote the Lord
gives in the prophecy against losing our first love is to come and Break
Bread.

> But I say to them (here is a secret), if you had attended My house on the
> first day of the week, around my Table … you would not have left your
> first love, for the love that was revealed on Calvary would be a burning
> love in your heart … In such gatherings [i.e. at the Breaking of Bread
> service, where Word and Sacrament are offered] I can reveal Myself in a
> greater way than I can do at any other time.[79]

Other Apostolics of previous generations simply pointed to the
practical reality that the Breaking of Bread keeps our preaching and worship
rooted in the Cross. We 'cannot stand at the Communion table, and take up
the Bread and break it, and pour forth the Wine and drink the Cup, without
… preaching the Cross. At the Table we see the Cross.'[80]

In addition to the New Testament pattern and the practical benefits of
weekly Communion, the early Apostolics also found the practice necessarily
flowing out of their theology of the sacrament. The Tenets of the Apostolic
Church confess our belief in 'The Sacraments of Baptism by immersion and
of the Lord's Supper.' We do not only believe in the practice of the Lord's
Supper, but we believe it is a *sacrament* (rather than an ordinance).[81] As a
sacrament, the Breaking of Bread is not simply our act, as a reminder of
Christ's death, but rather it is God's act: a means of grace by which the Lord
feeds, strengthens and builds us up. Therefore, it is not the Christian's table,
but the Lord's Table: it is not a private act of individual devotion, but rather
a feast to which the Lord invites us, and at which He both presides and

---

[78] Prophetical Ministry through the Prophet T.N. Turnbull, 'Loving the Lord', *Herald of Grace*, 3.8 (August 1943), 93

[79] Ibid.

[80] W.W. Watson, 'Evangelism: To Preach Christ', *Herald of Grace*, 3.9 (Sept. 1943), 100.

[81] This is a theological difference which explains why historically there have been certain differences in practice with regard to the Breaking of Bread between the Apostolic Church and the Elim Pentecostal Church and Assemblies of God. Elim specifically confess the Lord's Supper as an ordinance (rather than a sacrament) and the AoG merely confess their belief in the Breaking of Bread without specifying whether this is as an ordinance or sacrament.

feeds us. The bread and wine become the sacrament of Christ's body and blood when joined with Christ's Word.[82]

Our Apostolic forefathers confessed, in one of the earliest official explanations of their doctrine, that in the Breaking of Bread, 'the spirit, soul, and body of each believing saint partake, by faith, of the virtue of His Own Body and Blood, as substantial sustenance to the spiritual life.'[83] The founders of the Apostolic Church had a very high theology of the sacrament, believing that in it we feed on Christ and all His benefits.[84] With such an understanding of the sacrament, to withhold Christ's presence from the members of the church by not offering it every week was unthinkable to the early Apostolics. As the Reformation theologian Martin Chemnitz put it, less frequent communion means that 'these most beneficial comforts will be taken from us and snatched away.'[85]

The Lord's Table was also understood to be a place of physical healing. Because we feed on Christ, who is Life and Health, at the Table, 'one previously sick is able to rise from the Lord's Table healed.'[86] This healing provision was a further encouragement to ensure that the Breaking of Bread was available each and every Lord's Day, so that on any Sunday Christians might receive healing at the Table. They also sometimes made a similar connection with the Table and the baptism of the Holy Spirit.

Conclusion on the Frequency of Communion

The New Testament, Church history, and the century of the Apostolic Church's own theology and practice all point us to a position where the purpose of the church's meeting together is to Break Bread, and so the church Breaks Bread each and every Lord's Day.

---

[82] We'll look at what this means and how it happens in the next chapter.

[83] *Fundamental Truths Believed By the Apostolic Church*; for even stronger language in an official explanation of the Church's doctrine, see the *Athrawiaethau Sylfeinol* (although ignore the translation of this found in Worsfold's *Origins of the Apostolic Church in Great Britain*, as it deliberately and drastically changes the Eucharistic theology of the document).

[84] We'll look at this in the next chapter.

[85] Martin Chemnitz, *The Lord's Supper*, 193.

[86] Edwin Williams, *Riches of Grace*, vii.5 (May 1932), 214. In fact, Edwin Williams writes of healing not only for physical illness, but also mental illness, specifically referring to healing from depression.

Chapter 33

The Breaking of Bread:
This is My Body, This is My Blood

What Happens in the Breaking of Bread?

Commemoration

When He instituted the Lord's Supper, Jesus said, 'do this in remembrance of Me.' Nowadays it is often assumed that this means the sacrament is something we do to help us remember the death of Christ. And so these words, 'do this in remembrance of Me,' are central to the Memorialist understanding of the Supper. However, these words do not appear in all of the Biblical accounts of the institution of the sacrament. Only Luke and Paul use the words 'in remembrance' (*Lk 22:19; 1 Cor. 11:24-25*), and even Luke only records these words for the bread. Luke doesn't attach remembrance to the cup, and neither Matthew nor Mark mention the word at all. So although Jesus did speak of remembrance, it is not the key to understanding the central reality of the Supper.

Nor does the remembrance of which Jesus spoke necessarily mean what we generally assume it means. This remembrance is not just an aid to jog our memory, but something much more deeply rooted in Scripture. For Old Testament Israel, the Passover was given as a remembrance: 'So this day shall be to you a memorial; and you shall keep it as a feast to the Lord throughout your generations. You shall keep it as a feast by an everlasting ordinance' (*Ex. 12:14*). The Passover feast was not simply a memory aid to remind the people of that night in Egypt, but a powerful proclamation of the great deliverance which God had accomplished for His people.

> 'To remember God's mighty acts' or 'to remember the poor' is not simply
> to call them to mind but to assign to them an active role within one's
> 'world.' 'To remember' God (*cf. Deut 8:18; Judg 8:34; Ps 22:7*) is to engage in
> worship, trust, and obedience, just as 'to forget' God is to turn one's back
> on him. Failure to remember is not absent-mindedness but unfaithfulness
> to the covenant and disobedience. 'Remembering' the gospel tradition
> (*Rom. 15:15; 1 Cor. 15:3*) or 'remembering' Christian leaders (*Acts 20:31;
> Heb. 13:7*) transforms attitude and action. To 'remember' the poor is to
> relieve their needs.[1]

Therefore, 'those who reduce the Lord's Supper to an act of mental
recollection are imposing modern modes of thought on the text of
Scripture.'[2] In Christian worship, 'remembering is not so much fondly
recalling something that happened in the past as it is having that distilled
event from the past inserted into our present.'[3]

But it is not only we who remember. Jesus did not say 'do this so that
you will remember,' but 'do this in remembrance.' Yes, it is our
'remembrance'; but it is also God's remembrance, in which 'God remembers
His new covenant promises and bestows His gifts.'[4]

Proclamation

'For as often as you eat this bread and drink this cup, you proclaim the
Lord's death till He comes' (*1 Cor. 11:26*). In our remembrance of Christ and
His remembrance of us, the death of Christ is proclaimed at His Table. As
we've seen in the last chapter, the sacraments are visible words which
portray the gospel of Jesus Christ. And to be a sacrament, the elements must
be attached to the Word; so in the Supper, the gospel of Christ's death is
proclaimed in the Words of Institution: *This is my body, broken for you ... This
is my blood of the new covenant, which is shed for many for the remission of sins* (*1
Cor. 11:24 ; Mt 26:28*).

But not only is Christ's death proclaimed visibly, and in the Word
attached to the sacrament, but Christ's death is also proclaimed in the
preaching of the cross at the Breaking of Bread service. The gospel, 'should,
when preached, make us understand what the visible sign means.'[5] The

---

[1] Thiselton, *First Epistle to the Corinthians*, 879.

[2] Keith A. Mathison, *Given For You: Reclaiming Calvin's Doctrine of the Lord's Supper*, 232.

[3] Arthur A. Just, *Heaven on Earth: The Gifts of Christ in the Divine Service*, 227.

[4] Arthur A. Just, *Heaven on Earth: The Gifts of Christ in the Divine Service*, 228.

[5] John Calvin, *Institutes of the Christian Religion*, 4.14.4

proclamation of the Word must accompany the ministry of the sacrament, for 'the sacrament requires preaching to beget faith.'[6] Therefore, the Word should always be preached at the Breaking of Bread service, and this preaching 'should always be around the cross.'[7]

Anticipation

This proclamation of the Lord's death in the sacrament is carried out 'till He comes' (*1 Cor. 11:26*). As we feed upon the body and blood of Christ in the Supper, the church longs for the day when her heavenly Bridegroom will return and she will feast with Him in glory at the marriage supper of the Lamb (*Rev. 19:6-9*).

Heaven One Long Eucharist

Ian Macpherson is well remembered as one of the greatest preachers of British Pentecostalism in general, and of the Apostolic Church in particular. He was also quite a prolific author, principal of the Apostolic Church Bible College in Penygroes, and a hymn writer. And one of Pastor Macpherson's great interests was the Breaking of Bread. He was so concerned that we have suitable songs to sing around the Lord's Table that he compiled a new hymnbook, *Hymns at the Holy* Table, to be used as a supplement to the *Redemption Hymnal* for the Breaking of Bread service. In fact, he wrote several of the hymns for the new book himself,[8] and through his hymns he teaches us quite a bit about the Lord's Table.

One particular line is striking in the way it points us to the Breaking of Bread as an anticipation of the heavenly banquet. It's the final line of Macpherson's hymn 'Here at our Holy Feast'[9], where he writes, 'Heaven one long Eucharist.' The last verse of the hymn speaks of how, in the resurrection, we shall eternally dine with Christ, ending with this description of heaven as one long Eucharist.

---

[6] Calvin, *Institutes*, 4.14.4; cf. D.P. Williams, 'Shewbread' MSS, p.10.

[7] *Apostolic Church 1932 Council Minutes*, p.8; NB this is of the essence of true preaching, for preaching is proclaiming Christ biblically, and the biblical Christ is the Christ who was crucified. Cf. *1 Cor. 1:23; Col. 1:28*.

[8] With several also being included in the *New Redemption Hymnal*.

[9] *Hymns at the Holy Table*, 52

The description is striking; yet it isn't a one off in Macpherson's hymns. Elsewhere he describes how we'll feed on the Bread of God 'throughout eternity.'[10] The Lord's Supper, then, is an anticipation of the heavenly feast, not only in terms of feasting with Christ, but also in feeding on Christ, the true Bread of God. At the Table we look forward to Christ's coming, not to bring an end to the Eucharist, but to usher it in in greater fullness. Where now at the Table we have a foretaste of the love and joy of communion with the Trinity:

> Then at a higher feast
> In that abode Divine,
> Our love and joy increased,
> We shall sit down to dine
> With Father, Holy Spirit, Son,
> While the eternal ages run.[11]

And for Macpherson, that higher feast is the very central reality of heaven. Rather than an image of the saints in heaven bowed before a throne of power, Macpherson invites us to see the saints – to see our future – seated at the Table, and so to recognise that the Table is Christ's throne.

> Then when in heaven we sit around Thy table,
> Hunger and thirst for evermore unknown,
> We shall adore Thee as we're now unable
> And find that table an eternal throne.[12]

Yet the heavenly Table-Throne is not different from the Table around which we gather on the Lord's Day. There we will know it in fullness, but already we see in part. And so, as we gather around the Lord's Table in our assemblies, in reality we are gathering with the heavenly hosts around the Lamb upon the Throne, and 'we here inherit / all that heaven can bestow.'[13] At the Table, as we enjoy communion with Christ in His body and blood, we have a foretaste of the heavenly glory, and share in all the blessings with which God has blessed us in the heavenly places in Christ (*Eph. 1:3*). That's why we hear older Pentecostals speak of healing at the Table, or hear testimonies of those baptised with the Spirit in the Breaking

---

[10] *Hymns at the Holy Table* No. 18, in a verse Macpherson wrote and added to Bonar's hymn 'I heard the voice of Jesus say'

[11] *Hymns at the Holy Table No. 57, a verse by Macpherson added to Charles Wesley's 'Author of Life Divine'*

[12] *Hymns at the Holy Table* No. 46, 'O Bread of Life, this hungry world requires Thee'

[13] *Hymns at the Holy Table* No. 6, 'Saviour, seated at Thy table'

of Bread, for at the Table of the Lord, the blessings of the Throne are poured out on His saints in a foretaste of the heavenly glory.

Now we have the foretaste. After Christ returns we shall have the fullness. Then we shall enjoy 'heaven, one long Eucharist' as we know full communion with Jesus, and with His Father and the Spirit, one God in three persons, blessed Trinity.

Participation

The Breaking of Bread is much more than a commemoration. It's even more than a proclamation or an anticipation. The Breaking of Bread is also a participation in the body and blood of our Lord Jesus Christ who died and rose again for us. 'The cup of blessing that we bless, is it not a participation in the blood of Christ? The bread that we break, is it not a participation in the body of Christ?' (*1 Cor. 10:16, ESV*).

What does it mean to participate in the body and blood of Christ? For a start it means that at the Table 'more than a memory is sensed.'[14] This opposes the teaching of *Zwinglian Memorialism*, which sees the Lord's Supper as merely something which we do to remind ourselves of what Christ has done. Memorialists follow Ulrich Zwingli in re-interpreting Christ's words 'this is my body … this is my blood' as 'this represents my body … this represents my blood.'[15] This Memorialist understanding sees the Supper as our work for Christ (we remind ourselves of Him and demonstrate our commitment to Him), rather than Christ's gift to us (where we participate in His body and blood, as Paul teaches in *1 Cor. 10:16*). Memorialists do not view the Lord's Supper as a *sacrament*, but only as an *ordinance* (something commanded by Christ).

The Apostolic Church, however, confesses that the Breaking of Bread is a sacrament and a true means of grace. There were two main ways in which the early Apostolics understood our participation in Christ's body and blood in the sacrament. Some, like D.P. Williams and Andrew Turnbull, taught, like Luther, that in the Breaking of Bread 'we drink His Blood; we eat His flesh.'[16] Others, like Ian Macpherson, taught, like Calvin, that we

---

[14] Ian Macpherson, *Hymns at the Holy Table* No. 66.

[15] However, they go much further than even Zwingli; for he did not altogether deny the presence of Christ at the Lord's Supper.

[16] D.P. Williams, *Riches of Grace*, xi.1 (Sept. 1935), 205.

'taste by faith [His] flesh and blood.'[17] In the Lutheran understanding, all who partake of the sacrament eat Christ's body and blood which are sacramentally united to the bread and wine. This view is often referred to as the *Real Presence*. In the Calvinist view, those who eat with faith, partake by faith of Christ's body and blood at the same time as partaking by mouth of the bread and wine. As the Scottish Reformer, Robert Bruce, put it: 'As soon as you receive the bread in your mouth (if you are a faithful man or woman), you receive the body of Christ in your soul, and that by faith.'[18] The church is lifted up into heaven by the Holy Spirit, there to feed on the body and blood of the ascended Christ by faith. Therefore, Calvin's view is sometimes referred to as the *Spiritual Presence*. Both of these views were widely held by the early Apostolics.

Both the Lutheran and the Calvinist inclined Apostolics believed that 'the Lord's presence is the main thing' in the sacrament of the Breaking of Bread.[19] By participation in Christ's body and blood in the Supper, we have 'vital fellowship with Christ in grace' by 'partaking of Christ Himself.'[20] At the Breaking of Bread, 'we partake substantially … of His body and His blood, to be sustenance for the spiritual life.'[21] D.P. Williams wrote that, 'Christ declared if we eat His flesh and drink His blood we shall live. So there must be a participation.'[22] In the sacrament, there is 'a mystical union of eating His flesh and drinking His blood' as we feed upon 'the Unblemished Lamb who has been sacrificed for us.'[23] Christ is present not only in memory or by the influence of his divine power on the worshipping assembly, but substantially in His body and blood in the Breaking of Bread.

A third view arose much later in the movement's history. D.T. Rennie taught that 'as we partake in faith, discerning His body and blood, we can draw from the living, glorified Christ, present in our midst by His Spirit, all that we stand in need of.'[24] This is another type of Zwinglianism: not Memorialism, but a high Zwinglianism which still sees the presence of Christ as of central importance in the sacrament, just not directly connected to the bread and wine. Rather, Christ is seen as the Host who feeds us at His

---

[17] *Hymns at the Holy Table*, 7v3.
[18] Robert Bruce, *The Mystery of the Lord's Supper*, 44.
[19] *Apostolic Church 1928 Council Minutes*, 144.
[20] *Apostolic Church 1928 Council Minutes*, 141, 138.
[21] *Athrawiaethau Sylfeinol*, 10.
[22] D.P. Williams, 'Shewbread' MSS, 9.
[23] D.P. Williams, *Herald of Grace*, 6.3 (March 1946), 68; *Riches of Grace*, ii.3 (Nov. 1922), 20.
[24] D.T. Rennie, *Riches of Grace*, 13.6 (June 1960), 177.

Table, and blesses us with His presence as we fix our eyes upon His sacrifice on the cross.[25]

Now that we've seen that the Bible teaches a participation in Christ's body and blood, and also seen the three views of Christ's presence, let's look at what the Scriptures teach on the presence of Christ in the sacrament of the Lord's Supper.[26]

This is My Body ... This is My Blood

The Words of Institution: 'Is' Means 'Is'

Christ tells us what the sacrament is in the Words of Institution, and so it is to these words of Christ that we must look to see what is happening in the Breaking of Bread. As Luther said, 'the chief and foremost thing in the sacrament is the word of Christ ... everything else depends on these words.'[27] The Lord tells us in these words that the bread is His body and the wine is His blood. While Zwingli and some of his colleagues tried to redefine 'is' to mean 'represents', Luther simply insisted that 'is' means 'is.' For Luther, this was a question of the authority of Scripture: 'I am bound and held captive by the words of the Lord, spoken at the institution.'[28]

---

[25] One first generation Apostolic apostle, Thomas Rees, held to a Zwinglian view in discussions in Council, but refrained from teaching it publically as he considered his opinion to be out of line with the Church's official position. Most of the other apostles appear to have been bemused by his idea of the Breaking of Bread, which was very explicitly driven by a fear of any possible hint of the aroma of Rome. Both D.P. Williams and Thomas Jones (Llwynhendy) explicitly warned of the danger of over-reacting to Roman sacramental theology by going too far in the opposite direction.

[26] I follow D.P. Williams, Andrew Turnbull, Frank Hodges and Martin Luther in adhering to the Real Presence understanding of the Supper, so that is the view I will outline in the next section of the chapter. Williams, Turnbull and Hodges were the pioneering apostles of the Apostolic Church in Wales, Scotland, and the south of England respectively, so this view has a strong Apostolic pedigree.

[27] Martin Luther, *The Adoration of the Sacrament*, LW 36:277.

[28] Martin Luther, *Marburg Colloquy*; translation in Sasse, *This is My Body*, 260.

> Belief in the Real Presence ... was for Luther, and it is still today, the great
> test whether we are able to found our faith on the Word of our Lord alone,
> or whether we still have need of some support from human sources.[29]

The Words of Institution are:

> The words of the last will and testament of the very Son of God and not a
> game or place for exercising the mind by dreaming up unending
> interpretations that depart from the simplicity and proper meaning of the
> words. The mind should treat and consider these words with neither
> temerity nor frivolity but with reverence and piety and in great fear of the
> Lord.[30]

It's common for those who support Zwingli's redefinition of 'is' to argue that Jesus uses figurative language on other occasions, such as 'I am the True Vine' (*Jn 15:5*). Jesus, they argue, is not literally a vine, and therefore the bread doesn't have to actually be the body of Christ. However, the two statements are not parallel. Jesus is not saying 'I represent the vine', but rather, that the vine is like Him. The verb 'to be' isn't figurative, and the identification works in the opposite direction.

But how could Jesus, who gave the bread and wine to His disciples, mean 'is' when He said 'is'? Luther's answer is simple: 'God said, This is my body. God is omnipotent. Consequently the body is in the bread ... You must not look so much upon what is said, but rather who says it. Since God speaks thus you must embrace the Word.'[31] In other words, the right question is not 'how can this be the body of Christ?', but 'who always speaks a true and effective word?' What the Lord says comes to pass. When the Lord says to a lame man, who cannot possibly walk, 'rise up and walk', he gets up and walks. When He speaks the world into being from nothing, the world is. When He speaks over bread saying 'this is my body', the bread is His body.

> The sacramental words in the Lord's Supper are the words which Christ
> spoke at the institution and which He speaks at all times through His
> ministers, words of Him who is God Himself and who is, therefore, able to
> effect what they say. They are the words of institution which effect the Real
> Presence of the body and blood of Christ.[32]

---

[29] Sasse, *This is My Body*, 368.
[30] Chemnitz, *Lord's Supper*, 26.
[31] Luther, *Marburg*, cited in Sasse, 225, 235.
[32] Sasse, *This is My Body*, 371.

The Lord's words do what they say. His words were effective at the Last Supper, and they continue to be effective today as He speaks them at the Table through His apostles and elders. As we sing:

> At the last great Supper lying,
> Circled by His brethren's band,
> Meekly with the law complying,
> First He finished its command,
> Then, immortal food supplying,
> Gave Himself with His own hand.
>
> Word made flesh, by word He maketh
> Of His flesh a sign to be;
> Man by faith Christ's blood partaketh;
> And if senses fail to see,
> That same faith the true heart waketh
> To behold the mystery.[33]

Guilty of the Body and Blood

In Paul's teaching on worthy reception of the Lord's Supper, just after his account of the Words of Institution, he again shows us the Real Presence of Christ's body and blood in the sacrament. 'Therefore whoever eats this bread or drinks this cup of the Lord in an unworthy manner will be guilty of the body and blood of the Lord' (*1 Cor. 11:27*). Coming immediately after the Words of Institution, the 'therefore' with which this warning begins must refer back to them. Thus, Paul is saying, because the bread is Christ's body and the wine is Christ's blood, whoever eats or drinks unworthily will be guilty of Christ's body and blood. They are not guilty of misusing bread and wine, or of a symbol or rite. The guilt is against the actual body and blood of the Lord Himself. For it is His body they have eaten in an unworthy manner and His blood they have drunk in an unworthy manner.[34]

---

[33] Thomas Aquinas, 'Of the Glorious Body Telling', *Hymns at the Holy Table*, 44. Ian Macpherson seems to have lightly edited the language here for inclusion in the Apostolic Communion hymnal. I quote it here with Macpherson's edits, to show it in the form it would have been sung in Apostolic assemblies.

[34] The doctrine that unworthy partakers receive the body and blood of Christ in the sacrament is called the *manducatio impiorum* ('eating by the impious').

Not Discerning the Lord's Body

Those who eat and drink unworthily, and thus who are guilty of the body and blood of the Lord, are those who do not discern His body. 'For he who eats and drinks in an unworthy manner eats and drinks judgment to himself, not discerning the Lord's body' (*1 Cor. 11:29*). 'He is not speaking of discerning the human nature in Christ per se or in an absolute sense, but of the fact that what we eat in the Supper the Son of God calls His body.'[35] To discern is to distinguish one thing from another, so those who do not discern the Lord's body are those who 'do not distinguish between the bread of the Lord's Supper and other, common bread, so that they fail to recognize His true presence and to attribute to Him due honour.'[36]

Participation in His Body and Blood

'The cup of blessing that we bless, is it not a participation in the blood of Christ? The bread that we break, is it not a participation in the body of Christ?' (*1 Cor. 10:16, ESV*). The bread and wine of the Holy Supper are a 'participation' in the body and blood of Christ. Here we see both that we truly partake of the body and blood of Christ in the sacrament, and also that the bread and wine remain bread and wine. The Bible does not teach that the bread and wine are turned into Christ's body and blood, but rather that the bread and wine are sacramentally united to Christ's body and blood so that in and with the bread and wine we receive His true body and true blood.[37]

> Bread and wine are by no means changed into the body and blood of Christ. On the contrary, in the holy Supper, Christ's body is sacramentally united with the consecrated bread and is received by means of the same. Thus also is Christ's blood sacramentally received with the consecrated wine and is drunk by means of the same.[38]

In the Supper, heaven meets earth as Christ's body and blood are joined in the sacrament with bread and wine on the Lord's Table. Although we eat

---

[35] Chemnitz, *The Lord's Supper*, 28.
[36] Chemnitz, *The Lord's Supper*, 133.
[37] Thus, the Apostolic Church explicitly denies the Roman Catholic doctrine of transubstantiation.
[38] Gerhard, *Comprehensive Explanation*, 353.

and drink the body and blood of Christ with our mouths, we do so in a supernatural way in the bread and wine.

> But the union or presence is not physical in the sense of our secular reasoning. Therefore we can more easily show what the sacramental eating of the Supper of the body of Christ is not rather than what it is. That is to say, it is not physical in the sense that it consists of the chewing, mastication, swallowing, and digesting of the substance of what it eaten, because the presence of Christ's body in the Supper is not a natural presence in the sense consistent with the ordinary use of this term.
>
> And yet it is not something merely figurative or imaginary but true and substantial, even though it occurs through a supernatural, heavenly, and unsearchable mystery. Thus we must not doubt as true and sure what the Son of God Himself affirms in the words of His last will and testament, that those who eat in the Supper receive and eat with their physical mouths not only the bread but at the same time also that body which was given for us, even though this does not take place in a physical way as when we eat ordinary bread.
>
> Although we are not able to demonstrate or understand how this takes place, it suffices for faith simply to believe what the words of Christ teach us in their proper and natural sense – that the physical mouths of those who eat in the Lord's Supper are not eating common or plain bread when they receive the bread, but the bread which now has been given its name by God, that is, the body of Christ. That is to say, it is bread with which the body of Christ is truly and substantially (although in a supernatural way) present and distributed.[39]

True Food and True Drink: John 6

Although some people argue that *John 6:47-58* couldn't refer to the sacrament as Jesus spoke these words before instituting the Lord's Supper, this would not be the only time during His earthly ministry where Jesus spoke of something which had yet to occur. Furthermore, from John's point of view in composing the Fourth Gospel, the Breaking of Bread had not only already been instituted, but was also a familiar part of the life of the church. John does not record the actual institution of the sacrament, but he does record these sacramental words at another Passover-time (*Jn 6:4*), and thus links the two together to show us that Jesus is here teaching about the true meaning of the sacrament.

---

[39] Chemnitz, *The Lord's Supper*, 60-61.

Looking back on the life, ministry, death, and resurrection of Jesus as a whole, [John] saw Jesus' speech as directly connected to the later introduction of the sacrament. From his later authorial standpoint the two were in effect part of the same reality.[40]

Both the early church and the early Apostolics read *John 6* as Christ's teaching on the sacrament.[41] Here Jesus teaches that the He is Himself the nourishment which He gives us, through His once-and-for-all sacrifice in our place on the cross: 'the bread that I shall give is My flesh, which I shall give for the life of the world' (*Jn 6:51*).

Jesus' first hearers understood clearly what He was saying, and so were shocked and disgusted: 'How can this Man give us His flesh to eat?' (*Jn 6:52*). Some found these words so impossible to accept that they 'went back and walked with Him no more' (*Jn 6:66*). But our Lord's response was not to soften His words. Rather than say He was only speaking figuratively, Jesus actually intensifies the physical nature of His language. From *verse 54* onwards, Jesus uses a different verb for eat, switching from φάγω (*phagō*) to τρώγω (*trōgō*). While φάγω (*phagō*) simply means 'eat,' τρώγω (*trōgō*) is a much more evocative word, giving notions of chewing, crunching, or gnawing. By choosing this word, the Scripture points us to the physical nature of eating Christ's flesh. Only the sacramental eating of Christ's body in the Lord's Supper makes sense of such vocabulary.

Thus, *John 6* ties together faith in Christ and the Breaking of Bread. We feed on the one in whom we believe as we eat His flesh and drink His blood in the sacrament. While partaking of the sacrament without faith can only lead to judgment, those who eat and drink in faith partake of life in the one who feeds them with His body and blood. As John Calvin put it:

[Christ] shows that in his humanity there also dwells fullness of life, so that whoever has partaken of his flesh and blood may at the same time enjoy participation in life … The flesh of Christ is like a rich and inexhaustible fountain that pours into us the life springing forth from the Godhead into itself. Now who does not see that communion of Christ's flesh and blood is necessary for all who aspire to heavenly life?[42]

---

[40] Robert Letham, *The Lord's Supper: Eternal Word in Broken Bread* (PRP, 2001), 8-9.

[41] *Athrawiaethau Sylfeinol*, 10.

[42] John Calvin, *Institutes*, 4.17.9

The Reliquae

If the bread is Christ's body and the wine is Christ's blood, then we must give consideration to what we do with the *reliquae* when we celebrate Holy Communion. The *reliquae* are any left-over elements from the Lord's Supper. This is bread and wine which has been consecrated, and so sacramentally united to the body and blood of Christ. Therefore, we must take great care with how we treat the *reliquae*. The rules set out for the *reliquae* in the Apostolic Church are that:

> After the close of the meeting when the Breaking of Bread service has been held, anything left of the emblems (bread and wine) should be destroyed, so as to avoid desecration ... (*Ex. 12:10*).[43]

> The Breaking of Bread ... is administered by the Presbytery to set forth the dignity and holiness which should be associated with this [sacrament] and to preserve it from any abuse ... At the conclusion of the service emblems remaining should be destroyed for the same reason.[44]

Therefore, there are four things good Apostolics can't do with left-over bread and wine after the Breaking of Bread.

1.) The reliquae cannot be reserved for adoration. This is the practice in the Roman Catholic Church. Due to their doctrine of transubstantiation, whereby they believe that the substance of bread and wine are replaced by the substance of the whole Christ – body, blood, soul, and divinity. Therefore, they believe that by adoring the reserved consecrated elements they are adoring Christ. However, the Scriptures teach that the elements are both body and bread, blood and wine after the consecration, and teach us distinctly that they are to be eaten and drunk, not reserved, carried round in processions, or adored.

2.) The reliquae cannot be kept to distribute another time, at another service. Again, this is a Roman Catholic practice, on certain occasions to use pre-consecrated elements for the Communion. However, the Word must be heard along with the eating of the bread and the drinking of the wine. Christ's words over the bread and cup proclaim the gospel to us, and so we

---

[43] *The Apostolic Church: Its Principles and Practices*, 216.
[44] *Introducing the Apostolic Church: A Manual of Belief, Practice and History*, 44.

must hear them when we partake. 'The elements consecrated by the pastor can neither be preserved nor sent to those who are absent, which was an evil custom of some in the ancient church. For the sacramental action, which consists of consecration, distribution, and reception, must be completely uninterrupted.'[45]

3.) The reliquae cannot be thrown out with the rubbish. This is a more evangelical temptation. However, these are not simply some left-over crumbs of bread or dregs of wine at the bottom of a cup; Christ has said that this is His body and this is His blood. Therefore, they should not be treated irreverently as rubbish and thus desecrated, for that would not be to discern the Lord's body.

4.) The reliquae cannot be kept to re-consecrate again at next Sunday's communion. Consecrated bread and wine should not be mixed with unconsecrated bread and wine, as if they were one and the same thing and could be used together on another occasion. Christ's word is not undone by the closing hymn and final benediction. Luther wrote a letter to Simon Wolferinus, warning him not to 'mix the remains of [consecrated] wine and bread with [unconsecrated] bread and wine.' Instead, Luther advised Wolferinus to:

> Do what we do here [in Wittenberg], namely, to eat and drink the remains of the Sacrament with the communicants, so that it is not necessary to raise these scandalous and dangerous questions about when the action of the Sacrament ends, questions in which you will choke unless you come to your senses.[46]

Thus, any *reliquae* should be reverently consumed, as the body and blood of Christ. Anything that is impossible to consume should, following the example of any holy remains of the Passover, be burned with fire (*Ex 12:10*).[47]

---

[45] C.F.W. Walther, *Pastoral Theology*, 144.

[46] Martin Luther, *[First] Letter to Simon Wolferinus [1543]*, WA Br. X, 340-341.

[47] For example, where the wine has been spilt and absorbed into fabric. Cf. *The Apostolic Church: Its Principles and Practices*, 216.

The Benefit of the Breaking of Bread

The early Apostolics often spoke of the benefit of the Breaking of Bread in terms of receiving *virtue* as we partake of the body and blood of Christ, singing:

> May the virtue in Thy body
> Feed our souls with life divine,
> And Thy blood with cleansing vigour
> All our hearts and our lives refine.[48]

We've already looked at the role of the Breaking of Bread in our sanctification in chapter 25. So let's look now at some other aspects of this virtue we receive as we partake of Christ in the sacrament.

The Breaking of Bread and Theosis

The Table is the place of 'mystical union of eating His flesh and drinking of His blood … and by that communion [we are] made partakers of the Living Christ.'[49]

> When, in the sacrament, we receive the body and blood of Christ, we are most intimately joined together with Christ Himself through that nature which He has inseparably and hypostatically united to Himself, and through Christ we are united with the Father. For through the bread we are united with the body of Christ, and through the body with Christ Himself, and through Christ with the Father. Thus we are made partakers with the Father, the Son, and the Holy Spirit. These things are the results of salutary communion of the body and blood of the Lord in the Supper.[50]

So, in the Breaking of Bread, the Church participates in 'fellowship with the divine … a communion with the Three in One.'[51] Therefore, the Breaking of

---

[48] J.B. Clyne, 'Taste the Bread of Sweet Communion', *Gospel Quintet Choruses*, 10:480. See also *Apostolic Church Council Minutes 1928*, 143.

[49] D.P. Williams, *Herald of Grace*, 6.3 (March 1946), 68.

[50] Chemnitz, *The Lord's Supper*, 143.

[51] D.P. Williams, *Herald of Grace*, 6.3 (March 1946), 67.

Bread service is the ultimate place of encounter between the Church and her Head.[52]

> The Son of God, therefore, in order that He might become the second Adam, assumed our nature, but without sin, and in that nature condemned sin, destroyed death, and restored that nature to life. Thus first of all in His own person He sanctified, restored, and blessed human nature. And now, in order that we might be made certain that these blessings apply also to us and our wretched nature, and have truly been communicated to us, Christ in His Supper again offers us that very nature which He has assumed from us and in Himself first restored, so that when we receive it with our poor flesh we are no longer in doubt concerning the salvation also of our nature through Christ. For in this way He, as it were, grafts our miserable and corrupt nature into the holy and life-giving mass of His human nature, as Cyril says, so that our depravity and misery are cured and renewed through the remedy of this most intimate union. These concepts, which are filled with the most abundant comfort, diminish and disappear if we remove from us by an immense distance the assumed human nature of Christ in the Lord's Supper.[53]

Apostolic prophecy even connected this partaking of the love of Christ in his body and blood in the sacrament with the outpouring of God's love in the heart through the outpouring of the Holy Spirit (*Rom. 5:5*).[54] By supplying his Body with Himself in his flesh and blood in the Breaking of Bread, Christ's Church 'deriv[es]' from Him the blessings of our redemption',[55] including the uprooting of sin,[56] participation in the divine life,[57] and mystical union.[58] At the Table, the Church participates in the life of the Triune God and so the Table is the paramount place of theosis.

The Breaking of Bread and All Christ's Benefits

When we partake of Christ, we partake of all His benefits. For every spiritual blessing is found 'in Christ' (*Eph. 1:3*). Therefore, not only is the

---

[52] See 'Loving the Lord: Prophetical Ministry through T.N. Turnbull', *Herald of Grace*, 3.8 (Aug. 1943), 93.
[53] Chemnitz, *The Lord's Supper*, 188-189.
[54] *Herald of Grace*, 3.8 (Aug. 1943), 93.
[55] D.P. Williams, *Herald of Grace*, 2.4 (June 1942), 48.
[56] D.P. Williams, 'Bwrdd Yr Arglwydd', *Cyfoeth Gras* (*Riches of Grace*) ii.1 (Gorffennaf, 1921), 13.
[57] D.P. Williams, *Athrawiaethau Sylfeinol*, 10; D.P. Williams, 'Ministry of the Word', 171.
[58] D.P. Williams, *Herald of Grace*, 6.3 (March 1946), 68.

table a place of sanctification and theosis, but it is also a place where healing and the fullness of the Spirit can be found.

Healing at the Table

Jesus Christ is the Healer, and so as we feed on His life-giving body and blood at the Table, we may partake of healing in Him, and so 'there is healing at the Table.'[59] As Andrew Turnbull put it, when faith lays hold of Christ, 'faith appropriates everything' and therefore 'many have testified their bodies are healed when drinking of the cup.'[60]

For the early Apostolics, the idea of healing in the cup was such an important implication of Christ's presence in the Supper, that to refuse the common chalice due to any hygiene concerns was seen as a denial of the presence of the Christ:

> We cannot see how any true Christian can see danger (in the members using the same cup) at the Lord's Table. We are partaking of and communing with Christ, Who is Life and Health. How can we partake of Life and Health and Death and Sickness at the same time, from the same source? It is impossible. It is either Health or Sickness, one of the two, and to say that there is a danger is nothing more but to belittle the value of Christ's Atonement.[61]

The Fullness of the Spirit and the Table of the Lord

The early Apostolics also saw a connection between the Breaking of Bread and the baptism and fullness of the Holy Spirit. The Lord Jesus Christ is the one who has received the Spirit without measure (*Jn 3:34*), and so it is in Him, and in Him alone, that we may partake of the fullness of the Holy Spirit. Therefore, as we partake of Christ at the Table, we may partake of the blessing of the Spirit's fullness in Him. Andrew Turnbull pointed to *John 7* in connection with the Lord's Supper and the fullness of the Holy Spirit.

> On the last day, that great day of the feast, Jesus stood and cried out, saying, 'If anyone thirsts, let him come to Me and drink. He who believes in Me, as the Scripture has said, out of his heart will flow rivers of living water.' But this He spoke concerning the Spirit, whom those believing in

---

[59] W.A.C. Rowe, *One Lord, One Faith*, 211.
[60] Andrew Turnbull, *Apostolic Church Council Minutes 1928*, 139.
[61] Edwin Williams, *Riches of Grace*, vii.5 (May 1932), 214.

Him would receive; for the Holy Spirit was not yet given, because Jesus was not yet glorified. (*Jn 7:37-39*)

As we drink of Christ's blood in the Cup of the Lord's Supper, we come to Him and drink. Therefore, there is a connection between the baptism and fullness of the Spirit and the sacrament. As Andrew Turnbull put it, at the Lord's Table, 'you drink of Him and you keep filled with the Holy Ghost.' This is not magically, 'because of the bread and wine', but rather, through faith, because, in the bread and wine we have 'fellowship with Christ.'[62] D.P. Williams explains that this is because, as we eat Christ's body and drink His blood, 'we are through faith participating; we are taking through faith, out of the substance of Christ, His life and Spirit.'[63] As we partake of the Supper, we partake of 'a fresh infusion of the Spirit.'[64] So, in partaking of the Lord's Supper, because we there partake of Christ and all His benefits, believers may be baptised in the Holy Spirit or filled afresh with the Spirit's fullness.

The Breaking of Bread and the Resurrection of the Dead

The early church called the Breaking of Bread 'the medicine of immortality'[65] and 'the life-giving blessing.'[66] For, as Jesus Himself said:

> I am the living bread which came down from heaven. If anyone eats of this bread, he will live forever; and the bread that I shall give is My flesh, which I shall give for the life of the world … Most assuredly, I say to you, unless you eat the flesh of the Son of Man and drink His blood, you have no life in you. Whoever eats My flesh and drinks My blood has eternal life, and I will raise him up at the last day. For My flesh is food indeed, and My blood is drink indeed. He who eats My flesh and drinks My blood abides in Me, and I in him. As the living Father sent Me, and I live because of the Father, so he who feeds on Me will live because of Me. This is the bread which came down from heaven — not as your fathers ate the manna, and are dead. He who eats this bread will live forever. (*Jn 6:51, 53-58*)

---

[62] Andrew Turnbull, *1928 Council Minutes*, p.143. In other words, this is not *ex opere operato* (or automatic in receiving the bread and wine), but only as the body and blood of Christ are received in faith.

[63] D.P. Williams, *1928 Council Minutes*, p.143.

[64] Messrs Turnbull and Macpherson, *1928 Council Minutes*, 138.

[65] Ignatius, *Ephesians*, 20.

[66] Cyril of Alexandria

Jesus is the Bread of Life (*Jn 6:35*), and so, whoever feeds upon Him, partakes of this life-giving bread. Through eating His flesh, we abide in Him, and He in us, and so we are kept now in eternal life in Him. We 'derive life at the Lord's Table,' for 'we are partaking of the very life and everything that is in Christ.'[67] But this life-giving benefit is not only for this life. For Christ will raise up those who eat His flesh and drink His blood on the last day. Therefore, Jesus connects our participation in His body and blood in the Breaking of Bread with our resurrection at His return (*Jn 6:54*). As Johann Gerhard put it:

> This our body in which sin and death are dwelling in this life will be resuscitated from the dust of the earth to eternal life because it has been nourished with the vivifying body of Christ.[68]

Who is to be admitted to the Lord's Table?

There are five requirements for participation in the sacrament of the Breaking of Bread.

Prerequisite One: Credible Profession of Faith

The Lord's Supper is a meal for believers. The first partakers of the sacrament were Jesus' 'disciples' (*Mt 26:26*). It was the saved in Jerusalem, those who received 'the apostles' doctrine', who 'continued steadfastly … in the Breaking of Bread' (*Acts 2:42*). In Troas, it was the 'disciples' who met together to Break Bread on the first day of the week (*Acts 20:7*). It is the meal shared in by 'the church of God' (*1 Cor. 11:22*), and the meal through which the church is formed and united as one Body (*1 Cor. 10:17*).

The Bread and Wine are offered joined with the sacramental words, 'This is my Body which is broken for you' (*1 Cor. 11:24*) and 'This cup is the new covenant in My blood, which is shed for you' (*Lk 22:20*), so are only to be received by those who receive and believe those Gospel words – 'broken

---

[67] *Apostolic Church 1928 Council Minutes*, 141.
[68] Johann Gerhard, *Loci*, XXI, cap. 20, par. 213, cited in Sasse, *This is My Body*, 386. Cf. D.P. Williams, *The Trinity*, 2:32.

for you, shed for you.' In other words, the sacrament is given to those who are saved.

In *John 6* Jesus connects eating His flesh and drinking His blood with having eternal life, with abiding in Him and He in us, and with being raised from the dead on the last day (*Jn 6:53-58*). For the earliest Apostolic doctrinal documents these verses were of great importance to the understanding of the Breaking of Bread.[69]

Prerequisite Two: Baptism

The Lord's Supper is the sacrament of continuance in the Christian life, but it is Baptism in water which is the sacrament of the beginning of the Christian life. Biblically, it is in baptism that a new Christian publicly professes faith in Christ and is outwardly welcomed into the church (*Mk 16:16; Acts 2:38,41; 8:12,36-38; 9:18; 10:47-48; 16:15,33; 18:8; 19:3-5; Rom. 6:3-4; Col. 2:12; 1 Pet. 3:21*). Only those who have professed faith in Christ and are accepted as part of His Church can partake of the sacramental meal which Christ has entrusted to the Church, and thus baptism is a necessary prerequisite for admission to the Lord's Table. It is those who were baptised in *Acts 2:41* who then 'continued steadfastly ... in the breaking of bread' in the next verse. This has been the practice of the entire Christian church throughout all history all over the world.[70] As *Didache* 9:5 put it all the way back in the 1st Century: 'But let no one eat of your Eucharist except those who have been baptized into the name of the Lord.' From the very beginning of our movement, this has been the understanding and practice of the Apostolic Church: 'It is clear that Baptism precedes the Lord's Supper in order.'[71] 'In the Word, Baptism is the first sacrament, because faith in the Lord and baptism are always connected with one another in the Acts; and then the other sacrament follows on.' [72]

Prerequisite Three: Discerning the Lord's Body

Those who eat and drink unworthily, eat and drink judgment to themselves 'not discerning the Lord's body' (*1 Cor. 11:29*). Therefore, those who partake

---

[69] *Athrawiaethau Sylfeinol*, 10; *Fundamental Truths Believed by the Apostolic Church*, vii.a.

[70] Until some recent laxity in places over the last 20 or 30 years.

[71] 'Mae yn eglur fod Bedydd mewn trefn yn rhagflaenu Swper yr Arglwdd' (*Athrawiaethau Sylfeinol*).

[72] *Apostolic Church 1920 Presbytery Reports*, 65.

of the Supper must be able to discern the Lord's body. If someone is not old enough to understand that once joined to Christ's Word, this is no longer ordinary bread and wine, but 'a participation in the body of Christ' and 'a participation in the blood of Christ' (*1 Cor. 10:16*), then they cannot meet the prerequisite of discerning the Lord's body. John Calvin wrote that to give the sacrament to an undiscerning child would be to give them poison![73] Therefore, presbyteries are not to distribute the sacrament to children.[74]

Prerequisite Four: Examining Oneself

Those who are to partake of the Lord's Supper are first to examine themselves (*1 Cor. 11:28*). Again, if someone is not old enough to examine themselves, then they cannot meet the prerequisite for participation in the Supper. We'll look at what it means to examine oneself below.

Prerequisite Five: Not Excommunicated

Finally, in order to partake of the Supper, one must not be excommunicated or under suspension.

Excommunication

The Bible, Lifestyle and the Supper

The apostle Paul addresses the issue of lifestyle and admission to the Lord's Table in *1 Corinthians 5:6-13*. Paul sets his instructions concerning not keeping company with those who claim to be Christians yet continue to live in open sin, by connecting it to our keeping of 'the feast' of 'Christ our Passover' who was 'sacrificed for us' (*vv.7-8*). 'Malice and wickedness' are to be excluded from Christ's Feast (*v.8*), and therefore the church is 'not even

---

[73] Calvin, *Institutes*, 4.16.30

[74] *Apostolic Church 1920 Presbytery Reports*, 58, 64 – *Beidio cyfrannu yr Ordinhad i'r Plant* ('Do not distribute the sacrament to the children'). Cf. *Apostolic Church Council Minutes 2015*, 9.1: 'We agree that every local assembly adheres to the age limit of 12 years for participation in the sacraments of baptism and communion, and for membership in the Apostolic Church.'

to eat' with 'anyone named a brother, who is sexually immoral, or covetous, or an idolater, or a reviler, or a drunkard, or an extortioner' (*v.11*). While this 'not eating' extends beyond the Breaking of Bread, it begins precisely with the Breaking of Bread itself. Thus, professed Christians who live in open sin are to be excluded from the Lord's Table, and thereby from Christian fellowship with the people of God. This is excommunication.

The sins included in *1 Corinthians 5:6-13* are not limited to moral issues, but also include doctrinal issues. The church is not to eat with idolaters. Idolatry is a rejection of the identity of the true and living God as He has revealed Himself in the Scriptures. Thus those who claim to be Christians, but who reject the Bible's teaching on the Triune God, including the Incarnation of God the Son for us and for our salvation, are not to be welcomed to partake with us from the Lord's Table.

Therefore we should not give the sacrament to Trinitarian or Christological heretics.[75] Nor should we give the sacrament to those who deny the bodily Incarnation of Christ (*1 Jn 4:3*), His finished atoning work upon the Cross or the gospel of free justification in Christ (*2 Cor. 11:4; Gal. 1:8-9*).[76]

One of the ethical issues raised by Paul in *1 Corinthians 5:6-13* which is frequently discussed in relation to lifestyle and the Lord's Supper is sexual immorality. This whole discussion was introduced by Paul's dealing with the issue of a man who was sleeping with his father's wife at the beginning of the chapter. Excommunication was the necessary response on the part of the Church to such open and flagrant sin, with the ultimate goal of winning the sinner back to repentance and faith (*1 Cor. 5:5*). Christians who enter into a biblically invalid marriage after a divorce are living in open adultery and so have been denied participation in the sacrament in accordance with Paul's instructions in *1 Corinthians 5*.

Paul's list of sins warranting excommunication here also includes extortioners and the covetous. This should at the very least cause us to

---

[75] This would include Unitarians, Oneness Pentecostals, Arians, Mormons or Jehovah's Witnesses, etc.

[76] In practice, this means that the Apostolic Church has taken the position that, in our assemblies, the sacrament should only be offered to members and (communicant adherents) of the Apostolic Church in good standing, or members in good standing of other evangelical churches.

Technically, it is the responsibility of the local presbytery to be satisfied that any non-members of the Apostolic Church desiring to commune have a credible profession of saving faith in the Lord Jesus Christ and are in an appropriate spiritual state. For the Apostolic Church's understanding of what is meant by an evangelical church, see the *Statement of Doctrinal Belief* of Affinity (formerly the British Evangelical Council).

seriously consider if it is in any way appropriate to allow unrepentant, persistent teachers of a prosperity gospel to commune at the Table.[77]

What is certainly clear from Paul's teaching in *1 Corinthians 5* is that it is not sufficient for someone to consider themselves a Christian in order to eat at the Lord's Table (or be received into the fellowship of the Church). The Church is to withdraw fellowship and suspend from the sacrament, or even excommunicate those who claim to be Christians, but who are living an openly sinful lifestyle, either in terms of ethical behaviour or doctrine.

What type of sin debars from the Table?

All Christians sin. 'If we say that we have no sin, we deceive ourselves, and the truth is not in us' (*1 Jn 1:8*). So what sins debar from the Lord's Table? Either private sins where the sinner persists in unrepentance despite admonishment, or public sins (sins which give public and general offence). Johann Gerhard explains what sort of sins should and shouldn't stop us from receiving the Breaking of Bread:

> Accordingly, a distinction is to be made among sinners. Those who fall into sin unknowingly or in weakness and are overtaken by their failure (*Gal. 6:1*) – but who confess their sin, trust in the Lord Jesus Christ, and promise to amend their ways – such sinners one should not exclude from the Holy Supper, for Christ instituted it for the sake of anxious sinners. Also, if the sin is secret ... However, if the sinner lies in public and known sin, promises no amendment, and by deed indicates none, one should by no means admit him to the Holy Supper.[78]

Excommunication and Suspension

Literally, excommunication is to withdraw the privilege of participation in the Lord's Supper. As we see in *1 Corinthians 5*, excommunication was already a practice of church discipline in New Testament times, and has continued as an important form of church discipline ever since. However,

---

[77] It's true that some church members may, from time to time, be taken in by what they hear on TV from the false teachers of a prosperity gospel, but that doesn't mean they should be excommunicated. There is a significant difference between being misguided and persistently and unrepentantly proclaiming a false gospel. It is those who preach such a false message and who profit (or seek to profit) from it whom I would suggest would be automatically excommunicated by *1 Cor. 5:11*.

[78] Johann Gerhard, *A Comprehensive Explanation*, 424-425.

there are two types of *'excommunicatio'* – *excommunicatio minor* (which we normally refer to as Suspension) and *excommunicatio major* (which is what is normally called Excommunication). Suspension is prohibiting the sinner from partaking of the Lord's Supper (privately, not publicly) and goes along with repeated admonitions from the Presbytery in order to bring the sinner to repentance.[79] Excommunication (*Excommunicatio major*), on the other hand, is when the sinner is cut off from the fellowship of the church and publicly forbidden admission to the Lord's Table. It 'involves a formal and permanent exclusion from all spiritual communion with the ministers and members of the Church, and from all privileges, until such a time as the offender is completely repentant.'[80] Only the apostleship can excommunicate or readmit a repentant excommunicated person to the church.[81]

Excommunication and suspension are important biblical forms of church discipline and so participation in the Breaking of Bread is not simply something which is left up to the individual. The presbytery and apostleship have a role in determining who can and cannot be admitted to the Table. To remove any restrictions on who can partake, or to remove the duty of the presbytery to oversee communicants, would be to remove biblical church discipline.

Self-Examination and Discerning the Lord's Body

The Scriptures teach us to 'let a man examine himself, and so let him eat of the bread and drink of the cup' (*1 Cor. 11:28*). This self-examination is necessary because unworthy eating of Christs body and unworthy drinking of His blood lead to guilt (*1 Cor. 11:27*). Therefore, to eat and drink unworthily is a sin. So the time for self-examination is not just a quiet pause in the service, but a vital prerequisite to guard from sin. This important duty should be undertaken in advance of the Breaking of Bread service, for the

---

[79] See current Constitution of the Apostolic Church, 3.2 for this sort of Suspension as a means of church discipline. Suspension may be carried out by the local presbytery; see *Introducing the Apostolic Church: A Manual of Belief, Practice and History*, 36.

[80] *Introducing the Apostolic Church*, 37.

[81] *Introducing the Apostolic Church, 37; Guiding Principles*, 222-223, 299.

pause in the communion liturgy is only brief. Yet the invitation to examine oneself and these moments set apart in silence for it before we approach the Table serve as a reminder of this important duty of self-examination.

The sin of unworthy eating leads to judgment (*1 Cor. 1:29-30*). This judgment takes the form of weakness (whereas the sacrament is supposed to strengthen and sustain), sickness (whereas we should find healing in the cup), and even death (whereas the Breaking of Bread is supposed to be communion with Christ, who is our life). The judgment for partaking of the Supper unworthily is the opposite of what we receive when we partake worthily. Yet the purpose of such judgment is not condemnation, but rather it is 'chasten[ing] by the Lord, that we may not be condemned with the world' (*1 Cor. 11:32*).

We are to avoid coming under this judgment by judging ourselves (*1 Cor. 11:31*). Thus, examining ourselves before the Table is an important protection, for it is a reminder from God that the Table is not to be taken lightly. It is a merciful reminder from the Lord not to eat and drink in an unworthy manner.

Why is this all so serious? It's all so serious because of the very nature of the Supper. For the question of eating worthily or unworthily is tied up with our discerning the Lord's body (*1 Cor. 11:30*). To partake unworthily is not about how good or bad we've been during the week, but rather it's about discerning Christ's body and seeing that our worthiness depends, not on ourselves, but on Him who gave Himself for us, and who now feeds us with His body and blood at the Table.

So how do we examine ourselves? We examine ourselves by recognising and confessing our sin (*1 Jn 1:8-10; Mt 5:23-24*), and by looking to Christ, for the forgiveness of sin and to discern His body in the Supper (*2 Cor. 13:4-6; 1 Cor. 11:30*).

This examination is not designed to keep us away from the Table, but to lead us rightly to the Table: 'Let a man examine himself, and so let him eat of the bread and drink of the cup' (*1 Cor. 11:28*) Examination shouldn't leave us in our sin, but lead us to Christ and Him crucified, in whom we know forgiveness and justification. The call to examine ourselves before we come to the Table is an invitation to respond afresh to the gospel.

Tenet 8

*The Divine inspiration & authority
of the Holy Scriptures.*

Chapter 34

The Inspiration & Authority
of the Holy Scriptures

Timothy grew up with the Scriptures. He was taught the faith from the Word by his mother and grandmother (*2 Tim. 1:5*), and so knew the Scriptures from his childhood (*2 Tim. 3:15*). Yet, having grown up and been ordained to the ministry, the apostle Paul writes to him of his continual need for the Scriptures.

> But evil men and impostors will grow worse and worse, deceiving and being deceived. But you must continue in the things which you have learned and been assured of, knowing from whom you have learned them, and that from childhood you have known the Holy Scriptures, which are able to make you wise for salvation through faith which is in Christ Jesus. All Scripture is given by inspiration of God, and is profitable for doctrine, for reproof, for correction, for instruction in righteousness, that the man of God may be complete, thoroughly equipped for every good work. (*2 Tim. 3:13-17*)

The Greek word for Scriptures simple means 'writings'. But these writings are not just any writings; they are 'holy' writings. 'Holy' is not just a word on the cover of a Bible; 'holy' is the very nature of Scripture itself.

Holiness is how the Triune God's character is set apart and distinguished from everything else. But this does not mean distance and inaccessibility. Rather, as the New England Puritan, Jonathan Edwards, expressed it:

> God is God, and distinguished from all other beings, and exalted above [them], chiefly by his divine beauty.[1]

> Holiness ... is as it were the beauty and sweetness of the divine nature.[2]

---

[1] Jonathan Edwards, *Religious Affections*, *Works*, 2:298
[2] Jonathan Edwards, *Religious Affections*, *Works*, 2:201

> Holiness is a most beautiful, lovely thing. Men are apt to drink in strange
> notions of holiness from their childhood, as if it were a melancholy,
> morose, sour, and unpleasant thing; but there is nothing in it but what is
> sweet and ravishingly lovely. 'Tis the highest beauty and amiableness,
> vastly above all other beauties; 'tis a divine beauty.[3]

Therefore, if the Scriptures are holy, the Scriptures must display the beauty
and sweetness of the Triune God.

Holiness cannot be separated from God Himself. When Moses
removed his sandals on 'holy ground' (*Ex 3:5*), the ground was only holy
because it was the place of God's presence. Thus, the Bible is a holy book,
not independently, nor due to the reverence given to it by human beings,
but because it is the book of God's presence. The Triune God meets with
people in all His holiness – His beauty and sweetness – in His Word.
Scripture is the Word of God written; in it we meet the living Word of God
who shows us the Father.

Therefore, the Bible is not just a book about God, but a book in which
we meet with our Triune God. So, if anyone claims not to need the Word,
what he is really claiming is not to need to meet with Christ in His Word,
for avoiding the Holy Scriptures means avoiding the Holy God of the
Scriptures.

The Inspiration of Scripture

Paul tells Timothy that all Scripture is inspired – or breathed out – by God (*2
Tim. 3:16*). This means that every single word of Scripture is God's Word. In
contemporary English we might use the word 'inspired' to mean something
much less significant. A moving poem, a brilliant idea, or an intellectual
influence might all be called 'inspired'. (Even among Christians we can fall
into this mistaken view of inspiration, when we talk about things like God
inspiring the writer of a worship song, which is in no way comparable to
His inspiring of the Scriptures.)

When it comes to the written Word of God, the Scriptures are inspired
in that God Himself has breathed them out, so that whatever the Scriptures

---

[3] Jonathan Edwards, *Sermons and Discourses 1720-1723*, *Works*, 10:478

say, God says. These are His very words. And so, if the Scripture has spoken, God Himself has spoken. We do not have to wait to hear from God about something which He has already told us in His written Word. As Peter writes: 'No prophecy of Scripture is of any private interpretation, for prophecy never came by the will of man, but holy men of God spoke as they were moved by the Holy Spirit' (*2 Pet. 1:20-21*). The words of Scripture have not come to us by man's will, but through the inspiration of the Holy Spirit. Even before the Day of Pentecost, Peter reminds the church of this, saying: 'this Scripture had to be fulfilled, which the Holy Spirit spoke before by the mouth of David' (*Acts 1:16*). Peter goes on to quote from *Psalms 69* and *109*, and so shows us that the words of the Psalmist are not his own. These Psalms have not merely come from David, but the Holy Spirit spoke through David, inspiring his words so that they are in fact the words of God Himself. It was very clear to the apostles and the early church that the Old Testament Scriptures were the very words of the Holy Spirit.

Therefore, the Holy Spirit has spoken; for, where Scripture speaks, the Spirit speaks. To wait for the Holy Spirit to speak again to a matter on which He has already spoken in the Scriptures would not be a way of honouring the Holy Spirit. Rather, to wait for the Spirit to speak again is to distrust God the Holy Spirit.

The testimony of the Scriptures to their divine inspiration is constant: it is the Triune God who has spoken in the Scriptures. 'God has spoken by the mouth of all His holy prophets since the world began' (*Acts 3:21; cf. Zech. 7:12-13; Heb. 1:1; 1 Pet. 1:11*). And, although the writing of the New Testament was not yet complete before these statements of inspiration were made, they do not only apply to the Old Testament, but to the whole of Scripture. For the New Testament demonstrates that 'Scripture' is a technical category of writings, which is not limited only to the Old Testament, but includes the New. Peter refers to Pauls' letters as Scripture (*2 Pet. 3:16*), and Paul quotes from both *Deuteronomy 25:4* and *Luke 10:7* together in *1 Timothy 5:18*, writing, 'For the Scripture says, "You shall not muzzle an ox while it treads out the grain," and, "The labourer is worthy of his wages."' So he quotes from both the New Testament and the Old Testament together as 'Scripture.'

Jesus tells us that every part of the Bible is inspired by God – and not just the general gist of it, but the very words. Jesus' discussion with the Sadducees about the resurrection turns on the tense of a verb (*Mt 22:31-32; Mk 12:26-27; Lk 20:37-38*). And even more strikingly than that, Jesus declares that not 'one jot or one tittle' will pass away from God's Word (*Mt 5:18*). Jot was the smallest letter, and a tittle was a small part of a letter that distinguished it (a bit like what the cross on our letter *t* does). So here Jesus is talking about the inspiration of the very letters of Scripture. It's not just the big idea, or the general gist that's inspired by God, but every word of Scripture is God's word. We call this *verbal plenary inspiration*.

The Inerrancy of Scripture

Because the words of Scripture are God's own words, they are entirely truthful and trustworthy. The words we use for the complete truthfulness of the whole of Scripture are *infallibility* and *inerrancy*.[4] To say that the Scriptures are infallible or inerrant means that Scripture is entirely true and trustworthy in everything that it teaches. It is not because the Scriptures are infallible and inerrant that we believe that they are the Word of God; rather it is because the Scriptures are the Word of God that we believe that they are infallible and inerrant. 'Scripture is trustworthy because the God behind Scripture is trustworthy.'[5]

The Scriptures are the Word of the God who is Truth and cannot lie (*Num. 23:19; Titus 1:2; Heb. 6:18*). All the words of the God of Truth are pure and true (*2 Sam. 7:28; Ps 12:6; Prov. 30:5; Jn 17:17*). According to Jesus, 'the Scripture cannot be broken' (*Jn 10:35*), and 'till heaven and earth pass away, one jot or one tittle will by no means pass from the law till all is fulfilled' (*Mt 5:18*). There is to be no process of discernment to discover which parts of the Scripture are God's truthful word and which can be rejected; for not even the smallest letter will be removed from the Scriptures, as they are, in their entirety, the truthful Word of God. The Bible is inerrant and infallible. Whether in doctrinal and moral matters, or in the details of history and geography, whatever the Bible asserts is true, because it is the Word of the

---

[4] In the UK, these two terms tend to be used to mean the same thing, with the preferred term being the older and more traditional term: *infallibility*. Therefore inerrancy is understood as a synonym for infallibility. In North America, in recent decades, some writers have started to use infallibility with a less precise meaning, and so the term inerrancy has come to be preferred on the other side of the Atlantic. I'll be keeping with the older, and British, usage of using the terms synonymously. The early Apostolics tended to write of the infallibility of Scripture (as that was the standard term in Britain), but very clearly with the meaning of inerrancy.

[5] Carl Trueman, 'The God of Unconditional Promise', in Paul Helm and Carl R. Trueman, ed., *The Trustworthiness of God: Perspectives on the Nature of Scripture* (Grand Rapids: Eerdmans, 2002), 178.

God who is Truth and never lies. As the church has always believed, from its earliest days: 'holy Scripture can in no way lie.'[6]

The Apostolic Church has always strongly upheld the infallibility and inerrancy of the Scriptures:

> When we thus attribute infallibility to Scripture, we mean that it is in itself true and accurate and may be trusted implicitly. Our best reasons for this are that the Spirit of God has so inspired the Holy Scriptures that they are self-authenticating and bear witness to their unique origin; and also He enlightens the mind and understanding of believers to recognise and to believe this, giving them the assurance in their hearts concerning it. We accept therefore the infallibility of Scripture because we believe that the Holy Spirit, speaking through Scripture, requires us to do so.[7]

Jesus Himself confirms the truthfulness of historical events recorded in the Scriptures. Although it might not be an aspect of His earthly ministry that immediately springs to mind, Christ actually had rather a lot to say about Old Testament people and events. And when He did talk about Old Testament people and events, He referred to them as historical facts. He didn't talk about them as stories, myths or legends, but rather as concrete people and events that His hearers would know about.

And He started right at the beginning, confirming the historicity of God's creation of the world, and of mankind as male and female (*Mt 19:4; Mk 10:6*). He speaks of the murder of Abel, and when he does so it's in a context where it's very important for what he's saying that this is historical fact (*Lk 11:52; Mt 23:35*). Likewise historical truth is important when He speaks of Noah and the flood (*Mt 24:38-39; Lk 17:26*).

Still staying in Genesis, Jesus speaks of Lot and the destruction of Sodom (*Lk 17:29*) and of Lot's wife (*Lk 17:32*). The historicity of Abraham, Isaac and Jacob (which Jesus confirms together with Moses' call at the burning bush) is very significant, as Jesus uses it to disprove the Sadducees' disbelief in the resurrection (*Mt 22:31-32; Mk 12:26-27; Lk 20:37-38*).

Beyond Genesis, Jesus also confirms God's provision of manna in the wilderness (*Jn 6:31-51*), David's eating of the shewbread (*Mt 12:3-4*), the splendour of Solomon (*Lk 12:27*), the visit of the Queen of Sheba (*Mt 12:42; Lk 11:31*), Elijah and the widow of Zarephath and Elisha and the healing of Naaman the leper (*Lk 4:25*), Jonah's three days in the belly of the great fish (*Mt 12:40*), and Daniel's prophecies (*Mt 24:15-16*).

---

[6] Fulgentius, *Predestination and Grace*, 3.23

[7] A.H. Lewis, *The Divine Inspiration and Authority of the Holy Scriptures*, Tenets of the Apostolic Church, Vol. 8, 21.

Jesus treated the Scriptures as the truthful and trustworthy Word of God. He treated them as infallible and inerrant, and so should we. 'To Christ the Bible is true, authoritative, and inspired. To him the God of the Bible is the living God, and the teaching of the Bible is the teaching of the living God. To him, what Scripture says, God says.'[8]

The Authority of Scripture

Because the words of Scripture are God's Words, the Scriptures speak with the authority of God Himself. What the Bible says, God says. Everything the Bible says, God says. So the Bible has authority because it is God speaking. The Bible's authority is God's own authority. And so, if God is to have the sovereign place in our lives, then, because it is God's Word, Holy Scripture should have supreme authority in our lives.

This means that we cannot put ourselves in judgement over the Word of God. We cannot decide which portions of Scripture we will accept and which we won't; for to put ourselves in any way over the Word of God is to set ourselves up as a rival authority to the God who has spoken in the Scriptures. This was the very temptation which the serpent brought to Eve in the Garden of Eden: the temptation to judge and reject the Word of God instead of humbly accepting and trusting the Word in faith.

Our place is not to stand over God's Word in judgment, but to tremble before it: 'But on this one will I look: on him who is poor and of a contrite spirit, and who trembles at My word' (*Isa. 66:2*).Does that mean we're to fall down on the floor in fear every time we see a Bible? Certainly not. It means we're to believe God's Word and delight in obeying it. Jesus rebukes His disciples for not believing the Scriptures: 'Then He said to them, "O foolish ones, and slow of heart to believe in all that the prophets have spoken"' (*Lk 24:25*).

What the Bible says, God says. So when we don't believe the Bible, it's God Himself we're not believing. And when we disobey the Bible, it's God Himself we're disobeying.

---

[8] John Wenham, *Christ and the Bible* (3rd Edition), 195.

During His earthly ministry, Jesus tells us that when the Scriptures speak, God speaks. In fact, not only does Jesus call the Bible the Word of God, but He also refers to Scriptures as 'the commandment of God' (*Mt 15:3 referring to Ex 20:12; 21:17, and Deut. 5:16*). Even more clearly again, in *Matthew 22:31* Jesus asks, 'have you not read what was spoken to you by God'? Here he quotes the Angel of the LORD (which is Jesus Himself), but His question is not simply about a quotation in the Bible of something the LORD said, for He makes clear that what they should have read was spoken to them by God. He's not merely talking about the historical recording of an event - the Angel of the LORD speaking to Moses - but about God speaking in the written account of that event. The Angel of the LORD did not speak to them at the burning bush, for they weren't there – they weren't even alive yet. But in reading the written text of Scripture God is speaking to them. *Matthew 22:31* is very significant as it connects God's speaking with the written text of Scripture.

So, when Jesus calls the Bible 'the Word of God', He's not just using a fancy name for the book. No – He's telling us what it is in its very nature. According to Jesus the Bible is God's Word because it is God speaking. When the Scriptures speak, God speaks.

If the Scriptures are the Word of God, if when the Scriptures speak, God speaks, and if every single word, right down to the smallest letter is breathed out by God, then God's own authority stands behind the Scriptures. That's what we mean when we say that the Scriptures are authoritative.

In *John 5*, Jesus speaks to the Jews about the Scriptures. There He tells them that Moses stands in accusation against them for their unbelief (*Jn 5:45-47*). But how could Moses do that? He'd been dead for centuries. The chapter ends with Jesus making it clear that this authority of Moses to condemn is found in Moses' writings. In other words, it's not so much Moses the man who has the authority to condemn them, but rather the Scriptures which Moses wrote. That's how authoritative the books of Moses, and all the rest of the Scriptures are: they have the authority to condemn us if we don't trust in Jesus.

A few chapters later in *John 10:35*, Jesus tells us that 'Scripture cannot be broken' – so there is no higher authority that can cancel out the authority of Scripture. Why? Because the Bible's authority is really God's authority. It is God who speaks, so the authority is His.

Jesus' greatest demonstration of the authority of Scripture is the fact that He Himself submitted to the authority of Scripture. That might sound like a shocking statement, but just remember what we've already said about the authority of Scripture – it's really God's authority. And we know that Jesus submitted to the authority of Scripture, for we know that He always perfectly obeyed God and kept His law for us (*Heb. 4:15; 5:8*).

But that's not the only way He submitted to the authority of Scripture. He lived His whole life, not only in obedience to God's law, but also to fulfil the Scriptures. He did what He did, He ministered as He ministered (*Mt 13:14*), and He died as He died (and rose as He rose for that matter) in submission to the authority of God's Word in order to fulfil it (*Mt 26:56; Lk 24:44-47*).

The Purpose of Scripture

The Bible is not a utilitarian book. The Triune God has given us the Scriptures for a reason. As we'll see in the next chapter, the Word of God is a three-fold Word: Christ, Scripture, and Proclamation. Jesus is the Word of God. The Bible is the Word of Christ. Preaching is the Word of the Spirit in which Christ is proclaimed biblically. Therefore, ultimately the Bible is a book to do with Christ, the eternal living Word of God. The Bible is the Word *of* Christ, for it is His Word. The Bible is the Word *about* Christ, for it speaks of Him. And the Bible is *to* Christ, for it leads us to Him. Christ is the subject of all the Scriptures (*Lk 24:27*).

Writing to Timothy, Paul speaks of the purpose of the Scriptures: 'the Holy Scriptures … are able to make you wise for salvation through faith which is in Christ Jesus' (*2 Tim. 3:15*). In the context, Paul has been warning about deceivers and false teachers (*2 Tim. 3:13*). And so he points Timothy to the proclamation of the gospel (*2 Tim. 3:14*) and to the written Scriptures (*2 Tim. 3:15*), as the guard and antidote to the teaching of the deceivers. Yet, Paul doesn't start off by talking about the Scriptures with which you can refute all the arguments of the false teachers. Instead, he begins with the Holy Scriptures that take you to Christ for salvation. The most important thing about the Scriptures – the reason we need them above all else – is that they take us to Jesus for salvation. The chief subject of the Scriptures is Christ our Saviour.

Scripture doesn't just take us to Christ for conversion, but for salvation – the whole of the Christian life. Through the Scriptures we grow in Christ. The Lord sanctifies us by His Word (*Jn 17:17*), and by His Scriptural Word we die to sin as we receive His reproof and correction. But not only do we die to sin by His Word, but He also uses His Word in Scripture to raise us to live to Christ, as we receive His doctrine and instruction in righteousness (*2 Tim. 3:16*). Through the Scriptures Christ equips us to serve Him (*2 Tim. 3:17*). Therefore, Bible study and service are not alternative options. True Bible study leads to service and true service is rooted in growth in the Word. Scripture and service go together.

The Clarity of Scripture

Paul writes that Timothy has known the Holy Scriptures 'from childhood' (*2 Tim. 3:15*). Because the Scriptures are clear, even children can know, read, understand, learn, and benefit from them. For the Scriptures are 'a lamp to [our] feet and a light to [our] path' (*Ps 119:105; cf. Prov. 6:23*). They enlighten the eyes (*Ps 19:8*) 'as a light that shines in a dark place' (*2 Pet. 1:19*).

> For this commandment which I command you today is not too mysterious for you, nor is it far off. It is not in heaven, that you should say, 'Who will ascend into heaven for us and bring it to us, that we may hear it and do it?' Nor is it beyond the sea, that you should say, 'Who will go over the sea for us and bring it to us, that we may hear it and do it?' But the word is very near you, in your mouth and in your heart, that you may do it. (*Deut. 30:11-14*)

The word is near to us, in our mouth and in our hearts, in that we can read it, understand it, memorise it, and internalise what the Lord has spoken in His Word. It is not a mysterious word which we cannot understand, but a clear word, 'making wise the simple' (*Ps 19:7*).

Some people mistakenly think that the Bible is a very difficult book which is so hard to understand that it has to be left to the experts. Yet, Timothy knew the Holy Scriptures from childhood. And in the Old Testament, God's people were commanded to teach the Scriptures 'diligently to your children, and … talk of them when you sit in your house, when you walk by the way, when you lie down, and when you rise up' (*Dt 6:7*). Therefore children can know God's Word, so we shouldn't keep it from them.

Not only does this apply to young children, but to teenagers too. Sometimes well-meaning adults will say that Bible studies and sermons are too much for teenagers. When we send them to school, we expect our teenagers to cope with algebra, organic chemistry, foreign languages, and the causes of World War One; and yet we want to shield them from the very Word of Life. Timothy knew the Scriptures from childhood. So our teenagers can certainly cope with hearing the Word of God proclaimed and studying it carefully.

The Clarity of Scripture doesn't mean that we'll understand every single verse straight away. Even Peter said that Paul wrote 'some things hard to understand, which untaught and unstable people twist to their own destruction, as they do also the rest of the Scriptures' (*2 Pet. 3:16*). Some passages may be difficult to understand, but, when we compare them with other, clearer portions of Scripture, we see that Scripture interprets Scripture. And to help us, the Head of the Church has given teachers to His Church so that we do not remain 'untaught and unstable' (*2 Pet. 3:16*).

Martin Luther admitted that some passages in Scripture are hard to understand, but showed that this doesn't negate the clarity of Scripture:

> I certainly grant that many *passages* in the Scriptures are obscure and hard to elucidate, but that is due, not to the exalted nature of their subject, but to our own linguistic and grammatical ignorance; and it does not in any way prevent our knowing all the *contents* of Scripture. For what solemn truth can the Scriptures still be concealing, now that the seals are broken, the stone rolled away from the door of the tomb, and that greatest of all mysteries brought to light – that Christ, God's Son, became man, that God is Three in One, that Christ suffered for us, and will reign forever? And are not these things known and sung in our streets? Take Christ from the Scriptures – and what more will you find in them? You see, then, that the entire content of the Scriptures has now been brought to light, even though some passages which contain unknown words remain obscure. Thus it is unintelligent, and ungodly too, when you know that the contents of Scripture are as clear as can be, to pronounce them obscure on account of those few obscure words. If words are obscure in one place, they are clear in another.[9]

---

[9] Luther, *Bondage of the Will*, p.71.

The Clarity of Scripture doesn't mean that we'll always understand every single word. Yet it does mean that the Bible can make even a child 'wise for salvation through faith which is in Christ Jesus' (*2 Tim. 3:15*). And the clarity of Scriptures means that if we read it, seeking God's help, and with the desire to trust His Word and obey it, then the Lord will enable us to understand clearly enough to trust in Christ for salvation and to respond to His great love with lives of love and joyful obedience to Him.

The Sufficiency of Scripture

The Scriptures are 'able to make you wise for salvation' (*2 Tim. 3:15*). Thus the Bible is sufficient to bring us to saving knowledge of Christ. We don't need any other source of revelation to give us some other hidden part of the gospel message. The whole gospel is contained and set forth in the Scriptures. The Bible is enough to make us wise for salvation.

And, the Bible is profitable so that we may be 'thoroughly equipped for every good work' (*2 Tim. 3:17*). The Bible doesn't just equip us for some good works, but for 'every' good work. Therefore we don't need something else to equip us for the other good works which God has prepared in advance for us to walk in. The Bible is enough for living as God calls us to live.

Whether for salvation or for the good works of the Christian life, we don't need any secret, extra knowledge. God has revealed everything we need, for salvation and life in Christ, in His Word. If we have 'Moses and the prophets', we have all that we need for the knowledge of salvation (*Lk 16:29, 31*). Therefore, the Scriptures are sufficient.

The Scriptures are the very words of God, and as such they are authoritative, infallible, inerrant, life-giving, clear, and sufficient. The faith of the Apostolic Church is that 'the whole Bible is the inspired Word of God, infallible in its declarations, final in its authority, all-sufficient in its provision, and comprehensive in its sufficiency.'[10]

---

[10] *The Apostolic Church: Its Principles and Practices*, 218.

Chapter 35

The Three-fold Word
& the Ministry of the Word

When the church gathers around the Lord's Table on the Lord's Day, she hears the Word of the Lord proclaimed. But is the preaching of the Word just a tradition? Is it something that could be replaced in the life of the church? After all, there's no verse in Scripture which says 'thou shalt have a sermon each and every Lord's Day morning.' So does that mean that we could do something else instead and dispense with the sermon?

If preaching were just a tradition, it would be a very old one indeed. Back in the middle of the second century, Justin Martyr gives us the earliest description of Christian worship outside of the Bible:

> And on the day called Sunday, all who live in cities or in the country gather together to one place, and the memoirs of the apostles or the writings of the prophets are read, as long as time permits; then, when the reader has ceased, the president verbally instructs, and exhorts to the imitation of these good things. Then we all rise together and pray, and, as we before said, when our prayer is ended, bread and wine and water are brought, and the president in like manner offers prayers and thanksgivings, according to his ability, and the people assent, saying Amen; and there is a distribution to each, and a participation of that over which thanks have been given, and to those who are absent a portion is sent by the deacons. And they who are well to do, and willing, give what each thinks fit; and what is collected is deposited with the president, who succours the orphans and widows and those who, through sickness or any other cause, are in want, and those who are in bonds and the strangers sojourning among us, and in a word takes care of all who are in need. But Sunday is the day on which we all hold our common assembly, because it is the first day on which God, having wrought a change in the darkness and matter, made the world; and Jesus Christ our Saviour on the same day rose from the dead. For He was crucified on the day before that of Saturn (Saturday); and on the day after that of Saturn, which is the day of the Sun,

having appeared to His apostles and disciples, He taught them these things, which we have submitted to you also for your consideration.[1]

A large amount of time was given over to the reading and preaching of the Scriptures at the Breaking of Bread services of Justin's day: 'as long as time permits.' Justin was writing around the year AD155, but even then he wasn't describing something new, but something already very old. For what Justin describes is very similar indeed to the Breaking of Bread service at Troas in *Acts 20*. There Paul preached, and 'continued his message until midnight' and afterwards broke bread (*Acts 20:7-11*).

In fact, this pattern goes back even further than Paul, for it is the pattern of the very first Lord's Day (*Lk 24:27-32*). The Lord proclaimed the gospel from the Old Testament to the two disciples on the road to Emmaus and then revealed Himself in the breaking of the bread.

So preaching is not merely an old church tradition; preaching is the Scriptural pattern. The Scriptures show us Christian worship as a movement from Word to sacrament.[2] In the worship of the church, the Lord feeds us in His Word and at His Table.

Does that mean we preach in order to stick to the pattern? No; there is much more reason to it than that. For the reason for preaching lies in what preaching is, and what preaching does. The reason for preaching lies in our theology of the Word.

The Word and the Growth of the Church

The book of Acts tells the story of the growth of the early church. But how does Luke describe the growth of the church in Acts?

Then the word of God spread, and the number of the disciples multiplied greatly in Jerusalem. (*Acts 6:7*)

But the word of God grew and multiplied. (*Acts 12:24*)

---

[1] Justin Martyr, *First Apology*, 67.

[2] In the traditional order of an Apostolic Breaking of Bread service the sacrament follows the Word, although this is being steadily eroded by the contemporary evangelical reversal of Word and sacrament.

Now when the Gentiles heard this, they were glad and glorified the word of the Lord. And as many as had been appointed to eternal life believed. And the word of the Lord was being spread throughout all the region. (*Acts 13:48-49*)

So the word of the Lord grew mightily and prevailed. (*Acts 19:20*)

With these summary statements throughout the book, Luke highlights the role of the Word. It is the Word which grows the church. The Word spreads, grows, multiplies, and prevails. The Word brings gladness. And the Word is even glorified. Yet, how can the Word do all these different things? What is this Word? For if by the Word, Luke means the Scriptures, how do the Scriptures grow, multiply and spread? And would glorifying a book not be a form of idolatry? If, however, Luke meant preaching, we might be able to understand what he means by the word spreading and multiplying; but we're still left with the problem of how the word can be glorified. Luke points us to the power of this Word, yet he leaves us to ask just what this Word is.

What is the Word?

Often as evangelicals, when we hear the expression 'the Word of God' we think straightaway of the Bible. Yet, at the same time, we know that the Bible uses the same expression to speak about something else as well. For 'in the beginning was the Word, and the Word was with God, and the Word was God' (*Jn 1:1*). Jesus is the Word of God. So when it comes to the Word which grew the Church in the book of Acts, and when it comes to preaching the Word, which Word are we talking about: Jesus or the Bible? The answer is that this is the wrong question.

The LORD Reveals Himself by the Word of the LORD

Back in chapter 2 we saw how, the very first time we find the expression 'the Word of the LORD' in Scripture, Abraham saw the Word (*Gen. 15:1-6*).

The Word came to Abraham and spoke to Him. Abraham trusted in this Word, and it was accounted to Him for righteousness (*Gen. 15:6*). For Abraham, to hear God's Word was not simply to hear words about God, or even words spoken by God. To hear the Word of the LORD was to encounter the living Word who reveals the LORD and brings salvation.

When the prophet Samuel was a boy, 'the word of the LORD was rare in those days; there was no widespread revelation' (*1 Sam. 3:1*). Yet, the LORD came by His Word to speak to the boy Samuel (*1 Sam. 3:1-21*). The Scripture both tells us that 'the LORD called Samuel' (*1 Sam. 3:4*) and that it was 'by the word of the LORD' that 'the LORD revealed Himself to Samuel' (*1 Sam. 3:21*). The One who came and spoke with Samuel was the Word of the LORD who is the LORD and reveals the LORD. The One who spoke with Samuel was the eternal Word and Son of the Father.

And when the Word of the LORD spoke the Word of the LORD to Samuel, Samuel spoke the Word of the LORD, first to Eli (*1 Sam. 3:18*), and later to 'all Israel' (*1 Sam. 4:1*). There is a three-foldness to the Word: the One who appears and speaks is the Word (*1 Sam. 3:21*), the words spoken by the Word are the Word, and the prophets words transmitting the Word of the Word are also the Word. And this becomes the pattern in the Old Testament: the LORD reveals Himself by the Word of the LORD (who is the LORD), then the prophets proclaim that Word, and as the people heard the Word proclaimed, they encounter the eternal, living Word. And to know Him is salvation.

The Preaching of the Word of God is the Word of God

In the New Testament, it is not only the prophets who proclaim the Word of God. The writer to the Hebrews urges his readers to 'remember those who rule over you, who have spoken the Word of God to you' (*Heb. 13:7*). Here he is speaking of the elders and apostles of the church, yet he doesn't intend us to think that they simply go around quoting the Scriptures constantly. It is not because their answer to every question is a memory verse that he says they 'have spoken the Word of God.' The pattern we have seen in the Old Testament helps us to understand: just as the Old Testament prophets encountered the Word who spoke the Word and then sent them out to transmit the Word, so too in the New Testament, the elders who know the Word and His Word proclaim the Word to others. In other words, the elders know Christ, the living Word, and the Scriptures, the written Word of

Christ, and so proclaim the Word to others by preaching Christ from the Scriptures. They speak the Word by proclaiming the Living Word from the written Word. Thus the preaching of the Word is the Word.

We can see this where Paul writes to the Thessalonians about their conversion:

> So, affectionately longing for you, we were well pleased to impart to you not only the gospel of God, but also our own lives, because you had become dear to us. For you remember, brethren, our labour and toil; for labouring night and day, that we might not be a burden to any of you, we preached to you the gospel of God. You are witnesses, and God also, how devoutly and justly and blamelessly we behaved ourselves among you who believe; as you know how we exhorted, and comforted, and charged every one of you, as a father does his own children, that you would walk worthy of God who calls you into His own kingdom and glory. For this reason we also thank God without ceasing, because when you received the word of God which you heard from us, you welcomed it not as the word of men, but as it is in truth, the word of God, which also effectively works in you who believe. (*1 Thess. 2:8-13*)

The Word of God, which Paul, Silas, and Timothy preached, isn't the 'word of men', but really is 'the word of God' (*1 Thess. 2:13*). Yet what is this Word which isn't their own, but God's? It's not a matter of quoting memory verses. As we look in the earlier verses, we see that it is 'the gospel of God' (*v.8*), that this is the gospel which was 'preached' (*v.9*), and that, when this Word was spoken, they 'exhorted … comforted, and charged every one of you, as a father does his own children' (*vv.11-12*). This isn't prophecy, and it isn't the quoting of Scripture verses. This Word of God which is not the word of men, but God's own word, is preaching. So true, biblical preaching is the Word of God.

Therefore, during the Reformation, the Protestant Reformers confessed:

> The preaching of the Word of God is the Word of God. Wherefore when this Word of God is now preached in the church by preachers lawfully called, we believe that the very Word of God is proclaimed and received by the faithful.[3]

Calvin wrote that, 'when a man has climbed up into the pulpit … it is so that God may speak to us by the mouth of the man.'[4]

---

[3] *The Second Helvetic Confession*

[4] John Calvin, *Sermon on 1 Timothy 3:1-4*, cited in Scott M. Manetsch, *Calvin's Company of Pastors: Pastoral Care and the Emerging Reformed Church 1536-1609* (Oxford: Oxford University Press, 2013), 159.

And this preached Word 'effectively works in you who believe' (*v.13*). This true, biblical preaching, which is the Word of God, is not merely a transfer of information to the hearers. Nor is it merely an encouragement to act. This preached Word of God is neither education nor motivational speaking. Rather, the preached Word works powerfully (that is, if the word preached is the Word).

Jesus Himself had taught His disciples the same thing. Think about *Matthew 10:40* where Jesus says to His disciples, 'he who receives you, receives me, and he who receives me receives Him who sent me.' As we can see very clearly from the parallel in *Luke 10:16*, Jesus isn't simply talking about hospitality: 'He who hears you hears me, he who rejects you rejects me, and he who rejects me rejects Him who sent me.' People who reject the words of Christ's messengers (that's you and me when we share the gospel with them) are actually rejecting Christ. Those who receive our message don't just receive a message about Christ, they receive Christ.

So, the LORD reveals Himself by Jesus, the Word. The apostles and elders in their preaching, and all Christians in their evangelism, proclaim Jesus. And when people hear Jesus proclaimed, they encounter the living Word – Jesus – who is salvation and holiness.

Therefore, Jesus is the Word of God, Scripture is the Word of God, and proclamation is the Word of God. Yet, these are not three different Words, for they are all saying the same thing. For the written Word and the proclamation of the Word speak Christ, the living Word. So the Word of God is not three different Words, but a three-fold Word: a unified Word which comes to us in three forms. The Bible, Jesus and proclamation are distinct yet inseparable. The Bible is a book about Jesus which is to be proclaimed. Jesus is the subject of Scripture and the content of true proclamation. Proclamation, if it is to be true Christian proclamation, is proclaiming Christ biblically. The three go together. In the words of D.P. Williams:

> We must always combine the Written Word, the Incarnate Word, and the Spoken Word, because they are one … This Word, whether it be the Written, the Spoken or the Incarnate Word, this Word is Christ.[5]

Seeing this three-fold nature of the Word of God, now we can understand how the Word does all the things it does in the book of Acts. The Word can spread, grow, multiply, prevail, bring gladness, and be glorified, because it

---

[5] D.P. Williams, *Riches of Grace*, ii.9 (Aug. 1925), 25, 27.

is a three-fold Word: because Jesus is the Word of God, the Scriptures are the Word of God, and proclamation is the Word of God.

The Written Word Speaks the Living Word: Christ the Sum and Substance of the Scriptures

On the evening of His resurrection, Jesus appeared to two of His disciples on the road to Emmaus and preached to them from the Old Testament Scriptures: 'And beginning at Moses and all the Prophets, He expounded to them in all the Scriptures the things concerning Himself' (*Lk 24:27*). And through this encounter we learn how to read the Scriptures rightly, for *Luke 24:27* teaches us to properly read countless other verses.

This is a key verse. Not because it is itself some magic key, but because it points us to Him who is the Key – Jesus. For that's what we learn in *Luke 24:27*: the key to the interpretation of all of Scripture is Jesus Christ. It's not an idea, a philosophy or a doctrine which opens up the Scriptures to us, but a Person, and only one Person – Jesus.

This is the day of the Resurrection and Jesus is walking along the road to Emmaus with two of His disciples, but they don't recognise Him. They know all about the crucifixion, and they've heard reports about the Resurrection, but they're confused and don't really know what's going on. None of it makes sense to them. So what does Jesus do? He opens up the Bible to them and makes it all clear how the Scriptures had already taught that 'the Christ [ought] to have suffered these things and to enter into His glory' (*Lk 24:26*).

They're despairing, so He takes them to the Word. They're confused, so He takes them to the Word. But it's not some sort of sanctified pep talk He gives them from the Word. His expository sermon is not about how they need to buck up, cheer up or man up. No, 'He expounded to them in all the Scriptures the things concerning Himself' (*Lk 24:27*). He takes them to the Written Word to show them the Living Word. His message for their comfort, strengthening and equipping isn't about what they need to do, but about who He is and what He has done. In their distress and confusion, the message they need to hear is Jesus.

But not only is Jesus the message for the hurting, despairing, doubting and confused: Jesus is the message of the Scriptures. 'All the Scriptures', Jesus showed them, speak of Christ. And, of course, the only Scriptures that had yet been written down when they walked to Emmaus were the Old

Testament Scriptures. That means that the Old Testament is all about Jesus. And that means that if we read the Old Testament without seeing Jesus, we're missing the point. It's not just the odd Messianic prophecy that speaks about Him, but the whole of the Old Testament.

But the Old Testament isn't the whole of Scripture. Scripture is a technical term, and so what's said about Scripture as a category of writing applies not only to the then already completed Old Testament, but also to the New. In fact, Jesus not only demonstrates here that He is the subject of the whole of the Scriptures, but also teaches it in *John 5:39*: 'You search the Scriptures, for in them you think you have eternal life; and these are they which testify of Me.' That's simply what Scripture is: the written Word of God which testifies to Christ the Word of God. In fact, Jesus goes on to tell us in *John 5* that if we don't see and trust Jesus in the Scriptures, then we don't actually believe the Scriptures at all (*Jn 5:46-47*). If, in reading the Bible, we miss Jesus, then we've missed the point.

In *Luke 24:27* and *John 5:39-47* Jesus points us to the true key to unlocking the Scriptures: Jesus Himself. The Bible isn't a book about me, it's a book about Jesus, and if I want to truly understand the Word and know its power in my life, I need to see Jesus in His Word.

Theology of Preaching: Proclaiming Christ Biblically

The proclamation of the Word of God which is the Word of God includes preaching, prophecy, and evangelism. But let's focus our attention on preaching, for, as preaching is of such importance to the life of the church, we need to know what true preaching really is. Our society uses the verb 'to preach' of stern moral lectures. Christian culture often speaks of emotion-filled speeches as 'preaching.' Yet, as we've seen, the Bible presents preaching as neither of the above. In the Bible, preaching is speaking the Word of God (*Lk 10:16; 1 Thess. 2:13; Heb. 13:7*). In the Bible, preaching is proclaiming Christ from the Scriptures (*Lk 24:27*). So, biblically speaking, *true preaching is proclaiming Christ biblically.*[6]

---

[6] Thanks to Glen Scrivener for condensing the definition of preaching into three words.

Understanding that preaching is proclaiming Christ biblically guards us from a few errors when we think about the preaching of the Word of God as the Word of God. Firstly, preaching is not a new revelation. The preacher does not come to the congregation with a new word from God, but rather he comes to speak afresh the Word which God has spoken from the very beginning. The preacher does not suddenly reveal to the church something which God has never said before, but rather he holds fast 'the faithful word' (*Titus 1:9*), holding this Word out week after week to the people of God and those who come to hear the good news.

Secondly, if the preaching of the Word of God which is the Word of God is proclaiming Christ biblically, then there is no excuse for unbiblical preaching. The pulpit is not the place for the opinions of men. The pulpit is the place to display the true Christ of the Scriptures in all His biblical glory.

Thirdly, a right understanding of the preaching shows us that, when we say the preaching of the Word of God is the Word of God, this isn't something that gives infallible authority or power to men. Just because the preacher says something in the pulpit does not mean that it is the Word of God. For it is not the location or the person which gives the Word its authority. The authority of the preached Word isn't the preacher's authority: it is the authority of the Word itself – the three-fold Word. And so it is not because something is called preaching that it is authoritative. It is only when Christ is proclaimed biblically that preaching is truly the Word of God. As Martin Luther put it:

> It is a right and excellent thing that every honest pastor and preacher's mouth is Christ's mouth and his word and forgiveness is Christ's word and forgiveness. For the office is not the pastor's or the preacher's, but God's, and the word which he preaches is likewise not the pastor's or the preacher's, but God's.[7]

When the Word is truly preached – when Christ is proclaimed biblically – then people encounter Christ, and Christ works in saving power.

Christ Speaks Through His Word

As we've seen above from *1 Thessalonians 2:13* and *Luke 10:16*, true preaching doesn't consist of the words, ideas and opinions of the preacher, but of God Himself speaking. Whoever hears true preaching, hears Christ

---

[7] Luther, *Sermon on John 20:19-31, 1534*, cited in Karl Barth, *Church Dogmatics*, I/1, 96.

(*Lk 10:16*). And when Christ speaks, His sheep hear His voice: 'My sheep hear My voice, and I know them, and they follow Me. And I give them eternal life, and they shall never perish; neither shall anyone snatch them out of My hand' (*Jn 10:27-28*). This is how we receive eternal life: by hearing Christ speak in His Word. For, when God speaks, it comes to pass (*cf. Gen. 1*). Right from the beginning, God has always acted through His Word.

Christ Acts Through His Word

In *Genesis 1*, God spoke and it was. God's Words always do what they say. Sometimes that's hard for us to grasp, as we can say one thing, but do another. Yet, even in our lives there are moments when our words accomplish what they say. For example, at a wedding when the bride and groom say 'I will' and the minister declares 'that they be husband and wife together', or at the registration of a new baby, when the parents speak the child's name.

Christ's words do what they say. His life-giving word actually gives life: 'the words that I speak to you are spirit and they are life' (*Jn 6:63*). As Simon Peter declared, 'Lord, to whom shall we go? You have the words of eternal life' (*Jn 6:68*). Faith comes by hearing the Word of Christ (*Rom. 10:17*), and it is by hearing His Word that He gives us new birth (*Jas 1:18; 1 Pet. 1:23, 25*) and salvation (*Jas 1:21*).

And Christ's Word is not only powerfully effective in saving non-Christians; it's also powerfully effective in the lives of those who have already come to faith in Christ. This Word 'effectively works in you who believe' (*1 Thess. 2:13*), for it is through His Word that Christ sanctifies and cleanses His Church (*Jn 17:17; Eph. 5:26*).

This is why preaching is so important in the life of the church: for Christ is at work in His Word to save and to sanctify. Christ is at work in His Word to grow His Church, not only numerically, but in maturity and likeness to Him. But how does Christ work so powerfully in His Word? Because He is present in His Word.

Christ is Present in His Word

Remember Abram (*Gen. 15*) and Samuel (*1 Sam. 3*): how did the Word bring them salvation and the knowledge of God? Abram and Samuel did not merely read about Jesus, or hear someone describe Him: they met with the Living Word of God. Salvation is not found in words about Jesus; it's found in Jesus Himself.

On the night of His arrest, Jesus prayed for those who would believe in Him through the preaching of His disciples (*Jn 17:20-23*). Those who believe are united to Christ, and Christ is in them. And, as a result, they are united to the Father through the Son, and glorified with the glory of Christ. But how does this come about? Through the preaching of the Word (*Jn 17:20*).

> The reception through faith of the apostolic testimony to Jesus Christ, he prays, will have as its result the unity of believers with the Father through the Son ... The proclamation of Christ is the means through which believers are included in the personal union between the Father and the Son. This proclamation is no mere presentation of information about Christ, and neither is believing in Christ the mere reception of information about him. Rather, Christ is both presented and received in the preaching of the Word. The reception of the apostolic testimony to Christ is the reception of Christ himself: 'Whoever receives you receives me,' Jesus told the twelve, 'and whoever receives me receives him who sent me' (Matt. 10:40).[8]

It is not that preaching presents us with information, which then permits faith, which in turn permits union with Christ. Rather, Christ Himself, 'the Incarnate Redeeming Word',[9] is present in His Word, reaching down to us and drawing us up to Himself as He is proclaimed in the preaching of the gospel, and so uniting us to Himself. Christ gives Himself to us in the preaching of His Word and draws out our hearts to Him in faith. As Luther put it: 'To preach the gospel is nothing else than Christ's coming to us or bringing us to Him.'[10]

This is why the gospel itself is 'the power of God unto salvation' (*Rom. 1:16*). For salvation is Jesus (whose very name means 'the Lord is salvation'). Therefore, the gospel which is preached is God's power for salvation because Christ is present in the preaching of the gospel in His saving power.

---

[8] Johnson, *One with Christ*, 223.

[9] D.P. Williams, *The Prophetical Ministry in the Church*, 78-79; cf. *The Enduring Word*, 14; *Riches of Grace*, ii.9 (Aug. 1925), 26.

[10] Martin Luther, WA 10. I. 14 (translation from Paul D. L. Avis, *The Church in the Theology of the Reformers*, 89).

God Works by His Word: Preaching is a Means of Grace

If grace is Jesus, then the only way preaching can be a means of grace is if Christ is present in His Word preached. And so, preaching is a divine activity: it is God's work, not man's. When the Word is preached, it is not us reaching up to God, but God reaching down to us in Jesus, who is savingly present in the preaching of His Word. Therefore, 'If the Word were removed, eternal good, God, Christ, and the Spirit, would be removed with it.'[11]

God's 'Now-Word' is Jesus:
There's no such thing as a 'rhema' word

Somehow in recent years an idea has crept in among charismatics, which then makes its way over to Pentecostals, that God speaks two types of words, which can be distinguished by two different Greek words - *logos* and *rhema*.

According to this teaching, a 'logos' word is what God has spoken in the past, which we have written down in the Bible. The 'rhema' word, however, is supposed to be something new and fresh, which God speaks now: it's His 'now-word'. As a result, the impression often comes across that the 'rhema' word is somehow better or more desirable than the 'logos' word, with the 'logos' seen as rather like dry words on a page until the 'rhema' comes.

Now, it's true that there are two words in Greek, *logos* and *rhema*, which could both (depending on the context) be translated as 'word' in English. But does that mean we can build a doctrine of two different types of words spoken by God upon these two Greek words?

Well let's have a very brief tour of some of the evidence, which I think will make the answer to that question clear, and then I want to go on to think about why this matters so much.

---

[11] Luther, *Bondage of the Will* , 92.

The Evidence

So, first the evidence. One way that we can often learn a good bit about Greek words in the New Testament is how those words were used in the Septuagint (the Greek translation of the Old Testament). The Septuagint (or LXX) was the Bible used by the early church, and so its usage of Greek words would have been very influential at the time the New Testament was being written. So what can the LXX tell us about 'logos' and 'rhema'? Do they highlight an important distinction between two types of word in the Old Testament? Not at all. The LXX uses logos and rhema interchangeably to translate the same Hebrew word for 'word'. In other words, in the Bible of the early church, logos and rhema were synonyms for the same thing.

So this distinction between a logos word and rhema word just isn't there in the Old Testament. But is it something that suddenly appears in the New Testament? Does God suddenly start to speak in two different ways? Well, how does the New Testament use the words?

Well, the New Testament uses them the same way as in the LXX - as synonyms. There are a number of passages which even use the two words in the same verse with clearly the same meaning. So, for example, in *Acts 10:44* we read about what happened when Peter preached the gospel to Cornelius and his household: 'While Peter was still speaking these words [ρήματα - *from rhema*], the Holy Spirit fell upon all those who heard the word [λόγον - *from logos*].' Here rhema and logos are both referring to Peter's preaching of the Gospel - the two words for *word* are both talking about the same thing.

We can see the same in *John 12:48*: 'He who rejects Me, and does not receive My words [ρήματά - *from rhema*], has that which judges him—the word [λόγος - *logos*] that I have spoken will judge him in the last day.' Those who don't receive Christ's Word are judged by His Word. Again rhema and logos are referring to the same thing.

Hebrews 12:19 uses the two words to describe what happened at Mount Sinai when the Israelites heard God's voice speaking the 10 Commandments: 'and the sound of a trumpet and the voice of words [ρημάτων - *from rhema*], so that those who heard it begged that the word [λόγον - *from logos*] should not be spoken to them anymore.' They heard rhema and so begged not to hear logos. Very clearly the two words are used synonymously to refer to the same thing.

It's not only the verses that use these two words as synonyms that show us that the distinction between written logos and now-word rhema doesn't add up. Peter's use of the word rhema is particularly interesting in *1 Peter 1:25*: 'But the word [ῥῆμα - *rhema*] of the Lord endures forever. Now this is the word [ῥῆμα - *rhema*] which by the gospel was preached to you.' Peter is talking about the gospel, and tells us that this is the everlasting word of God. In other words, he's talking about what God has spoken, and what we have received in the written word of Scripture. This is God's everlasting word, not some momentary 'now'-word. And yet Peter calls it rhema, not logos. So Peter absolutely demolishes this artificial distinction between past-logos and now-rhema in this one verse.

And just as Peter uses rhema for the everlasting word, so Paul uses logos to refer to something that those who promote this teaching would undoubtedly expect to be called rhema. What could be more of a 'now'-word than the Word of Wisdom or the Word of Knowledge? And yet the word for *word* in the names of those two gifts is *logos* (*1 Cor. 12:8*).

Finally, God does the same things through logos and rhema. He created the world by rhema (*Heb. 11:3*) and logos (*2 Pet. 3:5*) and He sanctifies us by logos (*Jn 17:17*) and rhema (*Eph. 5:25-26*). All the evidence shows us that logos and rhema are two synonymous ways of referring to God's Word, not two different types of word.

Dangers of making the mistake of thinking there's such a thing as a rhema word

1. It Undermines the Authority of Scripture

There are some huge problems when we start to think that we need a rhema word in addition to the logos word, and the first of these problems is that it undermines the authority of Scripture. What Scripture says, God says. That means I don't need another word from God before I believe or obey His Word in Scripture. And yet, all too often many Christians are ignoring what God has spoken in the Bible while they wait for another word on the same subject. 'The Holy Spirit hasn't spoken to me about that yet', they say. But if it's in Scripture, then the Holy Spirit has spoken to you about it! You don't need to wait for a so-called 'now'-word; you have the everlasting Word of God in the Bible.

2. It Undermines the Sufficiency of Scripture

The Sufficiency of Scripture means that, in the Bible, we have everything we need for salvation and godliness. That means we don't need a 'fresh' word to tell us what we need for godliness in Christ; we already have it in Scripture. God has not left us in the dark, waiting until a rhema comes along to enlighten our path. No, He is not a God who doles out little portions of grace or illumination now and then, but rather a God who has lavished His super-abundant grace on us in Christ Jesus, and in His loving grace He has given us more than we need for each moment in His Word, in Scripture.

3. It Undermines the Clarity of God's Word

This time it's not so much the waiting for a rhema-word that's the problem, but rather just the idea that we need this teaching in the first place. You see, in reading the Bible normally, in comparing Scripture with Scripture, we'd never see this distinction (because it isn't there!). But this whole concept of rhema-words is premised on the idea that we need someone to teach us this distinction. It's some sort of new revelation or secret knowledge. (And that has to be admitted, for no one in the first 1950 years or more of church history had ever heard of such a distinction, so it must be new or secret.) Now any idea of 'secret knowledge' should, of course, put us on our guard; needing secret knowledge is gnosticism, not Christianity. But perhaps even more fundamentally, this undermines the clarity of Scripture – it tells Christians that they can't understand the Bible without someone coming along to show them secrets. And that is a very dangerous idea indeed!

4. It Leads to a Lack of Confidence in the Power of God's Word in Scripture

If we need a 'now'-word, a rhema-word, to hear from God and know His power at work here and now, then what does that say about the power of God's Word in Scripture? And this is a fundamental question. For, you see, my ministry as a pastor and teacher relies upon, and must rely upon, the fact that God's Word is powerful to do its work. I know that I don't have to rely on my own bright ideas or the latest marketing trend, because God's Word in Scripture is powerful. So, like Martin Luther, 'I simply taught, preached, and wrote God's Word; otherwise I did nothing... I did nothing; the Word did everything... I did nothing; I let the Word do its work.'[12] But if I have to wait for a fresh rhema-word, then I can't have that confidence in the written Word to do its work. If I have to wait for a fresh rhema-word, then the ministry no longer relies on the power of God's Word, but on my own ability to discern the rhema rightly. Suddenly it's all about me and how

---

[12] Martin Luther, *Sermon from March 10th 1522*, LW 51:77

good I am at getting rhemas, instead of all about Jesus and how good and gracious He is to us in the Scriptures.

5. It Changes the Focus of the Word

There's a fundamental directional shift that occurs when we buy into this rhema-word business. You see, Scripture, rightly understood, moves us in a very particular direction – out from ourselves to Jesus. All the Scriptures speak of Christ (*Lk 24:27*), and Jesus says that we cannot understand the Scriptures at all without seeing Him and coming to Him (*Jn 5:39-40; 46-47*). So Scripture both points us to Jesus and brings us to Jesus. The whole direction of Scripture is Christward!

But this whole 'rhema' business works in the complete opposite direction: it becomes about what I must do, and so drives me further back into myself (which is the opposite direction from Jesus). God's 'word' (in this 'rhema' understanding) becomes focused on me, instead of focused on Jesus. And that is very bad news indeed.

6. It Elevates Subjective Experience Over Jesus Christ

The rhema/logos distinction ends up elevating the supposed rhema over the logos. Now, it might not always be expressed in those terms, but that's what it does. For the logos is seen to need a rhema, otherwise it's so often thought of as simply words (often 'dry words') on a page. True spirituality and true power are seen to come through the arrival of the rhema. And so, understandably, whether or not it's expressed officially, in people's minds the rhema becomes the most important.

But what is this rhema? It's a temporary and subjective thing. The written Word, however, is everlasting and objective. But more than that, the written word (and the proclamation of that Word) holds out to us Christ the living, eternal Word. Jesus is God's Word to us now and at all times. And no temporary, subjective experience can ever compare to Him. The true 'now'-word which God is constantly speaking to us is Jesus. That's why true prophecy is the 'testimony of Jesus' (*Rev. 19:10*). That's why true preaching is proclaiming Christ biblically. That's why the Scriptures constantly turn us out from ourselves to Jesus.

To elevate and chase after some temporary supposed rhema-word at the expense of seeing Christ, God's Yes-Word, held out to us in Scripture, is folly, madness, and ultimately death. Christ is the Logos, and He is our life. And He constantly invites us, and appeals to us, to look to Him and live. So why would we look away to chase after something else?

Tenet 9

Church government
by apostles,
prophets,
evangelists,
pastors,
teachers,
elders
& deacons.

Chapter 36

The Ministry:
Five Gifts, Three Orders

The Lord Jesus Christ, the eternal Word and Son of the Father who took on our flesh and lived, died, rose and ascended for us, is the glorious Head of the Church, which is His Body. Therefore, Christ the Head governs and directs His Church. Yet, how does Christ express His Headship in His Body? The Scriptures tell us in Paul's epistle to the *Ephesians*:

> But to each one of us grace was given according to the measure of Christ's gift. Therefore He says:
>> 'When He ascended on high,
>> He led captivity captive,
>> And gave gifts to men.'
>
> (Now this, 'He ascended'—what does it mean but that He also first descended into the lower parts of the earth? He who descended is also the One who ascended far above all the heavens, that He might fill all things.)
>
> And He Himself gave some to be apostles, some prophets, some evangelists, and some pastors and teachers, for the equipping of the saints for the work of ministry, for the edifying of the body of Christ, till we all come to the unity of the faith and of the knowledge of the Son of God, to a perfect man, to the measure of the stature of the fullness of Christ; that we should no longer be children, tossed to and fro and carried about with every wind of doctrine, by the trickery of men, in the cunning craftiness of deceitful plotting, but, speaking the truth in love, may grow up in all things into Him who is the head — Christ — from whom the whole body, joined and knit together by what every joint supplies, according to the effective working by which every part does its share, causes growth of the body for the edifying of itself in love. (*Eph. 4:7-16*)

Christ has given gifts of men to the Church through which He ministers to His Body and builds it up. These men are the apostles, prophets, evangelists, pastors and teachers (*Eph. 4:11*), which we refer to collectively as the *ascension ministries* (because they are given after, and as a result of, Christ's ascension: *Eph. 4:8*) or the *Headship ministries* (because, through them, Christ expresses His Headship in the Body).

Ephesians 4 tells us two things about the timing of Christ's giving of the ascension ministries. Firstly, these ministries were given *after* Christ's ascension (*Eph. 4:8*). This is important as it tells us that Paul is not referring here to the twelve apostles Jesus chose during His earthly ministry (*Lk 6:12-13*) or to the Old Testament prophets. Rather, this Scripture is teaching us about apostles, prophets, evangelists, pastors and teachers given by the Ascended Christ after His return to heaven. That means that these are ministries given in the Church, after Christ's death, resurrection and ascension to God's right hand.

The second thing which *Ephesians 4* teaches us about the timing of Christ's giving of the ascension ministries is the duration for which they are given. They are given 'till we all come to the unity of the faith and of the knowledge of the Son of God, to a perfect man, to the measure of the stature of the fullness of Christ' (*Eph. 4:13*). This level of spiritual development has not yet been reached by the Church, and will not be reached while the Church remains in this world. Thus the ascension ministries will continue in the Church throughout the whole of history. It should also be noted that *Ephesians 4* does not make any distinction between apostles, prophets, evangelists, pastors and teachers in this regard; if one continues to be given until Christ's return, then so do the others.

However, some might object that *Ephesians 4:11* says 'He Himself gave some apostles,' arguing that this is a past tense and thus has nothing to do with today. The Greek original, however, does not use a past tense here, but rather the aorist, a tense which refers to a verb 'simply as happening, without any regard to its continuance or frequency.'[1] Thus it is not the verb 'gave' that tells us about the duration of the giving, but rather its context. Therefore, as it is *Ephesians 4:13* which tells us the duration of the giving of these five ascension ministries, that means that we should expect all five in the Church today.

The Purpose of the Headship Ministries

Ephesians 4 does not only tell us about the duration for which the ascension ministries are given, but also the purpose for which Christ gives these gifts

---

[1] J.W. Wenham, *The Elements of New Testament Greek* (Cambridge: Cambridge University Press, 1965; rev. ed., 1991), 96.

to His Church. There Paul makes clear that these five ministries are given for the benefit of the Church. The Head of the Church gives them 'for the equipping of the saints for the work of ministry, for the edifying of the body of Christ' (*Eph. 4:12*). As a result, the ascension ministries cannot exist outside of or apart from the Church; they cannot carry out their ministry except within the context of the Church. Christ uses the ascension ministries to build up (edify) His Body.

Today, while there has been a growth in acceptance among Christians of the titles of apostle, prophet, evangelist, pastor and teacher, this has not always been deeply rooted in the context of the Church. For example, Peter Wagner has advocated the ministry of apostles today, and yet his view of apostleship is essentially non-ecclesial.

Wagner defines an apostle as:

> a Christian leader gifted, taught, commissioned, and sent by God with the authority to establish the foundational government of the church within an assigned sphere and/or spheres of ministry by hearing what the Spirit is saying to the churches and by setting things in order accordingly for the expansion of the kingdom of God.[2]

In defining apostleship, Wagner talks about church government, about the Holy Spirit's work, and about sending by God. But actually, the way he talks about these things is somewhat worrisome.

Yes, Wagner talks about church government – but he seems to set the apostle outside of that government. The apostle can establish government in the church, but he doesn't appear to be subject to it. For Wagner, a single apostle has '"extraordinary" spiritual authority "to assume and exercise general leadership."'[3] Apostles, he insists, have 'exceptional authority.' This might be over a network of churches, over individuals, over a specialised ministry, or over a geographic territory.

Essentially, Wagner's apostles are non-ecclesial. Some of them might take authority over churches, but they don't seem to come under the authority of the church and seem to be able to exist far outside the structures of the church. What's more, they seem to be, to a large degree, lone-ranger apostles. He speaks of horizontal apostles who bring apostles together to cooperate in things, but this is essentially a coming together of

---

[2] The definition is from Wagner's book *Apostles Today*, cited in Benjamin G McNair Scott, *Apostles Today: Making Sense of Contemporary Charismatic Apostolates: A Historical and Theological Appraisal* (Eugene, Oregon: Pickwick, 2014), 66.

[3] McNair Scott, *Apostles Today*, 67; citing Wagner, *Churchquake*, 105.

individuals. It is not a collegiate apostleship (one of the fundamental marks of Apostolic apostleship).[4]

Apostolic apostles cannot be non-ecclesial, because our whole understanding of apostleship is tied up with Christ's Headship of the Church. Christ, the Head of the Church, is the true Apostle (*Heb. 3:1*), and He gives gifts of men to His Church, who, through their ministry in union with Him, express His apostleship. That's also why we need a collegiate apostleship – no one man by himself can express the fullness of the apostleship which is in Christ Jesus.

The non-ecclesial nature of Wagner's apostles comes across too in the way he links them with 'the expansion of the kingdom,' rather than the building of the church; and the attending idea that the church exists for the kingdom. Yet in Apostolic theology it's the other way round. Christ and His Church are at the centre of God's Eternal Purpose. As D.P. Williams wrote, 'There is nothing higher nor nearer the heart of our glorified Lord than His Church.'[5]

Wagner's talk about 'hearing what the Spirit is saying to the churches' is also somewhat troubling. Here we have a man, who is accountable only to God and perhaps any peer-to-peer apostle accountability that he has set up for himself, who comes to the church to tell them what the Holy Spirit is saying. Yet, when the true and living God speaks, He speaks an open Word. He doesn't give secrets to individuals so that the church must receive their secret knowledge. That sounds much more like Gnosticism than Christianity. When God speaks in prophecy, He encourages – in fact, commands – the church to weigh and judge it to make sure that it is God speaking. We are not to accept that something is of God just because one person says so, even if they claim the sort of divine authority Wagner seems to want to give to his 'apostles.'[6]

Biblical apostles didn't give themselves to bringing secret messages from the Holy Spirit to individual churches. No; they gave themselves to prayer and the ministry of the Word (*Acts 6:4*). That's how apostles tell churches what the Holy Spirit is doing – by preaching the Gospel Word of salvation in Jesus Christ (for that's what the Holy Spirit is doing – applying

---

[4] The 2016 'centenary' of the Apostolic Church is actually the centenary of a stand our apostles took over collegiate apostleship against an attempt by an individual to assert his own individual apostolic authority over the churches.

[5] D.P. Williams, in the Foreword to Thomas Rees, *The Divine Masterpiece: Bible Readings upon 'The Church which is His Body'* (Penygroes: Apostolic Publications, 1943), 2.

[6] For a similar verdict (arrived at by a different route) of Wagner's position as essentially Gnostic and as an aberration, see Simon Chan, *Pentecostal Ecclesiology*, 113.

the Redemption purchased by Christ). Such independence on the part of apostles together with a view of them as the people who alone hear what the Holy Spirit is saying to the churches opens up a very real danger of abuse.

Wagner also differentiates between the gift of apostleship and the office of apostle. McNair Scott summarises this: 'the gift is given by grace alone, but the office is attained "as a result of works that have demonstrated faithfulness in stewardship of the gift."'[7] This would appear to make God's Gifts (for the office is a gift to the church, even if Wagner wants to separate the two terms) dependent, not on grace alone, but on grace and our cooperation with grace. This, then, leads people's understanding of grace and gifts away from the Reformation evangelicalism to a much more Roman position (especially given the huge emphasis which Wagner places on apostleship; with such a view it's only to be expected that people would take it as a model of how God's giving of gifts works in general).

Ultimately, Wagner's view of apostleship leads to a theology of Glory (as opposed to a theology of the Cross) – looking for God and His works in the things that seem biggest, brightest and best to us, rather than looking at them through the Cross.[8] For example, Wagner's idea of a 'congregational' apostle is the pastor of a very big church – one that grows beyond 700 or 800 people. Now, maybe this shouldn't be all that surprising – after all, Wagner was the 'church growth' guru – but numbers are all that matters here. In worldly terms, it looks successful. And so apostleship is, for Wagner, associated with (apparent) success. He even advocates something he calls a 'workplace apostle' (the whole idea of which has no biblical support) whom he claims are business entrepreneurs who can be identified 'owing to their level of wealth.'[9]

Contrast that with D.P. Williams, who insisted that apostleship entails suffering in fellowship with Christ. The Church and her ministers 'can hold glory only to the extent that we are crucified.' Unless there is this sort of cruciform apostleship, they'll be like 'children playing on the seashore' with 'superficialities' rather than 'facing the rough seas' and so venturing into the deep waters of God's Eternal Purpose in Christ.[10] D.P. Williams and the early Apostolics recognised that the power of the apostleship was power 'to

---

[7] McNair Scott, *Apostles Today*, 70; citing Wagner, *Apostles Today*, 144.

[8] On the theology of the cross (*theologia crucis*) and theology of glory (*theologia gloriae*), see chapter 15.

[9] McNair Scott, *Apostles Today*, 69.

[10] D.P. Williams, *Riches of Grace*, i.9 (1920), 5.

toil, labour and suffer.'[11] And even this power is invested in 'the apostleship', not in a lone apostle.

The great danger is that Wagner's view of apostleship leads to a rather man-centred message. He places a great deal of emphasis on the importance of having (his version of) apostles – so much so that the church must restore them in order to experience a great end-times revival. He sees apostles as being able to 'take territory from the enemy and convert it to the kingdom.'[12] In fact, the statement of belief of Wagner's coalition of apostles states that the fivefold ministries (including apostles) will 'establish the Kingdom of God on earth'![13] Surely only Jesus can give reviving, not mere men, and certainly only Jesus can establish His Kingdom.

Apostles are not the hope of the church, only Jesus is. As D.P. Williams warned, 'If we put our trust in the gifts, and not in the Giver, we shall soon become prodigals from our Father's Home.'[14] So, Wagner might use the same word as us, but he means something very different. He says he believes in apostles today, and we believe in apostles today. But that doesn't mean we believe the same thing at all.

Christ the True Minister and His Ministers

The Relationship Between the Ascension Ministries and Christ

According to *Ephesians 4:11*, Christ 'Himself gave some to be apostles, some prophets, some evangelists, and some pastors and teachers'. The Lord Jesus Christ Himself is the giver of these gifts. The Church does not make or appoint apostles, teachers, or any of the other ascension ministries; rather, she receives them as a gracious gift from her living Head.

Paul writes here in *Ephesians 4* that 'to each one of us grace was given according to the measure of Christ's gift' (*Eph. 4:7*). This verse is then linked to the giving of the ascension ministries, showing that it applies also to

---

[11] D.P. Williams, 'Apostleship' (June 1924), 17.

[12] McNair Scott, *Apostles Today*, 70.

[13] International Coalition of Apostolic Leaders: Statement of Faith (http://www.icaleaders.com/about-ical/statement-of-faith/)

[14] D.P. Williams, *Riches of Grace*, xv.9 (Oct. 1940), 97.

them. Each ascension minister has been given grace 'according to the measure of Christ's gift.'[15] Thus, not only has Christ given the ascension ministries to the Church, but it is also through the grace of Christ that these men minister. Therefore Christ's choice of ministers is not based on merit, but flows from the grace of God, and furthermore, it is only as a result of Christ's grace in their lives – of their union with Christ – that they can function in their ministries. It is also Christ who decides in what measure to gift each of His servants, and so there should not be any jealousy in the Body, for it is Christ the Head who has determined who is gifted in what way and to what extent.

As the Head and Giver of grace and gifts, it is Christ who is the true source of all ministry. Therefore, it is really Christ who ministers through the ministers. The ascension ministries are 'a means of expression for the ministry and government of Christ, the living Head.'[16] We can see something of this in the fact that Christ is specifically referred to as *apostle* (*Heb. 3:1*), *prophet* (*Acts 3:22-23*), *pastor* (*1 Pet. 2:25; 5:4*) and *teacher* (*e.g. Mt 26:18*). Furthermore, although He is never specifically referred to as *evangelist* (εὐαγγελιστής), the verb εὐαγγελίζω (*to announce good news; to proclaim the gospel*) is used with Christ as its subject (*e.g. Lk 4:18, 43*). Thus Christ is the epitome of each of the five ascension ministries. This means that it is Christ who defines each of these ministries and who is their source. As Christ gives gifts of men to His Church as apostles, prophets, evangelists, pastors and teachers, He is giving men who are to express something of His own ministry. In the words of W.A.C. Rowe, Apostleship 'is the Apostle-Christ in action through human channels'.[17] The living Head ministers to His Church through these ministers whom He gives to express *His* ministry.

The fact that the ascension ministries are ultimately expressions of Christ's ministry to the Church also highlights the necessity for plurality in Church government. Christ alone is Head of His Church. This means that no individual can govern by Himself without usurping Christ's place. Rather, the biblical pattern is that of plurality; the local assembly is governed by a plurality of elders (*e.g. Acts 14:23*) and the Church at large is governed by a plurality of apostles (*e.g. Acts 15*). Christ ministers to and

---

[15] It should not be forgotten that, although *verse 7* is linked to the discussion of the ascension ministries (and thus applies to them), it refers directly to 'each one of us', and therefore cannot (and should not) be limited to the ministers alone.

[16] W.A.C. Rowe, *One Lord, One Faith* (Penygroes: Apostolic Publications, 1960; 2nd ed., 1988), 245.

[17] Rowe, *One Lord, One Faith*, 247.

governs His Church through the ministers collectively. As the ministers express Christ's ministry and government in the Church, they cannot govern individually, for no individual man can express the fullness of any one of these ministries of Christ. B.J. Noot explained this well:

> There is need to emphasize the fact that Christ, in whom all the fullness of the Godhead dwelleth bodily, is the pre-eminent Apostle and as such is the source, essence and fullness of Apostleship, He being the possessor of all its wealth and efficiency in endless supply. It will be seen that it is manifestly impossible for any one man however great in stature he may be to reveal the full-orbed Apostleship of Jesus. Hence, He gave some Apostles.[18]

This applies to the other ascension ministries as well.

In *Acts 1:17*, we read that Judas 'obtained a part in this ministry' of apostleship. A few verses later we read that the apostles prayed to be shown which of the candidates the Lord had chosen to 'take part of this ministry and apostleship' (*Acts 1:25, KJV*). The use of the word 'part' in these two verses shows that each apostle only had a part of the ministry of apostleship, not the whole, which is found only in Christ. Thus the apostles must work together in the apostleship, rather than simply as individuals.

The fact that each apostle only shares in a part of Christ's apostleship means that there will be variety among the apostles. This is why we see differences in the ministries of the New Testament apostles. While Paul travelled widely founding assemblies, James appears to have remained in Jerusalem. While we frequently encounter the miracles of Peter, John and Paul, Scripture doesn't tell us anything about Andronicus or Timothy performing miracles. The only one person who can serve as *the* model for apostleship is Christ Himself. Again, this applies to all the ministries.

The Five Ascension Ministries

Having looked at some general principles which apply to all the ascension ministries, let us now turn our attention to the specific ministries of apostle, prophet, evangelist, pastor and teacher themselves. While space will not

---

[18] B.J. Noot, 'Apostles and Prophets', in Hugh Dawson, B.J. Noot, & Thomas Napier Turnbull, *Church Government by Apostles, Prophets, Evangelists, Pastors, Teachers, Elders and Deacons* (Bradford: Puritan Press, n.d.), 13.

permit a detailed examination of each of these ministries, we will briefly look at the nature of each.[19]

Apostles

Apostles share in and express Christ's apostleship, and consequently, the church needs a plurality of apostles. These facts help us to see that it is Christ who is the model of apostleship, not any other biblical apostle alone, and also that each individual apostle will vary. Therefore we should not expect all apostles to be exactly like Paul (or any other apostle in the New Testament). Neither should we expect all present-day apostles to be the same as each other (or one from recent history). Rather than looking to one individual as our model, we must look to the whole of the biblical teaching on apostleship.

In *Acts 6* the first deacons were appointed. The reason given for this appointment was so that the apostles could 'give [themselves] continually to prayer and to the ministry of the word' (*Acts 6:4*). Even necessary tasks in the life of the Church could not be allowed to distract the apostles from these two activities. Thus prayer and the ministry of the Word are of the essence of the apostles' ministry. The Scriptures also tell us that the early church 'continued streadfastly in the apostles' doctrine' (*Acts 2:42*), and so, again, the ministry of the Word is closely linked with the apostleship. Prayer and the proclamation of the Word are essential to any apostolic ministry.

The ministry of the Word includes the preaching of the gospel. In fact, chronologically this is one of the first things the apostles did after the beginning of the Church on the Day of Pentecost. On that day, Peter preached the gospel and three thousand people were saved (*Acts 2:14-41*). Much of the book of Acts records the expansion of the Church through the apostles' preaching of the gospel.

The proclamation of the gospel by the apostles goes together with the establishment of assemblies. This is especially seen in the case of Paul and the other apostles who accompanied him (Barnabas, Silas and Timothy), who were involved in the founding of many new assemblies. However, even apostles who are not seen founding assemblies in the New Testament, are seen building them up and establishing them in the truth.

---

[19] We'll return to look at the apostleship in more detail in the next chapter.

Once an assembly has been founded, it needs to be set in order. In the New Testament, this setting in order is always done by the apostles. The major part of the setting in order of an assembly is the appointment of elders. In *Acts 14:23* we are told that it was the apostles Paul and Barnabas who ordained elders in assemblies which they had founded. Paul left Titus in Crete to 'set in order the things that are lacking, and appoint elders in every city' (*Titus 1:5*). Likewise he gave instructions to the young apostle Timothy on the appointment of elders (*1 Tim. 3:1-7*). Thus, biblically, elders are not elected or self-appointed, but rather ordained by the apostles, through the laying on of hands (*2 Tim. 1:6*). As the first office in Church government, the apostleship is responsible, not only for the appointment and ordination of elders, but of all ascension ministries.

The apostles also lay on hands for the baptism in the Holy Spirit. In *Acts 8:14-18*, the apostles Peter and John laid hands on the new Christians in Samaria and prayed for them, and, as a result, these Samaritans were baptized in the Holy Spirit. Paul too did the same thing in Ephesus (*Acts 19:6*). Yet, although there is a strong link between the laying on of the apostles' hands and the baptism in the Holy Spirit, it is not a necessary condition. In fact, when Paul was baptized in the Spirit, it was an ordinary believer, not an apostle, who laid hands on him. Paul also linked the laying on of the apostles' hands with the impartation of spiritual gifts (*2 Tim. 1:6; Rom. 1:11*).

Another aspect of the ministry of the apostles is the general oversight of the assemblies. Paul wrote of his 'deep concern for all the churches.' (*2 Cor. 11:28*). This 'deep concern' is manifested in various ways in Scripture. One of these is the doctrinal care which the apostleship exercises over the assemblies (*e.g. Acts 15*). This is also seen in the exercise of church-discipline, for, in the New Testament, we find that it is the apostles who excommunicate and who restore to fellowship (*1 Cor. 5:1-5 and 2 Cor. 2:5-11*; in each of these cases Paul is physically absent, yet it is he who makes the decision and gives instructions for the assembly to carry it out. See also *1 Tim.1:20; 3 Jn 10*).

An Apostolic catechism well sums up the ministry of the apostles, explaining that 'the Apostleship, in establishing assemblies, ordaining into office, [and] imparting spiritual gifts, reveals the mind of God in connection with the government of the Church.'[20] Or, in the words of D.P. Williams:

---

[20] J.B. Clyne, *Asked and Answered: A Catechism of Apostolic Principles* (Bradford: Puritan Press), 25.

The Apostleship is invested with power and authority to carry forth the Revelation committed unto them: in prayer, intercession, the ministry of the Word; to preach, teach and heal; to toil, labour and suffer; to ordain Elders, impart spiritual Gifts (confirmed of God with signs and wonders); to rule and govern with demonstration of Divine wisdom, knowledge and discernment.[21]

Prophets

The Prophets speak to the Church with words that come from God. The New Testament distinguishes between *prophets* (gifts of men given by Christ to the Church) and those with the *gift of prophecy* (one of the nine gifts of the Holy Spirit). We can see this distinction quite clearly in *Acts 21:9-10*: 'Now [Philip] had four virgin daughters who prophesied. And as we stayed many days, a certain prophet named Agabus came down from Judea.' Here we see the difference between the description of Philip's daughters, who had the gift of prophecy, and Agabus, who was a prophet. Yet, it is not enough to know that there is a difference; we must also ask what the difference is between the office of the prophet and the gift of prophecy.

The gift of prophecy is given for the 'edification and exhortation and comfort' of the Church (*1 Cor. 14:3*). The office of the prophet, on the other hand, is greater in scope, including also governmental prophecy. That is why the prophets are included in the government of the church, but those with the gift of prophecy are not.

God speaks through His prophets to reveal callings in the Church. In *Acts 13*, we read that as the teachers and prophets in Antioch 'ministered to the Lord and fasted, the Holy Spirit said, "Now separate to Me Barnabas and Saul for the work to which I have called them"' (*Acts 13:2*). It is only after this calling through the prophet that Paul and Barnabas are referred to as apostles (*Acts 14:14*). Timothy's call (or separation) to the ministry was also through prophecy. Paul encouraged him to 'neglect not the gift that [was] in [him], which was given ... by prophecy, with the laying on of the hands of the presbytery' (*1 Tim. 4:14*, KJV; see also *1 Tim. 1:18*). As we have already seen, it is the apostles who ordain men to the ministry, thus it is their responsibility to judge and act upon any calls which come through the prophets. It is the apostles, not the prophets, who have been set first in the government of the Church (*1 Cor. 12:28*).

---

[21] D.P. Williams, 'Apostleship' (June 1924), 17.

God can also speak through His prophets to direct His servants to certain locations for His service. We can see an example of this in *Acts 16* where the apostle Paul was travelling with the prophet Silas (*Acts 15:32*). *Acts 16:6-7* reads: 'Now when they had gone through Phrygia and the region of Galatia, they were forbidden by the Holy Spirit to preach the word in Asia. After they had come to Mysia, they tried to go into Bithynia, but the Spirit did not permit them.' Here the Holy Spirit tells Paul and Silas that they should not go where they had planned to go. Given the context and the language used, it would appear that the Holy Spirit made His will known through the prophet.

The prophets also have a connection with doctrine. They do not reveal new doctrine, as the canon of Scripture is complete and nothing can be added to it; the doctrine of the sufficiency of Scripture means that God has already revealed in the Bible all that we need to know. Rather, the prophets unveil doctrine already contained in the Scriptures. Prophecy can illumine the written Word, helping us to understand it. The Bible teaches that one of the reasons for prophecy in the Church is 'that all may learn' (*1 Cor. 14:31*). God can speak through His prophets to explain doctrines from the Scriptures which we have neglected or which we have had difficulty understanding.

In *Acts 15* we see an example where the apostles, guided by the Holy Spirit, reached a doctrinal conclusion on an important issue in the life of the assemblies. After the decision had been reached it was communicated to the assemblies by the apostles, who also sent Judas and Silas. 'Now Judas and Silas, themselves being prophets also, exhorted and strengthened the brethren with many words' (*Acts 15:32*). So it seems that the prophets confirmed to the people the doctrine taught by the apostles.

It must be stressed, of course, that it is the Scriptures which are our highest authority. Any ministry through the prophet must be in accordance with the Scriptures. As with the gift of prophecy, prophetical ministry through the prophets must be judged (*1 Thess. 5:20-21*). As the first office in the government of the Church (*1 Cor. 12:28*), the apostleship has a special responsibility for judging the prophecies of the prophets.

To sum up, in the words of the catechism, the prophets' 'ministry is to give forth the mind of God in the midst of the Church, which can be separating, foretelling, directing, warning, confirming and exhorting.'[22]

---

[22] Clyne, *Asked and Answered: A Catechism of Apostolic Principles*, 25.

Evangelists

The word *evangelist* is used only three times in Scripture. It is used in *Ephesians 4:11*, where the evangelists are numbered among the ascension ministries; in *Acts 21:8*, where Philip is called an evangelist; and in *2 Timothy 4:5*, where Timothy is told to 'do the work of an evangelist'. The meaning of evangelist is one who preaches the good news; therefore his specific ministry is the preaching of the gospel. We can see two very different examples of this in *Acts 8*, when Philip (the only man to be specifically called an evangelist in the New Testament) preaches the gospel to many people in Samaria, and then to one man in a chariot on the way to Ethiopia.

Yet, the ministry of the evangelist is not only directed towards non-believers. As we have seen, *Ephesians 4:12* makes clear that the ascension ministries are given for the benefit of the Body of Christ. Of course this includes new believers being added to the Church through the preaching of the gospel. However, we should not forget that evangelists are given 'for the equipping of the saints for the work of ministry, for the edifying of the body of Christ' (*Eph. 4:12*). This suggests that evangelists will help equip the saints to be involved in evangelism. They will also edify the Body by preaching the gospel to the Church. After all, the gospel is not only the entry way to the Christian life, but it is also the way in which we continue and grow in our Christian walk. Christians need the gospel too.

Pastors and Elders

The word *pastor* is only used once in most English translations of the Bible (*Eph. 4:11*). Yet, the Greek word simply means *shepherd*, and so is used when the New Testament talks about shepherds. In the book of Acts, however, we do see some shepherds of the assemblies. When Paul calls together the Ephesian elders, he tells them to 'take heed to yourselves and to all the flock, among which the Holy Spirit has made you overseers, to shepherd the church of God which He purchased with His own blood' (*Acts 20:28*). The verb *to shepherd* (ποιμαίνω, *poimainō*) that Paul uses here is the verb form of the word *pastor* (ποιμήν, *poimēn*). Quite literally, Paul is telling the elders to *pastor* the assembly. Although we ordain some men as pastors and others as elders, there is no difference in the *nature* of their office.[23] The elders and

---

[23] Rather, we use the different titles to indicate a difference in the sphere of responsibility. (See *The Apostolic Church: Its Principles and Practices* [Penygroes: Apostolic Publications, 1937],

pastor (along with any other ascension ministries in the assembly) *together* form the *presbytery* (or eldership), and the presbytery governs, feeds, and cares for the assembly. We'll look more at the ministry of eldership in the next chapter.

Teachers

'God has appointed these in the church: first apostles, second prophets, third teachers' (*1 Cor. 12:28*). It is the particular task of the teachers to teach the Word of God. In fact there is a special link between the teacher (διδάσκαλος, *didaskalos*) and doctrine (διδαχή, *didachē*; διδασκαλία, *didaskalia*). Thus we find that the three ministries which have been set in the first three places in church government (apostles, prophets and teachers) all have some link with doctrine.

Like the difference between the prophet and those who prophesy, there is also a difference between the teacher and those who are 'able to teach' (*1 Tim. 3:2*). Paul sets out ability to teach as one of the qualifications of elders (and, notably, this is the main difference between the qualifications of elders and those of deacons, thus highlighting its importance for all elders), thus all elders (and pastors) should also be able to teach in order to carry out their ministries. Teaching or doctrine is essential to the life of the church, for, as we see in *Acts 2:42*, it is one of the chief characteristics by which we know the church. After all, it is our doctrine which determines our life.

The Three Orders of the Ministry

Historically, the Christian church has recognised three orders of ministry: bishops (as successors to the apostles), presbyters, and deacons.[24] Is the Apostolic concept of the five-fold ministry antithetical to the historic three orders of ministry in the church? D.P. Williams certainly didn't think so. He

---

231-232, 250. Page 250 in referring to *Ephesians 4:11* makes clear that 'Pastor includes Overseer and Elder' and hence that elders are included among the ascension ministries.)

[24] *1 Clement* 42:1-43:1; 44:1-6; Ignatius of Antioch, *Magnesians*, 6:1; 7:1; 13:1-2; *Trallians* 2:1-3; 3:1-2; 7:2; *Philadelphians* 7:1-2; First Council of Nicaea, *Canon 18*.

had a strong concept of the three orders of ministry (apostleship, presbytery and diaconate). After carefully tracing the emergence of the various ministries through the book of Acts, D.P. Williams concludes, not only that the responsibility for the calling of ministers and their ordination to office rests with the apostleship, but also that the apostles set in office 'in three ways: – Firstly, as to Deacons … Secondly: Elders … Thirdly: Apostles.'[25] This was not a one-off, passing argument on Williams' part. Elsewhere he notes the distinction between the diaconate and the other two orders of ministry: the apostleship and the 'Bishops (Elders)'.[26] Even the 'Rules of Belief' of the Apostolic Church refer to the three orders of 'Apostles, Elders and Deacons.'[27] The difference between the Apostolic three orders of ministry and the traditional three orders is a matter of terminology; while the traditional enumeration of the three orders would assign the title of bishop to the apostolic ministry, Apostolic theology equates the title of bishop with that of elder for the order of presbyter. 'The lower office of a Deacon is always subject to the higher namely the Apostleship and Eldership.'[28] There is a clear distinction between the orders of ministry, for the deacon 'is not definitely called to the ministry of a Bishop,' although some deacons may 'emerge into [the ministry] of an Elder or Evangelist.'[29]

---

[25] D.P. Williams, *Riches of Grace*, ii.5 (Dec. 1923), 11.
[26] D.P. Williams, 'The Diaconate', *Riches of Grace*, vi.4 (March 1931), 155.
[27] *The Apostolic Church: Its Principles and Practices*, 'Guiding Principles', 252.
[28] D.P. Williams, 'The Diaconate', *Riches of Grace*, vi.5 (May 1931), 197.
[29] D.P. Williams, *Riches of Grace*, vi.5 (May 1931), 200; See also the distinction between the orders of deacon and elder in D.P. Williams, 'The Diaconate (Concluded)', *RoG*, vi.6 (July 1931), 237. See further Williams' distinction of the two governmental orders, that of 'apostle, which is universal in his setting, and that of Pastor or Elder, which are local in their setting.' Williams, *Prophetical Ministry*, 83.

Chapter 37

Apostles & Elders

The Apostleship

What is Apostleship? Of Revelation & Authority and from whence they come

'Just what is an apostle?' is a question which is often asked, but seldom answered clearly. However, two words are often linked to apostles when an explanation is given: revelation and authority. That's all very well, but what exactly do we mean by linking apostles with revelation and authority? What sort of revelation and authority are we talking about?

Authority always has a source. A judge gets his authority from the Crown and the law. His authority is not his own, but an authority which he holds on behalf of the Crown. Parents, on the other hand, have authority due to who they are: parents. Theirs is not a delegated authority, but belongs inherently to them. And they can even delegate a measure of that authority to the babysitter.

So what sort of authority does an apostle have? Is it a derived authority (like the judge) or an inherent authority (like the parents)? It has to be a derived authority; for the apostle is not Head of the Church, Christ is. As the only Head of the Church, Christ is the source of all authority in His Church. Christ is 'the Apostle' (*Heb. 3:1*) and it is He who expresses His apostleship through the men He has called. As W.A.C. Rowe put it, apostleship 'is the Apostle-Christ in action through human channels.'[1] Each apostle shares in 'part' of the ministry of apostleship contained in full only in Christ Jesus (*Acts 1:17, 25*). And that means that each apostle derives his authority only from Christ, *the* Apostle and Head of the Church. The authority does not come from the man himself, nor does it come from the title (nor is it delegated by the church), but comes from (and belongs to) Christ. Yet, that

---

[1] W.A.C. Rowe, *One Lord, One Faith*, 247.

still leaves the question of how do apostles get this authority that comes from Christ?

The authority of the apostle comes from revelation. And that revelation which gives authority to the apostleship isn't something vague: it's either the Written Word of God in the Scriptures or prophetic revelation (whether to the apostle directly or through the prophet). Ultimately, the apostles must always 'appeal to the Gospel and the Written Word.'[2]

The apostle gets His authority from Christ the Head, through the revelation of Christ. Put the other (and better) way round, Christ reveals Himself and sends His apostles to authoritatively proclaim that revelation. Here it is in diagram:

The authority does not come from the man, the title, or the church, but from Christ.

And that authority comes through and stands on Christ's revelation. That too is an important issue: just what is this apostolic revelation? It can be the Bible or it can be prophetic revelation. (This is not, of course, to equate Scripture and prophecy; the two are distinct and prophecy must fall under the authority of Scripture.) That means Apostolic revelation isn't some sort of mysterious type of revelation that no one understands (and of which the Scriptures tell us nothing), but rather it comes in the same way as all revelation from God. That's why the apostles are linked both with doctrine (*Acts 2:42*) and with prophets (*Acts 15:22, 32*) in Scripture. (That's not to say that the apostle always needs a prophet for prophetic revelation; God often gives prophetic revelation directly to the apostles - e.g. *Acts 16:9-10*). That's also why the main priorities of the apostles in Scripture are the Word and prayer (*Acts 6:4*).

Recognising Apostles

Apostles are given by Christ, the Chief Apostle and Head of the Church. 'The apostle, as such, is appointed by God alone.'[3] Therefore, apostles cannot be identified simply by what they do, but rather, must be identified

---

[2] *Apostolic Church 1928 Council Minutes*, p.36.

[3] Kenneth E. Kirk, 'The Apostolic Ministry', in Kenneth E. Kirk, ed., *The Apostolic Ministry: Essays on the History and the Doctrine of Episcopacy* (London: Hodder & Stoughton, 1946), 9.

by recognising that they have been sent by the Head of the Church. And so there is a need for revelation in calls to the apostleship (or any of the other ministries for that matter). As W.A.C. Rowe has written:

> We find no call or appointment in the New Testament except by Apostolic or Prophetic revelation or direction (*Acts 13:1-4; 14:23; 20:28*). Individuals may receive personal inward revelation previously as in the case of Saul of Tarsus. But even for the illustrious apostle there came the public and official call of God.[4]

If the distinguishing feature of apostleship isn't a function, but rather being sent by Christ, then we need to rely on His revelation of whom He has sent.

Identity, Activity and Apostleship

But does that mean that function isn't important? Can we simply stop asking questions about the role of an apostle? Not at all. Function is important to ministry. But by pointing to the importance of revelation in the call, I want to highlight the fact that ministry is much more than function. *Ephesians 4:11* doesn't tell us that the ascended Christ gave some to apostle, some to prophesy, some to evangelise, some to pastor and some to teach. No! The gifts are not functions, but people: apostles, prophets, evangelists, pastors and teachers. Now, clearly there are functions which are vital to these ministries, but the gift is the man, not the function. Thus ministry is about identity, and not simply function. In fact, the function flows out from the identity. I'm not a teacher because I teach, I teach because I'm a teacher.

This fits together with the way in which God works in our lives. What we do flows out of who we are. Our love for Christ flows out of the fact that we are loved by Christ. Our good works flow out of the fact that we have been declared perfectly righteous in Christ. We aren't God's children because we act like it; we act like it because we are His children. That's the way God works: identity leads to activity, and never the other way round

And that takes us back to God's grace. Our identity as Christians is a gift of God's grace in Christ. And so are the identities of the ministers mentioned in *Ephesians 4:11*. Men did not achieve apostleship; rather, Christ gave some apostles. He has triumphed victoriously through His sinless life, atoning death and glorious resurrection. And in doing so, He has led captivity captive and given gifts unto men (*Eph. 4:8*) — He has taken those

---

[4] Rowe, *One Lord, One Faith*, 246.

who were slaves to sin and set them free for His service. And from those He has redeemed, He has given some to be apostles.

In themselves, apostles are sinful men, and so, if activity had the priority over identity, we wouldn't have any apostles. But Christ in grace gives a new identity, and, by His grace, that new identity leads to new activity through Him. Christ sends His apostles, and because *He* sends them, they fulfil their ministry.

Apostleship in Christ

Where do we find apostles? If we're prioritising function and activity, then it would seem natural to say that we find apostles where we see the function and activity being carried out. And, in a way, that's fair enough. The problem is that this can easily turn into a check-list; so the place where we look for apostles ends up being a church with a numerically large and fast growing congregation. And sometimes, perhaps even often, that is where we find them. But, it's not the place to look. For, in the apostleship, *sentness* and identity take priority over (and lead to) function and activity. A man isn't an apostle because he acts like one; he acts like an apostle because he is one.

In that case, I'd suggest, the better place to look is the place from which apostles are sent – in other words, to look to Christ the One who sends His apostles; for, not only does Christ send apostles, but Christ is Himself *the* Apostle (*Heb. 3:1*). Christ is our true Apostle, and hence the source of all true apostleship. John 17:18 uses the verb *apostello*, of both Christ and His apostles; they've been sent as He was sent. Judas had 'a part of this ministry' (*Acts 1:17*) and his replacement was to 'take part in this ministry and apostleship' (*Acts 1:25*). Each apostle then only fills part of the ministry of apostleship. There is only One who has the fullness of apostleship – the Apostle Christ Jesus.

So then, Christ is the Apostle, and the men He gives as apostles share in part of His apostleship. That means that it is only through their union with Christ, only as Jesus ministers through them that they can minister as His apostles. Apostleship 'is the Apostle-Christ in action through human channels.'[5]

---

[5] Rowe, *One Lord, One Faith*, 247.

Therefore, apostleship is found *in Christ*, and so true apostleship should always direct our attention to Christ, its source. Thus, if we want to find apostles, then Christ is the One to whom we should look.

Apostleship Under the Cross

True apostleship should bear fruit. In *Matthew 7* Jesus teaches and warns against false prophets, concluding, 'therefore, by their fruits you will know them' (*Mt 7:20*). Although he specifically mentions *false prophets*, the context suggests that this applies more widely. So surely true apostles will lead to good fruit.

Yet, agreeing that we should see good fruit is one thing, but what we mean by good fruit is another thing entirely. In the climate in which we live, we very readily translate *fruit* into *success*. And *success* in our culture is something that's thought of as easily measurable. But is that an adequate interpretation of *fruit*?

If Isaiah, Jeremiah or even Paul were around today, how would our modern success-oriented mind-set rate their fruit? Would we abandon God's true servants because of their lack of mega-congregations? Would we stand with Jeremiah and Paul in their imprisonments? What would we do with Isaiah's clear gospel message which begins with the words 'Who has believed our report?' (*Isa. 53:1*). And what would we make of Paul's apostleship when he was beheaded? Or Isaiah's prophethood when he was sawn in half? Certainly these are not the trappings of what we think of as success.

The theology of the cross (*theologia crucis*) shows us that our ideas of success can look very different to God's true success.[6] The fruit we covet may be somewhat different from the true and lasting fruit which is brought forth in the branches by the True Vine. Luther warns us against preferring 'works to suffering, glory to the cross, strength to weakness, wisdom to folly.'[7] To ignore his warning would be to trade in the way of the cross for a theology of glory.

Can fruitfulness be measured? And if so, how? Does it look like the need to build a new church to fit in the crowds, or does it look like faithfulness to Christ's call no matter how adverse the circumstances? James was executed early in the life of the Church (*Acts 12:2*). The seal of Paul's

---

[6] For the *theologia crucis* (and contrasting theology of glory), see chapter 15.

[7] *Heidelberg Disputation*, Proof of Thesis 21.

apostleship was a problem church that nowadays probably no one would want to pastor (*1 Cor. 9:2*). And even they didn't seem to think much of his preaching (*2 Cor. 10:10*). John was rejected by Diotrephes, and hence the church he led (*3 John 9-10*), and eventually ended up in exile on Patmos (*Rev. 1:9*). Yet, it's a lot easier for us to focus on the crowds of the Day of Pentecost.

The true fruit of apostleship is fruit that will be there both in the times of revival and in the times of tribulations. That type of fruit can't be measured by bodies, buildings and budgets; but that's okay – it doesn't have to be. Yet such fruit calls for deep roots. Fruit is seen on the branches, but it's borne by the Vine. So if the branches are to be fruitful in all circumstances, no matter how fierce the storm, then they must be firmly anchored in the Vine. Christ, the true Vine and true Apostle, is the source of all fruitfulness we see among His apostles here on earth. So, Christ's apostles must be deeply rooted in Him.

The Gospel, Grace, and Apostleship

Paul opens his letter to the Romans with a greeting that teaches us something about his apostleship:

> Paul, a bondservant of Jesus Christ, called to be an apostle, separated to the gospel of God which He promised before through His prophets in the Holy Scriptures, concerning His Son Jesus Christ our Lord, who was born of the seed of David according to the flesh, and declared to be the Son of God with power according to the Spirit of holiness, by the resurrection from the dead. Through Him we have received grace and apostleship for obedience to the faith among all nations for His name, among whom you also are the called of Jesus Christ *(Romans 1:1-6)*.

Immediately he links his apostleship with the gospel — he was 'called to be an apostle, separated to the gospel.' These aren't two unrelated callings, for he goes on to talk about both (the gospel and apostleship) as his greeting proceeds, drawing the two together again in verse 5 when he writes of 'grace and apostleship' received through Jesus.

So, Paul's apostleship is connected with his call to preach the gospel. In fact, Paul's apostleship is meaningless in separation from his call to preach the gospel — to be called as an apostle is to be separated to the gospel.

And this gospel which is so linked to his apostleship isn't something vague; it's not simply any biblical teaching (as if we could somehow make it refer to 'church government by apostles, prophets, evangelists, pastors, teachers, elders and deacons'), but rather some very specific good news. It is God's gospel. It is the good news He promised in the Old Testament. It's the good news all about 'His Son, Jesus Christ our Lord.' It's the good news that involves Christ's incarnation ('born of the seed of David according to the flesh') and His death, resurrection, and vindication (which is our justification — *1 Tim. 3:16; Rom. 4:25*). In other words, apostles are separated to the biblical message of Christ, the Incarnate Son of God, who lived, died and rose for us and our salvation.

And this separation to the gospel is to be seen in proclamation of the gospel. 'Through Him we have received grace and apostleship for obedience to the faith among all nations for His name' (*v.5*). Here we see that apostleship is empowered by the gospel — that's where its strength and capability comes from — for it is only 'through Him': because of who Jesus, the true Apostle, is and what He has done, and because those whom He has called to share in His ministry of apostleship only truly minister as apostles in union with Him. Jesus is the source and strength of apostleship. All true apostleship is found only in Him and so it is only as He is at work through those who are united to Him that we see the ministry of apostleship. (And the same, of course, applies to prophets, teachers, pastors and evangelists too.) It's not the mere presence of apostles that brings about 'obedience to the faith among all nations,' but rather, as Paul will tell us later in this epistle, 'faith comes by hearing, and hearing by the Word of Christ' (*Rom. 10:17*). So it's as the apostles (and others) proclaim the Gospel Word of Christ crucified and raised that people from all nations come to faith in Him and He builds up His Church.

Apostles are not the gospel. But apostles are called to proclaim, to teach, to defend, to contend for, and above all to believe the gospel. When we lose sight of the glorious grace of God, the apostles should be first in line to point us back to Jesus. We don't need apostles for *their* great ministries of what *they* can do or show us to do — we need apostles who find their ministry and identity in Christ and who point us to Christ as they proclaim the grace of God in Christ in the Gospel.

Grace and apostleship go together. The gospel and apostleship go together. Thankfully, the gospel and the grace of God don't depend upon apostles, so we can have gospel and grace without them. But it doesn't work the other way round. Certainly, we can have titles; but we cannot have true apostleship unless it is rooted in, grounded upon, permeated with, and always pointing to the gospel of God's grace in Jesus. Apostleship isn't really about what we all too often think of as leadership, nor is it about administration — it's about Jesus.

The Life in Christ and Apostleship

Paul starts off his second letter to Timothy with the greeting, 'Paul, an apostle of Jesus Christ by the will of God, according to the promise of life which is in Christ Jesus' (2 *Tim. 1:1*), and this particular greeting in this particular letter tells us something important about the nature of Paul's apostleship.

Paul's apostleship is 'by the will of God.' In other words, Paul hasn't set himself up as an apostle. It's not a career-choice that Paul made, but rather the call of God. And it's not simply a choice of the church. The church didn't just say, 'Oh, you know what, we could be doing with an apostle to the Gentiles, so let's set up a committee to draw up a shortlist so we can pick someone for the job.' No, not at all. It wasn't the church's choice, but God's choice. Apostleship is not simply a job, title or position, but a calling of God according to His will. As *Ephesians 4:11* tells us, it is Christ who gives gifts of apostles to His Church, not the other way round.

However, that is not all that this verse tells us about apostleship. Not only is Paul an apostle by the will of God, but also 'according to the promise of life which is in Christ Jesus.' The promise of life that God gives us in Christ Jesus is salvation: eternal life in Christ. But what does that have to do with apostleship? Surely these are two completely separate things on two completely different levels of importance. And yet Paul connects the two here. Or rather, God connects the two here. Apostleship is somehow connected with life in Jesus.

Of course, this does not mean that you need apostles in order to have life in Jesus. But what this does show us is that apostleship (or eldership or the pastorate for that matter) isn't simply a 'leadership role' within an organisation. It's not even simply an office of the church. Rather apostleship finds its origin and source, as well as its vitality and power, not in the apostle, the governing structures, or even in the church itself, but rather somewhere much better, somewhere much more vital, somewhere much more powerful; apostleship finds its origin and source, as well as its vitality and power, in the life which is in Christ Jesus.

Christ is the true apostle (*Heb. 3:1*), and so all true apostleship is found in Him. Likewise, Christ is the true prophet, teacher, evangelist, pastor and elder. So all true Christian ministry is ministry in union with Christ. It is not that Christ has put some thing in me to make me a pastor and teacher, but rather that I am united to Christ, and so Christ in me is the pastor and teacher. And the same goes for apostleship.

So apostleship (like all Christian ministry) cannot be carried out apart from or independent of Christ. Our ministry is not something that we do *for* Christ and offer to Him, but rather something that we do *in* Christ, united to Him, relying on Him as the true apostle, teacher or elder (or whichever of the other ministries He has called us to by His grace).

Christian ministry is 'according to the promise of life which is in Christ Jesus.' It's not a way of working our way toward life, but rather an expression of the life of Christ to whom we've already been united. And therefore, Christian ministry isn't about me and my ministry; it's all about Jesus.

The Twelve Apostles of the Lamb & the Ascension Gift Apostles of the Church

The Scriptures give a particular prominence and role to 'the Twelve' (*Acts 6:2; 1 Cor. 15:5; Rev. 21:14; cf. Acts 1:26; Acts 2:14*), the apostles chosen by Christ during His earthly ministry, along with Matthias as the replacement for Judas (*Acts 1:15-26*). The Twelve are also called 'the apostles of the Lamb' (*Rev. 21:14*).

The apostles given by the ascended Christ to the church are not apostles in a lesser sense than the Twelve, for Paul (who was not one of the Twelve) writes that 'in nothing was I behind the most eminent apostles' (*2 Cor. 12:11; cf. 11:5*). In *Galatians 2:8-9*, Paul suggests an equality of apostleship between him (as an ascension-gift apostle) and the Twelve. Both he and Peter have received their apostleship from God (*v.8*), and there is full communion between 'James, Cephas, and John, who seemed to be pillars' and Paul and Barnabas in their apostleship (*v.9*). Furthermore, this James is not James the brother of John (one of the Twelve, who was now dead), but rather, James the brother of our Lord (who was not one of the Twelve).[8] Yet here the (ascension-gift) apostle James is placed on a par with Peter (Cephas) and John, the leading figures from among the Twelve. This is not

---

[8] We know that James, the Lord's brother, was an apostle from *Gal. 1:19*.

to suggest that there is absolutely no difference between the Twelve and the ascension-gift apostles. However, even though they form two distinct groups within the apostleship (the Twelve, who cannot be replaced or added to, and the continuously-given ascension-gift apostles), there is an equality in the nature of their apostleship.

So, if both groups of apostles share equally in the nature of the gift (which is found in Christ, the true Apostle), what then is the distinction between the Twelve and the post-ascension apostles? The differences appear to be connected to the timing of their giving, to the fixed number of the Twelve, to their qualifications, and to their role beyond the church. The Twelve 'were called in the days of our Lord's humiliation,'[9] whereas the ascension-gift apostles were given by Christ, 'when He ascended on high' (*Eph. 4:8*). The Twelve had to be twelve in number; when Judas fell, the number was made up with Matthias, but no more could be added to the Twelve after that. The ascension-gift apostles, however, have no fixed number in Scripture. The Twelve had to have been with Christ and His apostles from the time of Jesus' baptism in the Jordan to the day of His ascension (*Acts 1:21-22*). Yet the Scriptures show us (ascension-gift) apostles of the church who not only did not fulfil this criteria (e.g. Paul), but also could not possibly have fulfilled this criterion (e.g. Timothy, *1 Thess. 2:6; cf. 1:1*). Finally, the Twelve were sent first 'to the lost sheep of the house of Israel' (*Mt 10:6*), and 'in the regeneration, when the Son of Man sits on the throne of His glory, [they] will also sit on twelve thrones, judging the twelve tribes of Israel' (*Mt 19:28*). While the Twelve also have a foundational role in the Church (*Rev. 21:14*), their role also extends beyond the church in relation to Israel during both Jesus' earthly ministry and His millennial kingdom. The role of the ascension-gift apostles, however, is limited to the church and its mission.

As the Twelve have a foundational role in the church, the ascension-gift apostles are, in their churchly ministry, 'successors' of the Twelve.[10]

Ordination

One of the significant distinctive ministries of the apostleship is that of ordination. It is the apostles who ordain other apostles and other ministers within the church. In *Acts 6*, the men chosen as the church's first deacons

---

[9] D.P. Williams, *1928 Council Minutes*, p.28.
[10] *Apostolic Church Council Minutes, Oct 1929*, p.123.

were 'set before the apostles; and when they had prayed, they laid hands on them' (*Acts 6:6*). By prayer and the laying on of hands, the apostles ordained these men to the diaconate. Later, when the apostles Paul and Barnabas established new assemblies, they 'ordained … elders in every church' (*Acts 14:23, AV*).[11] Paul left Titus in Crete, in part, to 'ordain elders in every city' (*Titus 1:5*). 'That the apostles appointed elders is unquestionable … On the other hand, for the elders to appoint apostles is unheard of.'[12]

Acts 13 might appear to provide a counter-example to apostolic ordination. When Barnabas and Paul are called through the prophet to the ministry of the apostleship (*Acts 13:2*), it is the teachers and prophets in Antioch who 'having fasted and prayed … laid hands on them, they sent them away' (*Acts 13:3*). Yet, these are exceptional circumstances. When Paul and Barnabas were called as apostles, they were the only apostles apart from the Twelve in Jerusalem. As there were no apostles present to ordain, the second and third ministries in the church (the prophets and teachers, *1 Cor. 12:28*) acted in recognition of the call, and then the newly called apostles travelled to Jerusalem at the first opportunity to receive the official recognition of their ministry by the church, through the apostles (*Gal. 2:1-10*). Thus the ordination at the hand of the prophets and teachers in Acts 13 may be seen as a type of provisional ordination in exceptional circumstances.[13] In this case, the newly called apostle was 'not accepted as a true apostle until his credentials [had] been scrutinized by those who were apostles before him.'[14]

Ordination does not make a man a minister. As Paul reminded the Ephesians elders, it is the Holy Spirit who makes ministers (*Acts 20:28*), for it is Christ who gives these men as gifts to His church (*Eph. 4:11*), according to the Father's will (*Gal. 1:1, 15; 1 Cor. 1:1; 2 Cor. 1:1; Eph. 1:1; Col. 1:1; 2 Tim. 1:1*). However, ordination is the church's setting apart of those who have been chosen and called by the Triune God to the ministry. The five-fold ministry (including elders) 'are set apart through prayer and the laying on of hands and by anointing with oil.' Deacons and deaconesses are ordained

---

[11] The word 'ordained' (χειροτονέω, *cheirotoneō*) was a more general word for *selection* or *appointment*, but became a technical word in the Christian church for *ordination*. Although some authors have tried to argue that this word points to congregational election by a show of hands, that meaning had become obsolete long before the New Testament was written. In the New Testament it points to ordination by the apostles, not voting by the congregation.

[12] Kirk, 'The Apostolic Ministry', 9.

[13] And so should not be imitated in unexceptional circumstances.

[14] Kirk, 'The Apostolic Ministry', 10.

'by prayer and the laying on of hands' (i.e. without anointing with oil).[15]
Apostles and presbyters are anointed with oil because:

> This indicate[s] that the one anointed was called to a place of authority, and symbolized the anointing of the Holy Spirit who [gives] the necessary virtue, grace and power required. Its use by the Church also indicates that this office is a gift of the anointed Christ carrying with it His authority.[16]

The Eldership

The Bible uses a number of words for the ministry of eldership. The words *elder* (or *presbyter*), *overseer* (or *bishop*), and *pastor* (or *shepherd*), are all used interchangeably in the New Testament to refer to the same ministry. In *Acts 20:17-38*, when Paul meets with the Ephesian elders, he sends for them as 'elders' (*v.17*), but then addresses them as 'overseers' (*v.28*). With each of these words the Scripture refers to the same group of men: the elders in Ephesus are the overseers. And this also means that there is a plurality both in the eldership and in the oversight: there is not one *bishop* (*overseer*) set over a number of *presbyters* (*elders*). The bishops are the presbyters. The overseers are the elders.

In his letter to Titus, Paul writes:

> For this reason I left you in Crete, that you should set in order the things that are lacking, and appoint elders in every city as I commanded you — if a man is blameless, the husband of one wife, having faithful children not accused of dissipation or insubordination. For a bishop must be blameless. (*Titus 1:5-7*)

---

[15] *The Apostolic Church: Its Principles and Practices*, 250. In the British Apostolic Church, an exception has now been introduced so that an ordinand may forgo the anointing with oil in his ordination if he so desires. However, technically and theologically, anointing is a normative part of an Apostolic ordination to the five-fold ministry/to the orders of apostle or presbyter. The distinction between the ordination practice for the five-fold ministry and the diaconate is rooted in the distinction between the ordination of priests and Levites in the Old Testament. D.P. Williams argued that it is 'not of human institution but by the command of God the Holy Ghost, to use the oil of Consecration in the setting apart of Elders and Apostles, but not the Diaconate.' He points, not only to the Old Testament pattern, but also to prophecy and the practice of 'the Early Church.' D.P. Williams, *Riches of Grace*, ii.5 (Dec. 1923), 11.

[16] *The Apostolic Church: Its Principles and Practices*, 251.

Titus is to ordain elders, and yet the qualifications of these elders are the qualifications of bishops. And so once again, we see the two terms being used interchangeably.

Peter also demonstrates that these terms refer to the same ministry:

> The elders who are among you I exhort, I who am a fellow elder and a witness of the sufferings of Christ, and also a partaker of the glory that will be revealed: Shepherd the flock of God which is among you, serving as overseers. (*1 Pet. 5:1-2*)

Peter tells the 'elders' to 'shepherd' and serve as 'overseers.' For Peter, as for Paul, the elders are the overseers, and their task is to pastor (shepherd) the flock.

In *Ephesians 4:11* we find the only use of the noun 'pastor' for the pastoral ministry in the New Testament. On every other occasion where a noun is used of those who pastor, it is either *elder* (*presbyter*) or *overseer* (*bishop*). Yet, not only does *Ephesians 4:11* show that 'pastor' is an appropriate name for the ministry of presbyter, it also shows us that pastors are included among the five Headship ministry gifts of Christ. Hence, the historical doctrine of the Apostolic Church is that elders, overseers, and pastors are included among the five-fold ministry. Tenet 9 is specifically intended to be understood as including the elders under the term pastor.[17] The custom in the Apostolic Church is that the terms *pastor* and *elder* are used to indicate a difference in the sphere of responsibility, but that the ministry of pastors and elders is one and the same.[18] In the wider government of the church, those called as pastors function as representative elders.[19]

As a Headship ministry, the role of the eldership is 'for the equipping of the saints for the work of ministry, for the edifying of the body of Christ' (*Eph. 4:12*), which takes place through 'speaking the truth in love' (*Eph. 4:15*).

---

[17] The Apostolic Church, *Minutes of the Bradford Convocation of Apostles and Prophets, Jan. 19th-25th 1932*, p.6. See further, *Minutes of the General Council of the Apostolic Church, Half Yearly, February 1937*, pp.73c, 90-91; *The Apostolic Church: Its Principles and Practices* (Penygroes: Apostolic Publications, 1937), 231-232, 250. Page 250 in referring to *Ephesians 4:11* makes clear that 'Pastor includes Overseer and Elder' and hence that elders are included among the ascension ministries (in agreement with the 1932 doctrinal minute).

[18] *The Apostolic Church: Its Principles and Practices* (Penygroes: Apostolic Publications, 1937), 231.

[19] *Minutes of the General Council of the Apostolic Church, Half Yearly, February 1937*, p. 91.

The Origin and Calling of the Eldership

The Great Shepherd Shepherds Through His Under-Shepherds

The ministry of eldership finds its source and origin in Christ, the true Elder. It is the Lord Jesus who is 'the Shepherd and Overseer of [our] souls' (*1 Pet. 2:25*). He is the 'great Shepherd of the sheep' (*Heb. 13:20*) and 'the good Shepherd' who has given His life for the sheep (*Jn 10:11*). Christ, the Head of the Church, is 'the Chief Shepherd', under whom the elders exercise their ministry of oversight for the flock (*1 Pet. 5:1-4*). For all eternity, 'the Lamb who is in the midst of the throne will shepherd [His people] and lead them to living fountains of waters' (*Rev. 7:17*).

As we have seen in the previous chapter, Christ is the true minister who exercises His Headship ministries through the ministers He has gifted to the Body. Therefore, the ministry of eldership is found in sharing in Christ's eldership. The call to the eldership is a call of grace, as Christ lifts captives out of sin and death, and gifts them to His Body as elders and pastors to shepherd and feed the flock. This grace for the ministry of eldership is not a power given by Christ; it is Christ Himself, who ministers through His chosen elders to whom He is united.

The Holy Spirit Makes Overseers

Christ reveals His gifts of elders in the Body through the Holy Spirit. And by His Holy Spirit the Great Shepherd equips and leads His under-shepherds. As Paul reminded the Ephesian elders, it is the Holy Spirit who makes overseers (*Acts 20:28*). The eldership is a spiritual ministry, carried out through union with Christ through the Holy Spirit. Elders are not simply respected men or talented leaders. They are the men through whom the Head of the Church shepherds and feeds His people.

The Apostles Ordain Elders

When the apostles Paul and Barnabas planted new assemblies, they also 'appointed elders in every church, and prayed with fasting' (*Acts 14:23*). Through their ordination by the apostles, the whole church can see that the eldership continues steadfastly in the apostles' fellowship. And so the members of the church are in communion with the apostleship, even when no apostles are present, through their communion with the presbytery.

The apostles' ordination of elders also demonstrates the delegation of responsibility from the apostleship to the presbytery in the local assembly. There were no elders at the beginning of the New Testament church. At first there were only apostles, and then apostles and deacons (*Acts 6*). Elders are only mentioned in the book of Acts after the church spreads beyond Jerusalem. In other words, the eldership first appears with the commencement of assemblies where there were no apostles. A distinct presbytery was not needed until then, for there was a plurality of elders in the Jerusalem church in the form of the apostles themselves (*1 Pet. 1:5; 2 Jn 1; 3 Jn 1*).[20] Therefore, elders fulfil in local assemblies part of the ministry the apostles fulfilled when there was only one assembly. This is seen in how the eldership shares in the apostles' task of prayer and the ministry of the Word (*Acts 6:4*). Like the apostles, the elders have a particular responsibility for teaching (*1 Tim. 3:2*) and a particular association with prayer (*Jas 5:13-16*). Prayer and the ministry of the Word are key features of the apostleship, and apostleship's most important ministry; yet the elders share in it.

The Nature of the Ministry of Eldership

Paul tells us that the ministry of an overseer is 'a good work' (*1 Tim. 3:1*) or 'a noble task' (*1 Tim 3:1*, ESV). But what does this noble task involve?

Eldership is a Governing Ministry

The first mention of elders in the New Testament church is found in Acts 11:30, where we read of money being entrusted to them for the church. (At this point the eldership is already in existence; there is no record of the beginning of this ministry.) That money is entrusted to the eldership for the church shows us both that the eldership is a governing office, and that the presbytery represents the assembly. So, for example, it is the presbytery who carry out church discipline; and when a matter for discipline is brought to the presbytery, it is brought before 'the church' (*Mt 18:17*).

---

[20] In the doctrine of the Apostolic Church, an apostle is an elder among the elders (*1928 Council Minutes*, p.22).

As the governing ministry in the assembly, the assembly is to submit to the presbytery. Paul urges the Thessalonians 'to recognize those who labour among you, and are over you in the Lord and admonish you, and to esteem them very highly in love for their work's sake' (*1 Thess. 5:12-13*). It is for the sake of their ministry in the Lord that the elders are to be recognised and highly esteemed. Thus it is not the person of the man himself, but rather the ministry which he faithfully carries out through union with Christ, the Chief Shepherd, which warrants such respect and submission. It is as the elders are faithful to the Lord who has entrusted the flock to their care (*1 Pet. 5:1-4*), that the flock is called to 'submit yourselves to your elders' (*1 Pet. 5:5*). As the writer to the Hebrews reminds us, we are to submit to faithful elders who faithfully speak the Word of God to the assembly:

> Remember those who rule over you, who have spoken the word of God to you, whose faith follow, considering the outcome of their conduct ... Obey those who rule over you, and be submissive, for they watch out for your souls, as those who must give account. Let them do so with joy and not with grief, for that would be unprofitable for you. (*Heb. 13:7, 17*)

These are the faithful elders who 'take care of the church of God' (*1 Tim. 3:5*). Therefore, governing in the church means caring for the flock and speaking to them the Word of God, by proclaiming Christ biblically.

Some elders are also involved in a governing role beyond the local assembly (*Acts 15:2,4,6,22-23; 16:4*). In the Apostolic Church we distinguish between those elders with a purely local responsibility and those involved in a wider governing role by calling the former *elders*, and the latter *pastors*.

Eldership is a Teaching Ministry

Paul tells us that 'a bishop must be ... able to teach' (*1 Tim. 3:2*). This is the only qualification of the presbytery that differs from the diaconate. In fact, every other qualification for elders is elsewhere expected of all Christians. An elder is to hold 'fast the faithful word as he has been taught, that he may be able, by sound doctrine, both to exhort and convict those who contradict' (*Titus 1:9*). Not only must he be able to teach sound doctrine, but he must also be able to refute those who teach false doctrine and correct those who have been taken in by erroneous teachings. When the writer to the Hebrews tells us to 'remember those who rule over you,' he specifies that they are those 'who have spoken the word of God to you' (*Heb. 13:7*). Therefore, the primary way in which the elders rule and govern in the church is by speaking the Word of God: by teaching the Scriptures and preaching Jesus.

Eldership is a Plural Ministry

The assembly is not governed by a pastor or an elder, but by a presbytery. Therefore, there must be a plurality of elders and a collegiality amongst them. Paul and Barnabas ordained 'elders' (plural) 'in every church' (*Acts 14:23*). In Miletus, Paul met with the 'elders' (plural) of 'the church' in Ephesus (*Acts 20:17*). In Jerusalem, he met with James 'and all the elders' (*Acts 21:18*). Titus was to 'appoint elders in every city' (*Titus 1:5*). And, when Paul wrote to the assembly in Philippi, he addressed his letter to the church, 'with the bishops [plural] and deacons' (*Phil. 1:1*). Although there are indications of a leading figure among the elders in at least some assemblies, which we might refer to as the pastor, (*1 Tim. 5:17; Acts 21:18*), scripturally he could be seen as no more than *primus inter pares*.[21] The only example of a single ruling figure in a New Testament church is where things have gone wrong (*3 Jn 9*).

Plurality in the presbytery brings unity in diversity. Christ exercises His Headship of the Church through the different elders together. No one man can possibly take on the fullness of the ministry of eldership which is found in Christ (*cf. the apostleship: Acts 1:17, 25*).

The Qualifications for Eldership and the Headship Ministries

The qualifications for the eldership are of particular significance, because they are the highest set of criteria we have for any ministry in the New Testament. As the apostles are elders among the elders (*1 Pet. 1:5; 2 Jn 1; 3 Jn 1*), the qualifications for eldership apply to all five of the Headship ministries: apostles, prophets, evangelists, pastors and teachers. The full listing of qualifications for the presbytery are found in *1 Timothy 3:1-7* and *Titus 1:6-9*. The majority of these qualifications are matters of morality and character. However, we shall look at two of these in more detail.

---

[21] First among equals.

A Minister Must Be Apt to Teach

This is the key distinctive qualification of eldership. Elders (and the other ascension ministers) must be able to teach by explaining the Scriptures accurately to others in a way which will lead them to Christ, the Head of the Church. This may involve public preaching in the church, but need not do so necessarily; there may be elders who teach capably, but do not preach as part of the church's worship. Preaching certainly involves teaching, but isn't simply to be equated with teaching. True preaching is proclaiming Christ biblically.[22]

Paul makes clear that some elders labour in the Word and doctrine, in a distinct way from other fellow-elders (1 Tim. 5:17). Therefore, various elders have differing loads of responsibility when it comes to preaching and formal teaching.

The minister's ability to teach involves two components: aptitude and faithfulness. He must have an aptitude for speaking the truth of the Scriptures to others in ways which they will be able to follow, understand, learn, and benefit from. Knowledge and the ability to teach are not one and the same; baffling 'teaching' is not deep teaching.

And this aptitude for teaching also means an ability to teach in a way which will bring benefit to the spiritual life of the church. Therefore, it is not to be divisive, arrogant, disinterested or overly technical.

The second aspect of the minister's ability to teach is faithfulness. His teaching must be full of sound content, and this requires study and diligence. A minister must 'be diligent to present [himself] approved to God, a worker who does not need to be ashamed, rightly dividing the word of truth' (2 Tim. 2:15). He needs to know how to interpret the Scriptures, and must himself be grounded in the gospel. For the gospel is the fundamental teaching of the church. Therefore, it is imperative that the elders and ministers of the church be able to articulate, explain and defend the gospel.

> All authority in the Church belongs to Jesus Christ, and He mediates that authority to His under-shepherds through His Word. Since the authority of the elder is derived from his handling of the Scriptures, he does need to be able to teach publically, even if infrequently, simply in order that his authority might be shown to derive from the Word of God and his accurate

---

[22] See chapter 35 on the ministry of the Word.

handling of it (not from the strength of his personality or the success of his business ventures).[23]

The Husband of One Wife: Why Are Only Men Ordained to the Eldership and Five-fold Ministry?

Greek has two words for *man*: one of these, ἄνθρωπος (*anthrōpos*), refers to a human being in general, whether male or female, while the other, ἀνήρ (*anēr*), specifically refers to a man in distinction from a woman, thus to a 'male' man, and is also used for a husband. Paul writes to both Timothy and Titus using the word ἀνήρ (*anēr*) among the qualifications of elders, for an elder is to be 'the husband of one wife' (*1 Tim. 3:2; Titus 1:6*). Specifically here, the qualifications for eldership rule out polygamy, but as they do so, they also restrict the ministry to men.

Peter also uses the word ἀνήρ (*anēr*) in setting out the qualifications for an apostle to replace Judas (*Acts 1:21*). Here, unlike in *1 Timothy* and *Titus*, there is no mention of marriage or wives, so the restriction cannot in any way be viewed as related to marital status. Although many of Christ's most faithful disciples from the very outset had been women, only a man was eligible to be called to this office of apostleship.

It is Christ, the Head of the church, whose actions and direction are decisive for the order of the church. Thus, the church's calling and ordination of men to the ministry is rooted in Christ's own calling and sending of men as His apostles (*Lk 6:13-15*). The Incarnate Christ is the true revelation of the Triune God, and so His calling of men as apostles is not a mere curiosity of history, but the revelation of the will of God for apostleship in the church. This is then reflected by Peter's use of the word ἀνήρ (*anēr*) among the qualifications for the new apostle called in *Acts 1*.

This was not an accommodation on the part of the Saviour to the patriarchal culture of the 1st century. For Jesus did not treat women in the normal way for the culture, but rather demonstrated with His words and actions the sinful oppression of women in that culture.

> Christ's relationship to women around Him is marked on the one hand by a superior freedom over against human ordinances and conventional rules. He makes a clean break with any degrading of the woman. All His dealings proclaim the similarity of all men. On the other hand, there exists

---

[23] Mark Dever and Paul Alexander, *The Deliberate Church: Building Your Ministry on the Gospel* (Wheaton: Crossway, 2005), 146.

a dissimilarity of functions. Among the greatest of His disciples there are a number of women. They, too, followed Him on His journeys. But He does not entrust to them a special commission nor a place among those who are to hold office in the Church. He calls only men to be apostles and to them He entrusts the Missionary Command, the Proclamation of the Word, Baptism, the Lord's Supper, and the Power of the Keys.[24]

Jesus sent women to evangelise (*Jn 4:28-30; Mt 28:5-10*), but He sent His apostles to baptise and teach authoritatively (*Mt 28:16-20*), and it was to His apostles that He entrusted the sacrament of the Breaking of Bread (*Lk 22:14-20*).

The Scriptures tell us that only ordaining men to the ministry of apostleship, and the delegated ministry of presbyter, is not only the example of the Lord, but also His command (*1 Cor. 14:34-37*). The word Paul uses for command (*1 Cor. 14:37*) is ἐντολή (*entolē*), which is the word Jesus uses in the Sermon on the Mount for the unbreakable commandments of the law which will not pass away (*Mt 5:19*) and for the commandments of God in contrast to the traditions of men (*Mt 15:3, 6; cf. Mt 19:17; 22:38, 40*). 'The Greek word *entole* has the force of a divine decree that threatens punishment to all those who break it.'[25]

But what exactly is this divine decree of the Lord?

> As in all the churches of the saints, let your women keep silent in the churches, for they are not permitted to speak; but they are to be submissive, as the law also says. And if they want to learn something, let them ask their own husbands at home; for it is shameful for women to speak in church. Or did the word of God come originally from you? Or was it you only that it reached? If anyone thinks himself to be a prophet or spiritual, let him acknowledge that the things which I write to you are the commandments of the Lord. But if anyone is ignorant, let him be ignorant. (*1 Cor. 14:33-38*[26])

According to Paul, the commandment of the Lord is that women are to 'keep silent in the churches, for they are not permitted to speak.' However, just a few chapters earlier, Paul has made very clear that women may pray and prophesy in church (otherwise there would be no need for what he

---

[24] Bo Giertz, 'Twenty-Three Theses on the Holy Scriptures, the Woman, and the Office of the Ministry,' English Translation in Matthew C. Harrison and John T Pless, ed., *Women Pastors? The Ordination of Women in Biblical Lutheran Perspective*, (St Louis: Concordia, 3rd ed., 2012), 258.

[25] David P. Scaer, 'May Women be Ordained as Pastors?', in Harrison and Pless, ed., *Women Pastors?*, 312.

[26] Punctuation adapted between vv.33 and 34 (cf. ESV).

teaches about the head-covering: *1 Cor. 11:5-16*). Therefore, when he writes here of keeping silent, he cannot be referring to an absolute silence. So what does this Scripture mean?

Firstly, this command is only 'in the churches'; the whole context of *1 Corinthians 11-14* is dealing with the corporate worship of the gathered church. Christian women are called to evangelise and bear witness to Christ (*Jn 4:28-30; Mt 28:5-10; Acts 16:14-15*). Christian women are to teach the faith outside of the church service (*Acts 18:26; 2 Tim. 1:5; Titus 2:3*). So this command applies only in the one context for which it is given: 'in the churches.'

Secondly, Paul uses a particular Greek word for speaking in this command. Rather than λέγω (*legō*), the general word for speaking, the Scripture here uses λαλέω (*laleō*). This word, 'unless otherwise modified by adverbs, when used in connection with worship services, refers to religious speaking or speaking religiously in the public way.'[27] In other words, this prohibition is not on any speech in the church service (which is clear from *1 Cor. 11:5-16* where Paul explicitly writes of women praying and prophesying), but rather, on the public proclamation of religious truth, which in Christian terms is the authoritative public proclamation of Christ, or preaching the sermon and declaring Christ's word in the sacraments. Therefore, this command of the Lord restricts the ministry of Word and sacrament, and thus the ministry of elder and apostle, to men.

Paul writes to Timothy on the same issue:

> Let a woman learn in silence with all submission. And I do not permit a woman to teach or to have authority over a man, but to be in silence. For Adam was formed first, then Eve. And Adam was not deceived, but the woman being deceived, fell into transgression. (*1 Tim 2:11-14*)

The silence is the same silence which Paul taught in *1 Corinthians 14*, and so not an absolute silence, but rather one which Paul defines here in terms of a prohibition on teaching in the gathered church or having authority over men. And so the restriction here in *1 Timothy* is almost identical to what we have seen in *1 Corinthians*: it is a restriction of authoritative proclamation of the Word and governance of the church to men, and thus the Scripture here limits the ministries of apostle and presbyter to men. In fact, the qualifications of elders follow immediately from this in *1 Timothy*; so what Paul is, in effect, saying is that only men may be ordained as elders, but not every man.

---

[27] Scaer, 'May Women be Ordained as Pastors?', 311.

Paul roots this instruction in the order of God's creation (rather than in the culture of the 1ˢᵗ century or the particular circumstances of the assemblies for which Timothy has responsibility).

> When Paul bases his argument on the order of creation of Adam and Eve, it indicates that his command about women not teaching or having authority in the assembled congregation transcends cultures and societies. It applies to men and women as they were created by God at the beginning, and it is not due to any distortion brought on by sin or the Fall. It applies, then, to all churches for all time, and it is a means by which the beauty of manhood and womanhood as God created them to be can be manifested in the life of the church.[28]

Claire Smith explains the significance of this creation order:

> The man in Genesis 2 clearly had temporal priority to the woman. He was made first. And so he is the firstborn, with the responsibilities that go with that, whereas she was formed after him, to accompany him and help in fulfilling their common mandate. The first reason Paul gives for his instructions to women is based on the way things are meant to be; the way God originally created men and women.[29]

Thus, the Scriptural restriction of ordination to the apostleship or eldership, and thus to the fivefold headship ministries, is not limited to a particular time or place, but is rooted in God's order in creation (*1 Tim. 2:13*), and is the commandment of the Lord (*1 Cor. 14:37*) for 'all the churches of the saints' (*1 Cor. 14:33*), 'everywhere' (*1 Tim. 2:8*).[30]

Due to the command of the Lord in the authoritative Scriptures, the Apostolic Church, together with the worldwide church throughout most of history, only ordains men to the ministries of apostle, prophet, teacher, pastor, elder and evangelist. The stance of the Apostolic Church has always been clear that women are not 'included in the five offices.'[31] The original statement of faith of the English Apostolic Churches (before they fully joined with the Welsh assemblies and adopted their Tenets), stated:

> That out of saved, sanctified and baptised (with water and Spirit) believers Jesus Christ is building His Church, on the foundation of the Apostles and Prophets, Jesus Christ Himself being the chief corner stone. In this church

---

[28] Wayne Grudem, *Evangelical Feminism and Biblical Truth* (Wheaton: Crossway, 2012), 69.

[29] Claire Smith, *God's Good Design: What the Bible Really Says About Men and Women* (Kingsford: Matthias Media, 2012), 36.

[30] All the instructions concerning men and women in *1 Tim. 2:8-15* are in the context of this 'everywhere.'

[31] *Apostolic Church Council Minutes, Oct. 1929*, p.159.

there are Apostles, Prophets, Teachers, Pastors and Evangelists. Without these you cannot have a New Testament Church. Also in this church the nine gifts of the Holy Spirit are in operation, and in order under the control of the Apostles or the Overseer. Women are not allowed to teach or to usurp authority over the man, but women's ministry is recognised in the office of Deaconess.[32]

In fact, prophecy received in the early years of the Apostolic Church stated that 'there is nothing so definite as that which is written: "I suffer not a woman to teach" ... I am expecting you to abide by the ruling of my Word.' Yet, 'there is a scope in the ministry of women if you and if they will abide by the ruling [*i.e. 1 Tim. 2:12*].'[33] The definite command of the Lord restricts ordination to the apostleship and presbytery to qualified and called men. Yet women, though not called as apostles and presbyters, are called to witness to the resurrection of Christ (*cf. Mt 28:5-10*),[34] and to teach and disciple other women (*Titus 2:3*).[35]

---

[32] *Statement of Faith of the Apostolic Church of God*. This was a key distinction between the Apostolic Pentecostals in the north of England, and the Wigglesworth-associated Pentecostals, particularly those associated with Smith Wigglesworth, and, along with the Apostolic acceptance of directive prophecy, one of the major reasons the Bradford Pentecostals emerged into these two movements. Thus, this is a significant feature of the distinctive Apostolic identity.

[33] Prophetical Ministry through W.J. Williams, *Apostolic Church Council Minutes, Oct. 1929*, pp.159-160. This prophecy accords with what Paul says true prophets would say on the matter in *1 Cor. 14:37*.

[34] *Apostolic Church Council Minutes, Oct. 1929*, p.160.

[35] *Apostolic Church Council Minutes, Oct. 1929*, p.161.

Chapter 38

Apostolic Church Government

The Triune God directs how His Purpose for His Church is to be fulfilled

The Eternal Purpose is the Triune God's purpose for His Church. He planned it and He has accomplished it in Christ. So if it is God's purpose, then that means it is for Him to decide how it is to be outworked. Therefore it is God who directs us how His Eternal Purpose is to be fulfilled.

Biblical Pattern vs. Pragmatism

How does God show us how His purpose is to be outworked? First and foremost, in His Written Word: the Bible. The authority of Scripture isn't limited in any way; the Bible is authoritative on whatever subject it speaks. This includes when it speaks on the nature, mission and structure of the Church. Our practice, and not only our preaching, is to be as biblical as possible.

Our desire to follow the biblical pattern for the life and mission of the Church is, of course, rooted in our strong commitment to the authority of God's Word, for we know that when the Bible speaks, God speaks. However, this commitment to the biblical pattern is also linked to our understanding of the Church as central to God's Eternal Purpose.

Because of the value we place on the Church in God's purpose, we see the importance of the Church in its own right. It is important because it is God's chosen instrument. Those who don't place emphasis on the Eternal Purpose, may be more inclined to miss the importance of the Church and view it simply as a means to an end. As a consequence they often take a more *ad hoc* and pragmatic approach to the life of the Church. For example, they might see the church as a useful tool in evangelism or in encouraging holiness, but they don't see it as particularly important in its own right. This means that a pragmatic approach to ecclesiology can take root; if the Church is simply a useful evangelistic tool, then surely the best approach to church life would be the one which seems to work best evangelistically. When the Church is thought of in this way many decisions about church life are seen as pragmatic decisions about what works, rather than biblical/theological matters.[1] One of the big problems though, is that the end result of a pragmatic ecclesiology depends on the decision as to what is the ultimate goal. That means pragmatism can lead to very different results (an evangelistic gathering, a society for the promotion of holiness, a meeting for the expression of a particular religious experience, a study-group, etc.).[2]

However, in Scripture, the ultimate goal is God's Eternal Purpose, centred in Christ and His Church. Thus the Church has an importance in its own right, rather than simply as a useful means to an end. It is not we who are making use of the Church in the furtherance of godly ends, but God who is using His Church in the outworking of His Eternal Purpose. Therefore it is not up to us how best to make use of the church, but up to God. Hence, rather than taking a pragmatic approach to ecclesiology, we believe that the Bible teaches how the Church is to be ordered. Historically, this has been a very important aspect of being Apostolic. In the early days there was a lot of talk about 'setting in order'. When a new assembly was planted or if a local church decided to join the Apostolic Church, it had to be set in order. What was meant by this was ordering the assembly according to the Biblical pattern. So, for example, in the early 20th century, most other movements, taking a more pragmatic approach to ecclesiology, did not have elders. Therefore, if an independent church decided to join the Apostolic

---

[1] This can be seen, for example, in the decisions made by some churches/movements concerning church government or the observance of the Sacraments.

[2] Significantly, the American pastor-theologian Mark Dever has argued that 'The greatest threat to the gospel specific to today is the indirect challenge of pragmatism among evangelicals.' Ajith Fernando, leader of Youth for Christ in Sri Lanka writes that 'A major shift . . . has taken place in western evangelicalism where truth has been replaced by pragmatism as the major influencer of thought and life. This path is suicidal.' (Ajith Fernando, *The Supremacy of Christ* [Wheaton: Crossway, 1995], 112. John Piper is in agreement, writing: 'This is especially true about doctrine. We are pragmatic. We demand quick solutions. We define success in measurable quantities. We have little patience with doctrinal precision. And we pastors who are infected with the pragmatic virus tend to justify our indifference to doctrine mainly by the fact that such reflection is not what the audience is looking for. Besides, it is stressful for relationships... vague language and pragmatic concerns preserve hollow unity at the expense of theological substance and Biblical clarity and power.' (John Piper, *God's Passion for His Glory: Living the Vision of Jonathan Edwards* [Wheaton: Crossway, 1998], 23).

Church, elders had to be ordained in keeping with the biblical pattern of a plurality of elders in each assembly (*Acts 14:23; 20:17,28; James 5:14; 1 Tim. 5:17; Titus 1:5; Phil. 1:1*).

Thus, the Apostolic approach to the Church is rooted in the Biblical pattern rather than in pragmatism. Of course, this is not to say that there is no place for any pragmatic decisions whatsoever in church life; yet the big picture of the nature, mission, structure and worship of the Church are to be modelled on the Scriptural pattern.

Directive Prophecy

'*Surely the Lord GOD does nothing, unless He reveals His secret to His servants the prophets.*' (Amos 3:7)

From the beginning, one of the major distinctives of the Apostolic Church has been our belief in directive prophecy. D.P. Williams himself wrote that 'If we are called as an Apostolic Church to witness for some thing above another, we witness to the unassailable truth that we are a standing body that is an evidence of the existence and value of the prophetic ministry.'[3]

Historically, it was our high view of the ministry of the prophet that played a major role in setting us apart from other Pentecostal movements in the UK.[4] In fact, it was this dispute over the prophetic that brought about the beginnings of the Apostolic Church in the north of England. The world-famous pastor, Smith Wigglesworth, led an assembly on Bowland Street in the city of Bradford, and in about 1916 there started to be directive prophecy in the Bowland Street Mission. Smith Wigglesworth eventually declared 'I will have nothing to do with the prophetical word here. I cannot trust or believe it, and therefore it is not going to be here.' Immediately a young woman prophesied, 'Being that you have finished with Me and My Voice, I finish with you, and there is a day coming when you will see the door of this assembly shut, but I will have another place, and I have faith in the

---

[3] Williams, D.P., *The Prophetical Ministry in the Church* (Penygroes, 1931), 100.
[4] In reality, most aspects of our ecclesiology set us apart. The other Pentecostal movements didn't have a high ecclesiology, and this is even reflected in the differences of name between the three movements: neither the 'Assemblies of God' nor the 'Elim Foursquare Gospel Alliance' used the word 'Church' (in the singular) in the name of the movement. But much of the focus in debate and discussion was often put on our view of the prophetical ministry.

heart of some of the young in this congregation.' As a result, a number of families were asked to leave 'because of the prophetic gift in our midst'. (These were the families who accepted directive prophecy, and included some young men who would later play prominent roles in the leadership of the Apostolic Church.) So they left and started their own meetings. Initially they started with twelve people, but many were soon saved, healed and baptised in the Spirit. This quickly grew into a very large assembly which would be the mother assembly of the Bradford Area of the Apostolic Church. As had been stated in the prophecy, the Bowland Street Mission was soon closed.[5]

The prophetical ministry was of such importance to the early Apostolics that D.P. Williams declared at the 1937 Penygroes International Convention, 'The secret of our unity in the Apostolic Church is that God speaks in the Church. It is His Voice that has united us. It is His Voice that keeps us together.'[6] The previous year God spoke through Pastor T.N. Turnbull, the prophet, saying, 'one of the greatest needs of all in the government of the Church of God is the Spoken Word, and you will never be able to be the Church of victory and triumph that I desire you to be, unless my Word is with you, and unless you are walking on my Word, saith the Lord'.[7]

This importance of prophecy in the government of the Church is because we believe in directive prophecy. *Acts 13:2* is perhaps the favourite Apostolic example of directive prophecy in the New Testament church. Here God speaks, saying 'Now separate to Me Barnabas and Saul for the work to which I have called them.' The preceding verse tells us that there were prophets present, and commentators widely agree that God's speaking was through one of the prophets.[8] Later, in *Acts 16*, as Paul and Silas, apostle and prophet, were travelling together, God gave direction, forbidding them to preach in Asia or Bithynia (*Acts 16:6-7*). Although it is not explicitly said to be through prophecy, this revelation is contrasted with the call to Macedonia which came by a vision which appeared to Paul in the night (*v.9*), and the New Testament elsewhere uses the expression 'by the Holy Spirit' (*v.6*) to refer to prophecy (*Mk 12:36; Lk 2:26; Acts 13:4*).

[5] For an account of these events see Gordon Weeks, *Chapter 32*, 50.

[6] Cited in James Worsfold, *The Origins of the Apostolic Church in Great Britain*, 317.

[7] Prophetical Ministry through Ps. T.N. Turnbull, *Riches of Grace*, xii 1 (Sept. 1936), 23.

[8] E.g. David E. Aune, *Prophecy in Early Christianity and the Ancient Mediterranean World* (Grand Rapids: Eerdmans, 1983), 265; Ernst Haenchen, *The Acts of the Apostles* (Oxford: Blackwell, 1971), 396; F.F. Bruce, *The Book of the Acts*, The New International Commentary on the New Testament (Grand Rapids: Eerdmans; rev. edn., 1988), 245.

When Paul writes to Timothy he makes reference to directive prophecy. He urges Timothy 'according to the prophecies previously made concerning you, that by them you may wage the good warfare' (*1 Tim. 1:18*). Either he is referring to Timothy being called to the apostleship through the prophet and encouraging him in his calling, or he's referring to a prophecy where God told Timothy to do something and encouraging him to act accordingly. Either way it's directive prophecy.

Directive prophecy has been vital in the life of the Apostolic Church. Our missionary work was brought into being through prophecy. Pastor W.J. Williams prophesied in Bradford: 'I would have you to know that I am revealing my will concerning the missionary work. In unity I would have you to work in this matter. I would not have the three nations to raise each its own missionary work. I have those of my choice in the midst of the three nations, but you cannot send them if you act separately.'[9] Many of the countries to which we subsequently sent missionaries were opened up to us through the prophets. Likewise, many of our assemblies in the UK were planted due to prophecies, and it was due to directive prophecy that the Bible College was established.

Throughout our history many men have also been called into ministries and to new locations through the prophets.[10] In former times such prophecies often came publically at Conventions as well as in Council.[11]

The Headship of Christ and the Government of the Church

Another major distinctive of the Apostolic Church is our focus on the Headship of Christ. The Bible teaches that, as a result of His Cross-

---

[9] Cited in T.N. Turnbull, *Brothers in Arms*, 56.

[10] E.g. the September 1934 edition of *Riches of Grace* lists 11 pastors who had just been called to new locations 'on the Word of the Lord' (i.e. through prophecy) and 2 men who had been newly called to the apostleship through prophecy. 'Foreword', *Riches of Grace*, x.i (Sept. 1934), 4-5.

[11] Such prophetic calls came publically at Conventions until at least the 1980s, for in the year I was born (1982) my father was called to the eldership by a prophet who had come over from the mainland for the Easter Convention in Belfast. Dad had never met the prophet and wasn't even present in the meeting when he was called, but other people from the Londonderry assembly were.

Resurrection-Ascension, Christ has been given by God the Father 'to be head over all things to the church which is His body' (*Eph. 1:22-23; cf. Eph. 5:23; Col. 1:18*).[12] Christ's Headship in the Church speaks to us of His authority and the fact that He supplies her with all that she needs.

But this also means that the church is not just an organisation for the promotion of Christianity, but a living entity united to Christ her heavenly Head. The church doesn't just belong to Christ in the sense that it's made up of Christians and Christians belong to Christ; but rather, the Church belongs to Christ in the sense that it is united to Him as His Body. There is such a unity that to persecute the Church is to persecute Christ (*Acts 9:4-5*). We are even told that the Church is Christ's 'fullness' (*Eph. 1:23*), which means that the Church is filled by Christ. This is how the Church has such a central place in God's Eternal Purpose: because it is united to Christ her Head.

One Body

Christ's Headship highlights the unity of the Church, for just as there is only one Head, there is only one body (*Eph. 4:4-6*). There is only one Body as God is using it in the outworking of His one purpose (*Eph. 3:11*[13]). This means that assemblies are not independent of one another. Each local assembly is not a local body of Christ, but rather the local manifestation of the One Body. This means that the assemblies are connected. Rather than being independent of one another, they are interdependent. This oneness of the Body among all the assemblies is demonstrated in a number of ways:-

The Unity of the Faith

Ephesians 4:13 tells us that the Ascension Ministries have been given 'till we all come to the unity of the faith'. Earlier in the same chapter, at the same time as reminding them that there is only one Body, Paul reminds the Ephesians that there is only 'one faith' (*Eph. 4:5*). If there is only 'one faith' then, of course, we should all be united together in that one faith, as anything else is error.

Our fellowship and cooperation also depend to a great extent on our common faith. As Amos reminds us 'Can two walk together, unless they are

---

[12] See also *Eph. 5:23; Col. 1:18*.
[13] '*Eternal Purpose*' is singular.

agreed?' (*Amos 3:3*): the answer he intends is clearly 'No!' Thus our fellowship and our working together will be impaired if we aren't united in the faith.

So, each assembly can't come up with its own doctrine. There is only one faith, and one of the roles of the fivefold ministry is to guide us toward that unity of the faith. The faith doesn't come from below (the grass-roots level), but from above; God has 'once for all delivered' the faith (*Jude 3*), and has entrusted the fivefold ministry with the role of bringing His people, gathered in all the assemblies, into the unity of that faith. This implies that it is necessary for centralised decision making on doctrinal questions, for each assembly cannot decide independently and still keep the unity of the faith. This is why we have the Tenets: each assembly doesn't come up with its own doctrinal basis, but we're all united on the same doctrinal basis found in the Tenets.

Care and Support

Not only are the assemblies united doctrinally, but the unity of the Body also means that there is mutual care and support between assemblies. We see an example of this when the assemblies in Galatia and Corinth took up a collection for the needs of the saints in Judea (*1 Cor. 16:1-3*).

This mutual care and support is also seen in the sharing of ministry. The Colossians and Laodiceans were to share each other's letters from Paul (*Col. 4:16*) and Epaphras worked with both those assemblies, as well as the assembly in Hierapolis. The unity of the Body means that assemblies are to support one another in spiritual ministry, such as prayer, teaching and outreach.

Benefitting from all the ministries

Another important implication of the unity of the Body is that assemblies can benefit from the full range of the fivefold ministry. Christ has given apostles, prophets, evangelists, pastors and teachers to His Church, but not to each individual assembly. Yet the unity of the Body means that assemblies without a resident apostle, prophet, evangelist, or teacher can still benefit from those ministries as Christ has gifted them to the Body and not just to one assembly.

Not only can assemblies benefit from the minister of another assembly, but it's also (in theory at least) possible, due to the unity of the Body, to fund salaries for men who will serve the Church at large without being tied by the responsibility of leading a particular assembly. Yet, this is only possible through the unity of the assemblies in one Body.[14]

Headship Ministries

Although we tend to use the term fivefold ministry of apostles, prophets, evangelists, pastors and teachers, have often been referred to as the 'Headship Ministries'. This term points to the truth that the fivefold ministry expresses something of the Headship of Christ in His Body.

As the Head and Giver of grace and gifts, it is Christ who is the true source of all ministry. Thus it is really Christ who ministers through the ministers. The ascension ministries are 'a means of expression for the ministry and government of Christ, the living Head.'[15]

Plurality

The fact that the headship ministries are ultimately expressions of Christ's ministry to the Church also highlights the necessity for plurality in Church government. Christ alone is Head of His Church. This means that no individual can govern by Himself without usurping Christ's place. Rather, the biblical pattern is that of plurality; the local assembly is governed by a plurality of elders (*e.g. Acts 14:23*) and the Church at large is governed by a plurality of apostles (*e.g. Acts 15*). Christ ministers to and governs His Church through the ministers collectively. As the ministers express Christ's ministry and government in the Church, they cannot govern individually, for no individual man can express the fullness of any one of these ministries of Christ. B.J. Noot explained this well:

---

[14] In the UK Apostolic Church, we do this with the national leader, and one or two Areas have an apostle freed from the responsibility of leading a local assembly. Yet, at least in theory, this doesn't have to be limited to apostles. We could have evangelists, prophets or teachers free to function in their callings on a wider scope. In the past this was more common.

[15] W.A.C. Rowe, *One Lord, One Faith* (Penygroes: Apostolic Publications, 1960; 2nd ed., 1988), 245.

> There is need to emphasize the fact that Christ, in whom all the fullness of the Godhead dwelleth bodily, is the pre-eminent Apostle and as such is the source, essence and fullness of Apostleship, He being the possessor of all its wealth and efficiency in endless supply. It will be seen that it is manifestly impossible for any one man however great in stature he may be to reveal the full-orbed Apostleship of Jesus. Hence, He gave some Apostles.[16]

This applies to the other headship ministries as well.

In *Acts 1:17*, we read that Judas 'obtained a part in this ministry' of apostleship. A few verses later we read that the apostles prayed to be shown which of the candidates the Lord had chosen to 'take part of this ministry and apostleship' (*Acts 1:25, KJV*). The use of the word 'part' in these two verses shows that each apostle only had a part of the ministry of apostleship, not the whole, which is found only in Christ. Thus the apostles must work together in the apostleship, rather than simply as individuals.

This means we need the apostleship, and not just an apostle; we need the prophets, and not just a prophet; we need the evangelists, and not just an evangelist; we need the pastors and elders, and not just a pastor or elder; we need the teachers, and not just a teacher.

Central Responsibility & Local Responsibility

The plurality and collegiality we need among the headship ministries means that there must be some central responsibility. This isn't to say that all responsibility is centralised; but some is. This is a necessary consequence of the functioning of collegiate apostleship. Two ways in which this can be seen in Scripture are in the concepts of 'sending' and 'council'.

Sending

Peter and John were 'sent' by 'the apostles' to Samaria (*Acts 8:14*), because many people had believed the gospel, yet none of them had been baptised in the Holy Spirit. Barnabas was 'sent' by 'the church' from Jerusalem to Antioch (*Acts 11:22*) to lead the newly established assembly. Later, after the Jerusalem Council, two prophets, Judas and Silas, were 'sent' by the Council

---

[16] B.J. Noot, 'Apostles and Prophets', in Hugh Dawson, B.J. Noot, & Thomas Napier Turnbull, *Church Government by Apostles, Prophets, Evangelists, Pastors, Teachers, Elders and Deacons* (Bradford: Puritan Press, n.d.), 13.

to accompany the apostles Paul and Barnabas to Antioch with the letter about the decision of the Council (*Acts 15:22-23,25-27,32-33*). In each of these cases Ascension Ministers are sent by means of a central decision taken by the apostleship. In each case they are sent for a different reason and for a different length of time (Peter and John are sent for short-term ministry in Samaria, whereas Barnabas is sent to take up the pastorate of an assembly), but in all these cases the power to send rests with the apostleship. The Antioch assembly chose neither its new pastor nor the prophets who would come back to them from Council.

This is not to say that the Bible shows all sending to be completely centralised. Paul left Titus in Crete (*Titus 1:5*) without any involvement from Jerusalem.[17] Thus in some situations 'sending' can be done by a group of apostles in an Area or Region.[18] And yet some degree of centralism remains in the decision: it is still a 'sending', not a local assembly decision.

Is there any difference between Crete and the previous examples of central sending? The one major difference would appear to be that Antioch and Samaria were places of great strategic importance (the opening of the Samaritan and Gentile worlds to the gospel), whereas Crete was not so strategically important in terms of the wider mission (but still important in its own right in terms of the work to be done there).

Council

The major biblical example of Council, is the Jerusalem Council of *Acts 15*. The Jerusalem Council was held to decide upon an important matter of doctrine. Yet the actual manner of the convening of the Council is worth noting. Paul and Barnabas didn't go up to Jerusalem for Council because it was a specific time of year. They went up because there was a matter to be resolved. There was a major problem to be settled in the life of the church, and the response was to send up the local apostles to meet with the rest of the apostleship in order to resolve the matter. It was recognised that this wasn't something that could be decided locally; it was a matter of doctrine, of the one faith, and so any decision had to be made for the whole church. So it was necessary for a central decision to be made.

---

[17] This isn't to suggest either that 'sending' should be a unilateral decision on the part of one apostle. Although there is some debate, it seems likely that Titus was an apostle too, and in any case, Paul usually travelled with at least one other apostle, and sometimes two.

[18] See previous note. The necessity of collegial apostleship still remains.

In fact the decision made at the Jerusalem Council didn't only relate to doctrine, but also to the direction of the Church's mission. (The two have a tendency to go hand in hand.) Again, this was an important matter to decide centrally, for it wasn't about the outreach strategy of a local assembly, but rather, about the direction the outreach of the whole Church was going to take. So there is a biblical model for Council to make decisions relating both to doctrine and mission.

However, the Jerusalem Council is not the only biblical model that applies to our Council. *Acts 13:1-3* has always been a popular passage in Apostolic ecclesiology. When we consider this Scripture it's normally to show a biblical example of calls coming through the prophet. Yet, these verses also give us an example of a Council: it was a gathering made up of headship ministers.[19] There is no reason given for this Council; no important decision to be made like at the later Jerusalem Council. All we are told is that they 'were worshipping the Lord and fasting' (*v.2*). It seems the purpose of their gathering was to seek the Lord and His direction. And the result of that Council was two men called to the apostleship and a major turning point in the outreach of the Church (not just the local assembly).

A final biblical model concerning Council is found in the book of Galatians. In *Galatians 2:1-10* Paul recounts a visit he made to the apostles in Jerusalem which isn't recorded in the book of Acts.[20] On this trip the apostles in Jerusalem[21] 'perceived the grace that had been given to [Paul]' and gave both him and Barnabas 'the right hand of fellowship' (*v.9*). Paul isn't writing here about becoming a member of the church (this is 'after fourteen years', *v.1*), but about the recognition of his and Barnabas' ministry by the apostleship. What ministry is being recognised? *Verse 8* shows that this is the recognition of Paul and Barnabas' apostleship.[22] So, it would seem that Paul and Barnabas were called as apostles through a prophet in Antioch. As at this stage in the history of the church there weren't yet any apostles outside of Jerusalem, they were ordained by the Ascension

---

[19] Granted, until the call came, there were no apostles present, only prophets and teachers. However, at this early stage in the history of the church there weren't yet any apostles other than the Twelve in Jerusalem.

[20] This is a passage which has caused a great deal of discussion among New Testament scholars due to the difficulty in harmonising it with any of the trips recorded in the Acts. Some have tried to match this trip to *Acts 11* and others to *Acts 15*, yet the details of neither trip fit well with what Paul describes in *Galatians 2*, thus it seems preferable to view it as a trip unrecorded in the book of Acts.

[21] v. 2 *'those who were of reputation'*, v.9 *'James, Cephas and John'*.

[22] Thus the revelation referred to in *Gal. 2:2* would appear to be the prophetic revelation of *Acts 13:2*.

Ministers who were there (the prophets and teachers), yet the newly called apostles still travelled to Jerusalem at the first opportunity to receive recognition of their ministry by the Church from the apostleship.[23]

So what does this meeting in *Galatians 2* teach us about Council? Well, it shows that Council, or a group of apostles delegated by Council (in that context James, Peter and John[24]), can recognise calls to ministries.

So to conclude our consideration of Council, the Biblical models for Council show its role in doctrinal decisions, direction in mission, seeking God and His direction, calls to Ascension ministries, major changes, and recognition of calls which came elsewhere.

Local Responsibility & Initiative

Yet, although the Bible does show a pattern of central decisions in some areas, it also shows a pattern of local responsibility and initiative in many areas of the life of the church. Paul encouraged Timothy to 'do the work of an evangelist' (*2 Tim. 4:5*). Timothy was not to sit and wait for an evangelist to be sent to Ephesus. Neither was he to wait for instructions to be sent out on how to evangelise. Rather, he was to get stuck in with the work of evangelism. He knew the Biblical responsibility to evangelise and it was up to him with the local presbytery and people to put that commission into practice in their local context.

This seems obvious enough. Yet the Bible doesn't only show central authority and local responsibility. In *Acts 11:25-26* we learn that when Barnabas was leading the Antioch assembly he went to get Saul and brought him to Antioch. Saul was not sent to Antioch by the apostles in Jerusalem. Rather, the local minister, Barnabas, took the initiative to bring Saul. Barnabas was not yet recognised as an apostle, nor were there any apostles in Antioch. Barnabas didn't wait to run the proposal by the apostles on his next visit to Jerusalem: he went ahead and acted. This shows us that local responsibility isn't just a response to central authority (as if the local served the central), but that local responsibility carries with it the authority and scope for local initiative.

---

[23] This might seem a bit pedantic, but it's actually quite important, as this is the only time we see a call to either eldership or an Ascension Ministry where the apostleship isn't directly involved. Seeing it in the context of *Galatians 2* shows that it isn't really an exception to the general model that calls to ministries are recognised by the apostleship.

[24] In the context of the Apostolic Church in the UK, the Ministerial Appointments Board or the National Leadership Team.

Authority & Relationships

Such concepts as 'sending', collegiate apostleship, and Council point to lines of authority within the Church. However, the Bible does not only point to lines of authority linking apostles and pastors or local assemblies to the wider Body, but also places a great emphasis on relationships.

One place where this emphasis on relational links is seen very clearly is in one of the big arguments of the Bible. In *Acts 15:36-40* Paul and Barnabas begin to travel and minister separately because Barnabas wanted to take John Mark and Paul disagreed. Instead Paul 'chose' Silas as his fellow labourer (*v.40*). Even though the situation resulted in 'a sharp disagreement' (*v.39, ESV*), neither Paul nor Barnabas is stopped from going; neither is reprimanded, neither is said to be wrong. Council doesn't tell them who is to go with whom. The links between everyone involved are on a relational footing. And the relationship changes, for later Paul would tell Timothy to 'Get Mark and bring him with you, for he is useful to me for ministry' (*2 Tim. 4:11*).

The fact that Paul 'chose' Silas is also worth noting because Paul was an apostle and Silas a prophet. There were other prophets in Antioch and Jerusalem and any of them could have been sent with Paul. But none is sent; rather Paul chooses. So, in this case, Council doesn't mandate a particular pairing of apostle and prophet, but rather the apostle chooses the prophet to minister alongside. It is a relational link between the apostle and prophet.

Another way in which the balance between authoritative and relational links is seen is in the concept of spheres of ministry. *Galatians 2:7-9* notes the differing spheres of ministry of James, Cephas and John on the one hand, and Paul and Barnabas on the other. James, Peter and John were to go to the Jews and Paul and Barnabas to the Gentiles. Yet a few verses later we read of Peter coming to Antioch where Paul and Barnabas were (*Gal. 2:11*). We also see example after example of Paul and Barnabas preaching first to Jews when they came to a new town (*E.g. Acts 13:5, 14; 14:1; 17:2, 10, 17; 18:4, 19*). Peter and Paul would even write epistles to the same people (*2 Pet. 3:15*). So it would seem that, even though there is a general structure or framework for the division of ministry into differing spheres, these are not set in stone. The spheres of ministry are not rigid and there is flexibility to work along more relational lines.

Another place where the relational, as opposed to purely authoritative, nature of links is seen is in the connection between Paul and Timothy. When

Paul met Timothy in Lystra, the brethren there spoke well of him and, we are told, that 'Paul wanted to have him go on with him' (*Acts 16:3*). The very next verse tells us that 'they delivered to them the decrees to keep, which were determined by the apostles and elders at Jerusalem' (*Acts 16:4*). These two verses contrast the authoritative relationship between the Council and the assemblies in the matters of doctrine and missional direction with the relational link between an apostle and a young man he is going to equip for ministry. Council didn't tell Paul that he had to mentor Timothy; Paul 'wanted to'. Yet, the relational nature of the link doesn't do away with authority structures. At times Paul commanded and Timothy did as Paul commanded (*e.g. Acts 17:15; 19:22; 1 Cor. 4:17*).

The Apostleship as Focus and Sign of Unity

D.P. Williams saw the ministry of the Apostolic Church in terms of the three historic orders of ministry in the Christian church: the apostolic ministry, the presbyterial ministry, and the diaconate. In the tradition of the Christian theology, the apostolic order of ministry is a 'focus and sign of unity.' Therefore the apostleship is closely tied to the communion of the church. After all, the early church continued steadfastly not only in the apostles' doctrine, but also in the apostles' fellowship (*Acts 2:42*). The apostle not only stands *in persona Christi*, representing Christ, but he also represents the churches under his care. Thus the authority of the area apostle is an authority-in-communion: not an appropriation to the individual of authority, but the authority of the church expressed through the apostle in loving communion. This communion of the people of the churches with the area apostle also has an impact on the unity of the assemblies in the area, for while he is 'their' apostle, he isn't uniquely theirs. They share him with each of the other assemblies in the area. And so unity with the apostle brings with it unity between the assemblies.

Now, of course, it's not the apostle who creates this unity. It is Christ Himself who is the unity of the church and who brings this unity of the church as one in Himself about through His Holy Spirit. The church is one, has always been one, and will always be one. Yet, we do not always live out the unity which is ours in Christ. But again, we need to be careful here, it's not the apostle who enables us to live out this unity, but Christ the Head of the Church who ministers through the apostle. Christ is the true apostle, and so all true apostolic ministry can only be carried out in union with Christ. It is Christ the Apostle who is at work through his apostle.

So, as the area apostle draws the assemblies together in unity, it is Christ who is at work drawing his people together as one. This isn't an imposed unity, but a unity in loving communion, which then expresses itself in prayer, and care, and fellowship. As the area apostle moves about among the assemblies, the people of the assemblies hear of what's going on in each of the other assemblies – not through a formal report, but in the context of fellowship – and that leads to opportunities to pray for one another, to provide help and care for one another, and to join together in worship in united fellowship. As the area apostle shares in the life of each of the assemblies, then the assemblies share in each other's lives through him.

If people are looking for one sent from Christ, the Head of the Church, as a representative in the outworking of His purpose in the church, then what could be better than an apostle who builds up the churches in unity together in Jesus. After all, Christ's prayer for the church is 'that they all may be one, as You, Father, are in Me, and I in You; that they also may be one in Us, that the world may believe that You sent Me' (*Jn 17:21*).

An apostle who builds as the focus and sign of unity builds something that will stand strong and stable long after he's gone. Scripture speaks of the foundation laid by apostles and prophets (*Eph. 2:20*). If an apostle tries to lay a foundation in his own charisma, it won't last long after him. But a foundation laid in loving communion (which is, after all, the very nature of the Triune God) is a foundation laid deep in Christ, and so in Christ it will stand strong.

Yet the connection between apostleship and communion doesn't only apply internally within the life of the assemblies in one geographical area, but also externally, between the churches of the area and the wider church. Even when geography divides, and we never see fellow-believers in Brussels, Brisbane, Blantyre, or Belo Horizonte, we are still in communion with them as we share together in 'the apostles' fellowship.' While the apostles from Malawi may not regularly spend time in Bridgend or Belfast, in fellowship with the saints there, they do share fellowship with the apostles from those areas. The people in the Welsh assemblies are in communion with the people in Blantyre through our respective apostles. That communion manifests itself in some of the structures of the church (like Apostles' Councils), but goes beyond structures and exists even outside of them. The apostles in Nigeria have fellowship the apostles in Sri Lanka because they all minister as apostles in union with Christ, sharing together in His ministry of apostleship. For, ultimately, their communion is found in Christ the Head of the Church and True Apostle.

Tenet 10

The possibility of falling from grace.

Chapter 39

The Possibility of Falling from Grace

Scriptural Assurance and Scriptural Warning

The Bible is explicit in the assurances it gives of salvation. Jesus Himself said that no one could ever snatch us out of His hand (*Jn 10:28-30*). Paul gives thanks to God, 'being confident of this very thing, that He who has begun a good work in you will complete it until the day of Jesus Christ' (*Phil. 1:6*). God 'will also confirm [us] to the end, that [we] may be blameless in the day of our Lord Jesus Christ (*1 Cor. 1:8*). Peter writes that we're 'kept by the power of God through faith for salvation ready to be revealed in the last time' (*1 Pet. 1:5*). In fact, Paul even goes so far as to say:

> I am persuaded that neither death nor life, nor angels nor principalities nor powers, nor things present nor things to come, nor height nor depth, nor any other created thing, shall be able to separate us from the love of God which is in Christ Jesus our Lord. (*Rom. 8:38-39*)

Now that's assurance!

The Bible is also explicit in the warnings it gives about falling away from salvation. Jesus Himself tells us that it is 'he who endures to the end [who] will be saved' (*Mt 10:22; 24:13*). Paul likewise gives us warnings: 'Therefore let him who thinks he stands take heed lest he fall' (*1 Cor. 10:12*).

> And you, who once were alienated and enemies in your mind by wicked works, yet now He has reconciled in the body of His flesh through death, to present you holy, and blameless, and above reproach in His sight—if indeed you continue in the faith, grounded and steadfast. and are not moved away from the hope of the gospel which you heard (*Col. 1:21-23*).

(For a few more warnings from Paul's pen, have a look at *Rom. 11:20-23; 1 Cor. 9:27; 1 Cor. 15:1-2; Gal.5:4; Gal. 6:9; 1 Tim. 1:19-20; 1 Tim. 4:1.*)

John not only tells us of the branch which doesn't abide in Christ being cast out of the vine (*Jn 15:6*) and of names blotted out of the Book of Life (*Rev. 3:5; 22:18-19*), but also warns of a 'sin leading to death' (*1 Jn 5:16-17*).

James encourages us to go after those who 'wander from the truth' to turn them back, for 'he who turns a sinner from the error of his way will save a soul from death and cover a multitude of sins' (*Jas 5:19-20*). That sinner whose soul will be saved from death is one from 'among' us – a brother or sister in Christ.

Peter's warning is very strong:

> For if, after they have escaped the pollutions of the world through the knowledge of the Lord and Saviour Jesus Christ, they are again entangled in them and overcome, the latter end is worse for them than the beginning. For it would have been better for them not to have known the way of righteousness, than having known it, to turn from the holy commandment delivered to them. (*2 Pet. 2:20-21*)

Peter is writing about people who knew 'the Lord and Saviour Jesus Christ', people who had been saved from the 'pollutions of the world' and have gone back to it, turning away from the righteousness they had in Christ.

It is probably the writer to the Hebrews who gives us the most explicit, and well-known, warnings. We are to 'beware … lest there be in any of you an evil heart of unbelief in departing from the living God' (*Heb. 3:12*). You cannot depart from the living God unless you were with Him in the first place. We are to 'fear lest any of you seem to have come short of [His rest]' (*Heb. 4:1*). Those who 'have tasted the heavenly gift' but 'fall away … crucify again for themselves the Son of God, and put Him to an open shame' (*Heb. 6:4-6*). And 'if we sin wilfully after we have received the knowledge of the truth, there no longer remains a sacrifice for sins, but a certain fearful expectation of judgment' for such sin would mean one had 'trampled the Son of God underfoot, counted the blood of the covenant by which he was sanctified a common thing, and insulted the Spirit of grace' (*Heb. 10:26-29*). Now that's a warning!

So, if we have these strong assurances and we also have these strong warnings, how do they fit together? Does one set of passages cancel the other out? – Surely not! For this is the Word of God. It is the Lord Himself who speaks each of these assurances, as well as each of these warnings, to us. So we have to take both sets of passages equally seriously. And to truly take them seriously, means taking the assurances as true assurances, and taking the warnings as true warnings. We don't try to explain either away; both are true. So let's look at some of these Scriptures more closely and think about how and what it means to hold both together: the true assurance and the true warnings.

Holding the Assurance and the Warnings Together

But how can we have such strong true assurance if the warnings are true warnings? Or how could the warnings be true warnings if our assurance is so certain? Surely the two can't stand together! Well, that's the way many evangelicals approach these texts. On the one hand Calvinists will hold onto the assurances and explain the warnings. On the other hand Arminians will hold onto the warnings and explain the assurances. Some Calvinists argue that the warnings are hypothetical; others that they're aimed at people who are in the church but aren't really Christians. Some Arminians argue that the assurances are misread (either they're prayers/hopes/rhetorical expressions of confidence in God, or not actually speaking to the subject); others that they're to be taken conditionally.

But, although those are the common alternatives for reading these texts among British evangelicals, they are not the only ways they have historically been read by Protestants with a high view of Scripture. For, even back in the days when the Calvinists and Arminians started debating these things, there was another voice calling them to take both sets of texts at face value: the Lutheran voice.

Now, Lutherans are almost non-existent in Britain. We've never had a strong Lutheran presence here. And so the Lutheran contribution is easily forgotten. Historically, British evangelicalism has been moulded by Calvinism, and so even the questions we traditionally ask are moulded by that Calvinistic outlook. So we set up dichotomies like true assurance or true warnings and a Lutheran just looks at us as if we're mad, scratches his head, and says, 'But the Bible gives both!'[1]

A Lutheran approach finds no problem with seeing both true assurance – you have been saved from your sins, justified, have eternal life, and will be raised up with Christ in glory on the last day, because Christ has died for you – and true warnings – beware of 'an evil heart of unbelief in departing from the living God' – because a Lutheran approach tends to remember

---

[1] Incidentally, that explains why Lutherans often lump Calvinists and Arminians in together as 'the Reformed' even though we tend to think of Arminianism as the opposite of Reformed theology – for both work on the same set of questions. The fact that they both ask the same questions puts them closer together than you'd imagine.

much better than the Arminians and the Reformed that God has spoken two words: His word of Law and His word of Gospel.[2] So the Gospel says you have been saved, nothing can separate you from the love of Christ, nothing can take you out of His hand; while the Law reminds us that we can have no confidence or security in ourselves, and so sends us to flee to Christ our Saviour, in whom alone we can have true security.

The Law/Gospel distinction allows us to hold both sets of texts together and to believe with equal seriousness both the assurances and the warnings. Mueller puts it like this:

> The warnings set forth in Holy Scripture against defection ..., enforced by examples of temporary believers (Saul, Demas) do not militate against the blessed assurance of the Gospel that God will graciously keep the believer in faith to the end ... but rather sustain it. These warnings belong to the Law and must not be used to nullify the Gospel promises. St Paul, though aware of the possibility of his becoming a castaway, 1 Cor. 9:27, was nevertheless fully persuaded of his perseverance, Rom. 8:38,39; 2 Tim. 4:7. God warns us against defection through the Law in order that we may beware of carnal security, which destroys the certainty of salvation, and cling to the Gospel, which bestows and nourishes the assurance of salvation.[3]

We shall return to the matter of assurance below, but next we're going to have a closer look at some of the warning texts and see what it actually means to fall from grace.

What does it Actually Mean to Fall From Grace?

Let's have a closer look at some Scriptures to see what it actually means to fall from grace. A good place to start would be the text from which the expression comes – *Galatians 5:4*: 'You have become estranged from Christ, you who attempt to be justified by law; you have fallen from grace.'

Here we see what we are talking about and what we're not, which will help clear up a few misconceptions about the possibility of falling from grace. For a start, Paul is writing about Christians who go back to relying on attempts to keep the law for salvation. (Specifically here, it's about

---

[2] See above, chapter 9.
[3] John Theodore Mueller, *Christian Dogmatics*, 439.

Christians who decide they need to get circumcised.) Now, the whole point here is that he is writing to Christians. These aren't unbelievers. These aren't just people associated with the Church. They can only become estranged from Christ because they were united to Christ. They can only fall from grace because they were in grace. So this is a warning about true Christians losing their salvation.

But how? By attempting 'to be justified by law'. It's a case of people stopping relying on Christ and starting to rely on something they do instead. There's no mention of doing bad things here; it's not through committing certain sinful actions that these people fall from grace. Instead it's all a question of faith. Once their faith was in Christ alone; now their faith is in Christ plus their own attempts at keeping the law. Ironically, they're looking for assurance of salvation and that's what causes them to lose their salvation, because they're looking in the wrong place: *in* to themselves instead of *out* to Christ and Him crucified.

So, the very place where the expression 'fallen from grace' occurs in the Bible teaches us that falling from grace isn't a matter of what you do, but rather a matter of where your confidence lies. Is your confidence in something else other than Jesus? Have you stopped relying on Christ alone for salvation? So, it's not a case of being saved by faith but falling by (bad) works. No, we're saved by faith, and those who fall, fall through 'unfaith'.

We can see this connection between unbelief and falling very clearly in *Romans 11* as well. There Paul is writing about the Gentiles being grafted into the good olive tree. But he warns them about what happened to the natural branches:

> Because of unbelief they were broken off, and you stand by faith. Do not be haughty, but fear. For if God did not spare the natural branches, He may not spare you either. Therefore consider the goodness and severity of God: on those who fell, severity; but toward you, goodness, if you continue in His goodness. Otherwise you also will be cut off. And they also, if they do not continue in unbelief, will be grafted in, for God is able to graft them in again. (*Rom. 11:20-23*)

Those who stand, stand by faith. Those who are broken off are broken off by unbelief. Those who continue in God's goodness remain in the tree. Those who don't continue in unbelief are grafted into the tree. So, the difference between being in the olive tree and out of the olive tree is the difference between faith and unbelief. Faith is the way into the tree. Unbelief is the way out.

In Colossians we see that it is faith in the Gospel which keeps us in salvation:

> And you, who once were alienated and enemies in your mind by wicked works, yet now He has reconciled in the body of His flesh through death, to present you holy, and blameless, and above reproach in His sight — if indeed you continue in the faith, grounded and steadfast, and are not moved away from the hope of the gospel which you heard (*Col. 1:21-23*).

We have been reconciled through the death of Christ, and we will be presented holy, blameless and above reproach, but there is a condition here in the text: 'if indeed [we] continue in the faith.' Salvation and faith go together. We're not to be moved away from the hope of the gospel. Our confidence is to remain in Christ and Him Crucified for us. Salvation continues as faith continues. But to move away from faith, to move away from the hope of the gospel, is to move away from the salvation proclaimed in the gospel. In *1 Corinthians 15:1-3* Paul similarly tells us that we're saved 'if you hold fast that word which I preached to you – unless you believed in vain', that word being the gospel word of the death, burial and resurrection of Jesus.

In Hebrews again we're warned of unbelief.

> Beware, brethren, lest there be in any of you an evil heart of unbelief in departing from the living God; but exhort one another daily, while it is called 'Today,' lest any of you be hardened through the deceitfulness of sin. For we have become partakers of Christ if we hold the beginning of our confidence steadfast to the end. (*Heb. 3:12-14*)

Again, it's unbelief that causes one to depart from the living God. (And notice, it's not sinful actions on the outside that make a heart 'evil', but what's on the inside – unbelief.) We partake of Christ as we 'hold the beginning of our confidence steadfast to the end.' In other words, we partake of Christ through faith. But we depart from Christ through unbelief. We are Christ's dwelling, not if we're really good all the time and avoid sinning, but rather 'if we hold fast the confidence and the rejoicing of the hope firm to the end' (*Heb. 3:6*). It's not what we do that keeps us in the faith, but rather it's the One in whom we trust.

Hebrews goes on to give a very strong warning about falling away in chapter six:

> For it is impossible for those who were once enlightened, and have tasted the heavenly gift, and have become partakers of the Holy Spirit, and have tasted the good word of God and the powers of the age to come, if they fall

> away, to renew them again to repentance, since they crucify again for
> themselves the Son of God, and put Him to an open shame. (*Heb. 6:4-6*)

The people in view here were believers. How do we know? Well, they were
'enlightened', whereas unbelievers are in 'darkness' (*Jn 12:46; Acts 26:18;
Rom. 1:21; 2 Cor. 6:14; Eph. 5:8; Col. 1:13; 1 Thess. 5:4-5; 1 Pet. 2:9; 1 Jn 1:6*).
They've 'tasted the heavenly gift', which could either be a figurative
reference to experiencing salvation or a reference to partaking of the Lord's
Supper (which is only a heavenly gift to those who eat with faith; for those
who eat without faith, to partake of the Supper means condemnation and
judgment – *1 Cor. 11:29-32*). In either case, those who have 'tasted the
heavenly gift' are Christians. As Hohenstein puts it:

> To 'taste the gift from heaven' is to possess it and to *experience* it in the
> fullness of its sweet and saving power … [It] involves much more than a
> passing touch of its blessing. It involves much more than just 'catching the
> crumbs' which happen to 'fall from the Master's table,' the 'leftovers' of
> His meat of mercy and love. Tasting the gift implies a happy and hearty
> feast upon that 'living Bread which has come down from heaven.' Cf. John
> 6:50-55. This is a keenly conscious tasting of the sweetness of the Lord's
> grace (1 Peter 2:3).[4]

The same is true for those who 'have become partakers of the Holy Spirit.'
Those who do not have the Spirit do not belong to Christ; conversely those
who partake of the Spirit belong to Christ (*Rom. 8:9*). These people have
tasted of God's Word and found it to be good. The Greek phrase translated
'the good word of God' here is used in the LXX[5] in *Joshua 21:45* and
Zechariah 1:13 for comforting words from the LORD (rather than words of
judgment). So what they've received is the goodness and comfort of God's
Gospel Word. And, in the Holy Spirit, they have experienced the in-
breaking of 'the powers of the age to come.' (Also, they had previously
repented – otherwise it wouldn't make any sense to talk about renewing
them 'again' to repentance in *v.6*.) So, there can be no doubt that this
passage is speaking of Christians.

And yet, we're told, that it's possible for them to 'fall away'. And this
falling away is not a light matter. It's a crucifying again of the Son of God,
putting Him to an open shame. In fact, it's impossible to renew these people
to repentance, and their 'end is to be burned' (*Heb. 6:8*). In the context here,

---

[4] Hohenstein, 'A Study of Hebrews 6:4-8', *Concordia Theological Monthly*, xxvii.6, 438.
[5] The LXX (or Septuagint) is the Greek translation of the Old Testament used by the early
Christians.

to 'fall away' can mean nothing other than apostasy. This is the only time the word is used in the New Testament, but in the LXX it's used for people falling away from trust in the LORD or from worshipping the LORD. But what does it mean that they 'crucify again for themselves the Son of God, and put Him to an open shame'? These are the reasons they can't be renewed again to repentance, but what do they actually mean?

Well, remember, a huge focus in the letter to the Hebrews is the uniqueness of Christ's once-for-all sacrifice. So a re-crucifixion is just unthinkable! As O'Brien explains it: 'They totally reject the saving work of the Son, and show their contempt for him … putting themselves in the position of those who had him crucified.'[6] Or as Hohenstein paints the picture:

> Through the medium of faith, or lack of it, men transcend the boundaries of space and time and still stand before the Crucified. To that cross men may react in one of two ways. Either they will confess [Jesus is Lord] or say [Jesus is Anathema]. The first is faith, the second unbelief. And even as the believer benefits from the blessings bestowed in that redemption, so the unbeliever, by his rejection, actually repeats the same crime of [those who crucified Christ] and with them brands Christ as a cursed criminal and pseudo-Messiah. In this sense an unbeliever, a fallen Christian, can be said to 'recrucify the Son of God.' To recrucify Christ is to deny His claim as God's Messiah sent from above to reveal God and to rescue men from this present, perishable creation to that new world which knows no slavery to pain and death. To recrucify Christ is to say 'No!' to the 'Yes!' of God's Son. It is to attempt to enter life by another door, another way, another truth, apart from Christ. It is the futile effort to find salvation in a name other than Jesus.[7]

But not only do they crucify Christ again, they also 'put Him to an open shame.' So their recrucifixion is not just a private thing, but it publicly brings dishonour to Christ. When people fall away from the Gospel, the church sees it and the world sees it (and the principalities and powers as well).

So how do these people fall from grace? They fall from grace by going from clinging to the Crucified to crucifying Him all over again; by going from trust in Jesus who shed His blood for us to contempt for Jesus and His precious blood. In other words, by abandoning their faith in Christ and

---

[6] Peter T. O'Brien, *The Letter to the Hebrews*, Pillar New Testament Commentary (Nottingham: IVP, 2010), 227.

[7] Hohenstein, 'A Study of Hebrews 6:4-8 (Concluded)', *Concordia Theological Monthly*, xxvii.7, 541.

returning to unbelief. And that's just what we've seen in all the other texts we've looked at so far.

The writer to the Hebrews takes up the topic again in *Hebrews 10*. There we're encouraged to 'hold fast the confession of our hope without wavering, for He who promised is faithful' (*Heb. 10:23*). Our hope doesn't need to be shaken, for our God is the faithful God. At the end of the chapter the writer quotes from the LXX of Habakkuk: 'Now the just shall live by faith; but if anyone draws back, my soul has no pleasure in him,' followed by the assurance: 'But we are not of those who draw back to perdition, but of those who believe to the saving of the soul' (*Heb. 10:38-39*). In both the OT quotation and the assurance, the contrast is between faith and drawing back. Faith leads to life and salvation, but drawing back to perdition and God's displeasure. Again, then, here we see that falling away is associated with unbelief, the opposite of faith.

But, in-between the two sections of *Hebrews 10* I've quoted above, comes one of the strongest warnings in the NT about falling away:

> For if we sin willfully after we have received the knowledge of the truth, there no longer remains a sacrifice for sins, but a certain fearful expectation of judgment, and fiery indignation which will devour the adversaries. Anyone who has rejected Moses' law dies without mercy on the testimony of two or three witnesses. Of how much worse punishment, do you suppose, will he be thought worthy who has trampled the Son of God underfoot, counted the blood of the covenant by which he was sanctified a common thing, and insulted the Spirit of grace? For we know Him who said, 'Vengeance is Mine, I will repay,' says the Lord. And again, 'The Lord will judge His people.' It is a fearful thing to fall into the hands of the living God. (*Heb. 10:26-31*)

Now, you might be thinking that this seems to immediately go against all that we've been saying about unbelief, rather than bad things we do – sins we commit – being the cause of falling from grace. After all, this passage starts off by warning what will happen 'if we sin wilfully.' But what does it mean to sin wilfully? If it simply means having willingly sinned, then that would cast us all out into this 'fearful expectation of judgment', for 'if we say that we have no sin, we deceive ourselves, and the truth is not in us' (*1 Jn 1:8*). Thankfully for us all, sinning after we become a Christian doesn't cause us to lose our salvation, but instead we have a remedy for our post-conversion sin for 'if we confess our sins, He is faithful and just to forgive us our sins and to cleanse us from all unrighteousness' (*1 Jn 1:9*). So *Hebrews 10:26* can't in any way be suggesting that we need to lead sinless lives to avoid falling.

What then does it mean? Well, let's have a look at *Numbers 15:22-31* to find out. There we find a distinction between presumptuous sins (or sins committed with a high hand) and unintentional sins (or sins of ignorance). The Greek word used sinning 'wilfully' in *Hebrews 10:26* is the opposite of the Greek words used for sins of ignorance in the LXX of the OT. The sinner wasn't necessarily ignorant of his sins of ignorance, but rather they were essentially sins which flowed from weakness – for in this life the saved are always *simil iustus et peccator* (at the same time righteous and sinful) – but from which the sinner would want to repent and receive God's forgiveness. The presumptuous sins on the other hand were sins committed with a high hand raised against God – just imagine someone shaking their fist against the Almighty. These were sins committed in arrogance, defiance and unbelief: sins committed with a disdain for God and His Word. So, ultimately, to sin with a high hand was an act of apostasy. There was no sacrifice for sin committed with a high hand.

So, coming back to *Hebrews 10* we can see how that fits in. The writer to the Hebrews is talking about Christians: those who have 'received the knowledge of the truth' and were 'sanctified' by 'the blood of the covenant.' But now they sin by 'trampl[ing] the Son of God underfoot,' counting His blood 'a common thing, and 'insult[ing] the Spirit of grace.' So, even the way their sin is described here in Hebrews isn't in terms of bad stuff they've done, but rather in terms of apostasy in turning away from the Lord Jesus and His saving work, rejecting the grace of God. Their wilful sin is the sin of the high hand against the Lord: apostasy from gospel.

The result of this unbelief is the Lord's vengeance, for 'there no longer remains a sacrifice for sins' for those who have rejected the only sacrifice that can avail for sin. Instead, they are once again God's 'adversaries' who will be devoured by 'judgment and fiery indignation.' For, 'it is a fearful thing to fall into the hands of the living God.'

Peter also warns of the perils awaiting those who fall away:

> For if, after they have escaped the pollutions of the world through the knowledge of the Lord and Saviour Jesus Christ, they are again entangled in them and overcome, the latter end is worse for them than the beginning. For it would have been better for them not to have known the way of righteousness, than having known it, to turn from the holy commandment delivered to them. (2 Pet. 2:20-21)

Again, we might be tempted to think in terms of doing bad things here, when we read the warning against 'turn[ing] from the holy commandment.' But is that what Peter's talking about? Well, what's 'the way of righteousness'? It's not a life of our own righteousness, but rather trust in Christ for righteousness. Salvation is not found in obeying a legal commandment, so then how could falling from salvation come about by turning away from a legal commandment? I'd suggest that, in line with what all the other passages about falling away have taught us, Peter's not writing about keeping a legal commandment, but rather he's writing about the gospel command to repent and believe in Christ (see Peter's words in *Acts 2:38* and compare what Paul has to say in *Acts 17:30-31*). The holy commandment which they had received was the commandment to believe on the Lord Jesus Christ for salvation, and so to turn from that commandment would be to turn away from faith in Christ.

James encourages us to bring back those who wander from the faith:

> Brethren, if anyone among you wanders from the truth, and someone turns him back, let him know that he who turns a sinner from the error of his way will save a soul from death and cover a multitude of sins. (*Jas 5:19-20*)

The one who wanders here is a brother from 'among you'. He was in the truth and wanders from it. So this is a Christian that James is talking about. Yet the one who turns him back from his wandering saves 'a soul from death'! So this is someone who was saved, but has fallen away from eternal life to death. And how does he do that? By wandering from the Truth: turning away from Christ the Truth to unbelief. (John has a similar encouragement for us to pray for those 'sinning a sin which does not lead to death' so that God will 'give life' in *1 Jn 5:16-17*).

John writes in his first epistle of how we persevere. 'Therefore let that abide in you which you heard from the beginning. If what you heard from the beginning abides in you, you also will abide in the Son and in the Father' (*1 Jn 2:24*). We continue in our fellowship with the Father and the Son by abiding in what we have 'heard from the beginning.' And in case it isn't clear what that is, John has already told us in the opening verses of the letter:

> That which was from the beginning, which we have heard, which we have seen with our eyes, which we have looked upon, and our hands have handled, concerning the Word of life— the life was manifested, and we have seen, and bear witness, and declare to you that eternal life which was with the Father and was manifested to us— that which we have seen and heard we declare to you, that you also may have fellowship with us; and truly our fellowship is with the Father and with His Son Jesus Christ. (*1 Jn 1:1-3*)

We abide in the eternal life which is knowing the Father and the Son, by abiding in the Word of Christ – the gospel which we have heard. For faith comes by hearing.

This fits in well with the words of Jesus which John records in his Gospel about the vine and the branches:

> I am the vine, you *are* the branches. He who abides in Me, and I in him, bears much fruit; for without Me you can do nothing. If anyone does not abide in Me, he is cast out as a branch and is withered; and they gather them and throw them into the fire, and they are burned. If you abide in Me, and My words abide in you, you will ask what you desire, and it shall be done for you. By this My Father is glorified, that you bear much fruit; so you will be My disciples. (*Jn 15:5-8*)

The branches which don't abide in Christ are cast out and thrown in the fire. But not only that, we also see there that abiding in Christ goes together with having Christ's Word abiding in us. As we receive the Gospel word in faith, we entrust ourselves to Christ in whom is salvation. Those who no longer abide in Christ, and so are cast out of the Vine, then, are those who no longer have His Word abiding in them – those who have turned away in unbelief.

So, then, we've seen that, not only are the Scriptures rather clear about the possibility of falling from grace, but they're also rather clear about how that happens. Falling from grace is just that – falling from *grace*. So it's a rejection of God's grace in Christ by turning away from faith in him and back to relying on something we can do for ourselves. Which brings us right back, full circle, to *Galations 5:4*: 'You have become estranged from Christ, you who attempt to be justified by law; you have fallen from grace.'

Falling from Grace, Abandoning the Faith

Now that we've looked at what the Bible has to say, let's think about some questions that come up from that. We've seen that people fall from grace by turning away from faith in Jesus. We're saved through faith. But the warning is not to fall through unbelief.

Now, sometimes this all gets a bit confusing for us, because we often have a tendency to think of salvation as a state. Often we think that believing in Jesus is a 'decision' or a one-time thing that takes us out of the state of being lost and into the state of being saved. But that's not really how the Bible describes things. For a start, faith isn't simply a decision or a one-off thing. Faith is trust in Jesus, and that goes on from day to day. So it's not a case of I believed (on a specific day when I responded to a gospel appeal) and so I've been saved, but rather it's a case of I believe in Jesus, and so I have salvation in Him. Faith isn't a thing we've done to get saved; faith is simply the empty hand that clings to Christ for salvation. When we see it like that, that helps us avoid the temptation to either think of faith as something in the past (a decision) or to think of salvation merely as a state rather than an ongoing good relationship with Christ to whom we're united.

For grace is not simply something we got from God when we got saved. No, grace isn't a thing, it's a Person, and that Person is Jesus who has given Himself for us (on the cross) and to us (as we are united to Him by His Holy Spirit).[8] So to fall from grace, is to turn away from Jesus. You simply can't have God's grace if you turn away from Jesus who is God's grace.

Assurance of Salvation and the Possibility of Falling From Grace

Assurance of salvation is not found in ourselves, but in Christ and Him crucified for us. Jesus Christ, the Incarnate Son of God, is our salvation, and in Him we have every spiritual blessing (*Eph. 1:3*): not only the spiritual blessings of the past and present, but also every spiritual blessing we will enjoy in the future. And such spiritual blessings include our perseverance in the faith and our resurrection to eternal life. Therefore, as we look out from ourselves to Jesus, we find assurance, not only of present salvation, but of the consummation of our salvation in the future, in Him. In Christ, we have security of salvation, and so the Welsh Apostolics gladly sang:

> Truth and mercy like a flood
> Kissed in beauty at the Tree
> Thus I'm secure through Jesus' blood
> And rejoice in Calvary.[9]
> …
> No! Says Jesus, Never shall they be lost
> Not anyone who trusts in me;
> Not while the value of the blood endures
> That was shed on Calvary.[10]

---

[8] See chapter 22.
[9] D.P. Williams, 'Agorwyd drws ar Galfari', *Molwch Dduw*, 70.

Belief in the possibility of falling from grace need not in any way diminish our assurance of salvation in Jesus Christ. The law's warnings are true; but so is the assurance of the gospel.

Falling From Grace and Unconditional Election

It's often assumed that all Pentecostals are Arminians. But historically that's simply not the case for the Apostolic Church. Yes, much of American Pentecostalism had Arminian roots, but the same isn't true for Britain.

The roots of the early Apostolics were in Welsh experiential Calvinism. However, they did move away from that in a way by adopting a belief in 'the possibility of falling from grace.' But that doesn't mean they adopted Arminian theology. Far from it; they held strongly to a doctrine of unconditional election and a monergistic understanding of salvation.[11] They still held to an effective atonement, and some still even held to a doctrine of particular redemption (i.e. that Christ's death was for the elect).[12]

Most, however, adopted what was rather close to a Lutheran approach to salvation (although they probably wouldn't have seen the similarities, as there was very little Lutheran theological writing available in English or Welsh in the UK at the beginning of the 20th Century). The basic schema was something like this: God saves those who are dead in sin (*utter depravity*) and so incapable of doing anything to contribute to their own salvation, by granting them faith, through the atoning work of Christ. While it's God who grants faith and repentance and keeps us in His salvation, we can turn away from Him in unbelief and thus fall from grace. God will, however, certainly keep His elect.

The Calvinist approach to unconditional election follows the logical argument of 'an unbreakable chain' from election to glorification, which rules out the possibility of falling from grace. Thus, for Calvinism, the mystery of why some are saved and others are not is rooted in the inscrutable will of God.

---

[10] Parch. T. Levi, 'Ar y cefnfor mawr tymhestlog', *Molwch Dduw*, 490.

[11] See chapters 30 and 9.

[12] Even some of the early Apostolic catechisms taught this. E.g. 'Christ died specifically for the elect' (*Catechism upon the Tenets of the Apostolic Church*, 3.3.27).

The Lutherans and Apostolics both rejected the Calvinist appeal to logical necessity, arguing that the Bible teaches both unconditional election and the possibility of falling from grace. This does not jeopardise the certainty of God's election, for the elect will certainly persevere unto the end. The Lutheran, Pieper, writes that 'Scripture teaches that without fail all elect enter life eternal, or, in other words, that none of the elect can be lost.'[13] The Apostolics believed that the elect 'cannot fall.'[14]

The doctrine of unconditional election should not lead first and foremost to an attempt to read the inscrutable divine decree, but instead should point us forward to the certainty of the church's future hope in Christ and backward to the outworking of God's predestined purpose at the cross. Proper teaching on election should not lead to an introspective questioning of whether or not one is elect, for that puts 'predestination between the sinner and the cross' and that sort of unclear teaching has unfortunately led many to completely misunderstand and say 'if I am not predestined, chosen and elected, why should I bother about my salvation, and if I am elected I will be alright whatever happens.'[15] The solution to such misconceptions, according to D.P. Williams, is not to abandon or downplay the doctrine of election, but rather always to look at election in light of the cross (rather than in the context of an inscrutable decree). The Apostolics would agree with the Lutherans that we:

> Must seek eternal election in Christ and His holy Gospel, as in the book of life. For the Gospel excludes no penitent sinner, but calls and invites all poor, all troubled and afflicted sinners to repentance, to the acknowledgment of their sins, and to faith in Christ; it promises the Holy Spirit for their purification and renovation.[16]

When seen through the cross, election cannot be abstracted from Christ; God's election is found only in Him (*Eph. 1:4*). As another early Apostolic put it, 'God chose One,' that One being Christ together with 'all who place their faith in Him.'[17] The elect in Christ will abide in Christ and be kept in

---

[13] Francis Pieper, *Christian Dogmatics*, 3:479.

[14] 'The Eternal Security of God's Elect' (Prophetical Ministry through W.J. Williams, Bradford, Dec. 9th, 1933), *Riches of Grace*, x.5 (May 1935), 213; Cf. Prophetical Ministry through T.N. Turnbull, Penygroes, August 8th, 1926, in *Riches of Grace*, iii.1 (March 1927), 111. One of D.P. Williams' Welsh hymns goes: In the Divine Counsel of the Trinity / In loving predestination / He elected us. 'Etholodd Ni', *Molwch Dduw*, 139.

[15] D.P. Williams, *All Sovereignty is His*, 74.

[16] C. F. W. Walther, *The Doctrine of Election Presented in Questions and Answers in: Predestination in Lutheran Perspective* (White Horse Inn, 2006), 36.

[17] W.R. Thomas, *On Ephesians*, 5.

Christ to the end. The elect receive the gift of perseverance in Christ; yet there are those who receive grace in Christ, who later turn away from Him and fall from grace.[18]

Kept by God through Faith

The Saviour has taught us that 'he who endures to the end shall be saved' (*Mt 10:22; 24:13; Mk 13:13*). And yet, Christ also teaches us that it is only in and through Him that believers do endure to the end.

> My sheep hear My voice, and I know them, and they follow Me. And I give them eternal life, and they shall never perish; neither shall anyone snatch them out of My hand. My Father, who has given them to Me, is greater than all; and no one is able to snatch them out of My Father's hand. I and My Father are one. (*Jn 10:27-30*)

It is as we hear the Good Shepherd's voice that we persevere. It is as we are held by the Son, and by His Father, that we know security of salvation in Him. It is Christ's preservation which keeps us, rather than our own great work of perseverance.

> Kept by His pow'r,
> Kept by His pow'r,
> Jesus is keeping me,
> Now and eternally.
> I'm kept by His pow'r;
> Kept by His pow'r;
> Wondrous the mighty love
> That is keeping me.[19]

How does Jesus keep us? He says in *John 10* that it is as we hear His voice (*Jn 10:27*). The Lord preserves us in His grace through His means of grace: as we hear His Word proclaimed and see and taste His visible Word in the sacrament. Anyone who is trusting in Christ's Word will not perish (*Jn 8:51*). It is the Word which keeps our faith in Jesus, for 'faith comes by hearing, and hearing by the Word of God' (*Rom. 10:17*). It is no coincidence that the admonishment not to forsake the assembling of ourselves together

---

[18] This was also the position of Augustine. See Augustine, *The Gift of Perseverance*.
[19] Hugh Mitchell, 'Kept by His Power', *Gospel Quintet Choruses*, 3:93.

(*Heb. 10:24-25*) immediately precedes the strong warning passage of *Hebrews 10*, for it is as we assemble together as the church, that we 'exhort' one another with the Gospel Word of Christ by which He keeps us in the faith.

Jesus spoke of those who receive the word with joy and yet endure 'only for a while' in the parable of the sower (*Mt 13:1-9, 18-23*). According to the parable, there are those who receive the word in faith, yet fall away, by turning their gaze from Christ and His Word 'when tribulation or persecution arises because of the word' (*Mt 13:21*) or when 'the cares of this world and the deceitfulness of riches choke the word' (*Mt 13:22*). What leads to the falling away in the parable is what happens to the Word: it's when people start to view the Word as a bad thing, or when they start to view other things as more desirable than the Word of the Lord that they fall away. And that is exactly how our first parents fell in the Garden.

It is by His Gospel Word that Christ keeps us in the faith. As we continue to receive and trust in His Word, we abide in Him, and He in us. So the greatest thing we can do to persevere in the faith until the end, is to avail ourselves of the means of grace: not forsaking the assembling of ourselves together, but gathering together with the Lord's people, around the Lord's Table, under the proclamation of the Word of the Lord each and every Lord's Day.

Tenet 11

The obligatory nature of tithes & offerings.

Chapter 40

Of Christian Obligations: Good Works & the Law of God in the Life of the Christian

Of Good Works

Good works, in the true biblical sense, flow from love. In 21st century Western culture, we might be tempted to contrast obedience and love, but the Scriptures make no such contrast. Jesus says:

> If you love Me, keep My commandments … He who has My commandments and keeps them, it is he who loves Me. And he who loves Me will be loved by My Father, and I will love him and manifest Myself to him … If anyone loves Me, he will keep My word; and My Father will love him, and We will come to him and make Our home with him. He who does not love Me does not keep My words; and the word which you hear is not Mine but the Father's who sent Me. (*Jn 14:15, 21, 23-24*)

For Jesus, love and obedience belong together. If we love Him, we will keep His commandments. Our good works are our acts of obedience to Christ's commandments, and so good works flow from love for Christ. And such loving obedience is not only seen in our relationship with God, but also with other people.

> Beloved, if God so loved us [by sending His Son as the propitiation for our sins], we also ought to love one another … If we love one another, God abides in us, and His love has been perfected in us … God is love, and he who abides in love abides in God, and God in him … If someone says, 'I love God,' and hates his brother, he is a liar; for he who does not love his brother whom he has seen, how can he love God whom he has not seen? And this commandment we have from Him: that he who loves God must love his brother also. (*1 Jn 4:11, 12, 16, 20-21*)

The love of God abiding in us, as Christ abides in us and the Holy Spirit dwells in us, turns us out from ourselves, not only towards God, but also towards others in God's love. And so we lovingly obey this new commandment given to us by Christ.

> A new commandment I give to you, that you love one another; as I have loved you, that you also love one another. By this all will know that you are My disciples, if you have love for one another. (*Jn 13:34-35*)

Obedience flows from love, and loving obedience carries us out to serve others with good works of love, which God has prepared in advance for us to walk in (*Eph. 2:10*). This is true religion. For, although it may have become commonplace for Christians to contrast religion with a relationship with Christ, in the Bible true and pure religion is a very good thing; it simply cannot be separated from a good relationship with the Triune God through the blood of Jesus.

> Pure and undefiled religion before God and the Father is this: to visit orphans and widows in their trouble, and to keep oneself unspotted from the world. (*Jas 1:27*)

God's love to us leads us to love God in obedience, which results in love expressed in good works to those around us. And this is pure and undefiled religion before God.

We are not justified by our good works (*Rom. 3:24; 4:1-5; Gal. 2:16*). Yet good works are the inevitable result of the true faith by which we are justified (*Gal. 5:6; Jn 15:5; Jas 2:14-26*). For 'faith by itself, if it does not have works, is dead' (*Jas 2:17*). Living faith is faith which lays hold of the living Saviour, and through this living faith, the Holy Spirit unites us to Christ. Therefore, those who are justified are clothed with Christ and His love and righteousness, and indwelt by the Spirit of love. Therefore, our faith is demonstrated through loving obedience and the ensuing good works of love, for those who are justified by faith abide in God and God in them.

Therefore Christian obligations are not dry duties, but delightful expressions of love for our Saviour and for those around us. For, if we love Him, we will keep His word (*1 Jn 14:23*).

Of the Ten Commandments

Martin Luther sums up the whole classical tradition of Christian education, writing that the Ten Commandments, along with the Apostles' Creed and the Lord's Prayer:

> Are the most necessary parts of Christian teaching that one should first learn to repeat word for word … A person who is so rude and unruly as to be unwilling to learn these things is not to be tolerated. For in these three parts, everything that we have in the Scriptures is included in short, plain, and simple terms.[1]

The Ten Commandments (*Ex 20:1-17; Deut. 5:6-21*) summarise how we are to 'love and trust in [the Lord] and gladly do what He commands.'[2] They are 'the sum of the moral Law', which is eternal.[3] 'Surely as God's essence is eternal, so also God's holiness, mercy, and perfection are eternal, and the expression and representation of His holiness, mercy, and perfection are set forth in the Law.'[4] Therefore, while the ceremonial and forensic laws of the Old Testament were given for one nation only, the moral law, as summarised in the Ten Commandments, is universal. The moral law is fulfilled in the love of God and love of neighbour (*Mt 22:37-40; Rom. 13:8-10*).

When the Lord spoke the Ten Commandments to Israel, He rooted their loving obedience in the love He had first shown them, declaring at the very outset: 'I am the LORD your God, who brought you out of the land of Egypt, out of the house of bondage' (*Ex 5:2*). And still for Christians today, our loving obedience is rooted in the love which the Triune God has first shown us. It is because God has first loved us and sent His Son as the propitiation for our sins that we now love Him, and love one another, and keep His commandment (*1 Jn 4:10-11, 20-21*).

---

[1] Martin Luther, *Large Catechism*, Shorter Preface, 15, 18.

[2] Martin Luther, *Small Catechism*, Part 1.

[3] Johann Gerhard, *Loci*, XV §13-14.

[4] Johann Gerhard, *Loci*, XV §14.

Of the Lord's Day

The Lord's Day – the Christian Sabbath – is not an old-fashioned legalism, but a gift of God's grace.[5] The Lord calls the Sabbath 'my holy day' (*Isa. 58:13*), and so it is the day which He has sanctified and set apart from everyday use to be used exclusively in worship. Therefore, the Sabbath is not just a day of rest, but a day of worship.

This is a gift given by the Lord, for 'the Sabbath was made for man, and not man for the Sabbath' (*Mk 2:27*). The Sabbath-rest is not a work we perform to try to earn God's favour, but rather, we lovingly obey God's Word in receiving a day of rest and worship as a gift from Him. The Lord's Day is not about making rules and regulations of what can and cannot be done, like the Scribes and Pharisees of old, but rather, it's about the privilege of being able to put aside the work and cares of the week to fix our eyes upon our Saviour.

Like marriage and work, the Sabbath is a creation ordinance (*Gen. 2:2-3*). So it was not something introduced with the Mosaic Law. Some people point to *Colossians 2:16-17* as showing the abolition of the Sabbath, arguing that Paul is saying that the Sabbath, like the Temple and the sacrifices, just pointed forward to Jesus and His work, and therefore is now obsolete. However, in that passage, Paul is dealing with the problem that the Colossians had of trying to supplement their faith in Christ with Jewish practices which had been abolished by Christ's work. And so he is referring to the old, seventh-day Sabbath. Some believers (motivated by the same zeal as the Judaizers who wanted Gentile Christians to be circumcised) wanted to impose the Jewish feasts and festivals (including the seventh-day Sabbath) on all Christians. Paul isn't writing of the moral law to keep one day in seven, but the ritual law of the seventh day. There has been a transition from shadow to substance: the shadow of the Old Covenant seventh day is gone, and the Christ-centred substance is here on the first day – the Lord's Day. Paul is saying that a seventh-day Sabbath with its rituals and its prescribing and proscribing rules is gone. The Christian Sabbath is about grace, not ritual law.

The day has changed, but the principle remains. 'There remains therefore a [Sabbath] rest for the people of God. For he who has entered His

---

[5] In the Apostolic Church, 'it is expected that all members will observe the sanctity of the Lord's Day, namely Sunday, the first day of the week.' *Introducing the Apostolic Church: A Manual of Belief, Practice and History*, 29.

rest has himself also ceased from his works as God did from His' (*Heb. 4:9-10*). The word used here for 'Sabbath rest' is not the normal word for 'rest' used elsewhere in the same chapter. In fact, this is a unique noun, but the verb form is used elsewhere in the New Testament meaning 'to sabbatize': to keep the Sabbath. So *Hebrews 4:9* is telling us about Sabbath keeping; there remains therefore a Sabbath-keeping for the people of God. The writer is pointing forward to our eternal rest and showing that our earthly Sabbath rest is an anticipation of what is to come.

And this passage in Hebrews also establishes the day of the Sabbath. We know that the early church kept their Sabbath on the first day of the week from their example in Acts and the Epistles. But here we get the explanation of why. *Verse 10* begins with the word 'for', therefore the reason that we keep the Lord's Day is found in this verse: 'For he who has entered His rest has himself also ceased from his works as God did from His' (*Heb. 4:10*). Who is 'he'? Some translations try to interpret instead of translate here, putting 'anyone' instead of 'he', and so making it sound as if Hebrews is referring to believers. But the Greek is singular – 'the One who'; and the one who has entered His rest is Christ. Throughout these chapters, when the writer refers to the rest of believers, he uses the plural (e.g. *Heb. 4:3* – 'For we who have believed enter that rest'). But here he refers to an individual.

Furthermore, in *verse 11* the responsibility to enter into rest remains for the believer, but here 'the One' has already entered into rest. We have begun to experience God's rest; however we won't fully enter His rest until we're glorified with Christ in heaven.

So, here we learn that we keep the Lord's Day because of what Christ has done: because He has risen from the dead, having completed His atoning work. Jesus rested from His work of redemption on the first day of the week. In His resurrection He confirmed that eternal life had been purchased, and He entered into the enjoyment of His work. The old seventh-day looked forward to God's promised rest. But now the first day looks back to rest on what Christ has accomplished to bring God's rest.

Of Tithes and Offerings

The giving of tithes and offerings is an act of worship and an expression of love. From the beginning, the Apostolic Church has recognised through tithes and offerings, 'God in His Word has provided a way to care for the poor and needy, and those who are oppressed, so that there might be security for all the saints, the poor and rich alike,'[6] and also that through them 'God has set out in His Word an honourable plan to carry out His work.'[7] The church is not to seek support from the world, but rather is to be a source of blessing to the world.

As a good work of obedience flowing from love for God and for neighbour, the giving of tithes and offerings is not a form of legalism, but rather is rooted in the generosity of grace of the Triune God of love.

> Tithe giving is based on faith in the Grace of God, and this being so, its dismissal from all claim for consideration by us as being an essentially legal and Mosaic institution cannot be justified. In the Law minute instructions amounting to thorough systemisation of tithe giving are given, but neither the practice nor the spirit of tithe bringing owe itself in the least to Moses, for they were means of expressing the worship of the faithful heart centuries before he was born.[8]

Although tithing was codified as a legal system under the Mosaic Law, this was not the beginning of the tithe: both Abraham and Jacob explicitly paid tithes before the introduction of the Mosaic Law. Abraham gave 'a tithe of all' (*Gen. 14:20; cf. Heb. 7:2, 6*) to Melchizedek, 'the priest of God Most High' (*Gen. 14:18*), who had blessed Abraham with the blessing of God (*Gen. 14:19-20*). Abraham was not legally required to pay a tithe to this king-priest Melchizedek, but rather gave this tithe as an expression of thankfulness to, and dependence upon, the Lord.

> What was true of Abram's faith and of Abram's tithes is in principle true still of all who know God by saving grace. Tithe giving or bringing is not in response to any externally imposed demand, but a spontaneous upspringing of genuine thankfulness for grace received.[9]

The particular significance of this event comes from the way Abraham is set out as a model of Christian faith and obedience in the New Testament (*Rom. 4; Gal. 3; Jas. 2*) as well as the fact that Melchizedek, the King of Righteousness and King of Peace, who is the priest of God Most High, prefigures the true King of Righteousness and Peace, and Great High Priest

---

[6] Athrawiaethau Sylfeinol, 14.

[7] *Athrawiaethau Sylfeinol*, 15.

[8] J. Omri Jones, *The Obligatory Nature of Tithes and Offerings*, Tenets booklets, 11:14-15.

[9] J. Omri Jones, *The Obligatory Nature of Tithes and Offerings*, Tenets booklets, 11:16.

over the house of God: Jesus Christ our Lord. In *Genesis 14* the model believer freely brings a tithe to a type of Christ.

Jacob's vow of tithe-giving (*Gen. 28:20-22*) also flows from worship rather than necessity. It is because the Lord will be his God and protect and deliver him that Jacob vows to 'surely give a tenth' to Him. The giving of tithes is in response to who the Lord is and what He has done for us.

And just as tithing began before the giving of the Mosaic Law, so too tithing continues now in the New Testament church. Under the Old Testament law, 'mortal men receive tithes,' but now in heaven Christ 'receives them, of whom it is witnessed that he lives' (*Heb. 7:8*).[10]

In his woes against the scribes and Pharisees, Jesus chastised them that they had paid the 'tithe of mint and anise and cummin, and have neglected the weightier matters of the law: justice and mercy and faith' (*Mt 23:23*). Yet, He continues: 'These you ought to have done, without leaving the others undone.' Justice, mercy and faith do not undo the obligation of bringing our tithes (even of the smallest of God's gifts, like mint and anise and cummin) to the Lord, as an obedient expression of love.

The believers in the churches of the New Testament gave generously to the Lord. Special offerings were made for the poor (*1 Cor. 16:2; 2 Cor. 8-9*). Christians were encouraged to give regularly, and in proportion to their wealth (*1 Cor. 16:2*). Yet, it was not only the rich who were to give, but also the poor (*2 Cor. 8:2; cf. Mk 12:44*). Therefore, all Christians should contribute to the Lord's work and to the need of others through giving tithes and offerings. Yet wealthier Christians should give beyond a tithe, in proportion to how the Lord has prospered them.

Christians are to give 'not grudgingly or of necessity' but rather, joyfully, 'for God loves a cheerful giver' (*2 Cor. 9:7*). And the Lord will not allow his children to suffer lack through their generous giving out of love for Him. Rather, 'God is able to make all grace about toward you, that you, always having all sufficiency in all things, may have an abundance for every good work' (*2 Cor. 9:8*). It is the Lord Himself who is our sufficiency, and He is the one who provides not only for our needs, but for us to show His love in meeting the needs of others.

Tithes are to be given in the church. For it is to Christ, the Head of the Church, that we bring our tithes (*Heb. 7:8*). Therefore, we lay our tithes at His feet by giving them to His Church, the Body which He has established,

---

[10] Some commentators view *Heb. 7:8* as a reference to Melchizedek rather than Jesus. However, even in that case, it would imply that Jesus, as a High Priest after the order of Melchizedek, now receives our tithes as part of that priestly ministry.

which He is building, and to which He is united as Head. Other Christian organisations may do very good work, and may help the church in the fulfilment of its mission; but, unlike the church, they have not been divinely instituted by the Saviour. Offerings may be given to other organisations, but as human institutions they cannot receive tithes. Tithes are to be brought to the Lord's storehouse 'that there may be food in My house' (*Mal. 3:10*).

In the early centuries of the life of the Christian church, Christians brought their tithes and offerings to the bishop or presbyters (the overseer and elders), who would then distribute them according to need, for the ministry of the church and the needs of the poor. In the fourth-century *Apostolic Constitutions*, we read:

> Let him [the bishop] use those tenths and first-fruits, which are given according to the command of God, as a man of God; as also let him dispense in a right manner the free-will offerings which are brought in on account of the poor, to the orphans, the widows, the afflicted, and strangers in distress, as having that God for the examiner of his accounts who has committed the disposition to him. Distribute to all those in want with righteousness, and yourselves use the things which belong to the Lord, but do not abuse them; eating of them, but not eating them all up by yourselves: communicate with those that are in want, and thereby show yourselves unblameable before God.[11]

Presbyteries should take the same attitude to the tithes which they administer today, remembering that God our Father is the examiner of our accounts, and that we are only stewards of the finances the saints have laid at Christ's feet.

Of Financial Giving and God's Blessing: A Warning Against the New Indulgence Sellers

Tithing is not a business transaction with God. It is not to be mistaken for a financial investment. The saints do not secure God's blessing through their financial giving (*Acts 8:20-22*). God's blessing is found only by His grace in Jesus Christ who died and rose again for us, and who gives Himself to us by His Holy Spirit through faith, so that in Him we are blessed (*Eph. 1:3*). The association between tithing and blessing in *Malachi 3:8-12* is not the purchase of blessings through paying tithes, but rather the blessings which are found when we trust in the Lord and lovingly obey His Word. These

---

[11] *Apostolic Constitutions*, 2.4.25

verses should be understood in light of the fact that 'there are Christians who are poor because their uncompromising Christian faith has resulted in them suffering great loss.'[12]

For anyone to suggest that the saints will only receive blessings depending on the amount of money they give, or to teach that healing can be secured through financial giving, is to blaspheme the infinite worth of the blood of Christ. Such wicked teaching is a revival of the error of Tetzel, whose claim that 'when a coin in the coffer rings, a soul from purgatory springs' sparked Luther's *Ninety-Five Theses*. As Luther wrote in that document nailed to the castle church door, 'any true Christian, whether living or dead, participates in all the blessings of Christ and the church; and this is granted to him by God, even without indulgence letters.'[13] And even without a contribution to the account of the tele-evangelist. Instead, 'Christians are to be taught that he who gives to the poor or lends to the needy does a better deed than he who buys indulgences.'[14]

Wicked false-teachers, who as wolves in sheep's clothing prey upon Christ's little flock for financial gain, are not servants of Christ. Rather, they serve 'their own belly, and by smooth words and flattering speech deceive the hearts of the simple' (*Rom. 16:18*). And so they should be noted and avoided by the children of God (*Rom. 16:17*), for the light has no fellowship with darkness.

Of The Tithes and the Table: A Conclusion

Among the early Apostolics, the cry was 'Bring the tithes to the Table!'[15] The traditional Apostolic way of gathering the tithes is for the members to bring them forward during the closing hymn of the Breaking of Bread service and place them in a tithe bowl on the Lord's Table. There were two reasons for this practice. Firstly, it demonstrated that the tithes belonged to the Lord, not to the Apostolic Church or the presbytery or apostleship. Secondly, it was so that the Lord's people 'may realise, when they bring their tithes to the table, that they are worshipping the Lord in the beauty of holiness.'[16]

---

[12] *Introducing the Apostolic Church: A Manual of Belief, Practice and History*, 196.

[13] Martin Luther, *The Ninety-Five Theses*, 37.

[14] Martin Luther, *The Ninety-Five Theses*, 43.

[15] *The Apostolic Church: Its Principles and Practices*, 241 (quoting Prophetical Ministry, Glasgow, Feb. 1931).

[16] *The Apostolic Church: Its Principles and Practices*, 241-242 (quoting Prophetical Ministry, Glasgow, Feb. 1931).

In bringing our contributions to the Table, the Apostolic practice is in line with the historic practice of the early church. 'The Table is where, in the convergence of God's gift and ours, we taste what it is to be swept up into the eternal self-giving of Father, Son, and Holy Spirit.'[17] But one significant change has been made. While in ancient times (and in most other movements which still place the people's gifts on the communion table today) the tithes were brought before the Breaking of Bread, the Apostolic practice is to bring them after the sacrament, and therefore to avoid any impression that the blessings of God may be purchased with money. This Apostolic liturgical innovation safeguards the display of the gospel of God's free grace in Jesus in the Breaking of Bread service. Our giving flows in loving obedience out from what God has first given us, by sending His only-begotten Son, in His great love, to take on our flesh, and live, obey, die, and rise for us and our salvation.

Because of His great love to us, we keep His word in loving obedience. And so we bring our tithes and offerings to the Lord for His glory, and for the good of His people.

> According to the Word of the Lord, we believe and teach the truth of tithes and free-will offerings, not of constraint, but voluntarily ... The tenth of the believer's income is not his, but the Lord's, and should always be strictly recognised as such, and faithfully set apart for the Lord's work.[18]

All that we have belongs to the Lord. And in recognition of this, Christians act as stewards of what they have received from the Triune God, giving back to Him of the time and resources which He has generously given to us, by hallowing His Day, and bringing our tithes and offerings to His feet.

---

[17] Reggie Kidd, 'Tithing in the New Covenant', in David A Croteau, ed., *Perspectives on Tithing* (Nashville: B&H, 2011), 120.

[18] *Riches of Grace*, 1.1 (April 1916), 14. This statement appeared in every issue of the first volume of *Riches of Grace*.